THE PURSUIT OF LIBERTY

ORCHARD RIDGE BOOKSTORE

W9-AUD-161

THE PURSUIT

A HISTORY OF THE AMERICAN PEOPLE

Wadsworth Publishing Company

Belmont, California
A Division of Wadsworth, Inc.

OF LIBERTY

VOLUME ONE / SECOND EDITION

R. Jackson Wilson
Smith College

James Gilbert
University of Maryland

Stephen Nissenbaum
University of Massachusetts

Karen Ordahl Kupperman
University of Connecticut

Donald Scott
The New School for Social Research

History Editor: Peggy Adams
Production Editor: Leland Moss
Interior and Cover Design: James Chadwick
Art Editor: Marta Kongsle
Art Assistant: Roberta Broyer
Photo Research: Pembroke Herbert
Print Buyer: Barbara Britton
Compositor: Jonathan Peck Typographers
Copy Editor: Anne Montague
Editorial Assistant: Karen Moore
Cover Art: A Social History of the State of Missouri, by Thomas Hart Benton, Missouri State Capitol Building, Jefferson City, Missouri. Courtesy Missouri Department of Natural Resources, Missouri State Museum.

© 1990 by Wadsworth, Inc. All rights reserved. No part of this book may be reproduced, stored in a retrieval system, or transcribed, in any form or by any means, electronic, mechanical, photocopying, recording, or otherwise, without the prior written permission of the publisher, Wadsworth Publishing Company, Belmont, California 94002, a division of Wadsworth, Inc.

Printed in the United States of America **34**

1 2 3 4 5 6 7 8 9 10—94 93 92 91 90

**Library of Congress
Cataloging-in-Publication Data**

The Pursuit of liberty.

Includes bibliographical references.
1. United States—History. I. Wilson, Raymond Jackson.
E178.1.P985 1990   973   89-16712
ISBN 0-534-11694-9 (hardcover)
ISBN 0-534-11697-3 (pbk. : v. 1)
ISBN 0-534-11699-X (pbk. : v. 2)

Chapter opening photos are from the following sources: Chapter 1, John Carter Brown Library at Brown University; Chapter 2, British Museum; Chapter 3, Pennsylvania Academy of the Fine Arts, Joseph and Sarah Harrison Collection; Chapter 4, Yale University Art Museum; Chapter 5, Chicago Historical Society; Chapter 6, Brown University Library, Anne S. K. Brown Military Collection; Chapter 7, Woolarac Museum, Bartlesville, Oklahoma; Chapter 8, Cincinnati Historical Society; Chapter 9, The Metropolitan Museum of Art, Gift of I. N. Phelps Stokes, Edward S. Hawes, Alice Mary Hawes, Marion Augusta Hawes, 1937 (37.14.22); Chapter 10, New York Historical Society; Chapter 11, Culver Pictures; Chapter 12, Library of Congress, Brady Collection.

CONTENTS

6   The Republic on Trial

7   Beyond the Appalachian Barrier

11   Expansion and the Crisis of the Union

12   "His Terrible, Swift Sword"

AUTHORS' PREFACE

When the oldest of the authors of *The Pursuit of Liberty* was in the eighth grade, he had to take his first course on the history of the United States. His teacher was a legend in the school, a tough, slightly forbidding woman, who was determined that her students were going to learn *something* about the history of their country.

She gave her roomful of fourteen-year-olds a demanding task. They had to memorize any 200 facts about American history, including dates. When the final examination came, they had to write down their list of facts in the correct chronological order. You could choose any facts, as long as there were 200 of them and they were in chronological order. You might start with "1492—Columbus discovers America." Or you could begin with "1607—First English colony in America at Jamestown, Virginia." (In both cases, you would be a bit wrong. But that didn't matter. These "facts" were in the textbook, and the important thing was that you had learned them.)

Nowadays, of course, everything about learning history has changed. The authors' own children come home from history classes in schools and colleges with their heads full of "concepts." They don't think "1607—Jamestown" (or even "1587—Roanoke," which is closer to the truth). Instead, they are taught to talk about large and abstract events, such as "The Confrontation of European and Native-American Cultures." They study grand processes such as "Industrialization," "Immigration," and "Urbanization." They seem to learn history in a more sophisticated and better way than memorizing some list of 200 facts.

But there is a problem. Students who study American history today seem to know something in general, but nothing in particular. They discuss abstractions and generalizations, but these are not connected with any firm grasp of relevant factual information. Have our best and most innovative teachers and professors simply replaced 200 facts with 20 vague concepts? The old problem was that history was a grab bag of names and dates and places. Students learned something in particular and nothing much in general. But the new problem, knowing the general but not the particular, is just as serious. Either way, studying history runs the risk of being a plain waste of time.

This dilemma is partly the result of the nature of history itself. There *are* large and general tendencies and there *are* particular facts. The difficult thing is to see how the two fit together. We tend to look at history the way we look at a painting. We focus on the foreground—the facts. Or we think about the background, about the general way the picture is structured and the kinds of claims it makes on our imagination. But when we study history, it is difficult to put the foreground and the background, the facts and the general concepts, together. We seem to choose between foreground and background, unable to see how each makes sense in terms of the other.

When most history textbooks try to bring specific facts and general concepts together, they do so by simply *telling* readers that this or that fact is an example of this or that general tendency. First comes a heading, something like "The Contact of European and Native-American Cultures" or "Industrialization." Then comes a sentence or two of generalization. A little further on come the facts, such as "1607—Jamestown" or "The first transcontinental railroad was completed in 1869."

Some important things are lost in this way of writing history. We are not asked to see or understand the relationship between fact and general concept at all. Did something called "industrialization" *cause* the first transcontinental railroad or did a host of facts, such as the building of that railroad, cause industrial development? Concrete facts and general concepts merely coexist in such textbooks, each of them inert and incapable of giving any sort of life to the other.

Perhaps worse, when students study history in textbooks of this sort, they get no sense of the human *experience* involved in either the specific events they find listed there or the generalizations they read and underline to study for next week's test. Most history textbooks contain no narrative, no stories, no accounts of the dramatic, sometimes triumphant, often shameful efforts and struggles of human beings. Human action is squeezed out of history and we are left with dead "events" and equally lifeless generalizations.

We have written *The Pursuit of Liberty* in the belief that we have found ways to solve these kinds of problems. We started with two convictions. First, we had to make it possible for students to see and *understand* the ways that specific sequences of human action were related to the general setting in which they took place. Second, historians ought not to keep a secret of the remarkably exciting and dramatic ways people actually acted in the past.

These two convictions have shaped our book, and they explain its unusual structure. Each chapter has two different parts. In the first, we tell the story of a very specific and concrete episode: a witchcraft hysteria in Salem, Massachusetts, in 1692, for example; or the massacre of a band of the Native American Sioux at Wounded Knee Creek in the Dakotas in 1890; or the rending struggle for custody of the infant known as "Baby M" in the 1980s. Episodes like these are the human material out of which history is made.

But history is more than stories. It involves coming to understand how the stories could have happened. To do this, we have to know something about the general context within which a specific episode took place. So the second part of each chapter is a discussion of the historical setting of the chapter's episode. The narrative of Salem witchcraft is followed by a discussion of seventeenth-century New England Puritanism; the Wounded Knee massacre by an examination of the westward expansion of European-American society into the territories of the Native Americans; the story of Baby M by a discussion of the tangled relationships between private morality and public politics that characterized American life in the 1980s.

And so we go through *The Pursuit of Liberty*, alternating between the specific and the general, between narrative and explanation. In the end we think our readers will have a much better grasp of the way history works, of the way that all the specific actions of people are shaped by the historical setting in which they take place. And we have faith, too, that some of our readers will learn the most important thing that history has to teach all of us: We all live in history, profoundly shaped by the society around us, by what it has been as well as by what it is now.

If this lesson is learned, then our readers will have learned what we already know, that learning history is a way of discovering our kinship with all those real people who have come before us, who have acted out their struggles, terrors, and occasional exaltations with the same anxiety and effort that go so deeply into all our lives. The past is inescapable, for everyone, whether one knows it or not.

It is better to know it.

R. Jackson Wilson
James Gilbert
Stephen Nissenbaum
Karen Ordahl Kupperman
Donald Scott

ABOUT THE AUTHORS

R. Jackson Wilson is a Professor of History at Smith College. He is a graduate of the University of Missouri and received his M.A. and Ph.D. degrees from the University of Wisconsin. He has taught at an unusually wide range of institutions, including the University of Arizona, the University of Wisconsin, Columbia University, the University of Massachusetts, Hartford College for Women, Yale University, the University of Pennsylvania, and the Flinders University of South Australia. He has been a fellow of the Woodrow Wilson Foundation, the National Endowment for the Humanities, the Charles Warren Center, Harvard University, and the National Humanities Center. He is the author of *In Quest of Community: Social Philosophy in the United States* and *Figures of Speech: American Writers and the Literary Marketplace, from Benjamin Franklin to Emily Dickinson.*

James Gilbert is Professor of History at the University of Maryland and a graduate of Carleton College and the University of Wisconsin. He has also taught at Teachers College, Columbia University; Warwick University in Coventry, England; the University of Paris; and Sydney University in Australia. His books include *Writers and Partisans* (1968), *Designing the Industrial State* (1972), *Work Without Salvation* (1978), *Another Chance: Postwar America* (1981), and *A Cycle of Outrage: America's Reaction to the Juvenile Delinquent in the 1950s* (1986). He has been a Fellow of the Woodrow Wilson Foundation, the National Endowment for the Humanities, and the Woodrow Wilson Center. Currently he is finishing a book on Chicago in the 1890s.

Stephen Nissenbaum is a Professor of History at the University of Massachusetts, Amherst, where he teaches intellectual and social history and directs The Center for New England Culture. He has held fellowships from the National Endowment for the Humanities and the American Council of Learned Societies. He has taught at Smith College, Hampshire College, and Mount Holyoke College. He has been the James Pinckney Harrison Professor of History at The College of William and Mary. He has served as president of his state humanities council, the Massachusetts Foundation for Humanities and Public Policy. He is the author of *Sex, Diet, and Debility in Jacksonian*

America and (with Paul Boyer) *Salem Possessed: The Social Origins of Witchcraft*, which won the John H. Dunning prize of the American Historical Association. He is currently writing a book about Edgar Allan Poe, Nathaniel Hawthorne, and the social history of literature in the Jacksonian period.

Karen Ordahl Kupperman is Professor of History at the University of Connecticut. She is a graduate of the University of Missouri and holds an M.A. from Harvard University and a Ph.D. from Cambridge University. Her previous books include *Settling with the Indians: The Meeting of English and Indian Cultures in America, 1580–1640* (1980) and *Roanoake, the Abandoned Colony* (1984). She is also the editor of *Captain John Smith: A Select Edition of His Writings* (1988). In 1980, her essay "Apathy and Death in Early Jamestown" won the distinguished Binkley-Stevenson award of the Organization of American Historians. She has been a Mellon Faculty Fellow at Harvard, a fellow of the National Humanities Center, and senior associate member of St. Antony's College, Oxford.

Donald Scott is a Professor of History and Dean of Eugene Lang College of the New School for Social Research. He is a graduate of Harvard College and received his Ph.D. from the University of Wisconsin. He is the author of *From Office to Profession: The New England Ministry, 1750–1850*, and is co-author of *America's Families: A Documentary History*. He has been a fellow at the Davis Center for Historical Studies, Princeton University, and a National Endowment for the Humanities Fellow at the American Antiquarian Society. He is currently working on a book on democracy and knowledge in nineteenth-century America.

ACKNOWLEDGMENTS

We believe that everything that is said in *The Pursuit of Liberty* is true. Well, almost everything. But the book contains two unavoidable falsehoods, both of them on the title page. Both are formulas that are imposed by the powerful conventions that govern the publication of books in our society. The first is the suggestion that an abstract corporate entity named Wadsworth Publishing brought the book into existence. The second is that five individuals known as "authors" are responsible for all the words and ideas in the book. We would like to set the record straight on both these points.

The truth of the matter is that Wadsworth Publishing is really a set of very specific people who have generously invested efforts, care, and talent in this book. In particular, no one could have worked more diligently and effectively than Leland Moss, Margaret Adams, James Chadwick, Marta Kongsle, and Roberta Broyer. The book owes much to them.

The truth is, as well, that the writing of history is a collective enterprise. We owe an incalculable debt to generations of men and women who have labored to make the history of the American people comprehensible. We also owe a great deal to the people—many of them now mature men and women—who have been our students. We cannot repay them for all the history lessons they have given to us; we can only hope that some of *their* children may learn as much from our book as we have from them.

The Pursuit of Liberty is also the product of some fine advice from many extremely intelligent and dedicated people. We are grateful to them all, and particularly to: John K. Alexander, Stephen L. Berk, David Bernstein, Lee R. Boyer, Thomas J. Boyle, John C. Chalberg, Lawrence Foster, Paula Franklin, William Graebner, Pembroke Herbert, James Henretta, Donald W. Hensel, William C. Hine, E. Rusten Hogness, Cornelia Hopkins, Marvin L. Jaegers, George L. Jones, Stephen Kneeshaw, Neil B. Lehman, Gerald McFarland, Frank Nation, Gary Nissenbaum, Gregory Nobles, Thomas C. Parramore, S. Fred Roach, Chris Rogers, Philip R. Royal, Alan Schaffer, Rodney Sievers, John Snetsinger, Dennis Thavenet, Stephen Weisner, Nancy Woloch, and Phyllis Zimmerman. Sometimes their suggestions have posed formidable tasks for us. Although their criticisms have not always been gentle, even their sternest comments have been useful because they were obviously motivated by a genuine concern for history and for teaching.

THE PURSUIT OF LIBERTY

CHAPTER 1
FIRST ENCOUNTERS

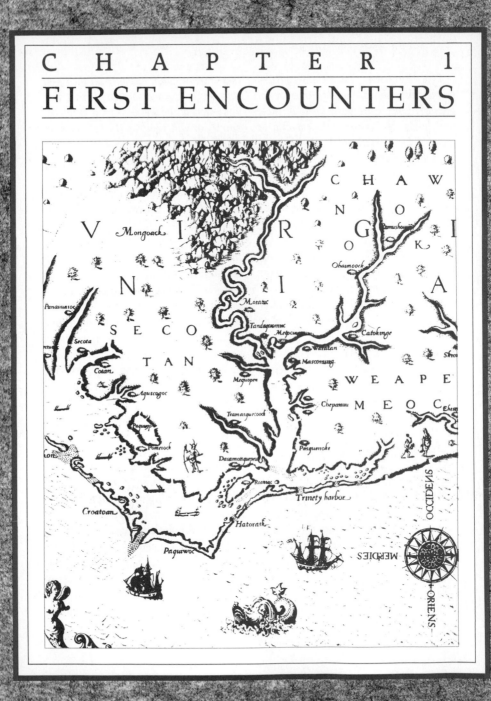

THE EPISODE: *Twentieth-century people take colonization of America for granted. Once Europeans knew of those vast lands, we assume, they would be eager to found settlements, looking forward to the growth of mighty empires and strong cultures. But the possibilities of America emerged slowly: Only decades after 1492 did Europeans develop a clear sense of the American continents. Colonization was not an obvious choice, nor did it promise much in the way of returns. Many possible investments were more promising than colonization.*

Only a few people like Sir Walter Raleigh in the 1580s were prepared to devote efforts to this new kind of endeavor. He had to convince his associates that colonization would pay off. Planting settlements in America soaked up money, and many investors saw nothing in return. Great empires did grow, but they rarely enriched those who founded them. Other, later, people reaped the benefits of the early efforts of the founders.

THE HISTORICAL SETTING: *The real question that must be answered is why European men and women put their money into exploration and colonization instead of more promising enterprises. Even more difficult is explaining why hundreds of thousands of men and women gave up their homes in Europe and braved the hazards of a grueling Atlantic voyage and of life in a strange, even hostile, environment. What did they expect? Why did*

they think it might be worth all the risks? Was life in Europe so difficult that they approached the gamble in a fatalistic spirit, or did they really believe they would make their fortunes in America?

What did the Indians make of the newcomers? The Native Americans' role was much more dynamic than modern readers realize. Popular culture has taught us to assume that once the Europeans arrived with their sophisticated technology— their guns, ships, and horses—the Indians were essentially forced to retreat in dismay. The story is actually much more complex. Although in some cases their predictions were not borne out by events, the natives made shrewd judgments on the evidence available to them and aided some plantations in order to get access to the European products they valued.

All the participants entered the new set of relationships with specific goals in mind. Often the situation turned out far different from their expectations. Many times events carried the participants into situations they never anticipated. Some results, such as the impact of European diseases on Native Americans, were completely unanticipated. Explorers, natives, and settlers were always reacting to unexpected circumstances. In many ways colonization was a constant series of improvisations, and America a giant laboratory for a great experiment in human relations.

SIR WALTER RALEIGH AND THE BEGINNINGS OF THE BRITISH EMPIRE

On October 29, 1618, Sir Walter Raleigh was publicly executed in London, a city he had loved. Raleigh had once been among the richest and most powerful men in the kingdom. At the height of his influence, he had originated English colonization of America. Even the prosecutor who called for his execution said of him, "He hath been a star at which the world hath gazed."

Raleigh, like many great men and women of his time, viewed the world as a theater and saw himself as acting out predetermined roles. Thus, he stage managed his own execution so that it would be remembered by all who saw or read about it. Onlookers marveled at his self-possession. As he was taken past the scaffold on which he was to die to the room where he was to spend his last night, he met a friend and asked him to come and witness the execution. He warned that there would be crowds: "I know not what shift you will make, but I am sure to have a place." When he was admonished for joking about such a serious matter, he answered, "Give me leave to be merry, for this is the last merriment that ever I shall have in the world: but when I come to the sad part, thou shalt see, I will look on it like a man."

He believed that he could go to his death calmly because he was innocent of the false charge of treason on which he had been convicted. No one had worked harder or devoted more of his life to serving England than he had; therefore, he could die with an easy conscience. On the morning of his execution he was "very cheerful." He ate heartily and smoked his pipe (his own settlers from the Roanoke colony had made smoking popular in England), "and made no more of his death, than it had been to take a journey; and left a great impression in the minds of those that beheld him."

It was customary for the condemned man to make a final speech on the scaffold. Raleigh first told the audience that the malaria he had caught on his American adventures might make him shake, but he would not shake with fear. When he saw some noblemen looking down from a window, he shouted so they could hear him; instead, they came down and sat with him on the scaffold. Next he went through the list of charges against him, maintaining his innocence of all of them.

So effective was his speech and manner, according to one eyewitness, that many of his enemies who had come to gloat at his death found their feelings completely changed, "and turned their joy to sorrow, [and] it filled all men else with emotion and admiration." At the end he asked the spectators to join him in prayer. Then he distributed some small presents to those around him, saying, "I have a long journey to go, and therefore will take my leave."

The spectators then left the scaffold and the executioner approached. Raleigh asked to see the axe. The executioner was upset and held back. Raleigh said to him, "I pray thee let me see it. Dost thou think that I am afraid of it?" As he tested the axe's edge with his finger, he remarked, "This is a sharp medicine, but it is a physician for all diseases." He then knelt down and put his head on the block. One of his friends said he should face east, toward Jerusalem, but he answered, "What matter how the head lie, so the heart be right." He refused a blindfold and controlled the event right up to the end. He said he would lift his hand when he was ready. The executioner, perhaps overcome with emotion, stood still despite the signal. Raleigh admonished him, "What dost thou fear? Strike, man!" Then the axe fell and Raleigh's life was over. The manner of his death would not be forgotten, even hundreds of years later.

Raleigh's fall was great because he had risen so high. No one could have guessed when he first made London his home, almost forty years before his death, that his life would follow a roller-coaster curve from obscurity to the heights of power and wealth, then down again to prison and a criminal's death. His life and death illustrate the grandeur and possibilities of the period of Queen Elizabeth I, England's great monarch. One of these possibilities was the creation of an English empire in America, which Raleigh worked tirelessly to bring about. Raleigh's career also illustrates the risks and dangers of the time: The schemes that helped build England's greatness and his own power also brought him to disgrace.

London was a powerfully exciting city at the end of the sixteenth century. Everyone felt it. The city was a magnet drawing the young in search of opportunities from all over England. Talented people came to find like-minded friends, and literary circles burgeoned. William Shakespeare and Ben Jonson created plays that drew high and low to the theater—a different play every day, sometimes two a day. Criers would travel through the city calling out the names of the plays, and fans would flock to the Globe Theatre and its rivals, where rich and poor jostled together.

On the Thames, ships set out for ports around the world, returning with unheard-of luxuries and exotic items—tobacco, chocolate, and sugar from America, silks and spices from the Orient. The whole world was opening up, and England was determined to be at the center. First Portugal and then Spain had been leaders in world exploration, but the English were determined to change this. No longer would they be an insignificant little country on the fringes of Europe!

The English were not just seeking glory for themselves, they were fighting for God and "true religion," by which they meant Protestantism. All Europe was involved in a great struggle over religion. As the sixteenth century opened, Europe was almost completely Roman Catholic, all countries paying homage to the pope in Rome. Beginning with Martin Luther's defiance in Germany in 1517, this unity was shattered.

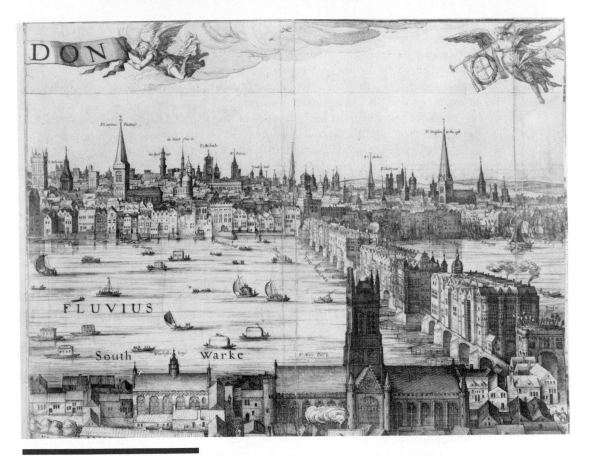

London Bridge. John Visscher's 1616 engraving shows the city teeming with life and projects, with the ship-filled Thames River as its central artery. (Trustees of the British Museum)

Luther argued not only that the Roman Catholic church was corrupt, but that it had misread the Bible. He asserted that faith, not good works and sacraments, was the way to salvation. The movement he began spread over much of northern Europe. England became Protestant, as did the Netherlands and the Scandinavian nations. Germany, which was made up at that time of more than 300 small states and principalities, was split, as was France, between Catholics and Protestants.

Spain, the leader of the Roman Catholic nations, led the fight to try to force the newly Protestant countries back into allegiance to the pope. England, a much weaker nation, took on the role of leader of the Protestants. The English believed that God had specially selected them to carry the truth around the world. Their sense of national pride and their belief that they were fighting for truth against Spain, "the sword of that Antichrist of Rome," gave impetus to their attempts to build a great empire.

The nation looked to Queen Elizabeth, who symbolized England for her subjects. She could make them believe that God really had called the English to greatness. When the pope excommunicated her as a heretic, it only made them prouder of her. She was smart, even crafty, in dealing with foreigners and managed to build her country's prestige while spending as little money as possible. She brought the most glittering people to her court to adorn it, and she was loved by her people.

Her Roman Catholic predecessor, her half-sister Mary, had been a cold, reserved woman. Elizabeth, in her formal procession through the city on the day before her coronation in 1558, told the crowds, "I will be as good unto you as ever queen was to her people. . . . And persuade yourselves, that for the safety and quietness of you all, I will not spare, if need be, to spend my blood." Raleigh compared her court to a "great theater," and all acknowledged that she played the role allotted to her well.

This scintillating London was the place Sir Walter Raleigh loved best. He was a man of many talents, and the city gave him the chance to show them off. The literary world prized him for his poetry. He could hold his own with the best of them in raucous evenings in the inns and taverns. He found a new world of interest in overseas ventures, and conferred with ship captains and mapmakers, who brought news of uncharted lands. He wanted a part in the great campaign to make the world acknowledge England's greatness. And, most important, the queen loved him. It was her love that made possible his great power and actions.

Elizabeth liked to have young, witty men at her court, and Raleigh, famous for his puns and clever verses, became her favorite soon after he came to live permanently in the city in 1582. The queen, who had now ruled for twenty-four years, was in her late forties; Raleigh was twenty years younger, but he courted her in his poems, writing that her eyes "set my fancy on fire" and her red hair held "my heart in chains."

The old story that he first caught her attention by putting his brand-new cloak on a puddle before her feet may very well be true. He wore beautiful and expensive clothes to please the queen and cultivated his dark, exotic good looks. He sported one huge pearl earring, which became his trademark.

Though he could play the lighthearted young suitor to the middle-aged Queen Elizabeth, Raleigh had already lived through a world of experiences before he came to London. He was certainly not born to that elegant world. His family was an old and distinguished one, but his father was not a rich man; Raleigh grew up on the family's farm in Devonshire in the west of England. This part of England looked out to the sea, and young Walter grew up hearing stories of great maritime exploits.

His mother had been married before, and Walter had older half brothers, John, Humphrey, and Adrian Gilbert. Humphrey was in his teens when Walter was born in 1554, and Raleigh looked up to him all his life. It was through Humphrey that Raleigh received introductions to many roles he would play as an adult. Humphrey was a pioneer in arguing for an empire that would make England great.

English men and women typically left home for good when they were about fourteen, and Raleigh was no exception. Whereas young people of humble origins started their careers as servants, working in someone's home, farm, or workshop, Raleigh prepared himself for the life of a gentleman by going off to war with a company of gentlemen from Devonshire to fight on the side of the French Protestants, called Huguenots, against the Roman Catholic French in 1568. It was a brutal introduction to life for a young teenager. The fighting was vicious. Young Raleigh returned home after four years a cynical eighteen-year-old.

When he returned to England in 1572, Raleigh registered at Oxford University, but apparently did not spend much time there. In 1575 he registered at the Inns of Court in London, which served as England's law school. Here, at the age of twenty-one, he became part of his older half brother Humphrey Gilbert's circle and was introduced to the plans being made for English exploration abroad. Gilbert was convinced that there must be a passage through the continent of North America that would allow the English to reach the riches of the Orient, and he was trying to find backers for a scheme to look for it. Raleigh was entranced to be a part of such big plans. He began to evolve his personal style. He published his first book of poetry in 1576, and he became known for his rowdy style of life. His drunken exploits were legendary.

This exciting time was not to last, however, for there was more war in Raleigh's future. In 1580, when he was twenty-six, he went to England's most difficult war, that in Ireland. Earlier, in France, he could believe he was helping honest Protestants to free themselves of Roman Catholic tyranny, but the Irish war offered no such justification. England had ancient claims on paper to Ireland, but actually bringing Ireland under control was quite another matter. The religious conflict of Protestants vs. Roman Catholics all over Europe made it imperative for England to control Ireland. The Irish had remained Roman Catholic when the English became Protestant, and the Irish hated the English. Therefore, if Spain or some other Catholic power wanted to invade England, the English feared that Ireland would offer them a good base. The English believed they had to conquer Ireland once and for all.

The fighting here was more vicious than in France. The Irish used guerrilla tactics. English commanders, perhaps because their cause was so suspect, called the Irish "barbarians," even "cannibals," then used these names to justify English actions. One commander wrote from Ireland that the Irish "live like beasts, void of law and all good order." He said they were "more uncivil, more uncleanly, more barbarous and more brutish in their customs and demeanors, than in any other part of the world that is known." Therefore, according to the English, the most severe tactics were acceptable.

Sir Humphrey Gilbert had been commander in the Irish province of Munster in 1570, ten years before Raleigh went, and he had become famous as the most ferocious and brutal of all the English. When Raleigh went to Ireland, he must have had his beloved brother's actions in his mind. Gilbert had instituted a system of total war, in which women and children were executed along with soldiers. It was said that when his troops moved through the country not a living creature was left behind. He lined the path to his tent with the severed heads of those he had slaughtered, in order to "bring great terror to the people when they saw the heads of their dead fathers, brothers, children, kinsfolk and friends, lie on the ground before their faces, as they came to speak with the said colonel."

Raleigh was plunged immediately into the slaughter that was still going on ten years later when he arrived. He participated in the conquest of the Irish fortress at Smerwick, which was garrisoned by 400 Spanish and Italian volunteers who had come to help their fellow Roman Catholics as the English had helped the French Protestants. In addition, the fort held about 200 Irish women and children. The English commander, Lord Grey of Wilton, decreed that all the captives be killed, despite the fact that he had apparently promised them their safety if they surrendered.

Lord Grey ordered Raleigh and another captain to oversee the slaughter. The 200 men they commanded carried out the executions of the 600 captives that day. It must have been a horrifying experience. As a commander, Raleigh would have had to deal with the hundreds of condemned men, women, and children, who pleaded in agony as they waited their turn during that long day. The English forces, in order to kill so many in one day, would have had to take great care that their swords did not become dull. If they killed the victims with a thrust in the stomach, that would preserve the sword's sharpness but result in a slower and more painful death. Highly skilled soldiers could strike a clean blow through the neck without hitting any edge-dulling bone. Lord Grey's report to Queen Elizabeth described the slaughtered garrison: "as gallant and good personages as ever beheld."

That Raleigh never spoke of his Irish service in his later life indicates he found the memory painful. He knew he would have been treated the same way had he been captured in France. He sent his own analysis of the Irish problem to the court—a daring thing for a junior officer to do. He argued that the war was all wrong, that the Irish should be wooed rather than battered into submission. Having seen two vicious wars in which religion was an issue, he hoped for better solutions to England's problems.

Finally, in 1582 Walter Raleigh came to London and found his natural home: the court of Queen Elizabeth. Raleigh's rise to preeminence among the queen's favorites meant fabulous wealth and power. Those she favored she showered with estates and monopolies over production or import of key commodities. Raleigh, in addition to estates in England and Ireland, won monopolies on the importation of sweet wines, the export of woolen cloth—England's most important product—and tin production in Cornwall. This meant his agents could rake off a percentage of profits, and Raleigh's men saw that he always got his cut. He soon became the equivalent of a modern millionaire.

These monopolies, which could easily degenerate into mere corruption, were Elizabeth's way of concentrating national resources in the hands of men such as Raleigh who could then use them in great ventures that would benefit the entire country. Raleigh, probably more than anyone in England, was ready to make use of the opportunities such wealth offered. He reinvested his wealth in projects to raise England to great-nation status. He had learned well the lessons gained while listening to the great plans of Humphrey Gilbert and his advisers. Now that he was the queen's favorite, he suddenly had the wealth and power to try to make those dreams come true.

Walter Raleigh, like many of his countrymen, was unhappy with England's lowly position. The great superpower of the age was Spain, the leader of the Roman Catholic nations. There was no mystery about the sources of Spain's preeminence: its great American empire and the fabulous riches of the Aztecs and Incas. While England had myopically focused on subduing the Irish threat, Spain had conquered half the New World and achieved unparalleled wealth and power.

The Spanish empire was a remarkable structure for the sixteenth century, because it was highly organized from top to bottom. All expeditions were sent out directly by the king, and the royal government required elaborate reports from everyone in the field, which were funneled through the Council of the Indies. These reports were actually read, often by the king himself, and new directions sent back. The empire functioned almost like a modern bureaucracy. All trade was licensed through the Casa de Contratación in Seville, which also kept accounts of all revenues. The empire was divided into two viceroyalties, New Spain and Peru, and each was divided into *audiencias*, which were again subdivided into *presidencias*, and so on. Everything went through the chain of command. No other American empire built by a European nation attempted anything quite like this.

When Raleigh looked at Spain, he saw clear lessons for England. Spain had become powerful through the riches the conquest produced. England was weak and backward because it had lagged behind. Nearly a century had passed since word of the newly discovered continents had spread over Europe. England had established claims to North America by the voyages of John and Sebastian Cabot, sent out within the first decade after 1492; yet the nation had done next to nothing to develop these claims. Raleigh and his associates, ashamed of English slackness, were determined to rectify that neglect.

With an American empire, England would also become a world-class power, and by doing so, it could both help itself and strike a blow at Spain. For the time being, nothing could be done about the Spanish possessions, but at least Spain could be prevented from taking over North America as well. And England could show the world how colonization ought to be done. Raleigh and his friends were disgusted by the Spanish example, which they interpreted as a ruthless search for gold to the exclusion of all else. When the Indians died out, the Spanish imported slaves from Africa in huge numbers to take their places on the plantations and in the silver mines.

A Spanish priest, Bartolomeo de las Casas, wrote a book vividly depicting the suffering of the Indians, *A Brief Relation of the Destruction of the Indies*, published in 1552. It was translated into English as *The Tears of the Indians* in 1583, just at the time Raleigh was becoming interested in founding a colony, and it horrified the English public. Raleigh and other English promoters believed they could show the world an empire that would not inflict such injustice, either on Indians or on Africans.

In 1584, when Raleigh began to plan for his first settlement at Roanoke, his associate Richard Hakluyt, a geographer, wrote a long treatise for Queen Elizabeth explaining why England needed colonies, and why she should help Raleigh. In this *Discourse of Western Planting* he quoted Las Casas to demonstrate that Spain's was an evil empire. Hakluyt and Raleigh strongly believed that the Indians and Africans who had been enslaved by the Spanish would rise up and greet the English as liberators, "to shake off from their shoulders the most intolerable and insupportable yoke of Spain." Hakluyt quoted numerous instances of torture and claimed 12 million Americans had died in the first forty years of Spanish rule, because of the Spaniards' "most outrageous and more than Turkish cruelties in all the West Indies, whereby they are everywhere there become most odious unto them."

This was mostly just big talk in the early 1580s. England had a long way to go before it could mount a successful challenge. The country was backward in every way. Though English ships went every summer to fish off the Newfoundland Banks, English mariners lacked the skill to navigate the much more difficult journey to the islands of the Caribbean and the coast north of Florida. When English ships sailed into those regions, they were forced to rely on Portuguese pilots to guide them, a humiliating experience.

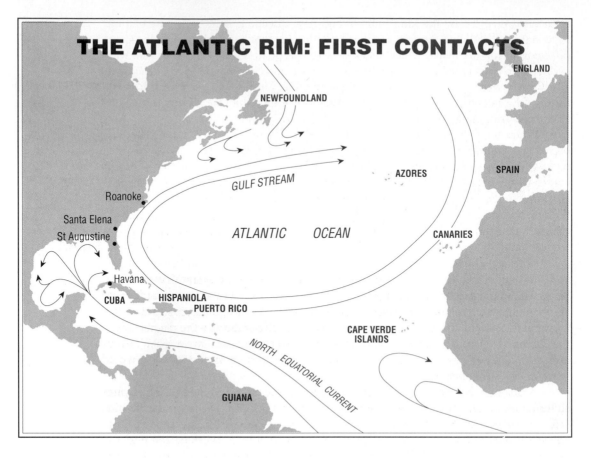

THE ATLANTIC RIM: FIRST CONTACTS

ENGLAND

NEWFOUNDLAND

GULF STREAM

AZORES

SPAIN

Roanoke

ATLANTIC   OCEAN

Santa Elena
St Augustine

CANARIES

Havana

CUBA   HISPANIOLA
PUERTO RICO

CAPE VERDE
ISLANDS

NORTH EQUATORIAL CURRENT

GUIANA

Nor were the English competitive with the Spanish and Portuguese in the theoretical knowledge needed to make the maps and charts essential to colonization. Whereas Oxford and Cambridge, the ancient universities of England, disdained mathematics and geography as mere "practical" subjects unworthy of their notice, Spain and Portugal had long since established academies where sea captains learned the basic trigonometry required for navigation by stars and sun out of sight of land, and surveyors learned how to make accurate maps.

Raleigh, whose new wealth and position at court made action possible, was determined to change all this. Durham House, a London mansion given him by the queen, became a center of experts planning a new role for England, a kind of "think tank" where they could pool their knowledge. Raleigh amassed his own fleet and hired a young scholar from Oxford, Thomas Hariot, to create a textbook on navigation and teach it to his captains. Geographer Richard Hakluyt was also part of this group. He went on to devote his life to gathering all the information available about America and published it in massive collections, the most famous of which was *Principal Navigations, Voyages, Traffics, and Discoveries of the English Nation*, which appeared between 1589 and 1600. All this was part of the campaign to focus the nation's attention on America.

Technical advances. Under the guidance and prodding of such pioneers as Sir John Hawkins, Sir Francis Drake, and Raleigh, English ship designers developed innovative new forms that laid the foundation for English mastery of the seas. This painting of shipwrights working out a new hull design is by Matthew Baker, himself a master shipwright. (Magdalene College, Cambridge, England)

The Durham House group generated an atmosphere of tremendous excitement. England was poised for takeoff as a colonial power. The key problem was finding the money to finance ventures. Establishing a colony cost enormous amounts of money—comparable to building a large and continuously occupied station on the moon today—and, given the fact that it would take years before settlers could even establish themselves and become self-sufficient, it was unclear what they could produce that would repay such outlays of money.

This was where the key difference between the Spanish and the English empires became important. Spain's great empire was funded and controlled by the Spanish crown. But Elizabeth and her successors never had the money to finance such grandiose projects. Colonization had to be underwritten by private investors, as a business proposition. Elizabeth gave Raleigh the exclusive right to colonize in North America. He could then attract investors and colonists and set up his colonies as he wished. As with all monopolies, Raleigh would expect to make money off his colonies. He saw nothing wrong with mixing public service and private gain.

Raleigh knew just how his ventures would make money. He would set up a colony as an American base for his fleet, which could then dart out and attack Spanish ships as they carried the wealth of the Aztecs and Incas home to Spain. He knew that all the treasure produced in the Spanish colonies was carried every year to Havana and from there loaded onto huge ships knows as carracks. Once a year a great convoy of these carracks, which were slow and clumsy, made its way from Havana to Seville. If English sailors could detach and capture even one ship, riches beyond belief would flow to the investors. This kind of piracy, known as privateering, was considered legal, even patriotic, because it was carried out against England's enemy.

An American colony, then, would allow Raleigh to do everything he wanted: strengthen England, enrich himself, and harm Spain. In 1584 he sent out a reconnaissance voyage to find a good location for his base. After a few weeks, his ships returned with the news that the Carolina Outer Banks offered the perfect site. The

Outer Banks are long sandbars along the coast, and sheltered within them was little Roanoke Island—hidden away and yet close to the Spanish islands. Arthur Barlowe, one of the captains, described Roanoke as almost a paradise: "We found the people most gentle, loving, and faithful, void of all guile, and treason, and such as lived after the manner of the golden age. The earth bringeth forth all things in abundance, as in the first creation, without toil or labor."

Barlowe told Raleigh what he wanted to hear, and immediate plans were drawn up to send a colony. Only later would Raleigh realize that such lavish praise could not be true and only set up the colonists for greater failure later. It turned out that Roanoke was a very poor site. The sandbars that made up the island and the Outer Banks lacked the fertility to sustain a large English population, and the surrounding waters were so shallow that the great ships had to anchor miles out to sea, exposed to furious Atlantic storms and visible to the enemy. Roanoke, the first English colony, was useless for the purpose for which it was designed, but only long and painful experience would make that clear.

In the spring of 1585 Raleigh dispatched the first contingent of English colonists to America. After choosing the location, the next problem was to select the people who would go. Raleigh made the most obvious choice: The settlement would be made up of young men, preferably with military experience. They could then defend themselves against both the Indians and the Spanish, and they ought to be able to spend the rest of their time exploring. Raleigh thought of setting up a colony as similar to sending an expedition to France or to Ireland.

Anyone would probably have made the same choice, but we now know this was the worst possible model for a colony. The young men tended to fall apart in the isolation and frustration, and they were difficult to control. Ralph Lane, who was the governor of this first Roanoke colony, said that while the American "savages" posed great challenges to the settlement, many of his worst problems stemmed from "the wild men of my own nation." Also, these men, many of whom were veterans of the religious wars in Europe or English campaigns in Ireland, always thought of force as a solution to all situations. They visualized Indian relations as basically a question of which side would dominate, and they wanted to make sure the English would always be on top. Their attitudes and methods destroyed any possibility of peaceful and friendly relations with the Indians.

The little fleet carrying England's first American colonists set out in early spring of 1585. When they arrived at Roanoke on June 29, they immediately found out that the Outer Banks were a poor place for a colony. The *Tiger*, the ship carrying almost all the provisions that were to feed the colonists over the winter, ran aground on the treacherous sandbars. Everything was ruined. It was too late to plant food crops. And all winter long the stormy Atlantic was too dangerous to cross. This meant that the colonists would have to get all their food from the Indians—and of course the Indians had had no advance warning that they would be expected to keep over a hundred extra people fed for almost a year. It was a situation set up for disaster.

Nonetheless, the colonists set to work building their settlement under the direction of Ralph Lane. Meanwhile, Sir Richard Grenville, commander of the fleet, took some of the smaller boats and explored the sounds between the Outer Banks and the

An Indian village. John White painted the Carolina Algonquian village of Secoton after his return from Roanoke. White was eager to demonstrate to European audiences that the Indians encountered by the Roanoke colonists were not nomadic savages, but lived a settled village life. He showed corn at three different stages of growth, and included scenes of Indian religious and family life. (The New York Public Library, Rare Book Division, Astor, Lenox and Tilden Foundations)

mainland. Grenville graphically taught the Indians what the coming of the Europeans would mean to them. One of his men kept a terse record of their stops:

> *The 12*. we came to the Town of Pomeiocke.
> *The 13*. we passed by water to Aquascococke.
> *The 15*. we came to Secotan and were well entertained there of the Savages.
> *The 16*. we returned thence, and one of our boats with the Admiral was sent to Aquascococke to demand a silver cup which one of the Savages had stolen from us, and not receiving it according to his promise, we burnt, and spoiled their corn, and Town, all the people being fled.

This is hard to believe. Grenville knew that the hundred-plus men he was leaving in Roanoke would be utterly dependent on the Indians for food. Yet here he was not only committing an incredibly hostile act, but destroying some of that food which would soon be in such short supply. Why would he do such a thing?

These colonizers saw all life as a struggle for domination. Grenville believed that either the colonists would dominate the Indians or vice versa. Despite what theorists like Hakluyt wrote in England, Grenville's thinking was much closer to the Spanish model. He and most of the leaders like him believed that if the colonists ever showed the slightest sign of weakness, the Indians would realize they had the upper hand and the English would be at their mercy. He honestly thought he was protecting the colonists in the most effective way.

Ralph Lane, fresh from service in Ireland, carried on in the same tradition after he and his colonists were left alone. When he wanted to ensure cooperation of an Indian leader, he kidnapped his "best beloved son" and held him hostage. Because of such behavior, but even more because the colonists' incessant demands for food pressed the Indians so hard, relations deteriorated. Lane had expected fresh supplies from England in April, but they did not arrive. Meanwhile, the Roanoke chief, Wingina, had become rich and powerful because he had acquired so much English copper and so many European goods in return for corn. Lane became convinced Wingina was forming a large coalition to wipe out the settlement, so he and his men planned a preemptive strike. In a surprise attack on June 1, 1586, the colonists began their "slaughter, and surprise of the Savages" with the watchword of the day: "Christ our victory." Wingina was killed and his severed head displayed on a post. All possibility of good relations with the Roanoke Indians was over.

Now the situation was truly desperate. Food supplies were almost completely gone. A week later, June 8, the lookout sighted ships, "but whether they were friends or foes, he could not yet discern, but advised me to stand upon as good guard as I could." They turned out to be English, but not the anticipated supply fleet. These were the ships of Sir Francis Drake, who had been privateering in the Spanish colonies for almost a year and had arrived at Roanoke hoping to inaugurate its role as a rest and repair center. Instead, he found the colonists desperate and in disarray, unable to feed even themselves, much less all of Drake's men.

After some discussion, Drake agreed to take them all home. They sailed June 19, after Drake's impatient sailors threw overboard almost everything the settlers had collected in their year in America: "the most of all we had, with all our Cards [maps], Books and writings, were by the Sailors cast overboard, the greater number of the Fleet being much aggrieved with their long and dangerous abode in that miserable road." Among the articles lost was a "fair chain" of native pearls Lane had hoped to present to Queen Elizabeth. This was the end of the first Roanoke colony. Raleigh's supply ships were already at sea, but they arrived to find the island deserted.

Lane's colony was not just a failure, however, nor had it ever been just a military outpost. Raleigh had sent along two men, his scientific adviser Thomas Hariot, and an artist named John White, to investigate the country and make a record of Indian life and culture and of the flora, fauna, and resources of the region. Hariot had prepared for the task by learning the Algonquians' language from two Indians, Manteo and Wanchese, who had been brought to England by the reconnoitering voyage in 1584. Hariot and White's report was the finest discussion of America's natural history and Indian life produced in the entire colonial period. They also created the most accurate map of any part of America done to that time. Moreover, an exploring party from

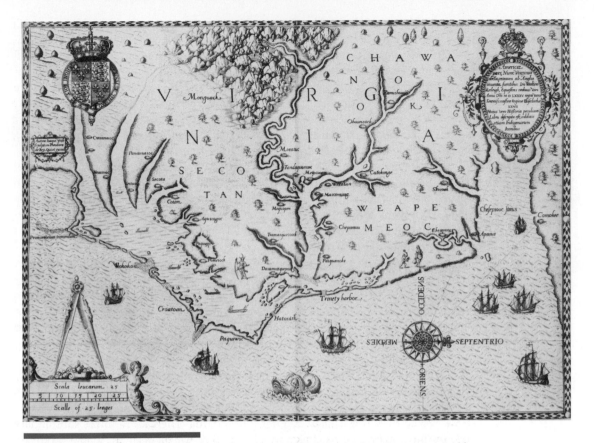

Roanoke and Chesapeake Bay. Theodore DeBry engraved this map, based on an original by John White, for his edition of Hariot's *Brief and True Report* (1590). The map demonstrates the sophistication of Hariot and White's survey of the immediate Roanoke area, and showed prospective investors that even though Roanoke was a poor site, Chesapeake Bay was nearby and was a good prospect for a permanent colony. (John Carter Brown Library at Brown University)

Roanoke had discovered a much better site for a colony to the north, along one of the rivers that fed Chesapeake Bay. This site had what Roanoke lacked: It could shelter a settlement from enemy eyes, yet was approachable by oceangoing ships; the James River was navigable for many miles. So deep was the river that the largest oceangoing ship could be tied up to a tree branch.

Raleigh determined to try again, and in his plans for the new colony, his real genius shone through. Instead of tinkering with this or that aspect of the old plans, he realized that a completely new approach was called for. He decided to put his colony on Chesapeake Bay, and to scrap the idea of sending soldiers. This new venture was to have families for its settlers. Men, women, and children would go to America and work to become self-supporting. Only then could they live in peace and harmony with the Indians. And only families working on their own land would have the incentive to put in the effort to make a colony successful. Raleigh was among the first to acknowledge that women's skills were as important as men's contributions in setting up new societies in America.

The backing for the new colony was also arranged differently. Raleigh now realized that a single individual, no matter how wealthy and powerful, did not have the resources to sustain a large colonial venture. He created a joint-stock company, a kind of corporation, to sponsor the colony. Joint-stock companies, just emerging in England during the sixteenth century, were used to sponsor all kinds of activities, from Shakespeare's Globe Theatre to privateering voyages. They made it possible to pool funds and spread risks involved in big ventures.

John White, the painter, was one of the few members of Lane's colony whose enthusiasm was undiminished, and Raleigh chose him to be governor of the "City of Raleigh in Virginia." White, in turn, recruited many of the new settlers, including his pregnant daughter, Eleanor Dare, and her husband, Ananias. Eleanor was one of two women on board the ships who were pregnant. The trip across was always bad for passengers; it must have been almost intolerable for these women, and for children. Sixteenth-century ships lacked bunks or cabins. Passengers rolled up in blankets and slept on deck or, in bad weather, belowdecks. During storms, passengers were forced to remain below, where the stench quickly became intolerable. There were no toilet facilities, and seasick passengers contributed to the stench. Rats and cockroaches, stirred up by the ship's motion in a storm, and fleeing the water that inevitably leaked in, made sleeping difficult. America must have indeed looked like a paradise to this set of passengers when they finally arrived.

The settlers set out in the spring of 1587 with great enthusiasm; each family was to have 500 acres, a huge estate by English standards. The new formula, substantial families who would work hard because they worked for themselves, would produce a nearly self-sufficient plantation. This was the formula that led to success in later plantations. John White's colony should have been a glorious success, yet it became the famous Lost Colony.

How could this have happened? The answer lies in the perennial search for money. Investors had to be repaid, and sources of quick income had to be found. Raleigh had solved this problem by having his ships go privateering, but it now became clear that colonization and privateering did not mix. The fleet carrying the settlers was, as usual, under the direction of a Portuguese mariner, Simão Fernandes. Fernandes and John White hated each other, and White was horrified that Fernandes started privateering on the way to America despite the risk to the women and children. Then, when the ships made a brief stop at Roanoke on their way to Chesapeake Bay, one of Fernandes's men "called to the sailors in the pinnace, charging them not to bring any of the planters back again, but leave them in the Island . . . saying that the Summer was far spent, wherefore he would land all the planters in no other place."

White and his colonists were stunned. Fernandes, putting privateering before the colony, was jeopardizing their lives and the entire enterprise. The colonists begged White to return and describe their situation to Raleigh. He at first refused, fearing he would be accused of desertion, but was "at the last, through their extreme entreating, constrained to return into England." He embarked August 27, 1587, shortly after the birth of his granddaughter, Virginia Dare, the first English child born in America. As he said goodbye, he could not know that no European would ever see any of the 114 colonists again.

The planters expected to be resupplied in the spring. Meanwhile, they told White they would attempt to move the settlement overland to Chesapeake Bay. As soon as he was back in England, White flew to Raleigh and infected him with his own sense of urgency. As White had expected, Raleigh received his news with great concern and authorized a large fleet and new supplies, which were gathered over the winter. Just as the fleet was ready to depart in the spring of 1588, word came from the Privy Council that no ships were to be allowed to leave English ports. Spain, fed up with English interference with its ships, had decided to invade England and bring that country to its knees once and for all. Because Queen Elizabeth "doth receive daily advertisements of the preparations of the King of Spain," the "intended voyage" to the aid of the Roanoke colonists was forbidden.

Raleigh's supply fleet was diverted to the national defense. Every ship was needed, because the "advertisements" reaching the queen's ears were correct. King Philip II of Spain had amassed the greatest armada the world had ever seen to finish off England's resistance to his power. In one of the most dramatic moments in English history, the Spanish Goliath was met by the English David. Queen Elizabeth, at Tilbury to review the troops massed to resist the threatened invasion, gave one of her most famous speeches, in which she said, "I know I have the body of a weak and feeble woman, but I have the heart and stomach of a king, and of a king of England too, and think foul scorn that Parma or Spain, or any prince of Europe should dare to invade the borders of my realm." Never had she been more popular with her people. Storms (some said the hand of God) scattered the Spanish fleet, and many of the sailors were lost. Philip II's dream of finishing off England was not fulfilled.

But the armada did help kill Raleigh's Roanoke colony. Just as privateering was the reason the colony had first come into existence, now it was privateering, or at least the outcome of privateering, that ended it. No supplies were sent to the settlers in 1588, nor in 1589. Raleigh's attention was increasingly diverted to other projects. Elizabeth granted him large estates in Ireland, and he was collecting colonists and supplies to be sent there while his Roanoke colonists were being neglected. Only John White continued to put the Roanoke settlement first in his concerns, working constantly to attract attention to their plight. Twice White managed to get passage on small ships that he hoped would look for the planters, but each time the mariners just went privateering instead.

Finally, in 1590, White returned to Roanoke Island. The landfall was made at evening, and "we saw a great smoke rise in the Isle Roanoke near the place where I left our Colony in the year 1587, which smoke put us in good hope that some of the Colony were there expecting my return out of England." As they anchored near the spot, White and the sailors "sounded with a trumpet a Call, & afterwards many familiar English tunes of Songs, and called to them friendly; but we had no answer." Next morning they found the village deserted. The smoke came from brushfires kindled by lightning.

White was disappointed, but not desolate. He and his party found the word CROATOAN carved on a post. A Maltese cross would have indicated that the colonists had left in distress, but just the one word had been carved. And the settlers had carefully buried everything they could not take with them. They clearly had not been

Queen Elizabeth I. This portrait, painted to commemorate England's victory in 1588 over the Spanish Armada, shows the country's inflated claims to mastery as the Spanish ships go down to destruction in a God-sent storm in the right corner, and Elizabeth's hand rests on a globe of the world under a representation of the serene English fleet. Pearls such as those adorning her dress and hair were one goal of overseas colonies. (Woburn Abbey Collection, by permission of the Marquess of Tavistock and the trustees of Bedford Estates)

wiped out, nor had they left in a hurry. Croatoan, the home of Manteo, who had spent time in England, and the sole village that had remained friendly to the Lane colony, would be a natural place for them to go. White was actually encouraged.

But as the ships prepared to make the short journey south to Croatoan Island, a great storm blew up. The *Hopewell*, White's ship, lost two of its three anchors in attempts to avoid being hurled against the Outer Banks. With only one anchor standing between the ship and certain disaster, the master insisted on leaving that dangerous area. The second, smaller ship had already deserted the cause. White and the *Hopewell*'s master agreed to seek aid in the West Indies before resuming the search for the colonists, but the vagaries of wind and weather pushed them toward home.

Inexplicably, that was the last attempt to find the families of the Roanoke Lost Colony until 1603, when one ship made a slender effort. When Jamestown was founded in 1607, twenty years after the Lost Colony's abandonment, the settlers heard vague rumors of people like them who had lived on Chesapeake Bay until they had been wiped out by Powhatan, the dominant Indian leader of the region, but nothing of theirs was ever found.

Why was nothing done? The answer to that question lies in the basic conception of the English empire. Two things would have to change before colonies would be successful. One was the practice of associating colonization with privateering. The 1590s, the period when the colonists might still have been found if anyone had looked for them, was the great age of privateering; English ships swarmed over the Atlantic and West Indies, and they found they could be highly successful without a base such as Roanoke. As long as privateering was the goal, colonies were unnecessary. Privateering could bring in vast wealth with a single lucky strike; a settlement would be nothing but a drain for a long time and might never have anything to offer but basic agricultural commodities.

The idea that a single great man could control colonization also had to be abandoned. Even at the height of his wealth and power, Raleigh never had sufficient resources to people and supply Roanoke for as long as would be necessary. More important, his position was never secure. In the early 1590s he began to be edged out of the favorite's role at Elizabeth's court. The tall, young, glamorous earl of Essex had appeared at court and caught the queen's eye. Moreover, Raleigh was maturing and longed for a family of his own. The queen could not tolerate disloyalty among her courtiers. When Raleigh's secret marriage to Bess Throckmorton, one of the queen's ladies-in-waiting, was revealed by her pregnancy, Elizabeth threw both of them into prison in the Tower of London. She soon freed the couple, but sent them into exile in their country home at Christmas 1592. Bess Raleigh was never again allowed to come to court.

Raleigh worked from his country retreat to be allowed once again to see his queen and take up his court position as captain of her guard. He also worked to develop his plans for a British empire. He had been so proud and arrogant when in power that many rejoiced in his disgrace, but he knew he had not yet finished his part in history. What he needed was a big strike, something that would restore his fortunes with the queen and continue his campaign for English greatness in one grand gesture. In the West Country, his mind returned again and again to a story told him by a Spanish grandee, Sarmiento de Gamboa, who had been captured by his privateers in 1586. According to this account, the wealth of the Aztecs and Incas was excelled by a third great center, the fabulously rich city of El Dorado, which lay in the region of Guiana on the South American mainland.

Raleigh determined to put together a great fleet and find that golden city and its mines. He knew that however much he had offended Elizabeth, she would not ignore him if he brought such riches to England. In 1595 the fleet of five ships set off.

Amazed at the strangeness and beauty of the country, Raleigh wrote one of the great classics of exploration literature about Guiana on his return, but the practical results of the voyage were small. Raleigh's men, like many before and after them, found the web of marshes and tributaries marking the mouth of the Orinoco River

Raleigh in the New World. Theodore DeBry published Raleigh's description of his 1595 Guiana voyage with woodcuts illustrating the action. This shows Raleigh directing the disposition of Don Antonio de Berrio, the Spanish commander taken prisoner when Raleigh's men attacked San Josef, Trinidad. (The New York Public Library, Rare Book Division, Astor, Lenox and Tilden Foundations)

extremely confusing. Raleigh interviewed many Indians and even some captured Spaniards who were also searching for the fabled gold, and he was thoroughly convinced that a rich mine existed, but though he wrote that "every stone that we stopped to take up promised either gold or silver by his complexion," none of the samples he brought back proved worthwhile.

He claimed this voyage had never been intended as anything more than a reconnaissance, and vowed to return. His quest was for the gold, but he was also attracted to the alien land and its strange people and beasts; Raleigh was convinced that the Amazons of ancient legend lived beyond the gold in the interior. He had gleaned this knowledge from his long and cordial talks with Indian leaders, who had also convinced him that the English would be welcome along the Orinoco. Raleigh, like Richard Hakluyt, believed the natives lived in terror of the cruel Spanish and that they would rise up to aid English liberators and would gladly share their wealth. The English, unlike the Spanish, would not come as parasites.

The Guiana voyage did not accomplish what Raleigh had intended; too many false hopes had been generated by other voyages. London had gone wild over tons of ore brought back by other voyages to other parts of America, and had turned against such ventures when it all proved worthless. Promises and rumors were not enough; provable ore or tangible gems were required to entice skeptical backers. Though Raleigh continued to nourish hopes of a gold mine in Guiana, he found no enthusiasm among those who would have to lay out money for another voyage.

The next year Raleigh turned his attention to the threat of Spain nearer home. In 1596 in association with his rival, the earl of Essex, and the lord admiral, Charles Howard, Raleigh became involved in a massive plan to attack the great Spanish port of Cadiz, humiliating Spain and cutting off supplies to Spanish America. Nothing shows England's scale of values more clearly than this venture. At a time when Raleigh and the businessmen who had backed the City of Raleigh corporation could not spare one or two ships to seek the Lost Colonists, a great fleet of ninety-six English and more than twenty Dutch ships carrying 10,000 soldiers was amassed to take and loot Cadiz.

The Cadiz expedition was not a great success. The city was taken, but the forces spent their energies in a frenzy of sacking and pillaging. Nothing of permanent importance was gained; after about ten days the fleet left for home despite Essex's contention that Cadiz should be held for England. Raleigh, wounded in the initial attack, limped painfully for the rest of his life.

All had been worthwhile from Raleigh's point of view, however, because he had regained the queen's favor. He would never be singled out as before, but he was welcome at court and once again the recipient of favors. But the old queen's reign was drawing to a close. With her death in 1603, the first phase of England's interest in America, and especially the virulent anti-Spanish emphasis, would end. Elizabeth's successor, James I, who was also king of Scotland and the first of the long Stuart line of monarchs, wanted to avoid war at all costs. He sought to conciliate England's enemies rather than defy them. At times he even seemed to be pro-Spanish.

Raleigh was out of tune with the new regime. Most courtiers, seeing that Elizabeth was dying, had secretly approached James in Scotland to secure a place of favor in the new regime. Raleigh was one of the few who remained steadfastly loyal to Elizabeth right to the end. In flattering and fawning over the man who was soon to be king, other men hoped not only to enhance their own status in the new reign but also to harm those who might be rivals. Raleigh's refusal to play this game cost him heavily. His rivals poisoned the new king's mind against him, convincing James that Raleigh was plotting against him. When they met, James, indulging in one of the puns he loved so much, said: "On my soul, man, I have heard rawly of thee." Raleigh was soon hit by a series of blows; one by one he lost the sources of income and many of the estates that had been Elizabeth's gifts.

Soon the greatest blow of all fell: Raleigh was committed to the Tower of London on a charge of high treason. The charge was ludicrous; he was said to have conspired with Spain against England. It was almost as if the government had looked for the most farfetched accusation they could have made. Even Raleigh's enemies considered it impossible that he, the leader of those who hated Spain, would have done anything to help that country.

But Raleigh did have many enemies; his arrogance in his days of power had alienated many. One courtier had said of him when he was at his most powerful that he was "the best hated man of the world, in Court, city, and country." Now, in 1603 his humiliation created deep satisfaction at court, and crowds gathered to jeer him on his way to trial. Though his dignity and courage were to win over the crowd, he was convicted as everyone knew he would be and sentenced to a traitor's death.

King James was too smart to create a martyr, though, and offered Raleigh his life, to be spent in imprisonment in the Tower of London. The original sentence remained in effect; James could have him executed at any time.

Raleigh remained in prison for twelve years. He had an apartment and could receive guests; the Raleighs had a son during the Tower years. In some ways these were the most productive years of his life, for he devoted them to writing and to scientific experiments. Much of his reputation as a Renaissance man stems from this period. The governor of the Tower allowed him to cultivate a garden for his medicinal experiments, and he and his fellow prisoner, the earl of Northumberland, set up a laboratory. Thomas Hariot brought them books and worked with them.

Among Raleigh's frequent visitors was Henry, Prince of Wales, son and heir of King James. Henry was only fourteen when he began to visit Raleigh, but he already showed signs of the intelligence and independence that gave observers hope the kingdom would be run very differently when he came to the throne. Raleigh began to teach the boy about statecraft and policy; for Henry's benefit he began his great prose work, *The History of the World*. Prince Henry respected Raleigh, and remarked that "no king but my father would keep such a bird in a cage." But Henry died in 1612 at the age of eighteen of typhoid fever he caught from swimming in the foul Thames River. Raleigh, completely discouraged, quit writing his *History* after completing just one volume. Though its immediate object had been lost, the book went through many editions within a few years and is considered one of the great classics of English literature.

During his imprisonment, Raleigh's thoughts turned again and again to Guiana. King James was chronically short of money, so even he could not be indifferent to the gold Raleigh was sure existed there. If only he could return to the Orinoco, he was certain he could locate the mine. Raleigh began a campaign to present his case to the king.

While Raleigh spun his dreams of a great gold strike, other patriotic Englishmen had founded Jamestown in 1607, the first successful English colony in America. The colonial scene had changed greatly under the new regime. James I had shut down the successful privateering war as soon as he acceded to the throne in 1603. National leaders were angry that England was completely out of America, except for the annual fishing voyages to Newfoundland, while Spain was now allowed a free hand in extracting treasure. Since James would allow no hostile acts against Spain, patriots had decided to do what they could. This peaceful colony would prevent Spanish expansion into North America, but would be far enough away from Spain's colonies to avoid conflict. On the other hand, if war were to break out, the new colony's location would prove useful as a base.

But the new colony's first decade was a dismal one. When Jamestown did begin to emerge from its poverty, the tobacco that was Virginia's gold seemed to many a poor commodity. King James hated to see England's American empire founded on smoke, and he hated the way the habit was spreading in England:

> It makes a kitchen of the inward parts of men, soiling and infecting them with an unctuous and oily kind of soot. . . . Is it not a great vanity, that a man cannot heartily welcome his friend now, but straight they must be in hand with tobacco? . . . that the sweetness of man's breath, being a good gift of God, should be wilfully corrupted by this stinking smoke?

So James was prepared to listen to Raleigh's rich dreams, and decided the possibility of a great gold strike that would bring immediate returns was worth a try. The king agreed to let Raleigh conduct another expedition to Guiana with one proviso: There must be no hostile actions against Spanish subjects. In accepting this restriction, Raleigh was walking into a trap. Guiana was in the heart of the Spanish empire. It would be virtually impossible to go there without some clashes. He did not know how bad a trap James had set for him, however. James gave the Spanish ambassador an exact description of each of Raleigh's ships and their armaments as well as his itinerary. The Spanish knew exactly where he would be and how well he could defend himself as his little fleet set sail in June 1617.

Raleigh was now in his early sixties and not in good health. His Cadiz wound and a series of strokes suffered in the Tower had left him unsteady and in constant pain. This kind of buccaneering venture was a young man's game. Once it was under way, the expedition was plagued by problems. Devastating sickness broke out, killing many. Raleigh was too sick to travel into Guiana himself. He was forced to stay with the ships in the Caribbean while the exploring party, led by his associate Lawrence Keymis and Raleigh's son Walter, nicknamed Wat, set out up the river.

Raleigh was pleased to find that the Indians of the region remembered him; the news confirmed his belief that they would support the English against their Spanish "oppressors." He wrote to his wife, "To tell you that I might be here king of the Indians were a vanity, but my name hath still lived among them." But none of his other expectations held up. The tangled web of streams at the mouth of the Orinoco confused Keymis, who never even approached the area where the mine was thought to be, and soon the inevitable clash with Spanish soldiers occurred. Hotheaded young Wat Raleigh rashly led an attack in which he was killed, and his father's doom was sealed. Keymis returned empty-handed to tell Raleigh that his son was dead and the expedition compromised, then committed suicide in his cabin. Everything was over. Raleigh wrote to his wife, "I was loath to write, because I knew not how to comfort you: and, God knows, I never knew what sorrow meant till now."

Raleigh considered escape to France or some other friendly country, but ultimately returned to face execution on his original death warrant. King James offered to allow the king of Spain to execute Raleigh in Madrid, but Philip III wisely decided to allow James alone to bear the blame. Because he was a knight, Raleigh was allowed to die by the executioner's axe rather than the horrible traitor's death.

With Raleigh's death in 1618, the Elizabethan plan for empire was ended for good. He lived on through his writings and as a symbol. When Charles I, James's son

Sir Walter Raleigh and his son Wat, 1602. Nine-year-old Wat clearly inherited his father's determination and recklessness. Once as a young man he told an unsavory story about his father at a dinner party. Raleigh slapped the young man across the face. Wat, who did not dare to hit his own father, immediately turned and hit the man sitting next to him, saying "Box about. 'Twill come to my father anon." (National Portrait Gallery, London)

and successor, was challenged by the new Puritan opposition, Raleigh was remembered as the man who had fought for the country's true destiny under England's great Queen Elizabeth and who had been brought down by the pettiness of a Stuart king. This opposition movement would ultimately bring Charles I to the same end as Raleigh on the executioner's block at the close of the English Civil War in 1649.

Puritan leaders also revived Raleigh's dream of a great English empire in America, but here they parted company with much of his legacy. The search for gold, already anachronistic when Raleigh set out on his last Guiana voyage, was abandoned.

Instead, the enduring legacy was the one outlined by Thomas Hariot and John White at Roanoke. The real foundation of the English empire would be true colonies, settlements of English men and women who would re-create their native culture in a new environment. These colonies would enrich England by trade in commodities.

Even in 1618 when Raleigh was executed, though many in England were doubtful about it, Virginia was building a sound economy on tobacco culture, and the colony's promoters had begun to encourage families there with the promise of free land. And Plymouth colony, composed of families each on their own farm, would soon be founded in New England. The British empire of which Raleigh had dreamed was already secure.

EUROPE'S NEW WORLD

Raleigh's attempt to found the Roanoke colony was part of a long process of transplantation to the American continents. The Spanish had been involved in colonization for almost a century when Raleigh began his efforts in 1584. Moreover, the Indians were also the descendants of immigrants transplanted to the Americas thousands of years before.

When Europeans "discovered" America, they stumbled on continents that had been occupied for thousands of years by people who had developed a rich variety of cultures. The earliest explorers and colonists wondered who the Native Americans were and how they had come to America. Some Europeans thought they were the descendants of the Ten Lost Tribes of Israel. Modern archaeology has demonstrated that the American Indians share a common set of ancestors with modern Asian people.

During the last Ice Age (which began about 50,000 years ago and ended about 10,000 years ago), sea levels were lower. The Bering Strait between Siberia and Alaska was sometimes dry land. The ancestors of the modern Indians must have crossed this "land bridge" as they followed the big game animals of the period, such as mastodons. They were not conscious "immigrants"; they simply moved as the animals moved. Prob-ably only small groups found themselves on the American side, and they would have been unaware that they had crossed from one continent to another. Since the interior of the continent was under a huge glacier, their track would have taken them down the coast.

As these hunters moved over the land bridge and along the margin of the cold land, the weak and diseased would have fallen by the way. Hardship acted as a "disease filter," and many of the pathogens that constantly threatened the rest of the world were not imported into the Americas. The big game was plentiful and unwise to the ways of hunters, so, despite the cold conditions, food must have been relatively plentiful for these nomads. Scholars believe this initial small population expanded rapidly.

Major changes occurred as the world began to warm up, about 10,000 years ago, and the great animals became extinct. The ancestors of the modern Indians gradually became more sedentary; that is, they remained in the same region all the time, although they may have moved according to the seasons within that region. They came to rely more and more on hunting small animals and gathering plants for food. This naturally led to cultivation of chosen plants, which reinforced a settled life.

The Great Serpent Mound from Adena near Cincinnati, Ohio. Early explorers were only dimly aware of these massive structures and the complex cultures needed to build and maintain them. This thousand-year-old mound measures seventy-five feet across the serpent's open jaws, and its total length from head to triple-coiled tail is one-quarter mile. (Richard Erdoes)

Native American Cultures

On the basis of the artifacts and other physical evidence these early Indians left behind, archaeologists describe a succession of increasingly sophisticated cultures that grew up in the center of what would become the United States. At the same time that Christianity was beginning to win converts in the Old World, these people began to build large mounds for ceremonial and burial purposes in the New. We do not know what ceremonies were conducted around the mounds, some of which are shaped like animals. Nor do we know much about these cultures, which scientists have named the Adena and Hopewell cultures. The reasons for their disappearance are equally mysterious.

These early cultures were succeeded by one scholars call Mississippian, which is better understood. Although its great period had passed when Europeans became aware of America, Mississippian sites were still in use. The Spanish explorer Hernando de Soto met the heirs of Mississippian culture and saw their great structures as he traveled through the Southeast in 1539–40.

This culture originated, as the name indicates, along the Mississippi River. Its most highly developed center was Cahokia, near modern St. Louis at the conjunction of the Mississippi and Missouri rivers. This city of 40,000 was the largest in North America not only then but for a long time to come. Boston held only 15,000 people when the American Revolution's first shots were fired. Cahokia was the center of a vast trade and cultural network. Things made there have been found across a wide territory, and many objects from all over the continent have been unearthed in Mississippian sites along the river.

The Mississippians centered their cities on enormous mounds built like flat-topped pyramids. In many cases the large central mound would be surrounded by many smaller mounds. Some sites were so extensive that they could not really be appreciated until airplanes flew over them in this century.

The size of their cities, and the fact that they were fortified, suggests that the Mississippians may have been developing political systems in which several villages became allied or even subservient to a stronger community. Spanish and French explorers who traveled through the Southeast described highly developed political systems along the Mississippi, such as among the Natchez Indians.

The English colonies were along the Atlantic coast, far from the great Mississippian centers. But English writers at Roanoke and Jamestown also described political groupings with strong Indian chiefs at their heads. Powhatan, the father of Pocahontas, was said to be building an empire when Jamestown was colonized in 1607. He had inherited the overlordship of six tribes from his father, and he was described as the emperor of thirty. Some scholars wonder whether, if Indian life had not been disrupted by European intrusion, North American Indians might not have developed nations with powerful political structures.

At the time of colonization, though, Indian life was far removed from a European-style empire. All the Indians with whom English settlers initially came in contact were Algonquians. Names such as Algonquian, Iroquois, Athapaskan, and Sioux refer to Indian language complexes; they point to similar sources of these languages, just as French, Italian, Spanish, and Portuguese are grouped as Romance languages. The groupings do not imply that Algonquians would always be allies, or that they would even recognize any common elements with Algonquians from far away. There were many, often mutually unintelligible, languages within each group.

Though the Europeans wrote about "nations" and "empires," much of that hierarchy was in their own imaginations. Along the eastern coast, Indians were often organized at the village level, with some means for cooperation between villages when that was necessary. Chiefs usually worked by consensus, by getting the agreement of the people, rather than through coercion. Even warfare was usually a matter of men getting together to conduct a raid rather than a political decision by either a chief or an entire tribe. European observers, who were greatly impressed by the order and self-discipline in Indian communities, simply could not believe that they functioned without the kind of concentrated authority and ruthless law enforcement necessary in the Old World.

Work roles were evenly distributed within the villages. Men were responsible for hunting, war, and ceremonial practices. Women were the agriculturalists, and their role was seen as so important economically that, among many Indians, women actually owned the land, and children reckoned their descent through their mothers and grandmothers rather than their fathers and grandfathers. In the fields the women worked together; throughout the villages the emphasis was on sharing. This was the thing Europeans found most difficult to understand about Indian life: Possessions were held in common and a person attained status by giving away goods rather than accumulating them.

Justice and war among the eastern Algonquians operated on the principle of equilibrium. Peace reigned when relationships were evenly

THE FIRST AMERICANS

balanced. If something upset the peace, balance had to be restored. If a person was injured, it was up to him or his village or clan to inflict an equal injury on the clan or village of the one who had done him the harm. Intent did not matter. An accidental wrong was avenged just as an intentional one was. Nor was the retribution necessarily visited on the one who had originally caused the trouble. The goal was not to punish the guilty party or make him suffer, but to restore the balance.

This principle of repayment extended to diplomacy, where gift giving was essential. When the first party of explorers at Roanoke encountered a single Indian courageous enough to board their ships, they "gave him a shirt, a hat, and some

Indians fishing, De Bry engraving after John White. Both the Roanoke and the Jamestown colonists were initially dependent on the Indians for food. White demonstrated the sophistication of Indian techniques, not only in fishing from their canoe at night with a fire to attract fish, but also in the complex traps they constructed along the rivers. (*Latin America*, Pars I, Latin, Plate XIII, "Incolarum Virginiae piscandiratio," William L. Clements Library, Ann Arbor, Michigan)

other things, and made him taste of our wine, and our meat, which he liked very well." Instead of hurrying home with his prize, the explorers were surprised to see,

> He fell to fishing, and in less than half an hour, he had laden his boat as deep as it could swim, with which he came again to the point of the land, and there he divided his fish into two parts, pointing one part to the ship, and the other to the pinnace: which after he had (as much as he might) requited the former benefits received, he departed out of our sight.

The explorers had had their first lesson in Native American diplomacy. Reciprocity, maintaining the balance, was the important thing.

First Contacts

For thousands of years after the glaciers melted, the two American continents were isolated from the rest of the world. Old sagas told of one brief break in this isolation when Norse voyagers led by Eric the Red and Leif Ericsson established short-lived settlements in Newfoundland about A.D. 1000. Archaeological investigation has established that these colonies, extensions of settlements in Greenland, really did exist. But they were not sustained, and the Americas remained isolated.

America was "discovered," made known to Europeans, only after 1492. Spain and Portugal led the way in exploring and exploiting the new find. These nations had come into close contact with advanced North African cultures during the Middle Ages, which had developed mathematical and geographical knowledge far superior to that of the Europeans. It was partly this technology borrowed from the "Moors," as the Spanish called the North Africans, that enabled Europeans to consider the possibility of sailing west, over enormous stretches of uncharted ocean, in search of new routes to the riches of the East.

COLUMBUS Many of the original explorers were Italian-born, but they looked for Atlantic nations to sponsor them. Columbus sought support in France and England as well as Spain. In 1492, Spain was prepared to back his voyage—intended to find a new route to the trade of the Orient—but other countries were skeptical of his plan.

Columbus returned with news that he had found land across the western ocean. Though we know his landfall was in the Caribbean, he believed (and maintained through all four of his voyages and to his dying day) that he had reached the Far East. Columbus's error symbolizes the problem confronting all of Europe in thinking about the discoveries. It would be a long time before many would realize that two huge, entirely new continents had been discovered.

The earliest landfalls were on islands. The Atlantic was dotted with islands and island groups, such as the Azores (discovered between 1427 and 1452), the Canaries, and Iceland and Greenland. Scholars naturally first thought that the newly discovered islands would be parts of such groups.

JOHN CABOT That the islands were in fact on the margins of vast continents slowly became apparent. Giovanni Caboto, an Italian from Genoa like Columbus but known to us by the name he adopted in England, John Cabot, had been seeking backing for a voyage to Asia at the same time as Columbus. Shortly after Columbus returned from his first expedition in 1493, Cabot had made the English city of Bristol, whose fishing ships had ventured far out into the Atlantic, his headquarters. In 1497 he sailed west from Ireland and made a landfall on the North American coast somewhere in the latitude of 42 to 54 degrees (northern New England or southern Canada) and established grounds for an English claim in America. Though he did not find the rich spices and silks of the Orient, Cabot did report seas filled with fish; his voyage started an annual stampede of ships from all over western Europe to the Newfoundland Banks for the rich fishing.

THE SPANISH The Spanish gradually mapped the coastline of South America, a process begun by Amerigo Vespucci's discovery of Guiana in 1501. In some ways it is appropriate that the New World should be named after Vespucci; he was the first to put forward the theory that new *continents* lay between Europe and Asia. South America's outline was fully known once Ferdinand Magellan's expedition had rounded the tip of the southern continent and crossed the Pacific to circle the globe, between 1519 and 1522.

As Spaniards began to investigate the newly found lands, they stumbled across the greatest Indian empires in America, those of the Aztecs in Mexico and the Incas in Peru. These Indians lived in highly organized state systems that even the ethnocentric Europeans recognized as genuine. Millions of people lived under Aztec control, which had been established around 1325, about 200 years before the Spanish arrived. The warlike Aztecs had succeeded earlier, more advanced people, the Mayas, whose culture was fading by the time the Europeans saw them. The Aztecs had inherited a form of written language, of numbers and calculation, and a calendar more accurate than any the Europeans had. The Incas, like the Aztecs, had advanced agricultural systems with irrigation networks. The Inca empire had built a remarkable web of paved roads superior to those in Europe. These Indian empires had large cities with huge public buildings, many constructed in the form of great stone pyramids. These Indians also possessed fabulous stores of wealth, rooms filled with gold tablets, and it was the gold that spurred on the conquest.

Conquest was not an occupation for the faint of heart. Most of the Spanish conquistadores were rough men ready to bear and inflict hardship in order to reach their goals. Millions were to die before the conquest was completed. The first settlers were left by Columbus on islands in the Caribbean, where little wealth was found. Central America was the next target. In 1513 Vasco Núñez de Balboa found that only the narrow Isthmus of Panama separated the Pacific Ocean and the Caribbean at that point.

Rumors of the riches of the Aztecs lured an army of about 600 under the command of Hernando Cortes to attempt the conquest of Mexico in 1519. Their first attack on Tenochtitlán, the Aztec capital on the site of present-day Mexico City, was repulsed by Aztec forces organized by the emperor, Montezuma. The Spaniards had brought something far more deadly than bullets, however: A smallpox epidemic broke out in the city. One of Cortes's companions recalled the events much later: "When the Christians were exhausted from war, God saw fit to send the Indians smallpox, and there was a great pestilence in the city. . . ." The Indians had no resistance to this European disease, and their ability to fight crumbled. When the Spanish entered the city they found "the streets, squares, houses, and courts were filled with bodies, so that it was almost impossible to pass. Even Cortes was sick from the stench in his nostrils."

The vast wealth discovered in Tenochtitlán spurred on further conquest. The Incas of Peru succumbed to a Spanish force under Francisco Pizarro in 1531–33. The Inca ruler was tricked into surrendering. His people paid a stupendous ransom—more than 40,000 pounds of pure gold and silver—but the emperor was executed nonetheless. The discovery of such amazing wealth led

to new conquests, always in the expectation of yet greater hoards. Expeditions invaded Ecuador, Chile, Argentina, and Bolivia. When no gold was found, leaders were tortured because the soldiers assumed they had hidden it away.

The conquistadores, who were largely ignorant of their own culture, had little appreciation for the sophisticated cultures they conquered, destroying artifacts, records, documents, and buildings in the search for riches. Gold was all that mattered. Some few priests and scholars worked frantically to save some artifacts, but little remained; these once-great cultures are mostly lost to us. By 1540 the conquest of Mexico, Central America, and Peru was largely accomplished.

The Spanish were interested in North America as well. In 1536 a Spanish gentleman named Cabeza de Vaca, survivor of an exploring expedition to Florida destroyed by shipwreck, turned up in Mexico City. He had been cast up on the Texas coast. With three other Spaniards, he had lived among the Indians there for six years. These four men had learned many of the Indians' skills, particularly in healing and the preparation of foods native to the region. They made their way on foot across the Southwest and down to Mexico; their stories of great cities, "populous towns and very large houses," seen on the way increased Spanish interest in exploration. Other early reports generated stories of seven golden cities of "Cibola" beyond the Rio Grande.

A huge expedition ventured out from Mexico in 1540 under Francisco Vasquez de Coronado, and these men quickly discovered a different reality. The environment was inhospitable; the Indians of the Southwest were superbly adapted to it, but it imposed real hardship on a large, roving expedition such as Coronado's. The great cities discovered by Coronado were the pueblos of the Zunis and Hopis. These pueblos were amazing feats, based on irrigation engineering that allowed the Indians to live a sedentary life year-round in that water-poor area, but they were not the gold-studded marvels for which the Spaniards yearned. Cibola (actually the Zuni pueblo Hawikuh) was, one of Coronado's men reported,

AMERICAN IMAGES

A New World, A New People

Europeans were surprised by their discoveries of the lands and seas to their west. It amazed them that the Atlantic Ocean was so broad, the new continents so enormous. The great stretches of the Pacific Ocean astonished them.

But the Europeans' curiosity about the "new" oceans and continents was mild in comparison to their fascination with the people they found there. Asians had been part of European lore and mythology for a long time; so had Africans. But the "red" people of North and South America were something else—a new "race," a sudden addition to the human species.

Almost all the explorers wrote descriptions of Native Americans. They tried to describe the food, the dress, the villages, and the temples of every native culture, from the

Plate 1. *A Tapuya Brazilian* (left). **Plate 2.** *Brazilian Woman* (right). Both by Albert Eckhout, 1641. (The National Museum of Denmark, Department of Ethnography)

Plate 3 (left and right). *Mexicans*, by Christoph Weiditz, 1529. (Germanisches Nationalmuseum, Nuremberg)

simplest Caribs to the impressive Aztecs. But what Europeans most hungered for were not descriptions but pictures of the new "savages."

Almost four centuries passed between the European discovery of America and the invention of photography. So the visual images the Europeans received were the work of artists—some good, some poor, some simply dishonest. Even the best artists looked at Native Americans with eyes that were far less honest than camera lenses. They projected their beliefs, hopes, and fears onto the Native Americans, creating a collective portrait of the men and women of the Americas that was one part depiction of American reality and two parts a mirror of the European mind.

In the luckiest of circumstances, an expedition might have a gifted artist along as part of the crew; the result could be superb and realistic renderings. The very best luck came when Albert Eckhout, an artist as talented as many of his more famous Dutch contemporaries, went to Brazil in the 1640s. His paintings of Brazilian men and women are works of rare skill and faithfulness (Plates 1 and 2). The dress, baskets, weapons, skin color, and decorations—all are as realistic as art could make them.

But even in Eckhout's work, imagination and exaggeration had their place. A man is shown in full battle

dress, not as he would have looked most of the time. The great snake at his feet can hardly have been there in all its ferocity without making even this warrior a bit nervous. Eckhout's Indian woman is a little too casual about the still well-shaped hand and foot she is carrying. Despite his attempt to be accurate, Eckhout was doing what every European artist before and after him did—emphasizing the bizarre and shocking aspects of this strange New World.

Eckhout's realism was unique: Only rarely did other artists draw or paint a Native-American figure in a way that paid more attention to reality than to fear or fantasy. Christopher Weiditz, a German artist who happened to see some Mexican Indians in Spain, was able to draw them in a reasonably realistic way (Plate 3), and Lucas de Heere's drawing of an Eskimo who had been brought to England in the 1570s is passingly convincing (Plate 4). But, for the most part, Europeans drew and painted not so much what they saw as what they wanted to see—or feared they might see. The artists were men of their age, sharing its prejudices as well as its forms of human blindness. The visual record they left behind hopelessly tangles together the fantastic with the realistic.

Perhaps the easiest and earliest way artists dealt with

Plate 4. *Eskimo*, by Lucas de Heere, 1576. (Universiteitbibliothek, Ghent)

Plate 5. *Adoration of the Magi*, by The Master of Viseu, c. 1505. (Museu de Grão Vasco, Viseu)

this whole new set of people was to paint them into an existing artistic reality. One of the earliest European attempts to depict a Native American was painted in Portugal about fifteen years after Columbus's first voyage (Plate 5). The artist begins with a conventional scene, the adoration of the Christ-child by the Magi (the three wise men). He paints a Brazilian Indian into the center position among the three Oriental kings—a spot that had, for centuries, usually been reserved for an African "wise man." It took very little imagination to replace a black figure with a copper-skinned one, dressed in feathers, wearing a feather headdress, and carrying a wooden weapon. But the strangeness of the Brazilian figure is incidental; on the whole, he adopts the usual aristocratic stance and gentle look of worship assigned to the other two Magi.

Another favorite conventional theme of European painting was the torments of the damned. The paintings showed men and women writhing under the fiendish tortures of demons, presided over by a grinning, beastly Devil. By the middle of the sixteenth century, it had become possible to show the Devil as a Native American. In The Inferno, an anonymous Portuguese painting of about 1550, the Devil wears the same Brazilian feather costume and headdress as the adoring king who visited the Holy

Family a few decades earlier. He also wears a purse of Native American beadwork (Plate 6).

Taken together, these two paintings reached the outer limits of the European capacity to invent meanings for the Native Americans—either as gentle, noble, nearly angelic, or as savagely demonic. More often than not, these contradictory ways of picturing Native Americans were found in the same paintings and drawings.

Gradually, a tradition took shape in Europe, from England and Holland down into Spain and Italy, which managed to combine two seemingly opposite points of view. On the one hand, the Native Americans were pictured in ways that incorporated them into what was already familiar to the European eye. They stood like Europeans; they had muscles, breasts, and genitals surprisingly like those

Plate 6. *Inferno,* anonymous Portuguese, c. 1550. (Giraudon/Art Resource)

found in Greek or Roman statues; and their women held babies in ways that could only remind Europeans of a conventional Madonna holding her infant son.

But, on the other hand, Native Americans were persistently shown as being very different from Europeans, either as more pure and innocent or (more often) as violent, savage, and cannibalistic. (William Shakespeare combined both aspects in his characterization of Caliban, the island native "tamed" by the European lord Prospero in The Tempest.)

This was the main paradox of the emergent European picture of the new people: They were shown as being impossibly like Europeans and yet as utterly different from Europeans. The more amateurish the artists, the more the Native American reality was submerged by the paradox.

For example, in a drawing of a Brazilian family made in the 1570s, the artist is at pains to show us everything that he finds different and surprising about the man, woman, and child (Plate 7). Naked, they are surrounded by the curious weapons and implements of their lives; the fruits and foods are strange and unreal. But there is something strikingly familiar about the statuesque pose of the man, the way his muscles are shown, and the conventionally artistic way his genitals are pictured—prominent but infantile, just as in the Greek statuary that European artists still worshipped and imitated. Most interesting of all, the woman and child adopt almost exactly the pose used by Raphael in a superb picture of Madonna and Child painted about half a century earlier (Plate 8).

These opposing habits—of picturing Native Americans

Plate 7. *Brazilian Family*, by J. de Lery, 1578. (New York Public Library)

Plate 8. *Madonna*, by Raphael, c. 1505. (The National Gallery of Art, Washington, D.C.: The Widener Collection)

Plate 9. *Camp-fire Ceremony*, by John White, 1586. (The British Museum, London)

Plate 10. *The Flyer*, by John White, 1586. (The British Museum)

in European, classical, and conventional ways, and at the same time emphasizing everything alien and incredible about them—came together in the first really popular books on America. Beginning in 1590, Theodore de Bry, a Belgian engraver and publisher, assembled a series of thirteen travel accounts. Copying the work of other artists and explorers, he created a set of superbly engraved pictures of Native Americans from Carolina to Cape Horn. The pictures consistently showed a "race" of men and women that Europeans could both recognize and marvel at, both familiar and fantastic.

De Bry's first volume, undertaken with the connivance of the English promoter Richard Hakluyt, was an account of the exploration of the area around the North Carolina island of Roanoke (where Sir Walter Raleigh's group had attempted to plant the first English colony in the Americas). De Bry agreed to publish Virginia first because he had a wonderful set of watercolors that had been done by an artist named John White, who went with the first exploring mission and later became governor of the short-lived colony—as well as being the grandfather of the first known English child born in America.

Some of White's watercolors—particularly *Camp-Fire Ceremony*—broke through artistic convention and presented a crude, naive, but probably reasonably realistic picture of the Carolina Indians. Others, such as *The Flyer*, fell into classical and Renaissance artistic conventions. In others, such as *Indian Woman and Child*, European conventions mix about equally with an emphasis on the bizarre and the "savage" (Plates 9–12).

On the last pages of *Virginia*, de Bry printed engravings taken from White watercolors showing not American "savages" but the savages of England in the fourth century—Picts and Britons. Bizarre, frightening, yet strangely familiar and classical figures, their wildness is counterbalanced by their delicate features and noble bearing. De Bry explained the matter simply: He had included these "figures . . . for to showe how that the Inhabitants of the great Bretainne have bin in times past as sauvage as those of Virginia."

Plate 11. *Indian Woman and Child*, by John White, 1586. (The British Museum, London)

Plate 12. *The Trwe Picture of a Woman Nigbour to the Pictes*, from Theodore de Bry, *Virginia*, 1590. (Courtesy of the John Carter Brown Library at Brown University)

Walpi Pueblo in Arizona. Spanish explorers were impressed by these cities. When the evidence of sedentary agricultural cultures was put together with legends of gold, Europeans easily convinced themselves that further exploration would lead to a big strike. (Arizona State Historical Library)

"a small rocky pueblo, all crumpled up, there being many farm settlements in New Spain that look better from afar."

Coronado met resistance as he marched, which he put down promptly with great cruelty; a picture of the Europeans was firmly fixed in the Indians' minds by this first encounter. His expedition traveled, gathering information all the way, through the Southwest as far as central Kansas, a journey of 1,500 miles. Had he been interested in geography as much as gold, Coronado might have realized that the Arkansas River, on which he camped, was part of a major river system. He could have followed it to discover the Mississippi River, the central artery of the continent. Instead, he returned to Mexico after two years, to report a land barren of riches.

Simultaneously, Juan Rodríguez Cabrillo ventured all along the coast of California as far north as Oregon in 1542–43. Cabrillo died on the voyage, and his crew returned in terrible condition to report no evidence of gold to the north, nor any sign of the western outlet of a passage through the continent. Concluding that the land north of Mexico not only offered no easy wealth, but exacted a heavy toll from those who attempted to travel in it, the Spanish largely ignored the Southwest for the next half-century. California was not to be colonized until the eighteenth century.

Spanish explorers were also curious about eastern North America. In the 1530s and 1540s, a Spanish party led by Hernando de Soto traveled through the Southeast. Their excitement grew as the expedition discovered the great mounds. Surely these Indians would possess riches like those of the Aztecs and Incas. No gold was found, but the search led the Spaniards all through the Southeast. De Soto's men crossed the Mississippi River, which he named Rio de Espíritu Santo, and were actually camped there while Coronado was nearby on the Arkansas.

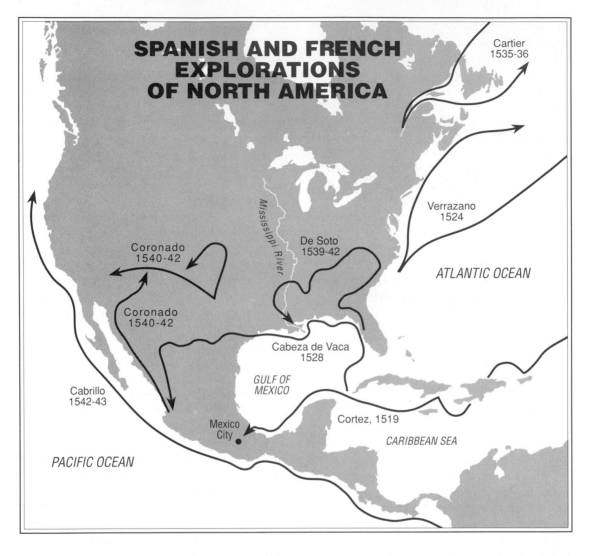

SPANISH AND FRENCH
EXPLORATIONS
OF NORTH AMERICA

Cartier
1535-36

Verrazano
1524

ATLANTIC OCEAN

Coronado
1540-42

Mississippi River

De Soto
1539-42

Coronado
1540-42

Cabeza de Vaca
1528

GULF OF
MEXICO

Cabrillo
1542-43

Cortez, 1519

Mexico City

CARIBBEAN SEA

PACIFIC OCEAN

Since each had taken a circuitous route and the two never met, the combined reports of the two expeditions did not make the extent of the continent clear. Wishful thinking prevailed, and geographers decided that North America was at most 1,500 miles across (about half its actual extent).

THE FRENCH France was also involved in exploration that revealed the shape of North America. Giovanni Verrazzano, an Italian from Florence who lived in France, sailed along the coast from south of Cape Fear, North Carolina, north past the mouth of the Hudson River. After a prolonged stop in what is now Newport Harbor, Rhode Island, "which we called 'Refugio' on account of its beauty," he continued to Newfoundland in 1524. So within a few decades of the first voyage of discovery by Columbus, the basic outline of the Americas was known.

Once Europeans understood that their New World consisted of two continents joined by a narrow isthmus, problems of conceptualization remained. Most thought of the great land masses, particularly the relatively unpromising northern one, as barriers to the trade routes they had hoped to chart, rather than as new opportunities to be developed. Adventurers now began to explore the coasts, looking for likely entryways to passages that might cut right through to the East.

One waterway that looked promising was the St. Lawrence River. Jacques Cartier had explored it for France in two voyages in the 1530s. Convinced that the land "was the finest and most excellent one could find anywhere," he returned at the head of a colony that was planted near modern Quebec in 1541. French backers hoped the settlement could support exploring voyages into the interior. The colony failed, partly because the planters were not prepared for the extreme cold of the Canadian winter, but the hope that the St. Lawrence might be the entrance to a system of rivers that would allow ships to travel right through the continent remained, especially when later explorers discovered the river's connection to the Great Lakes system. It would be centuries before the idea of a northwest passage was finally given up.

The Impact of European Diseases

So by the 1540s, the nature of the New World was becoming clear. What was less clear at the time was that exploration and the beginnings of colonization had produced a human event of massive proportions. The mixing of populations isolated from each other for 10,000 years brought consequences unprecedented in the history of the world, effects that can never be repeated as long as human beings remain on this planet.

The "disease filter" of cold through which the first immigrants to America had passed during the last Ice Age had been so efficient that most of the diseases present in the rest of the world did not exist in the Western Hemisphere. People acquire a degree of immunity to the bacteria and viruses that cause disease in their environment. Newborn babies inherit some resistance from their mothers. As that immunity wears off, they manufacture their own response to those pathogens that are always present. Even if they fall sick, they may have a milder case because they have some resistance. The Indians lacked acquired immunity to the pathogens the Europeans brought with them, and they were killed off by European diseases wherever the ships and their crews went. Plague, smallpox, and typhus, the great killers in Europe, felled many Indians. But others died of infections that were usually mild in Europe: influenza, colds, and measles. So devastating were these epidemics that scholars estimate 90 percent of the Indian population was destroyed in many places. One New England colonist wrote that "the twentieth person is scarce left alive."

The figures are horrifying. But the impact, physical and psychological, is incalculable. The process, initiated innocently by sixteenth-century explorers, was already well under way when the first colonists arrived, and may account for the ease with which Europeans were able to dominate. Powhatan told John Smith: "I have seen the deaths of all my people thrice." Three epidemics had swept through the Chesapeake *before* the Jamestown settlers even arrived. Alliances and political structures would have been in disarray. Religious systems, based on priestly power, including the power to heal, may have been assailed by doubt.

The diseases, because they affected the Indians but usually not the colonists, actually enhanced the reputations of the Europeans. One of the earliest Spanish accounts tells of how the Indians they encountered

did not dare eat, drink, or do anything else of this life, without first asking permission from the Christians. They did this because they thought that these Christians had the power to kill them, or to give them life. For this reason, they believed that they were dying because the Christians had been made angry.

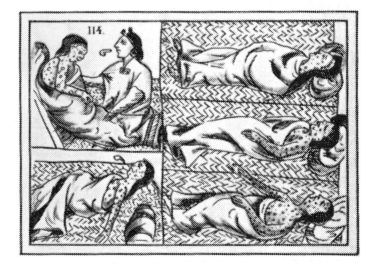

European disease struck the Indians with unparalleled ferocity. Fray Bernardino de Sahagun, who accompanied Cortes, included this illustration of the impact of smallpox in his *General History of the Things of New Spain*. (Fray Bernardino de Sahagun, *General History of the Things of New Spain*)

Each society was highly religious; both believed that events are controlled by God. Some Indians came to believe, as some colonists did, that the epidemics were, as one English colonist put it, "the hand of God" by which "the place is made so much the more fit, for the English Nation to inhabit in, and erect in it Temples to the Glory of God." No one understood how diseases are transmitted. In many cases the sickness would be carried by infected Indians to areas where the Europeans had never been. When the affliction broke out beyond the frontier, the Indians concluded that the colonists had the power to make sickness appear by remote control.

Navaho wall painting of the arrival of the Spaniards in the Southwest, Canyon del Muerto, Arizona. The expedition is accompanied by a priest dressed in black. The animals—horses, cows, pigs, and sheep—brought by the Europeans changed Indian life dramatically. (Richard Erdoes)

First Colonies

Spain and France took the lead in colonizing North America. Spain had followed up its early exploring voyages by settlements. Spanish colonists settled Florida as early as 1565, and sites were scouted on the coast of South Carolina, where the settlement of Santa Elena existed for a while (1572–75). And Chesapeake Bay was the site of a short-lived Jesuit mission established in the early 1570s. The bay, like the St. Lawrence River, looked as though it might connect with inland rivers to provide a passage through the continent, and Spain was the first European country to explore it.

THE SOUTHWEST In the Southwest, priests and soldiers, led by Juan de Oñate in 1598, began establishing a Spanish presence among the Indians in a huge territory the Spanish authorities called New Mexico. The southwestern Indians had adapted to their environment in different ways. Some, who later became known as Apaches and Navahos, had developed a roving culture that made use of the inhospitable land's changing offerings; these bands consisted of 50 to 300 people. Those whom we know as Pueblo Indians, including the Hopis and Zunis, had developed a sedentary life that harnessed the region's limited water supply. Their complexes of large, apartment-style houses were recognized by the Spaniards as true cities (*pueblo* is a Spanish word meaning either "town" or "people").

Though the pueblo-dwelling Indians cooperated with other cities for the immense irrigation projects that made their agriculture possible, neither they nor the Navahos and Apaches had a tribal identity. The names and the identity were imposed by the Spanish, who saw and labeled cultural similarities. Each village or band was completely independent; each was led by a person who was recognized as the moral leader of the community. The leader had no power of compulsion; persuasion was the only avenue to influence. The war leader, who organized defense and relations with outsiders, was much less important.

Oñate traveled among the pueblos, receiving expressions of fealty from their leaders, who knew from prior experience that resistance would be put down harshly. We do not know what they made of the ceremonies of submission, but it is clear that they did not sign over control of their lives to the Spanish. Throughout the region the Indians offered polite audiences, often adopting outward forms of Spanish life and religion while privately keeping their own culture intact. If pressure became too great, Indians would often simply move away from contact.

Oñate established his capital at Santa Fe by 1610 and sent out missionaries and soldiers to carry Spanish influence throughout the region. In those areas where the priests came first, the Indians recognized Spanish society as organized along proper lines, with the moral leader in charge. Because the pueblos were preexisting permanent structures, the priests were forced to set up their missions on the outskirts and to try to win the Indians over by making Christianity attractive to them. In many cases the priests were welcomed because they brought new agricultural technology that the Indians valued. Where military men set up forts and tried to compel Indian labor on their plantations, the Europeans looked alien and distasteful.

Spanish settlements north of Mexico were never more than peripheral to the main colonies, and Spain was never able to control the lands beyond the Rio Grande fully. Therefore, European influence was necessarily weaker, and these regions saw the development of a unique mixture of Indian and Spanish ways. Emissaries of Spanish culture found they had to adapt the religious, political, and social practices they offered to make them acceptable to Indian life; they were rarely in a position to impose their own ways. Often the Indians grafted outward forms and Spanish labels onto native government and religious structures. The resulting rich cultural mix is unique in the Americas.

FRENCH SETTLEMENTS France was also on the colonial scene early. In 1562 a group of French Huguenots (Protestants) erected a colony at Port Royal in South Carolina. Its life was cut short by a Spanish attack in 1565, but the French had more success in the far north. A series of voyages led by Samuel de Champlain, begun in 1602, followed up Cartier's discoveries. Champlain explored the coast of New England and the area around the St. Lawrence. Quebec, permanently settled in 1608, gave the French a key site for inland trade with powerful Indian confederations, particularly the Hurons.

France concentrated its colonial efforts on the fur trade. Quebec continued to be largely a trading post with a small population. In 1627 all of Canada held only 107 Frenchmen. The French presence was unique among European empires because they were able to construct a mutually beneficial relationship with the Indians with whom they traded. Champlain understood the ceremonial importance of the exchange of goods, and did not treat the Indians merely as trading partners. He gave them military assistance against their enemies, and, because the colony included few farmers, the French did not compete for land and resources. By following the traditions laid down by Champlain, the French influence was carried far into the interior in the course of the seventeenth century. French traders, often accompanied or preceded by missionaries, developed warm relationships with many of the Indians with whom they dealt. Their activities carried them all through the heart of the North American continent.

The English Approach to Colonization

So, by 1607, England was the only Atlantic power without an established presence in America. There had been many English voyages of exploration, and English ships went to the Newfoundland Banks to fish every year, but no colonies

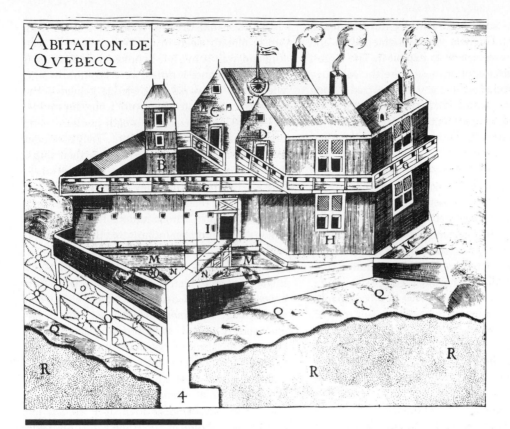

ABITATION. DE QVEBECQ

French habitation at Quebec. Samuel de Champlain left a lively visual record of his expeditions. His drawing shows the colonists' adaptation to the cold winters. One could move about the settlement keeping exposure to the outside to a minimum. (Public Archives of Canada)

existed. Individual exploits such as Sir Francis Drake's great voyage of 1577–80, attacking and plundering Spanish colonies on both coasts of South America and venturing up the west coast as far as California, did little to change the picture. Drake claimed California, as "New Albion," for England, but he and his men found it cold and unpromising, the coast shrouded in "most vile, thick, and stinking fogs . . . Besides, how unhandsome and deformed appeared the face of the earth itself! showing trees without greenness in those months of June and July." England seemed unable to make the effort to establish a continuing presence anywhere in America. Indeed, it was Drake himself who carried home the hapless first colony at Roanoke in 1586, as he returned from a second privateering voyage.

The problems England faced were of two sorts. First, the Roanoke colony had demonstrated that such ventures were very expensive, requiring support over a very long period of time during which they could not be expected to repay investors. The English crown, unlike the Spanish, was not prepared to put government money into colonization; therefore, a source of investment funds had to be found.

As Raleigh had realized in his final Roanoke venture, the joint-stock company was the solution to the problem of finance. By attracting many investors, the risk of investing could be spread and continuity of funding could be assured. The company would continue to exist even if one or more investors died. Joint-stock companies were founded to sponsor all kinds of ventures in sixteenth- and seventeenth-century England. Trade with the whole world boomed then and companies were set up to exploit it. The largest and most successful of these were the Muscovy Company, founded in the 1550s to trade along the northern sea route for Russian furs and wood products; the Levant Company, organized in the late 1570s to trade with the eastern Mediterranean nations for the spices and silks of the East; and the East India Company, chartered in 1599 to trade directly by sea with the Orient.

American colonies were naturally set up on the same lines, organized and paid for by joint-stock companies chartered by the government. But here the second problem arose. It centered on the expected rewards of colonization. Potential investors were hardheaded businessmen. The Muscovy, Levant, and East India companies were sure investments, with proven returns. What could America provide that would repay a massive outlay of capital? It was unlikely that the unpromising terrain of North America would ever furnish the silver and gold the Spanish had found in the south. Fish, as John Smith later pointed out, were a form of gold, but they could be obtained without the expense of colonies. France seemed to have the fur trade tied up. Even privateering did not require colonies; the English had demonstrated they could prey on Spanish shipping without permanent bases. There had to be a reason to assume the huge expense and problems of a colony.

Why did England finally become sufficiently interested in American plantations to support them all the way to success? There were many reasons, some old, some new. The old ones—the dream of gold and of finding a passage through the continent—continued to inspire explorers. Jamestown, the first successful colony, was placed in 1607 on the deepwater port discovered by the Roanoke colonists on Chesapeake Bay partly because it was hoped that the mighty James River or one of the other rivers flowing into the bay would link up with inland rivers to form the northwest passage. No one yet realized how extensive the continent was from east to west.

To these old dreams was added a growing sense, already seen in Sir Walter Raleigh, that England was being left behind while Spain and other European countries were building worldwide trade networks. Knowledge gained in the twenty-year privateering war, from the middle of the 1580s to Elizabeth's death in 1603, made English mariners more confident. They no longer needed Portuguese pilots to navigate their ships.

Religious reasons also grew in importance. The English boast that they were the leaders of the Protestant religion seemed hollow when they allowed Roman Catholic nations to colonize and convert the American Indians and the English did nothing.

Domestic reasons added their weight. Many English people feared that their society was entering a state of decay as Queen Elizabeth I was replaced by James I. The organization of English society seemed to be breaking down, especially the local networks that supported people in hard times, and the mechanisms by which men and women entered adult life, formed families, and settled on an occupation.

Traditionally, English men and women left their parents' home at about the age of fourteen. The lucky few whose parents could afford to pay became apprentices. The master to whom a boy was apprenticed promised to teach him his trade and to place him on the track that would allow him eventually to become a member of a guild. Guilds controlled the skilled professions. One could not enter them unless one followed the prescribed channels.

Most young adults became servants. Each fall, hiring fairs were held around the country, where servants and masters negotiated contracts that bound them together for one full year. A servant found away from his master's farm or shop at any time during the year would be whipped and returned. Similarly, the master, even if disaster befell him, was required to keep the servant on and feed, house, and clothe him for the entire year. This system gave servants a degree of control over their lives. If a master had a bad reputation, servants avoided him. The tradition was later adapted and became the indentured servitude that brought servants to the American colonies.

The system of servitude through annual contracts allowed men and women to prepare for adult life and learn a craft. Servitude was a stage of life rather than a social condition. Even families that could afford servants of their own might put their own children out as servants. After about a decade spent in such contracts, servants accumulated enough money to marry and set up a separate household. Young men and women, because they were on their own and often some distance from home by the time they married in their mid-twenties, chose their own marriage partners. The couple then built a new network of friends and neighbors when they settled down.

The upper 5 percent of the English population was the gentry and aristocracy. The other 95 percent ranged from the very poor without land to wealthy merchants. When the system was working well, most families had some land and a place to live. The landlord, often the local lord of the manor, would oversee the life of the area, dispensing justice and regulating relationships. Village life centered on the church, which offered social activities such as festivals and church ales as well as religious functions. Most English people identified with their local area. When they referred to their "country," they usually meant their county.

Now much of this order seemed to be breaking up. Since the early sixteenth century the population had been growing dramatically, and inflation of the money supply caused prices to rise. Incomes lagged far behind prices. More people were poor, and the poorest were poorer than before. The available land seemed insufficient for all who sought labor. Now "wandering poor," people with no place to go, threatened the social order. Cold weather and poor harvests—produced by conditions so hostile that historians have dubbed the sixteenth and seventeeth centuries the Little Ice Age—increased suffering. There were even occasional periods of famine. Many men and women were prepared to consider emigration to America now in hope of a better life and land of their own. Wealthy men were prepared to invest the money to send them over in hope of restoring order in England.

Most English people earned their bread by farming, but some were involved in trades. Textile manufacture, the most important industry in England, was in trouble as improved techniques in Europe outclassed English cloth. The industry needed access to new dyes and fibers from America and other parts of the world. Colonies could help put English industry back on a firm footing. Although there might not be gold in Virginia, other products, such as medicines, timber, foods, and metals, might be developed by the hard work of colonists. These would not only enrich colonial investors and the country, they would free England of reliance on other European countries for products it needed. Captain John Smith pointed out that even "that contemptible trade of fish" could be lucrative, and fish would never run out: "Let not the meanness of the word fish distaste you, for it will afford as good gold as the Mines of Guiana or Potosí, with less hazard and charge, and more certainty and facility." There were, it seemed, many good reasons to develop American colonies.

Jamestown

Heading off renewed French or Spanish attempts to settle in North America was a compelling reason for an English colony. The Spanish knew as well as the English that Chesapeake Bay was a good site. The English decided to plunge ahead in 1607 to keep others out. They hoped to create two new American settlements to mark out northern and southern claims. The name *Virginia* was applied to the entire coast of North America, so two Virginia Companies were set up to send out expeditions in 1607. One, based in London, was to found a colony on Chesapeake Bay. The other, headquartered in Plymouth, was to colonize on the Kennebec River in Maine. The Maine

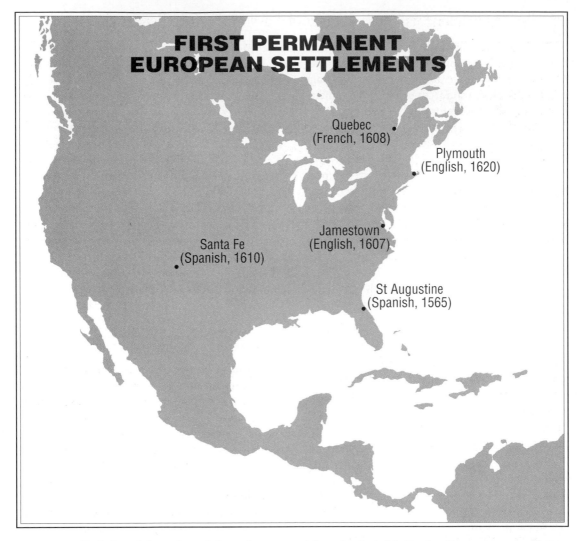

**FIRST PERMANENT
EUROPEAN SETTLEMENTS**

Quebec
(French, 1608)

Plymouth
(English, 1620)

Jamestown
(English, 1607)

Santa Fe
(Spanish, 1610)

St Augustine
(Spanish, 1565)

venture, called Sagadahoc, lasted less than a year, partly because of poor organization, but also due to the extremely cold winter "fit to freeze the heart of a plantation." The other Virginia colony lived on to become the first permanent English settlement in the New World, Jamestown.

Jamestown's planners had learned something from Roanoke's failure. A large joint-stock company was formed to ensure support over a long period of time. A massive propaganda campaign in favor of the colony was launched, with sermons, broadsides, and ballads carrying its message all over the country. English audiences were urged to "remember it is God's cause you have taken in hand." England's excess population would find a home in America, "our land abounding with swarms of idle persons, which having no means of labor to relieve their misery, do likewise swarm in lewd and naughty practices." The government authorized lotteries to help with finances. The country's attention focused on Virginia as it never had on Roanoke. Jamestown would not disappear from people's consciousness as the earlier attempt had.

Surprisingly, though, many of the same mistakes were repeated. Ignoring what Raleigh had learned from the Lane colony's failure, the Virginia Company sent an initial colony of soldiers

A Declaration for the certaine time of dravving the great ftanding Lottery.

Virginia lottery. King James I authorized the Virginia Company to launch a nationwide lottery to help finance the Jamestown colony. The lottery proved to be a successful device both in bringing in money and in publicizing the venture. (Society of Antiquaries, London)

of about the same size: a little over a hundred men. This group acted in many ways as Lane's had: They refused or were unable to grow food, so they tried to bully or cajole the Indians into selling them supplies. Their reliance on food from the Indians made them extremely vulnerable, so they often acted in a belligerent manner to prevent the Indians from taking advantage of that vulnerability. Their lack of self-discipline also meant the exploration they had been ordered to do—especially the search for gold and for a passage through the continent—was done poorly if at all.

Captain John Smith vividly described the colonists' disillusionment and disorder:

> Being for the most part of such tender educations and small experience in martial accidents, because they found not English cities, nor such fair houses, nor at their own wishes any of their accustomed dainties, with feather beds and down pillows, Taverns and alehouses in every breathing place, neither such plenty of gold and silver and dissolute liberty as they expected, [they] had little or no care of any thing, but to pamper their bellies, to fly away with our Pinnaces, or procure their means to return to England. For the Country was to them a miserie, a ruin, a death, a hell and their reports where, and their own actions there according.

Away from Jamestown, the colonists found that Indian aid sometimes vanished and they were left hungry and alone in an alien environment.

Many of the colonists found life in Jamestown more frustrating than they could bear. Throughout the first winter, more and more colonists fell sick and many died. Of the 108 colonists left in America in 1607, only 38 were alive the following spring. And this pattern was soon repeated. After its initial disappointments, the Virginia Company was reorganized in 1609 to try again on an even larger scale, demonstrating the power of a large joint-stock company. The newly reorganized company sent a huge fleet of nine ships with 500 new colonists to shore up the settlement. Part of the fleet—including most of the new government leaders—was shipwrecked on Bermuda, and did not arrive for an entire year (an event that inspired Shakespeare's play *The Tempest*). But most of the new colonists got through. These new settlers met disaster on an even larger scale than the first arrivals. Of the several hundred colonists left in Virginia in the fall of 1609, only 60 were alive the following spring.

CAPTAIN JOHN SMITH Something was clearly very wrong; if promoters could not find the reasons for such massive failure, any hope for a permanent English presence in America seemed lost. One man claimed to know the answer and seemed to have the evidence to back him up: Captain John Smith. He had been in charge of the colony in between the two starving times, and during his tenure very few had died. He wrote volumes pointing out his success and making his case. Despite the quality of his evidence, though, few in London would listen to him.

Smith was an unusual man, one of the few colonial leaders who was not born to high rank. Apprenticed to a merchant, he had run away at the age of sixteen to find fame and fortune. Like Raleigh, he learned much at the "university of war" in France and then in eastern Europe. When he finally returned to England in his middle twenties, he had traveled all through Europe and into North Africa and Russia. He had experienced the extremes the world had to offer: He had been knighted on the field of battle in Hungary and had been a slave in Turkey. The Virginia Company, impressed by his survival skills, selected him to be one of their governing council in Virginia with the first colony in 1607.

None of the other councilors liked Smith; he never ceased to remind them that he was the only member of the government who knew anything about dealing with alien situations. Smith became president of the council in Virginia, but he gained the position, in September 1608, literally over the other councilors' dead bodies. Only when the others were either dead or too sick to rule did they let Smith take control.

John Smith felt that Virginia's problems lay in the design of the colony, and the kinds of men chosen. There were too many gentlemen—six times as many proportionally as in England. Not only did the gentlemen expect to do no work, they expected to be attended by servants who would work only for them and not for the colony as a whole. Many of the other colonists were either soldiers or what the Virginia Company

Captain John Smith. Smith deliberately presented himself as a gruff, hardened, plain soldier in contrast to lavishly costumed courtier-explorers like Raleigh. (John Carter Brown Library, Brown University)

called "the scum of the earth," not a promising bunch with which to build a new society or convert the Indians. Smith told the Virginia Company that "a plain soldier that can use a pick-axe and spade is better than five Knights." Quoting the Bible, he commanded that "he who does not work shall not eat." Even the gentlemen went to work felling trees; their soft hands became so blistered, and the work so painful to them, that Smith had to discipline them for the oaths they uttered as their axes hit the trees.

Through his policy of enforced labor, President Smith solved many of Jamestown's problems. Just getting the colonists up and moving brightened their outlook, and the work gave them a sense of purpose and hope for the future. Through their work they made conditions in the settlement better. Deep wells were dug so the colonists would no longer sicken themselves by drinking groundwater, and secure houses were built. Food was planted, and Smith sent out expeditions to trade with the Indians for more supplies.

The proof of Smith's plan lies in his results: During his presidency the death rate fell almost to zero, and the few deaths were almost all from accidents. The upstart governor was replaced and forced out of the colony when the great new fleet came in 1609. The second wave of deaths, the reduction of the 500 colonists to 60, came after he had been expelled. He devoted the rest of his life to promoting colonization and analyzing what had gone wrong in Virginia.

The situation worsened in Virginia after 1609 under a series of governors. Finally, in 1611 Sir Thomas Dale arrived as governor and instituted a set of harsh new policies under a code called the Lawes Divine, Morall and Martiall. The colony's promoters may have thought the new system, carried on by Sir Thomas Gates after Dale left the colony, was similar to what Smith had instituted. In reality it was a code of the harshest severity, under which the colony languished. Virginia did manage to hold on, despite a prolonged war with the Indians, but just barely.

Indian Relations

The Indians' role, particularly that of the great confederacy headed by Powhatan, was crucial in the early history of Virginia. Powhatan, who controlled much of what happened around Chesapeake Bay, was perfectly aware that he could have eliminated the colony at any time during its first years. Not only were the colonists weak and ill-adapted to the environment, Powhatan's peo-

ple had wiped out a Spanish Jesuit mission near the same place in the 1570s. The question, then, is why did he allow the English to remain?

The answer seems to be that Powhatan, an extremely skillful strategist, wanted the trade goods the English brought with them, particularly metal tools and other equipment. Despite what the English believed, the Indians did not want to give up their own way of life in favor of a "superior" European way. But they did want tools that would make their *own* methods more efficient. Powhatan assumed that the English colony would remain a small trading post, and that he could always control the settlers by regulating their food supply. As the conduit for European trade goods, his power with his Indian clients would be enhanced. Powhatan told Smith that warlike acts would harm the colonists more than the Indians:

> What will it avail you, to take that perforce, you may quietly have with love, or to destroy them that provide you food? What can you get by war, when we can hide our provision and fly to the woods, whereby you must famish by wronging us your friends. . . . Think you I am so simple not to know, it is better to eat good meat, lie well, and sleep quietly with my women and children, laugh and be merry with you, have copper, hatchets, or what I want, being your friend?

Powhatan miscalculated on the future of Jamestown, but his reasoning on the information available to him was shrewd. After Captain Smith left the colony, relations deteriorated into a brutal intermittent war.

Powhatan's emissary in the early years was his "dearest daughter," Pocahontas, who was about ten years old when John Smith led the colony. She often carried messages back and forth between the Indians and the English. She was a "tomboy," and the soldiers in Jamestown loved her presence as a relief from the grim reality in the fort. When she reached the age of puberty, Powhatan, who was an extremely loving father, sent her away from the English. But she was

Powhatan speaking to his people. This is one of several inserts that adorned a map of Virginia published by John Smith. The figure of Powhatan was adapted from John White's portrait of a carved wooden idol he saw among the Carolina Algonquians. Artists and writers often borrowed from each other's accounts to enrich their own books about America. (Bodleian Library, Oxford, England)

discovered by an expedition out looking for corn, which kidnapped her and took her back to Jamestown as a prisoner. Pocahontas became a convert to Christianity, was baptized as Rebecca, and married John Rolfe. She went to England with her husband and young son, Thomas, in 1616, where she was received at the court of King James and reunited with John Smith. Next year, as her ship back to Virginia was leaving, "it pleased God to . . . take this Young lady to his mercy." Poca-

hontas was buried at Gravesend; she was twenty-one years old.

Pocahontas's marriage was followed by a cessation of the continuing hostilities between the English and the Powhatan confederacy, which had been draining to both sides. The truce gave the colonists the opportunity to move outside their fortifications and plan for the future. John Rolfe had helped bring peace to Virginia with his marriage.

Maioaks als Rebecka daughter to the mighty Prince
Powhatan Emperour of Attanoughkomouck als Virginia
converted and baptized in the Chriſtian faith, and
Wife to the worſl Mr Tho: Rolff.

Ætatis suæ 21. Aº 1616.

Pocahontas in London shortly before her death. Dressed as an English gentlewoman, she became the toast of London. (National Portrait Gallery, Smithsonian Institution, Washington, D.C.)

Economy and Society

Rolfe also helped bring economic security through his experiments with tobacco. Everyone knew that mere survival was not enough in Virginia. The colony, now almost a decade old, would have to develop some product of value that could be sold in Europe if the venture were ever to take off. Tobacco was to be that product. The native Virginia tobacco was considered too harsh, so Rolfe experimented with more acceptable West Indian strains until he found one that could flourish in Chesapeake conditions. When this tobacco began to sell in England, the Virginia economy entered a period of growth that was soon to produce a boom, a boom based, as the skeptics said, "on smoke."

Now that the economic future looked brighter, Virginia Company promoters in London began to consider how the settlement could be made secure. The backers knew that more immigrants to create a critical mass of colonists would have to be added to the 350 there in 1616. Tobacco culture was labor-intensive. If it were to succeed on the scale necessary, many hands would be needed. Moreover, if the colony were ever to be more than just an outpost, it would have to be filled with people who intended to stay, not temporary employees expecting to be rotated

Young Emissaries

The confrontation between the Indians on North America's eastern coast and the European colonizers is most often thought of in military terms. Great leaders like Captain John Smith and Powhatan hold center stage in most reconstructions. Less well known is the absolutely crucial role played in the Indian-European relationship by children and adolescents from both sides. Neither Smith nor Powhatan would have functioned so well without the children on whom they relied.

Pocahontas was one of these children. At the age of eleven or twelve, she formed a human link between Jamestown and the Powhatans, carrying messages and presents and soothing anger on both sides.

English boys played similar roles in early Virginia. Most ships and colonial forces carried a small number of boys, who could be called on to perform a variety of tasks. When Captain Christopher Newport came to Jamestown in January 1608, thirteen-year-old Thomas Savage was in his crew. Newport took Savage along when, only a month after their arrival, he and John Smith prepared to make a state visit to Powhatan. In order to cement the new English-Powhatan friendship, Newport "gave" Thomas Savage to Powhatan, telling him the boy was his son. The chief delighted in young Savage. Once after Powhatan, in a fit of rage at the English, sent him back to Jamestown, Pocahontas came to the fort and begged that he be returned, because both she and her father loved him "exceedingly."

Another English boy, Henry Spelman, a member of a distinguished family, was apparently sent to Jamestown at the age of fourteen because of his misbehavior. He arrived in 1609 and almost immediately found himself given to one of Powhatan's adult sons, Parahunt, as a token of peace. Spelman, who wrote one of the most revealing descriptions of Virginia Algonquian culture, noted that Parahunt "made very much of me, giving me such things as he had to win me to live with him."

Spelman later lived for a time among the Patawomekes, whose chief Japazaws also treated him as an honored guest. Spelman revealed a talent in caring for the chief's fretful baby: "None could quiet him so well as myself." When Japazaws found young Henry reading a Bible, he asked about a picture of the creation in it. Spelman explained the picture, "which the king seemed to like well of," and then Japazaws told him the creation story of his own people, which the boy judged "a pretty fabulous tale indeed."

These young emissaries were more than just pawns for truces, though that function was important. In living among the Indians, Spelman and Savage learned various native languages, just as Pocahontas learned English. The two English boys lived to be key interpreters as English settlements spread over the land, although Henry Spelman was killed in the fighting that followed the Indian attack of 1622. He was twenty-eight and had been "one of the best Interpreters in the Land" half his life.

The ties created by these young emissaries went beyond diplomatic relationships. Just as Pocahontas called John Smith "Father" when they met in London, the English boys were thought of as sons by the chiefs to whom they were given. Powhatan greeted Thomas Savage in 1614 after the colonists and the Indians had endured four years of warfare with these words: "My child, you are welcome. You have been a stranger to me these four years." But, the aging chief went on, "you are my child, by the [gift] of Captain Newport." The use of English and Indian youngsters as cultural emissaries allowed a level of contact and understanding that even warfare and the mistrust of military leaders could not entirely wipe out.

NOVA BRITANNIA.
OFFERING MOST
Excellent fruites by Planting in
VIRGINIA.

Exciting all fuch as be well affected
to further the fame.

LONDON
Printed for SAMVEL MACHAM, and are to befold at
his Shop in Pauls Church-yard, at the
Signe of the Bul-head.
1 6 0 9.

Advertising Jamestown. *Nova Britannia* was a pamphlet published in London in 1609 by Robert Johnson, part of a massive propaganda campaign designed to interest people in the reorganized Jamestown colony and to counteract the bad publicity generated by the high death rate of its first year. (New York Public Library, Rare Book Division, Astor, Lenox, and Tilden Foundations)

home after a tour of duty. So the Virginia Company began to think in terms of true transplantation of English society.

The transformation of Virginia into a successful agricultural colony involved more than just sending people. They would have to be the right kind of people, committed to a future of hard work. The promoters also realized (as Raleigh had thirty years before) that a settlement composed primarily of men would always fail. Only colonies that contained a fair proportion of women ever succeeded. The Virginia Assembly acknowledged this fact: "In a new plantation it is not known whether man or woman be more necessary." This was true partly because women's skills of food preservation and clothing manufacture were essential to survival. But it was also true that unless settlers had families to work for, they had no real commitment to the land. Families were encouraged to emigrate and women were recruited to go to the colony as servants and prospective brides.

Thousands of colonists went over in the years after 1618, attracted by a new set of offers the Virginia Company made, which introduced the principle of private property to the plantations. The Virginia Company realized that colonists would work hard to make the venture succeed only if they were promised land of their own. Why should they work to enrich investors in London? Most colonists went as indentured servants, which meant they agreed to work a specified number of years in return for their passage over. But now each servant, man or woman, was guaranteed fifty acres when the indenture was up. Also, those who paid the way of another or bought a share of stock in the Virginia Company were guaranteed fifty acres for each transaction as well. This "headright" system seemed to offer genuine opportunity, and many ordinary men and women took up the offer.

The Virginia Company realized that greater resources were needed to finance the colony's development. Groups of wealthy Englishmen were offered the chance to claim huge tracts of land in Virginia if they would take responsibility for sending over their own colonists and providing them with equipment and supplies. These "particular plantations" were like a series of small corporations within the main Virginia Company, and many who invested in them reaped handsome rewards.

With new incentives in place both for going over as a colonist and for investing in sending settlers, the population grew by leaps and bounds. Soon the plantations spread up the James River seventy miles on either side. The

Advertisement for tobacco. Despite the opposition of King James I and others, smoking quickly became a fashionable habit in England and tobacco a profitable crop for the colonies. This advertisement shows the popular identification of pipe-smoking with Raleigh. (Courtesy Ingham Foster Collection, Imperial Tobacco Limited)

company allowed the colonists to form a general assembly (later to become the House of Burgesses), the first representative body in English America, to discuss common problems. This momentous step was a practical solution to the colonial government's inability to impose laws on all the settlements; it was far better that the planters agree on what should be done. John Rolfe wrote a letter home giving news of the assembly's first meeting in June 1619. He also noted the arrival of twenty Africans sold to the settlers as servants.

As the plantations spread along the river, seizing the best land in Virginia, the pressure on the Indians became intolerable. Powhatan died in 1618, just as the tobacco boom began. He never

learned how badly his strategy had failed. His brother, Opechancanough, took over leadership of the confederacy and, by 1622, determined to do something to stop the English once and for all. He planned a great attack, timed to occur in all the plantations simultaneously at breakfast time on March 22, 1622. Though some of the planters had advance warning from Indians friendly to them, many were surprised and killed. Almost 350 English colonists fell that day.

News of the attack hit the Virginia Company hard. An investigation was launched that yielded far more stunning information. The 350 killed by Indians were just a fraction of total deaths. Of the thousands sent to Virginia under the new plan since 1616, most had died. The colony had been ill-prepared to receive them. Food and housing were inadequate. Moreover, the environment was unhealthy for newcomers throughout the Chesapeake. Malaria, introduced in a mild form by the English and later in a more deadly form by Africans, killed many throughout the seventeenth century. Most immigrants were sickly during their first two years, as their bodies became acclimated to the malaria parasite. During this period, known as the "seasoning," large numbers, sometimes up to half, of newcomers succumbed. If colonists survived two years, their chances of living a normal span were good, but most in the region were sickly all their lives, and even the normal life span there was short by the standards of English colonies to the north.

Only a portion of this picture could be seen in the 1620s. Much remained to be revealed. When the royal investigation looked at Virginia after 1622, it saw a situation in which, of 3,000 people sent to Virginia since 1618, less than a third were alive when the Indians attacked. Negligence and bad planning had killed many more English subjects than the Indians had. Gossips in England now said that the whole enterprise was nothing more than "a more regulated kind of killing of men." The king could not allow his subjects to be condemned to death through the bad management of a private company. He took the charter away from the Virginia Company and the government took direct control of the colony. Virginia became the first royal colony, with a governor appointed by the king. The phase of privately sponsored colonization was over in Virginia, though joint-stock companies would be allowed to found later settlements.

From the colony's standpoint, however, development went on as before. As long as economic conditions remained dismal in England, people would continue to take a chance on America. Terrible death rates were not enough to stem the flow of hopeful servants and planters, and tobacco production expanded at an incredible rate. In 1615, colonists had exported 2,000 pounds of tobacco; in 1620, it was 40,000 pounds; and by 1629, 1,500,000 pounds. Virginia was growing according to a pattern that would typify the South: concentration on a single crop, often to the exclusion even of growing their own food. Opechancanough had not stopped the process, and saw his people suffer through ten years of murderous warfare after 1622 while the plantations expanded at an even greater rate. In 1644 he tried again with another great attack. This time he was so old that he had to be carried out to watch the fighting on a stretcher. Again, casualties were high, but the colony was now too strong and the English population too large.

The Indians carried out this 1644 attack in a fatalistic spirit, preferring death to the life of a conquered people. Those who survived the colony's punitive warfare were forced to acknowledge the Virginians' dominion over them. Now no barrier remained to the rapid expansion of the English population throughout the colony in the search for new lands on which to plant tobacco.

Tobacco was the gold of Virginia. Though concentration on one crop brought problems, it provided a firm foundation for an English presence in America. The pattern was set, and the lessons learned. All future English colonies would be made up of families. All colonists would come expecting to mix their labor with the American soil to produce commodities to sustain them. Just as Virginia's tobacco economy was becoming established, in 1620 a colony of Puritan separatists and others, all grouped in families, were settling Plymouth in New England. A decade later the colony of Massachusetts Bay was founded at Boston, and the stream of immigrants, both to New England and to the Chesapeake, became a mighty flood.

Suggestions for Further Reading

SIR WALTER RALEIGH

Raleigh has been the subject of many biographies. Among the best recent ones are Robert Lacey, *Sir Walter Ralegh* (1973), and Stephen J. Greenblatt, *Sir Walter Ralegh: The Renaissance Man and His Roles* (1973). David B. Quinn has written a highly detailed history of the Roanoke colony, capping his lifetime of work on the subject: *Set Fair for Roanoke: Voyages and Colonies, 1584–1606* (1985). Karen Ordahl Kupperman, *Roanoke: The Abandoned Colony* (1984), offers a briefer history incorporating new work on English social history. The Roanoke documents are available in David B. Quinn and Alison Quinn, eds., *The First Colonists: Documents on the Planting of the First English Settlements in North America, 1584–1590* (1982). Thomas Hariot's *Briefe and True Report of the New Found Land of Virginia* (1588) has been republished in facsimile with the DeBry woodcuts of John White's paintings by Dover Books (1972). John White's paintings are available in *America 1585: The Complete Drawings of John White* (1984). On the connection between English activities in Ireland and American colonization, see Nicholas P. Canny, "The Ideology of English Colonization: From Ireland to America," *William and Mary Quarterly*, 3rd ser., 30 (1973), 575–98.

CHRONOLOGY

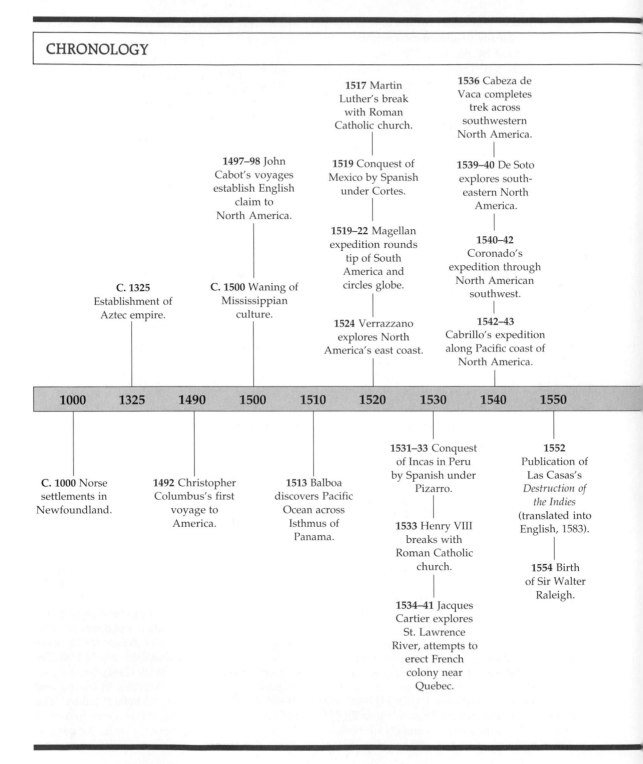

1517 Martin Luther's break with Roman Catholic church.

1536 Cabeza de Vaca completes trek across southwestern North America.

1497–98 John Cabot's voyages establish English claim to North America.

1519 Conquest of Mexico by Spanish under Cortes.

1539–40 De Soto explores south-eastern North America.

1519–22 Magellan expedition rounds tip of South America and circles globe.

1540–42 Coronado's expedition through North American southwest.

C. 1325 Establishment of Aztec empire.

C. 1500 Waning of Mississippian culture.

1524 Verrazzano explores North America's east coast.

1542–43 Cabrillo's expedition along Pacific coast of North America.

| 1000 | 1325 | 1490 | 1500 | 1510 | 1520 | 1530 | 1540 | 1550 |

C. 1000 Norse settlements in Newfoundland.

1492 Christopher Columbus's first voyage to America.

1513 Balboa discovers Pacific Ocean across Isthmus of Panama.

1531–33 Conquest of Incas in Peru by Spanish under Pizarro.

1552 Publication of Las Casas's *Destruction of the Indies* (translated into English, 1583).

1533 Henry VIII breaks with Roman Catholic church.

1554 Birth of Sir Walter Raleigh.

1534–41 Jacques Cartier explores St. Lawrence River, attempts to erect French colony near Quebec.

1558 Accession of Queen Elizabeth I.

1562–65 French colony at Port Royal on South Carolina coast.

1565 San Agustín founded by Spanish in Florida.

1582 Raleigh's appearance at court.

1584 Raleigh sends first reconnaissance voyage to Roanoke . Hakluyt writes *Discourse of Western Planting*. Manteo and Wanchese come to England.

1585 Roanoke colony set up as privateering base.

1585–1603 Privateering war between England and Spain.

1595 Raleigh's first voyage to Guiana.

1596 Raleigh participates in raid on Cadiz.

1598 Juan de Oñate establishes permanent Spanish presence north of Rio Grande.

1602–08 Champlain explores New England and St. Lawrence.

1603 Death of Queen Elizabeth, accession of James I. Sir Walter Raleigh arrested and sentenced to death.

1616–18 Introduction of headright system in Virginia. Women sent in large influx of new colonists after 1618.

1617 Death of Pocahontas.

1618 Execution of Sir Walter Raleigh. Death of Powhatan.

1619 First meeting of Virginia Assembly. First Africans in Virginia.

1620 Plymouth colony founded in New England.

1622 Concerted Indian attack on Virginia plantations led by Opechancanough.

1624 Virginia becomes first royal colony.

1560	1570	1580	1590	1600	1610	1620	1630	1640

1571–72 Spanish mission on Chesapeake Bay destroyed by Indians.

1572–75 Spanish settlement at Santa Elena on South Carolina coast.

1586 Death of Wingina. First Roanoke colony returns home with Sir Francis Drake.

1587 Second Roanoke colony. This group becomes the Lost Colony.

1588 England defeats great Spanish Armada.

1588, 1590 Publication of Thomas Hariot's *Brief and True Report of the New Found Land of Virginia* with paintings by John White.

1590 John White's expedition to Roanoke finds site deserted.

1592 Raleigh expelled from court because of his secret marriage.

1607 Jamestown founded on Chesapeake Bay. Sagadahoc founded in Maine.

1608 Permanent settlement of Quebec by French colonists.

1608–09 Captain John Smith president of Virginia.

1609 Virginia Company reorganized. Second starving winter.

1610 Santa Fe established in New Mexico territory.

1644 Second great Indian attack led by Opechancanough.

EUROPE'S NEW WORLD

Bruce Trigger, ed., *The Northeast: Handbook of the Indians of North America*, vol. 15, gen. ed. William C. Sturtevant (1978), contains very readable articles by specialists on individual Indian tribes as well as general topics. It covers Indians all over the Northeast, including as far south as the Carolinas. It is the starting place for any question about Indian life in the east. For an overview of evidence on prehistoric cultures, see George E. Stuart, "Who Were the 'Mound Builders'?" *National Geographic* 142 (1972): 783–801. See also the articles in R. Reid Badger and Lawrence Clayton, eds., *Alabama and the Borderlands: From Prehistory to Statehood* (1985). Charles Hudson, *The Southeastern Indians* (1976), offers a very full discussion of the culture of the Southeast, along with some material on the impact of European colonization. Edward H. Spicer, *Cycles of Conquest: The Impact of Spain, Mexico, and the United States on the Indians of the Southwest, 1533–1960* (1962), discusses the cultures in the Southwest and the major changes wrought by the coming of Europeans. Arrell Morgan Gibson, *The American Indian, Prehistory to the Present* (1980), is an overview, mostly focusing on European-Indian interaction. On the diseases that struck the Indians and other biological effects of the voyages to America, see Alfred W. Crosby, Jr., *The Columbian Exchange: Biological and Cultural Consequences of 1492* (1972).

The most thorough and informed overview of all European exploration and the beginnings of colonization is David B. Quinn, *North America from Earliest Discovery to First Settlements: The Norse Voyages to 1612* (1977). See also his *England and the Discovery of America, 1481–1620* (1974). Another very useful source is K. G. Davies, *The North Atlantic World in the Seventeenth Century* (1974). Kenneth R. Andrews, *Trade, Plunder, and Settlement: Maritime Enterprise and the Genesis of the British Empire, 1480–1630* (1984), describes the manifold overseas interests of English investors and places America within that context.

JAMESTOWN

On Jamestown and the settlement of Virginia, see Karen Ordahl Kupperman, ed., *John Smith: A Select Edition of his Writings* (1988). Edmund S. Morgan, *American Slavery, American Freedom: The Ordeal of Colonial Virginia* (1975), offers a challenging interpretation of the early colonial experience and the growth of slavery. Alden Vaughan, *American Genesis: Captain John Smith and the Founding of Virginia* (1975), describes the colony's first two decades. The essays in Thad W. Tate and David L. Ammerman, eds., *The Chesapeake in the Seventeenth Century: Essays on Anglo-American Society* (1979), take up important aspects of the problems of Virginia's founding.

Indian relations in early Virginia are the subject of Nancy Lurie's illuminating article, "Indian Cultural Adjustment to European Civilization," in James Morton Smith, ed., *Seventeenth-Century America: Essays in Colonial History* (1959), 33–60. The classic book on the controversial end of the Virginia Company and the transition to royal government is Wesley Frank Craven, *The Dissolution of the Virginia Company: The Failure of a Colonial Experiment* (1932).

CHAPTER 2
NEW COMMUNITIES
IN THE SOUTH

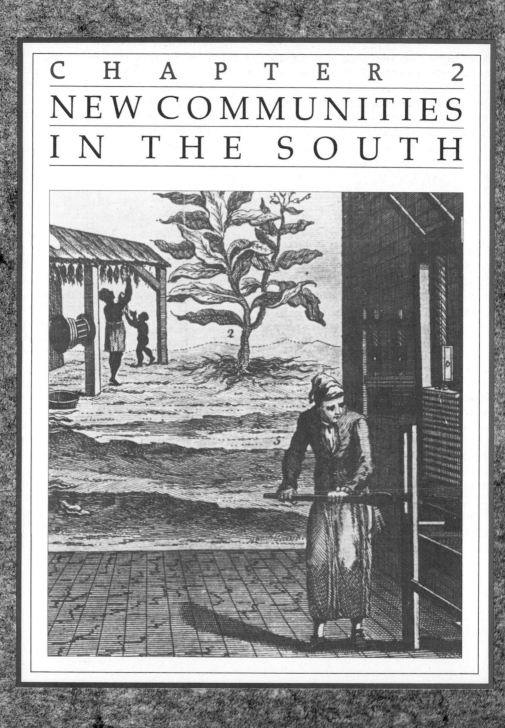

THE EPISODE: *In 1676, England's Virginia colony was in open and armed rebellion. The uprising became known as Bacon's Rebellion, after its youthful leader Nathaniel Bacon. Against Bacon and his rebels stood the king's government, led by the elderly governor Sir William Berkeley. Both men belonged, by birth and training, to the English elite. But historical circumstance made them enemies. For months, Bacon and Berkeley marshalled armed forces of white (and a few African-American) Virginians and struggled for control of the colony and its capital at Jamestown. In the process, they made peace more than once. But the struggle could not be settled by compromises or by official commissions or proclamations. Only threats, deceptions, and the force of arms could prevail.*

Bacon's Rebellion was complicated by another, parallel conflict, "the Virginia War." On one side were the Native American peoples of the area around Chesapeake Bay, trying to find ways of resisting or accommodating to the European invasion of their lands. On the other were the English people who thought they had come to "settle" Virginia—despite the fact that it was already settled. Bacon's "army," which sometimes had hundreds of armed and mounted men, spent as much time fighting the Native Americans as it did fighting Berkeley's forces. In the process, the rebels murdered and kidnapped, making little or no discrimina-tion between tribes that were supposed to be "friendly" or "hostile."

THE HISTORICAL SETTING: *At times, the rebellion seemed to be a contest between these two stubborn men. But history is almost never shaped by the obstinate will of one or two individuals. The historical forces that shaped Bacon's Rebellion were complex and involved two of the most profoundly important elements of America's history: race and class.*

The people who lived in Virginia and the other English colonies of the South were engaged in desperate struggles for domination. Those of English origin and descent were attempting to dominate Native Americans, even if the outcome was to be the extermination of whole tribes and cultures. The English and other European Americans were also seeking domination of Africans and African Americans, even if the outcome was the enslavement of tens or hundreds of thousands. And European Americans who had succeeded in getting wealth and power were trying to maintain their social and political domination of their poorer white neighbors and servants. Bacon's Rebellion came at a critical point in all these struggles for dominion. Its causes and outcomes can be understood only through an understanding of the way conflicts between races and social classes became the formative ground of the colonial experience in the Southern colonies.

Bacon's Rebellion

Thomas Mathew was a tobacco farmer with a small plantation on the south bank of the Potomac River in the English colony of Virginia. And he was worried. In 1675, he was watching what he believed were frightening "signs" that something terrible was about to happen. First came a great comet, "streaming like a horse tail, until it reached almost the horizon." Then flights of pigeons came into coastal Virginia from someplace in the vast and mysterious wilderness of the interior of the continent. There were so many of them that when they roosted at night, their weight broke even large tree limbs. The third "strange appearance" was "swarms of flies about an inch long and big as the top of a man's little finger, rising out of holes in the earth, which ate the new-sprouted leaves from the top of the trees, and in a month left us."

Mathew and his neighbors of the Virginia colony tried hard to decipher what these signs meant. They had good reason, for their situation was precarious. The English had been in Virginia for almost seventy years, but there still were only about 30,000 of them living and farming along the shores and riverbanks of the Chesapeake area. So they had to wonder what new disasters the comet, the pigeons, and the flies might foretell. Was there going to be another hurricane like the one that had devastated the colony a few years before? Or a terrible drought like the one that had ruined almost a whole year's tobacco crop? But the European-Americans in Virginia were most likely to read the signs as warnings of trouble with the Native Americans. According to Mathew, the comet "put the old planters under portentous apprehensions, because the like was seen when the Indians committed their last massacre." (Whenever Native Americans attacked Europeans, it was called a massacre; whenever the settlers attacked the Indians it was called something like "war.")

There were good reasons to worry and watch the skies for signs. There had been problems recently with the Doegs, a normally "friendly" tribe. They lived just across the Potomac in Maryland. Mathew himself had neglected to pay for some goods he had bought from the Doegs. In retaliation, the Doegs had tried to steal some of Mathew's hogs, but a band of Englishmen had tracked the Indians down and killed one or two of them. Mathew also knew that a band of Susquehanna Indians, much more warlike than the Doegs, had moved down from farther north to the Maryland side of the Potomac. Technically, both the Doegs and Susquehannas were friendly and lived under Maryland's protection. But the Potomac region was crowded—with

Virginians, Marylanders, Doegs, and Susquehannas. All the English who had lived through or even heard about earlier Indian wars expected trouble.

Trouble came to Mathew's door. He owned another plantation several miles up the Potomac, run by an overseer and a herdsman named Robert Hen. On a Sunday morning in July 1675, some people on their way to church passed near Hen's house and saw him lying in his doorway, hurt. An Indian lay nearby. Both men had been "chopped on their heads, arms and other parts, as if done with Indian hatchets." The Indian was already dead, and Hen was dying. But he had time to gasp, "Doegs! Doegs!" before he died. Then a boy who had been hiding under a bed in the house came out and told the people that "Indians had come at the break of day and done these murders."

Stealing hogs was one thing, but the death of an Englishman was much more serious. The Virginians had a militia to deal with such matters, and the local leaders called the farmers to arms. Years later, Mathew recalled what happened:

> Of this horrid action, Colonel Mason, who commanded the militia regiment of foot, and Captain Brent, the troop of horses in that country, having speedy notice, raised thirty or more men. They pursued the Indians twenty miles up and four miles over the river into Maryland. Landing at the dawn of day, they found two small paths. Each leader took a separate path, and either found a cabin, which they silently surrounded.

The English were not nearly so skilled at forest warfare as the Native Americans. But this time they were able to catch their enemy by surprise—probably because the Indians knew that it was against English law for Virginia militia to cross into Maryland.

> Captain Brent went to the Doegs' cabin. Speaking the Indian tongue, he called to have a *Matchacomicha Weewhip*, a Council, such being the usual manner with Indians. The king came trembling forth, and would have fled, when Captain Brent, catching hold of his twisted lock (which was all the hair he wore), told him he was come for the murderer of Robert Hen. The king pleaded ignorance, and slipped loose. Brent shot him dead with his pistol. The Indians shot two or three guns out of the cabin; the English shot into it. The Indians thronged out at the door and fled. The English shot as many as they could, so that they killed ten, and brought away the king's son of about eight years old.

So far, the Virginians' mission of revenge had been successful, at least by their own standards. They had taken ten Indian lives for one English life. And at this point they were not troubled by the fact that they had illegally invaded a sister colony. They did not even care that they had no way of knowing whether or not these particular Indians had actually been involved in the murder of Hen. But the other half of the company of militia was about to make a very costly mistake.

> The noise of the shooting awakened the Indians in the cabin which Colonel Mason had encompassed. They likewise rushed out and fled. The company shot fourteen before an Indian came and with both hands shook Colonel Mason (in a friendly way) by one arm, saying "*Susquehanougs Netoughs!* Susquehanna friends!" and fled. Whereupon Colonel Mason ran among his men, crying out, "For the Lord's sake, shoot no more! These are our friends, the Susquehannas!"

Mason and Brent took their militia back to the Virginia side of the Potomac. They had won a military victory, in which thirty Virginians had killed almost as many Indians. They had punished the Doegs. But in doing so, they had caused more problems than they had solved, for the Susquehannas would want revenge.

The Susquehannas who escaped Colonel Mason's troops went upriver to a fort their tribe had built on the Maryland side. The main body of the tribe had about a hundred warriors, plus their wives and children. They had built an English-style fortress with walls made of tree trunks sunk into the ground. At the corners were firing platforms, and the square was surrounded by a ditch.

With the Susquehannas safely inside their fort, the English had time to stop and think. The governor of Maryland sent a protest to the Virginia capital at Jamestown concerning the Virginians' illegal invasion of Maryland territory. A month passed without any serious trouble, and the governor of Virginia, Sir William Berkeley, ordered an investigation. He told two militia leaders to call together all the officers in the northern area of Virginia to conduct an inquiry. Berkeley wanted to move cautiously. He had kept peace with the Native Americans for over thirty years, and he did not want an Indian war now. But the militia leaders violated their orders. Instead of calling out the officers of the militia to make an investigation, they called out the troops. And, without authority, they asked for help from Maryland. Altogether, about a thousand men were quickly assembled from the two colonies. Before Governor Berkeley knew what was happening, they had set out up the Potomac to attack the Susquehanna fort.

The English arrived at the Indian fort in late September 1675, about two months after the murder of Robert Hen. The commanders asked the Indians for a council, just as they had done at the Doeg cabin. The Indians sent out four of their "great men." The English betrayed the truce by axing the Susquehanna chiefs to death; then they attacked the fort.

The Susquehannas were ready, however. They resisted the English successfully for several weeks, "shooting many of our men, and making frequent, fierce and bloody sallies. And when they were called to, or offered parley, they gave no other answer than 'Where are our four *Cockarouses* [Great Men]'"

The Indians kept themselves from starving by stealing English horses for food. But finally they had to escape. Seventy-five braves crept out of the fort at night, with their families, and killed ten sleeping English sentries in the process. In the morning the English militia awoke to find only three or four old people left in the fort. The Susquehannas, bitter at the murders of their chiefs, broke up into small bands of roving warriors, determined to take revenge. In a body, contained within their fort, they could have been controlled by the English. Now there was no way to keep track of them.

So far, every move the English had made was wrong. Governor Berkeley was outraged by the open murder of the Susquehanna chiefs. At the next meeting of the House of Burgesses (the lower house of the Virginia legislature), he declared: "If they had killed my grandfather and grandmother, my father and mother and all my friends, yet if they had come to treat of peace, they ought to have gone in peace!"

But more than the governor's sense of honor had been damaged. The militia had lost fifty men in its siege of the Susquehanna fort. (This loss in a colony of 30,000

The Susquehanna fort. After Bacon's Rebellion ended, the English sent royal commissioners to Virginia to investigate. As part of their report, the commissioners drew this rough map of the Susquehanna fort in Maryland. They pictured the siege of the fort as if it had been a formal battle between European forces. The Susquehannas' fortifications are impossibly square—as are the encampments of the "Virginians maine Garde" (marked with an "o") and the "Merrylanders maine Garde" (marked "n"). The overall effect is much more neat and geometrical than the rough and amateurish battle actually was.

inhabitants is comparable to the loss of more than 20,000 soldiers in the twentieth-century American population of over 200 million.) Moreover, the roaming Susquehannas soon began to make themselves felt. In January 1676, they raided some settlements on the upper Rappahannock and Potomac rivers and killed or captured thirty-six people.

Then the Indians surprised Berkeley by sending him a proposal of peace. The Susquehannas, too, had their idea of justice. The Susquehanna chief told the governor that since the Indians had now killed ten English settlers for every one of the murdered "great men," they were satisfied. There need be no more war. But if the English wanted war, the chief concluded, his people were ready to fight to the last man.

The "Indian troubles" had reached a critical point, and a policy decision had to be made. The murder of Hen, the attacks on the Doeg and Susquehanna cabins, the disastrous campaign against the Susquehanna fort, and the Susquehanna attacks of January could all be regarded as a series of small incidents. They had grown out of a misunderstanding between Thomas Mathew and the Doegs. All in all, about an equal number of Indians and whites had been killed. And the Susquehannas seemed ready to call off the fighting. Thus Governor Berkeley replied to them in a peaceful way, and during April and May the Susquehannas killed no whites, though they did steal some livestock.

There were really two conflicts in Virginia. The first, obviously, was between whites and Native Americans. The second was between small, frontier planters and the royal government. The small planters, like other frontiersmen throughout American history, believed that the solution to the first conflict was simply to wipe out all the Indians. Good land was already becoming scarce in the settled areas of Virginia, and whites were crowding north and west. The tobacco planters on the frontier had a very simple program. Every Virginian was armed, and most had horses. So volunteers would gather wherever there was the slightest hint of trouble and would kill as many Indians as they could find.

One difficulty with this policy was that it offered no real way of dealing with the many small tribes of friendly Indians that lived on permanent "plantations" (reservations) among the whites. These friendly tribes, such as the Doegs of Maryland, had technically become subjects of the English ruler many years earlier. They had a legal right to their lands, under English law, and they were a valuable source of beaver skins—a commodity second only to tobacco in economic importance in Virginia.

Governor Berkeley, as head of the royal establishment, wanted a policy of peace and order that would protect the friendly tribes and the beaver trade. He also wanted Indian policy to rest in the hands of the government at Jamestown, not in the hands of hundreds of small planters scattered along the edges of the wilderness. Berkeley's Indian policy, in other words, was generally defensive, while that of the small planters was offensive. The government's policy, which was slow and cautious, conflicted with the farmers' wish for drastic and immediate action.

The governor made the next move. He called the Virginia legislature into session in early March and had an act passed that declared war on the Indians and provided for defense against them. The colony would build a fort at the falls of each river and create a permanent army of approximately 500 men. Parties of horsemen would conduct regular patrols between the forts. To prevent a repetition of the murders of Indians that had occurred the preceding winter, the act provided that the governor's personal permission would be necessary for any attack on an Indian fort or village—a permission that might take days to obtain.

To the planters on the frontier, Governor Berkeley's plans made very little sense. The English forts would be separated by miles of forest, through which the Indians could move at will. The forts, with their permanent garrisons, would be expensive. Tobacco prices were very low, and many planters could hardly make ends meet. Paying taxes to support a useless military policy would only add to their economic troubles. Furthermore, it would not provide them with any real security from the Indians.

According to the report of a royal commission that later investigated the episode, the "vulgar sort" began to protest the governor's policy. Berkeley himself summed up the situation with classic simplicity and accuracy: "How miserable the man is," he wrote home to England, "that governs a people where six parts of seven at least are poor, indebted, discontented, and armed."

According to the report of the royal commission, the plain people of Virginia were near rebellion:

> The unsatisfied people finding themselves still liable to the Indian cruelties, and the cries of their wives and children growing grievous and intolerable to them, gave out in speeches that they were resolved to plant tobacco rather than pay the tax for maintaining the forts; that the erecting of the forts was a great grievance and cheat, and of no more use than another plantation with men at it; and that it was merely a design of the grandees [wealthy planters] to take all the tobacco into their own hands.

One group of angry planters from Charles City County went so far as to send out a call to arms against the Indians. When they brought a petition to the governor asking him to support an attack on the Indians, Berkeley angrily sent the petitioners away and "bid a pox take" them. The Charles City County men decided to gather in arms anyway, and they set up camp on the James River, where they were joined by men from Henrico County. They were now in open rebellion against the royal government. According to the report of the royal commission sent to investigate:

> The rout [the "giddy-headed multitude"] being got together now, wanted nor waited for nothing but one to head and lead them out on their design. It so happened that one Nathaniel Bacon, Jr., a person whose lost and desperate fortunes had thrown him into that remote part of the world about fourteen months before, was fit for such a purpose. [Actually, Bacon was wealthier than most Virginians.]

After months of trying to restore peace and maintain a cautious Indian policy, Governor Berkeley was faced with a collective force of about 300 rebellious men ready to defy his orders and follow a young and vigorous leader. In the weeks that followed, concern about the Indians became almost irrelevant, or at least secondary. Nathaniel Bacon and Governor Berkeley conducted a bitter and violent personal contest for control of Virginia, a contest known as Bacon's Rebellion.

Sir William Berkeley, the governor, and Nathaniel Bacon, Jr., the rebel, were in many ways very much alike. In fact, they were even cousins by marriage. Both came from wealthy English families. Each held a degree of master of arts from a great English university—Berkeley from Oxford and Bacon from Cambridge—in a day when most people could not even read. In addition, Bacon had traveled across Europe in the company of a tutor, and he had studied law in London for two years. Governor Berkeley, who had even written a play while still in England, was something of an amateur scholar and scientist. Most important, both men were enormously proud and quick to anger.

The two crucial differences between Berkeley and Bacon were age and position. Sir William Berkeley was almost seventy years old when the Indian troubles erupted. He had been governor of Virginia off and on since the early 1640s. In his youth, he had gained fame as a vigorous leader in the English wars against the Indians. Now he was tired. He wrote home to his king saying that his bones could not bear another six months in office. His age had also made him extremely irritable.

Sir William Berkeley. This portrait was painted sometime during Berkeley's long second term as governor, 1660–1676. His clothes and wig, his expression, and his way of posing all point up his claims to aristocratic status and cultivated manners. But his royal master Charles II did not always agree. After Berkeley hanged a number of Bacon's followers, the king compared the governor's actions to his own mild revenge on the group that had beheaded his father, Charles I: "That old fool has killed more people in that naked country than I have done for the murder of my father." (Courtesy of Mr. Maurice Du Pont Lee)

Nathaniel Bacon, on the other hand, was only in his twenties. According to contemporary accounts, he was extremely vain and ambitious, and he had a fortune and a career to make. The governor had an office: He was the king's principal servant in the largest and most profitable English colony in America. Bacon was a young planter with two plantations near the frontier, a born leader without an official position and without a following.

When the men of Charles City and Henrico counties gathered on the James River, Bacon had been in Virginia only a little over a year. But he had a great deal of money, and he was quite dashing. As soon as Bacon had come to Virginia, Berkeley had appointed him to the Governor's Council, the upper house of the Virginia legislature. His fortune, his dash, and his position—together with the fact that he lived near the western frontier—made him a ripe candidate for the leadership of the rebellious planters camped near his home. As the royal commission of investigation described him:

> He was said to be indifferent tall but slender, blackhaired and of an ominous, pensive, melancholy aspect, not given to much talk, or to make sudden replies, of a most imperious and dangerous hidden pride of heart, despising the wisest of his neighbors for their ignorance, and very ambitious and arrogant. But all these things lay hidden in him until he became powerful and popular.

This description, recorded after Bacon was dead, was written by the commissioners of a king whose authority Bacon had defied. The people whom Bacon led had kinder words for him, but both his friends and his enemies agreed that Nathaniel Bacon was a man of hot temper and quick to violence.

According to the report of the royal commission, Bacon was mildly tricked into taking command of the rebel army. He was

> in company of one Crews, Isham, and Bird, growing to a height of drinking, and making the sadness of the times their discourse. Crews and the rest persuaded Mr. Bacon to go over and see the soldiers on the other side of the James River, and to take a quantity of rum with them to give the men to drink. And (as Crews and others had before laid the plot with the soldiers) they all at once in the field shouted and cried out "Bacon! Bacon! Bacon!"—which, taking fire with his ambition, easily prevailed on him to head them.

After this staged and somewhat alcoholic demonstration, Bacon and his "soldiers" made a decision. They would ask the governor once more for a commission to go to war with the Indians. If Berkeley refused again, they would fight anyway.

> Bacon's friends told him they would go along with him to take revenge on the Indians, and drink damnation to their souls to be true to him. And, if he could not obtain a commission, they would assist him as well and as much as if he had one. He boasted what great service he would do for the country, and subtly and secretly seduced the vulgar and most ignorant people (two-thirds of each county being of that sort) so that their whole hearts and hopes were set now upon Bacon. Thus Bacon encouraged the tumult. And as the unquiet crowd followed him, he listed them upon a large paper, writing their names circular-wise, so that the ringleaders might not be found out.

During the next few days, Bacon recruited about 300 men to his cause. When Governor Berkeley angrily refused him the commission, Bacon led his troops into the forest. Berkeley rode out from Jamestown with a troop of "gentlemen" to try to stop Bacon, but he was too late. All he could do was to proclaim Bacon and his followers "rebels and mutineers."

In the meantime, Bacon and his men had marched off to the southwest. They found no Susquehannas. Gradually, as provisions ran low, the force dwindled to about fifty men, tired, restless, and hungry. Finally, they came upon a well-built fort belonging to a tribe of Indians called Occaneechis. The Occaneechis were friendly. In fact, they made their living partly by serving as middlemen in the beaver trade between the English and Indians who lived farther south and west. Their fort was many miles from the nearest English plantation, on an island in the Roanoke River. There was no evidence that they had been involved in the recent troubles.

The Occaneechis greeted Bacon and his followers warmly, sending out canoes to bring them to the island fort. Bacon explained that he was hunting Susquehannas. The Occaneechi chief informed him that there was a band of Susquehannas nearby and that, as a gesture of good will, the Occaneechis would wipe them out. Bacon agreed, and remained safe at the Occaneechi fort with his men while the small Susquehanna party was destroyed. A few prisoners were brought back to the Occaneechi fort and tortured to "entertain" the English.

Eyewitness accounts of what happened next are confused. For some reason Bacon ordered his men to surround the Occaneechi fort and keep as many Indian women and children outside as possible. This tense situation was broken by a shot

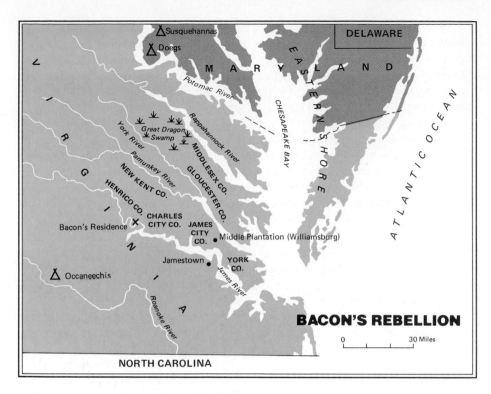

BACON'S REBELLION

0   30 Miles

NORTH CAROLINA

that killed one of Bacon's men. But the English were already at the fort walls, ready to fire in through the portholes. For a day and a half they poured shot in on the Indians. They also "fell upon the women and children without, disarmed and destroyed them all," according to a version of the event written by one of Bacon's own followers. When the battle was over, the Occaneechis had been destroyed. Bacon felt no need to justify the attack or make any distinctions between Indian friends and enemies. He said simply: "We fell upon a town of Indians, beginning our fight after midnight close at their portholes."

Bacon had not fired a shot at the Susquehannas. Instead, he had destroyed a friendly tribe—men, women, and children. But, like most of his followers, his aim was to kill Indians, not to conduct careful negotiations or make fine distinctions between friends and foes. He rode with his band of Indian fighters back to Henrico County, boasting of a great victory.

⌘

While Bacon was killing Occaneechis on the far-off Roanoke, Governor Berkeley was busily trying to repair his collapsing political popularity. He had not called for the election of a new House of Burgesses in more than fifteen years. Now he did so, and he even provided that all freemen could vote (the vote was normally restricted to property owners), a move designed to appeal to the "rabble" who supported Bacon.

The governor also offered to pardon Bacon, if Bacon would apologize. But Bacon refused, saying that "Indians in general were all enemies," and that he would not stop warring against them. The governor's policy backfired. As a result of the election, the new House of Burgesses was packed with Bacon men. The two commanders who had attacked the Susquehanna fort in the fall of 1675 were elected. Bacon himself was voted a burgess from Henrico County.

The new assembly opened on June 5, 1676. Bacon came cautiously down the river to Jamestown in a sloop with thirty armed men. He anchored out of gunshot range of Jamestown and waited to see what the governor would do. Berkeley, now angry and bitter, reacted in a way that Bacon might easily have anticipated. He sent a visiting ship, the *Adam and Eve*, to capture Bacon's little sloop. Bacon, the rebel, the wealthy young planter, and a recently elected member of the House of Burgesses, was taken into Jamestown as a military prisoner.

The governor now had Bacon in his power, but he also had to face the people of Virginia and their elected legislators. Berkeley's concern for order and calm won out over his anger: He decided to liberate Bacon and return him to his place on the Governor's Council. He also promised him a commission to fight the Indians. Bacon, in return, agreed at last to humble himself.

In a dramatic gesture Berkeley stood stiffly before the House of Burgesses and said, "If there be joy in the presence of the angels over one sinner that repenteth, there is now. For we have a repentant sinner before us. Call Mr. Bacon!" Bacon entered the chamber and knelt before Berkeley, begging the pardon of God, the king, and the governor. Berkeley paused for a moment and then said three times, "God forgive you; I forgive you!"

Both Berkeley and Bacon were probably just acting. Berkeley was not really interested in angelic rejoicing over a repentant sinner. He was trying chiefly to maintain peace and order until he became powerful enough to subdue Bacon for good. Bacon, on his part, was interested only in the commission that would officially make him "General of Virginia."

Neither man got what he wanted. Berkeley delayed the commission, and after a few days Bacon suddenly disappeared from Jamestown. For ten days rumors about his activities filled the air. Then, on June 23, Bacon reappeared, this time at the head of an army of about 400 men, all armed, with more than a hundred on horseback. He had not come to beg the governor's pardon this time. He had come instead to demand his commission, and to take it by force if necessary.

The scene that followed was part drama, part farce. Bacon approached the little statehouse between two files of his own foot soldiers. The governor, with his council, came out to meet him. Berkeley opened his coat and shirt and pointed to his chest, offering Bacon a coward's chance: "Here ! Shoot me! Before God, a fair mark! Shoot!" The governor repeated this insulting invitation several times. Bacon, with equal sarcasm, made a gentle reply: "No, may it please your honor, we will not hurt a hair on your head—nor of any other man's. We are come for a commission to save our lives from the Indians. You have so often promised it, and now we will have it before we go."

Berkeley once more refused to give him the commission; turning his back on Bacon, he began to walk toward his office at the other end of the statehouse. The members of the House of Burgesses, meeting inside, all had crowded to the windows to watch. Bacon followed the governor, shouting and waving his arms, and then suddenly commanded his men to aim their cocked flintlocks at the burgesses in the windows.

"God damn my blood!" Bacon swore. "I'll kill governor, council, assembly and all, and then I'll sheath my sword in my own heart's blood!"

The burgesses were terrified. Bacon gave an order for his men to fire if he drew his sword. Bacon's men were shouting, "We will have it! We will have it!"

Then one of the frightened burgesses waved a handkerchief from the window, shouting back, "You shall have it! You shall have it!"

Bacon had won in this showdown, simply by commanding a superior armed force. The governor had no alternative but to give in or lose his office, perhaps even his life, to the rebels. The assembly made Bacon "General of the Virginia War." A day or two later, the burgesses adjourned to go to their plantations. Berkeley went home to sulk. Bacon led his troops back west, this time with an official commission in his hands. He quickly set about appointing junior officers, to whom he gave the power to take horses, ammunition, and other goods from the plantations of Virginia for the Indian war he planned to wage. It was rumored he was preparing to fight any royal troops that might be sent over from England to put down his rebellion. For the time being, Bacon was in control of Virginia.

For the next few weeks Berkeley did nothing. Nor did Bacon seem to do much besides getting his army organized. Probably a few scouting parties searched for Indians, but there was no action. Bacon had become more interested in his rebellion than in fighting Indians. At the end of July he assembled all his forces at Middle Plantation, the future site of Williamsburg, a few miles from Jamestown. Berkeley, in despair, fled across the Chesapeake to a plantation on the Eastern Shore, abandoning the government.

At Middle Plantation, Bacon held what amounted to a political convention. He sent out an oath for all Virginians to swear, promising they would be loyal to him and even fight royal soldiers in his defense. On August 3 he also issued a "Manifesto and Declaration of the People" that stated the rebels' case against the Indians very clearly. All Indians were enemies and outlaws and ought to be wiped out. The governor had treated them as "darling and protected" subjects, as "quiet and honest neighbors." And, according to the manifesto, the governor had used the beaver trade solely to enrich himself and a small group of friends. This trade had enabled the Indians to arm themselves and murder English settlers. Bacon's solution was simply to put an end to the trade by putting an end to both groups of traders. He ordered the arrest of Berkeley and his associates and promised death to all the Indians.

Bacon's manifesto also introduced a new element into the rebellion. At Middle Plantation, for the first time, Bacon's movement took on the tone of a political revolution. Everyone who wrote about the rebellion at the time agreed on one fact: that Bacon's followers were of the "poorer sort," whereas Berkeley's were "gentlemen" or "grandees." The manifesto recognized this apparent class division for the first time.

The manifesto was full of brilliant political rhetoric, the product of Bacon's excellent education. "If virtue be a sin," Bacon began, then he and his followers were guilty. But, he continued, "we cannot in our hearts find one single spot of rebellion or treason." Instead, Bacon appealed to "the country" to examine its rulers, not its rebels. Over the years Governor Berkeley had gathered around him the wealthiest planters of the colony. These Virginians were a ruling elite—or so Bacon's rebels thought. This elite were men of "vile" education and background, Bacon charged. But they had been suddenly made into "grandees" by "mysterious wiles." Altogether, they were nothing but "sponges who have soaked up the public treasure, unworthy favorites and juggling parasites, whose tottering fortunes have been supported at the public charge."

Bacon marshaled "the people" against these so-called grandees. He insisted that the king would finally side with the people, once the political corruption of the ruling planters was exposed. Bacon demanded the surrender of Berkeley and nineteen of his "wicked counselors" within four days. After that time, he declared, anyone who hid or protected any of the "oppressors" would be considered "traitors to the people." Bacon signed the manifesto: "Nath. Bacon, Gen'l. by the Consent of the People."

Up to now, Bacon had been declared a "rebel and mutineer" by proclamation of the governor. But by marching back to Middle Plantation, sending out "Bacon's oaths" to all the counties of the colony, and issuing the manifesto and declaration, Bacon had become a rebel by even his own definition. In a conversation with John Goode, a Henrico County neighbor, Bacon tried to work out a strategy for resisting England and liberating the colony:

BACON: There is a report that Berkeley has sent to the king for two thousand red-coats.[1] Tell me your opinion. May not five hundred Virginians beat them, we having the same advantages against them the Indians have against us?

GOODE: On the contrary, I think five hundred redcoats may either subject or ruin Virginia.

BACON: You talk strangely. Are we not acquainted with the country, so that we can lay ambushes? Can we not hide behind trees? Are we not as good or better shots than they?

But Goode pointed out to Bacon that with their fleet the English could easily win.

GOODE: They can accomplish what I have said without hazard by landing where there is no opposition, firing our houses and fences, destroying our cattle, preventing trade and cutting off imports.

BACON: I am confident that it is the mind of this colony, and of Maryland as well as Carolina, to cast off their governors. And if we cannot prevail by arms, we may retire to the Roanoke [River] and establish our own government there.

By this time, both Bacon and Goode were becoming angry.

GOODE: Sir, this design will produce utter ruin. I hope you will excuse me from having any part in it.

BACON: I am glad to know your mind, but I think this proceeds from mere cowardice.

---

[1]English troops were given this name because of their scarlet uniforms.

At any rate, if a revolution was part of Bacon's plan, he seemed to have won easily. Berkeley had abandoned most of Virginia, and many of the planters appeared ready to follow Bacon. Without any real authority, Bacon ordered the election of a new House of Burgesses to meet in Jamestown on September 4.

When he had completed all these dangerous but successful political actions, Bacon gathered his troops and set out west in search of Indians. They were still supposed to be his principal concern. Once again, he did not pursue the Susquehannas, the real "enemy." Instead, he plunged his army into the Great Dragon Swamp to search for the village of a small, friendly tribe, the Pamunkeys. (Some suspected them, wrongly, of planning opposition to the English.) The swamp was a difficult place for Indians to maneuver in; it was nearly impossible for armed Englishmen. Bacon's army, which at first probably numbered a thousand, gradually dwindled to about 150 wet, tired men who were running low on food. Several times Bacon had to make fiery speeches to whip up the falling spirits of his men:

> I would rather my carcass should lie rotting in the woods, than miss doing the service the country expects from me. All you gentlemen that intend to abide with me must resolve to undergo all the hardship this wild can afford, and if need be to eat chestnuts and horseflesh before you return.

Finally, after days of marching back and forth across the swamp, Bacon happened on the Pamunkey village. His men immediately charged and opened fire. The Indians did not resist but simply ran. The English killed eight Pamunkeys and captured forty-five more. This was Bacon's second "victory" over the Indians. He stumbled out of the swamp toward Jamestown (expecting to find his House of Burgesses ready to meet). He had the captured Pamunkeys tied in a row as evidence of his success as an Indian fighter.

~♥

When Bacon emerged from the swamp, instead of finding a victory celebration, he was confronted with the shocking news that Berkeley had somehow managed to occupy Jamestown again. The governor had a thousand troops. Moored on the James were several large English ships with heavy guns, ready to defend the capital.

The shrewd old governor had played a sly trick. He had won control of Virginia's waterways. The colony in 1676 was as much water as land. Chesapeake Bay and rivers like the James, the York, and the Potomac led everywhere into the settled areas of the colony. Bacon too had realized this early in the rebellion, and he had captured two or three large merchant ships and armed them with cannon from Jamestown's fort. He hoped that these ships could capture any other vessels that might sail from England, including warships of the royal navy.

Early in September, while Bacon was hunting Indians in the Great Dragon Swamp, his little fleet sailed the thirty miles across the Chesapeake to attack Berkeley on the Eastern Shore. The rebel "navy" had 300 men, more than enough to capture Berkeley. But the governor shrewdly sent word to the captain of the fleet that he wanted to negotiate. The captain went ashore and unfortunately accepted too much of Berkeley's wine. While Bacon's captain drank, a small boatload of men loyal to Berkeley rowed out to the largest ship. With the help of the English sailors on board—who had been forced to join Bacon's troops against their will—Berkeley's men quickly

Nathaniel Bacon, a self-portrait. We often do not know how historical figures saw themselves, because their portraits were usually painted by artists (who often manage to get their own ideas about character into their portraits). But Nathaniel Bacon painted himself while he was still a young man in England. This engraved copy of his self-portrait shows a man who was very much the gentleman, dressed in the best fashion of the day. Only a complicated turn of history could cause such a man to lead a rebellion against Virginia's "grandees." (British Gallery of Historical Portraits)

captured the ship and disarmed Bacon's soldiers. By threats and promises, Berkeley quickly raised an army and sailed back to Jamestown. The detachment of men Bacon had left there abandoned the town, and Berkeley went ashore and fell to his knees to praise God for his mercy and help.

This was the situation Bacon confronted when he marched out of the Great Dragon Swamp. In bitter anger he led his troops on a forced march toward Jamestown, picking up recruits along the way. Finally, after a march of forty miles in one day, the men reached the outskirts of Jamestown. Bacon kept his tired men up all night, cutting down trees and digging a trench by moonlight, ready for the charge he was certain would come from the town and the cannon that would be trained on him from the ships in the river.

The next day, however, when no attack came, Bacon decided to move up heavy cannon of his own to fire at Jamestown's fortifications. To cover his men while they put the guns in place, Bacon sent scouts out to bring in the wives of some of Berkeley's leading supporters. He forced the women to stand between his men and Berkeley's guns while places were dug for the guns. Then they were released.

Finally, Berkeley decided to attack. Bacon described the battle this way:

Yesterday, they made a sally, with horse and foot in the van [the front]. The forlorn [the lead] was made up of such men as they had compelled to serve. They came up with a narrow front, pressing very close upon one another's shoulders, so that the forlorn might be their shelter. Our men received them so warmly that they retired in great disorder, throwing down their arms, as also their drums and dead men. They show themselves such pitiful cowards.

Bacon was right. Even the governor's supporters agreed that their men went out "like scholars going to school, with heavy hearts; but they returned home with light heels."

Once Berkeley's heavyhearted "scholars" were safely back inside Jamestown, they began to mutter of mutiny. Even the governor's officers encouraged the talk of desertion. Finally, Berkeley had no more than twenty men on whom he could rely. Under the safety of nightfall, he loaded his ineffective troops once more onto the ships and slipped off down the James.

Bacon had won again, or so it seemed. But all his victories added together meant nothing. He was finally forced to realize that in the long run, his situation was hopeless. In the first place, the governor still had the only useful ships in the colony, and he could take control of every other ship that sailed into Virginia from the Atlantic. This meant Berkeley could land forces anywhere in the colony.

Bacon had taught Berkeley a difficult lesson: Controlling the statehouse was not the same thing as controlling the colony. Now Bacon had to learn the same lesson. For him, occupying Jamestown was worthless as long as Berkeley was armed with ships and the title of royal governor. More important, Bacon realized that Berkeley would certainly have already sent home to England for help. Any morning tide might bring in royal warships and the king's redcoats to occupy the colony. Bacon might kill Pamunkeys. He might even drive the governor again and again to the Eastern Shore. But the entire colony of Virginia had fewer people than the city of London alone. And the English king had the world's greatest navy to pit against Bacon's army.

So despite his dramatic capture of Jamestown, Bacon was doomed. There would be no time to unite the people against Berkeley's supporters. The new House of Burgesses Bacon had ordered would never meet. Sooner or later, Bacon and his officers would either have to die in battle or be hanged as traitors. There was no way out. After occupying Jamestown, Bacon waited until night and then burned down every building in the town, even the church. From their ships down river Berkeley and his troops could see the fires light the harvest sky.

Over the next few weeks, Bacon tried to strengthen his position by issuing new oaths of loyalty and enlisting new recruits. But because Berkeley did not venture off the Eastern Shore, Bacon's men could do nothing. They grew disorderly and began to loot plantations, much to their general's dismay.

But Bacon faced an even more serious problem. In either the Great Dragon Swamp or the trenches outside Jamestown, he had become ill with dysentery—the "bloody flux," as it was called then. He may also have had malaria. He had also become so infested with lice that his clothes had to be frequently burned. He died in October.

Bacon's death brought about the quick collapse of his rebellion. While he was alive, it had no real chance of success, but with him dead, it simply did not exist. When Berkeley received the welcome news that his enemy had died, he began to attack the remainder of Bacon's followers with his ships. Here and there, small groups of rebels fought back. In one such battle a dozen or so rebels were killed. But on the whole, the rebels did not resist. Nevertheless, between the time of Bacon's death and March of 1677 the governor had twenty-three rebels hanged.

Finally, when it was no longer needed, help came from England. News of Bacon's Rebellion had caused great concern in London, and the king had sent over several warships, a thousand redcoats, and a royal commission of investigation. The English expected to find Bacon in command and Berkeley either dead or imprisoned. What they found instead was the governor securely in control and Bacon dead. Still, their instructions provided that if Berkeley was still alive, he should return to England as soon as possible. The governor delayed returning in order to hang rebels, but he finally set sail for London in March. He never returned to America. He reached London in June and died in July, without ever seeing the king to explain what had happened.

THE PLANTATION COLONIES

William Berkeley never stopped complaining that Nathaniel Bacon was a recent immigrant, a man who had been in Virginia less than two years when he became a rebel and mutineer. But the governor himself was an immigrant, as were most of the planters. Virginia was an immigrant society. The colony had existed for only about seventy years when Bacon's Rebellion occurred. Probably a majority of the people in the colony had been born not in Virginia but in England, not in the New World but in the Old. This fact, though obvious, is sometimes too easily forgotten, and it helps explain not only Bacon's Rebellion but much of the history of early America.

Like the Native Americans, who were the first immigrants, and like earlier Europeans, the English came to Virginia and the other colonies for one basic reason: to improve their lives. And, like the earlier immigrants, the English came without any real plans or much information. They had hopes instead: hopes of finding gold and silver as the Spanish had done in Mexico and Peru, or of finding a northwest passage to the wealth of the East. Some English people hoped to convert the Indians to Christianity. Then, too, the desire to make England a great and powerful nation moved many of the English either to go to Virginia or to give money and support to colonization. A straightforward itch to travel, to see new sights, was sometimes as important as any other motive for colonization.

All these motives—the desire for wealth, the missionary spirit, patriotism, adventure—were present, sometimes in the same person. But underlying them all, from the beginning of English colonization to the American Revolution—and probably to the present—was the idea that the New World meant wealth. To most Europeans, America meant gold, land, or profitable trade. Almost all the immigrants who came voluntarily thought of the New World as a place where they could improve their fortunes.

The problem that brought on Bacon's Rebellion was no different from the problem that existed in every part of America: *Whose* fortune was going to be improved first and most? And who was going to pay the price? There was an almost comic character to Bacon's marches to the west and back to the east, his inability to decide whether to fight Indians or his own government. But all the marching and countermarching grew out of one crucial fact. In Virginia, and all the other English colonies, there were three principal actors: Native Americans, English colonists, and England herself. Obviously, each had different ideas about how to divide the natural wealth of the New World.

Bacon and his followers were caught between two sets of interests that seemed to stand between them and wealth. On one side were the Native Americans, who held back agricultural expansion. On the other was the restraining influence of the Indian policy pursued by Berkeley and his supporters, and behind the governor stood the ultimate power of the English crown.

The Social Order of Plantation Society

The men who struggled for control of Virginia between 1675 and 1677 openly defined the struggle as a class conflict. The royal commission that investigated the uprising said it was the "vulgar sort" who had rebelled against the royal governor's authority. That governor, Sir William Berkeley, had no doubts about the underlying cause of *his* difficulties. He had to govern a colony "where six parts of seven at least are poor, indebted, discontented and armed." Bacon's supporters had no doubts either. Their struggle was against the "grandees," the rich and powerful planters who owned great tracts of land, had many indentured servants to produce their tobacco, and formed a ruling clique that, in collaboration with Berkeley, controlled almost every public office in the colony.

But Bacon's Rebellion was not a straightforward "democratic" uprising that pitted "the people" against an oppressive elite. The situation in Virginia was more complicated than that. To start with, the rebellion involved race as well as class. Bacon's forces spent as much energy killing Indians as they did trying to get control of the Virginia government. In fact, Bacon himself was probably unsure from week to week whether the main purpose of his men should be to conduct a race war or, as he put it, "throw off their governors." But there was an equation between race and class in the colony. Some Virginians owned small plantations in outlying areas, and knew that their only real chance at becoming rich was to open more and more land to settlement, land that they might take if it were not for the Native American "menace." These were the backbone of Bacon's "rabble." Others—the few grandees—had already made their fortunes and had great plantations in areas that were relatively safe from Indian attacks during times of trouble. The rabble had a very simple Indian "policy"—extermination. They were convinced that the grandees wanted to hold them back in order to prevent them from gaining land and wealth.

So the conflict was not a simple confrontation between rich and poor. It was between two groups of men (since women played almost no direct role in the Rebellion), one group already rich and the other determined to become rich. Bacon's Declaration of the People did not really complain about inequality in Virginia. Instead, it complained that the *wrong* men were wealthy, men who did not deserve their privileged position because their background and education were "vile." The grandees' rise had been suspiciously sudden, the declaration said, meaning that they had become wealthy through corruption, patronage, and influence.

The economic status of those followers of Bacon who can be identified was not much different from the economic status of Berkeley's defenders. But assessing the status of the members of any *failed* rebellion is a tricky business. The unsuccessful rebels whose names make it into the documentary record are almost always the more prominent members of the movement. The others, for obvious reasons, prefer to remain anonymous. There can be little doubt that the nameless rebels of 1676 were on the whole less wealthy than the defenders of the government.

Still, Bacon was indulging in a bit of political demagoguery when he talked about "the People." And Berkeley was speaking a kind of shorthand when he said that six out of seven Virginians were "poor." Neither Bacon's "People" nor Berkeley's "poor" was really meant to include the large class of indentured servants and tenant farmers that had emerged in Virginia during the preceding half-century.

Most of the work on Virginia plantations was still being done by men and women who had come from England under contracts of indentured servitude. Typically, they were bound to work for their masters for seven years, with the promise of fifty acres of land at the end of their term. The idea was a reflection of what had once been a customary assumption in England—that young men and women would work for a time as servants before marrying and getting some kind of farmstead or trade. But that practice no longer worked in England, and it did not work in Virginia, despite the relative abundance of land. In practice, most of the men and women who worked out their indentures were not able to succeed as farmers. They might have access to fifty or a hundred acres of land. But they needed a house and tools, they had to clear the land, and they had to eat. A majority of them failed, and had to make deals with some successful planter to live and work on his land as tenants.

Bacon's forces included a small number of these tenants, and even fewer indentured servants. In fact, his army was made up mostly of men who already owned farms. They had the property that made it *possible* for them to be in debt (for no one would lend money to the landless poor). Many of them probably had an indentured servant or two. They could afford to meet in taverns and drink to Nathaniel Bacon's good health. Each owned a horse and a gun, with the freedom to go marching about the countryside slaughtering Indians. One of their main battle cries was "No levies, no levies!"—meaning no taxes. But only men who owned property of some kind had to pay taxes. They were men who could dream of wealth, of becoming grandees themselves. They could also have nightmares about failing and falling into tenancy, joining the landless poor who were becoming every year more numerous in Virginia.

In Virginia, during the fifty years since the Virginia Company had failed, a distinctive class system had developed. It was the result of a peculiar kind of agriculture in an equally peculiar setting.

TOBACCO AND SOCIAL CLASS Economically, Virginia was one very simple thing: a place where tobacco was produced for export. The scale of production was something approaching an economic miracle. In the 1620s half a million pounds had been considered a remarkable achievement. But by 1663 Virginia was exporting 9 million pounds of cured tobacco a year. Production continued to increase. By the time of Bacon's Rebellion, the figure stood at over 11 million pounds.

Success in agriculture can have odd consequences. Growing more of any crop is the way an individual producer can hope to increase income. But every other producer has the same need, and flooding any competitive market with a product causes prices to decline, sometimes drastically. This is what happened in the 1620s, when rapid increases in tobacco exports broke the price on the London market, causing a drop of about 2,000 percent in a few years. After the 1620s, the price varied from year to year, but it averaged only about three pence per pound. This meant a planter had to grow, harvest, cure, pack, load, and ship an enormous quantity of the stuff if he wanted to live like a gentleman.

Growing tobacco was a very labor-intensive form of agriculture, requiring a great deal of hand cultivation and a complicated curing and packing process. One laborer could handle only about five acres of the crop. So only a man with a considerable amount of money could afford to buy the necessary labor contracts, build the curing sheds, and own the presses that packed the tobacco into great barrels ready for shipment. Tobacco culture was full of what economists call "economies of scale." That is, if it was produced on a large scale, tobacco was much more profitable. So tobacco agriculture had a built-in tendency to create large differences of wealth and class.

LAND AND LABOR On the other hand, two factors were at work in Virginia that could have promoted social and economic equality. First, there was an abundance of "free" land—an abundance that was quite staggering to the minds of English people, who came from a world where every square foot of ground that could be owned already was. This abundance of land could have produced a society characterized by a considerable degree of practical equality (as it did in parts of the British colonies in New England). It had been part of the vision of the 1618 system of headrights devised by the Virginia Company (see Chapter 1), which would have entitled a man who could pay the passage for himself, a wife, and three children to 250 acres of land.

Second, there was a distinct shortage of labor, which could have caused masters to offer high wages, good working conditions, shorter indentures, and more generous settlements at the end of a worker's term of servitude.

But the abundance of land and the shortage of labor did not have egalitarian consequences in seventeenth-century Virginia, for several reasons. To start with, the death rate in Virginia remained very high until the middle of the century. In a normal year in Virginia as large a portion of the population was likely to die as in London during an epidemic of the black plague. For decades after 1620, the life expectancy of a man or woman in Virginia was only about forty-eight years (compared to seventy in parts of New England during the same period). The premature deaths of many indentured servants meant that their masters got years of almost free labor, since all the master had had to do was pay a small initial charge for the contract, and then provide food and clothing. There was little reason to worry whether the food and clothing were good enough. Economically, it was advantageous for a master to have a worker die in the sixth or seventh year of a labor contract. The land the worker would have been entitled to would still belong to the master. A vicious gambling cycle was in operation, a cycle nobody planned, but which worked anyway. Poor food and harsh conditions for workers could help enrich their masters, and a rich master could afford to bring over more and more indentured servants to gamble their lives against the prospect of surviving to get fifty acres of land.

The relative abundance of land did not help much, either. The economics of producing tobacco for export meant that parcels as small as

fifty acres were not worth very much. Tobacco ruined the soil rapidly, so in a few years a farmer with so small a plot of land would no longer be able to produce a crop. Only two out of every ten ex-servants who lived long enough to win their gamble got land and succeeded in becoming self-sufficient, taxpaying citizens. The others failed quickly and had to sell out and become the working tenants of some grandee. This helped turn an "abundance" of land into a glut of real estate. The situation was so extreme by the 1660s that land in some parts of Virginia could be bought at a price of one pound of tobacco per acre. In any case, the best land in the settled areas had already fallen into the hands of a few planters. By the time of Bacon's Rebellion, thirty men owned over 100,000 acres of land along the south bank of the Potomac River.

GOVERNING THE SOCIAL ORDER The few Virginians who did manage to become wealthy also became politically powerful. And this power only made them richer. The normal assumption in both England and Virginia in the seventeenth century was that political office should be profitable. The assumption worked well in Virginia. At the top of the system of political profit stood the king himself. According to the law, Virginians could not ship their tobacco to any place but England. The customs duty charged on the tobacco was the largest single source of revenue for the king. By the time of Bacon's Rebellion, the royal purse bulged with income from the tobacco trade that averaged about £100,000 a year. Little wonder that his majesty's government was very anxious to maintain order in the colony.

In Virginia, the king's agent was his royal governor. The Virginia House of Burgesses regularly voted Sir William Berkeley an enormous salary of £1,000 a year (compared to £80 earned by the governors of Massachusetts). But Berkeley also was legally entitled to as many bushels of corn as there were adult males in Virginia—about 15 tons of corn a year. He had the right to claim any stray cattle in the colony. He got 200 pounds of tobacco for every marriage license issued, 350 pounds of tobacco for every tavern he licensed. He was paid handsomely for every ship that entered Virginia waters, and for every new settler who entered the colony.

The reason the planters who controlled the House of Burgesses were willing to vote such lucrative rights to the governor was very simple. He had the power to grant land—to them. He could appoint men—like them— to public offices that were very profitable indeed. The governor stood at the center of the grandees, who regularly taxed and took with an air of conspiracy among themselves. The position of colonial secretary was worth about 150,000 pounds of tobacco a year, about as much tobacco as could be produced by a hundred men working on 500 acres. Sheriffs took a 10 percent surtax on everything they collected. The burgesses paid themselves handsomely for their political participation, at rates ten to twenty times what the members of New England legislative bodies were paid. They could also hold other offices of profit while they served in the House.

The system reached all the way down to the most minor public offices. The man who beat the drum to summon the burgesses to their sessions (which usually lasted only a month or so each year) was awarded 3,000 pounds of tobacco a year at a time when this equaled the work of three men for a year.

Naturally enough, the men who had made it into this kind of rewarding political circle did not want to lose their position in it. They had no immediate interest in sharing the glory with others, either. The solution to maintaining this kind of "stability" was easy. Governor Berkeley had the authority to call for elections to the House of Burgesses, and for fifteen years before Bacon's Rebellion, he did not call a single election. Most of the men who ruled Virginia in 1675 had been in place since 1650. So when Bacon's "rabble" demanded new elections, they were demanding their chance to get a seat at this feast of profit and power.

The Founding of Maryland

The social situation in Virginia was complicated, but it was made even more so by the existence of a sister colony on the Chesapeake, Maryland. In some ways, Maryland was exactly like Virginia: a tobacco colony, with roughly the same social and economic features. So the colonies were able to cooperate, as when the "Merrylanders" helped the Virginia militia lay siege to that Susquehanna fort just before Bacon's Rebellion. But Maryland had a distinctive history that made it seem to some Virginians an alien and dangerous place.

For one thing, all Maryland belonged to one man. It had been carved out of Virginia in 1632. In an action that disturbed many speculators in Virginia land, Charles I had given away about 10 million acres of Virginia to a Catholic friend and supporter named George Calvert. Calvert was an aggressive man who had been a member of the London Company that founded Jamestown and had never given up the dream of making a fortune out of the New World. He was also a convert to Catholicism, and he hoped to found a colony in the New World that might serve as a haven for other Catholics, who were never quite safe in Protestant England.

The Stuart kings, James I and his son Charles I, both smiled on Calvert. (James's mother, Mary, Queen of Scots, a Catholic, had been deprived of her head on the orders of her Protestant cousin Elizabeth I.) They ennobled Calvert as the first Lord Baltimore, and they helped him in his efforts to promote a colony in America.

James I gave Calvert a grant in Newfoundland, but a winter's experience convinced him it was not a suitable place. Then, in 1632, Charles I gave Calvert an even more attractive grant in Virginia: almost all the land on the Eastern Shore of Chesapeake Bay, plus a curious strip north of the Potomac River, running west toward the unexplored Appalachians.

From generation to generation. This detail from a painting of the 1660s shows young Cecil Calvert and the hand of his grandfather, Lord Baltimore, both holding a map of TERRÆ MARIÆ—Maryland. The painter meant to give visual evidence of a secure line of family ownership over the proprietary colony. This effect is heightened by the superimposition of the family coat of arms onto the land. (The map has been painted on its "side," with north to the viewer's right.) (Enoch Pratt Free Library, Baltimore)

The Maryland charter of 1632 was quite different from the original Virginia grant. It did not create a modern commercial enterprise; instead, it seemed to look back to an older, feudal England. It made Calvert and his heirs "absolute lords and proprietaries" of their new colony. This meant, in effect, that they had the same kinds of powers in Maryland that the king himself had in England. They could grant large tracts of land to anyone they chose, making the grantees their "vassals." The only restrictions were that their laws had to conform to English laws, that they

had to have the consent of the "freemen" or their representatives (just as the king had to have the consent of Parliament), and that they had to pay the English crown each year a token of two arrowheads, plus a fifth of any gold or silver they discovered.

The new colony, which was named after Charles I's French Catholic wife, Maria, got off to a slow start. The old London Company, which still claimed some of its rights in Virginia, put legal obstacles in the way. George Calvert died before the grant even became effective. It then

Forced labor, white and black. The lines separating free people from those who were not free remained confused in the colonies throughout the colonial period. And this meant the lines separating African Americans and European Americans also remained somewhat blurred. This handkerchief was made in England late in the eighteenth century. In blue colors, printed on linen, it showed a white convict who had been "transported" to the colonies. He is at work in the fields with two black slaves, one male and one female. Like the slaves, the convict is barefoot. Like them, he is working with a hoe. But there is a difference. The artist— probably white and free—suggests that the convict is agonized by his condition while the slaves are not. The message seems to be that crime does not pay, that the worst thing that can happen to a white person is to be reduced to the condition of a slave. (Courtesy of the Colonial Williamsburg Foundation)

passed to his son Cecil, but he had to stay on in England to protect his rights. So it was not until 1634 that the first settlement of Maryland was made. Two ships, bearing the gentle kinds of names that were common among English colonizing vessels, the *Ark* and the *Dove,* sailed into the Chesapeake with about 250 settlers aboard. Once in Maryland, however, the colonists planted themselves without the horrors of massacre, starvation, and disease that had plagued the Jamestown settlement. Within a few years, the little town of St. Mary's, the "first seat" of Maryland, was the center of a thriving tobacco culture very much like that of Virginia.

Maryland also copied the Virginia system of land grants to induce settlement. Very little of the feudal vision of the charter was ever to find concrete expression in practice. In fact, the unique aspect of the new colony—and the thing for which colonial Maryland is still most famous— was not "feudal" at all, but rather modern in style. In 1649 Cecil Calvert prepared a law guaranteeing religious freedom to all Christians. The

Maryland legislature, the House of Delegates, passed it as the Toleration Act. But the law did not grow out of Calvert's modernity or liberalism, or out of the enlightened principles of the colonists; instead, it was the result of a fact of life: The colony was settled mainly by Protestants, who were fearful of their Catholic proprietor's power over them. The Toleration Act in fact made little difference in the patterns of immigration or religious practice.

In time, the Maryland "rabble" came to have the same sorts of complaints against their governors and masters that Bacon's men had, and with a religious issue to boot. An obscure rebellion arose in one Maryland county in 1676 that was probably an offshoot of Bacon's Rebellion. But social conflict in Maryland did not reach serious proportions until 1688, when news came that King James II, a Catholic, had been overthrown in what came to be called the Glorious Revolution. One of the results of the revolution was a law providing that only Protestants could become rulers of England. The Protestant farmers of

Maryland reckoned that they could have a little revolution of their own, overthrow the Catholic proprietary regime, and ensure a Protestant government in the colony. Several hundred men formed a Protestant Association, marched on the capital, and took over the government. The colony was not returned to the Calvert family until 1715—after the family had converted back to Protestantism. By then, Maryland had been transformed by the same social revolution that also changed the social and political fate of Virginia: slavery.

Plantation Slavery

Bacon's Rebellion came at a time when a profound decision was being made, the decision to replace white indentured laborers with African slaves.

The first shipload of Africans reached Jamestown in 1619. But they were brought as "servants," not slaves. English law had no formal definition of slavery, and for fifty more years after 1619, Virginia law would not have one either. For decades, Africans were only a very small part of the labor force in the two Chesapeake colonies. In 1650 there were still only 300 blacks in Virginia, some of them technically "free."

But a change was coming. In the next twenty years, the number of black laborers and their children increased to 2,000. In 1670 the House of Burgesses took the formal step of passing a law that declared, "All servants not being Christians imported into this colony by shipping shall be slaves for their lives." The tortured phrasing was intended to avoid the explicit naming of races. "Not being Christians" meant not being whites of European descent. "Imported into this colony by shipping" meant not being Indians, who had proved easier to kill than they were to enslave.

Virginians were becoming habituated to the idea of slavery. There was no English tradition for it, but it had become the dominant labor system in the British island colonies of the Caribbean, as it was in Spanish, French, and Portuguese colonies. During Bacon's Rebellion—just six years after slavery was formally legalized—the newly elected "reform" burgesses passed a law defining the privileges of the soldiers whom Bacon led against the Indians. They were to have "the benefit of all plunder either Indians or otherwise." (The phrasing was much more direct than in the 1670 slavery law. By "otherwise," the law meant everything: corn, furs, weapons, and so forth. By "Indians," it meant Indians.)

By 1680 the number of black slaves in the Chesapeake had risen to over 3,000. Twenty years later, the number stood at 8,000. The transition to slavery was not sudden and neat. No small group of powerful men ever sat in a room and made a deliberate decision to create slave societies. Social transformations of such magnitude are the cumulative outcome of thousands of individual decisions over a long course of time. White indentured servants continued to come to the area at the rate of about a hundred a month through 1690. But the choices were made. The English colonies, from the Chesapeake area southward, were destined to become societies built on the labor of Africans and their children, people who were not free. After 1700 the slave population exploded. By 1750 there were 100,000 slaves in Virginia alone, and many thousands in other colonies.

SLAVERY, CLASS, AND RACISM British colonists chose slavery for straightforward economic reasons. If some other labor system—indentured servitude or free labor—had been more profitable than slavery, few planters would have persisted for long in using slaves. But what people do for economic reasons they very often justify with arguments that have nothing to do with profit and loss. Virginians and Marylanders and other Southern colonists eventually worked out a justification for slavery that centered on the fact of race.

Processing tobacco. Tobacco was a product that required a lot of hand cultivation and special processing. These difficulties made it possible for planters to try to separate workers according to both race and sex. This picture, made around 1750, suggests that the planter or the artist thought it was all right for black males and females to do the same work, but that white women ought to work apart from men. The day is hot (the blacks, male and female, are shown topless) but the white woman and young girl are bundled up, even though they are working in the sunshine near mid-day. The artist has also emphasized the fact that the white females do not see the half-naked slaves. Pictures like this often say more about the way people thought things *ought* to be than about the way things really were. (Courtesy of the British Museum)

The central assumption of most forms of racism is that one people is "civilized" and the other "savage" or "barbaric." The conclusion is that the "superior" race has a right, even a duty, to dominate the "inferior" race in one way or another—sometimes by extermination, sometimes by enslavement, and sometimes only by denying rights and privileges. The white colonists settled

on extermination in the Indian case and slavery in the African case. And they used the same kinds of language to describe the despised others: Indians and blacks were "brutes," "filthy," "heathen," "lewd," "naked," and so on. But the most significant question for the historian is: Did white Europeans think Indians and Africans ought to be killed or enslaved because they were "sav-

Plantation boyhoods. This highly idealized painting, made in Maryland around 1710, shows a planter's son, Henry Darnall, III, and his young "servant." Henry has been hunting with his little bow and arrow, and the slave has carried the quarry back to the main house. Young Henry has been on horseback, for he holds a riding crop; the slave has no doubt walked. Henry's aristocratic pretensions are mirrored in the slave's decent clothing and in the silver collar around his neck. The collar is a sign of both the slave's captivity and of his young master's wealth. In such pictures of colonial masters and slaves together, the slaves often look intently at the masters, and the masters look just as intently in another direction. (Collection of the Maryland Historical Society, Baltimore)

ages"? Or did they need to think Native American and African people were savages because they meant to kill or enslave them?

The answers to such questions can never be neat or certain. But there are clues. For one thing, the way educated English people described blacks and Indians in the seventeenth century was similar to the way they described their own poor; the vocabulary of class and the vocabulary of race were almost identical. The white poor were just as "nasty," "brutish," "filthy," and "lewd" as any African or Native American. In England, there were many proposals that poor whites be enslaved, or at least bound to labor as indentured servants for very long terms. John Locke, who was one of the great "enlightened" philosophers of the age, proposed that the chil-

dren of the poor be bound to hard labor beginning at the age of three. Another great British philosopher, Bishop Berkeley, believed "vagrants" ought to be enslaved for an extended period of years. There was, in other words, no necessary connection between slavery and race in the English mind, at least not at the beginning.

As for the truly poor whites themselves, it is extremely difficult to discover what their attitudes toward race and class were. They left few records. There is no reason to *assume* that poor whites were as racist as their social "betters." In fact, being educated in the seventeenth century was likely to make a man or a woman more, not less, racist. There are a few surviving bits of evidence that the English poor understood that their social superiors believed them to be no better than Indians or blacks. In Virginia they may even have felt some sense of common identity with African laborers. Blacks and whites often ran away from their masters together. The last organized resistance in Bacon's Rebellion came from a small band of runaways who had joined the uprising. There were only a hundred of them, but they held out to the end—perhaps because they thought they had no choice. The group was composed of eighty blacks and twenty whites, who fought side by side.

It may even be true that in the early stages of racial contact, there was no taboo among the poor against interracial sex. Here, too, the documentary record is sparse. But in one Virginia county where records do survive, there were nineteen prosecutions one year against white servant women who had borne bastard children. Of the children, four were "mulattos"—as Europeans had decided to call the offspring of sexual encounters between whites and blacks, using the Spanish word for "young mules." The proportion of 20 percent was almost exactly the proportion of blacks in the male servant population of the county. The result is what would be expected if blacks and whites, male and female, were making random sexual choices, with no regard to race.

The behavior of the colonial legislatures also suggests that racism in the colonies did not flow from the bottom up. Time after time, the planter elite felt it necessary to pass laws against interracial sex. They legislated severe penalties against white women who bore mulatto children. They forbade interracial marriages (a law that would hardly have been necessary if whites had *all* been racists). They provided that being baptized did not change the status of a slave (a law that would not have been needed if there were no white ministers who were interested in baptizing slaves, making them fellow Christians).

Gradually, a legal code came into existence in the Southern colonies that made an extreme racism the official policy of the colonial governments. All legal limits were removed that restrained masters from punishing, maiming, or even killing their African-American slaves. The

main beneficiaries of such laws were the white elite, not "the People." But a kind of informal bargain was being struck between the elite and the white majority. The legislators passed laws making it a crime for any black to "insult" any white, no matter how poor. The implication was clear: There ought to be a unity of race that was more powerful than any unity of class. The legislators were saying that whites, rich and poor, the people and the "grandees," should have a common interest.

The planter elite hoped that such an informal social bargain could prevent the kind of class conflict that had erupted in Bacon's Rebellion. If slaves replaced indentured servants, the growth of a dangerous class of poor and near-poor whites could be slowed down or halted. Plantation societies could be built and expanded without the threat of violent struggle between men who had wealth and a white "rabble" that wanted wealth. In these societies, a few wealthy planters might continue to be the proud, dominant class. But the most extreme forms of domination and pride could be directed more against their slave labor force, not against their white neighbors. The form of wealth that those white neighbors would come to envy and aspire to would—from now on—include black slaves. Viewing African Americans as potential property rather than fellow servants could help give any aspiring white a sense of solidarity with the greatest planter.

The Carolinas and Georgia

At the height of his rebellious career, Nathaniel Bacon told a neighbor that he believed "Virginia and Maryland as well as Carolina" were all ready to "cast off their governors." And, he thought, if his rebellion failed, he and his followers might "retire to the Roanoke" and establish their own government there, safe from Berkeley and safe, for a while, from English power. Bacon's ideas were vague and half-formed, and it is difficult to know what he meant exactly. But to "retire to the Roanoke" probably meant to move into the area around Albemarle Sound, where the Roanoke River empties into the Atlantic.

In 1675 a motley group of Virginians was settled there, occupying what amounted to Virginia's southern frontier. They were a lawless lot and were regarded by people like Berkeley as a band of thieves and ne'er-do-wells. In fact, when Bacon's Rebellion finally collapsed, one of Bacon's chief lieutenants, John Culpeper, did flee to the Albemarle frontier and lead a brief "revolution" there. Eventually, Culpeper was taken to England and tried for treason. But he was acquitted on the curious ground that there was no settled government in Carolina against which a man *could* commit meaningful treason, no matter how hard he might try. What Bacon referred to as "Carolina" was a subject of considerable confusion. The colony had existed on paper for a long time, but it was not until the decades after Bacon's Rebellion that this paper existence was translated into another successful colonial experience.

THE CAROLINA PROPRIETARY On paper, Carolina was older than Maryland. In 1629 Charles I had granted the colony to his attorney general on more or less the same terms as his grant of Maryland to Calvert three years later. For twenty years, no settlements were made. And in the 1650s only a few hundred Virginians and a small group of migrants from Massachusetts tried to found communities. After his restoration to the throne in 1660, Charles II revoked the grant of 1629 and, in 1663, created a group of eight powerful proprietors, granting them an even larger territory. The grant included, approximately, what today comprises North and South Carolina and Georgia.

The Carolina proprietors, whose ranks included Governor Berkeley, were enormously powerful men. In fact, William Berkeley was very much the smallest fish in the pond. One of the eight was Edward Hyde, an earl and lord high chancellor. He also happened to be the father-in-law of James, duke of York, soon to be King James II. Another proprietor was General George Monck, the most important military figure in Charles II's England. A third was George Carteret, widely regarded as the richest man in England. Perhaps the most active proprietor of all was Anthony Ashley Cooper. In 1663 Cooper was on his way toward enormous fame, fame that made him eventually the earl of Shaftesbury and founder of what was to become England's most important political party, the Whigs. In 1663 Cooper was already chancellor of the exchequer—a post roughly comparable to that of the secretary of the treasury in the modern United States.

In the 1660s, then, the entity known as "Carolina" was a very curious thing. Its owners were a stunning representation of English power, wealth, and office. Its people were a few hundred Virginians hanging on to some rather poor land in the northeastern corner of the vast, vacant colony. Between owners and people, there was little or no common ground. The proprietors' plans were aimed at making large amounts of money for themselves, primarily from the disposal of their only real asset, the land itself. But they also had other purposes. For one thing, they were committed to slavery (several of them had investments in the African slave trade), and from the beginning they rewarded those settlers who brought slaves to the colony. For another thing, the proprietors had a philosophical commitment in common: They were deeply opposed to the development of a "numerous democracy" of the sort that Bacon's Rebellion represented. The Carolina proprietors tried to make their colony into a fortress of traditional feudalism against what they perceived as dangerous democratic tendencies in English life.

Their chosen instrument was an odd document known as the "Fundamental Constitutions." It was drawn up by John Locke, who was to be famous, later, as the philosopher of natural rights. But Locke was very far from being a democrat at this early stage of his life, and the constitution he proposed was perhaps the most conservative document to grow out of the English colonial experience. Carolina, according to the Fundamental Constitutions as issued in 1665, was to be governed ultimately by the proprietors. The chief among them would be known as the "palatine," the remainder as "seigneurs." Below them would be a class of nobles known as "landgraves," and below them, a class of minor nobles called "caciques." Finally, the rest of the free population, known as "leet-men," would live and labor on the estates of the nobility. At the bottom, of course, would be slaves. Along with titles would go grants of land and political power. The net result, the proprietors hoped, would be a feudal utopia—a much neater version of feudalism than had ever existed in actual fact in medieval England.

In practice, the settlers never accepted the basic ideas behind the Fundamental Constitutions—except for slavery. The proprietors kept the constitution suspended much of the time and actually made most of their land grants according to the Virginia pattern rather than according to their own visionary scheme. Northern Carolina, especially, attracted a variety of colonists—English Quakers, French Huguenots, Swiss and German immigrants, and the sort of Virginia emigrés that caused the Albemarle settlement to become known as "Rogues' Harbor." For various reasons, none of these groups cared a whit for the proprietors' vision. It was no accident, therefore, that when John Culpeper fled to Albemarle, he found supporters who were quite ready to "cast off their governors" (as Bacon had put it). In general, northern Carolina developed as a poor extension of Virginia tobacco society, kept from rapid development by the lack of good harbors.

The situation in southern Carolina was different—for reasons that had very little to do with the Fundamental Constitutions. After some delay, a successful colony was planted at Charleston in the 1670s. Charleston quickly grew into a trading town, with an excellent harbor, a fort, and a very modern street plan—in fact, the only real town in the Southern colonies. But the city depended on a staple agriculture and slave labor,

every bit as much as the Virginia economy to the north did. There was a ready market for agricultural goods in the nearby British West Indies, and South Carolina soon developed a busy trade with the islands, consisting mainly of various food exports.

Most important for the long run, however, was the successful experiment with rice as a cash crop. Soil and climate combined to create the conditions favorable for this difficult crop, and skilled slave labor was available to carry out the arduous work of planting, cultivating, and harvesting. Soon there was a plantation elite in southern Carolina that rivaled Virginia's in its pretensions to aristocracy. The only real difference was that the Carolina planters tended to live in Charleston rather than on their own plantations.

Carolina also developed (despite the Fundamental Constitutions) a "normal" type of government. There was a governor appointed by the proprietors, a council, and an assembly. The council in time came to function as the upper house of the legislature and was appointed by the governor. The lower house was composed of the "representatives of the people"—representing, in practice, the landowners of the colony. In the 1690s, Charleston became the capital of the colony. The governor resided there, and a deputy was appointed to govern the northern part of the colony. Finally, in 1712, the two colonies were separated, and each was given its own government. Then, in 1729, in keeping with its colonial policies in all of North America, the crown revoked the proprietary charter, and both North and South Carolina became royal colonies like Virginia, with governors, councils, and other officials appointed by the crown.

GEORGIA One of the lessons that could be drawn from the experiences of Maryland and the Carolina proprietorship was that the realities of the situation in each case turned out to matter more than the abstract aims and goals of English promoters and proprietors. Calvert's purpose may have been, in part, to create a refuge for Catholics and a quasi-feudal society; but in practice, other forces prevailed over these goals. The

Savannah, Georgia. This engraving shows Savannah after about a year of settlement. It is depicted as an astonishingly neat town with identical houses, each one having its own garden plot. The artist has also attempted to convey the impression that Georgia has a great deal of space for its people and is quite safe. Notice that the palisade at the left is barely begun. The real fortification is the battery of cannon at the left, on the riverbank, aimed not against Indians but against a potential Spanish attack. (New York Public Library, Picture Collection)

Carolina proprietors' Fundamental Constitutions were blown aside by the winds of actual experience, and their colony developed into a "normal" plantation society with a "normal" government structure. This relationship between founders' visions and actuality was even more striking in Georgia, the last British colony to be established on the mainland of North America.

Originally, Georgia was part of the Carolina grant of 1663. But the Carolinians failed to settle the area. Since both Spain and England claimed the land, and since the two nations were at war

much of the time, it was inevitable that the English government would eventually encourage settlement there—for military reasons in addition to the usual economic motives for colonization. In fact, the individual chiefly responsible for the colonization of Georgia was a military man, General James Oglethorpe.

Oglethorpe was also a politician, however, and his most telling political experience was as a member of a parliamentary commission investigating English prisons. Oglethorpe became convinced in the 1720s that simple poverty led many

James Edward Oglethorpe

James Edward Oglethorpe, founder of Georgia, was born into a world still dominated by seventeenth-century conflicts and antagonisms. He died after the American Revolution at the age of eighty-nine. Across this turbulent span of almost a century, he typified many of the main preoccupations—and some of the curious eccentricities—of eighteenth-century British colonialism.

Oglethorpe's family was dominated by its loyalty to James II and the Stuart monarchy. When James was deposed by the Glorious Revolution of 1688–89 and replaced by a new "constitutional" monarch, Sir Theophilus Oglethorpe remained stubbornly loyal to the old king. James Edward inherited this loyalty and spent much of his youth on the Continent, living as a freelance soldier and a member of the Stuart court-in-exile in France and Italy. Finally, even the most ardent supporters of James II ("Jacobites," they were called) gave up. Oglethorpe drifted home in 1722, at twenty-six, to take control of the family manor and to enter Parliament, as his father and older brothers had done before him.

In politics, Oglethorpe was a Tory, an opponent of the Whig party that had come to power after the Glorious Revolution and that dominated Parliament during the eighteenth century. But Oglethorpe's "conservatism" was much more than an echo of his family's Jacobitism. He, like many of the Tories, was also a reformer. He opposed slavery, rum, the impressment of sailors, and the mistreatment of convicts. He was also an ardent supporter of an aggressive military policy—chiefly against Spain—and he wanted an expansion of the empire—chiefly at the expense of Spain.

All these concerns came conveniently together in the late 1720s, when Oglethorpe became interested in Georgia. The colony could serve as a refuge for paupers and ex-convicts, he hoped, and also as a model society without rum or slaves. It could also welcome religious dissenters from England and the Continent. Most important, it would be an outpost against the Spanish in Florida. Oglethorpe's interests differed, then, from the commercial ones of the Virginia Company and the proprietary ones of the Calverts.

Oglethorpe came to Georgia with the first colonists in 1733. For the next ten years, he attempted to realize his vision, to combine social reform and military effectiveness. But he was exposed, all along, to difficulties. The settlers refused to cooperate and often threatened rebellion. The Spanish kept military pressure on Georgia and diplomatic pressure on London. Carolinians objected to Georgia's invasion of the profitable Indian trade. Even Oglethorpe's fellow "trustees" complained about his sloppy accounts and his failure to file adequate reports with them. In the seventeenth century, these difficulties might not have been serious, but the administration of the empire was becoming more and more organized and public. Finally, Oglethorpe was pushed into resigning. He was even subjected to a court-martial trial—though he was quickly acquitted of all charges.

After his resignation, Oglethorpe married an heiress and settled into a genteel life. He was promoted in military rank several times, finally becoming an inactive general. He lived much of the time in London, where he was part of the most sophisticated social and literary circles of the period. His colony went very much its own way, almost unmarked by Oglethorpe's vision and unwanted reforms.

Picture: New York Public Library, Picture Collection

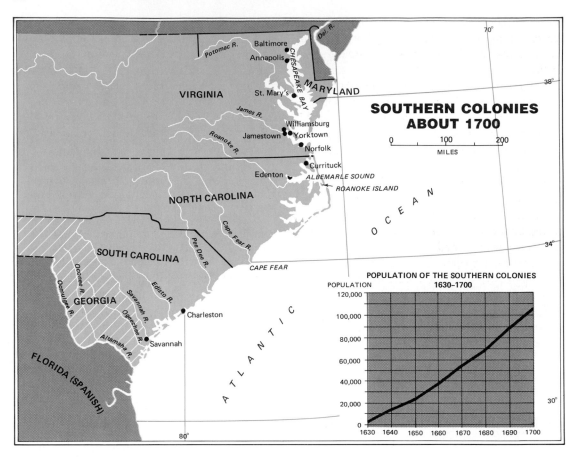

SOUTHERN COLONIES
ABOUT 1700

0   100   200
MILES

POPULATION OF THE SOUTHERN COLONIES
1630–1700

POPULATION

Englishmen to prison, often because they could not pay their debts. The solution to the problem, Oglethorpe and several wealthy friends believed, might lie in colonization. The result of their efforts was a unique charter issued by George II in 1732 that carved a new colony (named after the king) out of the Carolina grant. But the charter created neither proprietors, like those of Maryland and Carolina, nor a commercial company, like that of the original Virginia charter. Instead, the king named a board of "trustees" who would be in charge of the settlement of the colony for twenty-one years. They could make no money for themselves, and, after the period of trusteeship, the colony would automatically revert to the crown, to be added to the growing list of royal

colonies. In the meantime, the trustees were not required to create a colonial legislature; they could make laws themselves and could appoint a governor and other officials.

The enterprise got off to a quick start. In the fall of 1732, the first 130 settlers left England— so well provisioned by the trustees that only two of them died at sea. The immigrants who followed were of three main types. Some were free Englishmen, who were given grants of farms on the Virginia pattern of fifty-acre headrights. Many others were poor English people (though very few were actually convicts), who came as indentured servants and were promised twenty-acre grants after serving out their terms. Several hundred others were Protestant refugees from the Continent—most of them Germans. The trustees forbade Catholic immigration, for fear that Catholics would harbor secret sympathies for Spain.

The fear of Spain was behind a number of the trustees' policies. First, they wanted to make Georgia a colony of small farms, since this would provide the most militarily efficient population. So they restricted the size of individual grants to 500 acres and promised most immigrants only 20 or 50 acres of land. Second, they forbade slavery, not because they were opposed to it in principle, but because they believed a slave population would be militarily unsafe from Spanish subversion. They even forbade the importation of rum, not because they opposed drinking, but because rum might well mean unnecessary Indian troubles, and Indian troubles could expose the colony to Spanish intrigue or attack. In short, the trustees tried to create a disciplined military colony of sober, white, Protestant farmers.

The difficulty was that the interest of the colonists ran against those of the trustees. For one thing, the only profitable agriculture that seemed possible was rice farming on the model of South Carolina. But rice lands were also malarial lands. And this, in the eyes of Englishmen, meant that only Africans were a suitable labor force. The colonists also understood that quick money lay in the fur trade, which required a much freer hand with the Indians than the trustees were ready to allow. In addition, the colonists wanted a voice in the lawmaking process, they wanted larger farms, and they wanted rum. Several years before the expiration of the trustees' control, frustration among the colonists finally forced the trustees to relinquish control of Georgia. The forces of actual experience triumphed over the trustees' vision: Georgia began to develop the plantation agriculture, capitalist economy, slave labor, and mixed royal government that prevailed in all the other Southern colonies.

Suggestions for Further Reading

BACON'S REBELLION

A picture of Nathaniel Bacon as the leader of a "democratic" movement of small planters is presented in Thomas Jefferson Wertenbaker, *Torchbearer of the Revolution* (1940). A much less sympathetic account is Wilcomb E. Washburn, *The Governor and the Rebel: A History of Bacon's Rebellion in Virginia* (1958). There is an excellent discussion of the social background and consequences of the rebellion in Edmund S. Morgan, *American Slavery, American Freedom* (1975), the most important book on seventeenth-century Virginia.

THE SOCIAL ORDER OF PLANTATION SOCIETY

A seminal essay on the Virginia social order is Bernard Bailyn, "Politics and Social Structure in Virginia," in James M. Smith, ed., *Seventeenth Century America* (1959). T. H. Breen, in *Tobacco Culture* (1987), gives a lucid and well-argued picture of the society that took shape around the tobacco economy. An older but still useful study of the system of indentured servitude is A. E. Smith, *Colonists in Bondage* (1947). The same subject has been treated more recently in David Galenson, *White Servitude in Colonial America* (1982), and A. R. Ekirch, *Bound for America* (1987). Good coverage of the Maryland colony is to be found in two classic works on colonial history, the great three-volume labor of Charles M. Andrews, *The Colonial Period of American History* (1934–37), and Wesley Frank Craven's *The Southern Colonies in the Seventeenth Century, 1607–1689* (1949). Two more recent and quite useful treatments are David B. Quinn, ed., *Early Maryland in a Wider World* (1982), and Gloria L. Main, *Tobacco Colony: Life in Early Maryland, 1650–1720* (1982).

CHRONOLOGY

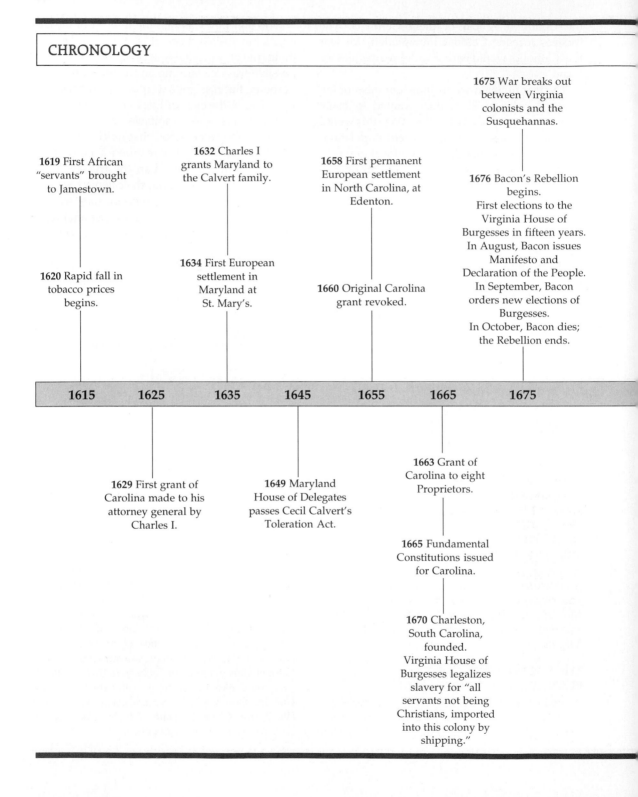

1675 War breaks out between Virginia colonists and the Susquehannas.

1619 First African "servants" brought to Jamestown.

1632 Charles I grants Maryland to the Calvert family.

1658 First permanent European settlement in North Carolina, at Edenton.

1676 Bacon's Rebellion begins.
First elections to the Virginia House of Burgesses in fifteen years.
In August, Bacon issues Manifesto and Declaration of the People.
In September, Bacon orders new elections of Burgesses.
In October, Bacon dies; the Rebellion ends.

1620 Rapid fall in tobacco prices begins.

1634 First European settlement in Maryland at St. Mary's.

1660 Original Carolina grant revoked.

1615   1625   1635   1645   1655   1665   1675

1629 First grant of Carolina made to his attorney general by Charles I.

1649 Maryland House of Delegates passes Cecil Calvert's Toleration Act.

1663 Grant of Carolina to eight Proprietors.

1665 Fundamental Constitutions issued for Carolina.

1670 Charleston, South Carolina, founded.
Virginia House of Burgesses legalizes slavery for "all servants not being Christians, imported into this colony by shipping."

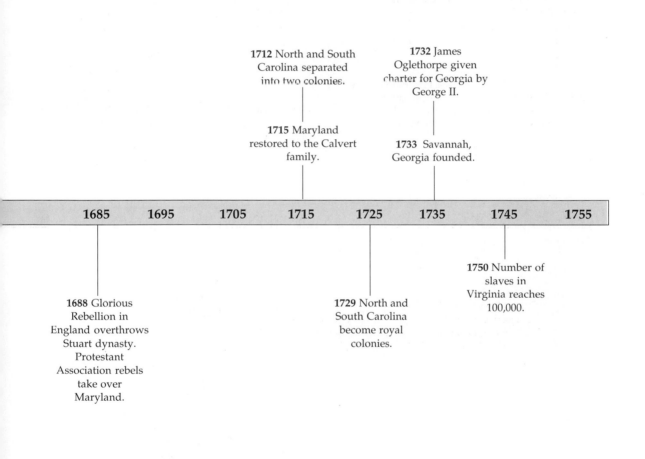

1712 North and South Carolina separated into two colonies.

1732 James Oglethorpe given charter for Georgia by George II.

1715 Maryland restored to the Calvert family.

1733 Savannah, Georgia founded.

| 1685 | 1695 | 1705 | 1715 | 1725 | 1735 | 1745 | 1755 |

1750 Number of slaves in Virginia reaches 100,000.

1688 Glorious Rebellion in England overthrows Stuart dynasty. Protestant Association rebels take over Maryland.

1729 North and South Carolina become royal colonies.

PLANTATION SLAVERY

Edmund S. Morgan, *American Slavery, American Freedom* (1975), has a compelling argument about the reasons behind the colonists' decision to make slavery their labor system. This book takes its place in a distinguished historical debate, which can be followed in Winthrop Jordan, *White over Black* (1968); David Brion Davis, *The Problem of Slavery in Western Culture* (1966); and Alan Kulikoff, *Tobacco and Slaves* (1986)

THE CAROLINAS AND GEORGIA

On South Carolina, Peter Wood, *Black Majority* (1974), is essential reading. Careful treatments of the Carolinas can be found in M. Eugene Sirmans, *Colonial South Carolina* (1966), and Hugh T. Lefler and Albert R. Newsome, *North Carolina* (1954). On the lower South generally, C. L. Ver Steeg, *The Origins of a Southern Mosaic* (1975), is quite valuable.

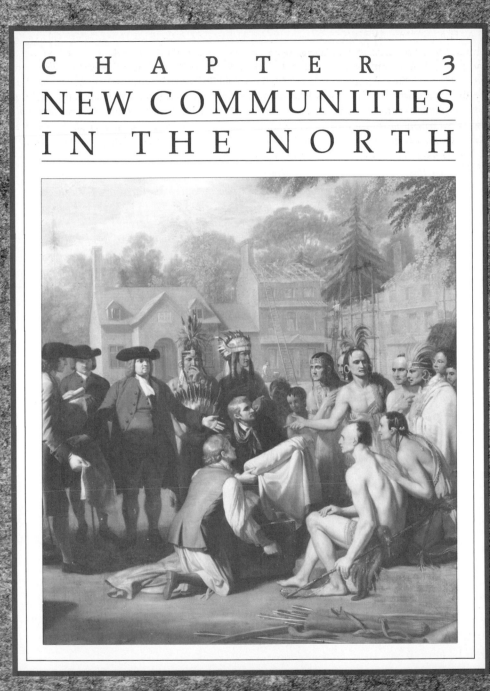

THE EPISODE: *In 1692, one of the most remarkable events in American history took place. It began in a small village just outside the town of Salem in the British colony of Massachusetts. A group of young people, most of them female, began to have what their elders called "fits." Then they started to accuse adults of being witches, tormenting them in league with the Devil. The little community was terrified. Almost everyone believed the Devil was real and that he could visit the earth and take possession of people's souls if they agreed to make a covenant with him. So the people of Salem Village set out to combat what they believed was a conspiracy, set afoot by the Devil himself. Within a few weeks, hundreds of women and men had been accused of being witches. Soon the highest authorities in the colony intervened, not to restore calm but to stamp out the Satanic conspiracy. Dozens of people were put on trial, and several "confessed." By the time the hysteria and the trials ended, nineteen supposed witches had been hanged.*

THE HISTORICAL SETTING: *This wrenching episode occurred on a very special historical stage. Just over sixty years before, a body of English men and women had migrated to Massachusetts. They attempted to found a new society that would be based firmly on their zealous form of Protestantism, known as Puritanism. The English Puritans were called that because they hoped to "purify" the Protestant Church of England by getting rid of the features of Catholicism it had retained. Most of them remained in England and struggled against the King and his bishops, even making a civil war and beheading a king. But one small group decided that the struggle could best be waged in America, where they could establish a new and "Godly" society. These American Puritans thought of themselves as chosen by God for a special errand into a wilderness, where they would build a holy "City upon a Hill."*

They were able, for a time, to create and maintain distinctive communities not only in Massachusetts but in Connecticut, Rhode Island, New Hampshire, Maine, and parts of Long Island. But by the 1690s, their utopian religious vision was deeply in crisis. The king and his judges had revoked their original charter, and they had been subjected to direct royal government. They believed their children and grandchildren did not have the same religious fervor that the first generations had had. Their ministers were incessantly warning them that the City upon a Hill had become more interested in commerce and material comforts than in holiness. The dark events of 1692 in Salem were an outcome of both the original vision of the New England Puritans and their fear that their errand into the wilderness was failing. The trials were the desperate, irrational attempt of a Puritan community to preserve the dream of a Holy Commonwealth against what they dimly perceived as the erosions of historical change.

WITCHCRAFT AT SALEM VILLAGE

The two girls were strangely sick. Betty Parris, who was nine years old, and her cousin, eleven-year-old Abigail Williams, often stared dully into space. Sometimes they went down on their hands and knees and made hoarse, choking sounds. At other times they simply fell to the floor and screamed. The girls lived in the house of Betty Parris's father Samuel, a minister, in a small settlement called Salem Village, Massachusetts. It was January 1692.

At first, Samuel Parris kept quiet about the girls' behavior. But as the minister of the town, he was more carefully watched by his neighbors than any other man. His house stood at the center of the village, just down a dirt road from the tavern and not far from the only meetinghouse, or church. Something had to be done, so Parris sent for the village doctor. Since the minister's family was considered the most important family in the village, the doctor proceeded seriously and carefully. He examined the girls, consulted his medical books, and tried various medicines. Nothing worked, and his books gave him no clue. Finally, he gave up. The girls, he told the Reverend Parris, were not physically sick at all but had been touched by "the evil hand."

No one in Massachusetts in 1692 needed to be reminded that the doctor was talking about witchcraft. Four years earlier, in Boston, an Irish woman called Witch Glover had been hanged for bewitching four children. One of Boston's most famous ministers, Cotton Mather, had taken one of the bewitched children into his own house to try to cure her. Mather had then published a book on witchcraft, a book read in every town of the Massachusetts Bay Colony. Samuel Parris had a copy.

Practically every citizen of the colony believed that the devil actually did visit the earth, persuading men and women to join him, and giving them a witch's power to torment innocent people. All over Europe at this time, witches were being accused, convicted, and hanged or burned at the stake. The people of Salem Village were just as superstitious as Europeans and other Americans. Cotton Mather was one of the best-educated men in the colony. Samuel Parris had attended Harvard College. The doctor who first examined Betty Parris and Abigail Williams was an educated scientist. All of these men believed in witchcraft. If such sophisticated community leaders accepted the idea that an evil hand was at work, what could be expected of the plain farmers of Salem Village?

Cotton Mather accepted the witchcraft trials of 1692 as an appropriate way to deal with people who had been possessed by the devil. Years later, though, he had second thoughts. He still believed in witches but had decided that fasting and prayer might "cure" a witch—a better solution than hanging. (Metropolitan Museum of Art, bequest of Charles Allen Munn, 1924)

As soon as gossip leaked out about Betty Parris and Abigail Williams, their young friends began to have similar fits. Between January and September of 1692 a group of about a dozen girls steadily acted bewitched. At nine, Betty Parris was the youngest of the afflicted children; the oldest of the group were two young women of twenty. Today they would probably all be called teenagers. This group of teenage girls was joined from time to time by other afflicted persons, some of them adults, but most of them young people. A few adults argued that the girls were only pretending and that a good spanking would cure them. But most of the people of Salem Village, of nearby Salem Town, and of the whole Massachusetts Bay Colony took the girls' fits seriously.

At first the girls did not name anyone as their tormentors. All over Salem Village, parents and other relatives prayed and fasted. Samuel Parris called in the ministers of several neighboring towns, and they too prayed and fasted. The questions in their minds were: Who was bewitching the girls? Whom had the devil persuaded to join him in witchcraft? Finally, on February 25, some of the girls called out three names. Whether the afflicted children had a plan or not, they were very shrewd—in the way that even truly disturbed or insane people can be shrewd. They named three women who were, for different reasons, not respected in the community.

The first was Tituba, a slave in the house of Samuel Parris. Tituba was from one of the islands of the West Indies, where Parris had worked as a merchant before coming to Salem to preach in 1689. She probably was part African American and part Native American. Tituba was married to another slave, John Indian, who also belonged to Parris. During dark winter afternoons in the Parris kitchen, Tituba had no doubt told weird stories of the islands to Betty and Abigail. She had also shown magic tricks to the village girls who were now afflicted.

The second person identified by the afflicted girls was Sarah Good. In her own way she was even more vulnerable than Tituba. Her husband was a laborer who had never held a job for long. Sarah herself was something of a hag. She smoked a pipe, muttered to herself, and often went begging from door to door in the village.

The third supposed witch was a prosperous old woman named Sarah Osburne. After her husband died, she had offended the town by living with an overseer on her farm. Although she eventually married the man, she had stopped going to church. She had a bad reputation.

In 1692 there were no regular judges in Massachusetts. Court cases were presided over by members of the colonial legislature known as assistants. So the parents and relatives of some of the afflicted children went to the two assistants of Salem Town and asked for the arrest of Tituba, Sarah Good, and Sarah Osburne on a charge of witchcraft.

March 1 was an exciting day for the village. The constables and uniformed military guard went out with drums to meet the two assistants coming from Salem Town. With this military escort the assistants marched into the meetinghouse, which had been converted into a courtroom. The assistants took their seats on a platform at the front of the church, with the afflicted girls facing them in the front pew. Almost everyone else in the village crowded in. Sarah Good was then brought forward for preliminary questioning.

One of the assistants, John Hathorne, was a stern, dark man who took his work very seriously. He leaned forward toward cranky Sarah Good and began to question her:

> HATHORNE: Sarah Good, what evil spirit have you familiarity with?
> SARAH GOOD: None.
> HATHORNE: Have you made no contract with the devil?
> SARAH GOOD: No.
> HATHORNE: Why do you hurt these children?
> SARAH GOOD: I do not hurt them. I scorn it.
> HATHORNE: Who do you employ, then, to do it?
> SARAH GOOD: I employ nobody.
> HATHORNE: What *creature* do you employ, then?
> SARAH GOOD: No creature. But I am falsely accused.
> HATHORNE: Have you made no contract with the devil?
> SARAH GOOD: No

Up to this point, Hathorne had not shaken this stubborn woman. She simply denied everything, saying in a tough old voice, "I scorn it!"

But Hathorne and the other assistant, Jonathan Corwin, had made a decision before opening the court. They would accept the testimony of the afflicted children about who it was that tormented them. Hathorne and Corwin believed that even if Sarah Good were standing innocently before the judges, her "shape," or spirit, might attack the girls. If the afflicted girls said that Sarah Good's shape was pinching or hurting them, then she would be put in jail for a full-scale witch trial and possible hanging.

According to the legal procedures of the day, Sarah Good was not told of this decision in advance. Nor was she represented by a lawyer. Hathorne's next move was very important. It established the pattern for all the hearings that would follow. The clerk's record of the testimony continued:

> Hathorne desired the children all of them to look upon her and see if this were the person that had hurt them. And so they all did look upon her, and said this was one of the persons that did torment them. Presently they were all tormented.

Here was the key to Hathorne's prosecution of the witches: "Presently they were all tormented." Here, for the first time, the afflicted girls learned that their moaning and screaming could attract favorable public attention. After a short time the girls quieted down. They said they were being tormented by the shape of Sarah Good, the cranky woman who at that moment was standing so still in the meeting-house. Hathorne returned to the attack. Sarah Good held her ground for a moment, but then she began to break down:

> HATHORNE: Sarah Good, do you not see now what you have done? Why do you not tell us the truth? Why do you thus torment these poor children?
> SARAH GOOD: I do not torment them.
> HATHORNE: Who was it, then, that tormented the children?
> SARAH GOOD: It was Osburne.

In her panic, Sarah Good tried to save herself by pointing an accusing finger at Sarah Osburne. But in doing so she sealed her own fate. Hathorne and Corwin reasoned this way: Sarah Good was not afflicted. Therefore, unless she were a witch, how could she know that Sarah Osburne attacked the children? Hathorne could see that Sarah Good was going to pieces, and he hurried the process:

> HATHORNE: What is it you say when you go muttering away from persons' houses?
> SARAH GOOD: If I must tell, I will tell.
> HATHORNE: Do tell us then.
> SARAH GOOD: If I must tell, I will tell. It is the commandments.

Hathorne sensed that she was lying. Sarah Good might still have saved herself if she could have repeated even some of the Bible's ten commandments. But when Hathorne asked her to name one, she hedged:

> HATHORNE: What commandment is it?
> SARAH GOOD: If I must tell, I will tell. It is a psalm.
> HATHORNE: What psalm?

As the clerk of the court recorded, "After a long time, she muttered over some part of a psalm." He also recorded: "Her answers were given in a very wicked, spiteful manner, with base and abusive words and many lies." Sarah Good was taken away, and her husband was questioned briefly. The clerk recorded his curious testimony:

> It was here said that her husband had said that he was afraid that she either was a witch or would be one very quickly. The worthy Mr. Hathorne asked him his reason why he said so of her. He answered that it was her bad carriage [attitude] to him, and indeed, said he, I may say with tears that she is an enemy to all good.

The "Witch House." This elegantly gabled building, constructed in 1675, is a fine example of seventeenth-century domestic architecture in New England. Its fame, however, is not architectural: It was the home of Jonathan Corwin and became known as the "Witch House." The painting on p. 107 was set in one of the rooms of this house. (Essex Institute)

Once finished with questioning Sarah Good, Hathorne and Corwin then called Sarah Osburne, who quickly panicked. She tried to claim that she herself had been bewitched. To save herself, she tried to throw suspicion on Tituba's husband, John Indian, by claiming that she had been attacked by a "thing like an Indian, all black." But the afflicted girls would not let her join their circle. They accused her just as they had Sarah Good, and she was taken away. The assistants then sent for Tituba, who was to be the star of the day.

Tituba's situation was frightening. Samuel Parris owned her as his slave. As the village minister, he claimed to own her soul, too. Between the time little Betty Parris first accused Tituba until she testified, Parris had sometimes beaten her and sometimes prayed for her. By March 1 she had worked out a shrewd plan. She would confess. But she would also save herself by throwing greater suspicion on others and by claiming that she was no longer working with the devil. Once more Hathorne took the lead in the questioning. At first, Tituba's answers sounded like Sarah Good's, and the afflicted girls behaved the same way:

HATHORNE: Tituba, what evil spirit have you familiarity with?
TITUBA: None.
HATHORNE: Why do you hurt these children?

TITUBA: I do not hurt them.
HATHORNE: Who is it then?
TITUBA: The devil for aught I know.

But then Tituba began to execute her plan. As soon as she began to confess, the afflicted girls calmed down. It was as though Tituba's confession released them from their spells for the time being.

HATHORNE: Did you ever see the devil?
TITUBA: The devil came to me and bid me serve him.
HATHORNE: Who have you seen?
TITUBA: Four women sometimes hurt the children.
HATHORNE: Who were they?

At this point Tituba had to be careful. For the moment, at least, the children were quiet. But she had to name names that the assistants and the village farmers would accept. She also had to try to protect her husband, John Indian. Sarah Osburne had testified that she was bewitched by "a thing like an Indian, all black." Tituba invented a "tall man from Boston," dressed in black, to throw suspicion off John Indian. She also accused her two codefendants. (When she named Sarah Osburne and Sarah Good as witches, Tituba called them Goody. This was an abbreviation of "Goodwife," a common way of addressing married women.) But she claimed that she did not know who the other witches were.

Then Tituba began to weave a tale of witches, devils, and strange animals. The citizens of the village listened in fascinated horror.

TITUBA: There is four women and one man. They hurt the children. And they lay
    all upon me and they tell me if I will not hurt the children, they will hurt me.
HATHORNE: What also have you seen?
TITUBA: Two rats, a red rat and a black rat.
HATHORNE: What did they say to you?
TITUBA: They said serve me.
HATHORNE: Why did you not tell your master?
TITUBA: I was afraid they would cut off my head if I told.
HATHORNE: What attendants hath Sarah Good?
TITUBA: A yellow bird. And she would have given me one.
HATHORNE: What meat did she give it?
TITUBA: It did suck her between her fingers.
HATHORNE: What hath Sarah Osburne?
TITUBA: A yellow dog. She had a thing with a head like a woman, with two legs
    and wings.
HATHORNE: What else have you seen with Osburne?
TITUBA: Another thing. Hairy. It goes upright like a man. It hath only two legs.
HATHORNE: What clothes doth the man [the "tall man from Boston"] go in?
TITUBA: He goes in black clothes. A tall man with white hair, I think.

At the mention of these creatures, the afflicted girls began to behave strangely again. The timing was perfect. Hathorne had to ask Tituba who was bewitching the girls. His question gave Tituba a chance to end her testimony in a helpful way. She could again throw suspicion on someone else. Doing so would prove that she wanted to help hunt down the witches. But then she could claim that she could no longer "see." This would prove that she was free from the devil's spell herself.

> HATHORNE: Do you see who it is that torments these children now?
> TITUBA: Yes, it is Goody Good. She hurts them in her own shape.
> HATHORNE: And who is it that hurts them *now*?
> TITUBA: I am blind. I cannot see.

Tituba, Sarah Good, and Sarah Osburne were questioned several more times during the next few days. On March 7 they were sent to jail in Boston to await a full trial. Sarah Osburne fell ill and died on May 10 without a trial. Sarah Good had a baby in jail, who died—confirming everyone's suspicion that she was an evil woman. With the three "witches" in jail, Salem Village might have calmed down. But Tituba had said that four women, plus the tall man from Boston, were tormenting the afflicted girls. And they continued to be afflicted. This meant more witches were on the loose.

Shortly after Tituba, Sarah Good, and Sarah Osburne had been taken away, Salem Village had a day of fasting and prayer. Once more the ministers of the neighboring towns came to meet with Parris. Once more the girls were watched, prayed over, and questioned. Finally, they called out a name, a name that shocked everyone and started the trials off in a new direction. The girls named Martha Cory, who was not a slave like Tituba, not a hag like Goody Good, and not a sinner like Goody Osburne. Martha Cory was an upstanding member of the village congregation. For the first time the girls had accused an adult with a solid reputation. If Martha Cory could be suspected, then no woman in Salem Village would be safe.

The warrant for Martha Cory's arrest was dated March 19, but because that day was a Saturday, she was not to be arrested until the following Monday. On the Sunday between she showed up at church, where a visiting minister, Deodat Lawson, was to conduct the church service. Lawson had once been the minister of Salem Village and was now living in Boston. He came to Salem to witness the witchcraft proceedings, and he had spent the night in Parris's house, where he watched Abigail Williams go through a violent fit of possession. The next morning, Lawson went to the meetinghouse to preach.

It was no ordinary Sunday service. Goodwife Cory herself came bravely into the meetinghouse, and there, during prayers and the sermon, the afflicted girls had fits. Ordinarily, it was a serious offense to whisper, doze off, or even look out the window during church services. In the meetinghouses men were assigned the job of patrolling the aisles during the sermon—which might last several hours—to prod or even hit people who misbehaved or did not pay attention. But the afflicted girls broke all the usual rules. Abigail Williams yelled out at the minister, and several of the other girls joined in. Finally, Abigail pointed to an exposed beam above the head of Martha Cory and called out, "Look where Goody Cory sits on the beam, suckling her yellow bird betwixt her fingers."

The girls had learned Tituba's lessons well. From the time of her confession to the end of the trials, they often mentioned strange animals, especially the yellow bird. Martha Cory, of course, was simply sitting in her pew. But when the girls cried out, all eyes looked overhead to the beam where her shape was supposed to be sitting with its sinister yellow bird. When Cory came before the assistants the next day, most of the villagers had already made up their minds that she was guilty.

The visiting minister, Deodat Lawson, wrote an account of Martha Cory's examination by Hathorne and Corwin:

> On Monday the 21st of March, the magistrates of Salem were appointed to come to the examination of Goodwife Cory. And about twelve of the clock, they went into the meeting house, which was thronged with spectators. Mr. Noyes [a minister from Salem Town] began with a very pathetic [sad] prayer. Goodwife Cory, being called to answer what was alleged against her, desired to go to prayer. This was much wondered at, in the presence of so many people.

Martha Cory was a very proud and rugged woman. When two officers of the town had first come to her farm to ask her about the charges of witchcraft, she had laughed at them. Now, in her examination, she was trying to beat the village at its own game. If they could pray, then she would pray herself. But Hathorne refused:

> The magistrates told her they would not admit it. They came not there to hear her pray, but to examine her in what was alleged against her. The worshipful Mr. Hathorne asked her why she afflicted these children. She said she did not afflict them. He asked her who did, then? She said, "I do not know. How should I know?"

Hathorne began with the same questions he had put to Sarah Good and Sarah Osburne. Once more, the suspected witch denied everything. Once more, the afflicted girls had fits. Every time Martha Cory moved an arm or bit her lip, the girls acted afflicted in the same parts of their bodies:

> The number of afflicted persons were about that time ten. Those were most of them at Goodwife Cory's examination, and did vehemently accuse her in the assembly of afflicting them, by biting, pinching, strangling, etc. And that they did in their fit see her likeness coming to them, and bringing a book to them. She said she had no book. They affirmed that she had a yellow bird that used to suck betwixt her fingers. Being asked about it, she said she had no familiarity with any such thing. She was a Gospel woman, which title she called herself by. And the afflicted persons told her, Ah! She was a Gospel witch.
>
> It was observed several times that if she did but bite her under lip in time of examination, the persons afflicted were bitten on their arms and wrists and produced the marks before the magistrates, ministers, and others. If she did but pinch her finger, or grasp one hand hard in the other, they were pinched and produced the marks before the magistrates and spectators.

Then the afflicted girls threw terror into the entire audience by saying that there was a gathering of witches that very moment in front of the meetinghouse!

> The afflicted persons asked her [Martha Cory] why she did not go to the company of witches which were before the meeting house mustering? Did she not hear the drumbeat? They accused her of familiarity with the devil, in the shape of a black

man whispering in her ear. They affirmed that her yellow bird sucked betwixt her fingers in the assembly.

She denied all that was charged upon her, and said they could not prove a witch. She was that afternoon committed to Salem prison.

Once the afflicted girls and their supporters had succeeded in their attack on Martha Cory, they were able to accuse anyone in the village. During the last week of March and the first days of April, several women with sound reputations were arrested and brought before the assistants. The village was in a deepening panic. Neighbors began to suspect each other, and people quickly forgot the difference between evidence and common gossip.

The panic spread from Salem Village to Salem Town, and then to the rest of the Massachusetts Bay Colony. By April 11, the examinations had to be moved to the larger meetinghouse in Salem Town. The deputy governor and several other leading citizens of the colony came up from Boston to observe the proceedings. The afflicted girls were no longer a local phenomenon. Now they were watched and wondered at by people from all parts of Massachusetts.

In the middle of April, with spring well on its way, the first break showed in the ranks of the afflicted girls. One of the women identified as a witch in early April was Elizabeth Proctor, whose husband owned a large farm in the southern part of the village. The Proctors' maidservant, Mary Warren, was one of the afflicted girls. But the Proctors did not believe in witchcraft at all, and they had the courage to say so in public. At Elizabeth Proctor's examination some of the girls had screamed out that her husband, John, was also a witch—or a wizard, as male witches were called. This accusation alarmed Mary Warren. She did not like Mrs. Proctor at all, but she seems to have had a twenty-year-old's crush on John Proctor, who was a middle-aged man. Outside the meetinghouse, she began to say that the afflictions were all a sport, that John Proctor was not a wizard at all.

When the other afflicted girls found out about Mary Warren's betrayal, they accused *her* of being a witch. On April 18 she was arrested and brought before the assistants. Suddenly, she had moved from the favored pew of the afflicted girls into the seat of fear where she had watched grown men and women collapse in panic. This was a crucial point in the trials. If Mary Warren could hold her ground against the screams of the afflicted girls, the stares of the audience, and the sternness of Hathorne, then the trials might come to a halt.

Samuel Parris himself kept the official record of the scene:

As soon as she was coming toward the bar, the afflicted fell into fits.

HATHORNE: Mary Warren, you stand here charged with sundry acts of witchcraft. What do you say for yourself? Are you guilty or not?

MARY WARREN: I am innocent.

HATHORNE: Hath she hurt you (speaking to the sufferers)?

Some were dumb. Betty Hubbard [one of the afflicted girls] testified against her, and then said Hubbard fell into a violent fit.

HATHORNE: You were a little while ago an afflicted person. Now you are an afflictor. How comes this to pass?

MARY WARREN: I look up to God and take it to be a great mercy of God.

HATHORNE: What? Do you take it to be a great mercy to afflict others?

This trick question of Hathorne's took Mary Warren by surprise. At the same time, all the afflicted girls began to howl. It was too much for the young woman to bear. She broke down and became incoherent. She struggled from time to time to regain control of herself, but it was no use. By now the fits may have become real hysteria, which Mary Warren and some of the other girls could no longer start or stop at will.

Now Mary Warren fell into a fit, and some of the afflicted cried out that Goody Cory and Proctor and his wife came in their apparition [shape] and struck her down.

Mary Warren continued a good space in a fit, and she did neither see, nor hear, nor speak.

Afterwards, she started up, and said, "I will speak," and cried out, "Oh I am sorry for it. I am sorry for it," and wringed her hands, and fell a little while into a fit again. And then she came to speak, but immediately her teeth were set, and then she fell into a violent fit, and cried out, "Oh, Lord, help me! Oh, Good Lord, save me!"

And then afterward she cried again, "I will tell! I will tell!" And then she fell into a dead fit again.

Mary Warren was taken to Salem to jail, where she was questioned again and again by the assistants and ministers. Finally, on May 12, she admitted that both the Proctors were witches. By then, she was probably completely out of touch with reality. She confessed that she herself had "signed the devil's book," and she wildly accused several other people of witchcraft.

What happened in Massachusetts in 1692 was really quite simple—though *why* it happened is complex. A group of teenage girls caused a brief revolution. In January they were ordinary girls, taking orders from adults, working very hard in their homes or as servants, listening to long sermons in church on Sundays and other days. By the spring of 1692 they held an enormous amount of power—even the power of life and death—over a large number of the adult citizens of Massachusetts. They had begun by accusing poor old women and slaves. But within a few weeks they were charging ministers, merchants, and other solid citizens. They were able to terrify tough old pioneer farmers. And behind them stood the power of the Massachusetts government to send innocent men and women to the gallows.

As panic gripped Salem and the rest of the colony during the summer of 1692, displays of both courage and cowardice could be seen, sometimes in the same family or individual. One such mixture of responses occurred in the case of George Jacobs, a toothless village elder who shuffled about with the aid of two canes. Jacobs's household included his son and daughter-in-law—"a woman crazy in her senses who had been so several years," according to local gossips. There were four grandchildren, the eldest a teenager named Margaret. Jacobs's servant, Sarah Churchill, was one of the afflicted girls.

Old Jacobs, like John Proctor, had scoffed openly at the girls' claims that they were possessed by witches. He even went so far as to mock his own servant Sarah as a "witch bitch." Unfortunately for Jacobs, no one in Salem in 1692 could make such

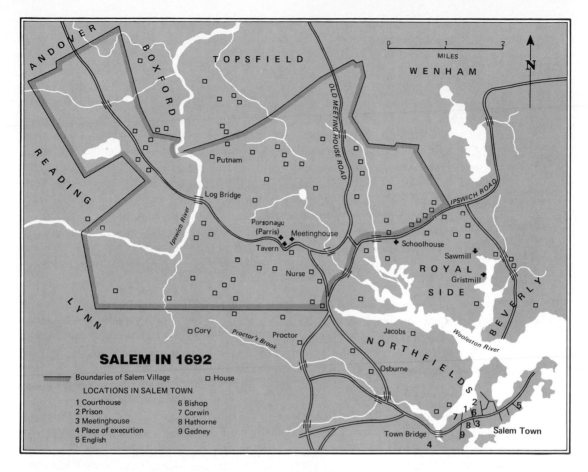

SALEM IN 1692

— Boundaries of Salem Village □ House

LOCATIONS IN SALEM TOWN

1 Courthouse 6 Bishop
2 Prison 7 Corwin
3 Meetinghouse 8 Hathorne
4 Place of execution 9 Gedney
5 English

remarks and escape reprisal. On May 10 Jacobs was summoned to answer to charges of being a wizard. Jacobs, like John Proctor and Martha Cory, was crisp and caustic in his examination, because he considered the accusation completely ridiculous:

HATHORNE: Here are them that accuse you of acts of witchcraft.

JACOBS: Well, let us hear who they are and what they are.

HATHORNE: Abigail Williams.

JACOBS: (Laughing) I am falsely accused. Your worships, all of you, do you think this is true?

HATHORNE: Nay, what do you think?

JACOBS: I never did it.

HATHORNE: Who did it?

JACOBS: Don't ask me. I am as innocent as the child born tonight. You tax me for a wizard. You may as well tax me for a buzzard.

But it was no use. Old Jacobs was sent away to the Boston jail. His son and namesake, George Jr., did not wait to undergo a similar examination. Instead, he fled the colony, leaving not only his crazed wife but also their four children to face the consequences of having a close relative declared a wizard. The consequences were not long in coming. The town officers soon dragged Mrs. Jacobs before the afflicted ones. At first the girls did not recognize her. Then one—probably her servant, Sarah Churchill—cried: "'Don't you know the old witch?' And then they cried out at her, and fell down in their fits." Mrs. Jacobs spent the next ten months in prison as a suspected witch, with her three youngest children left to the care of sympathetic neighbors.

Margaret, the eldest Jacobs child, had even worse luck. She was brought in to give testimony against her grandfather. Afraid that she would be denounced herself as a witch, Margaret confessed in order to save her life, accusing both her grandfather and the Reverend George Burroughs, a former village minister, of being wizards. Only after her grandfather and Burroughs had been put in prison did Margaret finally summon the courage to recant her confession. She wrote from prison, denying her previous accusations, but the court ignored this statement and Margaret remained in jail for another year, where she wrote or dictated this confession:

> The humble declaration of Margaret Jacobs unto the Honored Court now sitting at Salem:
>
> I was cried out upon by some of the possessed persons. The Lord above knows I knew nothing. They told me if I would not confess, I should be put down into the dungeon and would be hanged. But if I would confess, I should have my life. This did so afright me, with my own vile, wicked heart, to save my life made me make the confession I did, which confession is altogether false and untrue. What I said was altogether false, against my grandfather, and Mr. Burroughs, which I did to save my life and to have my liberty. But the Lord, charging it to my conscience, made me in so much horror that I could not contain myself before I had denied my confession, which I did, though I saw nothing but death before me, choosing death with a quiet conscience than to live in such horror.
>
> MARGARET JACOBS.

The girl managed to visit the Reverend Burroughs before his execution in August, however, and received his forgiveness. Old Jacobs was also told of her recantation before his own execution and, although his property had already been confiscated, he showed his pleasure at Margaret's brave act of conscience by including her in his will. After her grandfather's death, Margaret wrote from prison to her vanished father describing her experiences. She ended her letter by stating simply: "My Mother poor Woman is very Crazy, and remembers her kind love to you." Margaret's letter probably never reached her father.

By this time, almost two dozen more people had been arrested, and many more were being accused every day. By the last week of May, nearly fifty people had been sent to the dark, crowded Boston jail, waiting for their final trials. The accused were no longer outcasts or simple local farmers. One of those arrested in May, for example, was Philip English, the foremost shipowner of Salem. (He later escaped from jail and fled to New York.)

At last, on May 28, the afflicted girls named the Master Wizard. They had been questioned for weeks by the assistants and ministers about the "tall man from Boston"

George Jacobs on trial. During the nineteenth century, Puritan New England became a prime subject for historical novels—like Nathaniel Hawthorne's *The Scarlet Letter*—and paintings. This painting was made in 1850 and gives a highly romanticized impression of the trial of George Jacobs. Jacobs, the old man kneeling at the right, is hard to reconcile with the real George Jacobs, who laughed at Hathorne and Corwin and said, "You tax me for a wizard? You may as well tax me for a buzzard." (Photograph by Richard Merrill, 1972. Courtesy Essex Institute, Salem, Massachusetts)

Tituba had first mentioned on March 1. Everyone presumed he was the guiding hand behind the entire witches' plot. The magistrates summoned him to court, and on May 31 a tall man from Boston walked into the Salem meetinghouse. His name was John Alden. He was the son of the Plymouth Colony's famous lovers, John and Priscilla Alden. This John Alden was more famous as a soldier than a lover, for he was a sea captain who had fought bravely in recent battles with the Indians.

Alden would never have come to Salem by his own choice, since he thought that the accusation of witchcraft was insanely foolish. But the deputy governor of the colony, William Stoughton, ordered him to appear for questioning. So Alden marched into court to face his accusers. Later, writing in the third person, he gave an angry description of what took place.

John Alden was sent for by the Magistrates of Salem upon the accusation of a company of poor, distracted, or possessed creatures or witches. And being sent by Mr. Stoughton, arrived there the 31st day of May, and appeared at Salem Village before Mr. Gedney [a third assistant], Mr. Hathorne, and Mr. Corwin.

Those wenches being present, who played their juggling tricks, falling down, crying out, and staring in people's faces, the Magistrates demanded of them several times who it was of all the people in the room that hurt them?

Could the girls identify a man they had never seen before—except perhaps for his shape? For a moment the girls were helpless.

One of these accusers pointed several times at one Captain Hill, there present, but spoke nothing. The same accuser had a man standing at her back to hold her up. He stooped down to her ear. Then she cried out Alden, Alden, afflicted her. One of the Magistrates asked her if she ever had seen Alden. She answered, "No." He asked her how she knew it was Alden. She said the man had told her so.

The assistants had to be careful, for Alden was an important man and a war hero. They ordered a ring of men to stand in the street; then they took the girls outside to see whether they could pick Alden out of the ring. Somehow, the girls immediately selected him, and the assistants ordered him arrested. His sword was taken from him, and he was brought back inside. But Alden was no poor slave or hag of Salem Village. He stood his ground to the end:

Mr. Gedney bid Alden confess, and give glory to God. Alden said he hoped he would give glory to God, but appealed to all that ever knew him, and challenged any one that could bring in anything that might give suspicion of his being such a one [a wizard]. They bid Alden look upon the accusers, which he did, and then they fell down. Alden asked Mr. Gedney, what reason could be given why Alden looking upon *him* did not strike *him* down as well? But no reason was given that I heard.

Alden told Mr. Gedney that there was a lying spirit in them [the afflicted girls], for I can assure you that there is not a word of truth in all these say of me. But Alden was again committed to the marshal.

Alden spent the next fifteen weeks awaiting trial, not in prison but under guard at his Boston home. This special treatment was due to his friendship with the colony's leading ministers—men like Cotton Mather of Boston—and with crown officials like the governor himself. These ministers met with Alden from time to time in order to pray and fast for his deliverance, but whether they meant "deliverance" from the charge itself or from being a wizard was uncertain.

Although Alden was a strong and self-assured man, he began to doubt his chances of escaping trial. Finally, in September 1692, after several witches had been hanged, he fled to friends in neighboring Duxbury and pounded on their door at midnight, shouting: "The devil is after me!" His friends smuggled Alden to safety in New York. There he joined other well-to-do or prominent individuals who had left Massachusetts rather than face the Salem court. There was no democracy among "witches" in the Bay Colony. With wealth or influence one had a far better chance of reaching safety in colonies like New York than did the ordinary citizen accused of witchcraft. The following year, Alden was declared innocent by special proclamation,

Judge William Stoughton of the Court of Oyer and Terminer was a stubborn and overbearing man whose insistence that Rebecca Nurse be hanged was one of the low points of the vengeful trials. He was also a generous contributor to Harvard University. (Harvard University Portrait Collection)

and the tall man from Boston returned to Massachusetts, his person and property untouched.

Meanwhile, during the storm of arrests and imprisonments, a ship from England was bringing the man who would eventually control the outcome of events, Sir William Phips. He had recently been appointed the first royal governor of the Massachusetts Bay Colony.

Phips was born in New England, the son of a poor farmer in Maine. He had made a fortune in Boston and had added to it in the Caribbean islands, not far from where Samuel Parris had worked as a merchant and had bought Tituba and John Indian. Phips found a sunken Spanish ship near Haiti and raised a treasure in gold worth well over a million dollars. England's king at the time, James II, had knighted Phips as a reward. Sir William was also the hero of several battles against the Indians and the French in America. After a trip to England he was returning home as a wealthy hero and the governor of Massachusetts.

When Sir William's ship sailed into Boston harbor in May 1692, he knew nothing of the witchcraft trials because he had been at sea for weeks. He was horrified at the news. Like almost everyone else at the time, Phips believed in witchcraft, but he was determined to get to the bottom of things. Dozens of suspected witches were in Boston jail awaiting trial. At the end of May, Phips appointed a special court to try the prisoners. He named seven judges, with his deputy governor, William Stoughton, as the chief justice. The court was called a Court of Oyer and Terminer. (This old English term was derived from French words meaning "to hear" and "to end.") Verdicts of innocent or guilty were to be handed down by a jury picked from the men of Salem Town, where the trials were to take place.

The prisoners had to put their faith in the court. The judges were men of high standing in the colony. They would probably be very careful about hanging men and women who had been accused by a group of hysterical young girls. What the prisoners did not know, at first, was that most of the judges were just as severe as Hathorne.

Before they opened the Court of Oyer and Terminer, the judges made three decisions that hurt the chances of the accused witches. First, they decided to accept as evidence the records of the examinations Hathorne and Corwin had conducted in the village. These records—some of which were taken down by Samuel Parris himself—contained more than question-and-answer testimony. They also included vivid descriptions of the behavior of the afflicted girls. So the Court was ready to take their fits and screams as "evidence." The second decision the members of the Court made was to accept testimony about the "shapes" that could be seen only by afflicted persons. Third, and perhaps most important, the judges decided that anyone who *confessed* to being a witch would not be punished. They were reasoning that a confession was a sign that the accused person had broken the hold of the devil, and could be redeemed. But this meant that confession was rewarded, and it encouraged some, like Tituba, to accuse other innocent people in their confessions.

On June 2 the judges first tried a woman named Bridget Bishop. Stoughton probably chose her because the case against her was strong. She was the wife of a tavernkeeper in Salem Town and she had a very bad reputation. Also, several confessing witches had said she was one of their leaders. The jury quickly found her guilty, and the judges sentenced her to death. She was given a few extra days of life by an embarrassing discovery. There was no Massachusetts law providing the death penalty for witches. The colonial legislature, known as the General Court, quickly passed such a law. On June 10 the sheriff took Bridget in a cart to the top of Gallows Hill, where she was hanged. The first "witch" was gone.

But many more suspects were waiting, and Hathorne and Corwin were still conducting examinations in the village. Sometimes as many as fifty new witches were accused in a single day, no longer just in Salem Village but all over eastern Massachusetts. One week, then two weeks passed after the hanging of Bridget Bishop. But still the judges did not meet again. They were quarreling among themselves about the meaning of the afflicted girls' testimony concerning shapes. This kind of evidence, which was called spectral evidence (from "specter," meaning "ghost"), was considered all-important. Without it there would not be a case against a single suspected witch. The quarreling judges turned to the ministers of Boston and nearby towns to decide the question. The ministers finally decided that spectral evidence should be used, as long as the judges and jury were careful with it.

On June 28 the court met again, to try Rebecca Nurse. Goodwife Nurse was from a large and prosperous farm family of Salem Village. She was an old woman and nearly deaf. But she was a member of the church, and before the witchcraft panic she had been a respected old grandmother. The jury took the ministers' advice about being careful in admitting spectral evidence. This time, they ignored the shrieking,

The hanging of witches. This 1655 drawing shows women convicted of witchcraft being hanged in England. Four are dead already—at least the hangman is checking them to make sure they are dead. Three more are waiting below the gallows, and others are watching from the prison behind the barred window. ([R. Gardiner] *England's Grievance Discovered . . .* [1655]) (The Folger Shakespeare Library)

afflicted girls and brought back a verdict of not guilty. Chief Justice Stoughton quickly bullied the jury into reversing its verdict, however. Then Rebecca Nurse's relatives went to Governor Phips and persuaded him to stop the hanging. But it was no use. When Stoughton and others heard about Phips's action, they insisted that he change his mind.

Neither the jury nor the governor could save Rebecca Nurse, and on Tuesday, July 19, she was hanged. Four other women were hanged the same day. One was the hag of Salem Village, Sarah Good. When she was about to die, one of the ministers tried to persuade her to confess and save herself. Goody Good might well have done so. She had spent months in prison. One child had died there with her. A second child had been arrested as a witch, though she was only five years old. But these things had only toughened the old woman's will. "You are a liar," she spat back at the preacher. "I am no more a witch than you are a wizard. If you take my life away, God will give you blood to drink." With that, she went up the ladder to the waiting rope.

At the September meeting of the Court of Oyer and Terminer, one man refused to plead either innocent or guilty. He was Giles Cory, the husband of Martha Cory, who had already been condemned. Under an old English law, Cory was taken into a vacant field beside the prison in Salem Town and tortured. Heavy stones were piled on his chest, but he would not surrender and say either "innocent" or "guilty." Instead (according to legend), he said only "More weight!" By afternoon he had been crushed to death. Three days later, on September 22, the sheriff hauled eight more convicted

Samuel Sewall. Only one member of the Court of Oyer and Terminer ever openly admitted that the trial was an error and a sin. This was Samuel Sewall, who made a public confession in his Boston church in 1697—the same year the colony's legislature voted a fund to compensate the relatives of the victims. (Massachusetts Historical Society)

witches to the top of Gallows Hill to die, bringing the total executed to twenty—not counting the several who had already died in prison.

After the hangings of September 22, as suddenly as it had begun, the panic was over. The afflicted girls had gone too far. In the early fall of 1692 they began to accuse almost everyone, including the pious wives of well-known ministers. One girl even claimed that Cotton Mather, the colony's leading minister, was a wizard. Several of the girls began to see the shape of Lady Mary Phips, the governor's wife! These charges simply could not be accepted.

The trials that began in Salem Village were stopped by some of the leading citizens of the colony. They had finally become convinced that the entire affair had been a terrible mistake. On October 26, before the Court of Oyer and Terminer opened again, the General Court ordered a new meeting of ministers to consider the problem. Three days later, the General Court dismissed the trial court, and Governor Phips began releasing prisoners on bond. In November, following the advice of the ministers, the governor established a new court, with new rules. In the new trials spectral evidence would not be accepted. And, just as important, confessing witches *would* be hanged. Under these new rules there could be almost no convictions. One by one, the prisoners were tried and found innocent. Five still insisted on confessing, and they were sentenced to hang, but Phips overruled the court and allowed even these five to live. It was too late for Sarah Good, Martha Cory, John Proctor, old Jacobs, and the rest who had died. But the Salem witch trials were over at last.

Salem and the rest of the colony then started the impossible task of settling accounts. The released prisoners were required to pay for food and "rent" during their time in prison. Some remained in jail for several months until these charges were paid. Samuel Parris's congregation voted to dismiss him, and he left Salem Village in disgrace. No one knows what happened to little Betty Parris, but her younger brother went insane and died while still a young man.

In January 1697, five years after Betty Parris and Abigail Williams had first been afflicted, the General Court voted a fund of £598 (worth about $30,000) to be distributed among the relatives of the dead and the surviving "witches." The money proved small compensation for the terrible anguish people had endured. When it was divided up, the lives of Martha and Giles Cory turned out to have been worth about $50.

After any tragedy, people's minds eventually turn to other matters. In Salem Village the families of the dead gradually and painfully made peace with the families of the afflicted girls. By 1706 the little town was calm. But on August 25 of that year, the meetinghouse was once more filled to overflowing. A young woman named Anne Putnam had come to ask for admission to membership in the church. According to New England church custom, she had to make a public confession, after which the members of the church would vote on whether to accept her.

As a young girl of twelve, Anne Putnam had been one of the most active of the afflicted girls. Now, at the age of twenty-six, she was asking for full admission into the adult community. The congregation was seated while the new minister read her confession:

> I desire to be humbled before God for that sad providence in the year about '92. I, then being in my childhood, was made an instrument for the accusing of several persons of a grievous crime, whereby their lives were taken away from them. I now have good reason to believe they were innocent persons. What was said or done by me against any person, I can truly say I did not out of any anger, malice, or ill-will. What I did was done ignorantly, being deluded by Satan. I desire to lie in the dust, and to be humbled for it, and earnestly beg forgiveness of God, and from all those unto whom I have given just cause of sorrow and offence.

The minister finished reading, and then asked the congregation to vote. Sitting in the meetinghouse were many relatives of the innocent men and women whom Anne Putnam had helped imprison and hang. They must have scowled and clenched their hard farmers' fists. But they voted along with the rest of the congregation, unanimously, to accept Anne Putnam's plea for forgiveness. Shakily, she sat down. The story of the Salem witches had finally ended.

What happened in Salem Village in 1692 has puzzled historians, other scholars, and ordinary people for three centuries. Solutions to the puzzle have been many. Some people believe that it was an instance of mass hysteria or "possession." Others think that some of the villagers really were practicing witchcraft and were caught at it. There is even a theory that the episode was caused by a fungus that attacked the farmers' grain the summer before, producing a chemical hallucinogen that acted something like LSD.

But the Salem witchcraft trials were the outcome of a specific history, the history of English colonies in the part of America they decided to call New England. And it is only against the background of that specific history that the events of 1692 can be understood.

Ships and Shores

Like the history of the English colonies in the South, the story of the New England colonies had many beginnings. And, as in the South, these beginnings usually involved ships and strange encounters.

A LOST TRIBE AND A WANDERING COMMUNITY One such beginning came in 1614, when John Smith visited Cape Cod and stopped to explore. When one of Smith's ships left for Europe, it carried away 20 kidnapped members of the Patuxet tribe that lived on the Cape. Among them was a man about twenty-five years old named Squanto. During the next several years, Squanto saw worlds his people did not dream existed. He went first to Spain and then to England, where he learned the language. Then, in 1619, came what must have seemed a fantastic opportunity. An Englishman asked him to go along on an exploring voyage to America. He went but discovered that he had no home to return to. When he reached his old village, the people had vanished—something like the English colonists at Roanoake Island. They probably had been wiped out by one of the European diseases that were taking such a heavy toll all over the Western Hemisphere (chicken pox, most likely).

Squanto made a home with another tribe in the area. But his life was about to intersect with another voyage, another of New England's beginnings. A year after he came back to America, in September 1620, a tiny ship called the *Mayflower* set sail from England. On board—aside from sailors and laborers—were about 90 men

Governor John Winthrop. This portrait, by an unknown artist, captured much of Winthrop's stern, even ferocious, determination. The artist also caught Winthrop's tendency to brood darkly. The lace collar and cuffs, relieving a black suit, were usually the only bits of finery that English and Dutch radical Protestants permitted themselves. And this would have been Winthrop's most elaborate and ceremonial way of dressing. (American Antiquarian Society)

and women who were embarked not on an exploration, not on a trading or fishing venture, but on a religious pilgrimage (because of this, they would become known as "the Pilgrims"). They were fleeing what they believed was the deep moral corruption of their homeland, looking for a place to make a new beginning. Some of them had already made one voyage of escape to Holland, but things had not worked out there. Now they were headed for the New World, with permission from the Virginia Company to settle on its lands, hoping that their wanderings would come to an end.

The North Atlantic in September and October is a very rough ocean. It was nine hard weeks (during which two children were born at sea) before the *Mayflower* sighted the tip of Cape Cod. On November 11, they went ashore at the place that is now Provincetown, Massachusetts. They fell to their knees to give thanks to the "blessed God of Heaven" who had brought them safely "over the vast and furious ocean." After some exploration they moved down the Cape on the inward shore and founded their colony, Plymouth Plantation.

On the *Mayflower* only one person had died—something of a miracle by the standards of the day. But the colonists were weakened by malnutrition. Many of them had scurvy, a disease caused by deficiencies of vitamin C. When they arrived, winter was about to begin, and it was too late to plant crops. That winter, half of them died. They did better the next year, partly because Squanto came to Plymouth and in rough English explained how to plant and cultivate the Native American's main crop, corn. The next fall, in November of 1621, the Plymouth colony's governor even decreed a special feast of thanksgiving to celebrate a bountiful harvest. He called Squanto God's "special instrument." A year later, Squanto died. He was about thirty-two, probably the victim of one of the European-Americans' diseases.

A GREAT FLEET As it turned out, the Plymouth Colony was soon swamped by another migration, another new beginning. It came in 1630, when a great migration of English men and women to New England began. And that migration had its own beginning at sea. In the spring, a fleet of ships, led by the *Arbella*, set out from England for Massachusetts Bay carrying about a thousand colonists, the largest single English convoy to sail for America so far. On board the *Arbella* was the man who had been chosen to be the governor of a new colony, John Winthrop. And the governor kept a careful journal. On June 5, he noted that the crew took soundings and found the ocean's bottom at 80 fathoms (a little under 500 feet). This meant that land was near. The governor, the seamen, and the other passengers peered ahead through the Atlantic mist, straining for their first sight of America. Finally, late in the day, the mist cleared and they could make out the coast of what is now Maine.

During the next few days, the ships slowed and the men fished. (The governor was attentive to details, and noted that they caught sixty-seven large cod in less than two hours.) Finally, on June 11, the fleet turned south along the coast to look for a certain bay. It was described in the royal charter Winthrop kept locked away belowdecks as "Massachusetts, alias Mattachusetts alias Massatusetts Bay." (The present inhabitants of the place still use all these pronunciations, and others too.) Winthrop was acutely conscious of the extraordinary meaning of what was happening. He was not a sentimental man, but he made an entry in his journal that gave some small indication that he was moved:

> We had now fair, sunshine weather, and so pleasant a sweet air as did much refresh us. And there came a smell off the shore like the smell of a garden. There came a wild pigeon into the ship and another small land bird.

A few more days of sailing brought the fleet into Massachusetts Bay, to a tiny English fishing settlement known as Nahumkeck. But it would soon be given a biblical name, one the colonists thought more appropriate. They renamed it Salem. The history that would lead to the witchcraft trials of 1692 had begun.

Puritanism

Winthrop's fleet was the vanguard of a migration that would bring about 20,000 people to New England between 1630 and 1640. Most were part of a religious and political movement known as Puritanism. They shared some of the motives that

had led Europeans to all parts of the Western Hemisphere. But they had special motives of their own. They believed they were embarked on a mission much more important than finding gold or growing tobacco. They thought they had been chosen by God for an "errand into the wilderness." They hoped to create a purified Christian commonwealth, a place where godly men and women could lead holy lives, safe from the temptations and corruptions of the Old World. By the 1640s, they had succeeded in building a series of distinctive communities, clustering around Massachusetts Bay, but reaching north into Maine and New Hampshire, and south and west into Rhode Island, Connecticut, and Long Island. In many ways, the crisis of Salem Village was the crisis of sixty years of their effort—their successes and failures.

To be a "Puritan" in the sixteenth and seventeenth centuries was not a simple or clear-cut matter. There was no formal organization, no political party, not even a church called "Puritan." There was only a social movement—a movement that was often underground and revolutionary. And like most social movements, Puritanism was never clearly defined. The leaders of the movement themselves almost never used the term. "Puritan," in fact, was a word used most often by the enemies of the movement, a term of criticism or insult.

For many modern Americans, "puritanical" means nothing more than prudish, priggish, and repressive, especially in matters of sex. The concept of Puritanism has been so murky, ill-defined, and emotionally loaded that many historians have urged that it be abandoned. The history of New England might best be understood as just another episode in the colonization of North America, not fundamentally different from the history of Virginia, or Georgia, or Pennsylvania.

The problem with such a strategy is that the men who led and controlled society in New England in the seventeenth century did most certainly *believe* they were doing something different and special. From John Winthrop to Cotton Mather, several generations of religious and political leaders labored to keep alive a heightened consciousness of special purpose, mission, and divine errand. Samuel Parris still had some of it, and so did men like Hathorne, Sewall, and Stoughton. The ways people think about their lives are as much a part of their history as the things they actually do. The history of New England in its first century was very much the history of a set of ideals and attitudes—an ideology—that can still usefully be labeled "Puritan."

THE PURITAN SENSIBILITY Puritan ideology contained complex ideas about religion, politics, family and social life, economics, art, and science—indeed, about every aspect of human life. But somewhere near the center of all these ideas lay a relatively simple attitude toward the world—an emotional stance, a sensibility that in some way governed what the Puritan thought about everything else. The Puritan was a person stressed by what he or she saw happening in the world. England during the reigns of Elizabeth I, James I, and Charles I was a profoundly disturbing place and time. And the sense of disturbance went much deeper than the usual human grumbling about "the times." A few English people at first, and then growing numbers, began to feel basically detached and alienated from their own society. But, gradually, others— merchants, tradesmen, lawyers, country squires, workers in the small industries of the day— began to share the deep conviction that something had gone fundamentally wrong.

The typical candidate for involvement in the Puritan movement was literate and industrious, neither noble nor peasant. They had a sense of themselves as sober, hardworking, and responsible—or, as they would have it put, "godly." Such men and women felt trapped in a nation that was becoming every year more corrupt, disordered, and sinful. By the end of the sixteenth century, there was an identifiable style of thinking, writing, and preaching, a style governed by the central feeling of dismay, a style that was already being called Puritan.

This sense of embattled dismay had a historical dimension. Puritan preachers and writers gradually invented a contrast between what England had once been and what it was becoming. The old England, in their mythology, had been a land of simplicity, homely virtue, and order. The new society had corrupted these old values in every way. Even in matters as minor as dress and hair styles, the Puritan saw only decline.

Part of the problem, the typical Puritan felt, was that foreign influence had crept into English life. From France, Spain, and Italy had come habits, styles of dress, manners, and morals that were both corrupt and alien. These countries were the strongholds of Catholicism in Europe, so every influence from them was part of a vast intrigue to undermine Protestantism in England. And if the government itself fell under foreign influence, as it seemed to do under James I and Charles I, then the Puritan had to contemplate drastic action—such as emigrating or making a revolution.

Such attitudes marked the Puritan as a radical. This led many of the critics and enemies of Puritanism into the fatal error of viewing the Puritan as an agent of disorder and anarchy, an opponent of authority. In truth, however, the Puritan felt that there was not *enough* order, not enough law, not enough discipline. To Puritan eyes, the rich, the powerful, and the noble had developed a contempt for law and tradition. On the other side, the poor had lost their ancient ways of simplicity and deference and were leaving their ancestral plots and villages in alarming numbers to wander about the countryside or cluster in the slums of London. The net effect was that there seemed to be neither governors nor governed. In every area of life, the normal lines of authority and order seemed to have collapsed.

The Puritan solution to the problem was discipline. But (and here, again, the opponents of Puritanism often failed to grasp the point) discipline was not to be imposed by force. Instead, true order had to grow out of the free, voluntary decision of individuals to live "godly" lives. For corrupted people in a corrupted society, forceful control might be necessary. But the ultimate goal was to reform society, to create a purified commonwealth in which order would flow naturally from the will of the citizens. There would be no contradiction, in such a society, between freedom and order. (Here is an important clue to the odd decision in 1692 to send no confessed witch to the gallows. When even a slave like Tituba confessed, she signaled that she had regained her capacity for freedom and could now make a voluntary choice. A witch who refused to confess was still in the grip of the devil, still not free to rejoin the disciplined community.)

PURITANISM AS A RELIGION   The Puritans' distress, and their yearning for discipline and order, were almost as much emotions as ideas. Something more was required: a theory about nature and human society that would give coherent form to emotions. Fear and anger had to be translated into a more formal language. For any European of the period, the most obvious and easily available framework of language was religion.

For the most part, Puritan religious ideas were the ideas of the Protestant Reformation. Puritans pictured their age as one of climactic struggle between the old, Catholic order and a new, Protestant one. To them, the sins and errors of Catholicism were obvious. Like most other Protestants, they believed that many of the popes, bishops, and priests had fallen into sinful habits of luxury, cruelty, and corruption. The errors of Catholicism, which were even more numerous than the sins, could be classified under one main heading. For centuries, the church had been undermining the relationship between God and the individual. The church had, in fact, tried to stand between God and humanity—first as a bridge, but then as a barrier. As Puritans and other Protestants saw it, the church's multiplicity of rituals and sacraments, its complicated hierarchy, its insistence on the use of Latin as the only language of religion had removed God from individual

human experience. God could be reached, it seemed, only through the church—through the imposing cathedrals, the mysterious music, the Latin, the darkened confessional.

In general, the Protestant formula was to simplify the religious life and make it more accessible to the individual. The Puritans wanted to go further in this direction than most other Protestants. To them, religious experience ought to be as opposite to Catholic practice as possible.

The Puritans began with one of the most common Christian doctrines. An enormous gulf existed between God and humanity. God was all-powerful and all-perfect. Men and women were sinful, weak, and vile. But God, in his mercy and in the distant stretches of his own eternal time, had decided to save a fraction of the race. The others he had damned forever. No one deserved salvation. No one could earn it—not by any amount of prayer or good works. Salvation was the free gift of God's grace. And this gift of grace came directly, not through an earthly institutional church, not through any process of confession and absolution.

Because of God's merciful decision, those living at any given time included a number of the saved. These "elect," who were predestined for heaven, were the true church. They might not be organized, they might not have buildings and ministers. But they were the only real church, the church "invisible," as Puritans and other Protestants liked to call it. The error of Catholicism had been to ignore this invisible church of the true elect and to concentrate instead on building and maintaining the "visible," institutional church.

The Puritans' dream was to gather as many of the English "elect" as possible into congregations, to exclude all others from membership. These purified churches could then work to gain power in the world, to get the largest possible measure of control over society. For the Puritans, the only authentic religious institution was such a church of elected "saints." They did not admit the authority of any other religious power—neither bishops nor archbishops, popes nor kings.

The congregations of the elect, they thought, should have the power to admit new members, choose and dismiss their own ministers, hear confessions, and excommunicate sinners. (It was the Salem Village congregation that hired Samuel Parris, and it was they who fired him. And it was the whole membership of the church that heard Anne Putnam's confession and voted whether to accept it or not.)

The Puritans' ideal of congregation, then, was the basis for their religious life. Ordinary people, sinful and damned, should be required to attend church and should be forced by law to obey God's commandments, even though they could not be members. The elect *were* the church. They would "gather" themselves, sign their own compacts or covenants, and thus create their own religious institutions. After that, they would settle all important questions by vote. And they would recognize no other religious power on earth.

Theoretically, each congregation was free to go its own way. But there were certain principles upon which all the Puritans were agreed. Religion should be simple and comprehensible, stripped of mystery and confusion. There should be no instrumental music, and the hymns should be simple. The Bible should be read in English (not Latin) and by everyone. There should be no holy days, not even Christmas. Ministers should dress like everyone else and should marry like everyone else. Nothing—no stained glass or art, no ornate churches, carved pews, or organs—should distract the congregation from the direct worship of God.

THE ENGLISH REFORMATION The complex political-religious condition of England was a dreadful tangle for the Puritan. England was supposedly a Protestant nation. But the motives of the English monarchs who had created English Protestantism were more political than religious. Henry VIII and his daughter Elizabeth I would have been content with a "reformation" in which the only real change was that the king or queen replaced the pope as head of the church. For the rest, the Church of England was a compromise between Catholic and radical Protestant ideas. The hierarchy remained intact, with its bishops and archbishops. Prayers were still prescribed, not made up by individual ministers. Congregations still knelt in churches ornamented with stained glass before priests wearing elaborate robes.

In institutional terms, the Puritan was a person who wanted to "purify" this Church of England of its remaining "papist" practices. But the Puritans' insistence on the ultimate power of the individual congregation was a threat to the crown itself, since the king was the final religious authority. It was this fact that placed the Puritans in conflict with their own government. Elizabeth and James I regarded them as dangerous and annoying fanatics, and harassed them with fines and imprisonment. Charles I, who became king in 1625, carried the persecution further. He appointed William Laud archbishop, and Laud proceeded to dismiss ministers he suspected of Puritan leanings. In one famous case, a Puritan who published a book attacking Laud was fined and imprisoned and had his ears cut off as punishment.

The Laudian persecution (as the Puritans thought of it) only seemed to strengthen the movement. More Puritan books appeared, more and more Anglican priests were converted, new converts and allies were found in merchant groups and among lawyers and politicians. Finally, Charles I made a fateful mistake. He challenged the power of Parliament. This move created an alliance between the king's Puritan opponents and those who, for other reasons, wanted a strong Parliament able to resist royal authority. In 1629—just before Winthrop and the Massachusetts settlers set sail on the *Arbella*—Charles I finally dissolved Parliament and declared that he would rule England alone. The stage was set for a civil war between the king's forces and the supporters of Parliament. And this crisis, in turn, made even more converts to Puritanism.

City upon a Hill

A CHARTER In March 1629, Charles I overcame his fears and suspicions long enough to give Massachusetts to a group of Puritan gentlemen. The old Plymouth Company that had originally been given the northern part of "Virginia" had been dissolved. Subsequent attempts to colonize New England had achieved only small successes. Now Charles I granted the right to settle an area almost the width of modern Massachusetts to a new company "by the name of the Governor and Company of the Mattachusettes Bay in Newe England."

The Massachusetts Bay Company was, in structure, a regular joint-stock corporation, with shareholders (called, in the language of the day, freemen) and officers. The king appointed the first governor, but thereafter he was to be elected each year by the stockholders. These freemen, according to the charter, were to meet four times a year in a "general court" to vote on officers and policies for their business.

By some stroke of luck, oversight, or genius, however, the charter omitted one normal provision. The *place* of the General Court meetings was not specified. This meant that the company could take its charter anywhere and hold meetings anywhere. It was this lapse that made it possible for Winthrop, the second governor of the company, to bring the charter to America. This done, he and his colleagues could transform a trading company charter into what amounted to a political constitution.

Fewer than ten of the migrants of 1630 were stockholders of the Massachusetts Bay Company, and, technically, only they had the power to vote laws and elect their governor. Winthrop and the other stockholders quickly decided to do something that went far beyond the normal practice of English joint-stock corporations. They admitted all the adult male church members—the religious "elect"—to the status of freemen, or stockholders. This meant that all men admitted to full membership by a gathered congregation could vote for representatives to the General Court. By this stroke, the Massachusetts Bay Company was transformed from a corporation into a commonwealth.

Political participation in the new commonwealth was restricted to the saints elect. Thus the "invisible church" was made visible not only in congregations but in the political structure of the colony as well. Church and state were technically separate, but the same individuals would control both, and for the same goals and purposes. The stockholders' meetings in a General Court were transformed into a legislature of "assistants"— the position held by Hathorne and Corwin when they came out to Salem Village to hold hearings in 1692. Since the charter specified only a few small obligations to the king, the Bay Company was practically independent of England. The wide North Atlantic insulated the colonists from English failings and corruptions. No wonder, for a man like John Winthrop, the breeze off the Maine coast would seem "so pleasant a sweet air as did much refresh us."

A MODEL The transformed charter provided the Puritan migrants with a political structure. But they all were deeply convinced that *no* political structure would work without an emotional commitment to the community on the part of each of its members. It was just as important to spell out this commitment as it was to have a government. In mid-passage, with the charter safely locked below, Winthrop gathered his "company" on the deck of the *Arbella* and delivered a lecture about their mission. His title was "Christian Charitie: a Modell Hereof." His purpose was to remind the settlers of the supreme importance of their mission and of the kinds of "charity," or love, that mission would require of them.

In his lecture, Winthrop distinguished between two kinds of human situations. People live most of their lives in ordinary times, he said, but they also pass through "extraordinary seasons and occasions." In ordinary times, the main cement of society is status or class. Some people are rich and powerful, some poor and weak, but everyone is "knit together" by relationships of dependence, protection, charity, and law. Such is God's "providence." But extraordinary times and seasons, according to Winthrop, bring a suspension of God's normal providence. Familiar and comfortable lines of class and status fade or break down, encouraging anarchy. This was what he and the other Puritans thought had happened in old England. The only way to avoid such an outcome, to restore order and make society work again, was to find a different way of binding people together. Winthrop's solution was demanding but simple. In extraordinary seasons of crisis, Christians should be bound by love: the love of the Christian individual for the Christian community.

Of course, no "season" could be more extraordinary than the one the colonists were experiencing. They were a godly company chosen by God to perform a special work. This was their "commission." And it placed them under heavy obligations. They must abandon their normal concerns with their own private welfare and place their love of the community uppermost:

> We must be knit together in this work as one man. We must delight in each other, make others' conditions our own, rejoice together, mourn together, labor and suffer together—always having before our eyes our Commission and Community in the work, our Community as members of the same body.

If such a community of Christian love could be created, the bare skeleton of the charter would come to life. If that happened, Winthrop believed, God would cause the new colony to shine forth as a holy beacon for all the world. It would become, he said in words that would echo through American history for more than three centuries, "A City upon a Hill."

TOWNS AND CONGREGATIONS Armed with their charter, and with their ideal of Christian charity, the Puritan migrants set about building godly communities in the wilderness. The 20,000 or 30,000 settlers who belonged to Winthrop's generation came remarkably close to realizing their dream of a City upon a Hill. There was never enough "love," to be sure, but there was a good deal of luck and quite enough pious determination. Around Massachusetts Bay, and then outward into Connecticut, Long Island, western Massachusetts, New Hampshire, and even Maine, a society of Puritan towns was planted. These towns were highly integrated and disciplined communal units. In them, two public institutions functioned in close, almost drilled order: the town government and the congregation. For the individual, life was defined and regulated by these closely related public bodies.

In New England, as in all the English colonies, the primary economic resource was the land itself. But the Puritans devised their own curious system for parceling it out. They did not make grants or sales to individual "planters"; instead, the General Court granted land to towns. The towns could grant the land to individual heads of families, but they could also hold much of it in "common," as a reserve for the future. Each individual family, then, was ultimately dependent on its town. Town government, like church government, was a kind of democracy of the elect. Freemen gathered in town meetings to elect officers, vote on ordinances and taxes, and make decisions about roads, bridges, and similar details so important in any agricultural community. The towns also became the basic political unit of the colonies, since they elected the members of legislatures everywhere in New England.

Town government was, in effect, an extension of church government. The same "freemen"—adult male church members, usually the heads of families—ruled both in church meetings and in town meetings. The first-generation congregations were created with a great deal of care and deliberation. In some cases, the potential members would meet together each week for as long as a year, examining each other's spiritual state with what they called "loving" intensity. Only after this process did they decide who might be a member of the new church, a "visible saint." Then, with great deliberation, these saints, or the adult males among them, would draw up a "covenant" or compact, creating their church.

After the church had been carefully "gathered," new applicants for membership had to undergo a searching public examination before they could be voted in. And any member could be disciplined and even excommunicated if the congregation decided the individual was a "hypocrite inwardly."

From the beginning, then, the Puritans of New England had the habit of making public judgments about the states of their neighbors' souls. In Salem in 1692 this habit would show itself in a dramatic way. In fact, the witchcraft trials were a cleansing ritual, a kind of renewal of the covenant. Parris and his followers were trying to cast out people they believed were in league with the devil. But they were also trying to redeem those who would confess, and return them to the gathered community presided over by God's saints-elect.

Between them, the town and the congregation reached very far into the lives of every colonist in New England. Life had, by modern standards, an extraordinarily public character. And what was not touched and controlled by towns and congregations was often regulated by legislation in the General Court. Massachusetts, Connecticut, and Rhode Island all had laws governing such things as the prices of nails, the amount of flour to be used in bread, the amount of thread that each household had to spin every year. In the towns, there were numerous sets of rules and requirements: for church attendance, fence maintenance, the management of livestock, the number of days that men had to work on public roads, bridges, and dams. Blasphemy, Sabbath-breaking, fornication, and adultery were viewed not only as sins but as crimes, and perpetrators were prosecuted.

All this communal regulation of life is what gave the Puritans their later reputation for being authoritarian and repressive. They had no interest whatever in religious toleration or individual freedom. The idea that there was room for more than one opinion on any important question seemed foolish to them. There was only one true and godly answer to any question, and it would be a sin to "tolerate" any point of view or mode of behavior that was not God's way.

In their town meetings and church votes, the Puritans did not practice majority rule but argued and sweated their way toward a consensus. They hated the idea of factions or parties. They had been a faction in England, to be sure, but their hope had been to win out completely and to establish their way as the only allowable way. The very point behind the migration had been to win this kind of total victory in the New World. And, once it was won, the victory had to be protected by the most careful regulation of the details of life.

FAMILIES AND FARMS The Puritans of seventeenth-century New England wasted little or no time discussing such issues as "democracy" or religious "freedom." What they were interested in was the creation of a society that was close-knit and well regulated. They were operating within a set of myths about traditional English agricultural villages. In these old peasant communities, the Puritans believed, life had been tightly integrated and harmonious, simple and orderly. The typical Puritan town patterned itself accordingly. The families clustered in houses at the town center. The fields and pastures lay scattered in small plots throughout the town. Life was stable and closely controlled. Very few people came into the village or left it. In some ways, the situation was ludicrous. New Englanders were perched on the edge of a vast and tempting continent. But instead of expanding rapidly into it on individual terms—as Virginians and others did—they huddled together in communities that soon looked almost crowded, their version of the peasant villages in the worn world they had left behind.

Puritanism was in many ways a movement aimed at recovering a "lost" way of life. And, for a generation or two in America, it succeeded. The irony was that the old English way of life was almost as much an invention as it was a memory. Agricultural villages in England were not nearly as stable as Puritan towns. Despite the vast area of free land around them, the Puritans managed to hold their communities so tightly together that only about one person out of every hundred would leave their town in any given year. English villages, by contrast, lost about five people out of every hundred each year.

In the striking degree of cohesion they managed to maintain, Puritan towns went well beyond "traditional" English villages. The Puritans were in a curious position. They were deliberately *trying* to act out a traditional script. But when tradition becomes conscious effort, it is no longer tradition at all. Traditional English villages were not planned and "gathered" under covenants. They just happened. Puritan towns were deliberate, artificial creations—conscious choices. They did not grow "naturally" out of the environment; they were attempts to *defy* the environment, to create closed communities in a wide-open frontier setting. So long as men like Winthrop had their way, individuals were forbidden to strike out on their own into the wilderness as the Virginians did.

The Puritans' remarkable success at maintaining their communal towns for three or four generations was partly a result of pious determination. But determination was helped along by plain good luck. A civil war in England kept other, non-Puritan Englishmen from emigrating to New England, where they might have disturbed the towns. Soil and climate ruled out a staple crop like tobacco that might have encouraged a large-scale, individualistic, plantation-type agriculture.

Most important of all, they were able to maintain large families dominated by the original "saints" for unusually long periods of time. The original "elect" had another virtue: They lived a long time. The life expectancy of men and women in the first generation of Massachusetts settlers was about what it is today—seventy years or so. By comparison, life expectancy in England was only about fifty years. In New England, marriages occurred a little earlier in life, too, so women could expect to bear about twice as many children as their English sisters. In England, a man married at about thirty and died at about fifty. The odds were high that he would not live to see his grandchildren. John Winthrop's godly company married at a somewhat younger age and, by living to a ripe seventy, could expect not only to see their grandchildren, but to see them grow up and marry.

In New England—and this was not true anywhere in the European world—the three-generation family became "normal." Sons and grandsons remained in their towns, waiting to inherit their share of the family land. And while they waited, they were very much under the authority of the original settlers, the old saints. By the 1660s these aging saints had become surrounded by their own legendary past—the heroic past of migration and settlement. On their farms, in their churches, at their town meetings, they were the force that preserved the astonishing stability of their communities. They were what made the towns seem "knit together as one man."

A PRAISE AND GLORY For about thirty years, Winthrop's prediction seemed to come true. The Lord did seem to "dwell among us as his own people." There were problems, of course. About 200 people died the first winter. And, after a few years of uneasy peace, the Pequot Indians of the bay area finally lost patience with the encroachment of the growing settlements in the western part of the colony and made war. But problems like these could be solved. Even the "starving

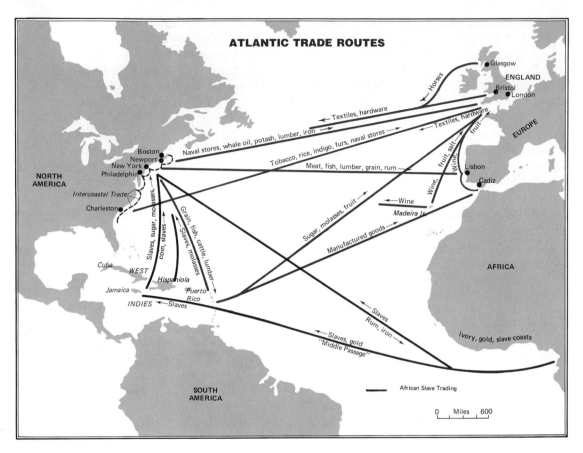

time" of the first winter was nothing compared to the Jamestown experience, and by the second year survival was not an important issue in New England. As for the Pequots, they could be dealt with, too. An angry Puritan army surrounded the main camp of the Pequots, set it afire, and killed about 400 of them. The few Pequots who survived were hunted down efficiently and either killed or sold as slaves. All the while, the preachers sang their thanksgiving that the Lord had lent his strength in battle.

Even the most severe economic problem, the lack of a staple crop, could be overcome. Colonists all over the New World were finding gold or silver or a crop they could send back to Europe. The Puritans found nothing of the sort, but they made ends meet from the start by trading in furs, taking wood from the forests, and, above all, fishing for the cod that Governor Winthrop had so carefully noted in his *Arbella* journal.

Even though the agriculture of New England was primarily one of subsistence, there were small surpluses of beef, pork, and beans almost from the beginning. And the New Englanders began almost at once to do something no other seventeenth-century colonists were able to do. They began to engage in trade, carried in their own small ships, instead of depending on English merchants and shipping. Within a half-century, merchants from Boston and Salem were shipping New England goods to Europe and the West Indies, bringing slaves from Africa to Vir-

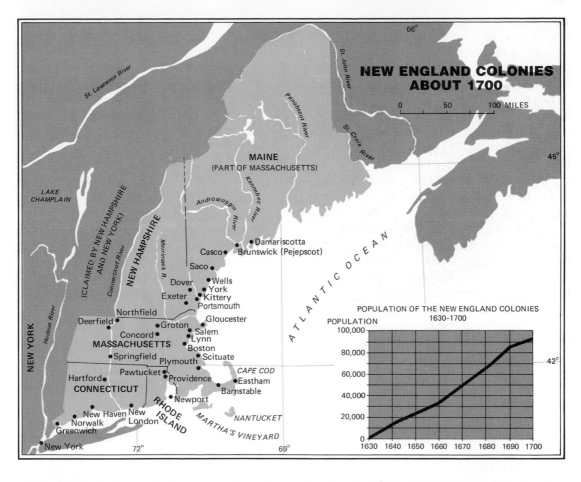

NEW ENGLAND COLONIES ABOUT 1700

POPULATION OF THE NEW ENGLAND COLONIES 1630–1700

ginia and the Indies, bringing sugar from the islands to be distilled into rum and reexported or consumed, and carrying tobacco from Virginia to England. The Puritans also launched into manufacturing, with a state-supported iron furnace and foundry, and they minted their own coin, a "pine-tree shilling." All this—the shipbuilding, the trade, the manufacturing—was aimed toward making New England as economically separate from the mother country as possible.

In other respects, too, the colony matured rapidly. In 1636 Harvard College was established, primarily to train new ministers. In 1647 the General Court created a public school system. Each town with 50 or more families was required to support a teacher, and each town of 100 or more families had to have a Latin grammar school to prepare young men for the college. Connecticut had a similar law, and from the 1640s on, New England probably had the most literate population in the Western world. No aristocrats came to New England—and none were wanted. But some quite well-to-do immigrants were attracted to the colony, as were some scholars with solid public reputations in England, like the minister John Cotton—especially as civil war between Puritans and royalists drew nearer.

Expansion was another sign of success and maturity. In 1635 and 1636, settlers under the leadership of another distinguished minister, Thomas Hooker, moved to the Connecticut Valley and established Hartford, then two other towns nearby. Another group settled around New Haven, on Long Island Sound. Dissenters expelled by the Puritans also established new settlements—in Rhode Island, New Hampshire, and Maine—and the Bay Colony claimed jurisdiction over these new colonies, too, despite the fact that they were founded by men and women who disagreed with the established government of Massachusetts. The disagreements usually were on minor points of theology, and the new colonies were, for all practical purposes, Puritan.

The English authorities were in no position to oppose this expansion. In the late 1630s the struggle between Charles I and Parliament broke into open war, with the Puritans gradually gaining control of the parliamentary side. Eventually, the royalists were beaten and the king beheaded, and from 1649 to 1660 a Puritan leader, Oliver Cromwell, governed England as "Protector" of the realm. During the first thirty years of settlement, then, the New England colonists created a mature, practically independent commonwealth.

Dissent, Decline, Dominion

The City upon a Hill did not last. It may have been doomed from the beginning, despite its early successes and seeming good luck. But from the very beginning, the Puritan communities were plagued by dissenters, people who would not conform to the beliefs and practices of the community. Later, especially after about 1660, there were two other enemies to contend with. The first was what the ministers called "declension" or decline—an apparent falling off of piety and religious energy among the people. The second was a reassertion of British authority after the Stuart monarchy was restored in 1660. Together, dissent, declension, and royal domin-ion created an acute sense of crisis in New England. By the beginning of the 1690s, many ordinary people had come to share their leaders' fear that the holy experiment was failing and that God's judgment would soon fall on them. This was the atmosphere in which Samuel Parris first discovered the two children having "fits" in his house.

ROGER WILLIAMS AND ANNE HUTCHINSON There was no simple Puritan creed. The members of the movement shared a general set of beliefs, but there were shades of opinion on a number of religious questions. The pressures of persecution and civil war in England demanded unity, and disputes were usually covered over by a relaxed policy of "toleration" within the movement. In America, these pressures were absent, and disagreement even over very narrow points of theology divided the towns from time to time. In a way, the Puritans were the victims of their own sophistication. Even a layman could follow theological arguments and see their implications. So a challenge as to the precise nature of "grace" might suddenly threaten to tear the commonwealth apart. The cases of Roger Williams and Anne Hutchinson illustrate this point precisely.

Roger Williams, everyone said, was a gentle man, a learned minister, and a devout Puritan. The problem was that he was almost too devout. When he came to Salem as minister, soon after the congregation was gathered, he began to fret publicly that the churches were "impure," even in the City upon a Hill. He argued, for example, that requiring the saints and the damned to attend church meetings together was corrupting. And he wanted the churches to declare themselves formally separated from the Church of England, to give up even the pretense of wanting to purify the established church. He insisted on a total separation of church and state—not to protect the government from religious influences, but to protect the church from the "worldly" influences of government. So, he argued, religious offenses ought not to be punished by civil authorities. From his Salem pulpit, he even began to suggest that there was something illegal about the Massachusetts charter. The king had no right to give away Indian lands, he said, and the English would never really own their homes and fields until they bought them from the Native Americans in fair bargaining.

Such talk threatened the entire basis of the commonwealth: the power of the saints to hold their land and to control the public lives of the nonsaints. Even John Winthrop liked Williams; he was, Winthrop said, "sweet and amiable." But by 1635 the Massachusetts authorities had realized that he was also dangerous, and they decided to send him back to England. Williams, however, sneaked out of Boston during the winter and went to Rhode Island. He bought land from some Narraganset Indians and established the town of Providence in 1636.

Williams was a Puritan. His disagreements with the Massachusetts establishment were caused by his demand that the Puritans' own churches be "purified" further. His principle was that the saintly should worship together, in seclusion from the rest of the world. In fact, later in his life, he reached the point where he could worship comfortably only when he was completely alone. The incidental result was a commitment on the part of Williams to religious "freedom." It ought not to matter, he thought, what the ungodly did. So at Providence, the rule was that any religious beliefs that did not disturb public order would be allowed. Paradoxically, a piety as deep and demanding as Williams's left the door open to a relaxed diversity.

No sooner had Roger Williams fled to Rhode Island than another dispute erupted in Boston. The cause this time was another gentle and devout person, Anne Hutchinson. She had come to Massachusetts in 1634 with her large family, a forty-three-year-old woman whose children eventually numbered fifteen. Her husband was a well-to-do merchant. To all appearances, she should have been a model citizen. She was a friend of John Cotton and other ministers, and she read the Scriptures avidly.

Like Roger Williams, Anne Hutchinson's problem was that she insisted too much on certain items of the Puritans' own faith. Specifically, she was preoccupied with the idea of people being saved by the free gift of God's grace, without any effort or "exertion" on their part. She began to accuse even ministers like John Cotton of deserting this principle and falling into a gospel of "works." The problem was aggravated by the fact that Anne Hutchinson did not keep her ideas to herself. She began to hold meetings, to examine sermons, and to attract a following that included many of the richest merchants in Boston.

The actual differences in theology between Anne Hutchinson and the Massachusetts establishment were very narrow. They too believed in "free grace." But it was important to them to be able to control social behavior, so they insisted, somewhat illogically, that everyone had obligations to God, even if fulfilling those obligations did not necessarily earn salvation. In a series of meetings with Anne Hutchinson, several ministers tried to get her to see her "errors." She seemed to soften, sometimes, but then to harden again.

Finally, the religious leaders declared the problem to be a governmental one, and Anne Hutchinson was brought before Winthrop and some of the other magistrates in Boston for a public trial. There she presented a skillful scriptural defense of her views. She might even have won, had she not lapsed into a dangerous claim. The Holy Spirit actually dwelt within the heart of a saint, she said, revealing itself directly, not through Scripture or miracles, but as a personal revelation.

This was too much. The image of a group of saints running loose, listening to their own private spiritual voices, alarmed men like Winthrop, who were committed above all to order. Hutchinson and a number of her supporters were banished in 1637.

Anne Hutchinson

The Puritan communities of Massachusetts Bay were, by modern standards, strikingly homogeneous. The first generation of settlers was all English. They were all Protestants, and almost all were serious in their piety. Still, there were some fundamental intellectual tensions in Puritanism that produced dissent even in such a homogeneous social order.

From time to time these ideological tensions found a concrete focus in an individual, as they did in the curious and precarious life of Anne Hutchinson. On the surface there was nothing in Anne Hutchinson's experience to set her apart from her fellow New Englanders. When she immigrated to Boston in 1634, she appeared to be a perfectly typical, middle-aged Puritan wife.

Anne Hutchinson took her own religious experience very seriously. She actually felt, she thought, an "indwelling" of the Holy Spirit, a kind of inward voice that made her certain she was one of God's elect. And she was just as certain that her salvation had been a result of God's pure grace, not of any of her own efforts or "works."

Anne Hutchinson was a fiercely committed woman with a quick mind. She began to attract not only attention but followers, and soon the Boston congregation was split into two factions. On one side were Hutchinson's disciples with their sweet slogans like "free grace," "gospel truth," and "glorious light." On the other side were her own minister, preachers from neighboring congregations, and Governor John Winthrop, with their concern for unity and order.

At first the authorities tried to reason with Hutchinson. But she stubbornly persisted. Gradually, people like Winthrop began to see her as a dangerous adversary—"a woman of haughty and fierce carriage, of a nimble wit and active spirit, and a very voluble tongue." Eventually, in November of 1637, she was charged with blasphemy and summoned before the General Court to be tried.

She defended herself skillfully, citing Scripture passage for passage against her chief prosecutor, Governor Winthrop. But then she made a fatal error. She admitted that she believed not only that the Holy Spirit dwelt within her, but that she actually experienced mystical revelations. The doctrine of free grace combined with the idea of personal revelations was too great a threat to social order. Winthrop personally delivered the sentence of the court: "Mrs. Hutchinson, the sentence of the court you hear is that you are banished from out of our jurisdiction as being a woman not fit for our society."

Roger Williams, that other thorn in the side of the Massachusetts establishment, offered Hutchinson sanctuary in Rhode Island. She and some of her followers moved there to found the town of Portsmouth. Four years later, after her husband had died, Anne Hutchinson migrated again, to New York, near Pelham Bay. In August of 1643, she and five of her children were killed by Indians—an event hailed by some in Massachusetts as a divine providence.

Picture: The Bettmann Archive

BAPTISTS AND QUAKERS The Church of England represented the most conservative wing of the Protestant Reformation in England. Most Puritans were somewhere near the center of the Protestant movement. But there were numerous other sects, most of them small, who wanted reforms that were more radical than most Puritans could accept. The two most important for the New England experience were the Baptists and the Friends, or Quakers.

The issue between Baptists and other Protestants was, as their name suggests, the rite of baptism. Anglicans, like Catholics, baptized the children of church members. Baptists wanted to reserve baptism for adults who had undergone conversion. There should be no halfway members of the church, they argued, no people who had been baptized but not converted. The Baptists, like Roger Williams, also wanted a much clearer separation of church and state than the Puritans practiced. In 1651, three Baptist preachers came into Massachusetts from Rhode Island. They made public attacks on the Puritans' standing order, and for their trouble were arrested and tried. They were found guilty, fined, and ordered to leave the colony. One of them refused to pay the fine, and he was publicly whipped.

The Quakers were even more dangerous. They denied the need for *any* churchly discipline and insisted that the state had no authority over individual religious beliefs. They even denied the need for ministers and sermons. And, like Anne Hutchinson, they preached that the Holy Spirit entered the soul of a converted Christian and dwelled there as an "inner light." During the 1650s and 1660s, Quaker missionaries, some of them women, began to come into Massachusetts to challenge the authority of ministers and magistrates. They refused to be silent during sermons and spoke out as they were inspired by their individual inner lights. When ordered to behave, they refused. When arrested and taken before assistants for trial, they would not take oaths and even refused to take off their hats in court. Their obstinacy was met with threats, banishment, imprisonment, and public whippings. As time passed, the punishments became more severe, and eventually the Massachusetts authorities resorted to mutilation. Cutting off an ear was a favorite device. Nothing seemed to work, however. Finally, in 1659, a Quaker named Mary Dyer was sentenced to be hanged. She was freed at the last moment as she waited at the gallows,

and ordered out of Massachusetts. But she returned the next year and this time *was* hanged, earning something like a sainthood among her fellow Quakers because of what they called her "double death."

The "witches" of Salem were not dissenters in the normal sense. They were not anything in particular but victims. But they were *seen* as the servants of an alien faith, as an organized group of spiritual servants of the devil. And this was precisely the way the Puritans looked on Baptists and Quakers. The occasional hanging of a witch was not unusual in Massachusetts—or in England or Virginia, for that matter. What was unusual at Salem was the fear that a large number of people had joined together in an organized conspiracy to undermine the peace and spiritual security of the commonwealth. In that sense, the witchcraft trials represent an extension of the Puritan experience in dealing with dissenters of all sorts—an experience that seemed to progress step by step from reprimand and banishment to mutilation and hanging.

DECLENSION Almost from the beginning, ministers and other leaders would complain from time to time that piety was waning, that the spirit of New England was declining. But after about 1660 this kind of complaint became a steady chorus. Ministers, especially, began to preach over and over again on the ways that New England had faltered, had forgotten its divine errand. God's special care seemed to have been withdrawn from the commonwealth, and new troubles tumbled one after another into the picture.

The ministers had a lot to complain about—or so it seemed to them. New conversions were few. The restoration of the Stuarts in 1660 threatened interference from outside. The invasion of Baptists and Quakers seemed to signal trouble. Even the Native Americans had become a major source of trouble. In 1675, under the leadership of a chief known as King Philip, they mounted

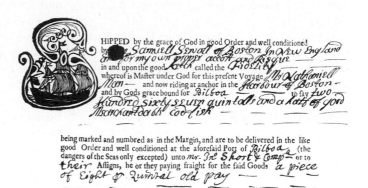

A Godly bill of lading. A good Puritan like Samuel Sewall of Boston believed that all human action—including trade for profit—ought to have a religious meaning. This 1687 bill of lading (loading) used a decorated printed form to declare that the salt codfish were being shipped to Spain "by the grace of God and in good order." The ship is called *Fidelity* and Nathaniel Man is its captain "under God." This merchant's document ends with a prayer: "And so God send the good Ketch to her desired Port in safety, Amen." (Massachusetts Historical Society)

a serious war against the colonists and destroyed about twenty towns. In the process, they killed off about one white male out of every sixteen. This time, the New Englanders had to use friendly "praying" Indians to help defeat their enemies. And it took three years of dark terror to complete the process—a far cry from the quick, unaided victory of 1637 over the Pequots.

All these specific troubles might have been seen as divine tests designed to strengthen the godly in their faith. However, the real issue was not the troubles themselves but what the ministers and other leaders thought lay behind them. The secret, they thought, was in the growing "worldliness" of the descendants of the founders of the City. Worldliness meant sin, of course, but it meant more. To the Puritans, worldliness had one underlying cause: a concern for the self as against the community. Any sort of self-seeking ambition or individualism was a betrayal of the spiritual welfare of the community. And there were many signs that individualism was gaining the upper hand.

For one thing, as the New England colonies prospered, more and more individuals tried to break out of the communal discipline of their towns and churches. The old practice of clustering a town's houses at its center gradually gave way to the building of farmhouses on the fields of individual families—the pattern displayed in the map of Salem Village on p. 105. Carpenters, shoemakers, and other artisans often were restless under the rigid control of wages and prices. Land speculation by individuals developed into a common practice, especially after the reassertion of royal authority that followed the Restoration. Perhaps most important of all, the rise of a merchant class threatened the spiritual integrity that the ministers believed so important.

There was a built-in tension between the desires and practices of merchant capitalism and the Puritans' concept of a controlled society. Merchant capitalism was a form of individualism; Puritanism was a communal ideology. It was no accident that Anne Hutchinson's supporters were drawn mainly from the ranks of the better-off merchants of Boston, whereas John Winthrop's support came mostly from the farmers of the outlying towns. It was no accident, either, that it was individual merchants who were often

The Mason children, 1670. This painting by an unknown artist shows three children of a
Boston family. It was made only forty years after Winthrop's fleet reached Salem, and twenty-
two years before the Salem witchcraft trials. The Mason family was not only prosperous but
anxious to display the signs of its wealth and status. The boy holds a silver-headed cane, and
one of the girls holds a necklace and an elegant fan. The girls' shoes have silver studding
around the soles. The children (whose ages are given in the painting as eight, six, and four)
are treated as though they were practically adults, able to assume moral responsibility for
any "sins" they might commit. (They also might be able, if the occasion arose, to accuse an
adult of witchcraft.) (Fine Arts Museums of San Francisco. Gift of Mr. and Mrs. John D.
Rockefeller, 3rd)

severely disciplined by their churches and even
by the General Court—for their attempts to get
the highest prices the market would bear. As
Boston and Salem and other towns along the
coast came to have larger and richer classes of
merchant-shipowners, it became clear that the
old Puritanism would eventually give way to a
new, more relaxed and liberal form of Protes-

tantism with which the new capitalists could feel
comfortable.

By the 1690s this process of accommodation
was well under way. But in outlying agricultural
communities like Salem Village, the resentment
of townsmen and traders was festering just below
the surface. One of the most startling facts about
the witchcraft episodes of 1692 is that so many

of the accused lived near or had strong connections with Salem Town. The afflicted girls had no knowledge of sociology or economic theory, but they did seem to have an instinctive sense that they could tap village resentment of the larger, more progressive, wealthier town. Samuel Parris often preached sermons against "worldliness," and no one could doubt that he meant economic self-seeking. He was, after all, a failed merchant himself. In this important sense, the witchcraft hysteria was an episode in the process of "declension"—its most violent episode, to be sure, but part of the larger process all the same.

The ministers presented declension as a general social problem. But, in a special way, it was their own narrow professional problem. The question for them was: Would they be able to maintain their position of profound authority as the colony became more and more "modern" and less and less a series of agrarian villages? In the long run, the answer was no. But the Puritan clergymen and their many supporters did not give up easily. Samuel Parris was an unusual man in a bizarre situation. But in effect, he was able to use the village hysteria to assert his authority.

The irony is, of course, that the key to Parris's efforts was children—his own Betty and the rest of the "afflicted." But even this was not unusual, for the ministers' preoccupation with declension had been focusing attention on New England's children for more than thirty years before 1692.

By the 1660s it had become clear that many of the children of the first-generation settlers were not having their own conversion experiences. They were baptized but not converted. This created a new difficulty when they had children of their own—the grandchildren of the original saints. Could these children be baptized? Theoretically, each congregation could make up its own mind. But the problem was so universal that the ministers of the colony tried to find a common solution. They devised what became known as the Half-Way Covenant of 1662.

The Half-Way Covenant recommended that the churches baptize any child descended from a church member—even a grandparent or great-grandparent. Since there were four grandparents and eight great-grandparents, this meant almost every infant had some claim to be baptized. The ministers' motives were obvious: They wanted to bring as many people under the umbrella of the church as possible. If they could not do it through conversion, they would accept baptism as a halfway measure. But most of the churches of Massachusetts and Connecticut refused to go along. There was a rift—the first one, really—between the ministers as a group and the churches. And it took thirty more years, until the end of the century, to heal it.

Gradually, reluctantly, the churches gave in, but only after a generation of quarreling. Little wonder that it seemed to the preachers "the heart of New England is lost, even in New England." To ministers like Cotton Mather it seemed that the Puritans had been able to brave every danger—the Church of England, the wilderness, the Indians, and the king—only to lose out because they could not conquer their own faintness of spirit. To the aging saints in their churches, the solution was not to make membership easier but to hold the line. Only after the 1690s did the ministers win out, but most of the meaning had gone out of their victory. The City upon a Hill had died.

ENGLISH DOMINION No matter how much the ministers might complain about internal spiritual decline, the most serious assault on the City came from the outside. In 1660 the Puritan colonies were the only English settlements north of Virginia, and they were practically free of London's control. Forty years later, there were English colonies all down the coast—in New York, New Jersey, and Pennsylvania. And the royal government had reasserted its authority in ways that staggered the independent New Englanders.

At first, all the home government tried to do was to control trade with the colonies in a series of laws called Navigation Acts. The first, passed in 1660, closed the colonial trade to all foreign ships—which did not bother New Englanders very much, since their ships qualified as English. But the law also listed certain "enumerated" articles that could be exported from the colonies *only* to England. If enforced, this provision would drastically interfere with the New Englanders' trading patterns with Europe and the West Indies. A second exertion of English power came in 1663, with an act providing that all goods imported into the colonies from any European country had first to be shipped into England and then reexported to America. The third Navigation Act, passed in 1673, imposed duties on goods shipped from one colony to another—a serious threat to New England merchants, who carried on a brisk trade with the British colonies in the West Indies. This law also provided for customs officers stationed in the colonies to collect the duties—the first royal officials to be stationed in New England, symbols of the power of the hated Stuart monarchy.

Much more serious and direct, however, was the king's assault on the charter. In 1660 the crown had the right to appoint a governor in only one American colony, Virginia. The first serious signal that all this would change came in 1679, when Charles II denied Massachusetts's claim to New Hampshire and established a separate, royal colony there. Soon after, Charles began the legal proceedings necessary to revoke the Massachusetts Bay Company's charter. The crown won its case, and in 1684 Massachusetts lost its separate existence as a corporate colony.

One year later, Charles died and James II became king. James was an ardent imperialist, having been heavily involved in taking New Netherlands from the Dutch and turning it into the royal colony of New York just a few years earlier. To the horror of the Puritans in all the New England colonies, he decided to create something called the Dominion of New England, including all the colonies east of New York. As royal governor of the Dominion (to which New York and New Jersey were eventually added),

James appointed Sir Edmund Andros. Andros was an Anglican, and, having set up his headquarters in Boston, he ordered regular services held for loyal members of the Church of England. He also tried to levy taxes on the colonists and denied their right to legislate freely in the General Court. He even threatened the validity of all the General Court's grants of land to the towns, thus calling into question the right of almost every farmer to his land.

Luckily for New England, James II was overthrown in the bloodless Glorious Revolution of 1688 and replaced by William and Mary, the new monarchs chosen by Parliament. Hearing the news, the citizens of Boston mobbed Andros and threw him into prison. For a brief moment, it looked as though the Lord had intervened. Cotton Mather's father, Increase, was dispatched to England to plead for the restoration of the old charter.

Mather failed. The ship that brought him back to Massachusetts in 1692 also brought the new, royally appointed Governor Phips and a new charter declaring Massachusetts a royal colony. (The new charter officially incorporated the remnants of the Pilgrim colony of Plymouth into Massachusetts. But this only confirmed in law what had long before happened in fact. For the Plymouth colony had ceased to have any meaningful separate identity.)

The new charter was better than Andros and the Dominion. It confirmed the powers of the General Court and secured land titles that derived from the old charter. But William and Mary cut into the heart of the Puritans' commonwealth by replacing the religious qualification for suffrage with the usual English property qualification. No longer could the saints rule their towns without opposition from the unconverted. The new charter also required religious toleration, not only for Anglicans, but for Baptists, Quakers, and others. On paper, at least, Massachusetts could no longer be distinguished from Virginia. Phips began a process of "royalization" in Massachusetts that lasted until the 1760s. And the process

New Amsterdam. The Dutch settlement at the southern end of Manhattan Island is shown here approximately as it was in 1660, just four years before the English fleet sailed in to conquer the entire colony for the duke of York. The whole town is walled on the north and east, and there is a great fort at the tip of the island. There are orchards and small gardens within the walls, but the larger plowed fields are outside. This drawing of the Castello, or castle area, is no doubt considerably idealized. (I. N. Phelps Stokes Collection of American Historical Prints, New York Public Library)

succeeded. It had taken the colonists less than a day to carry out the little revolution against Andros. When the next revolutionary movement against England began, in 1765, it took ten years to reach the point of open resistance to England and a long and difficult war to complete.

NEIGHBORS The Puritans of the 1630s and 1640s had hoped they could dominate not only New England but perhaps even most of "northern Virginia." Small bands of Puritans had settled on Long Island and even in Maryland, Virginia,

and finally in the Carolinas. But by the 1690s this hope of expansion was dead. The Puritans had been beaten in England, and they were about to be swallowed up in a burst of English colonization in New York, New Jersey, and Pennsylvania—which soon were being called the "Middle Colonies." New York was Dutch and Anglican. Pennsylvania had its beginnings as a Quaker colony. New Jersey was a mixture of Swedes, Anglicans, Puritans, and Quakers. But all these colonies had one thing in common: They had no interest in the Puritans' old dream of a City upon a Hill.

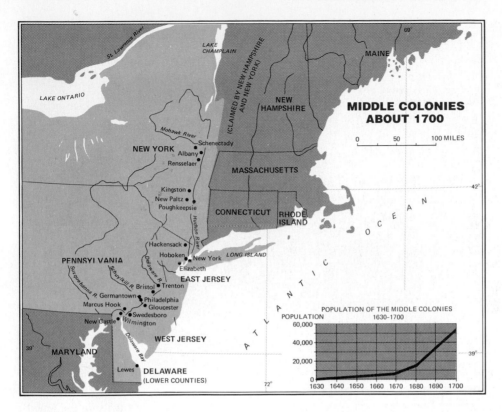

The Middle Colonies came into separate existence as a paper reality in 1664, a few years after the Restoration, when Charles II gave to his brother James, duke of York, all the lands between the Delaware and Connecticut rivers. Since 1609, the area had been claimed by both England and Holland. There were also a few Swedes and Finns settled on the Delaware. But the only important colony was New Netherlands, whose main center was on Manhattan Island, near the mouth of the Hudson. From this center, the Dutch exercised a weak control over the Delaware and competed with English colonists for the Connecticut Valley and Long Island. During the 1650s and 1660s, England and Holland fought a series of wars, and New Netherlands was one of the prizes. The English captured it easily in 1664. The Dutch won it back in 1673, but they lost it again the next year, this time for good.

The duke of York owned New York outright, as a proprietor. But when he became King James II, New York immediately became a royal colony. James, however, proceeded cautiously. He recognized the Dutch colonists' title to their lands, even though some of them owned vast personal estates, some as large as 700,000 acres. Though himself a Catholic, James recognized the fact that New York was peopled by a mixture of Dutch Calvinists, Anglicans, Puritans, and others. To encourage settlement, he decreed religious toleration and issued a Charter of Liberties and Privileges extending limited self-government to the colonists. At first, growth was slow. But by 1685, when New York became a part of the Dominion of New England, about 30,000 colonists lived there. It was clear that the colony would grow quickly and might well surpass Massachusetts as a trading and shipping center.

William Penn negotiates. About eighty years after the founding of Pennsylvania, the American artist Benjamin West painted this idealized version of William Penn's negotiations with the Delaware Indians. Penn's agents are offering the Indians cloth, while in the background the construction of the city of Philadelphia is already well under way. (Pennsylvania Academy of the Fine Arts, Joseph and Sarah Harrison Collection)

While still duke of York, James granted New Jersey to two tireless imperialists, Sir George Carteret and Sir John Berkeley, both of whom were also Carolina proprietors. Berkeley, in turn, sold off his half of New Jersey to two wealthy Quakers. The duke, meantime, in 1682 had given what was to become Delaware to another Quaker, William Penn, who was tireless in his attempt to create a haven for Quakers on both sides of the Delaware River.

Like the Calverts, Penn belonged to a religious minority that was often harassed. But, again like the Calverts, he also belonged to a distinguished family that often benefited from royal whims. Penn's father, Sir William, was an admiral and a great landholder in Ireland. Before his conversion to Quakerism, Penn himself had been educated

as a typical landed gentleman. But from the time of his conversion he was an active and controversial promoter of the Quaker cause—even if he sometimes had to promote it from prison.

Charles II was indebted to Admiral Sir William Penn, both financially and as an ally in the quest for the restoration of the crown. When Sir William forgave his son for becoming a Quaker, William Penn inherited the debt, and Charles II found it easier to pay off in land than in cash. He granted Penn the land west of the Delaware River in 1681. The duke of York had already cooperated by tossing Delaware colony into the bargain. And Penn and some fellow Quakers succeeded in buying the remaining half of New Jersey. A cluster of Quaker colonies had been inserted between New York and the Chesapeake colonies.

Penn took Pennsylvania (named by Charles II in honor of the old admiral, not the Quaker son) seriously. He came to the colony in 1682 and personally laid out the plan for Philadelphia. He was as much a utopian as the Puritans (the name Philadelphia means "City of Brotherly Love"). But, like other Quakers, he did not believe the state should interfere in religion. So he drew up a tolerant Frame of Government that guaranteed a considerable measure of self-government and religious freedom.

Like Roger Williams, Penn also took the Native Americans seriously, and he bargained fairly (though always successfully) with them for land. As a result, during his lifetime at least, the colony enjoyed a unique immunity from Indian troubles.

The Quaker colonies easily absorbed the Finns and Swedes already settled in the Delaware Valley. They absorbed the equally large number of Puritans who had settled in New Jersey. Within fifteen years, Philadelphia had grown to a city of several thousand people, and a shrewd observer might already have guessed that in the space of a lifetime it would surpass Boston as the largest and most successful American city.

Suggestions for Further Reading

WITCHCRAFT AT SALEM VILLAGE

The best book on the Salem episode is Stephen Nissenbaum and Paul Boyer, *Salem Possessed: the Social Origins of Witchcraft* (1974). Alternative points of view are presented in John Demos, *Entertaining Satan* (1982); Carol Karlsen, *The Devil in the Shape of a Woman* (1987); and Chadwick Hansen, *Witchcraft at Salem* (1985). For students who like to work with original documents, Boyer and Nissenbaum have assembled a fine and substantial set in *Salem-Village Witchcraft* (1972).

PURITANISM

The English background of the Puritan migration is well treated in Wallace Notestein, *The English People on the Eve of Colonization* (1954), and Carl Bridenbaugh, *Vexed and Troubled Englishmen* (1968). A brief and readable comparison of Puritanism in England and New England is Alan Simpson, *Puritanism in Old and New England* (1975). The transit of Puritanism to New England can be followed in T. H. Breen, *Puritans and Adventurers* (1980). But the most rewarding approach to the subject is probably through John Winthrop's own journal, published in a two-volume modern edition in 1908. A very readable account of a Puritan leader's decision to migrate is in Edmund S. Morgan, *The Puritan Dilemma* (1958).

CITY UPON A HILL

Two books by Perry Miller have become American classics: *The New England Mind: The Seventeenth Century* (1954) and *Orthodoxy in Massachusetts* (1959). Gentler introductions to Puritan religious ideas and practices are Charles Cohen, *God's Caress* (1986); Stephen Foster, *Their Solitary Way* (1971); and David Hall, *Faithful Shepherd: A History of the New England Ministry in the Seventeenth Century* (1972). The best study of Puritan relations with Native Americans is Neal Salisbury, *Manitou and Providence* (1982). On law and government, good places to begin are David T. Konig, *Law and Society in Puritan Massachusetts* (1979); T. H. Breen, *Character of the Good Ruler* (1970); and Bruce Mann, *Neighbors and Strangers* (1987). Philip Greven, *Four Generations: Population, Land and Family in Colonial Andover* (1970), is a fine example of what historians can accomplish through the intensive study of local communities. Others are Sumner Chilton Powell, *Puritan Village* (1963); John Demos, *A Little Commonwealth* (1970); and Kenneth Lockridge, *A New England Town, the First Hundred Years* (1970). L. T. Ulrich, *Good Wives* (1982), and Lyle Koehler, *A Search for Power: The "Weaker Sex" in Seventeenth-Century New England* (1980), are interesting analyses of the lives of women in Puritan New England.

CHRONOLOGY

1624 Dutch settlement founded at New Amsterdam (New York). First English settlements founded in New Jersey.

1635 Colonists begin to move into Connecticut. Roger Williams banished from Massachusetts Bay.

1636 Roger Williams founds Providence Plantation in Rhode Island. Harvard College established to train ministers.

1625 Charles I becomes king, appoints William Laud archbishop of Canterbury and head of the Church of England.

1614 Squanto kidnapped by English exploring party.

1637 English colonists in Massachusetts make war on the Pequots. Anne Hutchinson and some of her followers banished from Massachusetts Bay.

1610	1615	1620	1625	1630	1635	1640	1645	1650

1609 Dutch claim New Amsterdam.

1619 Squanto returns to Cape Cod.

1629 Charles I dissolves Parliament. Charles I gives charter for Massachusetts Bay colony.

1638 First Swedish settlement founded in Delaware.

1649 Charles I beheaded, and Puritan "Interregnum" in England begins.

1620 Pilgrims land at Provincetown, then found Plymouth Colony.

1640 Marcus Hook, in Pennsylvania, settled by Swedes.

1630 John Winthrop leads Puritan fleet to Massachusetts.

1642 Massachusetts General Court creates public grammar schools.

1674 English again take New Amsterdam from the Dutch.

1684 Massachusetts Bay Company charter revoked.

1664 Charles II gives New Amsterdam to James, duke of York. English capture New Amsterdam.

1675 English colonists conduct major war against Native Americans who are led by "King Philip."

1685 James I becomes king, and establishes Dominion of New England, with Sir Edmund Andros as governor.

1655	1660	1665	1670	1675	1680	1685	1690	1795

1659 Quaker Mary Dyer hanged in Boston.

1660 Puritan Interregnum ends; Charles II becomes king of England. Navigation Acts passed by Parliament.

1662 Half-Way Covenant adopted in Massachusetts, providing for baptism of any child with a church-member ancestor.

1663 Third Navigation Act passed by Parliament.

1673 Dutch recapture New Amsterdam.

1678 King Philip's War ends.

1679 Charles II takes New Hampshire from Massachusetts Bay colony, and establishes royal colony.

1681 Pennsylvania grant made to William Penn.

1682 Philadelphia founded.

1688 Glorious Revolution in England overthrows the Stuart dynasty. Reign of William and Mary begins. Sir Edmund Andros and Dominion of New England overthrown.

1692 New charter issued by William and Mary to Massachusetts. Plymouth Colony officially made part of Massachusetts. Salem witchcraft trials.

DISSENT, DECLINE, DOMINION

A dense and somewhat difficult book—but still essential reading—is Perry Miller, *The New England Mind: From Colony to Province* (1953). The development of commerce in New England is discussed in Christine Heyerman's excellent *Commerce and Culture* (1984). A good general discussion of dissent is Philip Gura, *A Glimpse of Sion's Glory* (1984). Emery Battis, *Saints and Sectaries* (1962), presents a challenging interpretation of the antinomian controversy. On Rhode Island, Carl Bridenbaugh, *Fat Mutton and Liberty of Conscience* (1974), is useful and readable. The early history of New York is traced in Robert C. Ritchie, *The Duke's Province* (1977), and Michael Kammen, *Colonial New York: A History* (1977). The career of William Penn and the founding of Pennsylvania can be followed in Mary Maples Dunn, *William Penn, Politics and Conscience* (1967). A fine example of what some historians call "the new social history" is Stephanie G. Wolf, *Urban Village: Population, Family Structure, and Community in Germantown, Pennsylvania* (1977). Another, also on Pennsylvania, is James Lemmon, *The Best Poor Man's Country* (1972). On the European migration in general, Bernard Bailyn, *The Peopling of British North America* (1986) and *Voyagers to the West* (1986), are ambitious pieces of work that may well become classics.

C H A P T E R 4
THE AMERICAN
REVOLUTION

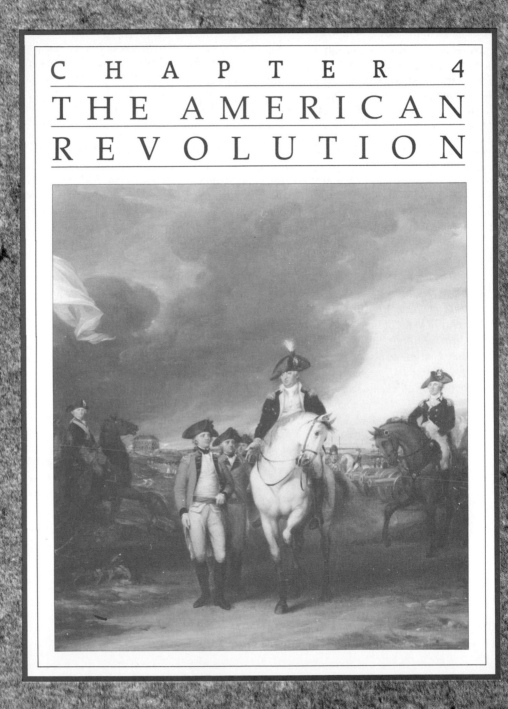

THE EPISODE: *American independence came about despite the best wishes of all involved. Eighteenth-century Americans viewed revolution with horror. They were proud of their membership in the great British Empire, whose government they saw as the most progressive on earth. Few believed that Americans could successfully defy Britain, or that a new nation could be forged to take a place among the nations of the world. These opinions persisted far longer than modern readers, knowing of the events of 1775 and 1776, believe. Despite Boston's defiance of the British army in 1770 that resulted in the Boston massacre, and right up to the outbreak of fighting at Lexington and Concord and the signing of the Declaration of Independence, most Americans hoped the cataclysm could be avoided; yet eventually most came to feel that they had no choice but to fight.*

THE HISTORICAL SETTING: *Britain's mainland colonies began a new stage of maturity as the eighteenth century opened. American-born colonists assumed leadership roles; many of the questions that brought turmoil to the seventeenth century seemed settled. Economically the colonies had found a comfortable niche within the British empire's vast trade networks. By mid-century a new standard of living allowed Americans to feel proud of their society.*

Signs of strain also appeared. Calls for religious revival, partly a response to growing economic success and its accompanying "worldliness," raised issues so fundamental that they threatened the rule of local elites. Population growth contributed to Americans' sense of success, but immigration, both forced and free, drew on new sources in Europe and Africa. These new Americans had no automatic loyalty to Britain; many had suffered in the past from English depredations. They would have little hesitation about joining in defiance.

When the crisis came, it grew out of Britain's imperial concerns. Britain's long-running rivalry with France reached a climax in the French and Indian War (1754–63), which saw the end of French claims in North America. British-Americans greeted the news with joy, but the British government decided to forge a new colonial relationship. Imperial efforts to police the new territories, to force the colonists to pay their share of the costs of empire, and to tighten the administration of trade led to defiance. Americans viewed every action within an interpretive framework that convinced them the empire sought to place them under a tyrannical government. The interplay of events and interpretations led the Americans to war.

How and why the "rude rabble" of Americans was able to confront and defeat the greatest military power on earth is the subject of this chapter.

THE BOSTON MASSACRE

March 1770. Boston was in the grip of ferocious cold. Snow and ice lay thick everywhere, the long winter subduing the people's spirits. Siege conditions prevailed in the city, which had been occupied by British troops since 1768. The inconceivable had come to pass: British soldiers were being used to control and spy on British subjects. Every passing day intensifed the hatred between Bostonians and the "lobsterbacks" in their red coats. As the long winter wore on everyone's nerves, the situation was primed for an explosion.

All the elements for combustion were in place. Action built slowly at first, as mobs of young Bostonians pelted the marching units of British soldiers with snowballs wherever they went. The crowds taunted the redcoats, daring them to fire. For their part, the soldiers swaggered through the town as if it belonged to them, treating its citizens as if they were rude provincials of no account. Everything the soldiers did seemed deliberately calculated to offend the Americans. For both sides, tension was reaching the breaking point. That point was passed in late winter 1770.

Massachusetts had agreed with the other colonies not to import British goods while the empire sought to impose taxes Americans saw as illegal. Not all merchants cooperated with these agreements, however, and they bore the brunt of the colonists' wrath. Many in Boston honored the nonimportation agreements at great personal cost. Merchants lost business, and artisans in the shipping industry found work scarce. Yet they were willing to accept such privation in honoring the greater cause of American rights. They had nothing but scorn for those merchants who put personal gain first. Sometimes rough measures were used to make their displeasure clear.

Ebenezer Richardson was one man around whom suspicions gathered. He was known to have turned in Boston traders to the customs officials for monetary rewards. He had made clear his contempt for the cause so dear to most Bostonians. When he returned to his home about ten o'clock on the morning of February 23, he saw a sign in front of the shop of his neighbor, Theophilus Lillie, identifying Lillie as one who had broken the nonimportation agreements. A crowd had gathered to see that no one did business with Lillie: "The whole Street filled with People who would suffer no person to go to his Shop."

A View of Part of the Town of Boston in New England and British Ships of War Landing their Troops, 1768. Paul Revere's engraving shows British ships controlling access to Boston, a city famous for its many churches whose spires rise above the skyline. In the lower right corner, an Indian woman sits with her foot on a British soldier. The Indian and the rattlesnake on the soldier's arm were both symbols of American identity. (Massachusetts Historical Society)

Richardson had boasted only the day before that he would see "a dust beat up" if he saw any more such signs, and said he hoped the soldiers would come and "cut up the damned Yankees." Gossip said he had also bragged that he was ready for the crowd, "for I've guns loaded." Richardson tried to pull down the sign in front of Lillie's shop, and the assembled people began pelting him with sticks and stones. Richardson fled into his house, saying to some members of the patriot organization, the Sons of Liberty, who had joined the throng, "By the eternal God, I'll make it too hot for you before night."

Richardson screamed to the people to disperse, but they knew they had every right to stand in the public street. He came to the door and shook a stick (many thought it was a gun) at the crowd, saying "By God! I'll make a lane through you!" A brickbat was thrown out of the house at the crowd. Before this, only fruit peelings and other soft items had been thrown at the building. Now the brickbat was thrown back through a window, and then a full barrage of rocks and sticks.

Suddenly, Richardson appeared with a musket at an upstairs window. He rested the weapon on the sill; everyone thought he was bluffing until he fired into the crowd. An eleven-year-old boy, Christopher Seider, lay dying with eleven pellets in his chest and abdomen. Seider, son of a poor German immigrant, became the symbol of the American people preyed on by a rapacious empire and its vicious toadies.

Samuel Adams took charge of events and staged the largest and grandest funeral ever seen in America for young Christopher Seider. Newspaper publicity called on patriots to turn out for the funeral. The *Boston Gazette* eulogized Seider as a "little hero." Those who knew him, the paper said, had "reason to think he had a martial genius and would have made a clever man. . . . Young as he was, he died in his Country's Cause, by the hand of an execrable Villain, directed by others, who could not bear to see the Enemies of America made the Ridicule of Boys."

The procession began at 5 P.M. on Monday, February 26, at the Liberty Tree near Boston Common. Despite huge drifts left by a great snowstorm just two days before, the procession of near 3,000 people marched over half a mile to the Old Granary Burying Ground, where the coffin was interred. Many would have agreed with Samuel Adams's cousin John Adams, who said, "My eyes never beheld such a funeral." It meant, he wrote, "that the Ardor of the People is not to be quelled by the Slaughter of one Child. . . ."

Increasingly, crowd action had emerged as a weapon against the frustrations created by the army's presence in Boston; leaders such as Sam Adams scrambled to get ahead of the developing tactic so as to control and shape it. Many of the moderate leaders of the resistance had been reluctant to associate themselves with something so distasteful as mobs. Adams, under the pseudonym Populus, had written in the *Boston Gazette* in 1768 that there must be "NO MOBS—NO CONFUSIONS—NO TUMULTS." But it soon became clear that any direction over the resistance movement would be lost unless the crowds and the Sons of Liberty became allies.

Between the troops' arrival in Boston in October 1768 and the Boston Massacre of March 1770, Samuel Adams emerged as a principal leader of the city's struggle to force the imperial government to reconsider its new policies.

Samuel Adams is one of the most interesting men among the great revolutionary leaders. He is the first man in American history who thought of himself as a professional politician, and his reputation has risen and fallen as Americans have changed their attitudes toward politicians. Loyalists among the colonists saw him as the sinister manipulator of the crowds, characterizing the people as simple tools of the "Machiavel of Chaos," Adams. There is a small grain of truth in this mostly false characterization: Adams alone among the Boston elite could speak the language of the artisans and had won their respect.

Adams allied himself with leaders who had risen through the ranks such as Ebenezer MacIntosh, a cobbler to whom Boston's workers had looked for leadership since 1765 and the Stamp Act riots. MacIntosh was passionately Protestant in religion and hated the Anglican, almost Roman Catholic, trappings that the empire was imposing on Boston. MacIntosh knew the poverty of the workers. He himself would be imprisoned for debt before 1770 was over. He despised the luxury and pretension of the great merchants and the army officers, and hoped that the radical movement would lead to a return to simplicity. He and his followers longed for the virtue and community solidarity of earlier times.

Proud of his descent from Puritan forebears, Adams saw the revolution as a chance to return to the virtue of the founders. Adams particularly liked the colonists' agreements not to buy or use British products, because these seemed to echo the covenants on which the early Puritan communities were built. He hoped that refusal

Samuel Adams, painted by John
Singleton Copley in the early 1770s.
(Museum of Fine Arts, Boston.
Deposited by the city of Boston)

to use imported products would bring back the simpler time before greed and acquis-
itiveness ruled everyone's lives. Far from being a rabble-rousing, power-mad boss,
Adams was always content to work behind the scenes and let others take the glory;
he remained a poor man till the day he died.

Adams was a politician in the sense that he believed in the political process. He
had faith that the people, given a free choice, would choose wisely, and he hated any
system that took away that freedom. He was also a politician in that he knew how
to get things done—how to work with people and keep his attention focused on the
main goal. Finally, he was a consummate politician in his use of publicity; he wrote
effectively in the papers and was able to stage great public events, joyful or solemn
as the occasion warranted, to focus attention on the resistance. The funeral of Christopher Seider was one such event.

As John Adams had predicted, the tensions did not die with young Seider. The
shock and horror of wanton killing, particularly when the victim was so young, made

many in Boston feel that the stakes had been raised at the end of February 1770. As the *Gazette* proclaimed on the day of his funeral, Christopher's blood "crieth for Vengeance, like the Blood of the righteous Abel."

An escalating series of incidents between townspeople and soldiers punctuated each day of the next week. The arrival of March did not lessen winter's grim hold on the city, and tempers were at the breaking point. On March 3 tension once again broke out into bloodshed. It began in a seemingly innocent way. An off-duty British soldier, Patrick Walker, came up to a rope and cable maker's looking for a job. The soldiers, whose pay was low, were allowed to "moonlight." By permitting off-duty work, the army could deflect pressure to raise salaries. William Green, one of the ropewalk workers, asked Walker whether he wanted a job. "Yes, I do, faith" was the reply. Green then retorted, "Well, then, go and clean my shithouse." "Empty it yourself" was Walker's reply.

The verbal sparring soon came to blows, and more of the workers got involved. Walker was humiliated when one man "knocked up his heels." He ran away, but soon returned with eight or nine other soldiers. The rope workers closed ranks and repelled the soldiers, who then returned with forty men armed with all sorts of clubs and weapons. The workers were armed with sticks used in rope twisting. Once again the soldiers were humiliated by the civilian rope makers. Authority stepped in on both sides to stop the fighting from escalating further, but the warring parties vowed the conflict was not ended.

Why did Private Walker's request for honest work lead to Green's surly reply and a battle? The answer lies in the relationship between the townspeople of Boston and the British army. Many different groups had reason to hate the presence of redcoats in the city, and all these different reasons built solidarity among the citizens. Workingmen had special reasons for resenting the army's presence. Life was hard and becoming harder for those who worked in Boston's industries, such as the building and outfitting of ships. The colonists had chosen to fight the new taxes imposed by the British government by refusing to import British goods. This was a good tactic. Merchants in Britain found their livelihoods in jeopardy because of it. But nonimportation also meant that ships did not come to Boston regularly. Therefore, the repair and refitting shops lost business, and workers were let go or took cuts in wages. The soldiers compounded this grievance by taking jobs in their off-duty hours for lower wages than the Boston men. Thus the workingmen found themselves in direct competition with the soldiers. The army's presence threatened their livelihoods.

George Robert Twelves Hewes was, like Ebenezer MacIntosh, a poor shoemaker who was drawn to the radical cause. Gray's Ropewalk was just down the street from his own shop, and he remembered the events of that day vividly to the end of his life. Hewes was one of many Bostonians who had viewed the British army up close and did not like what they saw. Most British officers, men whose patrons had laid out huge sums to buy their commissions for them, were arrogant, swaggering through the town as if they were members of an elite corps before which the citizens must bend their knees. The mercantile leaders deeply resented this intrusion of an alien aristocratic system.

British soldiers drilling on Boston Common outraged the citizens used to having the land for peaceful pursuits. This 1768 water-color drawing shows the Twenty-ninth Regiment in front of John Hancock's grand house. (Prints division, The New York Public Library, Astor, Lenox, and Tilden Foundations)

Rather than trying to adjust to the patterns accepted in Boston, the army made a display of flouting local custom. Traditional Sunday religious worship was disturbed by the sound of army bands playing as the soldiers marched in formation. The redcoats raced their horses on the Common on Sunday afternoons, and the troops brought open drunkenness and prostitution to the town. Hewes, like many of his fellows, belonged to a strongly Protestant evangelical tradition. Radicals of all economic classes were united in their devotion to Boston's Puritan ways and hated the foreign intrusion.

The army made Bostonians feel like prisoners in their own city. Soldiers were stationed around the city at night to keep the peace. Citizens were stopped by sentries as they moved around their own streets on their own business. When challenged by a sentry to identify himself, a person was supposed to answer "Friend," but Bostonians found it increasingly difficult to make that reply. They felt the soldiers were an alien and unfriendly force in their midst who had no right to challenge them at all.

George Hewes solved the problem by carrying a bottle of rum and offering a drink each time he was stopped. But many Bostonians reacted with hostility. If the sentries, ignored or taunted, attempted to enforce what they thought of as their just authority, they sometimes found themselves hauled into court on a charge of assault,

George Robert Twelves Hewes, painted near the end of his life in 1835 by Joseph G. Cole. (Bostonian Society)

to be tried before a jury sympathetic to the citizen. Often, even the judges were openly hostile to the soldiers and the practice of posting sentries. Crowds attended the trials to see that justice was done.

For Boston's workingmen, the soldiers represented unwelcome competition in hard times, but the radicals also saw that the soldiers were victims of an unimaginably harsh system of military discipline. Many soldiers had deserted from the army. Some of the radicals encouraged such desertions to lower the troops' morale. As they learned of the life the soldiers led, their sympathy grew. George Robert Twelves Hewes brought charges against a soldier who had picked up a pair of shoes Hewes had made for his commanding officer, Captain Thomas Preston. The soldier, Sergeant Mark Burk, pocketed the money Preston had given him and took the shoes without paying for them. Hewes appealed to Preston, who paid him and told him to register a complaint against Burk. Burk was convicted at the military hearing and, to Hewes's utter horror, sentenced to 350 lashes on his bare back. Hewes stood up and told the court "that if he had thought the fellow was to be punished so severely for such an offense, bad as he was, he would have said nothing about it." Both groups suffered because of what they saw as the British empire's unjust practices. Yet the army's presence repeatedly threw these groups into competition or conflict, and the solidarity that might have grown up between them withered.

By early March 1770, it was clear the soldiers should never have been brought to Boston. English tradition held that a monarch who keeps an army in peacetime is planning some kind of tyranny, because his intention must be to use military force against his own people. Now radical leaders saw their predictions coming true. When the Massachusetts governor felt a bit threatened, what did he do but immediately cry out for the support of the army? Military force was being used to prop up an unpopular governor. What was that but tyranny?

Commander in chief General Thomas Gage had sent the army into Boston in 1768 to deal with people he considered "mutinous" and "desperadoes." Now, early in 1770, he reflected on that mistake:

> The People were as Lawless and Licentious after the Troops arrived, as they were before. The Troops could not act by Military Authority, and no Person in Civil Authority would ask their aid. They were there contrary to the wishes of the Council, Assembly, Magistrates and People, and seemed only offered to abuse and Ruin. And the Soldiers were either to suffer ill usage and even assaults upon their Persons till their Lives were in Danger, or by resisting and defending themselves, to run almost a Certainty of suffering by the Law.

Benjamin Franklin had earlier warned the British against sending troops among the colonists: "They will not find a rebellion; they may indeed make one." John Adams demonstrated just how prophetic his words were:

> My daily Reflections for two Years, at the Sight of those Soldiers before my door were serious enough. Their very Appearance in Boston was a strong proof to me, that the determination in Great Britain to subjugate Us, was too deep and inveterate ever to be altered by Us: For every thing We could do was misrepresent[ed], and Nothing We could say was credited.

Law-abiding and loyal British subjects were radicalized by the army and the daily and constant affronts its presence generated.

All these feelings came to a head in the first week of March 1770. After the incident at Gray's Ropewalk on March 3, numerous small confrontations took place. Bostonians believed the situation was becoming increasingly serious. Rumors of an impending confrontation with the troops flew around the city. The soldiers also sensed a showdown was coming and prepared themselves for it. March 4 was a Sunday, and the city was quiet, but fears focused on the Monday.

About eight o'clock in the evening of Monday, March 5, an incident occurred that was to form the focus of that night's events. Small groups of civilians and off-duty soldiers patrolled the streets armed with clubs, and some minor altercations had already taken place. The *Boston Gazette* reported that "several soldiers of the Twenty-ninth Regiment were seen parading the streets with their drawn cutlasses and bayonets, abusing and wounding numbers of the inhabitants."

The main action was in front of the Customs House on King Street. A single private, Hugh White, was on guard at the corner of King Street and Royal Exchange Lane, but other, off-duty, soldiers were in the area. Edward Garrick, a young barber's apprentice, tried unsuccessfully to stop a passing officer, Captain-Lieutenant John Goldfinch, to collect an overdue bill from him. Garrick left, but later returned and began to shout that the officers of the Fourteenth Regiment were no gentlemen. Private White, outraged, rushed out of his sentry box to confront Garrick. When Garrick faced him, saying, "I am not ashamed to show my face," White hit him across the side of his head with his musket.

A crowd soon gathered, and Hugh White retreated from his sentry box to the steps of the Customs House, where he angrily fixed his bayonet onto his musket. White was nervous, but stood firm as the crowd insulted him, calling him a "damned rascally Scoundrel Lobster Son of a Bitch." The sentry held his gun level to keep off the crowd. Henry Knox, a bookseller, warned him not to shoot. White answered, "Damn them, if they molest me I will fire." When snowballs, some packed with ice, began to rain down on him, he called for support from the main guard, which was stationed just down the block.

The officer in charge of the guard, Captain Thomas Preston, who had been watching events with mounting concern, set out to rescue Private White about nine o'clock. He marched through the crowd at the head of a double file of six privates and a corporal, "the soldiers pushing their bayonets, and crying, make way!" The people parted to let them through, but once they had joined Private White in front of the Customs House, the rescue party found they were trapped there. With the threatening crowd in front of them, Preston ordered his eight men to form a semicircle with their bayonets and muskets pointed outward. He also apparently ordered the men to load their guns, though many in the street thought the muskets were loaded with powder alone to frighten the crowd, rather than powder and shot.

The atmosphere was charged with old hatreds. The civilians and the soldiers must have realized quickly that both the crowd and the little troop in front of them contained men who had been involved in the fight at the ropewalk two days before. Both sides felt there was unfinished business between them. The young men among the assembled townspeople, aware of the redcoats' predicament, taunted the soldiers. Some ran along their semicircle hitting the muskets with sticks, demonstrating that, despite their impressive uniforms and their weapons, they were powerless in this situation.

The church bells had been ringing since the trouble began. Since bells in the night usually meant fire, many men had come to help put out the flames. Others knew that this was a different kind of combustion and turned out to settle old scores. George Robert Twelves Hewes was there early: "I was soon on the ground among them," he later recalled. One of the soldiers, Matthew Kilroy, whom Hewes had caught and chastised when he mugged a Boston woman, struck Hewes on the shoulder with his musket as he passed. Samuel Gray and Nicholas Ferriter, both of whom had been at the ropewalk fight a few days earlier, hurried to the Customs House, not sure whether it was afire or not. When told there was no fire but "it is the soldiers fighting," Gray replied, "I will knock some of them on the head."

Some men joined the throng to try to calm this very different kind of conflagration that threatened the peace of Boston. Captain Preston was well known in the town and had won the people's respect as a gentleman. Henry Knox, the young bookseller, had from the beginning tried to prevent bloodshed. As Preston marched out with his little troop to rescue Hugh White, Knox said to him: "For God's sake, take care of your Men, for if they fire your life must be answerable." Preston answered simply, "I am sensible of it." The risks were very great on all sides.

The firing began in confusion. The throng pressed so close that "you could not get your hat betwixt them and the bayonets." One of the privates, struck by a piece of ice, slipped and fell just as Preston's attention was diverted by a quiet warning

The Boston Massacre.   Paul Revere's engraving made the deaths appear to be the result of a deliberate order to fire. This engraving, seen by many who knew little of the confusion of that night, was a powerful piece of propaganda. (Massachusetts Historical Society)

from another concerned Bostonian, Richard Palmes. As the private stood up, he fired his musket into the crowd. Soon after, the rest of the guard also fired. Witnesses described Private Kilroy taking careful aim and bringing down Samuel Gray. Eleven men were hit, with three dead on the spot and two dying soon after.

As the troops, having reloaded, once again leveled their muskets, Preston ran along the line, pushing up the guns with his arm shouting, "Stop firing!" Even after the shooting was over, some citizens, still believing the guns had been loaded only with powder, did not understand that men had been hit. Joseph Hilyer later recalled that when he first saw the bodies, "I thought they had been scared and run away, and left their greatcoats behind."

Samuel Gray, one of the ropemakers who had fought the soldiers the previous Friday, fell dead with a hole in his skull as big as a man's hand. Before he died, he may have recognized the three soldiers from the ropewalk fight, Privates William Warren, Matthew Kilroy, and John Carroll, who were in the line before him. He certainly saw Kilroy taking aim at him. A young mariner who was in Boston to learn the art of navigation, Samuel Caldwell, died immediately of a bullet in the chest. Crispus Attucks, a tall, proud man who was variously said to be black or Indian and may have been of mixed descent, fell dead with two bullets in his chest. Samuel Maverick, a boy of seventeen, was hit by a ricocheting bullet; he was carried home to his mother, dying. Patrick Carr, an artisan from Ireland, was taken to his master's house, where he died a few days later.

The dispersing crowd carried news of what had happened all over Boston: "Language cannot describe the horror and indignation which was excited through the town by this dreadful event." More and more people began to gather. With the clamor of church bells throughout the city filling the air, the sense of crisis grew. Boston had no street lighting, and the moon was slender. Though the thick snow reflected what little light there was, that reflection also created deep shadows. No one could be sure what was going on. Express riders had even gone to nearby towns, "and the inhabitants were called out of their beds, many of whom armed themselves but were stopped from coming into town by advice that there was no further danger that night."

John Adams, called to the scene by the firebells, went home convinced there would be no more violence. George Hewes gave a deposition the next day in which he told how he, like many of his friends, went home to arm himself. At about 1 A.M. he was back on the street carrying a cane. He met a troop of soldiers from the Twenty-ninth Regiment, all armed "with very large clubs or cutlasses." When one of the soldiers asked "how he far'd, he told him very badly to see his townsmen shot in such a manner, and asked him if he did not think it was a dreadful thing." The soldier, named Dobson, replied, "It was a fine thing" and that "you shall see more of it." When the soldiers tried to take his cane, Hewes told them, "I had as good a right to carry a cane as they had to carry clubs."

As crowds rumored to be in the thousands filled the streets, prevention of total disaster was up to Lieutenant Governor Thomas Hutchinson, in charge now that Governor Francis Bernard had returned to England. Concerned citizens appealed to Hutchinson, "For God's sake, . . . go to King Street," and warned that if something were not quickly done, "the town would be all in blood." Hutchinson responded quickly to the call. He first went to the scene of the massacre, despite the large and threatening crowd, and talked with Captain Preston. Hutchinson found Preston still backed by British soldiers in the street. "How came you to fire without orders from a civil magistrate?" Hutchinson demanded. Preston replied, "I was obliged to, to save my sentry." Hutchinson then countered, "These soldiers ought not to be here."

The crowd then began to push Hutchinson and the leaders with him toward the State House, the seat of the royal government on King Street. He addressed the crowd from the balcony, assuring the people that the law would see justice was done and imploring them to return to their homes. His words that night were the credo by which he lived: "The law shall have its course; I will live and die by the law."

Hutchinson then set immediately to work to see that the law did work. He began to take evidence that night. Witnesses were called, from their beds if necessary, to come and testify as to what they had seen. Though the evidence was conflicting, particularly on the source of the order to fire, Hutchinson issued warrants for the

Thomas Hutchinson at the age of thirty, painted by
Edward Truman. (Massachusetts Historical Society)

arrest of Captain Preston and his second in command, Lieutenant James Basset. By
two o'clock in the morning, as news of all the soldiers' arrests spread, Boston became
quiet and the people returned home. The barrel of tar that had been placed on Beacon
Hill which, when lit, would have alerted the neighboring towns that their assistance
was needed was carried away again.

Thomas Hutchinson's career forms a striking contrast to that of Samuel Adams.
Both men were descended from the Puritan founders of New England (Hutchinson
from the 1630s radical Anne Hutchinson), and each was devoted to his country. In
different circumstances these men could have been allies, but the issues of the 1760s
and 1770s divided them. Hutchinson, a merchant in a long line of merchants, had
been involved in public service since shortly after his graduation from Harvard and
had risen through the ranks of the colony's government. He had always been a strong
supporter of the interests of Massachusetts.

In the 1760s, as Britain's new imperial policies aroused American defiance,
Hutchinson felt divided within himself. He strongly opposed the new taxes, such as
the Stamp Act of 1765, but he believed America's best interests lay in membership in
the British empire. He was also a firm believer in the letter of the law. Therefore,
though he wrote to England strongly objecting to the Stamp Act, for example, he felt
that as long as it was the law it must be enforced.

When Thomas Hutchinson addressed the gathered people on the night of March
5, 1770, he, more than almost anyone else in Boston, had reason to fear the actions

of an angry mob. From the events of five years before, he knew the destructive power of a populace that acted to defend rights it thought were being violated. Bostonians had not appreciated Hutchinson's fine distinctions about obeying the Stamp Act while applying through legal channels for its repeal. Many believed it was an illegal imposition and that to give in to it would only lead to further incursions on their rights.

Riots forcing the issue had erupted in Boston, and one of the crowd's targets was Hutchinson. One night in late August 1765, a mob attacked his townhouse, destroying what they could not carry away. So thorough were the rioters that, according to an eyewitness, they spent three hours hacking at the house's cupola before they brought it down. Governor Bernard's report said that next day the lanes leading from the house were littered "with money, plate, gold rings, etc., which had been dropped in carrying off." Hutchinson estimated his losses at £2,218, a fortune in those days. Among the losses that night was a massive archive of papers dealing with colonial New England that Hutchinson, who was an accomplished historian, had put together for the commonwealth.

Hutchinson was no coward; no riot could deter him from his duty. When colonial pressure succeeded in getting the Stamp Act overturned, he believed that success demonstrated that adherence to the law would bring true justice. He continued to serve in his posts of chief justice and lieutenant governor; his advice was especially needed as the governor, Francis Bernard, was a man of very limited talent. Hutchinson served because he believed Massachusetts needed a man of his experience and ideas. When Bernard fled, Hutchinson shouldered all the responsibility, and brought his strict interpretation of the law to bear on the rising tension within Boston, a decision his Puritan ancestors would have understood. A more flexible man might have been more successful, but no one could have been more devoted to the good of the colony as he saw it.

Now, in 1770, the citizens were no more ready for fine legal distinctions than they had been in 1765. Boston was not satisfied with Hutchinson's demand that they allow the law to work its slow course. Until the troops were removed and the city was restored to full rights of citizenship, the people would continue to defy the empire and its representative, Thomas Hutchinson. A huge crowd, some said as many as 4,000 people, gathered in Faneuil Hall on the morning after the massacre and made their feelings clear.

Samuel Adams headed the committee that carried their demands to Hutchinson and his council in the State House. Adams reported the town meeting's insistence that all the soldiers be pulled out, and pointed to the large numbers of people all around Boston waiting to hear his reply and to force compliance with their will if necessary. Later, Adams wrote of the meeting with Hutchinson: "It was then I observed the Governor's knees to tremble. I thought I saw his face grow pale, and I enjoyed the sight."

The governor's council agreed that the army must leave: "Nothing can rationally be expected to restore the peace of the town and prevent carnage but the immediate removal of the troops." One councilor, Royall Tyler, warned that 10,000 men would come in from the countryside and force the troops out if they were not taken away. Delegates from Charlestown and Dedham confirmed this information. Hutchinson at first refused, saying he had no authority to command the troops to move, but finally

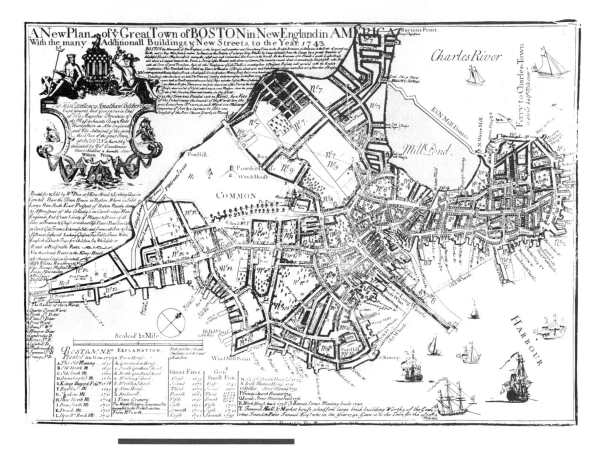

Boston in 1769. Engraving by John Bonner shows the site of the events of March 1770. The Boston Massacre took place at the Customs House directly up the street from Long Wharf. (Prints division, The New York Public Library, Astor, Lenox, and Tilden Foundations)

gave in. The news "gave Great Joy to the Inhabitants," who had been waiting at the Old South Church for word of the governor's decision. The soldiers were removed to Castle William, on an island in the harbor. Technically, they were still within Boston, but three miles of water separated them from the city.

In the days immediately following the incident, each side took its case to the court of public opinion. Radical leaders took depositions from many witnesses, including George Hewes, and published them to show, as the Boston committee contended, that the soldiers had been "instruments in executing a settled plot to massacre the inhabitants." In terming the deaths of five men a massacre, the Boston leaders called up images of brutal, irresponsible use of force.

They spread their message via newspapers and broadsides, and those who supported the royal government also put their case in print. The publicity campaign shows that what people thought, how the public viewed the actions of the British, was important. By default, the imperial representatives had already conceded the most crucial point. No flat declarations that the empire had the right to do this or that would suffice. The people of America must be convinced. American resistance to British authority had already had its effect. Newspapers throughout America and in England printed sensational stories about the event. The massacre came to be a crucial milestone on the path to defiance.

Paul Revere made an engraving of a drawing of the massacre done by a young artist, Henry Pelham, and copies of this engraving were widely circulated. It was not an accurate representation of the event (it made the musket fire seem to be the result of a deliberate order), but it was an effective representation of Bostonians' feelings about the presence of the army. Revere also prepared a more accurate plan of the affair that was probably meant to be used in the trials, which was not published.

On March 8, the first four "unhappy Victims" were buried. The funeral processions began from each of their four houses, joined at King Street, "the Theatre of that inhuman Tragedy," and marched to the burial ground. Business came to a standstill that day, and the church bells of Boston and all the towns around tolled "a solemn Peal." The citizens of Boston were joined by an estimated 10,000 people from the countryside, all of whom walked in the procession. According to one report, "The aggravated Circumstances of their Death, the Distress and Sorrow visible in every Countenance, together with the peculiar Solemnity with which the whole Funeral was conducted, surpass Description." Another great procession gathered to take Patrick Carr to his grave when he died a week later.

The Trial

All concerned in handling the proceedings against Captain Preston and his men were committed to the idea that justice must be done, and that the trials and verdicts be seen as fair. John Adams, a young cousin of Samuel Adams, took on the job of conducting the defense at the urging of the radical leaders, despite his anger at the army's presence in Boston. He later said that he instantly lost more than half his law business when his involvement in the case became known.

Adams took the assignment because he wanted to demonstrate that the resistance movement was not lawless and destructive, but that the Americans had acted in defense of the highest principles of English law. When asked to act for Preston, Adams answered, "If he thinks he cannot have a fair trial . . . without my assistance, without hesitation he shall have it." Ultimately, he took on the defense of all the soldiers. He himself had not been involved in the events of March 5, but had come to the scene in answer to the firebell after the shooting and had seen the blood of the victims thick in the street.

Like his cousin Samuel and Thomas Hutchinson, John Adams was also a descendant of the Puritan founders of Massachusetts and shared their high sense of morality and dedication to duty. John Adams did not inherit family wealth and position. He fixed on the law as the avenue to the position of influence and importance he hoped for. After a stint as a schoolteacher, he began his legal studies and aimed to become the most learned and accomplished lawyer in Massachusetts.

John Adams. Pastel by Benjamin Blyth, 1766. (Massachusetts Historical Society)

Adams was always an awkward man; he never felt he really fit in, and he determined to work to make himself into a successful person. The campaign of resistance to Britain gave him his opportunity to shine on a large stage, and he made the most of it. From his beginnings as a provincial lawyer, he went on to the Continental Congresses, to important roles in the revolutionary period, and finally to the presidency of the United States. Sam Adams was always content to work behind the scenes; John, though he never felt completely at home there, liked center stage. Late in life he wrote: "I am but an ordinary man. The times alone have destined me to fame." This was only partly true, for it was John Adams's preparation and knowledge of what must be done that made him able to grasp opportunities.

All this was in the future. In 1770, at the time he ventured to defend the redcoats in the Boston Massacre, he was a young man in his mid-thirties, just starting out. The trials, originally set for April, were subject to repeated delays, making Bostonians distrustful of Hutchinson's motives. They were eventually opened October 24 with *Rex* (Latin for "king") v. *Preston*. Though they had acted as agents of the royal government, the soldiers were prosecuted by the crown because they were accused of violating British law, which is the monarch's law.

John Adams faced the ethical problem of a possible conflict of interest between his various clients. Preston's best defense was that he had not ordered his men to fire, and was therefore not responsible. The soldiers, on the other hand, rested their defense on their duty to follow orders: They thought they had been commanded to fire. It would be hard for one man to argue both cases.

Testimony in Preston's trial revealed the same confusion as in the depositions taken the night of March 5. Many versions of what Preston was thought to have said were reported. Had he ordered his men to fire, or had he commanded, "Do not fire," or had the soldiers heard one of the many taunts from the crowd accusing the redcoats of being afraid to fire? Nothing was clear. Even Richard Palmes, the concerned citizen who had been talking to Preston when the firing began, was not sure. George Robert Twelves Hewes, interviewed many years later, remembered testifying at the trial on this very point:

> When Preston, their captain, was tried, I was called as one of the witnesses, on the part of the government, and testified that I believed it was the same man, Captain Preston, that ordered his soldiers to make ready, who also ordered them to fire. Mr. John Adams, former president of the United States, was advocate for the prisoners, and denied the fact, that Captain Preston gave orders to his men to fire; and on his cross examination of me asked whether my position was such, that I could see the captain's lips in motion when the order to fire was given; to which I answered, that I could not.

Clouding the whole proceeding was the widely shared conviction that, whatever the verdict, the king would see to it that Preston went free. In fact, Hutchinson had secretly been directed to ensure that no harm came to Preston until the king had a chance to issue a pardon. They need not have worried. The jury had been chosen from among men mostly sympathetic to the soldiers' cause, and Adams's summing-up was brilliant. Adams based his argument on the undoubted right of self-defense and the duty of an officer to protect his men if they appear to be in mortal danger, and he proceeded to tear apart the credibility of the crown's witnesses. He pointed out that Captain Preston was standing between his men and the crowd and was therefore in danger of being hit by the musketballs if he had ordered the guns fired. Adams reminded the jury that the law preferred to free many guilty men rather than wrongly to execute one who was innocent. On October 30 the jury announced its verdict: Not Guilty.

The soldiers' trial began in late November; much of the evidence focused on the provocations by townspeople that night and other times that had made the redcoats jumpy. Several witnesses testified that large, sharp pieces of ice had been thrown at the semicircle before the Customs House. Others agreed that many in the crowd had been armed with large sticks. Others spoke of the roughness and arrogance with which the soldiers had treated townspeople, particularly laborers.

But Adams refused to ground the soldiers' defense on the charge that the towns-people had acted outrageously. He would not smear his own people. Rather, he placed the blame squarely on the British government. While admitting that the soldiers might have thought they were in danger, he pointed to the greater responsibility of Britain for placing them and Boston in such an impossible situation. "Soldiers quartered in a populous town will always occasion two mobs, where they prevent one. They are wretched conservators of the peace." The government had acted stupidly by asking the army to do a job it was ill-suited to accomplish and then had refused to admit its error in time, causing loss of life and suffering all round.

The jury deliberated two and a half hours before returning with its verdict. Six of the men were acquitted. The two convicted were deemed guilty of manslaughter, not murder. Only they had been proved to the jury's satisfaction to have fired their guns. When they were brought to court for sentencing December 14, both claimed Benefit of Clergy. This loophole in the law went back to medieval times when anyone who could read was assumed to be a priest or monk. Since the government did not then have the right to take the life of someone under the control of the church, an accused person who could "prove" he was a priest by reading a selection from the Bible would be branded on the hand (this loophole could be used only once) and released.

The "neck verse," the passage that accused persons were asked to read, was Psalm 51:1, "Have mercy upon me, O God, according to thy loving-kindness: according unto the multitude of thy tender mercies blot out my transgressions." By colonial times, with the Bible translated into English and literacy much more widespread, Benefit of Clergy acted to allow many who had no official connection with the church to escape capital punishment. Though the law on the books was very harsh, such escape valves made its operation more lenient. The two soldiers were branded on the thumb by the sheriff and released.

Boston took the verdicts calmly; the great conflagration that many feared and some looked forward to was still in the future. The soldiers had been removed and, during the time that the trials had been pending, news of the repeal of all the Townshend Acts (which had imposed new taxes on essential commodities in 1767) except for the tax on tea had arrived. Colonists began to use imported products again, so business picked up and life returned to normal. Many people felt the crisis of the imperial relationship had passed for good.

Thomas Hutchinson's outlook was bleaker. He had been so shaken by his inability to control the situation that led to the massacre and his being forced to withdraw the troops that he had attempted to resign his post as lieutenant governor. He wrote to London that he was "absolutely alone." In his letter of resignation, he wrote, "I have not the strength of constitution to withstand the whole force of the other branches of government as well as the body of the people united against the governor." He could not uphold royal authority, and desired to retire to a more satisfying private life in his country house at Milton.

When the royal government begged him to reconsider, offering him the governorship in his own right, he agreed to shoulder the burden in a spirit that his Puritan ancestors would have approved. His insistence on observing the letter of the law would again cause trouble in the tea crisis of 1773. He did resign then, but the alternative of a quiet country life was no longer open to him. He lived the rest of his life as an unhappy exile.

Samuel and John Adams went on to roles of glory in the struggle that ended in the independence of the United States. John ever after remained proud of his role in defending the Boston Massacre soldiers, calling it "one of the most gallant, generous, manly and disinterested Actions of my whole Life, and one of the best pieces of Service I ever rendered my Country. Judgment of Death against those Soldiers would have been as foul a Stain upon this Country as the Executions of the Quakers or Witches, anciently."

George Robert Twelves Hewes lived on to 1840 to be celebrated every July 4 as one of the oldest survivors of the revolutionaries. After service in the Revolutionary War, he resumed his career as a shoemaker. He remained a poor man all his life, and died in Richfield Springs, New York. He was invited back to Boston for Independence Day celebrations in 1835. At ninety-three he was, briefly, a celebrated man and the center of all attention.

Every year March 5 was celebrated in Boston as a solemn day of remembrance. Orators recalled the day and drew its lessons anew. In the 1772 speech, Dr. Joseph Warren avowed:

> The fatal fifth of March, 1770, can never be forgotten—The horrors of that dreadful night are but too deeply impressed on our hearts—Language is too feeble to paint the emotion of our souls, when our streets were stained with the blood of our brethren—when our ears were wounded by the groans of the dying, and our eyes were tormented with the sight of the mangled bodies of the dead . . . our children subjected to the barbarous caprice of the raging soldiery—our virtuous wives, endeared to us by every tender tie, falling a sacrifice to worse than brutal violence . . .

Warren congratulated his fellow citizens on their restraint. The troops were removed, he reminded his hearers, "without one drop of blood being shed by the inhabitants."

Joseph Warren controlled his emotional picture of the horrors of March 5, 1770, by showing the Americans on the high ground of justice, refusing to meet violence with violence. As the crisis between the colonies and Britain again reached a critical point, the lessons drawn became more inflammatory. When Dr. Benjamin Church commemorated the massacre on its third anniversary in 1773, tensions were again rising to the boiling point. He told the crowd that "the sullen ghosts of murdered fellow-citizens haunt my imagination . . . the wan tenants of the grave still shriek for vengeance on their remorseless butchers."

Little did he know how fully that vengeance would soon be exacted, and how much more blood would be shed in the cause. Nine months after Church's oration, on December 16, 1773, patriots disguised as Mohawks dumped East India Company tea into Boston Harbor. The harsh punishment imposed on Massachusetts built colonial solidarity in reaction. All the colonies would soon feel the sense of outrage and fear for the future under British rule that the Boston Massacre had awakened and the commemorative celebrations had kept alive. John Adams, writing of the massacre in later life, reflected, "That night the foundation of American independence was laid."

THE COMING OF INDEPENDENCE

The defiance shown imperial officials by Bostonians in the days before and after the Boston Massacre of 1770 would have been unthinkable as the eighteenth century opened. British American society was constructed on principles of deference. Deference meant that the "middling" and "poorer sort" of people normally deferred to the judgment of the wealthiest and most established among them. In politics, deference meant that men from a few families were reelected to office again and again. There were no secret ballots; the voting was done in a body by show of hands, and men who were dependent on the patronage of those above them knew enough not to offend their "betters." Deference did not rest on fear, however. Much of the time, there seems to have been general agreement on who society's "natural leaders" were.

This sense of agreement came about partly because Anglo-American society had matured in some ways by 1700. For the first time, people of European parentage born in America outnumbered immigrants. Colonists were born into their roles in life and increasingly constructed their own ways of doing things. Deference gave elite officeholders confidence in the rightness of their judgment, and the colonial assemblies began to enlarge their sphere of operations, sometimes even in defiance of the royal governor and his council. Samuel Shute, governor of Massachusetts, wrote angrily in 1732 that the assembly had usurped his powers: It was "in a manner the whole Legislative and in a Good measure the Executive Power of the Province." Colonial merchants, planters, and artisans began to develop their own markets and internal trade structures.

In the family, deference also dominated, under a system historians call patriarchy. Fathers ruled their families. The flexibility of roles allowed women by the uncertainties of the seventeenth century had been submerged in a reassertion of male authority. Only very rarely did women have control over their own property, and public roles were largely denied them. There were some exceptional women, such as Eliza Lucas, later Eliza Pinckney, who ran her family's South Carolina plantation from the age of seventeen and developed methods for cultivation and processing of indigo, which became a major cash crop for the colony. Another female entrepreneur was Betsy Ross of Philadelphia, whose upholstery shop saw several young men working under her direction. For most, though, women's sphere was the home, where female roles were enlarged by the addition of spinning wheels and other equipment. Women's contribution to the family economy was crucial, and in newly settled parts of the colonies, women were still called on to do rough farm work at times. Despite the propaganda circulating in Europe, America was not a "Paradise on earth for women."

Deference was an accepted way of life in 1700. Yet seventy-five years later Americans would rise up in an unprecedented shattering of deference. Not only would the colonists defy Britain, but within the colonies established elites would be challenged by new groups dissatisfied with the way things were done. Over the course of those seventy-five years, a series of events and trends worked to break down deference and make possible the defiance of the American Revolution. The story of the eighteenth century in British America is largely the chronicle of that breakdown. As challenges to deference were played out, the Americans also developed an awakening consciousness of themselves as one people separate from Britain. Both were necessary to making the Revolution possible.

Religion and Colonial Elites

Religion played a major role in the development of an American consciousness in the eighteenth century. Religion had always been important in the colonies; many had been founded as refuges for persecuted groups and had continued to emphasize that special mission. In the eighteenth century, men and women fleeing religious persecution came to the colonies from many parts of Europe. But some Americans, descendants of earlier immigrants, felt that the religious fervor in the more settled regions had waned. Religion had become routine, a part of the social order rather than a deeply felt personal conviction. Growing prosperity had made people more concerned with taking advantage of new opportunities for amassing wealth than with the state of their souls.

Out of this concern emerged one of the most remarkable movements in American history, which historians have labeled the Great Awakening. It began with a series of small, local religious revivals as far back as the end of the seventeenth century in the Connecticut River valley. In the 1720s the Middle Colonies saw the beginnings of a series of revivals led by William and Gilbert Tennent, who worked primarily among Presbyterian Scots-Irish congregations in New Jersey and New York. Jonathan Edwards, a minister in Northampton, Massachusetts, led his congregation in a movement of religious renewal in 1734 and 1735. Edwards was a highly educated man who knew the work of the leading European philosophers of the day and wrote extensively on the psychology of religious conversion. He and his congregation became convinced that, though they had been going through the motions of a religious life, they had been spiritually dead. All the revivals stressed the *experience* of God's grace in daily life rather than adherence to specific doctrines.

Hundreds of Edwards's parishioners underwent the process of conversion, which began with a devastating examination of their own souls, leading to despair of ever being worthy of God's grace. Just at the moment when despair set in, most experienced a sense of God's forgiveness, of being flooded with light and grace. Edwards wrote a book about the revival, *Faithful Narrative of the Surprising Work of God*, describing how it affected "all sorts, sober and vicious, high and low, rich and poor, wise and unwise." Many people believed something great was about to happen. The movement spread to neighboring communities along the Connecticut River, but its excitement burned out by the end of 1735.

Soon "it pleased God to send Mr. [George] Whitefield into this land." Whitefield, a charismatic preacher recently arrived from England, traveled over the colonies, spreading the revival from Georgia to Maine as he preached several sermons each day. Nothing like it had ever been seen. Wherever he went, he gathered crowds too

Eliza Lucas Pinckney

Eliza Lucas Pinckney was a remarkable woman. In her long life (1722–93), she helped foster the massive changes that transformed America from an appendage of a great European empire to an independent union of thirteen states. Nor did recognition come to her only from later generations. So respected was she that George Washington himself asked to participate in her funeral as a pallbearer.

Eliza Lucas's independent spirit was evident from her earliest years. When she was only seventeen, she began to run her father's plantation, Wappoo, near Charleston, South Carolina. Her father, a lieutenant colonel of the British army, was stationed in Antigua, and her mother was an invalid. So, guided by her father's letters, young Eliza set out not merely to keep the plantation running, but to conduct experiments in growing and processing the valuable blue dye, indigo. Others had tried to cultivate indigo in South Carolina and failed, but Eliza Lucas, despite all manner of setbacks, stuck with the project and after four long years of frustration, succeeded in producing marketable indigo. Her London correspondent responded to the first samples sent to England in 1744: "I have shown your indigo to one of our most noted Brokers in that Way, who tried it against some of the best French, and in his opinion it is AS GOOD."

Eliza's next act shows her remarkable spirit. She gave indigo seeds to "a great number of people," providing the colony of South Carolina with one of its most important cash crops. Rather than monopolizing that wealth-producing commodity and profiting from the fruits of her own labors, she shared it with those around her.

The independence she showed as a plantation manager was equally reflected in her private life. Eliza Lucas rejected the marriage partners her father paraded before her beginning when she was eighteen. Of the first, an elderly man, she wrote to her father:

Pay my thanks to the old Gentleman for his Generosity and favourable sentiments of me and let him know my thoughts on the affair in such civil terms as you know much better than any I can dictate; and [I] beg leave to say to you that the riches of Peru and Chile if he had them put together could not purchase a sufficient Esteem for him to make him my husband.

Yet when she did marry, in 1744 at the age of twenty-two, she chose Charles Pinckney, a man of forty-five, the widower of a friend. She was a devoted wife and mother; her two sons, Charles Cotesworth Pinckney and Thomas Pinckney, like their father, played important roles in colonial and national politics. She also continued her economic experiments, hoping to make silk production profitable for South.Carolina. Her daughter Harriott became a competent plantation manager like her mother in her husband's absences and in her own widowhood. All three children inherited their mother's interest in scientific agriculture and instituted the latest techniques and crops on their plantations.

Eliza Lucas Pinckney lived through the Revolution as a widow (her husband died of malaria in 1758). Her letters record the sufferings of the home front during the war. In one to an English friend, she complained that her slaves had deserted her, and "my property pulled to pieces, burnt and destroyed; my money of no value, my Children sick and prisoners." The letter went on, "Such is the deplorable state of our Country from two armies being in it for nearly two years; the plantations have been some quite, some nearly, ruined—and all with very few exceptions great sufferers." The British army had brought smallpox to the region, which added greatly to the misery.

When she died of cancer in 1793, Eliza Lucas Pinckney's obituary said that it was impossible "to behold her without emotions of the highest veneration and respect," a judgment seconded by the president of the United States as he carried her casket to the grave.

George Whitefield. This 1742 English painting shows the enraptured congregation listening to his powerful sermon, and the painter indicates the central role of women in the early-eighteenth-century revivals. (National Portrait Gallery, London)

large for any building to hold, so he preached out in the open air. Nathan Cole, as he traveled to hear Whitefield preach in Middletown, Connecticut, in 1740

> saw before me a Cloud or fog rising; I first thought it came from the great River, but as I came nearer the Road, I heard a noise something like a low rumbling thunder and presently found it was the noise of Horse's feet . . . every horse seemed to go with all his might to carry his rider to hear news from heaven for the saving of Souls; it made me tremble to see the sight. . . .

Thousands heard Whitefield in Charleston, Philadelphia, and New York. When he came to Boston in 1740, his final sermon drew a crowd of nearly 30,000 to the Common—and Boston's total population was half that number.

At first the ministers, who had been preaching to half-empty churches, were overjoyed and vied to attract Whitefield and other touring ministers to their pulpits. As Benjamin Franklin wrote, "It seem'd as if all the World were growing Religious." Franklin went to hear Whitefield preach in Philadelphia and was amazed because the "Multitudes of all Sects and Denominations that attended his Sermons were enormous." But soon enthusiasm turned to suspicion; many wondered what the effect of such outpourings of emotion would be. How could the emotion be controlled and channeled? Parishioners began to compare their own ministers to the Awakeners and found them cold and unconverted. The faculty of Harvard College pointed out that because of Whitefield's example, "the People have been thence ready to despise their own Ministers."

Ben Franklin wrote that "the Clergy taking a Dislike to him, soon refus'd him their Pulpits and he was oblig'd to preach in the Fields." Closing the churches to Whitefield and other preachers who had adopted the Awakening forced people to choose. Many New England parishes split over whether they would follow the New Lights, as the Awakeners were called, or stay with the Old Lights, the established church. Old Lights pointed to the emotional nature of the conversion experience and doubted it would outlast the excitement of the revivals.

To some extent the Old Lights were right; the fervor of the Awakening faded. But the effects of the movement were long-lasting, and in some ways set the stage for the Revolution by breaking down habits of deference. Just the experience of attending one of the Awakeners' sermons had its impact. Ordinary men and women used to sitting in the meetinghouse or church—where every pew was assigned according to one's wealth and importance in the community, and where the minister preached a highly intellectual sermon—suddenly found themselves in an open field where everyone jostled together and the preacher reached out to them in emotional, everyday language. The Awakeners' message was: God wants *you* to be saved; *you* are important.

Conflicts between New Lights and Old Lights also produced important long-lasting effects. When parishioners chose the new churches over the established church, they were also refusing deference to the established order. Ordinarily, such middling people would "know their place" and would never have challenged those in authority, but the Awakening gave them sufficient assurance to make it possible even, as the Harvard faculty said, to "despise their own Ministers." It taught that the poorest and most ignorant may be chosen by God over the grandest Harvard graduate. Moreover, religious issues

were important enough to risk challenging the social order; where your soul was at stake, you could not stand by and duck responsibility.

The religious revivals became strong in the Southern colonies in the 1760s, as lively Baptist congregations grew up to challenge the established Church of England. In the Chesapeake the established church functioned as part of the social order. The great planters lived ostentatiously, in an aristocratic mode. Church services, like all other public meetings, offered opportunities to display their high status. They rode to church on their elegant horses and entered only when all the lesser people were seated. It was "not the Custom for Gentlemen to go into Church til Service is beginning, when they enter in a Body, in the same manner as they come out." Everyone who attended church received a dramatic demonstration of the social hierarchy.

Now the Baptists offered an alternative. Instead of elegant churches, they met in rough surroundings. Where the established church offered restraint in sermon and music, the Baptist meetings featured heartfelt, emotional preaching and singing. Instead of reinforcing the hierarchy, they insisted that all were equal in the sight of God. In a breathtaking break with Southern protocol, Baptists allowed slaves to join the church as equals. So outraged were the elite that they repeatedly tried to break up Baptist meetings with violence. Beatings were met with prayer and song, and ultimately only served to strengthen the new movement.

Women in all colonies were deeply affected by the revivals, which knew no distinction of age or sex. Many women experienced conversion, and many of the new churches allowed them a greater public sphere. Nathan Bowen, a Marblehead, Massachusetts, lawyer was disgusted because now "women and even Common Negroes take upon them to exhort their Betters even in the pulpit before large assemblies." At the same time, women's roles in the home took on new meaning. Sects such as the Quakers in the Middle Colonies had long emphasized that women's childrearing role was one of the most important functions of society. Children received their first knowledge of God and the world, as well as basic reading and writing skills, from their mothers. The future of the society was in the hands of women. Now, partly as a result of the revivals, childrearing received increasing emphasis and moved to the center of women's lives. Though in the short run this new emphasis made women content with their place, it also, by enhancing women's dominance of their own separate sphere, made future defiance possible.

Population and Immigration in the Eighteenth Century

Unparalleled growth transformed American life in the half-century before the Revolution. Because land was still available in the original grants, the settlements were able to perform a feat considered impossible: They absorbed huge numbers of new people without a drop in the standard of living. The population of the thirteen colonies doubled every twenty-five years in the century before the Revolution. Natural increase, an excess of births over deaths, was the source of much of the growth, particularly in the healthy North, but immigration was the great provider of new Americans, increasing the population tenfold from about 200,000 in 1700 to almost 2 million by 1770.

New towns filled empty spaces in the already settled areas, but most of the immigrants went to the frontier, where huge numbers settled in the west of Pennsylvania, Virginia, the Carolinas, and Georgia. On the day in 1769 when the land office at Fort Pitt began to open southwestern Pennsylvania to settlement, 2,790 people appeared to file applications; the rush into re-

gions further south was even greater. Georgia, the last of the thirteen colonies to be settled, saw its population increase by leaps and bounds.

Immigration was most intense between 1760 and the Revolution. New colonists came from the British Isles, many of them Irish, Scots-Irish, or Scottish Highlanders, and from the Rhineland and the Palatinate in Germany. The Scots-Irish may have been motivated to emigrate because of increasing economic hardship at home, but they and the Germans also responded to advertisements circulated in Europe promising property of their own and the chance to build for the future. Most from Britain came as individuals. The Germans arrived as families, in many cases with one family member signing a contract binding his labor for several years in order to pay his family's way.

Parts of America settled in this great mid-eighteenth-century immigration were very different in their ethnic composition from those settled in the earlier migrations. The influx of new ethnic groups contributed to the breakdown of deference. New people with different traditions were much less willing to agree on who society's "natural leaders" were than native-born colonists of English extraction.

In some frontier regions, farmers organized to challenge the rule of the eastern elites. As in Bacon's Rebellion almost a century earlier, they demanded protection from Indians, and roads and other government services in return for the taxes they paid. They knew the easterners looked down on them as "white savages" and considered their problems unimportant, so the frontiersmen organized to "regulate" their own lives. In the North Carolina and South Carolina backcountry, those in the movements in the 1760s called themselves Regulators to signal their concerns. The causes were different in every instance, but many of the colonies, including New York, New Jersey, Pennsylvania, and Vermont, found such movements on their frontiers in the 1760s and 1770s. Habits of deference were the first casualty of all such movements.

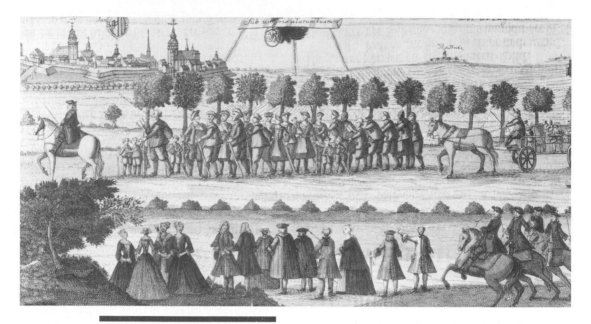

German immigrants to Georgia. The Salzburgers, persecuted Lutherans recruited to colonize the new colony of Georgia, are shown in this 1732 broadside. They were part of the flood of immigrants from all over Europe that flowed into Britain's American colonies in the eighteenth century. (New York Public Library, Rare Book Room, Astor, Lenox, and Tilden Foundations)

Economic Growth

The great bulk of the population lived by agriculture, which was a thriving, growing sector of the economy. Agricultural expansion allowed the colonies to be largely self-sufficient in food, and good incomes meant increasing importation of manufactured goods from England and from other countries.

Economic well-being led to a revolution in styles of life in eighteenth-century America. The homes of even the wealthiest planters in the seventeenth century had been no more than large farmhouses. Now rich Southern planters and city merchants began to build mansions with splendid downstairs rooms and great central halls and staircases. These homes were not only grander,

they were designed for a new style of life, one centered on society and entertainment. Pine furniture was replaced by fine cherry and walnut imported from Europe, and pottery dishes by china.

Though life in frontier areas was rough, the mid-century change in taste affected all levels of society in settled areas. Inventories, lists of possessions and their value, were often made when people died so that their estates could be divided up fairly. Inventories of humble farmers began to change about 1740 or 1750: Families that had formerly eaten their meals from wooden bowls began to have pottery. Chairs began to replace benches in these lists, and furniture of all sorts became more plentiful. Life at all levels became easier and more genteel for colonists from Europe and their descendants.

Benjamin Franklin recorded this transition in his own family. After describing how his wife worked with him in his printing shop, and scrimped to make the business a success, he wrote:

> My Breakfast was a long time Bread and Milk (no Tea), and I ate it out of a twopenny earthen Porringer with a Pewter Spoon. But mark how Luxury will enter Families, and make a Progress, in Spite of Principle. Being Call'd one Morning to breakfast, I found it in a China Bowl with a Spoon of Silver.

Franklin explained that his wife had bought the bowl and spoon without his knowledge,

> for which she had no other Excuse or Apology to make, but that she thought *her* Husband deserv'd a Silver Spoon and China Bowl as well as any of his Neighbors. This was the first Appearance of Plate and China in our House.

Prosperity did not extend to everyone. In the oldest and largest cities, especially the seaports of Boston, New York, and Philadelphia, those at the bottom of the economic heap were becoming poorer in the decades before 1776. Unemployment was widespread, and many jobs were only seasonal. Real wages (purchasing power of income) dropped for the poor, and the cities faced demands for public relief. Both prosperity and poverty helped to break down habits of deference, because both could make colonists dissatisfied with a static social order.

SLAVERY IN THE EIGHTEENTH CENTURY

Other groups were left out of the general prosperity. Good times were built partly on the backs of enslaved labor. The mainland Southern colonies had moved slowly and tentatively toward replacing the system of European indentured servants with slaves in the seventeenth century, although the number of enslaved Africans was still relatively small in 1700. In the eighteenth century, while indentured servants continued to arrive, there was a major shift to slavery as the preferred labor system, especially in the South.

Huge numbers of slaves, at least 250,000, were imported in the decades after 1700. These unwilling immigrants went through a series of terrifying and heartrending experiences. At least one-fifth died at sea. Many were sick when they arrived and would die early in their enslavement. The captains were careful to load their ships with cargoes from different parts of Africa so the captives could not talk together and plot rebellion at sea. In the eighteenth century most slaves destined for America came from Nigeria, the Bight of Biafra, and Angola. On their arrival, they went through the humiliating process of examination by prospective buyers. This poking, prodding inspection of their naked bodies might be repeated many times.

Then came transfer to a farm or plantation and unfamiliar work routines. Apparently, African slaves, faced with this overwhelming change, coped by denial, by running away repeatedly, or by refusing to understand what was required of them. Edward Kimber, who visited the Chesapeake in 1747, described the planters' frustration: A "new Negro must be broke . . . You would really be surpriz'd at their Perseverance; let an hundred Men shew him how to hoe, or drive a Wheelbarrow, he'll still take the one by the Bottom, and the other by the Wheel."

Slowly, the proportion of native-born slaves began to grow larger than those fresh from Africa, and the experience of slavery changed. Afro-American slaves responded to the demands made on them differently than did immigrants. Instead of denying the authority of the owners by running away or failing to understand orders, native-born slaves worked within the system to control it in their favor. In this they were able to have some success. The field hands worked in gangs of ten or twenty. If one of the gang were sick or old, the others would try to slow the work to a pace the weakest member could meet. While the master and his drivers literally held the whip hand, and beatings were common on the plantations, slaves had ways of frustrating the system's operation if they were driven too hard.

An Overseer Doing His Duty. This watercolor by Benjamin Henry Latrobe of a scene near Fredericksburg, Virginia, in 1798 graphically illustrates how the growing institution of slavery transformed Southern society. European-American female servants did not do field work; slave women did. Here the overseer takes his ease while he watches the women work. (Maryland Historical Society)

Native Americans' Response to Colonial Growth

Indians were also casualties of the rising prosperity. Absorption of huge numbers of immigrants from Europe and Africa was possible because of the decimation of Indian life east of the Appalachians. First devastated by European diseases to which they had no immunity, Indian populations were steadily reduced by war and expropriation, and even enslavement in the South. Tribes or tribal remnants moved away from the pressure of the European Americans and their marauding animals. Often, tribes that had grown too small to continue independently coalesced into new entities. Out of these movements great new Indian confederations grew up.

The South held large, powerful tribal structures. During the eighteenth century the Creeks withdrew from contact with the Europeans and worked through buffer tribes strategically placed between them and the colonists. Creek political structure was highly developed, based on a confederation in existence before the Europeans came. During the eighteenth century, annual council meetings of the Creeks brought together 4,000 to 5,000 officials and as many as 12,000 people. The Cherokees, placed in closer contact to the English frontier and the unscrupulous tactics of many of the traders and frontiersmen, suffered during the eighteenth century.

In the North, the Iroquois League, consisting of the Oneidas, Mohawks, Cayugas, Onondagas, Senecas, and, after the murderous Carolina frontier wars in the early eighteenth century, the Tuscaroras, built a strong confederation. The league formed a series of relationships known as the Covenant Chain with other Indian tribes and with many of the colonies. The colonies signed treaties with the Iroquois League and thereby joined the Covenant Chain in order to streamline their Indian diplomacy. Rather than attempt to understand and work through the hundreds of different Indian political relationships, the colonial governments preferred to conduct Indian affairs through one agency: the Iroquois League.

This relationship involved give-and-take on both sides, and very subtle diplomacy. Several times, representatives of most of the colonies met at Albany for great council meetings with the Iroquois that saw elaborate ceremony punctuated with exchanges of gifts. Council sessions with the Iroquois were the only times representatives of the colonies came together for any joint purpose. Working through the Covenant Chain meant that the colonial governments recognized Iroquois League sovereignty and protection of many tribes and much of the territory in the Northeast. Often the Iroquois, caught between their obligations to their Indian clients and the pressure exerted by the ever-expanding European frontier, forced Indians to give up land or were helpless to stop injustice. Ultimately, the Covenant Chain broke down under this pressure.

The Ohio Valley appealed to displaced Indians. Many groups, tired of being pushed west in small moves every few years as the European frontier grew, decided to move far beyond the line of settlement into this fertile region. Here an unprecedented development took place. Indians who had formerly been hostile to each other came to see that all shared a similar plight. A new pan-Indian sentiment grew up that promised concerted action in the face of the threat encroaching from the East.

As in the Great Awakening, this new sense of determination grew out of a religious revival. Neolin, the Delaware Prophet, had had a mystical revelation about which path the Indians must follow. He taught that they had brought on their misfortunes by giving up their old ways. They must strictly avoid alcohol, wear nothing but animal skins, and throw away their guns and live by hunting with bow and arrow. All the old skills must be re-created, and the old rituals reinstated. Neolin was able to weave together many disparate Indian traditions and included some Christian elements, such as the idea of one great God. His was the first of many such revival movements that responded to the Indians' losses. Often, by giving Indians a sense of renewed purpose, they sparked movements of armed resistance.

The restoration of native life called for by Neolin was not allowed time to develop. In moving beyond the frontier, Indians had hoped they would be able once again to take up their old ways, but the fertile Ohio Valley beckoned to the flood of settlers that soon filled the region east of the mountains. More important, the tribes found themselves in an arena of imperial conflict. Their fate was bound up in the policies of France and England and the continuing war between those empires.

The French and Indian War

England and France were engaged throughout the entire eighteenth century in a struggle for dominion. Each nation headed a European alliance system delicately calculated to balance that of the other. Time and again, competition erupted into war as events in Europe temporarily gave one or the other an edge. Because Britain and France each held extensive territory in North America and the West Indies, the colonists, much against their will, were drawn into these imperial wars.

The colonists' resentment can be seen in the names they gave the conflicts. While they were known in Europe by names that pointed to the imperial concerns for which they were fought, such as the War of the Austrian Succession, the Americans named the wars after the British monarchs who had forced the colonists into their fights: King William's War (1689–97), Queen Anne's War (1702–13), and King George's War (1744–48). The climax of this series, the French and Indian War (1754–63), which spread to Europe in 1756 and was called the Seven Years' War there, resulted in the expulsion of France from the continent of North America.

In the middle of the eighteenth century, on the eve of the French and Indian War, France

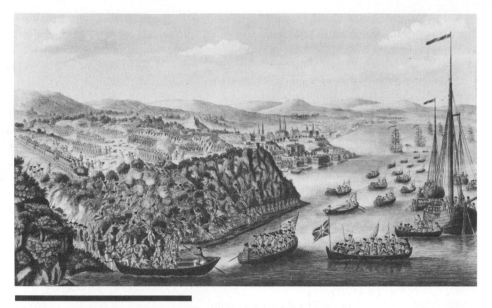

The Battle of Quebec, 1759. English reports celebrated the victorious surprise attack on the supposedly unscalable Plains of Abraham above the city where the French army was lodged. (Royal Ontario Museum, Toronto, Canada)

had looked much stronger in North America. Whereas the English colonies clung to the edge of the continent, France claimed much of the interior on the basis of early explorations. French fur traders moved throughout the vast interior of North America. French missionaries had converted many Indians, who became that empire's staunch allies. The French had access to the Mississippi River, the continent's central artery of trade and communications. Moreover, France was allied to Spain, whose American empire was even more extensive.

France's advantages, however, were more apparent than real. Its territories were thinly populated, and supply lines to the interior could be cut off by capturing Quebec. The English, with heavy and growing concentrations of population, were stronger than they looked. Pressure of numbers meant the colonists increasingly looked to the fertile land of the Ohio Valley beyond the Appalachian Mountain chain. It was here that the first clashes of the French and Indian War occurred. French agents began to build forts in the Ohio Valley to forestall English advance. A

Virginia militia force, led by the young George Washington in 1754, failed to push the French out, so regular British troops under Major General Edward Braddock were sent a year later to teach both the French and the colonists a lesson.

Indians in the Ohio Valley found themselves once again on the front lines. Tribes such as the Delawares had repeatedly been pushed back by the advance of European settlement and knew that an English victory over France would accelerate that process. However, the English were generous with trade goods, and the Indians knew the value of being on the winning side. The Delawares, still a numerous tribe, approached General Braddock to offer support against France if he would guarantee their right to live in the Ohio Valley after an English victory. Braddock, arrogantly underestimating both his allies and his foes, said: "No Savage Should Inherit the Land." The Delawares remained neutral, and Braddock, with most of his force, was slaughtered.

Meanwhile, representatives of six colonies, fully aware of the importance of Indian aid in the struggle against France, met with the Iroquois in

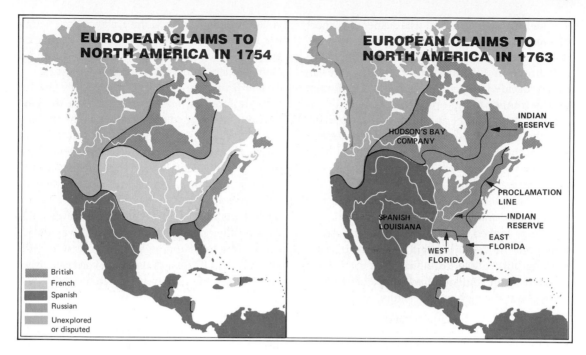

EUROPEAN CLAIMS TO NORTH AMERICA IN 1754

British
French
Spanish
Russian
Unexplored or disputed

EUROPEAN CLAIMS TO NORTH AMERICA IN 1763

HUDSON'S BAY COMPANY

INDIAN RESERVE

PROCLAMATION LINE

INDIAN RESERVE

SPANISH LOUISIANA

EAST FLORIDA

WEST FLORIDA

a grand council meeting in Albany in 1754. Though the Iroquois were initially unmoved by colonists' appeals, the conference provided an opportunity for colonial representatives to discuss their mutual problems. Here Benjamin Franklin unveiled the first plan to bring the European Americans together in a union through which they would meet periodically and build a sense of common commitment. The plan did not immediately bear fruit, but it laid the foundation for such planning in the future.

Braddock's defeat was followed by a series of British military failures in the Great Lakes and the northwest frontier that seemed to lay New York and New England open to French attack. At this point, British strategy changed dramatically. A brilliant young politician, William Pitt, was called to head the English government in 1757. He decided to reverse the plan of previous imperial wars and make North America the main focus of operations, leaving his allies to oppose France in Europe. Unprecedented amounts of money were raised, and troops and supplies were poured into America. A series of victories

was capped by the fall of the "invincible" fortress of Quebec in 1759. French bases in North America could now be "starved" into submission, as their access to weapons, ammunition, and other vital stores was cut off.

The Treaty of Paris, signed in 1763, recognized British control of all of North America east of the Mississippi River except for New Orleans, which went to Spain. The territory of British America was increased manyfold, and the British empire achieved new heights of glory. Twenty years later, in 1783, that empire lay in ruins.

EFFECTS OF THE WAR Signs of future trouble were evident even in the rejoicing of 1763, for the war had revealed to both the British and the American colonists that the empire had become in reality very different from what it was on paper. The British, believing the Americans unruly, sought to tighten the empire's control of colonial administration. Now, with the need to incorporate vast new territories into the colonies, and with the fear of France removed, such tightening would at last be possible.

The British government was desperately short of money. Not only had the war been tremendously costly, but George III, who had come to the throne in 1760 just after the American victories, decided to keep an army of 10,000 men on the frontier to police the vast new territories acquired from France and to control the Indians and the French who remained there. It seemed fair that the colonists pay part of the costs. After all, they were the beneficiaries of the war, and the army was for their protection. Moreover, the Americans were distinctly undertaxed. English citizens paid much heavier taxes.

Things looked very different from the American point of view. England's wars had meant nothing but trouble for the colonies. Many had suffered from Indian attacks on the frontier throughout the eighteenth century, and colonies had been called on time and again to provide troops and money for defense. The 10,000-man standing army also seemed potentially more dangerous than helpful. English tradition held that a monarch who maintained an army in peacetime was a potential tyrant. The army could just as easily be turned against the colonists.

The first test of the army's usefulness came as colonists began to pour into the newly won area beyond the Appalachians, and Indians responded to this encroachment. The frontier was inflamed in 1763 by a series of uprisings that together are known as Pontiac's Rebellion. Neolin's preaching gave Indians a sense of mission in this defiance.

General Jeffrey Amherst, commander of British forces in America, considered the old Indian diplomacy with its gift giving a symptom of colonial cowardice. Rather than "bribe" the Indians, he would force them, since they could no longer play off the French against the English, to obey his will. Amherst pursued a policy of "extirpation," ordering his men to "put to death all that fall into your hands." He introduced germ warfare, by sending blankets infected with smallpox among the Delawares. The captain who delivered the blankets remarked, "I hope it will have the desired effect." He was not disappointed, as a violent epidemic struck the Delawares. Though the Indian uprising was put down, it inflicted great destruction on the frontier and caused many settlers to retreat to established areas.

The British government, alarmed by the Indian warfare and not wishing to have the new territories developed haphazardly as the thirteen colonies had been, issued the Proclamation of 1763. This established a line of settlement, roughly equivalent to the edge of established farms and villages, beyond which the colonists were forbidden to go. It was meant to reassure the Indians and prevent expansion of the colonies until a fully thought-through policy was developed. Now the standing army was seen in a different light: It was preventing colonists from moving into the rich area they thought the war had won for them. The colonists wondered whose interests the British cared about.

The end of the French and Indian War in 1763 also brought changes in the feelings of the American colonists toward Britain. The colonists had been accustomed to thinking of themselves as British, and Americans looked to Britain for culture and trade. But the war brought individual Americans and Englishmen together, and the face-to-face meeting produced unexpected results. The British army was composed of aristocratic officers, who bought their commissions, and troops who were seen as the dregs of society. The troops were kept in line by a brutal system of discipline that prescribed the death penalty for relatively minor offenses and hundreds, sometimes even thousands, of whip lashes on the bare back for others. The Americans saw the officers as arrogant, brutal, and foppish, and the swearing, immoral troops disgusted the colonial militiamen who served with them. The revulsion Americans felt for the imperial army intensified when the troops were stationed in colonial cities, and culminated in the Boston Massacre.

For their part, the British came away with contempt for the Americans, who were seen as undisciplined, cowardly, and self-indulgent. Smuggling in wartime, sometimes even trading with the enemy, was seen as contemptible.

Despite the victories of the recent war, each side saw the other's army as deeply flawed, a miscalculation that may have led to a willingness to go to war in 1776. Each side thought the other incapable of mounting a sustained campaign.

Novel Taxation

The colonists did not have long to wait before they saw what England, now freed of the French menace, intended to do with its American plantations. The colonies had been founded as mercantilist extensions of England. Their purpose had been to serve the needs of the parent country by providing raw materials and buying finished products. Mercantilism held that the country which could fill most of its needs without going outside its own closed circle of relations would be the strongest. Dependence on outside countries for essential commodities spelled weakness.

The Navigation Acts, the laws made by the British Parliament through which the empire regulated colonial trade and collected customs duties, were regularly evaded in America both by smuggling and by paying bribes. When military officers returned to England and described American disregard for the law, the government determined to tighten American administration and see that the Navigation Acts were enforced. Efforts to pass more effective laws and provide more efficient administration brought Parliament directly into conflict with the claims of the colonial assemblies. The first clashes were over taxation.

Though trade between Britain and America was strong and growing, the government saw the colonial system as hopelessly out of control. Determined to bring order and rationality to the system, the royal government began to pass new laws for the colonies. The three immediate goals were to gain revenue to relieve the hard-pressed English taxpayer, to provide a degree of independence for English officials in America, and to see that the laws, especially those against smuggling, were enforced.

THE SUGAR ACT The Revenue Act of 1764, usually called the Sugar Act, sought to tighten up the customs service. To do so, it met one of the colonists' major objections: The Navigation Acts were such a tangle of regulations, and the duties so high, that if they were really enforced trade would stop altogether. The Sugar Act cut in half the tax on molasses, one of the staples of the New England–West Indies trade, and provided a new set of procedures to see that it was collected.

A swarm of officials entered the colonies to administer the new programs, and Americans increasingly felt the presence of the empire in their lives. Moreover, the tightening up of imperial regulation meant use of special vice-admiralty courts, in which judges made decisions without juries (colonial juries were notorious for refusing to convict smugglers), and the right of the accused to confront his accusers in open court was not honored. It seemed to colonists that the British government was setting up special procedures for Americans as if they were no longer full British citizens. Outraged colonists began an informal boycott of English goods in protest.

THE STAMP ACT Soon news came that a new form of tax was to be imposed on the colonies: a stamp tax on all sorts of documents, from deeds and court papers to newspapers and almanacs. The British government, in deciding to impose this tax in the Stamp Act of 1765, pointed out that not only were Americans taxed much less heavily than the English, but British subjects had been paying this form of tax for decades. In American eyes that was not the point. The Sugar Act and the Stamp Act were both troubling for the same reason: They were novel taxes imposed for new purposes. The colonists argued that all former taxation had been for the regulation of trade, which the British government had the right to do. Now the government wanted to collect taxes in order to raise revenue, and colonial leaders believed this was illegal without the colonists' consent.

Constitutional Challenges

New measures changing the colonial relationship forced the colonists to think about fundamental questions, especially about the place in the empire of the thirteen colonies and the governments they had evolved. In the changed situation after 1763, Americans began to develop a theory of their relationship to Britain that would fit the actual conditions of the 1760s rather than those of a century earlier. In this rethinking, colonial leaders drew on several English traditions concerning the British constitution and the rights of its citizens.

One of these was the English common law tradition, which guaranteed every British subject certain rights, such as the right to trial by a jury of one's peers in the district where the crime was committed. The colonists were firmly committed to the belief that they were full British citizens, although they lived across the ocean. Now it seemed that the king and his ministers sought to treat Anglo-Americans as less than citizens, to deprive them of some of those basic rights by the use of vice-admiralty courts, and by threatening to move trials away from sympathetic colonial juries.

Another fundamental tradition held that British citizens could not be taxed without the consent of their representatives. The British government recognized this right, but argued that the new taxes did not violate it. Parliament operated on the principle of virtual representation. This meant that even though most Englishmen and all women were denied the right to vote for members of Parliament, all were virtually rep-

resented because every MP spoke for the interests of the entire nation. Colonial experience had led to a different concept. The Americans argued for a theory of representation in which each member of the assembly represented the interests of a specific set of people who elected him. Therefore, the colonists could not consider themselves represented by the English Parliament. Their representatives sat in the thirteen colonial assemblies.

Over the previous half-century, the colonies had become used to a situation close to self-government. Most royal governors were controlled by colonial assemblies who paid their salaries. Colonial leaders had come to think of the assemblies as similar to the House of Commons. The Massachusetts Assembly declared in 1770 that it had "the same inherent rights in this province as the house of commons in Great Britain." The assemblies were seen as directly answerable to the king. Now the actions of Parliament and the king combined to challenge colonists' conceptions of representation and the place of their assemblies in the structure of royal government.

As novel taxes were imposed, concerned leaders all over the colonies formed groups known as the Sons of Liberty to meet and correspond to interpret British actions. Under this examination, England's policies looked sinister. Interpretation of government actions was based on a third fundamental tradition that sprang from the constitutional battles of the English Civil War of the 1640s and the Glorious Revolution of 1688. This tradition, developed in eighteenth-century England by a group of dissenting commentators known as the Real Whigs, argued that a powerful government headed by a monarch is always dangerous, because such governments have a strong, almost irresistible tendency to become tyrannical. The Real Whigs, especially John Trenchard and Thomas Gordon in their essays *Cato's Letters*, set up a series of signposts by which to judge whether a government was becoming tyrannical, and their writings were widely reprinted and avidly read in America.

Pro Patria
The first Man that either
distributes or makes use of Stampt
Paper, let him take Care of
his House, Person, & Effects.
Vox Populi;
We Dare

Stamps used by the English government in 1765. The Sons of Liberty's warning against allowing the stamps to be used was seriously meant, as people throughout the colonies discovered.

One sure danger sign was the creation of a standing army in peacetime. Another was increased and novel taxation. A third was attacks on the right of free assemblies to meet. Another symptom was attacks on the freedom of the press. Colonists seemed to see the Real Whigs' warning signs in every action of the royal government. The standing army, units of which were increasingly appearing in the East, in Boston and other cities, as well as on the frontier; the new taxes and regulations—especially the Stamp Act—all seemed to undermine basic rights. Why did the government, needing money, decide to tax newspapers with the Stamp Act, for example? Freedom of the press and the people's right to know what was going on seemed to be under attack.

Colonial leaders argued that the colonists had to make a stand, because an important principle was at stake. If they appeared to concede that Parliament could levy new taxes without the consent of those taxed, then no property was safe. If they could add a tax of a penny, they could add a tax of a shilling or a pound, or take away citizens' property altogether. This is what colonists meant when they said the British aimed to make slaves of them.

THE STAMP ACT CONGRESS Because such an important principle was at stake, the colonists, with the Sons of Liberty to coordinate activities, began to act. Representatives of nine colonies met in New York in October 1765. The Stamp Act Congress helped cement colonial resolve to resist. The Americans were already boycotting English goods. Mobs had threatened those men, many of them prominent, who had been selected by the British to collect the stamp tax. In some cases houses were destroyed, as Thomas Hutchinson's was in Boston, and many collectors were hanged in effigy. Virtually all got the message and resigned their commissions. By the time the Stamp Act paraphernalia landed in America, the tax was a dead letter. No one would administer it and life went on as usual.

Many in England were outraged by this defiance, particularly since it involved mob action, but others were sympathetic to the colonists' arguments. British merchants in particular called on Parliament to reconsider because their trade had been drastically cut by the boycott. Benjamin Franklin was in England in 1766, and he told Parliament that the Americans were not disloyal, nor were they unwilling to do their share. In attempting to calm the situation, he argued that colonists would willingly pay external taxes, those collected as cargoes entered the country, but found the new internal taxes, collected inside the colonies, offensive.

The government accepted this distinction and, partly because of political changes in London that had nothing to do with America, repealed the Stamp Act in 1766. Repeal was accompanied by a Declaratory Act that stated Parliament had the right to legislate for the colonies "in all cases whatsoever," but the Americans felt they had won a great victory.

Other problems remained, however. In 1765 the government had also passed a Quartering Act, requiring the colonies to provide barracks for the British army in America, and to furnish some provisions. This was a new tax in another form, and added to the colonists' unease about the presence of the standing army among them. When New York refused to comply, the royal government punished that colony, in 1767, by refusing to allow the assembly to meet. Once again, the Real Whigs' warnings seemed to be fulfilled. The royal government took the opportunity to cancel the right of the people's representatives to meet, an attack on fundamental rights. A meeting of Virginia freeholders denounced the forbidding of the New York Assembly as demonstrating "a fatal tendency . . . destructive of the Liberty of a free People."

The Townshend Acts, 1767

The British government was less effective than it might have been during the crisis period of the 1760s and early 1770s because of constant changes in leadership. Charles Townshend, a brilliant but erratic man, took control of the government early in 1767. He renewed the effort to make the colonies pay part of the expense of empire and to free British officials in America from control by colonial legislatures who paid their salaries. He decided to take the colonists

at their word, as given by Benjamin Franklin, and designed a new set of external taxes. These duties, on lead, paint, paper, glass, and tea, were to be collected at the point of entry into America and were to raise revenue that would be used to pay officials' salaries.

Now the trouble sown by Franklin's formula became apparent. The internal/external distinction had never been the colonists' concern. They objected to taxes for collection of revenue rather than regulation of trade. It was the new *purpose* of taxation rather than the way in which it was collected that mattered. Reaction to the Townshend Acts was surprisingly slow. Many hoped that merely petitioning the king and pointing out the acts' injustice would turn policy around. But as the new customs commissioners began to arrive in Boston, that city's radical leaders, Samuel Adams and James Otis, pushed a circular letter, to be sent to the legislatures of all the colonies, through the assembly. It did not suggest any particular program, merely that the colonies should once again prepare a joint reply. In response, the Virginia House of Burgesses sent around an even more radical letter calling for concerted action.

The year 1768 saw an outpouring of newspaper articles on resistance, and many popular demonstrations in Boston. Governor Francis Bernard, on orders from London, directed the Massachusetts legislature to rescind the circular letter. When they refused three times, he closed the assembly and called for troops to be sent to Boston to restore order, setting the stage for a new level of violence culminating in the Boston Massacre of 1770.

The immediate problem for colonial leaders was achieving repeal of the Townshend Acts. Failure to protest effectively would mean Britain could consider the principle of taxation for revenue to have been established. Agreements not to consume British goods were made fairly easily, but radical leaders wanted much more effective nonimportation codes. American merchants resisted, pointing out that importing and selling goods was their livelihood, but pressure grew until nonimportation became policy throughout the colonies. Local committees reinforced the agreements by seeking out anyone suspected of breaking them. Their names were published in the newspaper and their businesses boycotted. In extreme cases, offenders were tarred and feathered.

The nonimportation agreements were a rational use of economic power. American trade was important to Britain, and the colonists hoped to bring intolerable pressure on the government from injured merchants there. But there was more to the movement than that. Nonconsumption and nonimportation were used to build a new sense of purpose and of Americanness. British goods were associated with luxury and foolish chasing after fashionable "superfluities." Now Americans began to dress in homemade clothes made of homespun fabrics, and native food and drink replaced tea, wine, and other imported luxuries. Calls for the development of industries to free Americans of dependence on Europe echoed through the colonies. They were to be true to their own natures as sturdy, hardworking, independent citizens.

Women played important roles in this campaign. Most often they were the ones who coped with the problem of finding and preparing substitutes for imported goods. Women took up spinning and weaving as patriotic activities and made the boycotts work. Increasingly, women, both patriots and loyalists, became involved in the political debate. Patriot women's economic contribution was crucial to the resistance program, and women made informed choices as they took sides.

The boycott was successful, and it soon seemed that the colonists had won their point. In 1770 yet another new ministry, this time under Lord Frederick North, repealed the Townshend Acts, leaving only the tax on tea in effect. American rejection of British products had had an impact, but repeal also recognized that the law had been poorly thought through. To tax the products of British industry as they were exported into British colonies could only cut down on trade and revenue. In fact, the taxes had always cost more to collect than they brought in.

Most Americans thought the crisis was now over. Nonimportation was given up and the tax on tea accepted for three years. There were some danger signs to disturb the general peace. One was that the goal of greater independence for royal officials, now paid from the tax on tea, had been achieved. Royal governors no longer feared they would have their funds cut off if they displeased colonial assemblies.

Another danger sign grew out of an attack on a customs ship, the *Gaspée*, by a Rhode Island mob in 1772. Though the culprits were not caught, the ministry made clear that in future they intended to take such offenders into Canada or even to England to be tried away from lenient colonial juries. This was such a fundamental assault on the jury trial system, which required accusers to confront the accused in open court in the place where the crime was committed, that in 1773 the colonies, led by the Virginia House of Burgesses, appointed Committees of Correspondence. If Britain acted against the colonists' rights and liberties, the committees would be ready to interpret such actions and call for defiance.

The Boston Tea Party and the Coercive Acts

The Committees of Correspondence soon had something to interpret: the Tea Act of 1773. The British government, seeking to bail out the East India Company, which had a huge surplus of tea, gave it a monopoly of the tea trade with America. Since the company could now sell directly to America and avoid the payment of taxes and middlemen's fees in England, colonists would actually be able to buy their tea at a lower price. Everyone would benefit, or so the ministry thought. The colonists, already suspicious, fixed on the grant of a monopoly, however. They believed that elimination of competition meant, once again, the danger of enslavement. Eventually, the company could set the price at any

The Boston Tea Party, from W. D. Cooper's *History of North America*, published in London in 1789. The proud British lion on the ship's prow occupies the center of the picture, but the Americans, many symbolically dressed as Indians, control the situation. (Library of Congress)

level they chose and the Americans would have to pay. Today it was tea. Tomorrow it might be some essential commodity. The principle was important.

The colonists agreed not to accept any of the East India Company tea, and the ships carrying it were turned away all along the coast. Only in Boston did this strategy meet a stumbling block in the form of the royal governor, Thomas Hutchinson. Although Hutchinson was a native-born Massachusetts man, he was completely out of sympathy with the radicals' methods of operation. He thought the tax on tea wrong, and had repeatedly argued to the British government for its repeal, but he was determined to enforce the law, which held that once a ship entered harbor, customs duties must be paid on its cargo before it could be allowed to leave. The owner of the tea ships begged Hutchinson to allow him simply to leave the harbor as ships had done elsewhere,

but Hutchinson was adamant. The result was that in December 1773, a well-disciplined crowd of Bostonians, some "dressed in the Indian manner," boarded the ships and threw the tea into the harbor.

The tea was worth £10,000, a small fortune. Destruction of property on this scale took people's breath away on both sides of the Atlantic. Many Americans felt the owners should be compensated. Compensation would save the principle and make the action seem more legal. Other colonists drew back in horror. In associating themselves with the resistance movement, they had not expected such outlawry. In England even the friends of America were filled with revulsion and anger.

The royal government sought to take advantage of this feeling in punishing Boston for the tea party, and in doing so misread the nature of American public opinion. They began to visualize the radical movement as a kind of infection centered in Boston. If Boston could be cut off from the other colonies and fair punishment administered, the whole movement might simply die out. Lord North saw that the stakes were extremely high:

> We are not entering into a dispute between internal and external taxes, not between taxes laid for the purpose of revenues and taxes laid for the regulation of trade, not between representation and taxation, or legislation and taxation; but we are now to dispute whether we have, or have not any authority in that country.

When the punishment came, in a series of acts in 1774 known in England as the Coercive Acts and labeled the Intolerable Acts by the Americans, the extent of the ministers' miscalculation became clear. The acts were simply too extreme, and they came too long after the event. Rather than isolating Boston from more law-abiding colonies, the acts served to strengthen colonial solidarity. The cause of Massachusetts was seen as the cause of all.

The Intolerable Acts confirmed colonial suspicions that the underlying goal of the royal government was to do away with self-government and deny the colonists the rights of British subjects. The first act closed the port of Boston to all trade, a dire blow to the colony's economic life, which depended on commerce. The second took away two of Massachusetts's cherished rights of self-government by removing power to elect the governor's council from the assembly and giving it to the king, and forbidding town meetings, essential democratic institutions, except to elect town officials. The third act stipulated that any British official or soldier accused of a crime punishable by death could be sent to Nova Scotia or England for trial. Finally, the fourth act brought the army, removed after the Boston Massacre, back to the city. Not only were the troops back, but their commander, General Thomas Gage, was made governor. To colonists steeped in the Real Whig tradition, all the warning signs of tyranny were now present.

THE QUEBEC ACT The colonies rose to Massachusetts's aid in the face of what the Virginia House of Burgesses called a "hostile invasion," sending relief supplies overland to feed and sustain the settlers. The outpouring of support was fueled partly by another act passed early in 1774 by the British Parliament: the Quebec Act. England had spent eleven years designing a government for France's American territories acquired in 1763. Now, intending an enlightened policy, the ministry planned a regime that would be acceptable to the former French subjects. Accordingly, the Quebec Act accepted French law in the region, which extended south to the Ohio River, and gave the Roman Catholic church special status.

The colonists were horrified. Not only did the French system have no representative assemblies, the fundamental right to trial by jury was to be denied the territory's inhabitants. Added to these inroads on the rights of British subjects was recognition of the Catholic church, an institution that many of the colonists saw as going hand-in-hand with tyranny. Colonists who wanted to move into the rich Northwest Territory would do so at the expense of their liberties. No further proof that the British government intended to erect a tyranny in its American colonies was needed. Let the thirteen colonies beware.

The Continental Congress, 1774

So serious had the situation become that the Committees of Correspondence proposed a meeting of representatives from all colonies to discuss the next move. The first Continental Congress in Philadelphia in September 1774 was a momentous event, and delegates were aware of that fact. Most of the men present had only heard about their counterparts in other colonies, and the first weeks were spent taking each others' measure. Only nine of the fifty-six delegates had been at the Stamp Act Congress, and they had much to learn about one another. At first glance, they seemed to represent extremely different societies. The aristocratic planters from South Carolina were attended by liveried slaves. At the other extreme was Sam Adams, whose friends had gotten together and bought him a new plain black suit so he would not disgrace Massachusetts by his shabbiness. Uppermost in most minds as they got acquainted was whether they would actually be able to work together. Could they trust each other?

Delegates were not thinking in terms of war. Most feared that alternative, believing America could never win, though many talked of it outside the formal sessions. Their concern in 1774 was to find a way to live within the British empire. They wanted to enunciate a set of principles that would give the king his due, including the right to regulate the empire's trade, and at the same time protect colonists' liberties. Many leaders had begun to hope for a situation in which the colonies would be directly under the king, with the assemblies acting as separate parliaments.

Governor Thomas Hutchinson of Massachusetts believed such a status was impossible. He had told the General Court in 1773, "I know of no line that can be drawn between the supreme authority of Parliament and the total independence of the colonies." Delegates to the Continental Congress hoped to be able to prove Hutchinson wrong. They, like the people they represented, still believed the British constitution to be the foundation of the best and freest government on earth, and one within whose laws they wanted to live. Moreover, they continued to think of themselves as orderly, law-abiding people.

The most pressing problem facing the Continental Congress was to overturn the Intolerable Acts. Spurred on by the Suffolk Resolves, passed by Suffolk County in Massachusetts and carried to the congress urgently by Paul Revere, the del-

egates voted not only a return to nonconsumption and nonimportation, but also a ban on exports. This was a hard commitment to make. Merchants would suffer, as they had earlier, and those colonies that lived by exporting their crops to England, particularly the Southern agricultural colonies, would make a great sacrifice, but the congress agreed. Committees were to be set up in every village and town to see that the agreements were honored. The colonists continued to regard their self-denial as an exercise of virtue, an expression of their own special American strength of character. Where colonists did not accept this reasoning, dissent was crushed by the local committees.

The first Continental Congress dispersed in October 1774 with a sense of danger averted. John Adams confided to his diary as he left the city: "It is not very likely that I shall ever see this Part of the World again." Yet in a few short months the second congress was assembling in Philadelphia. Adams could not know that not only would the developing crisis bring him back to Philadelphia many times, but ultimately he would serve there as the president of the new nation.

First Shots

With the army back in Boston as ordered by the 1774 Intolerable Acts, the situation there grew more tense every day. General Gage, seeing indisputable evidence of the American militia's growing preparations for resistance, sent desperate reports to London, begging that the Intolerable Acts be repealed and that the army be enlarged. He pointed out that he lacked the forces to put down a rebellion, and hoped that the most radical leaders would be undercut by conciliation. The ministry treated his messages with contempt, telling him his enemy was merely a "rude

Lexington and Concord. Amos Doolittle did a series of engravings illustrating the British attempt to confiscate the arsenal at Concord and the resulting clashes with colonial militias at Lexington and Concord in April 1775. This plate shows the beleaguered soldiers leaving the scene of destruction, and marching back to Boston through the sniper fire of expert colonial marksmen. (Connecticut Historical Society)

Rabble" and therefore "cannot be very formidable." Fearing that Gage's nerve had broken, they sent three generals to work under him: Major Generals Henry Clinton, William Howe, and John Burgoyne. Howe would take over as commander in chief in October 1775.

To strengthen his position, Gage decided to secure the munitions stores in Concord and Worcester. His earlier drive to seize ammunition and cannon from Charlestown and Cambridge in September 1774 had almost precipitated a crisis, with militiamen coming in defiance from as far away as Connecticut. Now his move toward Concord in April 1775 resulted in the first exchange of gunfire between colonial militias and the British army. Paul Revere had organized a network

of unemployed Boston artisans who followed every movement of the redcoats. Thus the militias in Lexington and Concord were forewarned. The British soldiers were forced back to Boston through sixteen miles of sniper fire and were badly shaken by their first encounter with the "rude Rabble."

News of the shots fired at Lexington and Concord spread over the colonies. Each town that received the information rushed it to the next. Written across the packet arriving in Charleston, South Carolina, was: "We send you momentous intelligence, this instant received." The British began to realize that their estimates based on colonists' conduct in the French and Indian War might have to be revised. General Gage wrote that "these people show a spirit and conduct against us that they never showed against the French, and everybody has judged them from their former appearance and behavior, which has led many into great mistakes."

The second Continental Congress, called before the fighting broke out, assembled as the news was being absorbed, on May 10, 1775. Despite all that had happened, it was to be more than a year before the subject of independence was formally broached there, for, despite the fact that war was on, the goals for which they fought were still in doubt. Some new constitutional status within the British empire still seemed possible. Many still believed in the king, arguing that it was the ministers around him who persecuted the colonies. Accordingly, in July 1775 the Olive Branch Petition was sent to George III affirming American loyalty and asking him to take charge of finding a constitutional solution. The king's answer was to declare the colonies in "an open and avowed rebellion."

WASHINGTON TAKES COMMAND Meanwhile, the congress, still hoping for peace, prepared for war. A call for creation of an army went out, and on June 15, 1775, George Washington was named commanding general. As these decisions were made, violence once again flared up in Boston. General Gage decided to take and fortify the Dorchester Heights, which overlooked Boston and could render the city vulnerable. The Americans, hearing of the plan, decided to preempt him by seizing Bunker Hill and then moving to Dorchester Heights. When the two forces clashed, the British were successful, in that the Americans did withdraw, but the victory cost the redcoats dearly. This first full battle of the Revolutionary War resulted in 226 dead and 808 wounded on the British side, 140 deaths and 271 wounded among the colonial militia. One British general quipped that the "Americans' plan ought to be to lose a battle every week, till the British army was reduced to nothing."

George Washington arrived in Cambridge to take up his command two weeks after the battle of Bunker Hill, on July 2, 1775. He was conscious of the great problems facing the American side. The first necessary step was to whip the men besieging the British army in Boston into a recognizable military force. In a bold stroke, he and his men succeeded in taking and fortifying Dorchester Heights, arming the positions with heavy weapons taken by Ethan Allen and Benedict Arnold in daring attacks on British posts at Ticonderoga and Crown Point on Lake Champlain.

General Howe had long hated having his army cooped up in Boston. He had already decided to make the colonies' midsection his base of operations. Washington's seizure of the Heights hurried the British departure. They left in March 1776, hastily and in poor order. With the redcoats out of Boston, the first phase of British policy, the strategy of containing the infection of independence in Massachusetts, was over. At the same time, the Continental Congress was taking the first steps toward openly declaring separation from Britain.

Tom Paine's *Common Sense*

Thomas Paine arrived from England in 1774; he established himself among Philadelphia's artisan community and began to write articles and editorials for newspapers. Probably because he had come in from outside, and because he had seen the operation of the English system as a tax collector before emigrating, he was able to cut through the slowly developing debate and convince the Americans that independence, not some new status within the British empire, was

Thomas Paine. This 1783 mezzotint by James Watson is based on a painting by Charles Willson Peale. (National Portrait Gallery, Smithsonian Institution, Washington, D.C.)

what they wanted. His book *Common Sense*, published in January 1776, was the great best-seller of the eighteenth century. It was so popular because its points were made clearly in the language of the people (John Adams thought the writing coarse and offensive), and its price kept low. More important, *Common Sense* crystallized popular thought. Paine made people see that independence was already in their minds, though not yet formulated.

Tom Paine knew his audience; he set the pamphlet up in the form of a sermon, which he knew would suit Americans. The first step in his argument was to disabuse his readers of the notion that the British system was something special, that they should want to continue as part of the empire. Moderates had been hoping the colonies could remain as thirteen dominions under the king, with the colonial legislatures as separate parliaments. Paine exploded this hope. He placed the blame for the colonists' troubles not on Parliament or the ministry but squarely on George III, the "Royal Brute of Britain." The English royal

family was not ordained by God. Rather, Paine argued, it came to the throne with the invasion of William the Conqueror in 1066. Thus the king owed his title to "a French bastard landing with an armed banditti . . . The plain truth is, that the antiquity of English monarchy will not bear looking into." Paine used history, reason, and the Bible to argue that not only was the British system corrupt, monarchy was a bad form of government. He used Old Testament examples to demonstrate that God did not favor kingship.

The second step was to shift people's focus away from fear of consequences to looking at how much could be accomplished. America was not to be a stepchild of Europe. Rather, this continent was to give birth to a whole new system. Europe was worn out and degenerate. The Americans were the wave of the future. In one of his most memorable phrases Paine argued that "freedom hath been hunted round the globe." Only the Americans still had the power to rescue liberty from encroaching tyranny and thus realize their own destiny: "We have it in our power to begin the world over again."

Paine's genius was that he never forgot the practical concerns of his readers. While inspiring them with his vision of the American future, he also spoke to their needs. He argued that colonists need not fear being cut adrift if they became independent. They had already demonstrated that Europe depended on American trade. American products would always be in demand "while eating is the custom of Europe." America could have the best of the old relationship without the burdens of membership in the British empire.

From his vantage point in Pennsylvania, many of whose settlers were immigrants from Germany, Scotland, and northern Ireland, Paine was very aware that England was not the homeland of most Americans. All of Europe and Africa fed the colonial population. Moreover, not only did many of the flood of recent immigrants feel no special love for England, some, like the Irish, Scots, and Scots-Irish, had reason to hate that country for past imperial policies.

The Declaration of Independence

During the months after the publication of *Common Sense*, the Continental Congress came to share Paine's conclusions. In June 1776, Richard Henry Lee of Virginia moved: "That these United Colonies are, and of right ought to be, free and independent States." A committee was selected to draw up a statement. Thomas Jefferson wrote the first draft, and the Declaration of Independence follows his text closely. The Declaration, like *Common Sense*, places blame for the separation squarely on the king. There was a long list of specific accusations, many beginning with "He has."

The preamble to these charges is much more philosophical than Paine's work. Jefferson, a highly educated man, was very much aware of European intellectual currents. The Enlightenment of eighteenth-century Europe sought to examine the principles on which human society was erected. Rather than accept the notion that any particular government was ordained by God, these thinkers looked for natural reasons for government and tried to develop tests for judging whether a government was good. They argued that without government, human beings would be in a state of nature in which the strongest would rule, and there could be no progress because each family would be forced to devote itself to defense. Therefore, at some mythical time in the past, humans decided to form a government, to give it some rights over them, and to agree to abide by its decisions. Thus government is ordained by those who are governed, and its powers come from them.

Jefferson wrote these ideas into the Declaration of Independence. The truths in it were, he said, "self-evident" to human reason, not revealed by some mystical source. Government is set up to secure our rights, and this government derives its "just powers from the consent of the governed." It follows, then, that if a government does not offer the people protection but instead tramples on their rights, they have the right to change it. He said this would never be done lightly, but only after a "long train of abuses and usurpations." He then offered a lengthy list of "repeated injuries" that the colonies had suffered.

The Declaration of Independence shows how far the debate had moved along after the publication of *Common Sense*. Since 1763, Americans had been trying to convince England and its government of their sincerity and their suffering. In July 1776 the special relationship with Britain was treated as a dead letter. The Declaration was addressed not to England, but to "a candid world." And the arguments were not, as earlier, based on rights and privileges claimed under the British constitution, but on "the Laws of Nature and of Nature's God."

War

When General Howe moved his army away from hostile Boston in March 1776, they went to Halifax, Nova Scotia, and General Washington took advantage of the situation to move his troops to New York. In July, as the new states celebrated passage of the Declaration of Independence, Howe moved his much larger and better-trained army to New York and ousted the Americans in a series of battles. Superiority at sea gave the British the capacity to move their army quickly along the coast. While the British established themselves in New York, the rebel army slowly moved in retreat across New Jersey to Morristown. British forces set up outposts at Trenton, Princeton, and New Brunswick, New Jersey.

Washington's concern, at this point and throughout the war, was to keep his army together and supplied. Many of the militiamen signed up for short periods, and even the regulars tended to drift away. Men would sign on to

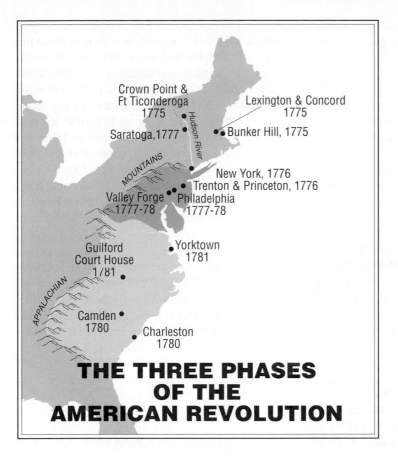

Crown Point &
Ft Ticonderoga
1775

Lexington & Concord
1775

Saratoga, 1777

Hudson River

Bunker Hill, 1775

MOUNTAINS

New York, 1776

Trenton & Princeton, 1776

Valley Forge
1777-78

Philadelphia
1777-78

Guilford
Court House
1781

Yorktown
1781

APPALACHIAN

Camden
1780

Charleston
1780

THE THREE PHASES
OF THE
AMERICAN REVOLUTION

defend their homes, but might stay behind if the army moved on. Discipline was the heart of the British army regime. The men were trained to behave like automatons under fire. Such unquestioning discipline could not be achieved in the citizen army of the American forces. When Baron von Steuben, a Prussian soldier who volunteered to work with Washington, trained the troops in the Valley Forge winter of 1777–78, he wrote to a European friend: "You say to your soldier, 'Do this,' and he does it, but I am obliged to say, 'This is the reason why you ought to do that,' and he does it."

In these circumstances, Washington was forced to conserve his troops, to choose the time and place of battle carefully. But the British were also concerned about conserving their armies.

Highly trained soldiers were a precious commodity, and replacements were both far away and expensive to acquire. Howe might have been able to crush Washington's army in New York in the summer of 1776, but he chose to protect his force, giving the rebels time to slip away and rebuild. Many times throughout the war the British, by acting cautiously, allowed the Americans to garner the resources to continue resistance.

Because the British army was such a mighty force, and the rebels seen as an undisciplined rabble, any American success was psychologically important. Washington led successful surprise attacks on the British outposts at Trenton and Princeton at Christmas 1776, which helped build morale both for the troops and the citizens among whom the armies were encamped.

Though neither site was strategically important, these victories reversed the impression of American weakness left by the retreat from New York. The British commanders could never get around the fact that, regardless of how great their victories were, their defeats counted more, as Washington pursued his strategy of attrition.

In the spring of 1777, the British adopted a new focus for the war effort. Howe decided to move his headquarters to Philadelphia, the rebel capital. His army moved by ship into Chesapeake Bay and marched up to the city. Meanwhile, British General John Burgoyne was to march his separate army from Canada down the Hudson Valley to meet Howe and the main force. This would have the effect of cutting the colonies in half and isolating New England. Once the Middle Colonies were firmly under control, then the South could, imperial strategists thought, be brought quickly into line, and New England's resistance would collapse.

Crucial to this plan was the assumption that the Revolution was actually being foisted on an unwilling population. Most Americans, the British thought, were really loyal to the empire, but were intimidated by the local committees and the militia. If the redcoats were present to protect these loyalists at heart, they would make their true allegiance known and the revolutionary movement would die out. Historians do not know how most Americans felt in their hearts. One rule of thumb divided the population into thirds: one-third was probably devoted to independence, one-third was at least secretly loyalist, and one-third was somewhere in the middle.

Whatever the true figures, the British strategy could never work, because the army was not a fit instrument for encouraging loyalist sentiment. Wherever the troops were sent, they created animosity. They tended to treat all the Americans with the contempt they thought rebels deserved. Even when they were strictly controlled, the fact that the armies lived off the land meant the people resented their presence. Even loyalists were disgusted. Sally Logan Fisher of Philadelphia initially welcomed the news that the British army was to make her city its headquarters, and looked forward to the arrival of Sir William Howe, "our beloved General." After just a few months, her opinion had changed completely. She was horrified by the army's plundering of Philadelphia citizens and the "wanton destruction" of the city.

Those with loyalist sentiments also soon learned that it was dangerous to trust in the protection of the British army. Sooner or later, the army would march on, and those who had publicly supported it were left to face angry neighbors. The great groundswell of sentiment in favor of reconciliation with the empire never materialized, but the British continued to hope for it.

INDIAN INVOLVEMENT One key group of loyalists in the colonies on whom the British relied heavily was the many Indian tribes that sided with the empire. The large confederations such as the Iroquois League in the North and the Creeks and Cherokees in the South were courted by both sides. Indian leaders understood very well what was at stake in this contest. Many saw that an American victory would be disastrous for them; the colonists already looked greedily at the Ohio Valley, and the Indians who had settled there knew their land claims would not be respected.

It is not difficult to see why many Indians saw their future as brighter with a British victory. Whereas the American leaders urged the Indians to remain neutral, presenting the fight as a "family quarrel," the British sought active Indian participation. The Iroquois League first decided to remain neutral, hoping to play the Americans off against the British, but most eventually fought on the British side. The Creeks were able largely to continue their policy of neutrality, but the Cherokees, suffering depredations all along the line of settlement, attacked frontier settlements. In the North and South, the frontier was unsafe because of Indian warfare, and the Americans' military strength had to be divided to meet this challenge. Iroquois aid was an essential part of Burgoyne's plan as he marched through New York.

Though participation on the British side was a rational choice, all Indians suffered for that role after the war. The British were treacherous allies, circulating stories that presented the Indians as ferociously brutal fighters who slaughtered women and babies as willingly as men, many of which were wholesale inventions. The redcoats used such atrocity stories to frighten the Americans, and threatened to "unleash" their "savage" allies on rebel settlements. After the war, all Indians reaped the bitter fruits of such propaganda, as the new American government compared the natives to wild animals who had to be rooted out to make way for civilized settlers.

Moreover, the British abandoned their Indian allies at the treaty negotiations. The Iroquois took the perfectly sensible position that the British Army had been beaten, but that the Iroquois forces were still in the field. To their shock, the British government signed over all the lands of their Indian allies, despite the fact that they had not been conquered, to the Americans and left the Indians to cope as best they could. The Indians of the Northwest fought on until the Battle of Fallen Timbers in 1794 against the forces of the president to whom they had given the name "Town Destroyer," George Washington.

Turning Point

Even with Iroquois aid, the second phase of British strategy, based in New York and Pennsylvania and aiming to cut the rebel states in two, was doomed to failure. The generals never did the necessary planning. Burgoyne and Howe did not coordinate their activities, and direction from London was poor. "Gentleman Johnny" Burgoyne began his march south from Canada in June 1777 in great style as the American forces retreated before him and he reclaimed Fort Ticonderoga. As one of his officers remarked: "We had conceived the idea of our being irresistible." Burgoyne issued a series of proclamations offering

to protect the Americans against the "tyranny" of the revolutionaries and predicting horrifying vengeance on those who held out.

The American forces, depressed at Howe's capture of Philadelphia, were soon heartened by the news that Burgoyne was in trouble, a situation that deepened as he moved farther from his supplies in Canada. Burgoyne's army was confronted and defeated at the battle of Saratoga in October 1777, an event many saw as the turning point in the war. For once, the Americans had met a major British force in a full-dress battle and won. The impact on American morale was tremendous.

FRANCE ENTERS THE WAR The effect in Europe was equally momentous. France, still smarting from its defeat in 1763, had been aiding the rebels secretly with much-needed supplies. After Saratoga showed the Americans to be a formidable opponent for Britain, France, despite great misgivings about aiding rebels, openly allied itself with the United States. Now the Americans not only received war material, the French navy challenged British superiority at sea. For the first time it looked as if the Revolution might succeed. Soon Spain declared war on Britain as France's ally, though it could never countenance befriending rebels. From this point forward, England was forced to fight all over the world as it sought to protect the empire from French and Spanish depredations.

The winter of 1777–78 was spent garnering strength for the future. The British in Philadelphia saw another change in command, with General Sir Henry Clinton replacing Howe in May. The main American army spent the winter at Valley Forge, Pennsylvania, drilling and preparing for new engagements. General Washington also drilled the soldiers on the principles for which they were fighting, and emphasized the necessity of sacrifice for the common good.

Washington was able to appeal to his soldiers' sense of commitment because the army genuinely thought in terms of a shared goal of great importance. Their dedication was grounded in the sense that they were fighting for their homes and families as well as the principles of the Revolution.

THE HOME FRONT These beliefs were shared by those on the home front. Men did the fighting, probably 200,000 in all on the American side, but women made the war effort possible. In doing so, they increasingly took on responsible public roles, running the farms and businesses of the absent men and providing the food and supplies the army required. Abigail Adams, wife of John Adams, ran the family farm so well that she aspired to have "the reputation of being as good a farmeress as my partner has of being a good statesman." When the fighting came to their regions, women cared for the sick and wounded.

The home front often presented a scene of suffering as great as that in the armies. Dysentery and smallpox were carried by the armies to civilian populations. After dysentery had killed many, including her own mother and niece, during the siege of Boston, Abigail Adams wrote that "the Desolation of War is not so distressing as the Havoc made by the pestilence." Soldiers' looting and, sometimes, raping of women whose men were off fighting created terror throughout the civilian population. Nonetheless, American women affirmed their devotion to the cause, and accepted deprivation willingly. Women throughout the colonies destroyed food supplies, even stocks on which they were dependent, rather than have them fall into the enemy's hands. Victory would not have been possible for the Americans without the contribution of women at home.

Victory

In the spring of 1778, the period of regrouping was over. General Clinton removed his army from Philadelphia to New York and prepared for the third and final phase of the war. British strategy was still based on the assumption that most Americans wished to be loyal to Britain. The focus in this third phase was on the South, which for several reasons was thought to be the most promising territory for the British. Not only were the Southerners, with their more aristocratic society, thought to have a natural affinity for England, but strategists thought they could be more easily intimidated. The South contained vast numbers of slaves, in some areas much more than half the population, and the threat of a slave rebellion armed and abetted by the British would surely bring Southerners around. There were also large and powerful Indian confederations, especially the Creeks and the Cherokees, who could be induced to ally themselves with the British.

This third phase of the war involved a plan for pacification of the countryside. The British would land in the far south and would then move north, sweeping the rebels before them and leaving the country in the hands of loyal self-defense forces. Accordingly, one force of redcoats seized Savannah, Georgia, in 1779, and Charleston, the key to the whole strategy, was besieged. The May 1780 fall of Charleston, the most important port in the South, marked the beginning of the pacification campaign.

Despite all the apparently favorable indications, British strategy failed here for some of the same reasons as earlier. Even if loyalist sentiment existed, luring it into the open was difficult. The plan called for the army to move north, and Southerners knew that those who had been friendly to it would suffer when the troops were gone. Again, the soldiers made enemies by their seizure of food and supplies and by their rough manner.

More important, the Southern strategy was based on fallacious reasoning. When the British appealed to slaves to rebel or leave, they offended white Southerners and thus alienated potential loyalists. Slavery offered the ideological weak point of the American campaign. Historians have long pointed to the irony that Thomas Jefferson, while writing the stirring words "We hold these

Lord Cornwallis surrenders at Yorktown, October 19, 1781. This painting by John Trumbull shows the French forces under Rochambeau on the left, with the Americans commanded by George Washington on the right. Lafayette and von Steuben are placed near Washington. (Yale University Art Museum)

truths to be self-evident: That all men are created equal; that they are endowed by their Creator with certain unalienable rights; that among these are life, liberty, and the pursuit of happiness," actually owned some 200 slaves, who had neither rights nor equality. Some have argued, like the early nineteenth-century English visitor Sir Augustus John Foster, that slavery actually made high-flown democratic theories possible, because of "the mass of the people, who in other countries might become mobs, being there nearly altogether composed of their own Negro slaves." Slavery represented a kind of blind spot for the American leadership, a part of American life whose implications they agreed to ignore for the time being in order to achieve the unity of purpose needed for the war effort. But slavery could not be ignored in the conduct of the war, because fear of slave rebellion rendered the South vulnerable.

Slaves, like Indians, seemed natural loyalists. In 1775, even before hostilities were formally declared, John Murray, Lord Dunmore, royal governor of Virginia, offered freedom to any slave who succeeded in getting through to the British lines. Several thousand slaves did manage to escape to the redcoats during the war, including large numbers of women with children who took advantage of the opportunity for freedom despite the great dangers and hardships involved. The men manned a regiment of Black Guides and Pioneers. Many runaway slaves left America with the defeated army when the war was over. But any call to the slaves was sure to alienate white Southerners, whose most fundamental fear was of slave rebellion.

The British Southern strategy was badly misconceived. It was not really possible to sweep the revolutionaries out of the countryside. Many Southern rebels waged a guerrilla campaign, striking at the British and then melting back into the population. An American force could be defeated and dispersed, but would coalesce again as soon as the British were occupied elsewhere.

The main American army in the South was first commanded by General Horatio Gates, whose incompetence was partly responsible for a massive defeat at Camden, South Carolina, on August 16, 1780. The rebels fared better when Nathaniel Greene took over and decided to conduct what he called a "fugitive war," one based on hit-and-run tactics. He was plagued by the necessity of constant supplication to the congress and the states for supplies. Meanwhile, the British army was suffering from sickness and the debilitating effects of the guerrilla activity. Far from finding a population filled with loyalists, the redcoats confronted people so alienated that the British were starved of information about local conditions and about movements of the rebel armies, and ignorance cost them very dearly.

Even British victories, such as the bloody battle of Guilford Court House, North Carolina, on March 15, 1781, involved losses so devastating that they shored up American morale. Finally, Charles Cornwallis, commander of the British army in the South, decided to head for the Virginia shore, where he could once again be in touch with supply ships from home. His march led through Yorktown, where he confronted a large army of Americans and Frenchmen under Washington and the Comte de Rochambeau, backed by the French fleet in Chesapeake Bay under Admiral François Joseph Paul de Grasse. Cornwallis had begged General Clinton to bring the northern and southern armies together in Virginia in vain. Now surrounded by superior Franco-American forces, he surrendered his entire army in October 1781. As the redcoats marched out to turn over their weapons, the bands, reflecting the soldiers' feelings, played an English music hall song: "The World Turn'd Upside Down."

Britain could have continued the war. The major American ports were still in British hands and the northern army was still intact, but this long and costly war had lost support at home. Peace negotiations now replaced the study of war. It would be two years before the Peace of Paris officially ending the war was signed in 1783 and the world recognized the independent existence of the United States of America.

Suggestions for Further Reading

THE BOSTON MASSACRE

See first Hiller B. Zobel, *The Boston Massacre* (1970). Zobel's study is criticized and set in context in Jesse Lemisch, "Radical Plot in Boston (1770): A Study in the Use of Evidence," *Harvard Law Review*, 84 (1970), 485–504. Dirk Hoerder, *Crowd Action in Revolutionary Massachusetts, 1765–1780* (1977), looks at the question of prerevolutionary violence from a perspective different from Zobel's. For the army's role as inciter of violence, see John Shy, *Toward Lexington: The Role of the British Army in the Coming of the American Revolution* (1965).

On men who took a leading role in the events of 1770, see Bernard Bailyn, *The Ordeal of Thomas Hutchinson* (1974), and "Butterfield's Adams: Notes for a Sketch," *William and Mary Quarterly*, 3rd ser., 19 (1962), 238–56; Pauline Maier, *The Old Revolutionaries: Political Lives in the Age of Samuel Adams* (1980); Peter Shaw, *The Character of John Adams* (1976); and Alfred F. Young, "George Robert Twelves Hewes (1742–1840): A Boston Shoemaker and the Memory of the American Revolution," *William and Mary Quarterly*, 3rd ser., 38 (1981), 561–623.

POPULATION AND ECONOMY

Bernard Bailyn, *Voyagers to the West: A Passage in the Peopling of America on the Eve of the Revolution* (1986), is a definitive statement on the migration from Europe that peopled America during the eighteenth century.

The essays in Jack P. Greene and J. R. Pole, eds., *Colonial British America: Essays in the New History of the Early Modern Era* (1984), offer an excellent discussion of developing interpretation of American social, economic, and political relationships in the period before 1763. John J. McCusker and Russell R. Menard, *The Economy of British America, 1607–1789* (1985), is an encyclopedic, but very readable, overview of colonial economic and social development and its relationship to the Revolution. These two books make an excellent starting point for understanding Anglo-America in the eighteenth century.

EIGHTEENTH-CENTURY CHESAPEAKE

Rhys Isaac, *The Transformation of Virginia, 1740–1790* (1982), Allan Kulikoff, *Tobacco and Slaves: The Development of Southern Cultures in the Chesapeake, 1680–1800* (1986), and T. H. Breen, *Tobacco Culture: The Mentality of the Great Tidewater Planters on the Eve of Revolution* (1985), together offer a brilliant, sometimes conflicting picture of the mature Chesapeake culture of the mid–eighteenth century. All these books deal with both white and black society. For a full treatment of slavery in that culture and in the Revolution, see Duncan J. MacLeod, *Slavery, Race, and the American Revolution* (1974).

AMERICA AND THE WAR FOR EMPIRE

On the experience of the French and Indian War and the changes in consciousness it wrought, see Francis Jennings, *Empire of Fortune: Crowns, Colonies, and Tribes in the Seven Years' War in America* (1988), and Fred Anderson, *A People's Army: Massachusetts Soldiers and Society in the Seven Years' War* (1984).

THE GROWTH OF AMERICAN RESISTANCE

The developing debate over English actions and their meaning for colonists is illuminated by Bernard Bailyn, *The Origins of American Politics* (1967); Pauline Maier, *From Resistance to Revolution: Colonial Radicals and the Development of American Opposition to Britain, 1765–1776* (1972); David Ammerman, *In the Common Cause: American Response to the Coercive Acts of 1774* (1974); and the essays in Alfred F. Young, ed., *The American Revolution: Explorations in the History of American Radicalism* (1976).

SOCIETY AND REVOLUTION

Gary B. Nash, *The Urban Crucible: Social Change, Political Consciousness, and the Origins of the American Revolution* (1979), analyzes urban development and its relationship to revolution. Robert A. Gross, *The Minutemen and Their World* (1976), and Richard D. Brown, *Revolutionary Politics in Massachusetts: The Boston Committee of Correspondence and the Towns, 1772–1774* (1970), discuss the coming of the Revolution in Massachusetts. See Edward Countryman, *A People in Revolution: The American Revolution and Political Society in New York, 1760–1790* (1981), Sung Bok Kim, *Landlord and Tenant in Colonial New York: Manorial Society, 1664–1775* (1978), and Eric Foner, *Tom Paine and Revolutionary America* (1976), for the Middle Colonies.

WOMEN'S ROLES

Women's roles as they affected and were affected by the movement toward independence are the subject of two fine recent studies: Linda Kerber, *Women of the Republic: Intellect and Ideology in Revolutionary America* (1980), and Mary Beth Norton, *Liberty's Daughters: The Revolutionary Experience of American Women, 1750–1800* (1980). For an overall interpretation of changes in women's place, see Mary Beth Norton, "The Evolution of White Women's Experience in Early America," *American Historical Review*, 89 (1984), 593–619.

WAR

Robert Middlekauff, *The Glorious Cause: The American Revolution, 1763–1789* (1982), is a detailed history of the background and conduct of the Revolutionary War treated purely as a conflict between Britain and its colonists. Edward Countryman, *The American Revolution* (1985), is a shorter, very readable overview that incorporates more of the recent findings of social and intellectual historians. Charles Royster, *A Revolutionary People at War: The Continental Army and American Character, 1775–1783* (1979), and John Shy, *A People Numerous and Armed: Reflections on the Military Struggle for American Independence* (1976), discuss the military experience and its impact.

CHRONOLOGY

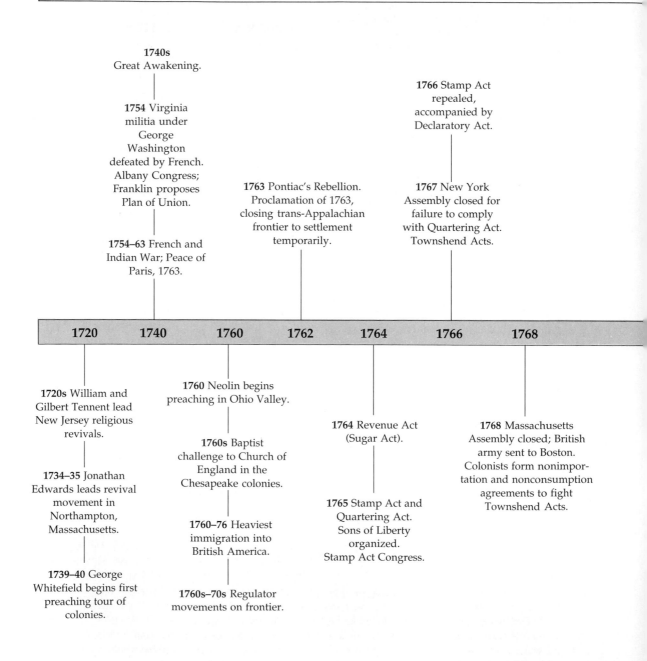

1740s
Great Awakening.

1754 Virginia militia under George Washington defeated by French. Albany Congress; Franklin proposes Plan of Union.

1754–63 French and Indian War; Peace of Paris, 1763.

1763 Pontiac's Rebellion. Proclamation of 1763, closing trans-Appalachian frontier to settlement temporarily.

1766 Stamp Act repealed, accompanied by Declaratory Act.

1767 New York Assembly closed for failure to comply with Quartering Act. Townshend Acts.

| 1720 | 1740 | 1760 | 1762 | 1764 | 1766 | 1768 |

1720s William and Gilbert Tennent lead New Jersey religious revivals.

1734–35 Jonathan Edwards leads revival movement in Northampton, Massachusetts.

1739–40 George Whitefield begins first preaching tour of colonies.

1760 Neolin begins preaching in Ohio Valley.

1760s Baptist challenge to Church of England in the Chesapeake colonies.

1760–76 Heaviest immigration into British America.

1760s–70s Regulator movements on frontier.

1764 Revenue Act (Sugar Act).

1765 Stamp Act and Quartering Act. Sons of Liberty organized. Stamp Act Congress.

1768 Massachusetts Assembly closed; British army sent to Boston. Colonists form nonimportation and nonconsumption agreements to fight Townshend Acts.

1774 Coercive, or Intolerable, Acts, accompanied by Quebec Act. First Continental Congress. Nonconsumption, nonimportation, and nonexport agreements adopted.

April 1775 Shots fired at Lexington and Concord.

Winter 1777–78 American army at Valley Forge.

May 1775 Second Continental Congress meets, calls for organization of army.

1770 Townshend Acts repealed. Tax on tea remains in effect. Boston Massacre.

June 1775 Battle of Bunker Hill.

1783 Treaty of Paris recognizes American independence.

July 1775 Olive Branch Petition. King declares colonies in rebellion.

1779 British take Savannah.

November 1775 Lord Dunmore offers freedom to Virginia slaves.

1770	1772	1774	1776	1778	1780	1783

January 1776 *Common Sense* published.

March 1776 British evacuate Boston.

1772 *Gaspée* attacked. British government announces that trials in such attacks will be held in Canada or England.

July 4, 1776 Continental Congress endorses Declaration of Independence.

May 1780 Charleston falls to British.

July 1776 British forces take New York from American army.

August 1780 Americans defeated at Camden, South Carolina.

December 1776 Surprise attacks on British forces at Princeton and Trenton.

March 1781 Battle of Guilford Court House, North Carolina.

1773 Committees of Correspondence formed. Boston Tea Party.

Spring 1777 British forces under Howe occupy Philadelphia. Burgoyne begins march down Hudson Valley.

October 1781 Cornwallis surrenders at Yorktown, Virginia.

October 1777 Burgoyne defeated at Saratoga.

Indians as a factor in both the cause and conduct of the American Revolution have attracted a good deal of recent scholarly attention. Barbara Graymont, *The Iroquois in the American Revolution* (1972); Francis Jennings, *The Ambiguous Iroquois Empire* (1984); Isabel T. Kelsay, *Joseph Brant, 1743–1807: Man of Two Worlds* (1984); and Anthony F. C. Wallace, *The Death and Rebirth of the Seneca* (1969), illuminate the position of the Iroquois League and its fate in the war and its aftermath. James H. O'Donnell III, *Southern Indians in the American Revolution* (1973), deals with the South. See also Francis Jennings, *Empire of Fortune* (1988).

CHAPTER 5
THE TRANSITION
TO NATIONHOOD

THE EPISODE: *When Charles, Lord Cornwallis surrendered his British army to the combined American and French forces at Yorktown, the Revolutionary War was effectively ended. For many years, the leaders of the revolutionary movement had talked and acted as though the colonies had only one serious problem: British "interference" in their affairs. Now, most of them believed the thirteen states could go about their business in peace and harmony, tied together by a loose machinery of national government. But during the next few years, many political leaders became convinced that a much stronger framework of national government was needed if the country was to survive.*

In this chapter, we follow one such leader, George Washington, through the steps that led him to this conclusion. Washington yearned for "retirement" from public life at the end of the Revolution. But his own experience seemed to teach him two things as time passed: that a new government ought to be created, and that he could not escape participating in this new government, perhaps even leading it. In some ways, Washington was a unique man. But the perceptions that led him to join the movement for a new constitution were far from unique. They typified the kinds of hopes and fears that would eventually lead the men Americans came to call their "Founding Fathers" to write the Constitution of the United States.

THE HISTORICAL SETTING: *At the end of the Revolution, the United States was governed by the same Congress that had declared independence in 1776. Then it had been a voluntary assembly, legitimated only by its own declarations. Now it had a new kind of legitimacy in the first constitution, the Articles of Confederation. This document, which was finally ratified by all the states near the end of the Revolution, was written on the assumption that the states were willing to grant the national government only those powers they would have been willing to see the British Parliament exercise over the colonies. They did not give the Congress certain crucial powers, such as the power to tax or the power to regulate foreign or interstate trade. Nor did the Articles provide for any executive or judicial branches; the national government was, in effect, only a national legislature.*

The chapter examines the way the Articles of Confederation worked in practice and assesses the achievements of the Congress. It also explains the kinds of difficulties Washington and other political leaders came to believe could not be solved under the Articles. Then it analyzes the complex set of compromises the Constitutional Convention of 1787 reached in order to create a new frame of government. Finally, the chapter spells out how the process of getting the Constitution accepted by the states resulted in the creation of the Bill of Rights.

GEORGE WASHINGTON, FROM GENERAL TO PRESIDENT

General George Washington had had enough of destroying towns, armies, and even empires. After he forced Cornwallis to surrender his forces in the Battle of Yorktown in 1781, Washington wanted very much to go home to his beloved plantation, Mount Vernon. He did manage to spend a week there—his first time home in six years. But the war was not officially over. Not until April 1782 did American, French, and British representatives begin to negotiate a peace treaty in Paris. And there was still a British garrison in the city of New York. So he moved his army to Newburgh, New York, to keep watch over the enemy. A year and a half passed before the American Congress finally ratified the Treaty of Paris in April 1783. But then Washington had to wait six more months because the British did not begin to evacuate New York until November. At last, early in December, Washington decided that his war was finally over. He asked his officers to meet at a Manhattan tavern to say goodbye. One of them wrote this account of the moving scene of farewell:

> The time now drew near when the Commander-in-Chief intended to leave for his beloved retreat at Mount Vernon. On Tuesday, the fourth of December, it was made known to the officers then in New York that General Washington intended to commence his journey on that day.
>
> At twelve o'clock the officers repaired to Fraunces' Tavern in Pearl Street, where General Washington had appointed to meet them and to take his final leave of them. We had been assembled but a few moments when His Excellency entered the room. His emotion, too strong to be concealed, seemed to be reciprocated by every officer present.
>
> After partaking of a slight refreshment, in almost breathless silence, the General filled his glass with wine, and turning to his officers, he said, "With a heart full of love and gratitude, I now take leave of you. I most devoutly wish that your latter days may be as prosperous and happy as your former ones have been glorious and honorable."
>
> After the officers had taken a glass of wine, General Washington said, "I cannot come to each of you, but shall feel obliged if each of you will come and take me by the hand."

Washington's farewell. In this 1805 painting, Washington's tearful 1783 farewell to his officers in a New York tavern is given that combination of deep sentiment and dignified restraint that was thought to be part of the ideal character of a gentleman. This scene played an important part in remaking Washington's public image from that of the military leader to one as the civilian head of a republic. (Courtesy Chicago Historical Society)

General Knox, being nearest to him, turned to the Commander-in-Chief, who, suffused in tears, was incapable of utterance, but grasped his hand, when they embraced each other in silence. In the same affectionate manner, every officer in the room marched up to, kissed, and parted with his General-in-Chief.

Such a scene of sorrow and weeping I had never before witnessed, and hope I may never be called upon to witness again.

Washington rode south to Philadelphia, then on to Annapolis, Maryland, where Congress was in session. (After the Continental Congress was forced to leave Philadelphia, it met in several towns for varying lengths of time. It held sessions in Annapolis for a year, beginning in November 1783.) The "general-in-chief" was by far the most popular and respected man in America. The new nation had a weak government, few traditions, and almost no leaders of national stature. Washington might have tried to claim political powers equal to his military powers. But he chose to resign. He went to Annapolis to turn in his commission as general of all Continental forces. In a draft of a speech to the Congress, he spoke of an "affectionate and final farewell" and of taking "ultimate leave" of public office.

For some reason, though, when Washington actually delivered the speech to the Congress on December 23, he struck out the words *final* and *ultimate*. At the end of his address, Washington said only that he was taking "leave of all public employments." His farewell was only "affectionate," not "final."

The General Washington who resigned his commission was in many ways the simplest and most straightforward of men. Even his very few enemies recognized his almost perfect honesty and forthrightness. But Washington also embodied some important paradoxes of the American Revolution and the American situation in general. He was, to begin with, an aristocrat who (along with other aristocrats) had somehow led the first modern revolution, a revolution with many democratic overtones. Furthermore, history had placed Washington at the absolute center of the revolutionary stage. If he had been killed or captured or become ill, the Revolution might have collapsed very quickly. Washington was not, at heart, a dedicated revolutionary. He had been involved in the movement for revolution in Virginia almost from its beginnings in the 1760s. But he did not have the flaming philosophical dedication of the men whose words and ideas had been so important: Thomas Jefferson, Thomas Paine, Samuel Adams, and others like them. Before 1776, Washington had been a minor figure in the Virginia movement. Even during the war, he was often dismayed to find himself so constantly at center stage. When the war was over, he appeared to want nothing more than to return to Mount Vernon by Christmas Day 1783, and to stay there.

These paradoxes in Washington point to some larger problems of his country. In the last analysis, his power and influence had been military. He was not a great general in the tactical sense. But he was the only general, over the long haul from 1775 to 1783, whom everyone could trust. Now the fighting was over, the army broken up, and Washington back at Mount Vernon. Could Americans create a political unity to replace the fragile military unity that had won the Revolution? Would political leaders come forward who could unify the former colonies the way Washington had managed to hold the Continental army together at Valley Forge? And would political institutions be developed to replace the war as a means of making Virginians and New Yorkers, Carolinians and New Englanders, into one people? These were the questions that were raised, indirectly, by Washington's retirement to Mount Vernon.

When Washington rode home at the end of 1783, he had no wish to raise any such questions. Indirect or direct, they simply were not much on his mind. He was a public figure, and he knew it. From the time of the Revolution on, his life would always be full of public affairs. His days would be taken up with receiving distinguished visitors in his Virginia home. And an incredible amount of his time would always be absorbed with writing to important political figures, in both Europe and America. (His letters fill thirty-nine thick volumes.) But thinking about public affairs, entertaining important visitors, and keeping up a steady correspondence on the issues of the day— all these did not necessarily involve a direct participation in politics and government. What Washington wanted in 1783 was time—time to rest, time to build his plantation and attend to the thousands of acres of land he owned in the West. He wanted time for his wife, Martha, and the rest of his family, time for riding, fox hunting, and the other preoccupations of a leisured, slaveowning Virginia planter.

At first it seemed to work. Washington enjoyed his self-imposed retirement. Since it was winter, there was little farm work to supervise. The roads were bad, and not very many visitors came. The general seemed to believe he could turn himself into a gentleman planter again. To old military comrades he wrote: "The tranquil walks of domestic life are now beginning to unfold themselves. I am retiring within myself." He described himself as a "wearied traveler," home at last "after treading many a painful step with a heavy burden on his shoulders."

Turning inward for Washington had always meant Mount Vernon. This great estate was the center of Washington's conception of himself as a private man. It was his refuge and sanctuary, the visible, touchable focus of his private life.

But another focus—that of politics, revolution, war—always pulled him away from Mount Vernon, out into the world of Virginia and American politics. When Washington resigned his commission in 1783, not only had he left the army, he had also returned home in a very special sense. He was fifty-one years old and healthy (except for the bad teeth that bothered him all his life). Yet he was on the downhill side of middle age. For all he or anyone else could tell, he had already reached the peak of his fame, public service, and involvement in politics. If he had never again left Mount Vernon, he probably would still have been known as the Father of His Country.

There were two flaws, however, in the picture Washington had of himself. More than any other man in the country, he *was* the American cause. In an almost unique way, vanity and patriotism were the same emotion in him. He identified himself so closely with his new country that any ambition for it almost amounted to an ambition for himself—and vice versa. In an odd sense, Washington could actually have no private life. The second flaw was that he was in some ways a poor man. He would have to build his fortune rather than retire on a fortune ready-made. The war had been expensive for him and his plantation. Slaves had been sold and crops had spoiled. Also, Washington had accepted no salary during his years as commanding general, though he had been reimbursed for his actual expenses.

As Washington added up his accounts in 1784, he found himself short of money. At the end of the year he could not have put his hands on more than £86 in cash (about $500). In land and slaves he was rich—at least on paper. Besides Mount Vernon, he owned well over 30,000 acres in the West, which he had bought before the war. Some of this land was just west of Pittsburgh. More was farther down the Ohio River, near the present city of Cincinnati. The land was a speculation, however, only a potential source of wealth. It was worth very little at this time. Mount Vernon with its slaves was a great plantation, but the land had become too poor for successful tobacco agriculture. (From Berkeley's time on, tobacco had been a great depleter of soil.) The plantation was simply not a paying proposition in any substantial way.

Washington's wealth made him one of the richest men in America. But it was an odd form of wealth. Either it was impossible to turn into ready cash, like Mount

The hero at home. This painting is the only contemporary picture of Washington and his family at Mount Vernon. He is wearing his general's uniform. The two young people are Martha Washington's grandchildren, who grew up as part of Washington's household. The black man at the right bore one of Virginia's proudest names, Billy Lee, and had been the general's "body servant" during the Revolutionary War. The painting must have been made after 1791, because the map shows the site of the future capital in the District of Columbia. In the background is the Potomac River. (The National Gallery of Art, Washington, D.C., Andrew Mellon Collection)

Vernon itself or its slaves, or it was potential wealth, like the western lands. Washington's other assets—fine horses, clothes, furniture, and dogs—were all luxuries, not real wealth.

In many respects, Washington's financial future rested on the lands in the West. The value of those lands, in turn, depended on getting settlers there, improving road and water transportation, and extending orderly government into the Ohio Valley. In a very concrete way, then, Washington's future was tied to the nation's. He was not a narrow man, and he was certainly not selfish. But it was clear to him that he had a great stake in the new republic. If it prospered, so would he. And if it became a respectable nation among nations, his work in shaping it would have been worthwhile and his reputation and honor secure.

These kinds of concerns and reflections drew the retired general back toward public life. Mount Vernon could not be walled off from the world. Nor could Washington daydream for long on "the tranquil walks of domestic life." He had too much energy and too much of the habit of participation and power. These traits were reinforced by his great pride in himself and his country. When Washington's economic circumstances were added to such a picture, almost anyone could easily have predicted that his "retirement" would be either very short or very incomplete.

The most direct temptation to involvement beyond Mount Vernon led west, to the Ohio Valley lands. Several things were on Washington's mind. He was angry that land speculators were illegally offering his Ohio land for sale in Philadelphia and New York markets. Trespassers, or "squatters," were living on his land near Pittsburgh, without paying rent or recognizing Washington's title. Also, several Virginians, including Thomas Jefferson, were talking about opening up a trade route from the Chesapeake Bay area to the West. They planned to use the Potomac River and some of the branches of the Ohio for water transportation, possibly building canals or new roads across the short stretches between the eastern and western rivers. Washington was very interested in such schemes. They would help his state and the nation. And, obviously, opening the West for settlement and trade would also be to his own economic advantage.

All these concerns put Washington on horseback in early September 1784 for a trip west. He was accompanied by his nephew, and an old friend and his son, plus three African-American "servants." The group started northwest along the Potomac toward the Allegheny Mountains and Pittsburgh. From there they planned to go by boat to the lands down the Ohio. On the way, Washington traveled over what was known as Braddock's Road, through territory he had scouted, surveyed, and fought in as a young soldier thirty years earlier in the French and Indian War. Now the French were gone, the country was filling with farmers, and the British were surrendering the entire Ohio Valley to the Americans.

Washington traveled as the first citizen of the United States. But he traveled to argue with plain farmers who were living on his land and who were not ready to surrender what they thought of as their "rights," even to the revolutionary general-in-chief. Trying to maintain a pace of five miles an hour, he finally reached his land on September 18. In his diary, he kept a running account of his encounter with the squatter farmers:

> *September 19th*: Being Sunday, and the people living on my land *apparently* very religious, it was thought best to postpone going among them till tomorrow.
>
> *20th*: Went early this morning to view my land, and to receive the final determination of those who live upon it. Dined at David Reed's, after which Mr. James Scot and Reed began to inquire whether I would part with the land, and upon what terms. They did not conceive they could be dispossessed, but to avoid contention they would buy if my terms were moderate. I told them I had no inclination to sell. However, after hearing a great deal of their hardships, their religious principles, and unwillingness to separate or remove, I told them I would make a last offer: the whole tract at 25 shillings per acre. Or they could become tenants upon leases of 999 years.

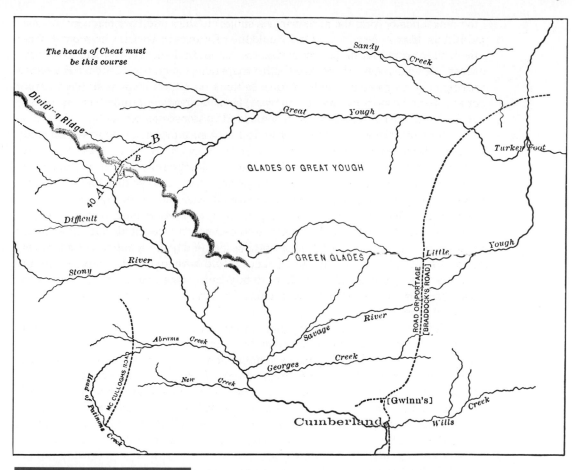

Washington's West. On his trip to the West in 1784, Washington paid very close attention to the geography of the area, especially to the rivers and creeks that might provide a basis for a transportation system. When he returned home, he had this map printed. It shows Cumberland, Maryland, on the Potomac at the lower right. The "Glades of Great Yough" are in Pennsylvania. The general was particularly interested in passages across ridge lines, like the one he drew running north and west from the center of his map. (Virginia State Library)

The potential "tenants" discussed the question among themselves for a long time, while Washington sat gravely to one side. Then they turned back to him and said they would not buy, move off, or pay rent. Washington would have to sue them:

> They had a long consultation. They then determined to stand suit for the land. I told them I would receive their answers individually, and accordingly I called them by name as they stood. They severally answered that they meant to stand suit, and abide the issue of the law.

Washington had come face to face, on a very practical level, with a problem that was worrying many wealthy Americans who lived in the East: Would the settlers in the new lands beyond the mountains be subject to rules and laws made in the East? Could the frontier be governed? Or would the new areas be lawless and separate from the United States? Theoretically, as educated Americans looked toward the Mississippi River, the wilderness seemed to be both a tremendous opportunity and a tremendous problem. But Washington did not have to think on a theoretical level. (He was not much of a philosopher by nature, anyway.) He had already encountered the problem, and it had the most direct and worrisome kinds of consequences for him. If the time came for using governmental power to deal with such problems, he would be ready to see that power put to use.

The question of power and the western lands presented itself in yet another way on Washington's trip. The general had planned to go down the Ohio to his other lands, but every traveler he met coming east advised him to stay away. The Native Americans, they said, were on the "warpath." He was told over and over that it would be dangerous to travel much farther into the Ohio country. He decided to head for home, having accomplished almost nothing. Some day, he thought to himself and later wrote to his friends, the United States would have to deal aggressively with the Indians. The government would have to buy land, make treaties, and, if necessary, use force. The problems and opportunities of westward expansion seemed always to demand more power and stronger government.

So far, Washington had met only disappointment. But his return trip had its rewards. He decided to head for home by a southern route up the Cheat River, a tributary of the Monongahela that cuts south into what is now West Virginia (see map, p. 241). From there he would cross the mountains to the upper reaches of the Potomac, looking for places to build connecting roads between the two rivers. If such roads were possible, all the future produce of the Ohio Valley could come down the Potomac to Virginia instead of going north and east to New York or down the Mississippi to New Orleans. Virginia could become the commercial center of the new nation.

Washington headed up the Cheat September 23. His trip took eleven days. Along the way he carefully noted every twist and turn of the rivers, every rapids, every stretch along which roads might be built. The going was rough. The discomfort, however, was worth it, for Washington felt that he had found the key to the future of the West, of his own lands, of Virginia, and of the struggling economy of his young nation.

When Washington reached Mount Vernon on October 4, he went to work on a series of detailed reflections about his trip:

> 4th: Reached home before sundown, having travelled on the same horses since the first day of September, by the computed distances, 680 miles.
>
> And, 'tho I was disappointed in one of the objects, namely to examine the land I hold on the Ohio and Kanawha, and rescuing them from the hands of land jobbers and speculators, I say notwithstanding this disappointment, I am well pleased with my journey.

Page after page in his diary he filled with his thoughts and calculations—detailed estimates of distance, of what rivers were navigable and how far, and where the lines of trade might eventually run.

Pennsylvania countryside. As he made his way from Mount Vernon to the West in 1784, Washington would have passed through settlements very much like this one outside York, Pennsylvania. The road, which leads toward Baltimore, is very wide and would have been used to drive herds of livestock to market. The one-room houses are made of logs, but they have good brick chimneys, and the large fields suggest a growing prosperity. It would have made perfect sense for Washington to believe that his own lands down the Ohio River could be transformed into something like this agrarian miracle in a short time. (Library of Congress)

He began with an analysis of river transportation in northern Virginia. All the rivers, taken as a network, "could afford water transportation for all that fertile country between the Blue Ridge and Allegheny Mountains." This filled Washington with proud confidence about the economic future of Virginia. But his thoughts ran well beyond the boundaries of his state, far to the west. The trade of western Virginia, great as it might become, was still "trifling, when viewed upon that immeasurable scale which is inviting our attention!"

Here was the key, to Washington and to many others like him in the new nation. They had won independence. Now they were free to concentrate on the richest kinds of visions about the future of their country—especially, a new empire to the west! Part of Washington's mind may have been tied to Mount Vernon and plans for retirement. But he was also thinking of expansion.

Nor were his reflections vague and abstract. Washington rummaged among all the maps and papers in his possession and worked out in surprising detail a scheme for connecting the Ohio Valley to the Atlantic, preferably through Virginia—past his own great mansion, in fact, down the Potomac to Chesapeake Bay. Detroit, he calculated, would be the critical point in the Ohio Valley. It would control all the commerce of the Great Lakes region—as far west, Washington figured, as the Lake of the Woods in northern Minnesota. According to Washington's estimates, the total distance from Detroit to Alexandria, Virginia, was only a little over 600 miles. The distances from Detroit to Philadelphia and New York were over 700 and 900 miles, respectively. So

Virginia had the advantage. It would not be Philadelphia, New York, or Boston that would become the economic and commercial capital of the republic. It would be Alexandria. (This city is just across the river from Washington, D.C., today—though Washington had no idea in 1784 that the federal capital would ever be created.)

All these calculations were of great importance for Washington. His mind ran in large strategic channels:

> Hitherto, the people of the western country have had no excitements to industry; they labor very little. But let us open a good communication with the settlements west of us, and see how astonishingly our exports will be increased.
>
> No well-informed mind need be told that the flanks and rear of the united territory are possessed by other powers, and formidable ones too. It is necessary to apply the cement of interest to bind all the parts of the country together by one indissoluble band, particularly the Middle States and country back of them.

Washington had focused on a problem that would occupy him for a long time to come: how to apply the "cement" of economic interest—trade—to hold the nation together and make it powerful. If the United States failed to achieve this unity and power, the West might very soon form a new nation and separate from the United States, or it might even join with Spain or Great Britain.

As a result of this trip, Washington could see more clearly than before just how closely his own life was related to such large questions. His patriotism, which was intense and powerful, was not merely a notion or an ideal. It was also directly tied to his own stake in the future of the republic that he had done so much to bring into existence.

All these reflections led to a simple set of questions: Would Americans have the good sense to see how much was at stake and what had to be done? Would the governments of Virginia and the other states support projects to make the new commerce come to life? Would the central government be stable and powerful enough to maintain the unity of the nation and hold the West in line? The symbolic questions that had ridden with Washington from New York to Virginia in 1783 were gradually becoming more and more real.

For Washington himself, a chain of events had begun that was to lead him eventually to join in overthrowing the existing government of the United States, creating a new constitution and government, and becoming the nation's first president. The chain ran clearly from his farmhouse confrontation with his Pennsylvania squatters in 1784 to the presidency five years later. One link in the chain was the observations he had made on the trip home. Another was his careful reflection on western trade. Now came the next link: an attempt to get Maryland and Virginia to cooperate in opening up the Potomac to trade.

When Washington reached home in October 1784, he moved quickly from reflections on the West to practical action. He traveled to the new capital of Virginia at Richmond to lobby for his Potomac project. It was clear that Maryland would have to cooperate, since the Potomac formed the border between the two states. So Washington was appointed commissioner to arrange for similar legislation in the two states.

It took him only three days to hurry to Maryland's capital, Annapolis, even though it meant missing his second Christmas at home since the war. Mount Vernon suddenly became a political clearinghouse. Washington was acting the politician in ways he had not practiced since he was a young man.

By the end of December everything was falling into place. Washington worked far past his usual nine o'clock bedtime on the project. As he wrote to his young friend James Madison on December 28, 1784: "It is now near 12 at night, and I am writing with an aching head, having been constantly employed in this business since the 22nd without assistance."

The "business" was complete by the first week in January. The legislatures of both Maryland and Virginia had appropriated money and joined in creating a joint-stock company to open up river transportation to the West. Washington was soon named president of the Potomac River Company, as it was called. Throughout the next two years he paid very close attention to its affairs. He fussed over the details of planning and surveying and fretted when there were delays. He went about the project with such energy that Madison shrewdly observed: "The earnestness shows that a mind like his, capable of grand views, and which has long been occupied with them, cannot bear a vacancy."

Commissioners from Maryland and Virginia met several times, at least once at Mount Vernon itself. Then, in January 1786, just a year after the Potomac Company was formed, the Virginia legislature took a surprising step that would soon have even more surprising consequences: It suggested that delegates from all the states meet at Annapolis to discuss trade, taxes, and other matters of common concern. Such a meeting seemed innocent enough, but in fact it bypassed the existing central government completely. Washington thought carefully about the proposal. In many ways, it had grown directly out of his own work on the Potomac Company. But it raised large questions about the political future.

Washington was optimistic about the country. He wrote a French friend:

The country is recovering rapidly from the ravages of war. The seeds of population are scattered far in the wilderness. Agriculture is prosecuted with industry. The works of peace, such as opening rivers, building bridges, etc., are carried on with spirit.

But despite the apparent prosperity, there was a problem of government, a problem that made Washington and many of his friends increasingly uneasy. During the Revolution the states had written a constitution, the Articles of Confederation, to bring a central government into being. This government was weak, Washington thought, too weak to fulfill his grand vision of empire. If the central government was weak, the states would constantly quarrel with one another. All during 1785, Washington's letters were filled with complaints:

Contracted ideas and absurd jealousy are leading us from those great principles which are characteristic of wise and powerful nations, and without which we are no more than a rope of sand. The Confederation appears to me to be little more than a shadow without the substance. If we are afraid to trust one another, there is an end of the Union. We are either a united people, or we are not. If we are not, let us no longer act a farce by pretending to it.

Because of these fears and doubts, Washington was intensely interested in the meeting at Annapolis, which was finally scheduled for September 1786. But the result of the meeting was only more anxiety. Only five states sent delegates. None at all came from New England. Here lay one source of Washington's frustrations. Out in the country, there was activity and opportunity. A great nation was waiting to be built, as it had waited in 1775 to be born. But the state governments, Washington felt, seemed to care nothing for the opportunity. Still, the few delegates who did come to Annapolis accomplished one thing. They recommended another meeting—a convention to begin in Philadelphia in May 1787—to consider what ought to be done to strengthen the Articles of Confederation.

Washington's reaction to the Annapolis Convention was a mixture of frustration and hope—frustration because more had not been accomplished and hope for a more promising result in Philadelphia that following year. Other news soon burst in to trouble him further. An armed rebellion of some kind was under way in Massachusetts. Most of the rebels were farmers, who seemed to come mainly from the western part of the state. (They probably were men much like the tenants on Washington's Pennsylvania lands.) In September, bands of these men had kept courts from sitting in many sections of Massachusetts. Memories of 1776 crowded in on Washington. This time, however, it was an *American* government that was being threatened by mobs.

Friends sent Washington warped reports of the rebellion: It had a leader, a Revolutionary War captain named Daniel Shays. It was well organized and might even have foreign support (from old loyalists, probably). Shays and his followers believed in some kind of radical division of all private property. They wanted all debts canceled, all taxes abolished. They were threatening to raid the federal arsenal at Springfield. Then they planned to march on Boston and bring down the established government!

These reports were wildly exaggerated, though Washington had no way of knowing it. Daniel Shays was not so much a leader of an organized movement as a surprised farmer who somehow found himself signing statements drawn up by the "rebels." The farmers did not believe in abolishing private property, debts, or taxes. They were protesting more personal economic difficulties—namely, the seizure of their farms to pay their debts. The only time they threatened the Springfield arsenal, in January 1787, they were fired on by government cannon and ran away without returning a single shot. Once it reached the Springfield area, the Massachusetts militia easily put the rebellion down without a real battle.

To Washington, however, and to most men of wealth all along the eastern coast, Shays's Rebellion was like a sudden thunderclap. Washington's informants were in near panic, and he shared their fears. The leaders of the revolutionary movement in the 1770s had always exaggerated the dangers of British actions, as though every new tax meant tyranny or slavery. Now Washington and many of his friends exaggerated the significance of Shays's Rebellion. A few hundred farmers turning out to close some country courts seemed to spell the eventual downfall of the whole federal republic.

On the last day of October, Washington sat at his writing table working on two long and important letters. The first was addressed to an organization of former Continental officers, the Society of the Cincinnati, of which he had been president for three years. They were scheduled to hold a general meeting and elect a president in

Daniel Shays and Job Shattuck. This contemporary woodcut was part of a pamphlet published in 1787 that mocked Shays's Rebellion. The author gave Shays's rank as "General," and made Shattuck a "Colonel." The artist gives them uniforms, a flag, and artillery (none of which they had). The picture was accompanied by a poem saying, "Thro' drifted storms let SHAYS the Court assail / And Shattuck rise, illustrious from the Jail. / In coward Hands let legal Powers expire, / And give new subjects to my sounding Lyre." (National Portrait Gallery, Smithsonian Institution, Washington, D.C.)

May 1787 at Philadelphia. (The time and place were exactly those chosen for the new convention to revise the Articles of Confederation.) Washington's letter was a careful defense of his decision not to attend the meeting and not to serve again as president of the Society. He cited his heavy correspondence, his work on the Potomac Company, and problems with his health. All these increased his determination to pass the rest of his days "in a state of retirement." More than anything else, the general said, he wanted "tranquility and relaxation."

Washington's second letter was about Shays's Rebellion. It seemed to say that no matter how much he wanted retirement, Washington would not be able to stay away from politics:

> I am mortified beyond expression when I view the clouds that have spread over the brightest morn that ever dawned upon any country. You talk of employing influence to appease the present tumults in Massachusetts. Influence is no government. Let us have a government by which our lives, liberties and properties will be secured; or let us know the worst at once.
>
> These are my sentiments. Let the reins of government be braced and held with a steady hand. If the Constitution is defective, let it be amended, but not trampled upon whilst it has an existence.

Washington's canal project, and his hopes for the West, had made it clear to him that the Confederation had its problems. Shays's Rebellion pushed him over the line. To him, the rebellion proved that even in the older states the Confederation could not guarantee public order. How could such a government hope to make western expansion orderly and secure? Washington was now convinced that the Articles of Confederation were not workable. The central government was almost bankrupt, barely able to meet its current obligations. More important, it could not even begin to pay off the huge debts that Congress had run up while fighting the war—debts owed to foreign governments as well as to American citizens. And there was little

Washington presiding. This rather crude contemporary engraving shows Washington and the delegates to the Constitutional Convention in Philadelphia. The artist has contrived the scene in a way that suggests Washington was much more active than he actually was. He is shown standing, though he usually sat. He is shown with parchment in one hand, and in the other the longest quill pen in sight, as though he were literally writing a constitution himself. (The Library Company of Philadelphia)

hope that the debts would ever be paid, since the Articles did not give the central government the power to tax. It was very unlikely that this lack of taxing power would be remedied, either, since the Articles could be amended only with the agreement of every state.

There was another side to things, of course. Many people and political leaders believed that the problems of the Confederation could be solved in the course of time. They were confident that the West would be settled. They were equally sure that the roads and canals men like Washington dreamed of could be built. They knew that the sale of public lands would eventually bring in the money needed to pay off the debts. They were confident the governments of the states were strong enough to keep public order. (After all, Massachusetts had been able to handle Shays's Rebellion with ease.)

People who thought this way believed that people's first loyalties belonged to their state and local governments, not to any national government, strong or weak. And there was always the possibility that a strengthened central government might turn out to behave like George III and his Parliament before the Revolution. Might not the liberties of the people depend on keeping power out of the hands of the national government?

Washington, however, thought otherwise. All his experience, his ambitions, and his interests conspired to convince him that nationalism was the solution. And if he had questions about America's future, many Americans had questions about *his*. He had more prestige than any man in America. No one else had anything like his reputation as a man of honor, good sense, and character. If he wanted a stronger national government, how could he hold back from sharing in the movement to abandon the old constitution and write a new one?

The Virginia legislature nominated Washington as a delegate to the Philadelphia Convention. Some of his most faithful young followers, among them James Madison and Alexander Hamilton, kept urging him to join the movement. Others advised him to hold back, not to risk his flawless reputation on a venture that might prove an embarrassing failure. Month after month, Washington made excuses. Some were valid. He did have an aching rheumatism that forced him to go around the Mount Vernon farms with one arm in a sling. There were deaths in the family, financial troubles, and even a brief quarrel by letter with his mother. All these things reminded him that his life was full enough without involving himself in the creation of a new constitution.

In the end, though, Washington had no choice. The pressure from his friends was too powerful. His fears for his country were too strong. And, in the last analysis, he wanted to be part of a great event, to stand somewhere near the center of activity. In his letters of the spring, Washington referred often to his reputation. He was as close to being vain as he had been in twenty years. It may have been this vanity that provided the final tiny weight needed to tip the balance toward Philadelphia and away from Mount Vernon—though his rheumatism was better, too.

Philadelphia was miserable in May. It rained day after day. Most of the delegates were late in arriving. On the day the Convention was set to open, only Virginia and Pennsylvania were represented. Gradually, enough delegates drifted into town to conduct business. To no one's surprise, Washington was unanimously elected president of the Convention. Week after week he sat in the chair, presiding over the secret discussions, listening and wondering whether or not a new government could be created. Would the people accept this new Constitution? Would it work?

When the sections of the Constitution outlining the powers of the new office of president of the United States were being discussed, Washington must have listened with special care. Not a man in the room doubted that the office would belong to him if he would have it.

During the whole Convention, Washington made only one speech. He had a talent for knowing when to be quiet and follow the lead of others who were quicker with words and ideas than he could ever be. Washington was always alert. He could follow a point in political theory or philosophy very well, but he made few points of his own. If he was a leader in Philadelphia, it was because other people trusted in his character, not because he led the way toward the new frame of government.

The first inauguration. This engraving is the only contemporary depiction of Washington's inauguration as president in New York, April 30, 1789. The artist, Peter Lacour, has paid more attention to the building than to the people, as though he were anxious to emphasize its grandeur. It had been renovated by Pierre Charles L'Enfant (who later designed the national capital). The image is dominated by the heraldic symbol of the eagle, above the clouds, with a sunburst behind, and holding the arrows of war in one claw and the olive branch of peace in the other. The capital would eventually move to the District of Columbia. But this view is from Wall Street, which would later be the center for a different kind of capital. (Stokes Collection, Miriam and Ira D. Wallach Division of Art, Prints, and Photographs, The New York Public Library, Astor, Lenox and Tilden Foundations)

After the new Constitution had been created, Washington hoped for its ratification. Once more he did not actually lead. Younger men with more interesting minds—especially men like Madison and Hamilton—carried the burden of trying to explain the Constitution to an extremely suspicious public.

After a precarious struggle, the Constitution was ratified by the required number of states. The Articles of Confederation were set aside. A presidential election was held, and Washington was, almost inevitably, given all the electoral votes.

The new president left Mount Vernon for New York City (which was the first capital of the United States) in mid-April 1789. From town to town—Alexandria, Wilmington, Philadelphia, Princeton—the citizens and the militia turned out for ceremonies. The trip took seven days. Finally, on April 23, Washington took a barge across the Hudson to Manhattan. There were more salutes, bells, and cheers as he reentered the city he had left six years before from Fraunces' Tavern. A week later, Washington was inaugurated on an open balcony that looked down on a crowd in Wall Street. The judge who administered the oath turned to the cheering crowd and shouted, "Long live George Washington, President of the United States!"

THE MAKING OF THE AMERICAN CONSTITUTION

In 1799, George Washington died. It was the middle of December, cold and wet, but he was back home, at Mount Vernon. For eight years he had served as first president of the new republic, and then had come a brief and final period of retirement. Washington's health had been good almost to the end, and he died gently. "I am just going," he said to a friend. "Have me decently buried and do not let my body be put into a vault in less than two days after I am dead. Do you understand me?" "Yes, sir," answered the friend. "'Tis well," said Washington, and soon he was dead. His body had to be measured for the coffin, and the doctor recorded that he was "in length, six feet, three-and-one-half inches, exact."

Washington's height, which was unusual in a day when most men were much shorter than they are today, was in keeping with the gigantic reputation he had acquired. There have been times, during his lifetime and the centuries since, when he seemed more than human, when he seemed to rise above his surroundings just as his enormous monument does today. And Washington's last statement, "'Tis well," says a good deal about the kind of philosophical calm he seems to have won for himself during the long, difficult period between the Revolution and his death. About a month before he died, Washington heard from a friend about recent political troubles in the nation's capital. He would say nothing, Washington replied, because "the vessel is afloat, or

very nearly so, and considering myself as a passenger only, I shall trust to the mariners whose duty it is to watch, to steer it into a safe port."

Washington had come a long way since he took command of the straggling little army outside Boston in 1775. Now, at the end of the century, the vessel was afloat. The Revolution had been won, difficult times had been endured, and the country had a government that looked promising. Washington had survived two presidential terms. John Adams, the second president, was now completing his term. The next year, the first year of the new century, a third president would be chosen. There had been two constitutions. There had been times when war with Britain, France, or Spain looked inevitable. But somehow the vessel had stayed afloat. And the man who had piloted it in the turbulent quarter-century was indeed entitled to congratulations at the end.

It had not been easy. At times it had seemed impossible. Every single year of the twenty-five years between Lexington and Washington's death had held out hope and fear. Washington and his political colleagues had acquired what amounted to a habit—hoping for the best and fearing the worst at the same time.

There was plenty to fear. The Revolution might be lost, and its leaders might, as Franklin had joked, "hang separately." Or the Americans might win the Revolution only to lose their country. They might not be able to create a stable

215

Independence Hall. What Americans now know as Independence Hall was known in the eighteenth century as the Pennsylvania State House, or the state capitol. This view was drawn and engraved in about 1778, during the American Revolution. This was the hall where the Constitutional Convention would meet. (Historical Society of Pennsylvania)

national government to hold the old colonies together. Or the new nation might be carved up by hungry European powers, just as all of North America had earlier been divided among several empires. Many people believed that they were living at a moment of profound historic significance. They thought they had a chance to create a nation built on the principle of liberty. They dreamed of a West where they might expand to fill half the huge continent that they thought of as "empty"—except for the Native Americans, who could surely be crushed and swept aside, as they had been for almost two centuries. They dreamed, too, of a new, more innocent world where the ancient tyrannies and corruptions of the Old World might be cast away. A new kind of nation, a republic, might be brought forth,

whose people would be citizens and not subjects. There were even many Americans—some who had European roots, and some whose origins were African—who hoped that something might be done about the institution of slavery.

In the minds of most Americans who thought about their national future, the fears and the dreams were mingled. This mixture of anxiety and hope was the backdrop against which a critical period of history was acted out. There seemed to be only one real certainty in Washington's mind and in the minds of other citizens: The fate of America was being decided in the years after 1775. Some held an even more extravagant opinion: that it was not just the fate of America but the fate of humanity that somehow hung in the balance.

Debate about such matters was a major pastime of an entire generation during and after the Revolution. Gradually, in Congress, state legislatures, and the conventions at Annapolis and Philadelphia, debates grew more and more skillful. Painfully, voting Americans piled up experience in political theory. Their leaders became as sophisticated and adept as any generation of politicians in any nation's history. The questions were simple and classic: What form of government best preserves the liberties of its citizens? Can a national government exist without destroying individual states? How are powers to be split among legislative bodies, executive officers, and courts? What is the relationship between a national constitution and the laws of the states?

The real problems may have been practical ones, such as Washington's problem with his western lands. But American political leaders had earned a generation's experience at translating practical problems into political theory and then retranslating the theory into practice through constitutions, treaties, and legislation. If Washington could relax somewhat at the end, it was because he and his generation of Americans had survived a revolutionary quarter-century with an astonishing mixture of stubbornness, skill, and plain luck.

The Confederation Period

The First and Second Continental Congresses were revolutionary governing bodies. They had no real legal standing. To the British, especially, they were little more than collections of outlaws and traitors. But they were engaged in an act of frightening significance: creating a government where none had existed before. They exercised powers, such as making war, that usually belong only to established governments. Even before the Declaration of Independence was drawn up, the Second Continental Congress appointed a committee to draft a new constitution in order to give the government legitimacy. The Congress debated the draft constitution until November 1777, when it agreed on the new Articles of Confederation. Another year passed before a majority of the states accepted the Articles.

In the meantime, the revolutionary government, the Continental Congress, simply kept on exercising power the way it had from the beginning. The arrangement was quite undemocratic in a way. The Congress had no direct "consent" from the people. But there was a war on, and politics had to be adjusted to reality. At last, in the spring of 1781, Maryland, the last state, finally ratified—four years after the original committee had been appointed. The Articles were official. They created a new government, bearing the name "The United States of America."

GOVERNMENT UNDER THE ARTICLES In most ways the new Articles simply confirmed the practices of the old Congress. The Constitution created a confederation of states, each of which was to retain its "sovereignty, freedom and independence." The states were the real political entities. It was a government that was somewhat like a national government but also somewhat like a treaty relationship among sovereign powers. The legislatures of the states chose delegates to the Congress, where voting was by states, with each state having one vote regardless of its population. Small states such as Rhode Island and Delaware had as much legislative power as large states such as Virginia and Massachusetts. A state might choose to send as few as two delegates to the Congress or as many as seven. No matter how many delegates it had, each state had an equal vote.

The Congress had some of the powers that normally belong to national governments. It could declare war and raise armies and navies.

It could borrow funds. It could coin money, issue paper money, and operate a post office. It could send ambassadors to and negotiate treaties with foreign nations. In essence, the states gave the Congress the power to do all the things they had willingly allowed the king and Parliament to do before the Revolution.

But the states kept for themselves powers they had refused to allow the king and Parliament: regulating commerce and raising money through taxes. The Congress could not control the conditions of trade among the states or with foreign nations. And when the United States needed money—as every government does—it had to ask the states for it in a request called a "requisition." If a state did not pay its requisition, the Congress was powerless to enforce the issue.

The states had recently been in the midst of a revolution against the central authority of Parliament and the crown. They did not want to create a new central government that might subvert their liberties the way many Americans felt the British had tried to do. To the average American, his or her "country" still meant Virginia or Pennsylvania or Massachusetts. So Americans were ready to face the peace with the same kind of government that had conducted the war. This meant a government of states. They would work together to solve problems after they arose, but not before.

There was no permanent federal judiciary under the Articles and no Supreme Court to make final decisions about constitutional questions. The Congress had the power to settle disputes among states. This power was to work through a complicated system of arbitration, however, not through a national court. The state courts were expected to enforce federal law at the local level. There was no executive, either, although the Articles did provide for a number of secretaries who might eventually develop into a cabinet system like that of the British.

Obviously, there could be no separation of powers among legislative, judicial, and executive branches under the Articles. The colonists had long been familiar with the idea of separation of powers, for they had had ample experience in the conflicts between governors and assemblies. All the state constitutions had elaborate schemes of checks and balances—that is, the executive, legislative, and judicial departments were separated in function but balanced in power. At this time, though, the states thought of the Confederation as an instrument to be used only for certain very limited purposes.

Even the limited powers of the Congress were difficult to exercise. On all important questions, nine votes out of thirteen were necessary for passage of a bill. This meant a few small states could block any piece of legislation. It was almost impossible to amend the Articles. An amendment had to have the consent of *every* state. It was obvious that new states would soon be admitted to the Confederation, which would make amendments even more difficult to ratify.

The Confederation did have one excellent possibility of making itself financially independent of the states. An energetic group of nationalists, led by Robert Morris, James Madison, and Alexander Hamilton, proposed in 1781 that the Articles be amended to give the Congress the power to put a five percent duty, or impost, on imports. The Revolutionary War was almost over, but although twelve states were willing to approve the amendment, the approval had to be unanimous. So when Rhode Island rejected the proposed impost, it died. Morris and his supporters tried again in 1783, just as the peace treaty with Britain was ratified. Washington himself published a passionate plea for the ratification of the impost. But this time the state governments were less willing to go along than they had been two years before. Again the impost failed. Morris quit politics. A dejected Madison "retired" to Virginia. Hamilton, too, gave up on the Confederation and waited for better days.

ACHIEVEMENTS UNDER THE ARTICLES
Political leaders and historians have often dismissed the Articles of Confederation as a weak and ineffectual frame of government. After all, from Maryland's ratification in 1781 to the Philadelphia Convention, the Articles lasted only six

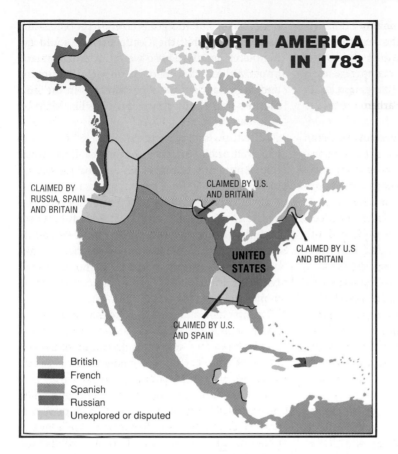

NORTH AMERICA IN 1783

CLAIMED BY RUSSIA, SPAIN AND BRITAIN

CLAIMED BY U.S. AND BRITAIN

CLAIMED BY U.S AND BRITAIN

UNITED STATES

CLAIMED BY U.S. AND SPAIN

British
French
Spanish
Russian
Unexplored or disputed

years. And, in retrospect, it seems obvious that the Articles had so many flaws that a new constitution was almost inevitable.

But when the question is put into proper perspective, and when the partisan opinions of victorious nationalists like Washington are set aside, it is equally obvious that the confederation system made some remarkable achievements. For one thing, the Confederation was not actually born in 1781 but in 1775, with the Second Continental Congress. This means Americans were able, within the framework of a confederation, to declare their independence and conduct the war. They made a major alliance with France and wrote a treaty of peace with Britain. For a dozen violent and eventful years, internal peace and a reasonable level of cooperation among the states were maintained.

Most important of all, the Confederation was able to take control of the vast territory between the Appalachians and the Mississippi and to provide for orderly settlement and government there. In a series of laws, climaxed by the Ordinance of 1787—the Northwest Ordinance—the Congress established the basic set of rules under which new land could be organized into territories and finally become new states. A clear-cut survey system was created. Land in the territories—one thirty-sixth of the whole—was set aside for the support of a public school system. A General Land Office was formed to sell the remaining land. Finally, in what may have been its most significant action, the Congress prohibited slavery in the Northwest Territory—the area that eventually became the states of Ohio, Indiana, Michigan, Illinois, and Wisconsin.

Any assessment of the Articles of Confederation must take into account the fact that they were a product of history, not just of abstract political theory. For almost two centuries, each of the colonies had strained for a larger and larger degree of independence. Only when there was trouble—war with France, or with Native Americans, or with Britain—did the colonies admit their dependence on each other or on a central government. All this experience taught the same lesson: The real, day-to-day business of governing was a matter for the individual states.

Within the states, in fact, political leaders displayed great legislative and constitutional skill. Between 1776 and 1780, with no real help from the Congress, eleven of the thirteen states wrote new constitutions. (Rhode Island and Connecticut kept their old colonial charters with a few changes.) The methods varied from state to state, but some common characteristics emerged in all the constitutions. The powers of government were divided among executive, legislative, and judicial branches. Explicit limits on the powers of government were set. The rights of citizens were listed. And the consent of the people was recognized as the only ultimate source of governmental authority.

All in all, then—despite the restless impatience of critics like Washington—the period of confederation was one of rather spectacular accomplishment, both at the national level and within the states. A revolution had been won, and some of its principal results had been written into constitutions and laws. And all this had been gained despite almost overwhelming odds. Men like Washington might be shocked and frightened by something like Shays's Rebellion, but any partisan of the Confederation could point to the other side of the coin: The rebellion had been brief, and Massachusetts was able to restore order without the help of any powerful central government.

FIVE MAJOR PROBLEMS OF THE CONFEDERATION The Articles of Confederation created a government that was equal to its immediate tasks, but there were other problems and opportunities that the Confederation could not handle efficiently. These were the problems and opportunities that had disturbed Washington and many of his fellow participants in the Revolution—especially younger figures like Madison and Hamilton.

The first, and in a way the most severe, problem was public finance. During the Revolution, the Continental Congress had issued mountains of paper money. This paper currency was really a debt. It amounted to a vast number of promises by the government to pay off, at some future time and in "real" money, the dollar value of each bill. The states followed the same practice, so the country was flooded with paper money of all types. The real value of this paper money depended on the hope that the national or state government would eventually be able to pay off all or part of the debt.

The Congress simply could not meet its obligations. This meant the paper money of the United States was practically worthless. In 1783 and 1784 a United States dollar could buy about fifteen cents' worth of goods. The government was nearly bankrupt. There was no effective national currency in circulation. The states paid only about a sixth of the requisitions made by the Congress. They were trying to pay off their own individual debts by buying back state-issued paper money. The result was a shortage of cash. People found it difficult to conduct ordinary business.

Only a stronger government, with the power to raise money through taxes, could solve this problem. It was this realization, as much as any other, that moved political leaders in the various states to think of revising the Articles. The movement that led to the Annapolis Convention, the Philadelphia Convention, and eventually to a new government was fed by fear of financial anarchy and bankruptcy.

A second problem involved commerce. Under the Articles, the states were free to make most of their own trade regulations, both with foreign nations and with other states. Foreign trade, always extremely important in the American

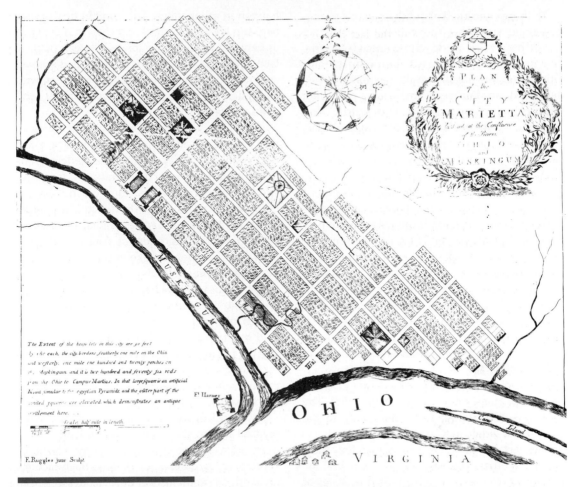

A town in the Northwest Territory. This was the town plan for the first major European-American settlement in the Northwest Territory, Marietta, in what is now Ohio. The main reason for its early importance is typical for new towns in the West: It was at "the Confluence of the Rivers Ohio and Muskingum." Older towns in the East tended to be built helter-skelter (with some notable exceptions, like Savannah and Philadelphia, which came late in the colonial period). But most western cities were surveyed before they were settled, so their street patterns could be a rectilinear grid. (The American Antiquarian Society)

economy, depended, of course, on relations with foreign nations. The Revolution had not altered the basic economic relationship between America and Europe. Europe was still the principal market and manufacturing center. But the Revolution had removed the British government from the picture. Now the Americans were free from British restrictions—but they were also "free" from British protection.

Sensing American weakness at the national level, the British put restrictions on American trade that were more severe than those of the old colonial system. For example, they barred American ships from other British colonies in the New World. Old patterns of trade were completely broken. New avenues of direct trade with nations like France and Spain did not take up the slack—at least not fast enough.

To those concerned about the nation's future, it seemed clear that the national government would have to be made strong enough to write new treaties of commerce with European nations. Otherwise, Americans would be ruined. They depended on European markets to sell their tobacco and other agricultural products. And they had to be able to buy European manufactured goods on a reasonable basis in order to survive.

A third difficulty was political stability. This was what people like Washington wanted most of all. If stability could be achieved, then Americans could seize the opportunities open to a new nation. The western lands furnished an important example. A stable political situation would allow people to move west, create new states, grow more crops, and import new quantities of manufactured goods. In doing so, they would be building a great new empire. But if stability was not gained, the British would refuse to evacuate their military posts in the Ohio Valley (which they did). The Spanish would try to break up American control of the Southwest by closing the Mississippi to American traffic (which they did). The frontier settlers might feel little loyalty to the nation and would refuse to pay debts and recognize eastern law and control (which they did).

Still another troublesome problem was the possibility of quarrels among individual states or different geographic regions of the country. Boundary quarrels had produced scattered armed conflicts between citizens of different states. Almost any law or treaty would have different effects on the North and the South, since one section depended heavily on commerce and the other was almost purely agricultural. Unless the states surrendered their sovereignty, sooner or later some issue would cause the nation to fly apart into competing regions.

Within the individual states, too, there were potential conflicts among groups that could tear state governments apart. Washington felt that Shays's Rebellion was frightening. It was even more frightening as an indication of what might

happen in other states. There might be disputes between western farmers and eastern merchants or between religious groups or between political factions. If the country was to survive, it seemed essential to create a national government with enough power to settle problems among and within states.

Added to all these issues, in the minds of many political leaders, was what might be called the "problem" of democracy. The leaders of the Revolution were not democratic in ways we would recognize. That is, they did not believe everyone should participate directly in government. All the states had some kind of property or tax-paying qualification for voting. Only people with an economic stake in society could take part in government (and of these, only free white males almost everywhere). All the states had complicated barriers to popular control of any branch of the government. The political theory held by almost all the Founding Fathers taught that the people were sovereign only in an abstract sense; individuals were equal only in theory. In practice, they believed government ought to be in the hands of men of education and property.

In almost every state, however, there was a political faction that wanted more democracy—a broader suffrage, more frequent elections, shorter terms of office for leaders. Such factions demanded laws that would protect debtors from their creditors. They tried to get the states to print more, not less, paper money. With more money the farmers could pay off their debts to bankers and merchants in cheap, almost worthless, currency. These factions demanded equal representation in the legislatures for the farming areas outside cities like New York, Boston, and Philadelphia. They talked, in other words, of what Washington would have scorned as "democratical" government. To Washington—and to most of the wealthy, educated leaders who came from the eastern seaboard—such talk could lead only to anarchy. The inherent danger in the Articles was that in any given state the "democratic" faction might get control of the government. If this

Noah Webster

The efforts of men like Washington to forge a more independent and secure political structure for the new nation were paralleled by similar preoccupations in every area of life. Poets and novelists set out to create a new, "American" literature. Others attempted to create an "American" style in religion or dress or manners or even diet. Noah Webster—whose name became almost synonymous with *dictionary*—tried to devise an American language as different as possible from the English language of England.

Webster's efforts began when he was a modest schoolteacher in the tiny town of Goshen, New York. In 1782 (the year the British and Americans began to negotiate the peace treaty), Webster published a little spelling book. The title eventually became *The American Spelling Book*, but for several generations of Americans who learned from it, it was known universally as "the Blue-backed Speller." Together with a grammar book he wrote in 1784 and a reader of 1785, Webster's speller created a common language for a society with the world's highest literacy rate.

Webster's purposes were mixed, but all of them were common to his age. He believed that literacy was closely tied to character. In fact, a common slogan about the Blue-backed Speller was that it "taught millions to read and not one to sin." But virtue, for Webster as much as for Washington, was closely tied to nationality. He was not interested solely in creating virtuous character, but virtuous national character. This, he thought, required a language that was uniform, that cut across regional lines and class differences.

The main principle behind Webster's speller was simplicity. He changed British endings like *-our* in such words as *honour* and *labour* to the *-or* in *honor* and *labor*. The mysterious *-re* in British words like *theatre* and *centre* became *-er* for Webster's generations of pupils. The double middle consonants in British words like *waggon* became single, as in *wagon*. Ambiguous spellings like *gaol* became phonetically recognizable as *jail*. Similarly, *plow* replaced *plough*. (There were limits to reform, however, and some of Webster's proposals—like *wurd* for *word* and *iz* for *is*—did not catch on.)

After the successes of his speller, Webster was preoccupied with two grand projects. The first was his dictionary. He spent years collecting notes on the ways Americans spoke and wrote English. In 1828 he finally published the result. His dictionary was in two volumes and included about 12,000 "new" words—words, that is, that had not appeared in any English dictionary published previously.

Webster's second great preoccupation was reminiscent of Washington's ambition to build a canal system connecting Virginia to the West. Webster wanted a national copyright law to protect the interests of authors by preventing printers from simply copying books without paying authors any royalties. Webster was not a nationalist *because* of his concern for the economic interests of writers—any more than Washington was a nationalist merely because he owned western lands. But in both cases, there was an intimate connection between ideas and interests, a harmony of ideological and practical concerns, that made a strong nationalism seem the only appropriate option.

Picture: The Metropolitan Museum of Art, bequest of Charles Allen Munn, 1924 happened, there would be no national power to intervene in behalf of the state's republican government. There would be no national constitution forbidding the states to abolish debts, private property, and political privilege.

During the few years between the peace of 1783 and the Philadelphia Convention, all these problems, domestic and foreign, gradually came together. The concerns might differ from person to person. John Adams might fear democracy more than Thomas Jefferson. Washington might be more concerned with western lands than Alexander Hamilton, whose principal worry was public finance. But sooner or later, in much the same way the revolutionary movement had built up in the colonies, the movement to revise or repudiate the Articles of Confederation grew. People in one state corresponded with their friends and relatives in another. Soon most of those who had led the Revolution were involved in a movement to make a second, peaceful revolution. They would throw off their government, just as they had done in 1776, and replace it with another.

Washington's interests, plans, and fears led him to Philadelphia in exactly the same way that dozens of other people were led by their interests, plans, and fears. Most of the delegates went to Philadelphia sharing the conviction that something had to be done. The Articles had to be drastically altered or else thrown out. If the Articles could have been amended more easily, the Philadelphia Convention might well have simply changed them, leaving the government basically intact. But the delegates decided to start afresh, to draw on the experience of making state constitutions, and to build a new United States.

The Philadelphia Convention

The fifty-five delegates who straggled into Philadelphia in the summer of 1787 were an extremely interesting group of politicians. As statesmen go, they were young. More were under thirty than over sixty. Together they represented an enormous amount of experience—in war, in the Congress, on foreign missions, and in state governments. Thirty-one had college educations—at a time when many people could not read, and only a tiny fraction of the population went to school for more than a few years. In fact, every delegate who spoke in the Convention was college educated. Most of them were wealthy men who were as interested in maintaining social order as they were in experimenting with political forms. They were, in short, a political, economic, and social elite.

Perhaps the most interesting fact about the Convention was that almost all its delegates had decided the main question before coming to Philadelphia. They were already committed to building a national government to replace the Confederation. Before the first hour of debate in the hot hall where they met, most of them had agreed on another point: Their essential goal was to create a government that would operate on *citizens of the United States*, rather than on the *states* as the old Congress had done. Since this goal was more or less taken for granted, the real questions involved methods. How would the interests of the small states and large states be reconciled? How would power be divided among various branches of government? How would the question of slavery be handled, if at all?

For all its importance in American history, the Constitutional Convention spent much of its time in what might be called tinkering. The delegates' work was a kind of political carpentry, in which they arranged and rearranged parts to satisfy the most people. Very little discussion of high-flown political theory took place. Whenever a word like *democracy* was mentioned, it was used as a scare word, to provoke fear.

All the tinkering had one objective. Delegates wanted to create a political structure that would not alarm the people, who were very much afraid of strong central government. They also wanted to avoid putting any particular state or geographic section of the country at a disadvantage. The Founding Fathers needed a consensus, a common acceptance of what they accomplished.

THE VIRGINIA AND NEW JERSEY PLANS The Convention spent much of its time discussing the virtues and faults of two different plans. The first, called the Virginia Plan (drafted by Virginian James Madison), would have made voting in the national legislature dependent on population. Virginia or Masachusetts, for example, would have had more votes than Rhode Island or Delaware. The second plan, the New Jersey Plan (proposed by delegate William Paterson of New Jersey), would have continued the system used in the Articles, giving each state the same number of votes.

There were several other important differences between the Virginia and New Jersey plans. The Virginia Plan provided for an executive with a veto power over acts of Congress. In other words, it proposed creating a strong executive, with power balancing that of the legislature. The New Jersey Plan proposed an executive, too, but it would have been composed of several people elected by the legislature, like a cabinet, and it would have had no veto power.

Both plans provided for a national judiciary, separated from and working in balance with the executive and the legislature. But there was an important difference. The Virginia Plan called for both a national supreme court and other, lower federal courts. The New Jersey Plan, in contrast, provided for a supreme court only. Under this plan, therefore, the national court in most cases could only act on appeals from the state courts.

Though there were some exceptions, generally the delegates from the small states supported the New Jersey proposal, while those from large states favored the Virginia Plan. The reasons were obvious. The Virginia Plan would give the large states almost complete control of the national government. The New Jersey Plan would have made the states equal in Congress; it would have made Congress much more powerful than the other branches of government. No great principles of "liberty" or "democracy" were involved in this conflict. The issue was simple and practical. How could the new constitution be adjusted to give equal protection to the interests of both the large and the small states?

The New Constitution

Out of the debate over the Virginia and New Jersey plans came a series of compromises, sometimes known as the Great Compromise. As with many compromises, the solution to the main problem was really very simple. The Convention delegates created a Congress consisting of two houses. The upper house, which they named the Senate, would have equal representation, with each state sending two senators. In the lower house, the House of Representatives, representation would be by districts, apportioned according to population.

The Senate was essentially the kind of legislature proposed in the New Jersey Plan. It protected the interests of the small states. In fact, the Convention provided that this feature of the Constitution could never be amended unless every state consented to have the number of its senators reduced. The House of Representatives, on the other hand, was a reflection of the large-state bias of the Virginia Plan.

As a concession to some of the smaller states and to states where slavery was not common, the South agreed to count a slave as only three-fifths of a person. This meant the number of representatives for a state like Virginia or South Carolina would not be so large as originally suggested by the Virginia Plan. (Slaves were not mentioned as such anywhere in the Constitution. Instead, they were referred to as "other persons" or "such persons.")

POWERS OF THE FEDERAL GOVERNMENT The powers given to Congress were about the same as those exercised by the old Congress under the Articles. Congress could declare war and coin and borrow money. But two important new powers were added, powers whose absence had crippled the old Congress. The new Congress could raise revenues through taxation, and regulate commerce with foreign nations and among the states.

A more significant revision of the old Articles was the creation of an executive branch, independent of Congress and on an equal footing with it. The chief executive would be called the president. (Everyone at the Convention assumed, as they drew up the article on executive powers, that the first president would be Washington.) The president's principal duty was to execute the laws passed by Congress, but he was also given some of the powers that the British king exercised: being commander in chief, for example, and conducting foreign policy.

The Constitution also provided for a judicial branch. There would be a Supreme Court with final power to enforce federal laws and interpret the Constitution whenever legal questions arose. In addition, Congress had the power to create other federal courts to ensure that federal law and the Constitution remained what the Constitution said they should be—the "supreme law of the land."

CHECKS AND BALANCES Among these three branches of the new government was to be a complicated system of relationships. Each branch was to have some independence from the others. That is, there was to be a separation of powers. The judges of the federal courts would serve for life. This would presumably make them independent. The president would owe his office to no other branch of the federal government but to the electors of the electoral college. Senators would be elected by and therefore responsible to state legislatures. Congressmen would answer to their constituents. All the officers of the new government, in other words, would have separate bases of power and support.

These separations were far from complete, however. Judges were to be nominated by the president and approved by the Senate. They could be removed from office through a process of impeachment by Congress. Nor was the presidency altogether separate. Obviously, presiden-

tial programs of almost every type would eventually require money. Funds would have to be voted by Congress. Also, presidential appointees, such as ambassadors or cabinet officers, would have to be approved by the Senate. Finally, as a last resort, a president could be removed from office through impeachment.

Despite the creation of the executive and judicial branches, the framers' minds were still dominated by their own experience. The legislature was, for most of them, still the basic, lawmaking centerpiece of the new government—as it had been in the states and in the Confederation. But the powers of Congress were subjected to new checks. The president was given the power to veto any law unless a two-thirds majority in Congress overturned a veto. The members of the Convention assumed in their debates that the courts, especially the Supreme Court, would have the power to declare any act of Congress unconstitutional. (In the end, the Constitution did not explicitly give the courts this right, and a good deal of argument was to take place on the question of whether the courts actually had this ultimate power. In practice, however, no Congress and no president ever defied a Supreme Court ruling—at least not for long.) Still, within the constitutional limits of its powers, a two-thirds majority in Congress was given about as much freedom of action as Parliament had ever had in England.

In these and other ways, the powers of government were separate yet interdependent through a system of checks and balances. The idea behind this system was that no part of the government ought to become powerful enough to override the other branches or violate the Constitution. At any one time a strong president, a runaway Congress, or a determined Supreme Court might take the initiative on a policy question. But the other two branches would always be watching carefully—at least in theory. Each would thus protect its own powers and defend the basic structure of government as laid down in the Constitution.

FEDERALISM The Constitution created a federal system of government—that is, one in which power is divided between the national government and state governments. In keeping with their general approach, Convention delegates wanted this division of powers and responsibilities to be a balanced one.

On the one hand, the Constitution itself limited the powers that the national government could exercise. And the states were protected by retaining control over the processes of electing senators and congressmen.

On the other hand, nothing was said about state sovereignty in this new Constitution. The states were forbidden to do two very important things: issue paper money or "impair the obligation of contract." This meant no state legislature could pass any law that significantly altered existing property relationships. The specter of Shays's Rebellion lay behind these two provisions.

ATTITUDES TOWARD DEMOCRACY The Constitution that came out of Philadelphia contained few guarantees of individual liberties. The states and the federal government were forbidden to create titles of nobility. The federal government—but not the states—was forbidden to set up any religious qualifications for holding office. Except for these provisions and one or two others, the Constitution was remarkably silent about the great question of liberty, the question that had rung out so loudly and clearly in 1776.

As for democracy, the Constitution had nothing at all to say. Only one group of officials in the new government would be elected by the voters directly: members of the House of Representatives. Even in this case the states were given complete control of property or religious qualifications for voting. Senators were to be chosen by the state legislatures. The president would be selected by the electoral college. Justices of the Supreme Court and other federal judges would be appointed by the president (who had been chosen by the electors). Then judges would be confirmed by the Senate (chosen by the state legislatures).

Almost every member of the convention would have agreed that these provisions were much better than direct popular election. The people might rule, in theory. But they would be allowed to rule only at a distance and through machinery complicated enough to slow down or stop any movement toward popular democracy at the national level. Furthermore, the federal government guaranteed each state a republican form of government. This protected the states from any attempt to establish monarchial governments. But it also meant that any move toward "anarchy"—like Shays's Rebellion—could be met by federal force.

Was there, then, no genius to the Constitution? Was it nothing more than political tinkering resulting from a desire to protect order from the "democratical" elements in society? Many of the delegates would probably have answered yes. They were practical, hard-bitten men who had been burned more than once by popular movements that threatened to get out of hand.

But for a few others, notably Madison, there was another aspect to the Constitution that not many people noticed at the time. The opening words of the document are "We the People." This Constitution, unlike the Articles and many of the state constitutions, would rest, in some sense or other, on the popular will. And it would operate directly on the people, with minimal intervention of state power.

The new government could tax individual citizens. It could try them in its own courts under its own laws. The federal courts might even declare state or local laws unconstitutional—though this possibility was hardly discussed at all in Philadelphia. Finally (the most inspired maneuver of all), the Constitution would be ratified by specially chosen conventions in the states, not by the state legislatures. Thus the new government would be created not by the states but by "We the People."

The Struggle for Ratification

The new Constitution was drafted and approved by a majority of delegates by mid-September. (For the complete text, see the back of this volume.) At this point, the delegates at Philadelphia must have felt somewhat uneasy. They had been told by their state legislatures and by the Congress to amend the Articles of Confederation. But they had scarcely considered this as a possibility. Instead, they had created a new government. They had held secret debates about a scheme that amounted to a coup d'état. They knew they had very little chance of getting all the states to accept the new government, at least not for several years. So they proposed their most radical idea of all: The new Constitution would go into effect as soon as nine state conventions had accepted it.

The proponents of the Constitution had some important advantages. For one thing, almost everyone agreed that something had to be done about the Articles. Another advantage was the prestige of men like Washington and Franklin. A third was the method of ratification. The state legislatures might have rejected the document in order to preserve their own powers, but a series of conventions elected for the specific purpose of judging the plan would give it a better chance of adoption. As for the document itself, delegates argued that their complicated structure of checks and balances left little to fear from the new central government.

Despite all these advantages, ratification was an uphill fight. A shrewd observer of American politics in 1787 would probably have predicted that the Constitution would be rejected. There was opposition in the Congress. Why, some of its members argued, should that body roll over and play dead? Some members of the Constitutional Convention itself, alarmed by the final result, had refused to sign the document and

Alexander Hamilton. One of the great leaders of the Federalist cause, and secretary of the treasury under the new government, was Alexander Hamilton. He was the author of more than half the essays in *The Federalist*. At the Constitutional Convention, Hamilton argued for an overwhelmingly powerful executive. (Library of Congress)

were ready to mount opposition. Finally, there were the old traditional state loyalties to overcome. The Constitution, much more than the patriot leaders of the Revolution, much more than the Articles, asked people to think of themselves as Americans, not solely as citizens of a state.

Generally, those who favored the Constitution were more aggressive than its opponents. They were richer and better educated. They wrote more, spoke more, and lobbied more. Three young men—Madison, Hamilton, and John Jay of New York—produced a remarkable series of newspaper essays in favor of the Constitution. (The essays were later published as a book, *The Federalist*.) These essays have become so much a part of history that they have even been cited as evidence in Supreme Court opinions. Madison, Hamilton, and Jay also managed to acquire the

John Jay. John Jay, like Hamilton, was a New York politician who distrusted the principle of democracy. He wrote a number of the articles in *The Federalist*. He would become an important diplomat in George Washington's administration and then chief justice of the United States. (Yale University Art Gallery)

name "Federalist" for their political faction. ("Nationalist" would have been more accurate.) This seemed to leave no name for the opposition but the clumsy and empty "Antifederalist."

The first state convention to act, that of Delaware, did so swiftly. After that, the fight for ratification was close, tough, and full of bargaining. The decisions of the four largest states—Massachusetts, New York, Pennsylvania, and Virginia—were crucial. Theoretically, the Constitution could have been ratified without the participation of any of them. Actually, however, the new government would have been crippled without all of them. Pennsylvania fell into line in December 1787. But when the Massachusetts convention first met, the vote on the Constitution was 192 against, 144 in favor. The prospects for ratification were also poor in Virginia and New

York. Eventually, in February 1788, the Federalists managed to win in Massachusetts, which voted 187 to 168 in favor of the Constitution. In Virginia the convention ended by supporting the Constitution 89 to 79 at the end of June 1788. Meanwhile, New Hampshire had ratified on June 21, becoming the ninth state to do so and thus officially putting the Constitution into effect. But New York still stood outside, along with North Carolina and Rhode Island.

The Antifederalists were very strong in New York, but Virginia's ratification helped turn the tide. With it, ten states had already ratified. It looked as if New York, the only large state not to do so, might stand alone. The essays of *The Federalist* also had a strong impact. New York ratified July 26, a month after Virginia's vote. North Carolina and Rhode Island hung back until 1789 and 1790, respectively, but there was no need to wait. The old Congress simply closed up shop and ordered new elections for early in 1789.

Things Left Unsaid and Undone

To Washington, Madison, Hamilton, and the other Federalists, it was clear that a crisis had been averted. They had acted with care and energy, they believed, and saved the nation from itself. The uphill struggle for ratification had been the final critical stage, but they had won. To many Antifederalists, however, a world had been lost. Now they could only engage in opposition politics in the new Congress when it finally met. Regarding the choice of president there was no question; Washington was the only conceivable man for the job. But the fight over ratification had caused men to band together into factions, with the beginnings of platforms or programs.

But the Constitution was silent on the question of political parties. This was not because the framers were naive or inexperienced men. Many

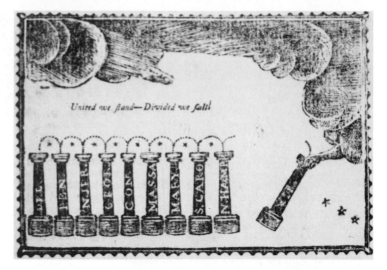

The ninth pillar raised. After New Hampshire became the ninth state to ratify the new Constitution (by a narrow margin of 57 to 46), *The New Hampshire Gazette* celebrated with this woodcut. It represented each ratifying state as an independent column, but joined by a starry bond to the others, giving mutual support. Virginia, the tenth state, is being raised up by what would seem to be the hand of God. "Fame," the *Gazette* trumpeted, "claps her wings and sounds it to the skies." (The American Antiquarian Society)

of them had been forming and leading political factions for twenty years, and they were acutely aware of how rapidly political parties had taken shape in the states in the years since the Revolution. But they all said they despised the "spirit of party," maintaining that no "gentleman" could ever take up the career of politician and believing that political parties usually became the instruments of men who were interested only in office and power, men who would trick and mislead the voters.

One of the main hopes of the men who wrote the Constitution was that they had created a system of government so remote from the voters that no national parties would be formed. This was one of the reasons behind the cumbersome machinery of the electoral college, instead of direct election of the president. This was also the motive for stipulating that the six-year terms of senators be staggered, with only a third up for election every two years. And the fear of parties was an important reason for having senators chosen by state legislators rather than in direct elections.

The framers did not accurately foresee the future. Within a few years after 1787, they themselves would form political parties and contend for control of the national government. The organized efforts in favor of and against ratification

began the process. But it went on with a vengeance in the 1790s. During the decades after 1800, there would be intermittent periods when the struggles between political parties were subdued. But in the long run, parties became the most prominent and permanent fact of American political life. What Americans like to call "the two-party system" became part of their culture—but it was a part that the Founding Fathers would have regarded with fear and dismay.

The Constitution said nothing about another important feature of national life. Except for the so-called three-fifths clause and provisions relating to the slave trade and fugitive slaves, it was nearly silent on the issue of slavery. During the decades after 1787, the two most prominent features of American history were the rise of political parties and a series of crises involving slavery. The Founding Fathers were great political leaders, but they were not prophets. If they were trying to guess at the future, they badly misjudged what it held.

In the final analysis, the Constitution represented only a political structure, a kind of skeleton on which history would have to build a political and social body. The "vessel was afloat," as Washington said. But only experience would tell whether its compass, sails, and other equipment would be able to provide the order and stability that the Philadelphia Convention wanted so badly. Soon challenges would come from directions and from people the delegates at Philadelphia could hardly have imagined, much less prepared for.

THE BILL OF RIGHTS Another subject on which the Constitution was almost silent was "liberty"—all those rights that individuals have *against* governments. This question was fiercely debated during the ratification process, and the Federalists responded by promising to add amendments spelling out the rights of citizens under the new government. The result of this promise was a series of amendments—twelve, at first, but reduced to ten—that came quickly to be known as the Bill of Rights.

The task of drawing up the amendments fell to James Madison. He sifted through a large number of recommendations, some proposing as many as forty different provisions. He also worked through precedents in the state constitutions, particularly the Declaration of Rights adopted in Virginia in the first year of the Revolution. Finally, Madison boiled the proposals down to seventeen. The Senate dropped five of these, and what finally emerged were the first ten amendments to the Constitution. They contained the now familiar guarantees of freedom of speech, press, religion, assembly, trial by jury, the right to bear arms, and so forth, plus a general amendment stressing that the federal government had *only* those powers explicitly granted in the Constitution. (Two other proposals, concerning the proportioning of representation and the salaries of members of Congress, were quietly dropped.)

The amendments were quickly ratified—though three of the original states did not get around to doing so until 1941. One of the main objections of the Antifederalists had been met, and the Constitution had at last some genuine claim to originality and historic significance.

Suggestions for Further Reading

GEORGE WASHINGTON

A very readable introduction to Washington is Marcus Cunliffe, *George Washington, Man and Monument* (1958). Serious students will want to look into Douglas Southall Freeman's massive and adoring seven volumes, *George Washington* (1948–59). Washington's career as commanding general, both during and after the Revolutionary War, can be seen in context in Robert Middlekauff, *The Glorious Cause* (1982).

THE CONFEDERATION PERIOD

Gordon Wood, *The Creation of the American Republic, 1776–1787* (1969), is a fine place to start. Two books by Merrill Jensen, *The Articles of Confederation* (1940) and *The New Nation* (1950), are still essential reading for serious students. Jackson Turner Main, *The Sovereign States* (1973), is equally important. The functioning of the Congress can be followed in J. N. Rakove, *The Beginnings of National Politics* (1979). A particularly fine state study is Edward Countryman, *A People in Revolution: The American Revolution and Political Society in New York, 1760–1790* (1981).

THE CONVENTION AND THE CONSTITUTION

A long debate on the nature of the movements for and against the new Constitution was begun in 1913 by Charles Beard, *An Economic Interpretation of the Constitution*. Part of Beard's argument—that the Founding Fathers expected to benefit directly from the new government because they held large quantities of government securities—has been subjected to searching scrutiny by later historians, most aggressively by Forrest McDonald in *We the People* (1958). But Beard's more general point, that the Constitution was the product of a distinctive consciousness of the relationship between politics and social class, remains an important one. Fine examples of

CHRONOLOGY

1781 The Articles of Confederation ratified by the last state. Cornwallis surrenders his army at Yorktown, Virginia. Congress proposes duties on imports; the amendment to the Articles of Confederation fails when it is rejected by Rhode Island.

1783 The Congress ratifies the Treaty of Paris, recognizing American independence. Congress proposes a five percent impost on imports; again, it fails. Washington surrenders his commission to the Congress.

1777 Continental Congress completes draft of Articles of Confederation.

1776	1777	1778	1779	1780	1781	1782	1783

1782 Peace negotiations begin in Paris among representatives of France, Britain, and the United States. Noah Webster publishes *The Little Spelling Book.*

1786 Shays's Rebellion breaks out in Massachusetts; it is quickly suppressed. Annapolis Convention meets to discuss revisions to the Articles of Confederation.

1790 Rhode Island ratifies the Constitution. The first amendments to the Constitution, the "Bill of Rights," are approved by Congress and submitted to the states for ratification.

1784 Washington travels to Pennsylvania and the West.

1788 The Constitution is ratified by New York, the necessary ninth state.

1784	1785	1786	1787	1788	1789	1790	1791

1785 Washington named head of the Potomac River Company.

1787 The Confederation Congress passes the Northwest Ordinance. The Constitutional Convention meets in Philadelphia. Madison, Hamilton, and Jay begin to write *The Federalist* essays. The first of the states ratify the new Constitution.

1789 The first national elections. Washington inaugurated president. North Carolina ratifies the Constitution.

its continuing vitality are Jackson Turner Main, *The Anti-Federalists* (1961), and Gordon Wood, *The Creation of the American Republic* (1969). There are a number of good modern editions of the essential papers that became known as *The Federalist*.

THINGS LEFT UNSAID AND UNDONE

The best approach to the question of political parties is Jackson Turner Main's extremely careful study, *Political Parties Before the Constitution* (1973). On slavery during this period, the indispensable book is David Brion Davis, *The Problem of Slavery in the Age of Revolution, 1770–1823* (1975). Arthur Zilversmit, *The First Emancipation* (1967), is a valuable study of the ending of slavery in some of the states. The later chapters of Winthrop Jordon, *White over Black* (1968), are also relevant. A good account of the first amendments to the Constitution is Robert A. Rutland, *The Birth of the Bill of Rights* (1955).

CHAPTER 6
THE REPUBLIC
ON TRIAL

THE EPISODE: *One of the most striking features of the movement that led to the American Revolution was that so many of its leaders were quite young men. And when the war for independence finally began, even younger men were catapulted from lives as farm boys, clerks, or students into positions of military authority. And this sudden leap from obscurity to what they called "glory" led a whole generation of these young men to pursue very ambitious careers in public life after the war. From the end of the Revolution down to 1820, the United States was, in effect, governed by the cohort of youths that had declared and won independence.*

One such man was Aaron Burr, who at the beginning of the Revolution found himself a captain at the age of twenty. After the war, he became a lawyer—and a very good one, too. But, as for so many of his contemporaries, the law was only an aspect of his real career, politics. He helped form a political party, served as a senator, then became Vice President of the United States in 1800. But then one of the most curious episodes in American history brought his spectacular career into crisis—eventually bringing him to trial for treason.

THE HISTORICAL SETTING: *The revolutionary generation had its heroes and its villains. The heroes—the Washingtons, Jeffersons, Hamiltons, and Franklins—are revered, and their faces adorn even our currency. The villains are less well known. Aaron Burr has become one of them, lost to the fame that might have been his. But our purpose is not to judge Burr; through understanding his career, we can understand the main forces at work in the history of the United States during its first decades.*

From 1790 to 1820, the new United States took shape. Its government became a reality rather than a constitutional projection. Its first political parties were formed. Its western lands began to be settled by European Americans. It confronted the strains of regional and sectional dissension. The new nation also had to find its way through a difficult thicket of foreign affairs, complicated by the French Revolution and the Napoleonic Wars in Europe. While trying to survive in this difficult international setting, the United States acquired a territory in the West that doubled its size, fought an undeclared war with France, almost went to war with Spain, and fought a declared war with Britain. The forces at work in all these events were also at work in the rise and fall of Aaron Burr. In a sense, he was always on trial, from the time he became a revolutionary soldier to his formal trial for treason. But the new Republic was also on trial. And the nature and outcome of these twin processes, one individual and the other national, depended on the same kinds of historical realities.

AARON BURR, CONSPIRATOR

Early on the morning of July 11, 1804, a pair of small barges carried two duelists across the Hudson River from New York to the New Jersey town of Weehawken. The two seconds for the duel, and the usual doctor, were also aboard. The two parties in the duel went to a level spot along the river, cleared away some of the summer brush, and carefully loaded the pistols. After the two men had taken up positions ten paces apart, one of the seconds called out "Present!" Each man raised his pistol in a salute similar to a fencer's "En garde!" Without any further ceremony or signal the two men fired, one a little after the other. One of the men spun partly around and fell forward. The small, round shot had lodged in his spine, and he was bleeding internally. The other man started to rush forward as if to help or offer a gentleman's apology. But he was pulled away by his second and taken quickly back across the river to New York. The wounded man went home more slowly, lapsing in and out of consciousness. He lived with pain, doses of opium, and a grieving family, into the next afternoon. Then he died.

The dead man was Alexander Hamilton, a hero of the Revolution. He had been first secretary of the treasury, and he was a leader of the Federalist party. He had achieved a remarkable career in his forty-nine years. As he lay dying, his doctor released frequent public bulletins on his condition. After his death, the city of New York went into official mourning. Mass meetings demanded the arrest of the "murderer," who escaped from the city after a few days. Finally, in both New York and New Jersey, Hamilton's opponent was indicted for murder. He fled first to Philadelphia and then south to Georgia and out of the country to Florida (still a Spanish possession). Much of the time, he traveled under an assumed name, like any ordinary fugitive from justice.

Sooner or later, however, this particular outlaw had to come out of hiding. For he was, in fact, the vice president of the United States, Aaron Burr. He could afford to spend the late summer and early fall in the South, but Congress would soon go into session, and it was his constitutional duty to preside over the Senate. He was fairly certain that the murder charges would eventually be dropped. In the meantime, he would not be arrested if he stayed out of New York and New Jersey. Even though New York was his home, he had no reason to go there. His handsome house had been sold at auction to pay off some of his debts, and his other creditors were howling for the rest of his money. So, on November 4, the vice president, over his head in debt and wanted for murder, took his seat as the president of the Senate. One senator, shocked at Burr's display of nerve, wrote angrily to a friend, "We are indeed fallen on evil times!"

It was not really the Senate that had fallen on evil times. The main victim (aside from the dead Hamilton, of course) was Burr himself. He was a gentleman and had fought an honorable duel—still the custom among some gentlemen of the day. He had won. But he had lost, too.

Burr had enjoyed as spectacular a career as Hamilton. Like Hamilton, he had been one of the young heroes of the Revolution. A brilliant lawyer, he was said never to have lost a case. He was also a very shrewd and successful politician. He had already been a senator from New York.

But now, in the fall of 1804, Burr was in disgrace because of the duel and his debts. His term as vice president was expiring. He had just been defeated in an attempt to become governor of New York—a defeat that Hamilton had helped bring about and that was the cause of their duel. Hamilton had been criticizing Burr privately for many years. During the campaign for governor, remarks by Hamilton were released publicly that referred to Burr as "a dangerous man and one who ought not to be trusted with the reins of government." When Hamilton refused either to deny the remarks or to apologize, Burr had challenged him to the duel.

Burr was still in his forties, but it seemed his career might be ruined. He never allowed himself to become publicly flustered, so he kept up an appearance of calm. In a letter to his married daughter, Theodosia, he even made a joke of the entire affair:

> You have doubtless heard that there has subsisted for some time a contention of a very singular nature between the states of New York and New Jersey. The subject in dispute is which shall have the honor of hanging the Vice President. A paper received this morning asserts, but without authority, that he has determined in favor of New York. You shall have due notice of the time and place. Whenever it may be you may rely on a great company, much gayety, and many rare sights, such as the lion, the elephant, etc.

To his daughter's husband, Burr hinted that the situation was more serious. The duel would not cost him his life, to be sure. But his career was a shambles, and so he wrote, "I shall seek another country."

~≈

One thing was certain. During that winter the vice president's mind was not on Senate business. He was busy instead with mysterious maps and a dangerous partnership. An old friend of Burr's was in Washington that winter. He was James Wilkinson, the highest-ranking general in the army of the United States. The general also happened to be a spy. For years he had been Agent 13 on the Spanish espionage rolls. He was very much interested in the same sorts of maps and plans as Burr.

James Wilkinson. General Wilkinson eventually testified against Burr in a treason trial. But the government prosecutors never quite trusted him. In the War
of 1812, Wilkinson performed poorly, then retired to
write a long and pompous autobiography. (Independence National Historical Park Collection)

The vice president who was wanted for murder and the general who was a spy
had known each other many years. In fact, they had been twenty-year-old captains
together during the first year of the Revolution. Their paths parted when Wilkinson
was forced to leave the army after joining a plot against George Washington. Burr
went on to become a major on Washington's staff.

Like many others in trouble, Wilkinson had gone west. He made a career in
politics in western Pennsylvania and Kentucky, and he began his secret occupation
as a Spanish agent. In 1791 Wilkinson was able to reenter the army and fight against
the Native Americans in the Ohio Valley. He rose rapidly in rank, and by 1796 was
the highest-ranking general in the army.

From about 1794 on, Burr and Wilkinson had carried on a secret, coded correspondence. Now, together again in Washington in the winter of 1804–05, they made
new plans and copied maps of Spanish possessions in the Southwest and of the
western territories of the United States.

At this time, Spain still ruled the American West and Southwest, as well as
Mexico. (The term *Mexico* was often used to refer to all these North American regions.)
The Spanish also owned East Florida—the peninsula itself—and what was called West
Florida—the area west of the peninsula, north of the Gulf of Mexico. The United
States had just purchased the territory known as Louisiana, the vast region between
the Mississippi River and the Rocky Mountains (see map, p. 269).

In the area between the Mississippi and the Appalachians, change was the order of the day. So far, only Tennessee, Ohio, and Kentucky had been admitted to statehood. But from Michigan to Mississippi, settlers were on the move, driving out Native Americans and clearing land. If these western states and territories decided to secede from the Union, there was little chance the federal government could use force to hold them.

Two very dangerous but exciting possibilities occupied the imaginations of Burr and Wilkinson. One was an invasion of Spanish territory. The other was an attempt to separate America's western lands from the rest of the Union. A private attack on Spain would be a crime. Separation of the West from the rest of the United States would be treason. If only one of the plans worked at first, then Burr and Wilkinson might try to combine the two. The result could be magnificent—a new nation stretching all the way from Ohio to Panama. The two plans had one very practical advantage: They required the same kind of preparation. If money could be found for it, a private army might be raised in the West. This army would travel downriver by way of the Ohio, the Cumberland, the Tennessee, and the Mississippi to New Orleans. Only then would a final choice have to be made between the conquest of Spanish possessions and the separation of the West.

These schemes made a great deal of sense in 1805. After all, the United States was a small and relatively weak nation. The government exerted little control over the states and territories west of the Appalachians. It had even less control over the lands west of the Mississippi. It seemed only a matter of time before Mexico and the Southwest broke away from Spain in a revolution such as the Americans had recently fought against Britain. The United States and Spain had been on the verge of war for some time. If war came, the conquest of Mexico and the Southwest would become a patriotic duty. Burr and Wilkinson had influence and friends in high places. Some friends could be brought into the plan, and others could be tricked into helping. There was little need to fear the American army, even if Wilkinson had not been in command. Its strength consisted of only about 3,000 troops scattered along the Atlantic coast and through the West. Burr and Wilkinson had every reason to believe that one scheme or the other, conquest or secession, would work. It was just possible that both plans might succeed, with thorough preparation, careful timing, and a run of good luck.

～◒

The first step was to obtain money and military support from some foreign power. When Burr fled New York after the duel with Hamilton, he sent a message to the British minister in Washington, Anthony Merry. Merry reported to his government that Burr had made an astonishing proposal.

> I have just received an offer from Mr. Burr to lend his assistance to his majesty's government in any manner in which they may think fit to employ him, particularly in endeavoring to effect a separation of the western part of the United States in its whole extent.

In late March of 1805, after a winter of planning with Wilkinson, Burr went to Merry in person. This time he had a more detailed scheme. Merry reported home in a dispatch marked "Most Secret":

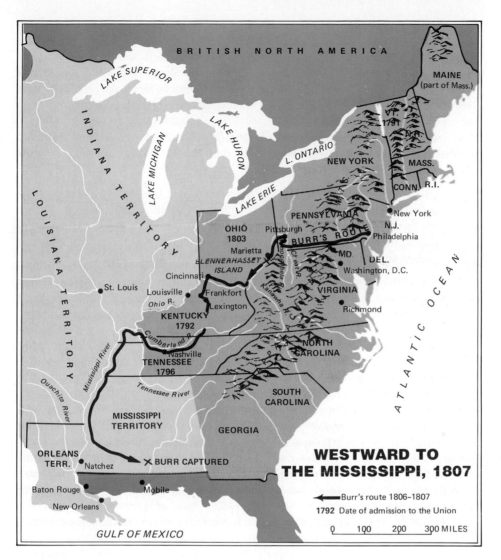

WESTWARD TO THE MISSISSIPPI, 1807

◄— Burr's route 1806–1807
1792 Date of admission to the Union

0   100   200   300 MILES

Mr. Burr has mentioned to me that the inhabitants of Louisiana seem determined to render themselves independent of the United States, and that the execution of their design is only delayed by the difficulty of obtaining assurance of protection from some foreign power.

Burr wanted the British to station a squadron of ships at the mouth of the Mississippi in order to immobilize the American navy. And he wanted a "loan" of half a million dollars. Merry was hooked. His secret dispatch ended by recommending Burr in the most favorable terms:

He certainly possesses, perhaps in a much greater degree than any other individual in this country, all the talents, energy, intrepidity, and firmness which are required for such an enterprise.

The response from England was painfully slow, so Wilkinson and Burr went ahead on their own. They managed to persuade President Jefferson to appoint Wilkinson governor of the Territory of Louisiana, which was created in 1805. Wilkinson would make his headquarters in St. Louis. Burr, meanwhile, would take a tour down the Ohio River and travel for several weeks in Kentucky and Tennessee. Then he would go down the Mississippi to New Orleans, making plans and enlisting support along the way.

Burr left Washington on horseback April 10, 1805. Three weeks later he arrived in Pittsburgh to begin his work. He embarked on the Ohio River in style. He wrote to his daughter, Theodosia, on April 30:

> Arrived in good order yesterday. Find my boat and hands ready. My boat is, properly speaking, a floating house, sixty feet by fourteen, containing dining room, kitchen with fireplace, and two bedrooms; roofed from stem to stern; steps to go up, and a walk on the top of the whole length; glass windows, etc. This edifice costs one hundred and thirty-three dollars.

On this elaborate "ark," as he called it, Burr went everywhere and saw everyone of any importance. He visited the senators and congressmen he knew from Washington. He stopped at plantations and country houses. Everywhere he was treated as a celebrity. At each stop, the story was the same. There might be a concert or a traveling play. There was certain to be a dinner or two with the leading citizens. Most important, there would be at least one long and guarded conversation among the men only, flavored with whiskey, secrecy, and cigars. Then Burr would hint at his plans and sound out his hosts for their possible future support.

Burr left the Ohio River at Louisville, Kentucky, then rode south across the state and into Tennessee. He visited Andrew Jackson in Nashville. For four days he filled Jackson with the exciting prospect of a war against Spain, in which Jackson's hill-country militia could help drive the Spanish out of Florida and then off the entire continent. From Nashville, Burr went down the Cumberland on one of Jackson's boats to rejoin his own great houseboat. He met Wilkinson at a small fort where the Ohio empties into the Mississippi.

Wilkinson gave Burr a military escort (even though Burr was no longer the vice president) and an "elegant barge" for the trip downriver to Natchez and New Orleans. In New Orleans Burr continued to hint at his purposes and find potential supporters. Then he headed north on horseback, through Nashville for another visit with Jackson. In St. Louis, Wilkinson's headquarters, Burr reported on his trip. Then he made the hard, slow journey back east, arriving in Washington in November. Though only a little over a year had passed since Burr's duel with Hamilton, his life had taken on a new direction, a new style, and new goals.

The next year was frustrating. Minister Merry's appeal to the British government for funds got nowhere. With a new collaborator—Jonathan Dayton, a senator from New Jersey—Burr tried to trick the Spanish themselves into financing the secession of the West. But the Spanish minister was cautious and would provide only $1,500, hardly enough to finance an army. Wilkinson was strangely silent, perhaps sensing that the time was not ripe. Burr began to suspect his colleague of being fainthearted.

Worst of all, both Spain and the United States were doing everything possible to avoid a war. Against such obstacles, no amount of preparation, cunning, or timing could win out. Burr wrote Wilkinson a coded letter complaining, "Nothing has been heard from Brigadier [Wilkinson] since October." The bad news, Burr said, was that the "execution of our project is postponed till December; want of water in Ohio renders movement impracticable."

"Want of water in Ohio" was the plotters' code phrase for "lack of necessary money." Without money they had no chance, unless there was a war with Spain. Unfortunately for the conspiracy, the administration of President Jefferson grounded its foreign strategy on the simple principle "Peace is our policy." Then, just at the moment when everything looked hopeless, the Spanish made a curious decision that almost led to the war Burr wanted so much.

When the United States bought Louisiana from France in 1803, its western boundary was left undefined. Technically, the United States could have claimed everything east of the Rio Grande. But the Spanish claimed the Texas region and sent in about 1,500 troops to occupy the area. Since Jefferson believed that Americans might never settle west of the Mississippi, he decided not to quarrel over Texas. Instead, he set the border with Mexico at the Sabine River. But the Spanish placed the border east of the Sabine, at a small stream named the Arroyo Hondo (see map, p. 269). In the fall of 1805, after Burr had returned east from his trip, the Spanish moved a few troops—twenty-nine men and one officer—across the Sabine. In February 1806 an American troop of sixty soldiers forced the Spanish to evacuate their post and return across the Sabine. These border incidents were small and not very dangerous, and Burr probably did not know about them. In fact, it took the government about six weeks to receive emergency messages from the border.

The country between the Sabine and the Arroyo Hondo was virtually uninhabited, and either the United States or Spain could have given it up with no loss to national interest or security. But both sides were stubborn. Jefferson, when he finally learned of the problem, announced that he intended to hold the Sabine line. The Spanish authorities in Mexico then reinforced their garrison and once more crossed the Sabine. The American commander in the area reported to his government that the situation was desperate. He had only 200 men fit for duty, six old guns, and a shabby fort. The Spanish refused to answer his request to withdraw.

Jefferson was determined. He ordered the frontier reinforced. Early in May the president told Wilkinson himself to move his headquarters to New Orleans and take personal command of the troops in the disputed area. Now the general was in an awkward position. All along, he had been trying to juggle three roles: commanding general of the army, spy for Spain, and plotter with Burr. The problems on the border brought the three roles into painful conflict and put him in a predicament.

In a crisis, Wilkinson could choose to combine any two of his three roles, but at least one of them had to be dropped. In case of war with Spain, he could be both commanding general and Burr's collaborator in the conquest of Mexico. The roles of spy for Spain and collaborator with Burr could work together if the goal were the secession of the West. Wilkinson's third option was to remain commanding general and spy for Spain. This would require him to keep peace with Spain along the Sabine but also to desert Burr and thus prevent either the conquest of Mexico or the secession of the West. The choices were extremely difficult. They depended on circumstances

UNDER MY WINGS EVERY THING PROSPERS

New Orleans. This illustration of New Orleans was made in 1804, shortly after the Louisiana Purchase. It was meant to suggest that under the American eagle, agriculture and commerce could flourish as never before. To the left is the great bend in the Mississippi River that made New Orleans a port city, even though it is many miles from the Gulf of Mexico. (The Historic New Orleans Collection)

that Wilkinson could not completely control, such as the movements of Spanish troops and the aggressiveness of Jefferson. Like many men confronting hard choices, Wilkinson moved slowly. Jefferson ordered him to leave St. Louis in May. The general hung back until August, when he finally started downriver to New Orleans.

Burr's problem, as he fretted through the spring of 1806, was just the opposite of Wilkinson's. Wilkinson had too many roles to juggle; Burr had no role and was trying to find one. During the months when it seemed there would be no war with Spain, Burr had been raising money among his friends and relatives. He had also decided to buy part of a huge land grant on the Ouachita River in what is now the state of Louisiana. If nothing else worked, he could bring in settlers and become a private prince. The preparations for the Ouachita plan—boats and armed men—were exactly the same as for the conquest of Mexico or the secession of the West.

When Burr heard the news of the border incidents on the Sabine River and learned that Jefferson had ordered Wilkinson to go to New Orleans, he made a fateful decision. On July 24 he sent a messenger west with a secret letter to Wilkinson written by Senator Jonathan Dayton. Dayton began by trying to convince Wilkinson that Jefferson was about to replace him as governor of the Louisiana Territory. He ended by urging Wilkinson to act:

> It is now well ascertained that you are to be displaced in the next session [of Congress]. Prepare yourself, therefore, for it. You know the rest. You are not a man to despair,

Jonathan Dayton. Senator Dayton (after whom Dayton, Ohio, is named) was eventually indicted for treason but was never put on trial. He may well have been the author of the famous "cipher letter" (see p. 246) that Wilkinson turned over to government authorities. (The Corcoran Gallery of Art, gift of William Wilson Corcoran)

especially when such prospects offer in another quarter. Are you ready? Are your numerous associates ready? Wealth and glory! Louisiana and Mexico!

The message was almost clear. Burr and Dayton were trying to get Wilkinson to commit himself. But to what? Dayton's words (which Burr probably dictated)—"You know the rest. . . . Louisiana and Mexico!"—left all the options open.

Burr had Dayton write another letter July 29 in the code he and Wilkinson had always used. It was much more elaborate, but it still left the choice of destinations open. This letter tried to trick Wilkinson by falsely claiming that all the pieces had fallen into place and by implying that success was certain:

Your letter postmarked 13th May is received. I have at length obtained funds and have actually commenced. The eastern detachments from different points and under different pretences will rendezvous on the Ohio, 1st of November.

The letter was exaggerating. The "eastern detachments" did not exist on July 29, except perhaps in imagination. This exaggeration was small, however, compared to the lies that followed immediately:

Every thing internal and external favors our views. Naval protection of England is secured. It [an English naval force] will meet us at the Mississippi.

The promise of English naval support was simply a lie. Minister Merry had not succeeded in getting a promise of help from London. The letter continued trying to excite Wilkinson's imagination:

It will be a host of choice spirits. Wilkinson shall be second to Burr only, and Wilkinson shall dictate the rank and promotion of his officers. Burr will proceed westward 1st August, never to return. Our object, my dear friend, is brought to a point so long desired. Burr guarantees the result with his life and honor, with the lives, and honor, and the fortunes of hundreds of the best blood of our country.

The cipher letter. The most famous piece of writing ever attributed to Aaron Burr was this jumble of numbers. Burr may have written it, or he may have inspired it; it is much more likely that it was written by Jonathan Dayton. The code was a simple one: the numbers stood for entries in a dictionary owned by the writer and Wilkinson. The third paragraph reads: "Burr will proceed westward 1 August—never to return. With him go his daughter and grandson. The husband will follow in October with a corps of worthies." The letter refers many times to Burr, always as Burr or as *he*. But it also uses the word *me* several times. This alone suggests it was not written by Burr at all. (Newberry Library)

Then came a few details of planned movements:

> Burr's plan of operation is to move down rapidly from the Falls [of the Ohio—that is, Louisville], on the 15th of November, with the first 500 or 1,000 men, in light boats now constructing for that purpose, to be at Natchez between the 5th and 15th of December, there to meet you, there to determine whether it will be expedient to seize on, or pass by, Baton Rouge.

After setting down these details, the letter hinted at the key to the entire scheme:

> The people of the country to which we are going are prepared to receive us; their agents, now with Burr, say that if we will protect their religion, and will not subject them to a foreign power, that in three weeks all will be settled.

What "country" did Burr, Wilkinson, and Dayton have in mind? The Louisiana Territory or Mexico? There probably were no agents of either Louisiana or Mexico with Burr at the time. Both areas were Catholic, so the protection of their religion would be a problem in one as well as the other. The most important clue may be the timetable of three weeks. Burr could hardly have hoped to put together a fleet, sail across the Gulf of Mexico to Veracruz, and conquer Mexico in such a short time. On the other hand, capturing New Orleans and proclaiming a new western nation probably could be done in three weeks, with Wilkinson's help. What Burr probably planned to do was to gather his forces, meet Wilkinson at Natchez, and then decide whether to invade Mexico, take over New Orleans, or peacefully settle the Ouachita lands. The simple fact was that his future was in Wilkinson's hands, and those hands became more unsteady every day. The letter closed with a last attempt to coax Wilkinson into action: "The gods invite us to glory and fortune; it remains to be seen whether we deserve the boon." A few days later, Burr set out for the Ohio, never to return—or so he believed.

Shortly after Burr left for the West, Wilkinson started downriver from St. Louis. He reached Natchez early in September and started up the Red River to the main American fort at Natchitoches. He arrived there September 22 to find a small, unprepared garrison, with no cannon or horses ready for duty. For thirty hot, frustrating days the general bargained and hesitated and tried to reinforce his little army. At first he was tough. He wrote the Spanish military commander of Texas that his orders were "absolute." The border was the Sabine River, and the Spanish must withdraw or face the consequences. But the Spaniard was just as tough. His orders were to enforce the Spanish claim east to the Arroyo Hondo, he said, and the choice of peace or war rested with Wilkinson.

While Wilkinson carried on his correspondence with the Spanish officials, he wrote very excited letters to his American friends. For a crucial two weeks at the end of September and the beginning of October, he became convinced that war with Spain was certain. He was ready for much more than a squabble over the border between Texas and Louisiana. At last, his dream of conquering Spanish Mexico seemed about to come true. On September 26 he wrote to a friend, Senator John Smith of Ohio:

> I have made the last effort of conciliation. I shall be obliged to fight and flog them. Five thousand mounted infantry may suffice to carry us forward as far as the Grand River [the Rio Grande]. There we shall require 5,000 more to conduct us to Monterrey [Mexico], and from 20,000 to 30,000 will be necessary to carry our conquests to California and the Isthmus of Darien [Panama].

To another friend Wilkinson exclaimed, "A blow once struck, and away we go!"

It was at this critical point—with the Spanish refusing to retreat and war seemingly certain—that Wilkinson finally received Burr's coded letter of July 29. The letter had taken two months to catch up with him, and it hit him at an awkward moment. If a war did begin, Wilkinson would be pinned down in a land action in Texas. There was no way to control what Burr might do in New Orleans. If Burr did have a thousand men and a British fleet, he could undoubtedly have his way in New Orleans. Then he could probably invade Mexico by sea before Wilkinson could get his troops assembled, much less advance to the Rio Grande. The moment had finally come when Wilkinson must choose. He received the crucial letter October 8. He waited and thought for two agonizing weeks. He also drank more whiskey than was his usual custom, for his situation was difficult indeed.

Blennerhassett's mansion. Blennerhassett's dream of re-creating the life of a European country gentleman in America lay behind this aristocratic structure. One of the participants in the scheme described Blennerhassett as a man with "every kind of sense except common sense." He was taken to Richmond for trial, but the prosecution dropped the case against him. He died in Europe, in near poverty. (Cincinnati Historical Society)

Meanwhile, Burr was traveling in the Ohio country, having boats built and recruiting volunteers. Sometimes he said that he was going to settle the Ouachita land grant. At other times he talked of raising a force of volunteers for the war with Spain that was sure to begin soon. He visited Cincinnati, Frankfort, Lexington, Nashville, and all the settlements in between.

Burr also established a base of operations. In the Ohio River near Cincinnati was an island owned by a wealthy Irish immigrant named Harman Blennerhassett, who had become involved with Burr during the winter of 1805–06. He seems to have had a vision of himself as minister to England in the new government of Mexico that Burr would establish. Whatever the vision, Blennerhassett was willing to put himself into debt and danger to help Burr. According to the timetable, boats would be built at Blennerhassett Island and at other points along the river. From the island, around the beginning of December, the fleet and the volunteers would start south.

All during September and October, preparations went fairly smoothly. Many boats were completed. Dozens of volunteers were recruited, many of them the young sons of leading planters, politicians, and military men. In Kentucky, Ohio, and Tennessee, Burr's expedition—whatever its destination—was the main subject of gossip and speculation.

Some talk was good for Burr. Like any enterprise, his needed advertising. But the talk began to filter back to Washington. Jefferson's administration became first suspicious and then alarmed. Early in November a Kentucky district attorney even attempted to have Burr arrested for planning an invasion of Mexico. Most Kentuckians interpreted this action as a political move. The district attorney was a member of the Federalist party, and Burr was a Republican. In addition, the district attorney had so admired Hamilton that he had taken the name as his own legal middle name. Two sympathetic juries, one in November and another in December, found Burr innocent of any crime. Still, it was clear that Burr's preparations could not go on much longer without forcing the government into some kind of response.

～

Burr did not know as he completed his preparations that he had already been betrayed. Wilkinson decided to do whatever was necessary to make peace with the Spanish on the border, and then he would turn against Burr. He could thus gain credit with the Spanish for protecting their interests. At home he could claim he had saved his country from Burr's intrigues.

On October 20 Wilkinson put his plan in motion. He wrote President Jefferson two very strange letters. In the first, he enclosed an "anonymous" document—which he had actually written himself. In it Wilkinson sounded an alarm against "a numerous and powerful association" illegally organized for the invasion of Mexico. The general had to be careful not to appear involved. He claimed:

> It is unknown under what auspices this enterprise has been projected, from whence the means of its support are derived, or what may be the intentions of its leaders.

In his second letter Wilkinson again warned the president. Again he tried to appear innocent and confused:

> The magnitude of the enterprise staggers my belief. I have never in my whole life found myself in such perplexity. I am not only uninformed of the prime mover and ultimate objects of this daring enterprise, but am ignorant of the foundation on which it rests.

Wilkinson knew that when the president received these letters, he would have no choice but to move against Burr. This left only one nagging problem. If the Spanish insisted on starting a war, then Burr and his force might suddenly appear to be heroes on their way to fight the enemy. To cover this possibility, Wilkinson added an incredible postscript to his second letter to Jefferson:

> Should Spain be disposed to war seriously with us, might not some plan be adopted to correct the delirium of the associates, and by a suitable appeal to their patriotism engage them in the service of their country? I do believe that I could accomplish the object.

Here was Wilkinson's escape hatch in case something went wrong. If war with Spain did come, he would simply rejoin Burr in the plan to conquer Mexico.

Now everything depended on the Spanish, and on this front Wilkinson had extraordinary luck. On October 23, three days after he wrote Jefferson, he mounted his troops to begin a slow, tense march toward the Sabine. He did not know at the time that the small Spanish force had already withdrawn west of the river. When he met no resistance, Wilkinson proposed a neutral zone between the Sabine and the Arroyo Hondo. No Spanish forces would cross the Sabine, and no American troops would cross the Arroyo Hondo. The Spanish accepted the agreement, and Wilkinson was finally free to confront Burr. He immediately headed east for Natchez and New Orleans.

Before marching east, Wilkinson sent a messenger to the Spanish authorities in Mexico asking for a payment to Agent 13 for keeping peace and stopping Burr's plan to conquer Mexico! The Spanish government refused to pay this particular bill. But the resourceful Wilkinson did finally manage to get Jefferson to pay the messenger $1,500 in "expenses" for the trip.

Burr was now in deep trouble, though he did not know it. There was still a slender chance he might salvage something, but only if he moved quickly. Even by fast express, Wilkinson's letters would take six weeks to get to Washington. Burr thus had until early December before the federal government could act. Wilkinson would also need several weeks to travel to New Orleans and put the city's defenses in any kind of order. If Burr could get to Natchez by his original deadline of December 15, he might still have a chance to trick or surprise Wilkinson. This meant that Burr and his collaborators had to get their boats into the water by the middle of November. Any delay would give the government time to act and Wilkinson time to prepare. News that there was to be no war with Spain would soon reach Ohio and Kentucky, and this would threaten every version of Burr's scheme. He did not know that Wilkinson had written to Jefferson, made peace with the Spanish commanders, and turned for New Orleans.

Burr's plans were certainly ambitious enough to attract intense suspicion. He was having fifteen boats built at Marietta, Ohio, near Blennerhassett Island. Andrew Jackson was building five more at Nashville on the Cumberland River. At least eight others were being bought or built in Pittsburgh and other settlements on the Ohio. These twenty-eight boats could carry at least a thousand men and their supplies—a force several times larger than the army Wilkinson would command in New Orleans. But the boatbuilding went more slowly than Burr had planned, and he showed no hurry to get into action.

The first four boats were launched in Pittsburgh December 4. By this time any hope Burr might have had was gone. Ohio officials had been watching preparations at Marietta for many weeks, and they now knew of Wilkinson's treaty with the Spanish. On December 9 they seized the fifteen boats at Marietta. Harman Blennerhassett and a few other men got away down the Ohio in the four boats that had just arrived from Pittsburgh.

Burr knew nothing about these events. After his second trial in Kentucky he went to Nashville. He did not start down the Cumberland until December 22. By that time it was already much too late. Burr finally made his tardy rendezvous with Blennerhassett and the others on December 27, at the junction of the Cumberland and Ohio rivers. There were only ten boats and fewer than a hundred men.

Burr would surely have quit at this point if he had known of Wilkinson's betrayal. But he still believed that a small force at New Orleans could accomplish a great deal, if Wilkinson helped. Burr had learned that Wilkinson had made peace with the Spanish. He must have thought that either the peace would be temporary or that he and

Wilkinson would capture New Orleans instead of Mexico. In any case, he went on down the river, completely out of communication with the rest of the world. On January 10, 1807, he pulled to shore at a small settlement just north of Natchez. A man quickly showed him a newspaper that told the story of Wilkinson's treachery. He also learned that President Jefferson had ordered his arrest. The former vice president was once more a fugitive from justice.

General Wilkinson had already declared martial law in New Orleans and had begun to arrest Burr's friends there. Burr decided to take his chances with civilian courts in the Mississippi Territory. There he hoped to be out of Wilkinson's grasp. But after a few weeks of legal maneuvering, Burr learned that Wilkinson had sent troops north to arrest him. He fled and hid with friends for about two weeks. Finally, on February 19, he was surprised and captured near Mobile. He was then taken east under military arrest for trial in Richmond, Virginia.

Burr's trial began March 30, 1807. It lasted five months and attracted more attention than any other criminal trial in America up to that time. Some of this attention was simply a result of Burr's prominent political position and the fact that he was charged with one of the worst of all crimes, high treason. But his trial also had great political significance. President Jefferson committed himself actively to prosecuting Burr, and so he became almost a party to the trial. Many Federalists, on the other hand, became partisans of Burr in order to align themselves against the Republican president. The trial was presided over by none other than the chief justice of the United States, John Marshall. He was a Federalist and a bitter enemy of the president. Jefferson, Burr, and Marshall had last been together on March 4, 1800. Then Marshall had administered the oaths of office to President Jefferson and Vice President Burr. Now all three were locked in ugly and curious political combat over whether the president's legal staff could force the chief justice to convict the former vice president of treason.

Almost everyone believed that Burr was guilty of *something*. The president had publicly declared that Burr was guilty before the trial even began. The question was, however, guilty of what? Before the Revolution, British law had made conviction in treason cases fairly easy. The framers of the Constitution, in order to protect citizens from the power of the federal government, had defined treason quite narrowly. Only two things, the Constitution clearly said, were treasonable: giving "aid and comfort" to enemies of the United States and "levying war" against the United States. Since the country was at peace, it technically had no enemies. So Burr had to be convicted of "levying war." (What the term "levying" actually means was one of the main issues of the trial.)

The Constitution contained another important provision. There had to be two witnesses to an overt act of treason. The government would have to prove that Burr had actually participated in an act of war against the United States—not just that he plotted or encouraged it. And the government would also have to have at least two eyewitnesses to the specific act.

Jefferson anxiously ordered the government's lawyers to do everything necessary to get a conviction. Still the prosecution had trouble putting a case together. At first,

Marshall refused even to begin a trial for treason because the government could produce so few witnesses. The strongest witness would probably be Wilkinson, but weeks passed and he did not show up. One of Burr's lawyers pointed out, "In Europe, a general had been known to march the same distance at the head of his *army* in a shorter time than General Wilkinson has had to pass from New Orleans to this place." The court recessed, one hot June day after another, to wait for the general. The writer Washington Irving, who was covering the trial for a New York newspaper, commented sarcastically on the delay. Members of the court, he wrote, used the opportunity to go home, see their wives, have their clothes washed, and "flog their Negroes."

However the citizens of Richmond may have passed the time, they finally were treated to a sight of the general. On June 15 Wilkinson strode into court, as Irving described him, "booted to the middle, sashed to the chin, collared to the ears, and whiskered to the teeth." Wilkinson described his own courtroom appearance in a letter to Jefferson:

> I saluted the bench and my eyes darted a flash of indignation at the little traitor. This lionhearted hero, with haggard eye, made an effort to meet the indignant salutation. But it was in vain. He averted his face, grew pale, and affected passion.

Irving's newspaper story of the same meeting was a bit different:

> Wilkinson strutted into court and took his stand, swelling like a turkey-cock and bracing himself for the encounter of Burr's eye. Burr turned his head, looked him full in the face, and then coolly resumed his position. The whole look was over in an instant, but it was an admirable one.

Whoever won the exchange of looks, Wilkinson's pretrial testimony was enough—barely enough—to have Burr indicted for treason. The trial began August 3.

The first task was the selection of a jury. Virginia was Jefferson country, and it was difficult, if not impossible, to get an unbiased jury. Even the ghost of Hamilton rose up to haunt Burr. Burr and his lawyers questioned one juror very closely, and the man turned to the courtroom and said, "I am surprised that they should be in such terror of me. Perhaps my name may be the terror, for my first name is Hamilton." (He was excused.) Finally, Burr accepted an obviously biased jury, since he hoped to win on questions of procedure and law. These would be decided by the judge, not the jury.

The government lawyers received instructions directly from the president almost every day. Determined to prove that Burr had intended to make war, they held that he had assembled an armed force at Blennerhassett Island for this purpose. According to the prosecutors, this action was what the Constitution meant by "levying war."

The strategy of Burr's defense was to make the prosecution prove its accusation. As Burr sarcastically observed, Mr. Jefferson was having a great deal of trouble even *finding* a war:

> Our President is a lawyer, and a great one, too. He certainly ought to know what it is that constitutes a war. Six months ago he proclaimed that there was a civil war

Aaron Burr. This painting of Burr was done by a New York artist, John Vanderlyn. The painter was at pains to suggest a cool dignity and a respose that would surely not stoop to conspiracy. And the columns in the background are meant to associate Burr with the loftiest ideals of Republican and Roman virtue. (Courtesy of The New-York Historical Society, NYC)

[between Burr's forces and the government]. And yet, for six months have they been hunting for it, and still cannot find one spot where it existed. There was, to be sure, a terrible war in the newspapers, but nowhere else.

Day after day, Burr and his lawyers tore holes in the government's case. The prosecution had proved only that thirty or forty men congregated at Blennerhassett Island in early December 1806. But Burr was not even present on the island at the time.

Burr's lawyers were brilliant and cutting in their cross-examination of government witnesses. Burr, acting as his own lawyer, was even more brilliant and more cutting. One by one, the prosecution witnesses were broken. One had to admit, under Burr's questioning, that he had just been paid $10,000 by the government. Another ended by testifying *for* Burr; he admitted that, as far as he knew, Burr's force had been gathered for use only if the United States declared war against Spain. A third testified against Burr, only to have his own son follow him to the stand to swear that his father was "old and infirm, and like other old men, told long stories and was apt to forget his repetitions." Another witness, who knew Blennerhassett well, revealed that the latter was so nearsighted that it was ridiculous to imagine his participating in a military action.

The outcome depended on how Chief Justice Marshall defined treason. If he ruled that treason could mean participating in a *plan* that eventually led to treason, then the jury might find Burr guilty. But Burr's lawyers argued that the government would have to prove Burr had been personally present and had participated in the act of levying war. For days lawyers for the government and for Burr argued the point. On the last day of August, Marshall made his ruling. He decided in favor of Burr. To prove treason, he said, the government would have to prove by two eyewitnesses that Burr had been present and taken part in a specific act of war against the United States. Since the government had not made such a case, the jury had to deliberate only briefly. On September 1, Burr was found not guilty.

Burr had won the case, just as he had won his duel with Hamilton. But once again he seemed to lose in winning. He was still in legal trouble in several states, and he was now more deeply in debt than ever. Also, much of the public was convinced that Marshall, the Federalist, had let Burr go free just to embarrass the Republican administration. Burr's career was finished. Once more, he decided to "seek another country," and he went to Europe in a self-imposed exile that lasted four years. In 1812 he came home to practice law in New York. Many years later, at the age of seventy-seven, he married a wealthy widow; she soon sued him for divorce (charging him with adultery!). The divorce became final September 14, 1836. Burr died the same day, at the age of eighty.

DISSENT AND CONFLICT IN THE NEW NATION

The career of Aaron Burr was a strange one. In many ways his life was an expression of a unique, ambitious, and unpredictable personality. But when Burr's duel with Hamilton, his western scheme, and his trial for treason are considered today, they make sense as part of the larger history of the United States. The generation that made the Revolution and the Constitution continued to govern the United States until the 1820s. The public lives of this generation were controlled by four main tendencies. Each of them was very much present in the life of Burr.

First, the development of party politics and the first two-party system occupied the minds and energies of just about every politically active American during the period after 1789. Burr was, first and last, a politician. He was deeply involved in almost every political battle until his duel with Hamilton. In fact, political conflict between the two men was a major factor behind the duel.

Second, the history of the United States during the decades after Washington's inauguration was tied very closely to foreign affairs. Relations with France, Spain, and Britain tended to dominate national and even local politics. Many leading politicians and military figures were involved in secret intrigues with one foreign power or another. Burr sensed this situation clearly, especially after his duel. His mind was filled with thoughts of war with Spain and secret arrangements with Britain.

Third, the years between 1789 and the 1820s were marked by rapid expansion of territory and population. During this period the territory of the United States doubled. Thousands of pioneer settlers pushed over the Appalachian Mountains into the valleys of the Ohio, the Tennessee, and the Mississippi rivers. Burr's thoughts ran west with this expansion.

Fourth, the United States was involved in a serious test of whether the new federal system would work. Each section of the country had its own special interests and institutions. It was not clear whether the nation could survive. Would the western farmers secede? Would the question of slavery divide the North from the South? Would New England leave the Union and try to go it alone? These questions were quite real and important, not just to Burr but to other leaders.

The Development of Party Politics

The framers of the Constitution knew conflict between organized groups was bound to occur. Farmers would be pitted against merchants, slaveholders against nonslaveholders, the rich against the poor. Such divisions in society would

255

inevitably lead to factions, which would struggle for domination of state governments. These struggles would bring out people's worst failings: selfishness, intrigue, ambition, and deceit. In order to gain the advantage, political parties and their leaders might stop at nothing. They might mobilize their supporters by appeals to fear and greed. And people's loyalties would be not to their country but to their party.

To try to prevent the rise of parties, the authors of the Constitution tried to design a government that would be beyond the reach of factions and interests. They believed the system of checks and balances would make it impossible for any group to gain control of the whole federal structure. The president would not be the tool of a political party because he was elected by the electoral college, not the people. Since federal judges were to be appointed for life, they would not depend on party support for their offices. If a party formed in the popularly elected House of Representatives, then surely the Senate would counteract it. (Senators, elected for long terms of six years, would be more independent than members of the House, who had to run for election every two years.) The Constitution forbade the states to do certain things, such as coin money and regulate interstate commerce. So the worst effects of party politics in the states could be controlled from the national capital.

The political history of the first forty years of the United States is, among other things, the story of the failure of these hopes. The national government did not prove to be above party. The presidency did become a party office. Control of the national government became the highest prize in the conflict between one party and another. Supreme Court justices, senators, and congressmen did become party men with party loyalties. In fact, the very men who had written the Constitution to guard against parties became partisan leaders themselves. Even Washington, who had seemed in 1789 to stand loftily above all conflict and ambition, was drawn into the struggle and made a symbol of party conflict.

At first, Washington's dignity was his greatest asset. The friends of the new government knew that only he could be the first president. Only he could convince the people that the power of the central government would not operate in favor of any section or class, but in a generous and truly national way. Washington strained to create an appearance of majesty. He rode a white horse with a striking saddlecloth made from a leopard skin. He also had an elegant coach, bearing his crest and drawn by a matched team of six cream-colored horses. His house in New York, fully staffed with servants, was one of the grandest in the city. Almost everything Washington did was calculated to give an impression of regal state-liness, far above ambition and partisanship.

Some men in Congress wanted to put an official seal upon Washington's kingly manner. Just after the first inauguration, Washington's friends in Congress drew up a message of congratulations. There was a debate over how to address the president. One of Washington's admirers went so far as to propose the title "His Highness, the President of the United States and Protector of Their Liberties." After a heated debate, men of simpler taste won the day, and the letter was addressed to "George Washington, President of the United States."

In his appointments, Washington tried to fill offices with people from different states and with different interests. He hoped his administration could be representative of the country at large. His secretary of the treasury, Alexander Hamilton, was from New York. The secretary of state and the attorney general, Thomas Jefferson and Edmund Randolph, were both planters from Virginia. The fourth member of what eventually became known as the cabinet was Henry Knox of Massachusetts, secretary of war. (Although Washington did consult with the heads of his executive departments, they did not hold regular meetings. The cabinet as a formal institution did not develop until the administration of Thomas Jefferson.)

HAMILTON'S FINANCIAL PROGRAM The only man in the new government who had a clear political program was Alexander Hamilton. When he took office as secretary of the treasury, his job was to try to make some sense out of a confused financial situation. The United States was more than $54 million in debt. It could not operate effectively until it could pay off what it owed.

Most of the debt was in the form of certificates, like the United States savings bonds that are sold today. They had been printed during the 1770s and 1780s to finance the Revolution. Many of them had gone to soldiers of the Continental army as pay for their services. The certificates were promises that the government would some-day, somehow, pay back in real money what it owed private citizens and foreign governments.

No one expected the federal government to be able to pay back the entire debt, so the worth of the certificates had declined. Speculators bought them for a fraction of their face value. For example, a soldier who held a certificate worth ten dollars might sell it to a speculator for one dollar, on the theory that a dollar in the hand is better than ten in an uncertain future. All over the country, millions of dollars in certificates had been bought up or taken in trade. The government theoretically owed the entire $54 million. But no one expected it to pay back more than a few cents on the dollar.

Individual states had also printed certificates, and they were in debt, too. Some states were paying off what they owed. Others were not.

Hamilton laid out his plan in a series of brilliant reports to Congress in 1790–91. Concerning the federal and state debts, he made two unexpected proposals. One, known as "funding," called for the government to pay off the entire federal debt at its full, or par, value. The other proposal was termed "assumption." The federal government would take over (assume) the states' debts and pay them off at par. The money would be paid to whoever actually held the certificates at the time. The original holders, many of them ordinary farmers who had fought in the Continental army and the state militias during the Revolution, would get nothing. The effect would be to create, by government power, a class of very rich men, men who had bought federal or state certificates for as little as a few cents on the dollar.

Hamilton did not propose to pay off federal and state debts with cash. Instead, holders of certificates would receive newly issued govern-ment bonds. Funding and assumption, plus interest on the new bonds, would cost a great deal of money. Hamilton called for two new taxes. One was a tax to be paid by distillers of alcoholic beverages. The other was a tariff on imports, which would not only raise money but also encourage American manufacturing. The secretary of the treasury also proposed a national bank to help the government make all its financial transactions.

Some parts of Hamilton's program were acceptable to most people. Others aroused op-position. One group of congressmen, led by Madison, attacked the funding plan. Madison believed that speculators who had bought federal certificates should be paid half their face value. He felt the original holders should get the other half. Madison also opposed the assumption plan. Vir-ginia had been paying off its own debt, while some other states had not. Why should Virgin-ians be taxed to pay off the debts of other states?

Madison's congressional opposition to Ham-ilton's plan was powerful. He was soon joined by Jefferson, the secretary of state. But Hamilton had strong backing, too. The disagreement over funding and assumption was settled by a classic political bargain. Madison and Jefferson prom-ised to deliver enough votes in Congress to pass Hamilton's proposal. In return, Hamilton would deliver the votes of *his* followers for a measure providing that a new national capital would be created in the South rather than the North. The city would be called Washington, and it would be located on the Potomac River in a district that would bear the name Columbia. The funding and assumption measures were passed in July 1790 and were soon signed by Washington.

THE WHISKEY REBELLION One part of Hamilton's financial program was a tax on dis-tilled liquor, which meant mainly whiskey. At this time the cheapest and most economical way for most western farmers to transport their grain

GENERAL GEORGE WASHINGTON.
Reviewing the Western army at Fort Cumberland the 18ᵗʰ of Octobᵣ 1794

Washington in arms again. During the Revolutionary period, American leaders and heroes were seldom painted on horseback. But here, sometime after October 1794, a primitive painter chose to put the president on horseback, armed, and at the head of his army, ready to put down the Whiskey Rebellion. (Painted by F. Kemmelmeyer. Courtesy the Henry Francis Du Pont Winterthur Museum)

crops to the East was to turn the grain into whiskey. So Congress was taxing not a "luxury" but a basic economic product.

Many farmers in western Pennsylvania resisted the tax. In the summer of 1794 they even mobbed tax collectors, much as Americans had attacked Stamp Act tax collectors a generation before. The rebellion was small, much smaller than Shays's uprising had been eight years earlier. But President Washington reacted with a series of steps that went well beyond what was needed. He called out 15,000 militiamen and marched them west toward Pittsburgh with himself at their head. This excessive display of federal military power worked immediately, of course. The rebels were totally intimidated. In his zeal

Washington revealed the depth of his old concern about maintaining law and order in the West.

After the rebellion had been suppressed, Washington delivered an address to Congress in which he condemned not only the rebels but national political clubs called Democratic Societies. The societies had been formed in enthusiastic support of the French Revolution. Most of them were the local bases of an emerging political opposition to Washington's administration. But to Washington's mind the sectional question of East vs. West was closely tied to the question of political opposition. Anything that threatened national unity, whether it was a sectional uprising or an opposition political group, was an evil to be dealt with quickly.

REPUBLICANS VS. FEDERALISTS By 1792, Hamilton had succeeded in getting the new taxes he wanted and in establishing a national bank. But the groundwork had been laid for organized conflict between two major factions on the national level. From 1790 on, every major decision on domestic and foreign policy caused a quarrel. Jefferson and Madison, year after year, organized their forces. Slowly, almost against their wills, they formed a political party. They studied local and state elections throughout the country and supported candidates for Congress who they thought would be sympathetic to their views.

The followers of Jefferson and Madison were mostly small farmers and debtors. Many of them were former Antifederalists who thought Hamilton's program was a scheme to create a powerful federal government at the expense of states' rights. Gradually, this group adopted the name Republicans (or Democratic-Republicans). This term emphasized their avowed dedication to the interests of the people at large.

Hamilton's strongest supporters were mainly merchants, bankers, and speculators. They gradually began to call themselves Federalists. This name was derived, of course, from the term for supporters of the Constitution in 1788.

The support for both Hamilton's group and Jefferson's group was mixed. Only a small minority of Americans voted anyway, so both parties' claims to represent "the people" were false. In practice, voting support for the Republicans was only slightly more "democratic" than for the Federalists. But Jefferson was successful in creating the lasting myth that his was the party of the "people" against the rich and the well-born. Every new party created since has tried to lay claim to the same myth.

In 1792 Washington still stood "above party," and both sides joined in reelecting him. During his second term, he gradually identified himself with the Federalists. He still talked of disliking parties more than any feature of government, but he was under constant pressure from Hamilton and his friends to support their positions. Bit by bit, Washington's second term took on the appearance of a real administration—that is, it was staffed by members of one party whose goal was achieving a specific political program.

Yet, when Washington finally gained his longed-for retirement, he prepared a farewell address that contained a severe condemnation of political parties. Paradoxically, however, the address was itself a highly partisan political action. It was published in September 1796— almost six months before Washington was scheduled to leave office. The Republicans claimed (rightly) that the timing was meant to influence the voters in the presidential election in November. They also suspected (again, rightly) that Hamilton had a hand in both the content and timing of the farewell address. Still, what Washington had to say about political parties was bitter and eloquent:

Let me warn you in the most solemn manner against the baneful effects of the spirit of party. This spirit serves always to distract the public councils and to enfeeble the public administration. It agitates the community with ill-founded jealousies and false alarms; kindles the animosity of one part against another; foments riot and insurrection. It opens the door to foreign influence and corruption.

In theory, at least, Madison and Jefferson might still have agreed. But by 1796 they had had six years of experience in opposition politics. And they had formed, like it or not, a party. The Republicans nominated Jefferson for the presidency, to run against Federalist John Adams. Despite the short time available to mount a campaign, Jefferson was a close second in the electoral college. According to the awkward provisions of the Constitution, the runner-up in the electoral vote became vice president. So for the next four years the United States was governed by a Federalist president and a Republican vice president.

During Adams's term of office, party conflict reached a high pitch. Everywhere, Republicans

Washington vs. Jefferson. This cartoon, published in 1795—the year following the Whiskey Rebellion (see p. 257)—shows a determined but dignified Washington leading his volunteers out to put down rebels, who are the tools of French "cannibals." Jefferson and two of his followers are trying to hold back the chariot of republican order. In a French accent, Jefferson is shouting "Stop de wheels of de gouvernement." (Courtesy of the New-York Historical Society)

were organizing for the election of 1800. The Federalists could sense the tide running toward Jefferson. In anger and desperation they managed to ram through Congress a series of laws designed to stifle political opposition. Three of these Alien and Sedition acts were directed against new immigrants from Europe, most of whom became Republican voters. (One of them, for example, increased the period of residence from five to fourteen years before an alien could

become a citizen.) The fourth was a law making it illegal to "oppose any measure of the government of the United States." This Sedition Act of 1798 in addition made it a crime to publish any "false, scandalous and malicious writing against the government of the United States or either house of the Congress or the President." Under the Sedition Act, federal judges (appointed by a Federalist president) attempted to silence Republican criticism. One Republican candidate for

Party strife. The dignity of George Washington and the peaceful grace of Thomas Jefferson's Monticello represented Americans' best hopes for republican order. This fight in the House of Representatives, which took place in 1797, represented their worst fears. Roger Griswold, a Federalist from Connecticut, is attacking Matthew Lyon, a Republican from Vermont, with a cane. Lyon has grabbed the fireplace tongs to defend himself. In the Speaker's chair sits an amused Jonathan Dayton of New Jersey. The cartoon is clearly the work of one of many Americans who deplored the rise of political parties. (Library of Congress)

Congress was even sent to prison for speeches made against Adams during the campaign of 1798.

Madison and Jefferson were able to use opposition to the Sedition Act to unite their party and the state governments against the Adams administration. Madison wrote a resolution for Virginia and Jefferson one for Kentucky. These so-called Virginia and Kentucky Resolutions denounced the law as unconstitutional. They held, too, that the states could resist any federal law they judged to be a violation of the Constitution. These resolutions drew the lines very clearly for the election of 1800, and they put the Republicans firmly on the side of states' rights against federal power.

THE ELECTION OF 1800 The Republicans organized an intense campaign in the summer and fall of 1800. New York was a typical and important state. The Republicans had to win if they were to take the presidency from Adams and the Federalists. New York political affairs were in the hands of none other than Alexander Hamilton for the Federalists and Aaron Burr for the Republicans. In the state elections of 1799, Hamilton's party had won an impressive victory. But Burr, Jefferson's candidate for the vice pres-

idency, now went to work in the city of New York. He got Republicans to the polls by every means possible, and the result was a victory in the state legislature. Since the legislature in New York chose presidential electors, New York delivered all its electoral votes to Jefferson. Virginia, the largest state, also went to Jefferson. Although Adams held all the New England states, the Jeffersonians got more than half the votes in Pennsylvania.

The result should have been clear, but it was confused by the fact that the Constitution recognized no distinction between presidential and vice presidential candidates. All the electors who had voted for Jefferson also voted for Burr, so there was, technically, a tie. This meant the election would have to be decided by the House of Representatives.

Once the election was thrown into the House, the situation was even more confused. In the first place, voting was by states and each state was allowed one vote, no matter what its population. In the second place, the House was free to choose *any* of the candidates, even though Jefferson and Burr had both beaten Adams in the electoral college. The voting quickly settled down to a contest between Jefferson and Adams. Burr stood rather coyly to one side, refusing to shift his political support to Jefferson. Thirty-five ballots were cast before Hamilton threw *his* support to Jefferson. Hamilton did this because, although he disliked Jefferson, he hated Burr. His action settled the election. It also made the relationship between Burr and Hamilton impossible, and, together with events in New York, led the two men finally to the dueling ground at Weehawken.

JEFFERSON, A MAN OF NEW IDEAS After the election, Jefferson tried to soften party divisions, as Washington had always done. He announced, "We are all Federalists; we are all Republicans." But nothing could hide the fact that a political changeover had taken place. Jefferson himself called it the revolution of 1800. He believed the victory of his party over Hamilton, Adams, and the Federalists would cause a basic reversal in the direction of American history. His principles were different from theirs. And his party had committed itself to ideas of liberty and democracy that probably did have a profound and long-term effect on the lives of ordinary Americans.

Jefferson's conception of the good society rested on one fundamental opinion. As he put it, "Those who labor in the earth are the chosen people of God." Plain farmers, he felt, ought to be the backbone of any society. And the plain farmers of the Republic ought to have as much political power as they had virtue. They ought to control the government in a more or less direct and democratic way.

The central government ought to be devoted above all to republican simplicity. It should be small and relatively weak, so that it could not interfere with the liberties of the people. Power should be decentralized—that is, divided up among smaller authorities such as state and local governments Then people could keep a close eye on their elected representatives.

It sometimes seemed that Jefferson's political philosophy was based on a conflict between two simple ideas: power and the people. Whatever contributed to governmental power injured people's control over their own private lives. Jefferson wanted a "government which shall restrain men from injuring one another." But government should do no more than this. It should leave men "otherwise free to regulate their own pursuits of industry and improvement."

Such a government ought to practice the strictest economy. The number of federal officers should be cut to the bare minimum. The national debt should be quickly liquidated. (It had ballooned from $54 million to about $83 million as a result of Hamilton's program of funding and assumption.) In fact, Jefferson promised to pay off the entire debt within sixteen years. To save on expenses, Jefferson reduced the army from 4,000 to 2,500 men. He cut the navy back sharply to a defensive force of coastal guns and small gunboats.

Jefferson's was a political program that promised *not* to do things: not to maintain a powerful government with a large standing army and a powerful navy; not to allow the federal government to become powerful at the expense of the rights of the states and the people; not to pursue a financial policy that would benefit only a small class of merchants, bankers, and speculators. The heart of Jefferson's idea of government was his belief that the American people—most of whom really were plain farmers—could build a great nation if only they were let alone. Jefferson himself was a cultivated aristocrat, a highly educated man, and a wealthy slaveholding planter. But his political philosophy was one of democratic simplicity and an almost religious faith in the good sense of the people.

In the long run, Jefferson and the other Republican presidents who followed him were the captives of history. They were forced to expand, not contract, federal power in order to meet emergencies and opportunities that came their way. But their revolution was one of ideas, not acts. Jefferson and his successors made words like *liberty* and *democracy* the most important words in

John Marshall

For thirty-four years, from 1801 until his death at the age of eighty, John Marshall was chief justice of the United States Supreme Court. He was a firm nationalist, a Federalist in politics, and a rigorous and skillful interpreter of law and the Constitution. More than any other individual, he gave shape and meaning to the Constitution.

Marshall was born on the Virginia frontier in 1755. Like Hamilton, Jefferson, and Burr, he grew up just in time to serve in the Revolutionary War. He then became a lawyer (after only six weeks of formal training), and almost as quickly got himself elected to the Virginia legislature. He also became a leading champion of the Federalist cause in the Virginia fight over ratification. In 1800–01 he was appointed, in quick succession, secretary of state to Adams and then chief justice.

Three cases of outstanding importance decided by Marshall and his fellow justices were *Marbury* v. *Madison* (1803), *McCulloch* v. *Maryland* (1819), and *Gibbons* v. *Ogden* (1824). *Marbury* v. *Madison* grew out of some last-minute appointments of judges and other judicial officers under the Judiciary Act of 1801. The appointments were part of a final effort by Adams to extend Federalist control of the government, despite their loss of the election. The commissions were given the Seal of the United States by the acting secretary of state—Marshall himself. But in the hectic transfer of power to the Jefferson administration, some of the commissions never left the State Department.

One of these was a commission issued for William Marbury to be a justice of the peace for the District of Columbia. He sued the new secretary of state, James Madison, for his commission. The suit went directly to the Supreme Court under a provision of the Judiciary Act of 1789, giving the Court the power to order federal officials to carry out their legal duties.

Marshall's strategy was brilliant. He ruled that Marbury *did* have a legal right to his commission, but that the Supreme Court should not issue the order. The Constitution gave the Court original jurisdiction in a number of specific types of cases. Therefore, the section of the Judiciary Act that added to the Court's jurisdiction was unconstitutional. Marbury would have to go to another court first. Marshall had thus laid out the principle that the Supreme Court could rule on the constitutionality of acts of Congress.

McCulloch v. *Maryland* (1819) set forth a parallel principle with respect to state laws. The state of Maryland passed a measure that threatened to tax a federal agency, the Bank of the United States, out of existence. The bank refused to pay, and Maryland sued James McCulloch, a bank officer. When the case reached the Supreme Court, Marshall declared that any state law that was in conflict with a federal law was null and void.

Gibbons v. *Ogden* (1824) gave broad meaning to the commerce clause of the Constitution. New York State had granted a monopoly of steamboat commerce on the Hudson River to the steamboat's inventor, Robert Fulton, and his associates. Aaron Ogden had eventually acquired the monopoly. Thomas Gibbons challenged the state's power to grant such a monopoly. The Hudson River steamboat trade involved a great deal of interstate commerce, Gibbons argued, and the Constitution gave Congress, not the states, power to regulate interstate commerce. Marshall accepted Gibbons's arguments and ruled that the monopoly was unconstitutional.

Picture: The New York Public Library, Picture Collection

Monticello. This painting of Monticello shows how the leaders of the revolutionary movement tried in their lives, their writing, and their architecture to put together several seemingly contradictory principles. This grand mansion, planned and built by Thomas Jefferson, seems to argue that there was no incompatibility between his wealth and his principle that "all men are created equal." Greek grandeur is tucked into a simple, pastoral landscape. Geometrical order and child's play go together here, as do the gentleman's learned solitude and homey family closeness. Most of all, slavery is kept carefully offstage. (Thomas Jefferson Memorial Foundation)

the political language of Americans. And, after 1800, a professed faith in the people became the most prominent and unique feature of American political rhetoric.

Jefferson continued to believe political parties were evil. True, he had helped build a party that had turned the Federalists out of office. But he had done so because he believed the Federalists were a bad party and the Republicans were a good one.

After 1800 the Republicans were committed to making their party the only party, to driving the Federalists out of existence altogether. Jefferson was easily elected to a second term in 1804. Madison won the presidency in 1808 and 1812, and he was followed into office by another Virginian, James Monroe, in 1816. By this time the Federalist party had collapsed and did not even run a candidate. Monroe won again in 1820. By 1824 the fall of the Federalists was so complete

that the son of John Adams, John Quincy Adams, won the presidency as a Republican.

After 1824 a new party structure would emerge, with two new parties replacing the Republicans and the Federalists. But for the time being, it appeared that the Republicans had actually realized the hopes of the Founding Fathers by creating a unified government with no contending parties.

Foreign Affairs

During most of the twenty-five years after Washington's first inauguration, Europe was at war. Britain and France fought everywhere in Europe, around the Mediterranean, and in almost every other corner of the world. In the process, other

European nations and the United States were drawn into the conflict.

Events in Europe had a profound effect on the United States in two fields. One was the economy. Americans imported most of their manufactured goods from England, and they in turn sold many agricultural products, like tobacco and cotton, in Europe. This transatlantic trade was crucial to farmers in the southern and western states. Merchants in eastern cities also depended heavily on a brisk trade across the Atlantic. European nations at war needed the American trade, but at the same time they tried to cut their enemies off from American shipping. By turns, the English and the French attacked American ships. They even kidnapped American seamen for service in their own navies and merchant marine, a practice known as impressment.

The other field affected by European affairs was American politics. The conflict between Britain and France was an old one, going well back into the eighteenth century. Indeed, the Americans had fought their Revolution against the British with French help. But there was a new element in the conflict after 1789. In that year the French began a revolution against their monarchy. They proclaimed France a republic in 1792, and from then on they fought their wars for ideological reasons, as well as for the more traditional military, political, and economic ones. In fact, the French regarded themselves the agents of "a war of all peoples against all kings."

In the beginning, many Americans favored the French Revolution. To them it meant another monarch deposed, another republic created. America's old ally, the Marquis de Lafayette, even sent Washington the key to the Bastille, the notorious Paris prison whose capture was one of the opening events of the revolution.

Gradually, though, the French Revolution seemed to take a dangerous turn. At the height of revolutionary fervor, in 1793 and 1794, thousands of Frenchmen, including the king and queen, were guillotined. To many Americans (especially those with Federalist sympathies), this experience was a lesson in the excesses of democracy. But others—the political disciples of Jefferson—followed their leader in stubborn sympathy with the French Revolution and its democratic changes. Thus politics in America felt the impact of politics in Europe.

Out of this situation arose a crucial question: Could the United States remain neutral, since her trade and her politics were tied so closely to events in Paris and London? From George Washington to John Quincy Adams, American presidents and their administrations had to devote at least as much attention to foreign as to domestic questions. In fact, much of the time it was impossible to draw a line between the two.

This long episode in foreign policy involved almost every American political leader, from Washington, Hamilton, and Jefferson to men like Burr and Wilkinson. Burr's plans and intrigues were not the schemes of an isolated individual. Rather, he could claim the company of dozens of other public figures, all constantly involved in speculation, secret plans, and even spying. In the 1790s at least two cabinet officers were actively working for European governments. Many senators, congressmen, and lesser politicians were so sympathetic to one European side or the other that they lost sight of American purposes and goals.

For almost twenty-five years, Americans had no real independence of Europe. They were tied to France, Spain, and Britain by every ship that left America for Europe, by developing systems of party loyalty, and by tough, troublesome issues of war and peace. Only after 1815, with peace in Europe, did Americans find release from European entanglements.

A SHAKY NEUTRALITY Several forces pushed the United States toward a new war with Britain during the 1790s. Ill feeling still lingered after the Revolutionary War. The British refused to evacuate their military posts in the Northwest Territory. They also refused to return American slaves whom they had freed during the Revolution. Many Americans sympathized with the

French because of their aid during the war. In addition, there was the treaty of 1778, in which the United States pledged to come to the aid of France in case of conflict with Britain.

When France and Britain went to war in 1793, Washington's administration faced its first difficult decision in foreign policy. Partly under the influence of Hamilton, who despised the French for their democratic republicanism, Washington decided to ignore the alliance of 1778 and remain neutral. But the British made it very difficult for him. They used their position in Canada to stir up hostile Indians against American settlers, and British warships began to stop and even seize American merchant vessels trading with French islands in the West Indies.

At the same time, the French lost a chance to cement their relations with Americans by sending over a blundering diplomat, Edmond Genêt, who made the mistake of acting as though France and the United States were already allies. He did things that no representative of a foreign government can get away with for long. He set up French courts to take charge of captured English ships. He tried to talk a group of Americans into an armed attack on New Orleans (since Spain sided with Britain at the time). Worst of all, he interfered in domestic political matters. Even Jefferson, the ardent supporter of the French Revolution, could not stomach such behavior. Washington ended by demanding Genêt's recall to Paris.

In the meantime, despite Genêt's clumsiness, anti-British feeling was running high in America. There was real danger of war. Washington wanted to avoid it and settle old questions. He sent John Jay, a Federalist leader and a close friend of Hamilton's, to London to negotiate a treaty.

Jay returned home in 1794 bearing a document that became known as the Jay Treaty. The British agreed to give up their Northwest posts. They made a few other concessions of a minor nature. In general, though, the treaty was unfavorable to the United States and offered no real protection to American shipping. It immediately became a political issue. Republicans opposed it and Federalists supported it. Even Washington, who wanted desperately to avoid a war, was reluctant to sign it, but he finally did so.

NEGOTIATIONS WITH FRANCE The Jay Treaty made American relations with France more difficult, since the French believed that anything that helped the British hurt them. Late in Washington's administration and in the early months of Adams's presidency, the French began to intercept American shipping. Furthermore, they treated American sailors serving on British ships as pirates to be hanged. Like Washington, Adams tried to meet the crisis by insisting on neutrality and opening negotiations. He sent a team of three negotiators to Paris to try to arrange a treaty recognizing American trading rights and somehow putting an end to the embarrassing alliance of 1778.

The American mission failed. The French foreign minister, a shrewd and corrupt man named Charles Talleyrand, demanded a bribe of $250,000 for himself. He never met the Americans. Instead, he communicated with them through three anonymous go-betweens known only as X, Y, and Z. Through these agents, Talleyrand also demanded that the Americans pay the government of France several million dollars as the price of peace and a treaty. Two of the three American commissioners returned angrily to America to report to a shocked president and Congress. For a time, war seemed inevitable.

Adams's position was delicate. Many members of his party wanted war with France—partly to discredit the Republicans and partly to solidify their own hold on the national government. Adams moved considerably in their direction. He called for a stronger navy, better coastal defenses, and the arming of American merchant ships. He also gave in to Hamilton's demands that the army be strengthened. The retired Washington even agreed to take charge of the army in case of war, with Hamilton as his second in command. For several years American and French ships fought an undeclared war in the Atlantic known as the "Quasi-War."

But Adams was determined to avoid an unnecessary war, even if it hurt his position among the Federalists. In 1799 he sent another American mission to France with orders to negotiate an agreement. There the Americans found a new government in control. Its leader, Napoleon, was anxious to establish good relations with the United States. He agreed to scrap the 1778 alliance and also to end French interference with American shipping. For the time being, Adams had preserved American neutrality once more.

Territorial Expansion

One of the most obvious facts of life for the generation of Americans who lived after the making of the Constitution was growth. In 1790, at the time of the first census, there were fewer than 4 million Americans of European or African ancestry, and most of them lived on the eastern seaboard. Only about one person in every twenty-five lived over the mountains in Kentucky, Tennessee, and Ohio. But the spirit of expansion was everywhere. Every year, thousands of families set out for the Ohio Valley to make new homes. This growth and movement were very much on the minds of American political leaders. George Washington felt that strenuous efforts would have to be made to tie eastern and western peoples together. Burr, on the other hand, believed the federal government could not hold the loyalty of the western settlers.

By 1810 the population of the United States had almost doubled, to over 7 million. And by 1820 it was almost 10 million. As it grew, the population shifted steadily westward. In 1820 one of every ten citizens of the United States lived west of the Appalachian Mountains.

Everyone who looked carefully at the United States in the 1790s knew that the future lay in the West. Benjamin Franklin's calculations for the future always took for granted that the Ohio and Mississippi valleys held the key to the nation's destiny. Washington thought along similar lines, and so did Jefferson. After Hamilton's death had disgraced Burr, he simply followed an American reflex: When in trouble or in doubt, look to the West for new opportunities and answers.

THE LOUISIANA PURCHASE According to the peace treaty of 1783, the western boundary of the United States was the Mississippi River. This seemed to provide enough land to absorb the people and energies of the infant nation for decades to come. There was only one sore point. Spain still held most of the western half of the continent—and Spain controlled the Mississippi River and its outlet at New Orleans. The farmers west of the Appalachians depended almost entirely on the river to get their crops to market. (It was this traffic that George Washington had long wanted to divert to the East, through Virginia.)

It came as a bitter shock when the United States learned in 1801 that Spain had given Louisiana to France in a secret treaty. Now New Orleans and the vast Mississippi Valley would be in the hands not of weak Spain but of powerful and ambitious Napoleon. In 1802 the Spanish—still theoretically in control of New Orleans—caused another shock when they declared that Americans would no longer have the right to use New Orleans as a port.

Jefferson summed up the horror of most Americans when he said there was "on the globe one single spot, the possessor of which is our natural and habitual enemy. It is New Orleans." As was his custom, Jefferson turned immediately to negotiation. He made Napoleon an offer to purchase New Orleans for $2 million. The American negotiator, James Monroe, was greatly surprised and pleased when the French offered to

Lewis, Clark, Sacajawea, and York. Even before the purchase of Louisiana, Jefferson began to plan the exploration of the West. He chose his own private secretary, Meriwether Lewis, and William Clark to lead an expedition to the Pacific. For two years, their party made its way to the seacoast. They were helped enormously by a Native American woman, Sacajawea, who functioned as a guide, and by an African-American slave, York, an accomplished linguist who acted as interpreter. Nonetheless, the expedition has always been known by the name "Lewis and Clark." And in this painting, Lewis, standing, and Clark, armed, confidently hold center stage. A somewhat downcast Sacajawea and a somewhat frightened York are in the wings. (Montana State Capitol Building)

sell not just New Orleans but the entire territory of Louisiana—about 800,000 square miles of lush but practically uninhabited country—at least as whites defined "uninhabited."

In April 1803, the Americans closed the deal. They bought all of Louisiana for $15 million—a price that averaged out at about $20 per square mile for one of the richest areas in the world.

The purchase created some problems for Jefferson. He believed in what is called strict construction—a strict interpretation of the Constitution. Basic to this theory of government was the idea that the president and Congress could do only those things that the Constitution expressly gave them power to do. The Constitution nowhere gave the president the power to acquire new territory. In contrast to Jefferson's position was loose construction, favored by the Federalists. They felt that the government could do not only the things mentioned specifically by the Constitution but also other things that were merely implied. Thus, they would have argued,

the power to make treaties implied the power to acquire territory, since acquisition was in the nature of a new treaty arrangement. (This difference of interpretation first came up when President Washington was deciding whether to sign Hamilton's bank bill in 1791. Jefferson, a strict constructionist, argued against it; Hamilton's loose constructionist views carried the day.)

After some quarreling, mainly with himself, Jefferson gave up on what he called "metaphysical" questions. He asked Congress to appropriate the $15 million. The United States took formal possession of New Orleans in December of 1803, just seven months before the duel between Hamilton and Burr.

TROUBLE WITH BRITAIN After his victory in the presidential election of 1800, Jefferson began to dismantle the army and navy that Washington and Adams had expanded. Europe was temporarily at peace, and it looked as if the

THE TRANS-MISSISSIPPI
WEST, 1807

———— Lewis and Clark 1804–1806
– – – – Pike 1806–1807
⚲ Spanish missions

0   100   200   300 MILES

United States could achieve the promises of independence, freed from foreign involvements. In
1803, however, Europe again donned the familiar
mask of war. The major player this time was the
commanding figure of Napoleon. Over the next
dozen years Napoleon's incredible ambition sent
French armies all over Europe and as far as Egypt
and Russia.

The French emperor contemplated an invasion of England, and he even thought of moving

some of his armies into North America. The British were locked in what they regarded as a deadly
struggle for survival. For Americans the questions were the same old ones: Would they be able
to carry on their vitally necessary trade with
Europe? Would they be able to preserve their precious neutrality?

Beginning in 1805, British and French warships both began to intercept American merchant
shipping again. The British controlled the seas,

so they stopped more vessels. The British followed one practice that the French did not. They would board American vessels, pick out men whom they suspected of being British subjects, and force them into service in the Royal Navy. This practice of impressment, which to most Americans seemed little short of kidnapping, added to the fury that gradually built up in the United States.

Jefferson was committed to peace, to a small army and navy, and to a policy of negotiation rather than threat and bluster. But between 1805 and 1807 the British seized about 1,000 American ships, and the French about 500. No administration, no matter how devoted to peace, could permit American ships and sailors to be treated like this.

Another crisis occurred in the summer of 1807. A British warship, the *Leopard*, fired three broadsides into an American frigate, the *Chesapeake*, within view of the Virginia shore. The *Chesapeake's* guns were out of order, and it could return only one cannon shot. Three Americans were killed and eighteen wounded before the *Chesapeake* limped home.

Facing an aroused nation, Jefferson tried to ward off a war with Britain by a device used in pre-Revolution days. He asked Congress for a law, the Embargo Act, which simply prohibited Americans from exporting *anything* to foreign countries. It also forbade all ships to leave American ports bound for any other nation. In short, the embargo was designed to halt foreign trade altogether. Jefferson hoped that the British need for American markets, plus the French desire to import American goods, would force the two nations to behave more respectfully toward American commerce.

The embargo failed. It hurt Americans more than it hurt either the British or the French, because American farmers could not export their products. The law lasted until the end of Jefferson's second administration, when he happily left the capital for his plantation, Monticello. His successor, James Madison, then had to grapple with the problem. Madison's efforts at first were only modifications of Jefferson's policy. For the embargo, Madison substituted a modified policy of trade restriction with the Non-Intercourse Act of 1809. He reopened foreign trade with all nations *except* Britain and France. And he promised to resume commerce with either country if only it would respect American rights on the seas.

THE WAR OF 1812 The Madison administration experimented with one form of trade restriction or another for more than three years. Finally, Madison asked for a declaration of war, citing impressment and trade interference. Congress responded on June 18, 1812. Just two days earlier, the British had announced a favorable change in policy. But it was too late.

The War of 1812 produced frustrating and inconclusive results for the United States. There was a stalemate on what the Americans hoped would be the main front in the North. Then the British sailed almost unopposed into the Chesapeake and burned much of Washington. By the second year of the war, the British navy had total control of the North American coast. A final, spectacular American triumph in New Orleans came only after the treaty of peace had already been signed.

But the war did produce a couple of future presidents, several cherished slogans, a national anthem, and an important myth.

The Americans began with a shining confidence that they could quickly capture Canada. It was, Jefferson remarked, a "mere matter of marching." But it was not to be.

The Canadian front was divided by geography into three corridors. The first, in the east, ran up from Fort Ticonderoga across lakes George and Champlain, and on toward Montreal. The second lay across the Niagara River, between Lakes Erie and Ontario. The third ran eastward from Detroit, between lakes Huron and Erie.

In 1812 the Americans mounted assaults through all three corridors. All three failed miserably—two of them when New York militiamen simply refused to cross the border into Canada.

The burning of Washington, 1814. The British burned a number of major government buildings in the capital on August 24, 1814, though they did not occupy the city for long. Their action was a retaliation for the American burning of the capital of Upper Canada, York (which was later renamed Toronto). (Brown University Library, Anne S. K. Brown Military Collection)

The following year, the Americans again tried all three fronts. Once more, the result was defeat in the eastern and central corridors. But in the west, United States forces had a bit more luck. A young naval officer, Oliver Hazard Perry, sailed a small fleet of newly built ships from the eastern end of Lake Erie. Perry met and defeated the British at Put-in Bay, near Detroit. He reported his victory with one of the war's few lasting results, a slogan: "We have met the enemy, and they are ours."

Perry's victory made the position of British forces near Detroit untenable, so they began to withdraw. An American force under the command of William Henry Harrison—a future president who had already won a battle against Indians in 1811 at Tippecanoe, Indiana—gave chase and won the Battle of the Thames in October 1813. (One of the casualties of the battle was the great Indian leader Tecumseh, who had become a general officer in the British army. See p. 282)

Meanwhile, the Americans had won a few victories at sea in engagements between single ships, most notably a string of victories by the frigate *Constitution* ("Old Ironsides"). And one American defeat gave rise to another slogan. When the United States frigate *Chesapeake* was about to be taken by the British *Shannon*, the American captain, James Lawrence, supposedly uttered a famous dying order: "Don't give up the ship! Blow her up!" The order was not obeyed.

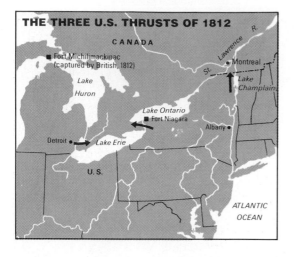

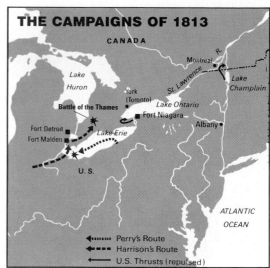

The *Chesapeake* surrendered. But the slogan took hold of a public imagination badly in need of heroes and good news.

In the end, British naval superiority was overwhelming—800 warships against a few dozen vessels in the American fleet. By 1814 the British completely controlled the American coastline. This was an ominous fact. But it was joined to another fact even more ominous. In 1814, when Napoleon was defeated and sent into exile, crack British regiments were freed to join the American war. The British now took the offensive.

Their first and largest assault came down the Lake Champlain–Lake George corridor from Canada. In the summer of 1814, about 10,000 British regulars began the attack. But they were turned back—as they had been at Saratoga in the Revolutionary War—by a desperate American victory on Lake Champlain, a victory managed by a skillful young officer, Thomas McDonough, in the Battle of Plattsburgh.

The second British attack came in August, up Chesapeake Bay. The British easily captured Washington and burned most of its major public buildings, including the White House. Then they set out to raid Baltimore. But here they were stood off by the resistance of a well-placed American fortification, Fort McHenry. The British bombardment was watched by an American, Francis

Scott Key, whose eyes searched the early light of the dawn for the American flag. He later set his thoughts to the tune of a bawdy British tavern song and gave the Americans a national anthem. With Washington in disarray, and Baltimore out of reach, the British could hope for little else in the Chesapeake.

Their third attack came in the South, at New Orleans. The Tennessee soldier-lawyer-planter-politician, Andrew Jackson, had marched an American force of militia down through the Mississippi Territory. He subdued the Creek Indians at the Battle of Horseshoe Bend. Then he invaded Spanish Florida and captured Pensacola. Then on to New Orleans, where he threw together a force of pirates, vagabonds, militia, and free blacks (blacks made up about 10 percent of his army) to defend the city against an invading force of British regulars.

The British commander, General Sir Edward Packenham, decided to throw his seasoned men in a close-ranked assault on the rough fortifications Jackson had built. The result was carnage. Jackson's well-placed artillery raked the British formations over and over again. Within about half an hour, some 500 British soldiers were dead, including Packenham, and about 1,500 others were wounded.

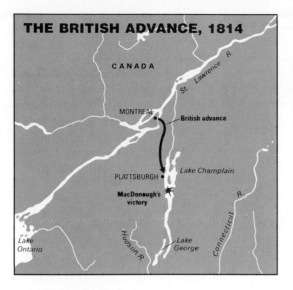

THE BRITISH ADVANCE, 1814

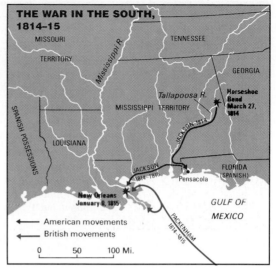

THE WAR IN THE SOUTH, 1814–15

(Jackson's riflemen had also shot a few of the enemy. But these "hunters of Kentucky" received much of the credit for the victory. This reinforced the myth of the frontiersman with his rifle as the soul and sinew of the republic and, incidentally, did more than anything else to make Jackson president in 1828. The myth of the rifleman was, clearly, much more attractive than the reality of a numerous and cunningly placed line of cannon.)

By the time Jackson defeated Packenham, the war was actually over. A treaty of peace had been signed in Europe, though news of it did not come until after the battle. But the flow of news was as important as the flow of events. Americans who heard first of Jackson's victory, and then of the peace treaty, were able to believe that the United States had "won" this inconclusive war.

The Treaty of Ghent provided only that the situation between Britain and America would remain just as it was in June 1812. No concessions or promises were made, and no territory changed hands.

The War of 1812 made little sense at the time, and it settled no real problems. Three years after it began came Napoleon's final defeat at Waterloo. From that time, Britain was not involved in a war with any Continental nation for a hundred years. If the Americans could have held out for three more years, British harassment of their trade would probably have stopped, and the war could have been avoided.

But at least the war was over, and the United States had not lost. In fact, many Americans, encouraged by Jackson's victory, thought of the war as a successful defense of American independence and neutral rights. They called it a Second War for Independence.

THE HARTFORD CONVENTION The Louisiana Purchase was approved in the Senate by a wide margin, twenty-four votes to seven. But the opposition was significant because it pointed toward a powerful and underlying problem in American life. Most of the opponents were from New England. People there realized that the westward movement would sooner or later result in a basic shift of people, economic power, and political control away from the East to the western territories and states. The Founding Fathers had worried about whether one government could control a nation as large as the United States. The future would be full of tests of the American motto, *e pluribus unum*—"out of many, one."

CHRONOLOGY

1789 Washington inaugurated as first president. Congress passes Judiciary Act. Revolution in France.

1790 Hamilton's proposals for funding, assumption, and a national bank are adopted. District of Columbia created. Wilkinson rejoins army.

1794 The Whiskey Rebellion suppressed.

1796 Wilkinson becomes highest ranking officer in U.S. Army. Washington publishes farewell address. John Adams defeats Jefferson in presidential election.

1800 Jefferson and Burr win the presidential election. House of Representatives decides technical "tie" between Jefferson and Burr in favor of Jefferson.

1801 Congress passes second Judiciary Act. John Adams appoints Marshall chief justice of the United States. Jefferson becomes president, Burr vice president. U.S. learns that Spain had given Louisiana to France in secret treaty.

1783 Wilkinson forced to resign commission in army for plotting against Washington. Treaty of Paris ends Revolutionary War.

1783	1786	1789	1792	1795	1798	1801

1792 Washington re-elected for second term. France declared a republic.

1797 John Adams becomes president, Jefferson vice president. Adams tries to negotiate an end to the French alliance of 1778; the XYZ affair follows. The Quasi-War with France begins.

1793 The "terror" of the French Revolution begins. France and Britain go to war. Washington demands recall of French ambassador Genêt.

1798 Alien and Sedition acts become law. Jefferson and Madison write Kentucky and Virginia resolutions.

1799 The Quasi-War ends. Hamilton's party defeats Burr's in New York elections.

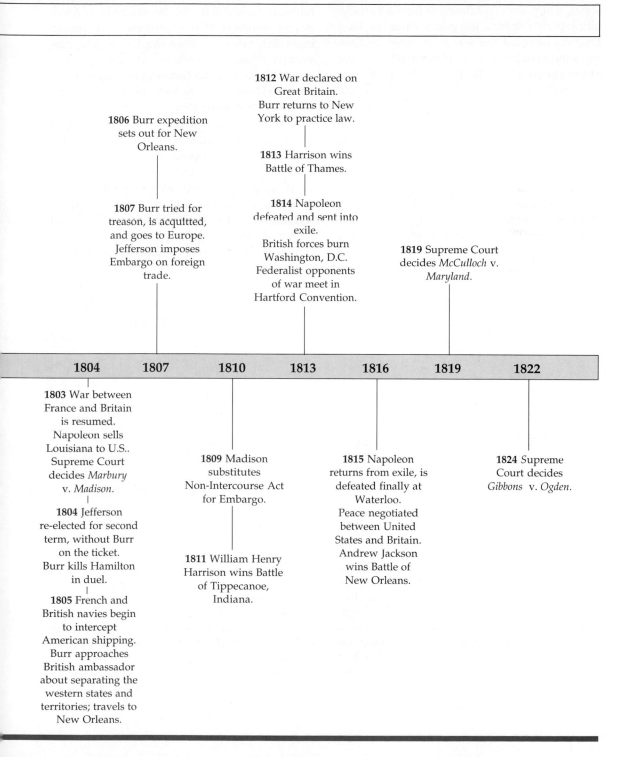

1806 Burr expedition sets out for New Orleans.

1807 Burr tried for treason, is acquitted, and goes to Europe. Jefferson imposes Embargo on foreign trade.

1812 War declared on Great Britain. Burr returns to New York to practice law.

1813 Harrison wins Battle of Thames.

1814 Napoleon defeated and sent into exile. British forces burn Washington, D.C. Federalist opponents of war meet in Hartford Convention.

1819 Supreme Court decides *McCulloch* v. *Maryland*.

| 1804 | 1807 | 1810 | 1813 | 1816 | 1819 | 1822 |

1803 War between France and Britain is resumed. Napoleon sells Louisiana to U.S.. Supreme Court decides *Marbury* v. *Madison.*

1804 Jefferson re-elected for second term, without Burr on the ticket. Burr kills Hamilton in duel.

1805 French and British navies begin to intercept American shipping. Burr approaches British ambassador about separating the western states and territories; travels to New Orleans.

1809 Madison substitutes Non-Intercourse Act for Embargo.

1811 William Henry Harrison wins Battle of Tippecanoe, Indiana.

1815 Napoleon returns from exile, is defeated finally at Waterloo. Peace negotiated between United States and Britain. Andrew Jackson wins Battle of New Orleans.

1824 Supreme Court decides *Gibbons* v. *Ogden.*

Before the War of 1812, the New England states, which were tied closely to Britain by trade, had bitterly opposed Jefferson's embargo. New England opposed the war even more. In Congress the strongest voices for war had been those of the so-called War Hawks—congressmen from the frontier regions who wanted to invade and annex Canada, adding even more land to the western domain at the expense of the East. Politicians and businessmen all over New England felt the government had betrayed them and was willing to sacrifice their interests to the war fever of the rest of the country.

In opposition to the war, New England resisted militia calls and wartime taxes and continued to trade with the enemy in Canada. In 1814 the New England governors called a convention in Hartford, Connecticut, to raise the same kinds of questions that the Annapolis Convention had raised about the Articles of Confederation in 1786. In calling the convention, the governors asserted that the Constitution had failed, that the New England states were not receiving "equal rights and benefits," and that the frame of government would have to be seriously revised. A few members of the convention demanded immediate secession from the Union. The convention drafted a series of proposed amendments to the Constitution—all of which would have weakened the federal government—and sent them to Washington to the next Congress.

Time, however, cured problems that might not have been solved otherwise. When the Hartford Convention proposal reached Washington, news of Jackson's victory had just arrived, and the news of the peace treaty was not far behind. As was to happen so often in American history, sectional crisis had been resolved by events and not by statesmanship. Despite its lack of positive results, the Hartford Convention had raised what was to become the basic political question for the next generation: Would the United States be able to resolve sectional differences, or would some crisis sooner or later divide one part of the country from the other?

Suggestions for Further Reading

AARON BURR

The best place to begin is still Thomas P. Abernethy, *The Burr Conspiracy* (1954). An attempt to "clear" Burr of the conspiracy charge is in the second volume of the biography by Milton Lomask, *Aaron Burr* (1982). Students who like to read original documents can follow Burr's trial in V. B. Reed and J. D. Williams, eds., *The Case of Aaron Burr* (1960). Perhaps the best way to see Burr's downfall, in the end, is as part of an interplay of monumental egos, as in J. Daniels, *Ordeal of Ambition: Jefferson, Hamilton, Burr* (1970). Anyone who prefers fiction to fact will find good summer reading in Gore Vidal, *Burr, A Novel* (1973).

THE DEVELOPMENT OF PARTY POLITICS

A richly meditative book on the meaning of parties is Richard Hofstadter, *The Idea of a Party System* (1973). A beautifully written brief account of the development of the parties is Joseph Charles, *The Origins of the American Party System* (1968). Richard Buel, *Securing the Revolution* (1972), is a fine study of party ideology in the 1790s, as is Lance Banning, *The Jeffersonian Persuasion* (1978). Ronald Formisano, *The Transformation of Political Culture: Massachusetts Parties, 1790s–1840s* (1983), is a model state study. So is Alfred Young, *The Democratic Republicans of New York* (1967). The Federalist collapse can be followed in David Hackett Fischer, *The Revolution of American Conservatism* (1965).

EXPANSION, FOREIGN AFFAIRS

A very readable place to begin is Felix Gilbert's fine little book, *To the Farewell Address* (1961). Jerald A. Combs, *The Jay Treaty* (1970), puts that affair into a comprehensible context. Alexander De Conde, *The Quasi-War* (1966), is a fine account of the undeclared war with France. A standard account of the diplomacy leading to the Louisiana Purchase is Alexander De Conde, *The Louisiana Affair* (1976). Reginald Horsman, *The Frontier in the Formative Years, 1783–1815* (1970), is a good general book on the West.

Malcolm Rohrbough, *The Land Office Business* (1968), is the definitive account of the management of the public domain by the federal government during the early decades. The origins of the War of 1812 can be traced in Reginald Horsman, *The Causes of the War of 1812* (1962). A charmingly presented account of the impact of the war on Americans is in Marcus Cunliffe, *Soldiers and Civilians: The Martial Spirit in America, 1775–1860* (1973). The standard discussion of the arch-Federalist response to the war is James Banner, *The Hartford Convention* (1970).

CHAPTER 7
BEYOND THE
APPALACHIAN
BARRIER

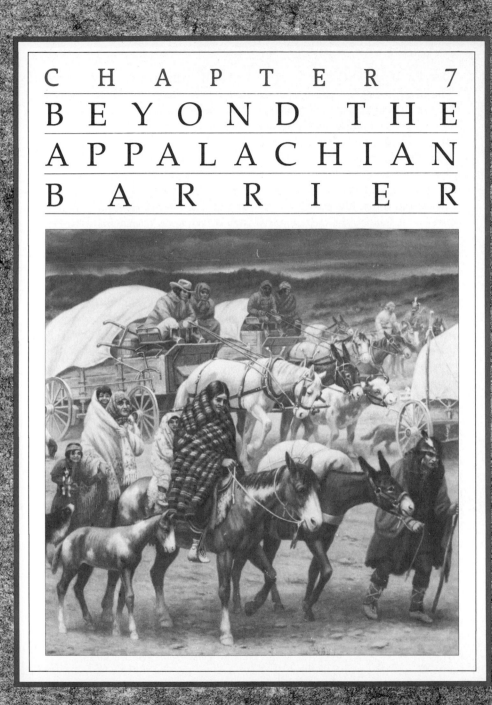

THE EPISODE: *On October 1, 1838, about 13,000 people set out from their homes in the southeastern United States. Most of them were on foot for their journey, which would not end until they had crossed the Mississippi River, hundreds of miles to the west. They were joining a westward trek that thousands of European Americans were also making to new homes on the frontier. But they were not ordinary pioneers. They were escorted by units of the United States army, and most of them did not want to go where they were going. They were members of the Cherokee tribe, and their land had been taken from them. The state of Georgia had declared that the tribe was "extinguished." Now they were setting out on the path they would come to call "The Trail Where They Cried" or "The Trail of Tears." By the time the last group of Cherokees reached the area known to white people as "Indian Territory" (now Oklahoma), thousands of them had perished of cold, exhaustion, and disease. Their terrible travail had taken many months, and they got to their destination in the midst of winter.*

The Cherokees' forced march to Indian Territory was the culmination of a long story that had begun toward the end of the eighteenth century. It was the outcome of a bitter struggle to protect their homes and farms against the mounting and relentless pressure of white "settlement." This chapter tells the story of that struggle.

THE HISTORICAL SETTING: *The Trail of Tears was a tragic event with its heroes and villains, but it cannot be understood only as the outcome of heroism and villainy. It did not result only from some particular individuals' choices, actions, or personalities. It was part of a larger history. The removal of the Cherokees has to be understood as one moment in the history of two closely related processes. The first was an astonishing expansion of the market economy in European-American society during the first decades of the nineteenth century. The second was the emergence of a new political style in the United States, a style that gave rise to new kinds of leaders with new kinds of ideas about what could and should be done. This chapter explains how the rapid geographical expansion of the market economy was related to the rise of new notions of democratic politics and political leadership. It provides the context within which the tragedy of the Cherokee people can be understood and judged.*

This is the first of two chapters that analyze the American political system during the period between the 1820s and 1840s. In this chapter, the emphasis is on the relationship between economic development and politics. In the chapter that follows, the emphasis will be on the development of a new system of political parties. Taken together, the two chapters provide the basis for a clear understanding of the way a novel political culture was taking shape in the United States.

THE TRAIL OF TEARS: THE TRAGEDY OF THE CHEROKEE NATION

Cherokees received their permanent names only after they reached adulthood. They were named for some aspect of their behavior or appearance that seemed characteristic: Thick Legs or Woman Holder. So when one young Cherokee warrior told his friends that he always returned home from the hunt by walking along the top of the mountain, it was only fitting that he began to be called Kahnungdaclageh, or The Man Who Walks on the Mountaintop. Later, when Kahnungdaclageh became well known to many white people, they called him simply The Ridge.

Now, as a young chieftain of thirty-six, The Ridge was about to commit a murder. It was August 1807—while Aaron Burr, hundreds of miles away, was on trial for treason. With an accomplice, The Ridge waited in a Georgia tavern for the arrival of his intended victim, an important Cherokee chief known as Doublehead. It was well after dark when Doublehead finally arrived and sat down to drink. A candle burned nearby; according to plan, someone moved it closer to Doublehead. The Ridge quietly approached the table and blew out the candle. Then, while Doublehead was startled and momentarily unable to see, The Ridge drew a pistol, shot him in the face, and quickly left the tavern. But, although the bullet had smashed through Doublehead's jaw, he was not dead. All night The Ridge and his accomplice searched the area for Doublehead, but it was not until daybreak that they finally found the house where he was hiding. The pair rushed in, yelling war whoops, and aimed their pistols at the wounded man. Another failure: This time their guns misfired. With a strength born of desperation, Doublehead leaped at The Ridge with a knife, and the two men struggled. Finally, the murder was done: The Ridge's accomplice reloaded his pistol, shot Doublehead, and finished him off with a crushing blow to the head with a tomahawk. The Ridge had to place his foot on the dead man's head and pull hard with both hands before the tomahawk could be removed.

Later, in the words of a white official of the United States government, The Ridge "addressed the crowd who were drawn together by this act of violence, and explained his authority and his reasons." But there was only one reason that he thought really mattered: Chief Doublehead had betrayed the Cherokee Nation.

It was under Doublehead's leadership that the Cherokees had surrendered ever-larger portions of their territory to the United States, in four separate treaties signed between 1798 and 1806.[1] Doublehead himself had profited handsomely from each of these treaties: He had received tracts of land from the government, and he had begun to purchase thoroughbred horses and black slaves. By 1802 Doublehead was addressing the government's agent (through a translator) as his "friend and brother," and requesting the gift of a large boat "for the purpose of descending the river to New Orleans" so that he could "open up a trade with the western wild Indians." By 1806 the United States secretary of war was so sure that Doublehead could be bought off that he instructed federal agents to negotiate specifically with him for the immense tract of land that the tribe would cede later that year. In 1807 still another land cession was in the works. Because of Doublehead's murder, the deal fell through. It would be almost ten more years before the Cherokees yielded any more territory.

In the meantime, the tribe was deeply troubled, and their problems were further complicated by Doublehead's death. Like all Native Americans east of the Mississippi, the Cherokees were caught up in a process as old as European expansion and as relentless as white "progress." For over a century they had been trading with white men—mostly in animal pelts, and often in return for alcohol. Increasingly, the tribe had come to depend on this trade, and white traders—often with official encouragement—had taken advantage of their dependence. After the American Revolution, the federal government continued the same policy. President Thomas Jefferson, for instance, instructed federal agents to lure the Indians into debt and then to offer to take their land as payment. A vicious cycle of poverty, alcoholism, and corruption had been set in motion, and the Cherokees had either to break the cycle or die as a tribe.

In 1811 an Indian chieftain from the north named Tecumseh urged all the Native Americans in North America to join together in an unprecedented alliance against the power of the United States. Such an alliance might well mean war—and Tecumseh darkly hinted that he spoke "in the name of the British." Tecumseh found ready ears among the neighboring Creek tribe to the south. But when his spokesmen, known as "prophets," came to organize the Cherokees, they met more resistance—a resistance that was finally led by The Ridge himself.

When a local "prophet" brought Tecumseh's message to a responsive Cherokee audience, and threatened that the Great Spirit would strike dead anyone who denied Tecumseh's words, it was The Ridge who took up the challenge. He said to the crowd:

> My friends, the talk you have heard is not good. It would lead us to a war with the United States, and we should suffer. It is false; it is not a talk from the Great Spirit. I stand here and defy the threat that he who disbelieves shall die. Let the death come upon me. I offer to test this scheme of imposters!

The Ridge survived. And when the United States went to war with Britain the next year, he and his friends persuaded the Cherokees to side with the Americans, even though that meant fighting against the neighboring Creeks, many of whom had heeded Tecumseh's call and attacked American citizens.

---

[1]The Cherokees had already had to cede much of their land to the United States after the Revolutionary War, in which they supported the British side.

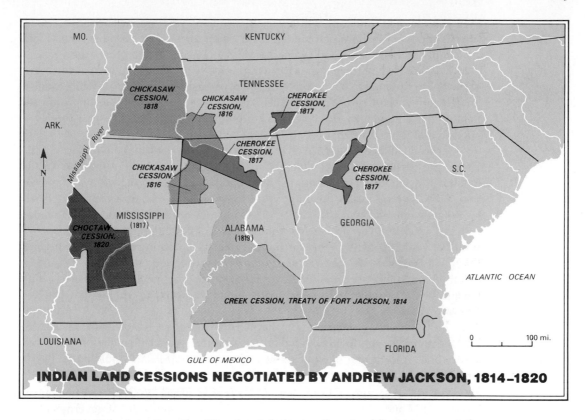

INDIAN LAND CESSIONS NEGOTIATED BY ANDREW JACKSON, 1814–1820

At The Ridge's urging, the Cherokee tribal council sent soldiers to support the United States against the Creeks. Early in 1814 a Cherokee regiment under the command of General Andrew Jackson played a key role in the crucial Battle of Horseshoe Bend, a bloody clash that ended in the death of some 800 Creek warriors—more Indian deaths than in any other battle in the history of Indian–white warfare.

The Ridge distinguished himself at Horseshoe Bend, and he hoped his role and that of his fellow Cherokees would make their lands safe forever. But it was not to be. First, General Jackson forced the Creeks (even those who had remained neutral) to cede more than 20 million acres of territory—an area encompassing most of what would soon become the state of Alabama, plus a large part of southern Georgia. Then, after he had disposed of his Creek enemies, Jackson proceeded to turn upon his Cherokee allies. He forced the tribe to sign two disastrous treaties in 1816 and 1817, surrendering more than 3 million acres for a token price of about 20 cents an acre.

The Cherokees did what they could to resist these cessions. They reminded Jackson of their previous loyalty and service to him. They tried to boycott the meetings at which he pressed his demands. They even sent delegations to Washington to argue their case. But to no avail. In the face of Jackson's barrage of patriotic pleading, threats, and bribery, Cherokee resistance withered.

First, Jackson would cajole the Indians:

Receive the offering of your beloved father the President of the United States [Madison]. Give him proof that you return his love and that you wish to join hearts and heads and live like our people, one family in peace and friendship.

Then Jackson would turn ugly and warn the Indians what might happen if he—or other white men—should become "irritated" with them: "Look around," he would say, simply and tellingly, "and recollect what happened to our brothers the Creeks." Finally, Jackson would dispense bribes with a free hand to any influential Cherokee who would accept them. He reported these bribes tersely enough to his white friends: "In concluding the treaty with the Cherokees, it was found both well and polite to make a few presents to the chiefs and interpreters." In fact, the "few presents" amounted to more than $5,000 in 1817 alone.

Jackson's ultimate purpose, even at this time, was the complete removal of the tribe. "The cession of land obtained is not important," he wrote of the 1817 treaty, "but the principle established leads to great importance." The "principle" was removal. The 1817 treaty promised the tribe, in return for the 2 million acres it ceded, an equivalent amount of land west of the Mississippi. Each Cherokee who chose to move to the new territory would receive "one rifle and ammunition, one brass kettle, or, in lieu of the brass kettle, a beaver trap." To be sure, nothing in the treaty *required* individual Cherokees to move west, but Jackson was confident that the pressure to emigrate would soon become too powerful to resist. The inevitable course of white expansion would surely, Jackson wrote to a friend, "give us the whole country in less than two years."

Only Jackson's timing was off the mark. While the Cherokees did make one final territorial cession in 1819, it would take not two years to remove the tribe, but twenty-one. And during eight of these years, Andrew Jackson would again play a central role—this time as president of the United States.

The delay stemmed from new and effective forms of Cherokee resistance. Between 1817 and 1827 the Cherokees devised a new form of tribal government. It was modeled on the government of the United States, and it undercut the old clan-based leadership that had made the tribe so vulnerable in its treaty negotiations. The new government replaced the traditional tribal council of local chiefs and headsmen with a two-house legislature. Members of the lower house were elected on a geographic basis, and they in turn designated thirteen men to serve as members of the upper house. It was this group of thirteen, known as the National Committee, that assumed ongoing responsibility for most tribal affairs (including negotiations with the United States). Its members were chosen to serve the tribe as a whole, and not the clans to which they belonged. Many of them were able to speak English. A system of courts and salaried administrative officials completed the new arrangement.

The Cherokees had been transformed from a tribe into a republic. The climax came in 1827, with the adoption of a written constitution, which resembled the Constitution of the United States. It provided for universal male suffrage and made the principal chief of the tribe (elected by the legislature to a four-year term) the Cherokee "president" in all but name.

This political transformation might have come about even if the Cherokees had not been trying to protect themselves from the incursions of the whites. Many Cherokees had come to adopt the manners of white "civilization." By the beginning of the nineteenth century, there were no longer enough game animals left in Cherokee country to permit the tribe to continue living on the fur trade. "Their hunting was nearly over," one Cherokee remarked, and the Indians were now "scratching after every bit of raccoon skin that was big enough to cover a squaw's ——."

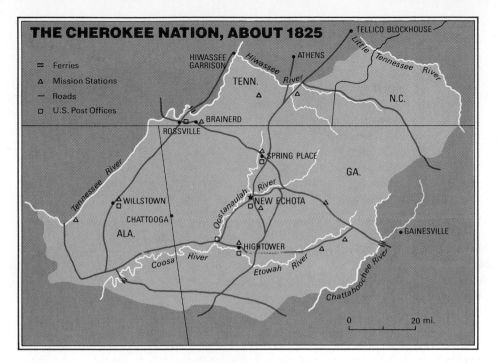

THE CHEROKEE NATION, ABOUT 1825

= Ferries
△ Mission Stations
— Roads
▫ U.S. Post Offices

TELLICO BLOCKHOUSE

Little Tennessee River

HIWASSEE GARRISON

Hiwassee River

ATHENS

TENN.

N.C.

BRAINERD

ROSSVILLE

Tennessee River

SPRING PLACE

GA.

Oostanaulah River

NEW ECHOTA

WILLSTOWN

CHATTOOGA

ALA.

GAINESVILLE

HIGHTOWER

Coosa River

Etowah River

Chattahoochee River

0   20 mi.

In place of the fur trade, the Cherokees had established a thriving agricultural economy. An 1825 survey of Cherokee property listed the results: 22,000 cattle, 7,600 horses, 46,000 pigs, 2,500 sheep, 762 looms, 2,488 spinning wheels, 172 wagons, almost 10,000 plows, 31 grist mills, 10 sawmills, 62 blacksmith shops, 8 cotton gins, 18 schools, and 18 ferries.

These economic changes were inevitably accompanied by cultural ones. Christian missionaries of several denominations, especially Congregationalists from New England and Methodists from the South, established schools within tribal territory. A portion of the tribe, including several prominent chiefs, became converts to Christianity, and a few even went on to become missionaries themselves. In 1824 the tribal legislature proposed the establishment of a Cherokee National Academy, complete with classrooms, library, and lecture hall, to serve as an educational and cultural center for the Nation. The legislature also planned to erect a museum designed to display artifacts of Cherokee history and craftsmanship. (The Ridge himself donated an old ceremonial pipe to the proposed museum.) In 1825 the legislature resolved to build a permanent capital city, New Echota, complete with municipal square, main street, and impressive government buildings. The new capital even contained a printing press, which, after 1828, published a bilingual national newspaper, the *Cherokee Phoenix*.

To be sure, much of this transformation touched only a minority of the tribe. The handsome frame houses and government buildings of New Echota were probably never seen by most Cherokees, who continued to live in log huts and who never learned the language or the customs of white Americans. In fact, the lavish reports of astonishing Cherokee "progress" were part of a deliberate campaign by tribal leaders

The Ridge. The Ridge began his career as a hunter. By the time this portrait was painted in 1834, he had become every inch the Southern gentleman. But he never learned to speak English. (Western History Collections, University of Oklahoma Library)

and their white supporters to arouse sympathy for the Cherokee cause among the American public.

Still, for an important minority of privileged Cherokees, the transformation was very real—and very comfortable. And it meant something more than becoming "civilized" in some vague sense. It meant that they modeled their lives on one particular group of privileged white Americans: the Southern ruling class—the plantation gentry, complete with its racehorses and its black slaves. And one man who adopted this style was The Ridge himself.

It had been sometime around 1800, as a young man, that The Ridge had made the shift from hunting to farming. By the 1820s he was prosperous enough to erect an elegant two-story "mansion," built for him by a white carpenter from Tennessee. The house boasted four brick fireplaces. All eight of its rooms were finished with hardwood floors, panels, and ceilings. Its thirty windows were set in walnut frames, and one of them, a large arched triple window, overlooked the commercial ferry that The Ridge owned on a river nearby. Behind the house were outbuildings that included two kitchens, a smokehouse, and a pair of stables. Then there was a group of cabins that housed The Ridge's thirty black slaves. These slaves labored in eight separate fields that produced corn, tobacco, wheat, indigo—and cotton. The slaves also worked on the plantation's vineyard, its ornamental garden, and its extensive orchards (which contained more than a thousand peach trees, alone). The Ridge even gave his plantation a name: He called it Chieftains.

One element of white culture that The Ridge never did absorb was the English language. But he made sure that his family acquired the white education he lacked.

John Ridge. Son of The Ridge, who sent him to be educated at a mission school in Connecticut, John Ridge impressed one New England girl as a "noble youth, beautiful in appearance, very graceful, a perfect gentleman everywhere." He returned to the Cherokee Nation and eventually took his father's place as a tribal leader. (National Anthropological Archives, Smithsonian Institution)

He sent his son (who was known as John Ridge), along with one of his nephews, to a mission school on tribal territory. Then, when the two boys became teenagers, he sent them off to distant Connecticut, where Congregationalists had recently started a school in the small town of Cornwall, "to educate the male aboriginees of all nations." There the two boys completed their adjustment to white culture in triumphant fashion. The Ridge's nephew, who had come to Cornwall with the Cherokee name Gullageenah, soon came to call himself Elias Boudinot, after a wealthy white man of that name who had made a $500 donation to the school. Young Boudinot proved such a brilliant student that after his graduation he was sent on to receive advanced training at Andover Theological Seminary in Massachusetts. (Boudinot would later serve as editor of the *Cherokee Phoenix*, and single-handedly translate the New Testament into the Cherokee language—from the original Greek.)

John Ridge and Elias Boudinot triumphed socially as well as academically in New England. To one Cornwall girl, they were "so graceful and genteel that the white pupils appeared uncouth beside them." And when the two young men returned to the Cherokee Nation in the mid-1820s, they brought with them the white women from Cornwall they had married. Both wives were members of locally prominent families; Elias Boudinot's new father-in-law was even a graduate of Yale.

Elias Boudinot. Both John Ridge and his cousin Elias Boudinot married white women from Connecticut. The day before Boudinot's wedding, an enraged white mob burned him in effigy. Even the Reverend Lyman Beecher, the most prominent New England minister of his day (and father of Harriet Beecher Stowe), protested the marriage. The scandal was so serious that the mission school closed the very next year. (Western History Collections, University of Oklahoma Library)

In the Cherokee Nation, intermarriage between Indians and whites had been taking place for nearly a century, and the mixed-blood offspring were accepted as full members of the tribe. The Ridge himself had married a half-blood Cherokee woman, whose father was probably a local white judge—so that his son John Ridge was himself partly white.

In fact, as a full-blooded Native American, The Ridge was a rarity among the new Cherokee leadership. By the 1820s the tribe was coming to be dominated, politically and economically, by mixed-blood Cherokees who were able to speak English and who were known by names like Joseph Vann, George Lowery, and Elijah Hicks. The white ancestors of these leaders had come to America in the eighteenth century, mostly from Scotland, moved west to make their fortunes by trading in furs and other goods with the Indians, and often married Indian women. Prosperous to begin with, the children of these traders found it easy to adjust to the change from hunting to agriculture when the supply of game ran low. They built large farms, generally near navigable rivers so they could sell their produce in white markets. Many of them also ran stores and taverns that allowed them to profit from the trade of their poorer full-blooded fellow tribesmen. They became, in short, a Cherokee upper class.

Usually, these mixed-blood Cherokees were not traditional clan leaders or headsmen. But they were the most prosperous members of the tribe. They already knew about farming and marketing when the rest of the tribe was just turning from the hunt to agriculture. They were able to operate easily in the white people's world at the very point when the Indians desperately needed leaders who could understand

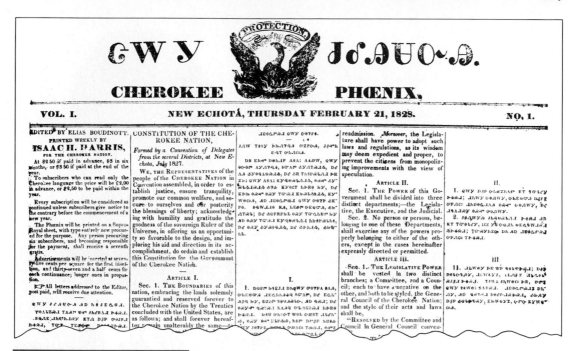

The *Cherokee Phoenix*. The *Cherokee Phoenix*, a bilingual newspaper edited by Elias Boudinot, used the alphabet devised a few years earlier by a Cherokee named Sequoyah. The left-hand columns were printed in English; the right-hand columns in Cherokee. The paper was intended partly to appeal to the tribe's white sympathizers. This first number contains the Cherokee constitution of 1827. (American Antiquarian Society)

the fine print in white men's treaties and who could hold their own—if any could—against men like Andrew Jackson. And they were accepted, by Cherokee law and tradition, as full members of the tribe. It was only natural, then, that these men came to win political power in the Cherokee Nation in the years after 1815. When the Cherokees began to reorganize their government in 1817, it was the mixed-bloods who initiated the move; from the start, it was they who dominated the National Committee that took charge of tribal affairs. And it was one of them—the "whitest" of them all—who was chosen president of the National Committee, who wrote the Cherokee constitution in 1827, and who was elected the following year as the principal chief of the tribe. His name was John Ross, and he proved to be the key figure in the struggle of the Cherokees.

John Ross was only one-eighth Indian. He was a Scotsman with only a touch of Cherokee ancestry. His maternal great-grandfather had immigrated from Scotland in the mid–eighteenth century, become a trader with the Cherokees, and married a Cherokee woman. The half-blood daughter of this couple married another Scottish immigrant in 1769. During the 1780s *their* quarter-blood daughter married still another Scotsman, Daniel Ross; he, too, was an Indian trader among the Cherokees. It was to this couple that John Ross was born in 1790.

Chief John Ross. Although he was only one-eighth Indian by "blood" and never even learned to speak the Cherokee language, John Ross was universally accepted as a member of the tribe and as its principal leader. In general, Indians were not concerned with ancestry or skin color but with loyalty when there was a question of tribal membership. (National Anthropological Archives, Smithsonian Institution)

Until he was in his mid-twenties, John Ross gave no hint that he would become a champion of the Cherokee Nation, or even that he would identify himself as an Indian at all. He was educated at a white boarding school in Tennessee and received his business training with a wealthy white merchant and planter there. (To the end of his life, Ross remained unable to speak or understand the Cherokee language with any fluency—he was forced to use an interpreter whenever he addressed his own people.) In 1813, as a young man of twenty-three, Ross left Tennessee to follow in the footsteps of his white father, grandfather, and great-grandfather: He moved to Cherokee country and became an Indian trader. The War of 1812 was under way, and Ross quickly managed to win lucrative government contracts to supply food and blankets for the Cherokee regiment that fought under Andrew Jackson at Horseshoe Bend. After the war, he set up a store and ferry on the Tennessee River at the edge of the Cherokee Nation and established there a flourishing trade. (One of his ventures—an especially ironic one, in light of his later role—involved selling supplies to those Cherokees who decided to move to the West.) Ross speculated in Tennessee land on the side. As late as 1817 he was asking the federal agent to the Cherokees to award him a certain contract on the grounds that it would be "more satisfactory to the Indians" if they were dealing with him rather than with some other merchant, because he was a man "they could confide in." This was the language of an Indian trader—not of an Indian.

From these beginnings, John Ross came slowly, during the 1820s, to assume a new identity as a member and a leader of the tribe he initially regarded as a source of financial profit. He may have sensed there was greater opportunity to win lasting success and glory as the political leader of an independent nation—a patriotic "chief" in every sense of the word—than as a private merchant. (That was exactly what happened to another Tennessean, the son of a Scottish immigrant, who also started as a planter and land speculator—Andrew Jackson.) In any case, in 1827 Ross abandoned his thriving business at the edge of the Cherokee Nation and built an elegant new house at its very heart, just a few miles from the new national capital at New Echota. The same year, he began to receive instruction in the oral traditions of the tribe. Despite the color of his skin and his white man's clothing and manners, John Ross soon came to receive the unquestioning support and adulation of the great mass of ordinary Cherokees. They knew he had staked his life on their interests, and they were right. He had come along in the nick of time.

Armed with their new tribal structure and "civilized" leadership, the Cherokee Nation squared off against the whites with real success during the 1820s. Andrew Jackson was no longer a military commander, and he was not yet president. Until the end of the decade, most of the pressure on the tribe to cede its remaining territory came from the land-hungry state of Georgia, which claimed most of what remained of the once-extensive tribal lands.

From the white point of view, there was a semblance of legality to Georgia's claims. Back in 1802, when the state had ceded *its* extensive western lands to the United States, the federal government had promised Georgia to "extinguish the Indian title to all lands lying within the limits of the State." The time limit on this promise had been left deliberately vague (in part because it conflicted with existing federal treaty obligations to protect the Cherokees against outside intruders). All that the government had agreed to do was to give Georgia the land "as early as [it] can be peaceably obtained upon reasonable terms."

During the 1820s the government of Georgia began to press the government of the United States to make good its promise. In the face of this pressure, Presidents James Monroe and John Quincy Adams each appointed agents to try to wring further concessions from the Cherokees. These agents resorted to the traditional techniques— private persuasion and bribery—but the new leaders like John Ross were able to resist these tactics and even to make them backfire against the whites. On one occasion, John Ross received a letter offering him $2,000 if he could persuade the tribal council to make a cession and assuring that "nobody shall know about it." Ross made a dramatic gesture: Addressing the tribal council, he not only refused the bribe, he even recited the offending letter aloud to the assembled council. The episode sealed John Ross's prestige among the Cherokees and enhanced the tribe's growing unity and pride. It was Ross who wrote what soon became the Cherokees' standard answer to the periodic white attempts to win territorial cessions: "It is the fixed and unalterable determination of this Nation never again to cede *one foot* more of land."

But the Cherokee leaders knew it would take more than pride and determination to protect their borders. They sent brilliant young Elias Boudinot, fresh out of theological school, on a tour of the United States to lecture about the tribe's "progress"— and to display himself as its prime example. They circulated their bilingual newspaper, the *Cherokee Phoenix*, through white America. And almost every year during the 1820s they sent delegations to Washington, to lobby with federal officials—and to impress influential whites with their "civilized" manners. John Quincy Adams, serving as Monroe's secretary of state in 1824, recorded his amazement at a four-man Cherokee delegation that included both John Ross and The Ridge. The Indians, Adams confided to his diary, "dress like ourselves" and behave like "well-bred country gentlemen." The Ridge especially—dressed in a satin-collared overcoat, buff vest, and silk cravat—made a "great impression" on Washington society with his "fine figure and handsome face."

While The Ridge impressed Washington society with his physical appearance, John Ross handled the serious negotiations with the federal government. And he did well. After several meetings, President Monroe publicly acknowledged that the United States government was under "no obligation to remove the Indians by force." John Quincy Adams, who succeeded Monroe as president, proved even more reluctant to apply strong federal pressure against the Cherokees.

As the decade went by, the Georgians became increasingly impatient. And when the Cherokees went so far as to adopt their written constitution in July 1827, the Georgians correctly interpreted the move as a blatant assertion of Cherokee sovereignty. If the tribe could get away with this move, it might become an independent nation in fact as well as in name. In December 1827 the Georgia legislature resolved that the land on which the Cherokees lived belonged to Georgia alone. The "Indians are tenants at her will," and the state had "the right to extend her authority and her laws over her whole territory and to coerce obedience to them from all descriptions of people, be they white, red, or black, who may reside within her limits." The resolution closed with a veiled threat that the state would use violence to secure its rights if peaceful means failed. The legislature set no time limit, but the federal government had been put on notice to act. Two years later, when nothing had been done, Georgia finally set a deadline: June 1, 1830. On that day the Cherokee Nation, with all its laws and institutions, would cease to exist. The tribal land itself would be formally annexed to Georgia—new county lines were already drawn—and it would be opened to white settlement.

By this time the Georgians had finally found themselves a powerful friend in Washington: In the election of 1828, Andrew Jackson had been chosen president of the United States—and many people had voted for him partly because they knew he would take a hard line on Indian removal. As president, Jackson was at last in a position to finish the job he had set out to do a dozen years earlier. Within weeks of his inauguration, the new president notified the Cherokees that he would not tolerate the existence of a "foreign and independent government" within the boundaries of an existing state, and he all but invited the Georgians to take over the Cherokee Nation by letting them know he would not stop them. Jackson flatly denied that the 16,000 Cherokees were entitled to hold the land they continued to inhabit. These unsettled people had no right to claim lands as their own "merely because they have seen them from the mountain or passed them in the chase."

But even Andrew Jackson had to operate within the framework of United States law. Before the Indian removal program could proceed, he needed Congress to authorize him to negotiate with the Cherokees and other tribes to "exchange" their existing homeland for land west of the Mississippi—land as yet unsettled by whites. Early in 1830 he submitted to Congress a bill which would allow him to do just that.

Jackson's Indian Removal Bill became one of the most controversial questions to come before Congress in 1830. Many legislators were already sympathetic to the Cherokee cause, and others were prepared to oppose the bill simply because they disliked Andrew Jackson. The opposition to removal was led by such prominent politicians as Daniel Webster and Henry Clay. Even the famous frontiersman Davy Crockett, who was serving in Congress from Jackson's home state of Tennessee, spoke out against the injustice of Indian removal. A senator from New Jersey argued for three days in behalf of the Native Americans. "Do the obligations of justice change with the color of the skin?" he asked.

> As the tide of our population has rolled on, we have added purchase to purchase. The confiding Indian listened to our professions of friendship: we called him brother, and he believed us. Millions after millions he has yielded to our importunity, until we have acquired more than can be cultivated in centuries—and yet we crave more. We have crowded the tribes upon a few miserable acres on our southern frontier; it is all that is left to them of their once boundless forests: and still, like the horse-leech, our cupidity cries, "give! give!"

But the proposed bill had powerful support, and, in a very close vote (102 to 97 in the House), it was approved. Jackson signed it into law immediately, on May 28, 1830.

The Indian Removal Law, like the treaties Jackson had forced on the Cherokees in 1816 and 1817, did not actually require the Indians to leave their homeland. It would take a new treaty to do that—a removal treaty, duly signed by Cherokee leaders, which would create the illusion that the migration was a free act. "This emigration should be voluntary," Jackson piously assured Congress. But in his very next sentence, Jackson made clear what freedom of choice would really amount to for the Cherokees: "They should be distinctly informed that if they remain within the limits of the States, they must be subject to their laws." In plain words, Jackson would let the Georgians do the dirty work while he himself posed as the Cherokees' friend and protector.

Georgia had already launched into the task with enthusiasm. The state law that "extinguished" the Cherokee Nation and placed its land and people under Georgia's control was due to go into effect June 1, 1830—just four days after Jackson signed the Indian Removal Bill. But months earlier, Georgians had already begun to move in large numbers onto Cherokee territory. Confident that they were acting with the support of both the state and federal authorities, some white families even occupied houses that had been abandoned by fleeing Cherokees.

The Indians made a desperate attempt to resist. For one last time, The Ridge daubed himself with war paint and led a raiding party of some thirty Cherokees to force the white intruders out of the houses they were occupying. As they came to each house, the raiders permitted the white occupants to leave, then burned the structure to the ground. But although The Ridge's men carefully avoided hurting anyone (even the war paint was a purely symbolic gesture), the raid proved to be a mistake. The Cherokees had neither the means nor the will to make war. And the Georgians, for once, were able to get some favorable publicity: One newspaper sarcastically pictured "the enlightened leader of the Cherokee Nation, Major Ridge,

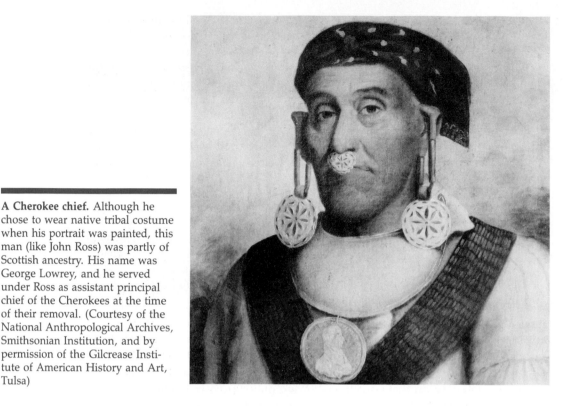

A Cherokee chief. Although he chose to wear native tribal costume when his portrait was painted, this man (like John Ross) was partly of Scottish ancestry. His name was George Lowrey, and he served under Ross as assistant principal chief of the Cherokees at the time of their removal. (Courtesy of the National Anthropological Archives, Smithsonian Institution, and by permission of the Gilcrease Institute of American History and Art, Tulsa)

dressed in his buffalo's head and horns, brandishing his tomahawk over suffering females and children."

Meanwhile, during the spring of 1830 Jackson pressed the tribe with all the power of the presidency. He ordered the removal of the federal troops that had long been stationed on Cherokee land (according to treaty) to protect the Indians from white intrusion. He told his agents to withhold from the Cherokees the $6,000 that the government owed the tribe each year in payment for its previous land cessions. And, ominously, he invited the Cherokee chiefs to meet with him privately that coming summer at his Tennessee plantation in order to discuss the terms of their removal.

But the tribe would not yield. They refused to meet with Jackson, and they drafted an appeal for support directly to "the good people of the United States." Finally, they decided to take their case to the one branch of the U.S. government that might still protect them: the Supreme Court. The Court was controlled by men who were hostile to Jackson. The old patrician John Marshall, who had led the Court during the conspiracy trial of Aaron Burr, was still chief justice. And Marshall had privately let it be known that he was sympathetic to the Cherokee cause. In addition, a prominent anti-Jackson politician and lawyer named William Wirt offered his legal services to the tribe. (Wirt would run for president against Jackson in 1832.) He proposed a test case that would challenge the right of Georgia to extend its laws over the Cherokees.

For a brief moment, the strategy even seemed to work. Early in 1832 the case of *Cherokee Nation* v. *State of Georgia* was heard by the Supreme Court. And Chief Justice Marshall issued a ringing decision in favor of the Cherokees:

> The Cherokee Nation is a distinct community, occupying its own territory, in which the laws of Georgia have no right to enter. The acts of Georgia are repugnant to the Constitution, laws, and treaties of the United States.

"It is glorious news!" wrote Elijah Boudinot. But the glory was short lived. John Marshall's words did nothing to help the Cherokees, because both Georgia and President Jackson simply refused to put the Supreme Court judgment into effect. (According to one of Jackson's opponents, the president said: "Well, John Marshall has made his decision: *now let him enforce it!*") The Cherokees had plenty of sympathizers in white America, but by the 1830s those sympathizers had lost national political power.

Meanwhile, in the absence of a removal treaty the Georgians continued to move into the Cherokee Nation and to dismantle its institutions. The tribal government was forced to abandon its bustling capital of new Echota and to meet at a makeshift site called Red Clay across the state line in Tennessee. And the Georgia government ordered a survey of Cherokee land so that it could be divided into 160-acre parcels. In October 1832 the state began to distribute these parcels by lottery. First, numbered cardboard tickets were sold; then the spin of a gambling wheel determined the lucky winners. Displaying their winning tickets in place of title deeds, hundreds of white Georgians began to take "legal" possession of Cherokee farms and houses. Many of them evicted the resident families without notice; some even demanded back rent from the Indians. The luckiest ticket holders won title to opulent plantations like that of Chief John Ross, who arrived home late one night from one of his thankless visits to Washington to find his house, fields, and ferry in the hands of a stranger, and his family turned out. (Ross moved with his family into a two-room log cabin in Tennessee, where he remained until the final removal of the tribe.) By 1835 there may have been as many as 40,000 white intruders living in the Cherokee Nation—well over twice the number of Indian residents.

These white invaders may have been thinking only of themselves as they claimed their new homesteads, but, back in Washington, Andrew Jackson was using them as part of a larger plan. It was Jackson's strategy to make life so intolerable for the Cherokees that they would finally agree to give him what he still needed: a formal treaty that would legalize removal by clothing it in the garb of a free contract. Congress had passed Jackson's Indian Removal Bill with a guilty conscience, and only on the assurance that the federal government would not "compel" the Indians to leave their homeland. Without a treaty, Jackson would have to rely on the piecemeal migration of demoralized or displaced Cherokees—not the mass migration he had in mind. And the Cherokee leaders knew that their last, faint chance of keeping their ancestral land lay in holding out collectively against a treaty until Jackson finally left office. Even after the president was elected to a second term in November 1832 (defeating Henry Clay, who had helped lead the opposition to the Indian Removal Bill), the Cherokee National Committee continued to resist. Visiting Washington early in 1833, John Ross defiantly told Jackson that his people remained "unshaken in their objections to a removal."

But Ross was wrong. Now, for the first time, he was not speaking for a united Cherokee leadership. The heavy blows that had fallen on the tribe had finally broken down its hard-won unity. A small group of important Cherokees had reluctantly concluded that removal was inevitable. Even as Ross was arguing with Jackson in Washington, one of the members of this group wrote Ross a letter that pleaded with him to reconsider his position: "We all know that we can't be a nation here. I hope we shall attempt to establish it somewhere else! *Where*, the wisdom of the Nation must try to find."

This letter must have been particularly discouraging for Ross, for it was signed "John Ridge." And young Ridge was speaking not only for himself but also for his distinguished father and for his cousin Elias Boudinot. These three men were highly respected within the tribe, and, except for Ross himself, they were its most influential spokesmen to white America. Boudinot now proposed to use the *Cherokee Phoenix* as a forum for arguments in favor of a removal treaty.

Ross was alarmed. He was sure Boudinot and the two Ridges were speaking for only a small minority of the tribe. But he also knew that the *Phoenix*, which was printed in English as well as in Cherokee, was the tribe's main channel of communication with white supporters everywhere. Ross pleaded with Boudinot to back down, at least in public. "On all important questions," he wrote, "the sentiments of the majority should prevail. The duty of the minority is to yield." When Boudinot refused to yield, Ross forced him to resign from the *Phoenix*, and the animosity between the opposing groups intensified. Soon, each side was openly accusing the other of self-interest, demagoguery, even treason.

That was just what Andrew Jackson had been waiting for. From his agents and spies, the president learned that John Ross continued to command the unquestioning support of almost the entire tribe, and that the protreaty Ridge faction was limited almost exclusively to a small minority of mixed-blood Cherokees. But this information did not discourage Jackson. It had always been his practice when dealing with Indians to lure a handful of chiefs into accepting his demands and then to deal with them as if they represented the tribe as a whole. And Jackson also knew that the Cherokees' white supporters thought of John Ridge and Elias Boudinot as the tribe's official spokesmen. If he could get a treaty with the Ridge faction and confirm it with even the flimsiest appearance of tribal support, he knew the Senate would ratify it and the American public would accept it as a legitimate agreement.

Early in 1834 Jackson decided the time was ripe. He authorized his secretary of war, John Eaton, to enter into secret negotiations with the protreaty Cherokees. When word of these negotiations filtered back to the Cherokee Nation, the bitter animosities between the two factions finally exploded into violence, and a member of the negotiating team, a mixed-blood named John Walker, Jr., was murdered. (Back in 1829 the tribe had passed a "blood law" which provided that any Cherokee who engaged in unauthorized negotiations with the whites would become an outlaw, and "any citizens of this nation may kill him, in any manner most convenient, and shall not be held accountable for the same.") When Jackson learned of the murder, he dashed off an angry letter to his agent:

> I have been advised that Walker has been shot and Ridge and other chiefs in favor
> of emigration threatened with death. The government of the United States has prom-

ised them protection. It will perform its obligations to a tittle. Notify John Ross and his council that we will hold them answerable for every murder committed on the emigrating party.

For the present, there would be no more murders. (In any event, John Ross was personally committed to nonviolence.) But while the federal government promised to protect the Ridge faction against physical attack, the Georgia authorities assisted them in other ways. The governor of the state made sure that their property was kept out of the state land lottery, and he ordered his mounted police to "assure Boudinot, Ridge, and their friends of state protection under any circumstances." It was clear that the Ridges had now become collaborators with their former enemies.

Toward the end of 1834 the pace of events quickened. In November eighty-three members of the removal faction met at the comfortable home of John Ridge and organized themselves into a "Treaty party." Early in 1835 two rival delegations arrived almost simultaneously in Washington: One was headed by John Ross, the other by John Ridge. The "National party," as Ross's antitreaty forces were now known, was received politely enough by Jackson. But it was with Ridge's Treaty party men that the administration negotiated. By March a provisional treaty was drawn up. It provided 13 million acres of land across the Mississippi in modern-day Oklahoma, along with $4.5 million in cash and various additional benefits—in exchange for the entire Cherokee Nation.

John Ridge was pleased with the treaty. It was financially "very liberal in its terms," he wrote to his father, and it would permit the tribe "to enjoy our own laws in the west." By agreeing to such a generous settlement, he added, "Gen. Jackson has demonstrated his ancient friendship and truly paternal benevolence to the Cherokees." (When John Ridge's Connecticut-born wife bore a son in 1835, the couple gave him a name that demonstrated the sincerity of his new outlook: They called the baby Andrew Jackson Ridge.)

But even now, before the removal treaty could go into effect, it had to be approved—somehow—by the Cherokee tribal council. John Ridge knew that Chief Ross would do everything in his power to block that approval. "The Ross party," Ridge warned Jackson, "will try to mislead the poor ignorant Indians, and may for a while succeed." He wrote to his father and their allies:

> Ross has failed before the Senate, before the Secretary of War, and before the President. He tried hard to cheat you and his people, but he has been prevented. In a day or two he goes home—no doubt to tell lies. But we will bring all his papers, and the people shall see him as he is.

And Ridge wrote to the governor of Georgia: "John Ross is unhorsed in Washington, and you must unhorse him here."

But it proved easier to "unhorse" John Ross in Washington than among his own people. When the tribal council met in May 1835, it refused even to consider the treaty that John Ridge had brought with him from Washington, and it unanimously passed a vote of confidence in Ross, giving the chief "full power to adjust all difficulties in whatever way he might think most beneficial to the people."

Once again, a snag had developed in Jackson's plans. But a solution was quickly proposed by the president's newly appointed agent on the scene, a minister named

John Schermerhorn—a particularly sleazy character whom Ross's followers called, in an obscene reference to his habit of fondling Cherokee women, "The Devil's Horn." The Reverend Schermerhorn pointed out that no tribal elections had been held for almost seven years. (In fact, there was no way elections *could* have been held, since they were now prohibited by Georgia law.) Schermerhorn concluded that under the terms of the Cherokee constitution of 1827, John Ross was technically no longer the chief of the tribe. There *was* no chief. Any Cherokee could call a council meeting.

John Ridge took Schermerhorn's hint: He called for a special council to assemble that July at his own house. Ridge expected John Ross to order a boycott of the meeting. That would allow members of the Treaty party to approve the pact in the name of the whole tribe. But instead, Ross had the meeting packed by his own followers, and once again the treaty was defeated. It was voted down still a third time at the regular annual meeting of the tribe in October 1835.

Undaunted, Schermerhorn personally announced a fourth meeting, to be held in December at the former Cherokee capital of New Echota. Elias Boudinot translated Schermerhorn's announcement into Cherokee and had it posted around the Nation. The announcement ended with an ominous warning: Any member of the tribe who stayed away from the meeting would be counted as voting in agreement with whatever might be decided there. Early in November, John Ross was arrested by Georgia authorities and jailed for more than a week, and after his release his movements were carefully watched. Ross was on his way to Washington to lodge a protest when the council assembled at New Echota late in December. For whatever reason, the fateful meeting was attended by only 300 or 400 Cherokees, many of them mixed-bloods or white men who had married into the tribe.

The serious negotiations at New Echota were performed by a Cherokee committee of twenty, chaired by The Ridge himself, that met with Schermerhorn at the house of Elias Boudinot. The treaty was signed by both Schermerhorn and the committee at midnight on December 29, 1835, and it was ratified by the "tribe" the following day by a vote of seventy-five to seven. Schermerhorn, exuberant at his success, wrote to Washington:

> I have the extreme pleasure to announce to you that yesterday I concluded a treaty. Ross, after this treaty, is prostrate. The power of the Nation is taken from him as well as the money, and the treaty will give general satisfaction.

But the military official whom President Jackson had appointed to superintend Cherokee removal was so outraged by what Schermerhorn had done that he angrily wrote this account of the proceedings to the secretary of war:

> Sir, that paper is no treaty at all, because [it was] not sanctioned by the great body of the Cherokee and made without their participation or consent. I solemnly declare to you that it would be instantly rejected by nineteen-twentieths of them. There were not present at the conclusion of the treaty more than one hundred Cherokee voters, although the weather was everything that could be desired. The Indians had long been notified of the meeting, and blankets were promised to all who would come and vote for the treaty. Mr. Schermerhorn's apparent design was to conceal the real number present. The delegation taken to Washington by Mr. Schermerhorn [in March 1835] had no more authority to make a treaty than any other dozen Cherokee accidentally picked up for the purpose.

The Ridge was the first to put his mark to the treaty. He said simply: "I expect to die for it."

The United States Senate approved the treaty of New Echota on May 16, 1836, thirty-one to fifteen—only a single vote more than the two-thirds required for the ratification of any treaty. The last legal barrier to Cherokee removal had been crossed.

It would still be two and a half years before the people of the Cherokee Nation would leave their homeland. The treaty itself allowed two full years from the date of ratification before the tribe had to be gone. John Ross used much of the time to continue his lobbying efforts in Washington and around the country. He refused to acknowledge that the treaty was legally binding, and he made no effort to prepare the Cherokees for their inevitable departure. Ross's opponents accused him of leading the tribe to destruction. Elias Boudinot wrote in despair:

> [Ross] says he is doing the will of the people. The will of the people! This has been the cry for the last five years, until that people have become a mere wreck of what they once were: all their institutions and improvements utterly destroyed; their energy enervated; their moral character debased, corrupted, and ruined.

But one federal agent who was on the scene insisted that Ross was indeed expressing the will of his people:

> Were he to advise the Indians to acknowledge the treaty, he would at once forfeit their confidence, and probably his life. Opposition to the treaty among the Indians is unanimous and sincere. It is not a mere political game played by Ross for the maintenance of his ascendancy.

When the official deadline, May 23, 1838, finally came, only some 2,000 Cherokees had left. The rest, close to 16,000 in all, simply went about their ordinary business. It was becoming obvious that the federal government would have to use coercion, perhaps actual violence. In the middle of May, General Winfield Scott arrived in the Cherokee Nation to take charge of the removal operation. The general immediately made his intentions known:

> The full moon of May is already on the wane, and before another has passed away, every Cherokee man, woman, and child must be in motion to join their brethren in the far west. I come to carry out that determination. My troops already occupy many positions in the country that you are to abandon; thousands and thousands are approaching from every quarter, to render resistance and escape alike hopeless. Will you, then, by resistance, compel us to resort to arms? God forbid! Or will you, by flight, seek to hide yourselves in mountains and forests, and thus oblige us to hunt you down? I am an old warrior, and have been present at many a scene of slaughter; but spare me, I beseech you, the horror of witnessing the destruction of the Cherokees.

General Scott's threat proved unnecessary: John Ross had always preached a nonviolent form of resistance, and no violence occurred now. Nevertheless, Scott had his troops construct a series of twenty-three concentration camps, scattered around the Nation—stockades built of logs that had been split, sharpened, and set in the ground. In these camps the Cherokees would be held until their departure. Beginning May 26, 7,000 soldiers fanned out across the Nation to round up every Cherokee man, woman, and child.

Winfield Scott. After he superintended the removal of the Cherokee Nation in 1838, General Scott became nationally famous as a hero of the Mexican War. His military record made him an obvious presidential candidate. Nominated for that office by the Whigs in 1852, Scott was overwhelmingly defeated by the Democrat Franklin Pierce. (Culver Pictures)

The roundup was completed with impressive efficiency. Almost 15,000 Cherokees were captured in just twenty-five days and impounded in the concentration camps. Because of summer heat and drought, General Scott agreed to postpone the tribe's departure until cooler weather arrived. Crowded into the stockades, the Indians were easy prey to disease. As many as 500 may have died over the summer.

John Ross returned from Washington in mid-July to find his people in despair. At last, he too was forced to accept the fact that further resistance was useless. With the approval of the federal government, Ross now decided to take into his own hands the terrible responsibility of organizing the migration. He became the official "superintendent of removal and subsistence"; it would be his job to arrange for transportation, food, and other supplies. All against his will, Ross became once again just what he had been at the beginning of his career—an Indian trader.

The migration got under way October 1, 1838. There were thirteen separate groups altogether, each about 1,000 strong, departing at irregular intervals throughout the month. Twelve of the groups made the 800-mile journey by land; the thirteenth, Ross's own, went by boat via the Tennessee and Arkansas rivers.

The trip was a disaster. For most of the march, neither roads nor lodging was available. Most of the Indians traveled on foot and without shoes. Few had tents or any other form of shelter. November brought hard rains; December, blizzards; and January followed with bitter cold. The Mississippi River was covered with ice that proved too thick for boats to break and too thin for people to walk on. One unfortunate group of Native Americans was forced to camp out on its exposed bank for more than a month, while hundreds of people lay sick or dying on the ground, with only blankets for protection.

When the travelers did encounter people along the route, they proved as unpredictable as the weather—and often as cruel. Many of these white pioneers were not willing to let the Indians stay on their land, or even to cross over it. (One marcher recorded in his diary: "Sunday, very cold—Jason Harrison, a mean man—will not let any person connected with the emigration stay on his property.") Other white land-

The trail of tears. On the surface, this wagon train is reminiscent of many others that carried migrants westward in the middle of the nineteenth century. But the presence of armed soldiers in this twentieth century artist's rendering hints at the difference. (Courtesy, Woolaroc Museum, Bartlesville, Oklahoma)

owners collected outrageous tolls for permitting the caravans to cross their land—$40 on one occasion. The Cherokees had to purchase most of their food and supplies from some of these same men, and often at prices double or even triple what the goods were worth. "They rob us in open daylight," one participant lamented; "they know that we are in a defenseless situation."

Once in a while, there was unexpected hospitality. One farmer let the passing Indians sleep in his barn; he fed them fresh eggs and even entertained them with a pet dog that had been trained to "sing, dance, and talk." This time, at least, the Cherokee children "talked and laughed all night."

But joking and laughter were not often heard on the long march. A far more frequent sound was crying, brought on by pain and hopelessness. One Cherokee later remembered how first his father, then his wife, and later his mother collapsed in the snow and died of exposure. ("She speak no more; we bury her and go on.") By the end of the trip, this same Indian had lost his brothers and sisters as well:

> One each day, and all are gone. Looks like maybe all be dead before we get to new Indian country, but always we keep marching on. Women cry and make sad wails. Children cry, and many men cry, and all look sad when friends die, but they say nothing and just put heads down and keep on go towards west.

In Cherokee society it was a terrible humiliation to cry in public. But the survivors came to refer to their tragic winter's journey as "The Trail Where They Cried"—or "The Trail of Tears."

The Indians finally arrived in Oklahoma between late January and March 1839. They had buried some 1,500 on the trail; perhaps another 1,500 were missing. All told, including the summer of internment that preceded the march, close to 4,000 Cherokees—almost one-fourth of the tribe—may have died.

It was the white people who were responsible for everything that had happened, but the embittered Indians were able to vent their rage only on their own brethren. On June 22, 1839, in Oklahoma, three more Cherokee leaders died—this time at the hands of assassins. John Ridge was hauled from his bed by masked intruders and, in the presence of his wife and children, stabbed twenty-five times. A few hours later, four strangers accosted Elias Boudinot as he was directing the construction of his new house. One of them stabbed him in the back, another drove a tomahawk into his skull. At about the same time, The Ridge himself, now almost seventy years old, was ambushed on the road by gunmen who riddled him with bullets. The three murders were committed after a secret "trial" under the blood law of 1829, which called for the execution of any Cherokee who gave up tribal land to the white man. Thirty-two years earlier, The Ridge had killed Chief Doublehead for the same offense.

The murderers were never identified, and no evidence was found that John Ross was in any way responsible for them. At no time had Ross advocated violence against anyone, white or Indian. He would remain as principal chief of the deeply divided Cherokee Nation until his own death twenty-seven years later, in 1866. Ross died in bed, of natural causes. His death occurred in Washington—where he had gone to lobby against still another treaty that the United States was trying to impose on his broken and divided tribe.

EXPANSION, THE MARKET ECONOMY, AND THE JACKSON PRESIDENCY

There was nothing new about the removal of the Cherokee Nation. For more than two centuries, Indians had been killed, subdued, displaced, and even enslaved by the white invaders. It could even be argued (in fact, it *was* argued) that Cherokee removal was carried out with unprecedented humanity and compassion—with no war and very little violence, at federal expense, and with generous provision for economic compensation. As President Jackson himself pointedly asked, "How many thousands of our own people would gladly embrace the opportunity of removing to the West on such conditions?"

Still, there was something different about the whole tragic episode—something that has etched it on the conscience of many Americans at the time and since. During the colonial period, the slaughter of Indians had generally been carried out in a haphazard, often informal manner, without any plan. In those days, the point had been to subdue Indian populations until they posed no further military threat to white life or property, and then to allow the Indians to live—their territory reduced, their morale shattered, their culture destroyed—on the edges of white settlement or even in its midst. And in the past, from the time of Governor Berkeley of Virginia in the 1670s (see Chapter 2) to the presidency of John Quincy Adams in the 1820s, the authority of the government had most often been applied as a restraining influence to counteract the impulsive violence of the whites. But now, in the Jacksonian period,

five tribes—some 60,000 people in all—were displaced from their territory and systematically transported to land a thousand miles away.[2] And the entire process was conceived, organized, and carried out by the military and bureaucratic machinery of the federal government. There was relatively little violence, to be sure. But the systematic relentlessness of the enterprise was something quite new. It was a massive undertaking, and one that could not have happened any earlier than it did. In a sense, the removal of the Southern Indians between 1815 and 1840 was the first large-scale peacetime undertaking of the government of the United States. And it reveals a great deal about what was happening to American society in the Jacksonian period.

The Expansion of Southern Agriculture

WAR Indian removal did not take place before the War of 1812 for a very simple reason. Before the end of that war, much of the area west of the Appalachians had been constantly threatened by

---

[2]In addition to the Cherokee, four other Southern tribes—the Choctaws, Chickasaws, Creeks, and Seminoles (in part)—were removed in the 1820s and 1830s.

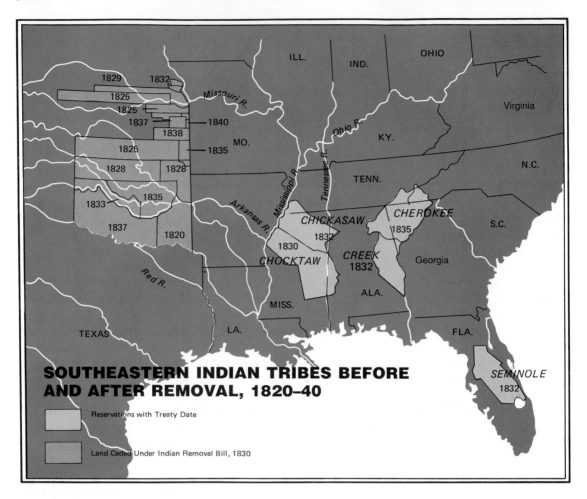

SOUTHEASTERN INDIAN TRIBES BEFORE AND AFTER REMOVAL, 1820–40

Reservations with Treaty Date

Land Ceded Under Indian Removal Bill, 1830

European powers—the English, the French, and the Spanish. And the Indian tribes—especially the relatively powerful ones like the Creeks—had been able to retain some vestige of independence by threatening to forge military alliances with one or more of these European powers. It was this strategy that the great Tecumseh had attempted just before the outbreak of the War of 1812.

But with the end of the war, and with Andrew Jackson's conquest of East Florida in 1819, the European nations lost their influence in the area—and the Indians lost their last strategic advantage, their last remaining room for maneuver.

By themselves, without the possibility of European support, the Indians were finished.

They lacked the numbers, the weapons, even the unity of the whites. The ending of the War of 1812 made it possible to remove the Indians from the area with little risk to the white population. The lands they still inhabited—the future states of Alabama and Mississippi, along with the western part of Georgia—were now available for white occupation. Mississippi became a state in 1817, just two years after the end of the war, and Alabama followed two years later.

LAND HUNGER: THE RISE OF "KING COTTON"　One of the excuses white Americans used to justify taking Indian lands was that there were simply too few Indians living on too much land—and too many whites living on too little land. The white population of the United States increased by nearly 10 million between 1810 and 1840, and the increase was accelerating all the time. In 1790 virtually all the white (and black) people of America had lived on a thin ribbon along the east coast. But by 1840 one-third of them lived in states west of the seaboard. And by 1860 the figure had risen to one-half.

Until the 1830s, the four western states that grew fastest were Alabama, Mississippi, Tennessee, and Kentucky. And most of the people who moved into this region came from the crowded seaboard states of Georgia, the two Carolinas, and Virginia. Andrew Jackson himself was a case in point: He was born in North Carolina in 1767 and moved west to Tennessee when he was twenty-two. For Jackson as well as for thousands of other Americans, the seaboard had become too crowded.

The land itself was causing problems that intensified the sense of overcrowding in the coastal states. Many of the farms in the region had been cultivated for a century or more, and the soil had become exhausted. In the headlong drive to grow as much as possible, and as fast as possible, farmers had neglected to rotate their crops or to rest their fields every few years. In many cases, they had seen their topsoil disappear by constant erosion, the result of plowing and planting in straight lines, often up and down hills, ignoring the contours of the land. The once-prosperous tobacco fields of Virginia and North Carolina and the rice plantations of South Carolina had come to yield small, stunted crops. Ineffective farm management reduced three early Virginia presidents—Jefferson, Madison, and Monroe—to embarrassing debt and near-poverty in their old age.

North Carolina was particularly hard hit. By 1815 the state contained as much land that had been abandoned to weeds as was still under cultivation. All along the seaboard, land was decreasing in value. In Georgia, more than in any other state, people were farming their land intensively and carelessly for a few years, then selling it or simply abandoning it in order to move on—to the West.

And in the West were Indians. It was a favorite argument of whites that the Indians did not "use" or "improve" their lands. Even when some did become farmers (as the Cherokees and the other Southern tribes had done), the Indians had left vast areas out of cultivation. They did not exploit the land with the same intensity as the increasingly desperate whites now pressing upon them from the East. But to many whites this attitude of the Indians was only one more argument for their removal. Land-poor whites were moving west; what was wrong with urging land-rich Indians to do the same?

The western lands, fertile and unspoiled, were alluring and valuable for yet another reason. It had suddenly become incredibly profitable to raise a single crop on these lands. This crop was cotton. Before about 1800, cotton had not been grown on a large scale in the United States because it was slow and difficult to separate the valuable fibers from the worthless seeds so that the fiber could be spun and woven into cloth. But in 1793 Eli Whitney and others had developed a simple mechanical device, the cotton gin (short for "engine"), which permitted one person—generally a slave—to clean as much cotton as several people had previously been able to do.

Suddenly, there was a new use for the new land. By the 1820s the United States was producing more cotton than any other nation, and by 1850 more than two-thirds of the world's cotton came from American farms and plantations. Most of it was grown in the very places that had been Indian land barely a generation earlier: western Georgia, Alabama, Mississippi, and eastern Texas. It was the removal of the Southern Indians that was directly responsible for the rise of the "Cotton Kingdom," the rich belt of large plantations, worked by black slaves, that was the heart of the new South.

Cotton did not become "king" simply on account of the invention of the cotton gin. The invention of various other machines—machines that could spin the cotton fibers into thread, weave the thread into cloth, and cut and sew the cloth into garments—contributed to its ascent. These new machines in turn depended on the

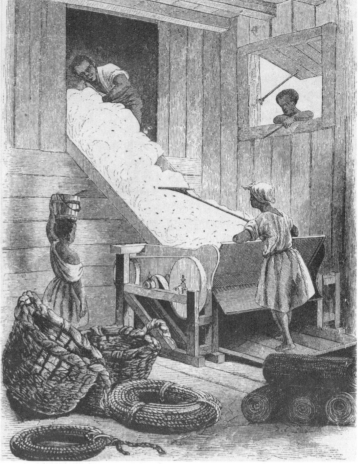

Cotton gin. The magazine artist has drawn the cotton gin in operation on a rather idealized Southern plantation. A young girl slave is tending the machinery, and a male slave standing in the loft gathers the cleaned cotton. An even younger girl and a boy are watching the process with curiosity. The baskets on the floor lie empty, and the ropes are neatly coiled. The work seems easy, even relaxed. All in all, the artist has deliberately conveyed a misleading impression that the cotton gin made the life of a slave easier and more pleasant. (New York Public Library)

need and ability of large numbers of people to purchase the manufactured cloth and clothing. The value of cotton lands ultimately depended on the existence of a technology to process the cotton, and of a ready market to consume it. And both these elements were present.

In the beginning they were British. It was British textile mills that first purchased most of the raw American cotton, and British consumers who bought most of the finished clothing. It was also British capital that provided American planters with most of the credit to begin producing cotton on the new western lands. But from the 1820s on, New Englanders increasingly competed with the British for Southern cotton, by building their own factories and providing their own customers.

One final ingredient was needed: efficient low-cost transportation that would enable cotton farmers to get their bound bales to market in ports like New Orleans and New York. Here they were fortunate in two ways. First, unlike food crops such as wheat or corn, cotton did not spoil easily, so it did not have to be harvested and shipped to market in a very short time. Second, the South was blessed more than any section of the country with many navigable rivers along which goods could be shipped. This was a matter of utmost importance at a time when there was no such thing as a paved road, and—for the time being—no railroads. To be sure, it was difficult for sailboats to navigate the intricate turns of these rivers, but this problem was neatly solved in the 1810s with the invention of the steamboat. Within a few years, steamboats were proudly plying the Mississippi and other rivers, carrying cotton and other goods below decks and passengers above.

But no matter how fast Southerners converted virgin land into fields of cotton, they were unable to supply enough of this miracle crop to keep pace with the ever-increasing demand. As a result, the price of cotton kept going up, and so did the price of slaves, and of land itself. (This was at a time of little general inflation, when the price of most goods remained generally stable.) Hundreds of British and New England capitalists got rich investing in Southern agricultural expansion. Thousands of Southerners got rich growing cotton.

Thousands of others got rich without even growing cotton, just by speculating in land and in slaves. Both land and slaves had, along with cotton itself, become *commodities* to be traded for profit. These men were land speculators and slave traders.

Indian removal, westward expansion, cotton production, technology, population growth, and the slave market—these were all bound together in an interconnected system. It was this system that produced the land-hungry Georgians who descended on Cherokee lands in the 1830s. It was this system that produced Andrew Jackson himself. The system was market capitalism, of a distinctively American type.

The struggle for Indian removal was a struggle between two dramatically different attitudes toward living on—and off—the land. By the end of the War of 1812, the Cherokee Nation had become for white people a tremendously valuable piece of real estate; it was worth a great deal of money in the marketplace. But the Cherokees held so steadfastly to their land not because of its exchange value but simply because it belonged to them and they belonged to it. They farmed and hunted in order to feed, clothe, and shelter themselves and because their ancestors had done much the same. The land was for their *use*, and not for its cash value in the market. In this sense, the struggle for Indian removal was not simply a racial struggle between Indians and whites: It was between a premarket system and a market system. This is what distinguishes the events of the Jacksonian period from earlier episodes in the long history of conflict between whites and Indians.

The Expansion of Northern Agriculture

LAND HUNGER: THE RISE OF WHEAT In some ways, the North changed in a very different fashion from the South. It eliminated black slavery. It developed industry, not plantations. Without question, the North and the South were far more distinct from each other in 1850 than they had been in 1815; the Jacksonian years represented an era of clear new regional identities— new identities that would make it possible for the two sections to go to war with each other in 1861.

Still, the North was responding in its own way to pressures that were similar or even identical to those that characterized the South. Like the South, the North in 1800 was a farming area along a thin coastal strip whose agricultural potential was not sufficient to sustain its growing population. The problem here was not soil depletion but the fact that, except for a few fertile valleys like that of the Connecticut River, most of the land in New England and in much of the Middle Atlantic states was too hilly, rocky, and infertile to support farming at anything much above a bare subsistence level. West of the Appalachians, on the other hand, in the Ohio Valley, the land was invitingly flat and clear, with deep topsoil.

By the end of the War of 1812, the Northwest was essentially free of Indians—at least, of Indians who might pose a military threat. In the South, Andrew Jackson's massacre of Creeks at Horseshoe Bend in 1814 marked only the beginning of massive Indian removal. But in the North, General William Henry Harrison's victory at Tippecanoe in present-day Indiana in 1811 (a battle fought while Chief Tecumseh was away visiting the Southern tribes) virtually ended Indian resistance and earned Harrison his lifelong nickname of "Old Tip."

Northern farmers swarmed west out of New England and the Middle Atlantic states, first into upstate New York, then into Ohio and on west toward the Mississippi. Indiana and Illinois achieved statehood in 1816 and 1818, respectively—during the same period as Mississippi and Alabama. Like the Southerners, the new northwestern farmers soon found a valuable cash crop—wheat—that was suited to the soil and climate and also found a demand in the marketplace. A better-quality wheat could be grown in the new lands than along the seaboard, and it could be grown more cheaply.

GETTING TO MARKET: THE ERIE CANAL There was only one thing that could hold back the rapid development of the Northwest: For all its advantages, the farmers who moved into this area lacked convenient access to markets on the coast and in Europe. Unlike the South, the Northwest did not contain a system of navigable rivers leading to the Atlantic. For those farmers who lived in the lower Ohio Valley, the long way to market lay down the Ohio and Mississippi rivers to New Orleans. For those who lived in upstate New York and northern Ohio, it lay across the Great Lakes and down the St. Lawrence River to Montreal. Each of these routes was difficult. Both threatened to shift the commercial benefits of the Northwest away from New England and New York and into the hands of the South—or worse, into the hands of a foreign power, British Canada.

It was no accident that, in the North, the War of 1812 was seen primarily as a war for Canada— and thus for access to the trade of the Northwest. The Americans had mounted six separate invasions of Canada in the course of the war; all of them failed (see pp. 270–73). What followed the failure to conquer Canada was an even more massive enterprise, this time a purely economic one:

to deny the British the fruits of the western trade. It was the Erie Canal, begun in 1817 (just two years after the end of the war) and completed eight years later. The Erie Canal was just as daring a venture as the Battle of New Orleans, and its success proved as important to the North as Indian removal was to the South.

Early in the nineteenth century, the mayor of New York City, DeWitt Clinton, described a vision: "The trade of almost all the lakes in North America," he wrote,

> would centre at New York for their common mart. This port would be left without a competition in trade, except by that of New Orleans. In a century its island would be covered with the buildings and population of its city. Albany would be necessitated to cut down her hills and fill her valleys in order to give spread to her population. The harbor of Buffalo would exchange her forest trees for a thicket of marine spars.

But in order for this to happen, the canal would have to reach west all the way to Buffalo, a distance of 364 miles from the Hudson River at Albany. (A shorter canal to Lake Ontario would have been much easier to construct. But such a canal would only have continued to divert most of the western trade to Canada.) The technological problems were extreme. Lake Erie is fully 565 feet higher than the Hudson River at Albany. That meant building a set of stairs, a series of eighty-three locks that would raise and lower boats. At one point, at a town aptly named Lockport, there were five of these locks in a row, rising 60 feet, like a huge, watery escalator. At other places, construction of the canal meant cutting deep into the hills that formed an obstacle to its passage—and occasionally blasting through solid rock. The most difficult of these deep cuts went through "seven miles of limestone, thirty feet thick and harder than a tax collector's heart." At eighteen other places, the canal had to be raised above valleys and streams. Here, the canal literally became a series of bridges that crossed over the rivers in its path on elaborate viaducts that resembled modern overpasses.

Lockport, New York. The town of Lockport owed its existence to the Erie Canal. This picture, drawn eleven years after the canal opened, shows a barge leaving the series of five locks that raised boats by a total of sixty feet. (Courtesy of the New-York Historical Society)

Construction of the Erie Canal obviously involved a massive and systematic application of technology, labor, and money. The money—over $26,000 per mile—was put up by the government of the state of New York, on the assumption that the canal would pay for itself within a few years and then bring a steady profit to the state. Contracts for the construction were given to private entrepreneurs on the basis of low bids, who assumed responsibility for short sections of the canal. Contractors hired laborers at the average rate of 50 cents a day. They worked in gangs under close supervision. Many of these laborers were young men who lived near the areas they worked, but since western New York was still sparsely populated, it became necessary to import workers from New York City and even from Ireland.

The technology of the construction, while ingenious and innovative, was entirely preindustrial in nature. Most of the work was done by hand (in this sense, the gangs of workers who dug the canal resembled the gangs of slaves who picked cotton in the South). The explosives that excavated the rocky areas were simply a modified variety of gunpowder provided by E. I. duPont of Delaware. The "machines" that removed tree stumps and rocks from the canal pathway involved levers and pulleys pulled by the same horses and oxen that worked the upstate farms.

The canal was completed and opened in several separate sections between 1819 and 1825. It was 364 miles long (the longest canal in America before this had been only 27 miles!), but it was only 40 feet wide and a mere 4 feet deep. Only small boats could travel the canal, pulled by horses or mules that trudged along towpaths constructed on the canal's edges. The boats were able to move at a speed of only 4 miles per hour, and it could take a full week to travel from Buffalo to New York City.

But, primitive as the canal may seem today, it was a staggering improvement at the time. A ton of wheat could now be shipped from Buffalo to Albany at a tenth of the previous cost and in a third of the time. Travelers themselves could make the same trip in a mere four to six days at the rate of only four cents per mile, meals included.

The Erie Canal opened up the Ohio Valley to agriculture, commerce, and industry, and it ensured that New York City would win the benefits of that prosperity. Struggling farmers from the hill towns of New England filtered west during the 1820s and 1830s. In 1817, as canal construction was starting up, Rochester was an isolated village of barely 300 people; by 1828 it was a city of 13,000—the most rapidly growing city in the entire country, in the middle of the most fertile wheat-producing area. Its ten flour mills had already made it the flour-milling center of the nation. Buffalo grew from 2,000 in 1820 to 42,000 in 1850.

The Expansion of Market Agriculture

In 1800 most Americans lived on farms, and most of their work involved producing food and other goods that never left the farm—or at least the community in which they lived. In fact, about three-fourths of their produce was untouched by the market. It was outside the economy, for their own subsistence or that of their neighbors. By the middle of the century, the situation was reversed. Roughly three-fourths of the productive work that Americans did had now entered the market economy. Labor, shoes, cotton cloth, passage on a steamboat—all were now for sale in the market. The family farm, on which most Americans lived as late as 1840, had formerly been a largely self-contained operation, raising (whatever its size) a variety of grains, livestock, and timber, which fed, clothed, and even housed its members. But now farms began to specialize. A farmer in Georgia might grow only cotton, while his counterpart in Kentucky might plant nothing but corn; a third farmer in upstate New York might grow only wheat, and a fourth in the hills of Vermont might do nothing but raise sheep.

Specialization meant that farmers no longer raised crops for their own use and that of their neighbors but rather for sale in the market economy. Most Southern planters had to devote all their land and energy to raising cotton—they could not afford to do otherwise. Farmers in New York's Genesee Valley, along the Erie Canal, grew wheat right up to their doorsteps—wheat they had to sell to merchants in Rochester, to be milled and shipped to New York City. The clothing they wore was no longer homespun. It was woven in Massachusetts factories (or British ones) from cotton grown in Alabama or Georgia—probably on land recently seized from the Cherokees or some other Indian tribe. The sheep raised by a farmer in Vermont were probably of a specialized breed imported from Spain, the Merino, which grew an especially heavy coat of wool—but their meat was tough and tasteless. The Vermont farmer might therefore have to buy most of his meat—perhaps pork shipped from Cincinnati (or "Porkopolis," as it was jokingly known). The commercialization of agricultural production meant that many people devoted all their labor to the production of a single item, intended for sale rather than for use. It meant, also, that they were forced to buy an increasing number of goods that they had formerly made for their own use.

Market agriculture demanded new levels of efficiency and productivity. A new cast-iron plow, for example, cut in half the labor required to prepare the soil for planting. Before seedtime, a farmer increased his productivity by treating his fields with fertilizer—a largely new development. At harvesttime, the automatic reaper (invented by Cyrus McCormick in 1831) made it possible for a single farmer to cut twelve acres of crops each day—about twenty times as much as he could have harvested with a traditional hand-held scythe. All in all, agricultural productivity increased 10 percent per capita in the period 1800–40, and perhaps another 20 percent in the 1850s alone.

M'Cormick's REAPER.

PATENTED 1845.

M'CORMICK'S REAPER

McCormick's reaper. Reaping, the first step in harvesting grain crops, was traditionally a time-consuming process performed by hand—a Northern equivalent to removing the seeds from cotton plants. The invention of a mechanical reaper (in England in 1828) made the process much faster and more economical—much like the cotton gin in the South. Cyrus McCormick patented the first American reaper in 1831. (State Historical Society of Wisconsin)

A revolution was under way. Farming had always had two purposes. People grew food and fiber for their own use or for sale. But now the balance had tilted dramatically, from use to marketing. It was a worldwide revolution. And in the United States, it was combined with something distinctive: westward expansion. Commercial agriculture and the conquest of the frontier went hand in hand. Together they redefined the shape and style of American politics.

Jacksonian Democracy

During the quarter-century between 1812 and 1837, a new order was created in the United States. Astride the entire development stands the imposing figure of Andrew Jackson. The beginning of the period is marked by his two great military victories in the War of 1812—against the Indians at the battle of Horseshoe Bend and against the British at the battle of New Orleans.

At the end of the period stands the completion of his second term as president and the final defeat of the Cherokees' attempt to retain their homeland. The generation between these two moments saw a set of social, economic, and political changes that bear the symbolic name "Jacksonian democracy."

The term, like most such terms, is an oversimplification. Andrew Jackson was president of the United States for only eight of the twenty-five years in question. And the democracy Americans created in those years was really quite limited. To be sure, most states opened up the franchise to the poor by reducing or doing away with voting qualifications based on property (see Chapter 5). But outside New England, the only people eligible to vote were adult white males. In fact, in five northern states that originally *had* permitted black men to vote (Ohio, New Jersey, Connecticut, New York, and Pennsylvania), that right was taken away—at the very time it was given to poor white men. And not a single state that entered the union after 1819 permitted African-Americans to vote. In 1807 women lost the franchise in New Jersey, the one state where they had once held it. Furthermore, even for white males, many states still maintained property restrictions on just who could vote for what offices. And men of wealth and standing were still the only sort apt to be elected to public office.

Even Andrew Jackson himself was not really a democrat or an ordinary man of the people. To be sure, he had been born in a log cabin and orphaned as a boy. But as a young man Jackson had become a rich planter, and he fought ruthlessly to protect his own interests—against anyone. He regularly instituted lawsuits against people who owed him money; once he sued 129 of them in a single case! When Jackson fought to rid the West of its Indian population, he did so not for the sake of "the people" but for the sake of land speculators like himself who could get rich by selling land to the people.

But "Jacksonian democracy" is still a useful concept. To begin with, the idea that *all* white men had the capacity to choose those who governed them—and to expect those men to do their bidding—was novel from a European perspective, and even from the perspective of the American past. But even more useful is the way Jacksonian democracy describes another right: the right of all men (at least all white men) to get rich, and to do so with a minimum of interference from their government.

Andrew Jackson's own career is a striking case in point. He was a self-made man, the first president who did not inherit wealth and status. Jackson was born in the Carolina backcountry in 1767 (he was the first future president born west of the Appalachians), the son of poor Scotch-Irish immigrants. Orphaned as a child, Jackson left home at the age of seventeen. Four years later, in 1788, he moved west to the frontier town of Nashville, Tennessee, then a stockaded log village. Young Jackson became, in short order, a lawyer, a district prosecutor, a congressman, and (in 1797, when he was barely thirty years of age) a U.S. senator. He resigned this last position just a year later and returned to Tennessee, only to be elected to a state judgeship. In 1802 he

resigned this position too in order to devote all his energy to the economic empire he had managed to accumulate.

Jackson's hard work led to wealth from virtually the moment he set foot in Tennessee. As a new lawyer, he specialized in collecting debts. (In his first month of legal practice, he issued almost seventy writs to delinquent debtors.) With his earnings, he began to speculate heavily in sparsely settled Tennessee lands, and he was able to use the public offices he held to befriend some of the wealthiest and most influential men in the state. On his large plantation near Nashville, worked by more than a hundred slaves, he built one of the greatest mansions in the United States, which he named the Hermitage. Even before Jackson left private life once again in 1812 to assume the military command that would win him national fame at New Orleans, he had become a great Southern aristocrat.

Politics and the Panic of 1819

Jackson continued to fight for his own economic interests even after he became a national figure. But by now those interests had become enmeshed in the new market economy. The effects of that economy would soon lead him, and many other men in Tennessee and around the nation, into a new involvement in politics. It was a financial crisis of national proportions, the Panic of 1819, that set the stage for much of what would happen to the country, and to Andrew Jackson himself, during the following decades. The great boom in money and land from which Jackson himself had benefited suddenly skidded to a halt.

The boom had been fueled by risky credit arrangements, not by "real" money that took the form of *specie* (a technical term for cash coined

A Presidential Scrapbook

An American who sat down to look through a presidential scrapbook in 1824 would have found a series of familiar and similar-looking pictures. From George Washington's election in 1789 down through the next thirty-five years, some rather striking continuities are evident: Most of the presidents wore wigs, knee breeches, and shoes with gold or silver buckles. Their portraits all show them seated or standing—although Washington might be shown riding in a coach. If the pictures had captions, some other similarities would quickly become obvious: The presidents were all from the two states that had led the way to the Revolution—and, incidentally, the two first successful British colonies. All except John Adams, who came from Massachusetts, hailed from Virginia. There was even a slang name for the presidential group: the Virginia Dynasty.

It was like a dynasty. There was a regular rule of succession that had been kept unbroken since the time of Washington: John Adams had been Washington's vice president; the third president, Thomas Jefferson, had been secretary of state to Washington and vice president to Adams; Jefferson's successor, Madison, had been his secretary of state; and the last in line, James Monroe, had served as secretary of state to Madison.

Plate 1. Here, in a portrait made by Charles Willson Peale in 1776, the first year of the Revolution, the commanding general is shown in the typical pose of a perfect eighteenth-century gentleman, English or American. Peale was striving for an effect of repose rather than action. Even the portraits of Washington as a soldier almost never showed him on horseback or holding a sword or pistol. (Courtesy of the Pennsylvania Academy of Fine Arts, Gift of Maria McKeon Allen and Phoebe Warren Downes through the bequest of their mother, Elizabeth Wharton McKeon)

Plate 2. This astonishing marble statue of Washington was begun in 1832 by Horatio Greenough and was supposed to sit in the Capitol. It suggests the godlike proportions the first president had assumed by the Jacksonian period. No one would have dreamed of calling this figure anything like "Old Hickory" or "Honest Abe." And this Washington is clearly shown as a lawgiver, not as a representative of a democratic mass. (National Museum of American Art, Smithsonian Institution, Transfer from the United States Capitol)

Plate 3. This portrait of John Adams was painted a short time before the ex-president died in 1826. The artist was Samuel F. B. Morse (who also invented the Morse code). Morse showed Adams as a man of marked reserve and dignity, a gentleman in politics, far from a "man of the people." (The Brooklyn Museum, Gift of Miss Harriet H. White)

The members of the dynasty had all been, in the new political slang, Founding Fathers—men who had made their political careers as revolutionaries, whose first taste of fame, power, and politics had come in the days of struggle against Great Britain. They had conducted foreign policy for the Revolutionary government. They had written its most basic documents: Washington had presided at the Constitutional Convention; Jefferson was the author of the Declaration of Independence; Madison had written much of the Constitution and the Bill of Rights and played a large role in producing the Federalist Papers; *Adams was virtually the author of the Massachusetts state constitution.*

In their portraits, these men all wore the look of gentlemen. They came from important families, they were well educated and polished. They all knew each other; they represented the closest thing the nation had to an aristocracy. In their public addresses, they strove for dignity and elegance—always being careful, of course, to add a republican touch here and there. They were also always careful to maintain the attitudes of gentlemen toward politics: They would not campaign openly and publicly; they

Plate 5. Gilbert Stuart's portrait of Madison emphasizes not only his gentlemanly elegance but his commitment to learning—a portrait of the ideal statesman of the Revolutionary generation: wealthy, dignified, scholarly. (Amherst College: The Mead Art Museum, Bequest of Herbert L. Pratt, 1895)

Plate 4. Rembrandt Peale painted this great portrait of Thomas Jefferson in 1805. The president, who was sixty-one at the time, was seen by Peale as anything but a "common man." With his look of learning and dignity, he is plainly an aristocrat. None of his supporters would have dreamed of giving Thomas Jefferson a nickname, though he himself made a point of walking to his inauguration rather than riding in a coach or on horseback. (The New-York Historical Society)

Plate 6. In one sense, John Quincy Adams—who was elected president in 1824—had a very literal claim to be considered part of the Virginia Dynasty: He was the son of John Adams. However, his election, unlike those of his predecessors, was far from guaranteed. He ran in a four-way race in which no candidate won a majority of either the popular or the electoral vote; in fact, Andrew Jackson won a plurality of both. The election was thus thrown to the House of Representatives, where opposition to Jackson was strong enough to give the presidency to Adams. (Metropolitan Museum of Art, Gift of I. N. Phelps Stokes, Edward S. Hawes, Alice Mary Hawes, Marion Augusta Hawes, 1937)

Plate 7. This portrait of Andrew Jackson, done in 1833 by Ralph E. W. Earl, shows him as a man of considerable dignity but emphasizes his military career. (Memphis Brooks Museum of Art, Memphis, TN; Memphis Park Commission Purchase 46.2)

Plate 8. This great statue of Jackson, which stands in Jackson Park in New Orleans, captures the fascination that military prowess and *machismo* held for Americans of the mid-nineteenth century. It is difficult to imagine a sculpture more determined to emphasize aggression and stereotyped masculinity. (Historic New Orleans Collection)

Plate 9. Martin Van Buren was one of the few Easterners to become president after the end of the Virginia Dynasty. However, his election had far less to do with geography than with the fact that he was Andrew Jackson's hand-picked successor. (Library of Congress)

believed, or at least said they believed, that the office should seek the man, not the man the office.

Nor did they have to go directly to the people for their offices. After Jefferson, they had all been chosen by a "caucus" of congressmen meeting in Washington. After 1800, their elections were really not party contests at all, because the Republicans were the only effective party in existence. And they were finally elected not by popular vote but by electors, most of whom, in turn, were not voted for by the people but by the state legislatures.

Collectively, the dynasty approved of the way national politics worked. They all feared political parties: Except in times of severe crisis and change, they did not think that two-party competition was healthy. And all were suspicious of any form of politics that forced leaders to appeal to the voting masses for support. It was well enough for

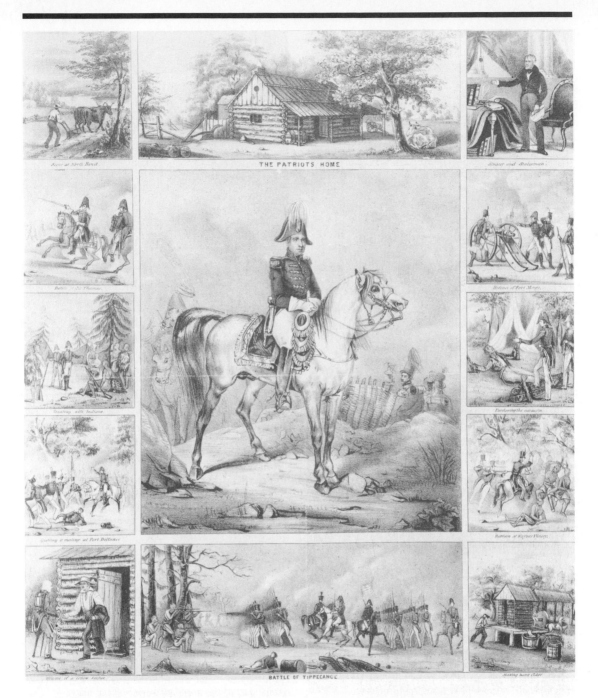

Plate 10. In 1840, the Whig party deliberately ran a candidate whom they could advertise as being very much like Andrew Jackson: William Henry Harrison was born in a log cabin and was a successful general in Indian wars and the War of 1812. The Whigs also gave Harrison one of the most curious presidential nicknames of the period, "Tippecanoe"—the name of the most famous battle in which he was involved. This poster typified what had become the ideal presidential candidate—the mounted soldier. (Library of Congress)

Plate 11. James K. Polk of Tennessee, nicknamed"Young Hickory," was the first "dark horse" candidate to win the presidency. During his term of office, 1845–49, the United States realized its "Manifest Destiny," resolving the Oregon border dispute with Britain and winning California in the Mexican War. (National Portrait Gallery, Smithsonian Institution; Gift of the James Knox Polk Memorial Association of Nashville and the James K. Polk Memorial Auxiliary of Columbia, TN)

Plate 12. In 1848, the Whigs once more set their hopes on a military hero, just as they had successfully done in 1840. They chose Zachary Taylor, a Mexican War general who went under the undignified name "Old Rough and Ready." Taylor died in office in 1850. (National Portrait Gallery, Smithsonian Institution; Gift of Barry Bingham, Sr.)

the people to elect the lower houses of the state legislatures and the House of Representatives. But above that level, they believed, the political leaders themselves ought to choose senators, judges, governors, and presidents. For the dynasty, politics was essentially the business of gentlemen; and the things gentlemen valued—such as decorum, gravity, and honor—could be preserved only if the "sovereign people" were kept at a respectful distance.

If the same American, now an old man or woman, pulled a presidential scrapbook off the shelf thirty years later, it would be clear that the dynasty had ended. By 1864, a new type of leader had emerged. For one thing,

there were no more wigs: James Monroe (who had been elected for two terms, in 1816 and 1820) was the last man to wear that powdered symbol of the upper class. And there were no more knee breeches, satin hose, or buckled shoes. Many pictures would show the presidents on horseback, not seated or standing in calm and dignified poses. The captions might even include nicknames that had become part of the president's semi-official image— "Old Hickory" for Andrew Jackson, elected in 1828 and 1832; "Young Hickory" for James K. Polk, elected in 1844; or "Tippecanoe" for William Henry Harrison, the man who won the office in 1840. The scrapbook would end with a picture of the current president, Abraham Lincoln, who was quite happy to be called "Abe."

Plate 13. After the Virginia Dynasty ended, Easterners became president only through political maneuvering or by accident. In 1852, for example, a deadlock among the three leading Democratic contenders for the presidency led to the nomination on the forty-ninth ballot of Franklin Pierce, an obscure New Hampshire politician. Pierce defeated General Winfield Scott, who—although a Mexican War hero—lost credibility because of his vague political views. This was the last election in which the Whigs ran a presidential candidate. (National Portrait Gallery, Smithsonian Institution; Transfer from the National Gallery of Art; Gift of Andrew J. Mellon, 1942)

What did the horses and the nicknames mean? One clue would lie in the names of the states from which this second generation of presidents had come. Not one had made his adult career in either Virginia or Massachusetts; in fact, almost all were identified with states west of the Atlantic seaboard. Jackson had been born in North Carolina but had made his life in Tennessee; Polk likewise. "Tippecanoe" Harrison was born in Virginia but had become a political leader in Ohio. Lincoln was from Kentucky and Illinois. The few Eastern presidents had come

into office as the result of political maneuver or accident: Martin Van Buren, elected in 1836, was a New Yorker who would never have become president if he had not been picked by Andrew Jackson. John Tyler was a Virginian, but he became president in 1841 because he was vice president when Harrison died. Similarly, Vice President Millard Fillmore, a New Yorker, became president on the death of Taylor, the Louisianian, in 1850. The lesson of the scrapbook is clear: As a rule, an Easterner could become president only by coming in a side door.

The names and the dates might bewilder anyone looking at this second-generation scrapbook. It was easy to memorize the names and dates of the Virginia Dynasty: With one exception (John Adams), they all served two terms. Starting with Washington in 1789, and taking note of Adams's one-term presidency, one could make simple, eight-year jumps. Then, in the second generation, between Monroe and Lincoln only Andrew Jackson was elected for two terms. (To make matters more complicated, Harrison and Taylor died in office, adding two new names to the list.) The old appearance of dynasty and regular succession was gone; the presidency had become a crazy quilt of names and dates. And when one looked a little closer—at the ways in which the men became president—this impression would be confirmed. The old pattern of secretary of state to presidency has disappeared; one would see instead the portraits of men who had had little or no executive experience in Washington prior to becoming president.

Partly because of their lack of Washington experience, the members of the second-generation scrapbook did not know one another. But the reason ran deeper. These were not American aristocrats; many had come from poor or plain families. Their public addresses did not achieve dignity or republican elegance; unlike their predecessors, they boasted about having been born in log cabins and being "men of the people."

Their attitudes toward the people—at least their public attitudes—were different, too. They campaigned hard for votes, and they were proud to refer to themselves as the direct representatives of the common people. Many even ran under a new party label—Democrats. They were proud that they had been nominated by national party conventions, not by congressional caucuses. And they were just as proud that the electors were now chosen by direct election, not by state legislatures.

One other item in the scrapbook captions would have caught the eye of the curious observer in 1864. Many portraits would have been labeled "General Jackson" or "General Harrison." A surprising number of the second-generation presidents had made their fame as soldiers—not in the Revolution, of course, but as "Indian fighters." "Tippecanoe" was the name of the Indian battle that Harrison had won in his middle age against the Tecumseh forces. General Zachary Taylor was elected in 1848 without a single day's political experience. Just as the old presidency was colored by the Revolution, the new presidency was colored by military struggles to possess the continent, to wrest control of the land from Native Americans, Spaniards, Britishers, and Mexicans. Even presidents who had not actually fought in the campaigns, like Polk, were war leaders in the White House—planning and approving campaigns to extend the national domain.

And so, although the names and the dates may be hard to memorize, this new presidential group makes its own kind of sense. It is Western; its rhetoric is that of parties and direct democracy; its style is informal. Its careers are tied firmly to westward expansion and military conquest. If the new presidents are not a dynasty, they are at least a recognizable group with common traits and manners.

Plate 14. George Caleb Bingham's *The County Election* (1854) captured much of the essence of the political culture that emerged between the 1830s and the Civil War. His Missouri voters—all white and male—are mostly plain farmers and artisans. Some are obviously quite drunk. But a candidate stands at the top of the stairs, smiling, half-bowing, and tipping his top hat. This eager appeal from a gentleman to a much poorer man who is not even wearing a jacket and tie would have astonished and appalled the Founding Fathers. But the banner proclaims the central premise of the new political logic: "The Will of the People The Supreme Law." (Collection of Mr. and Mrs. Wilson Pile)

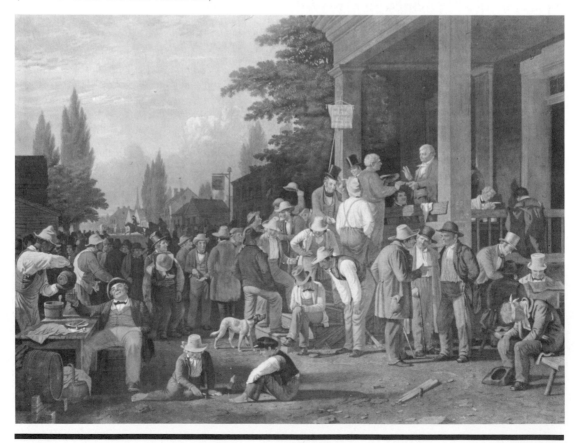

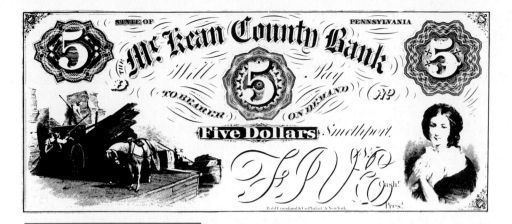

Bank note. This five-dollar note resembles modern money, but it was privately issued by the Mt. Kean County Bank in Pennsylvania. The small line of print at the bottom even gives the name of the private company that printed the note. A well-stocked lumber yard is pictured at the left, and at the right is a fashionably dressed woman holding a dove. Taken together, the two pictures suggest commercial prosperity and domestic comfort—just the kind of situation a bank would have an interest in presenting. (Print Collection, Miriam and Ira D. Wallach Division of Art, Prints and Photographs, The New York Public Library, Astor, Lenox and Tilden Foundations)

from gold or silver). Specie was in very short supply in the early decades of the nineteenth century. As recently as a generation earlier, hard cash had not been required on a large scale, since most economic transactions involved trading goods or work among neighbors of long standing. And a generation or two later, cash would be more readily available, whether as specie or in the form of dependable paper currency. But in the 1810s and 1820s, cash was both important *and* difficult to come by, especially in boom areas like the Southwest.

In place of cash, there emerged a whole set of shaky arrangements that functioned as currency. Almost any group of men could set up shop as a "bank," issuing "notes" that could pass from hand to hand as money. Many of these "banks" were completely unregulated. At any one time, literally hundreds of competing brands of "money" were circulating in the United States. (In Pennsylvania alone, different currencies were issued by forty-eight legal banks, twenty-two illegal ones, and thirty-nine private citizens in 1817.)

These *bank notes*, as they were known, could be exchanged for hard cash at the bank of origin—in theory. In fact, most banks issued notes in amounts that were far, far greater than what they could pay out in hard cash. People knew that, and so a five-dollar bank note might actually be worth much less than five dollars.[3] Bank notes

---

[3]Bank notes, which are no longer used, were like a cross between personal checks and modern paper money. Like a personal or company check, a bank note was a piece of paper that could be exchanged for actual money. (It was issued by the bank itself, though, not by an individual or some other company.) Accepting a bank note, like accepting a check today, involved an act of trust—trust that the issuing party (in this case, the bank itself) had enough money on hand to pay out when the note was presented for "cashing." People are not supposed to write checks for amounts in excess of what they have on account. But the banks of the 1810s did just that: They often issued bank notes for *far* more cash than they really owned, in the expectation that only a few of these notes would be cashed at any one time, and that the rest would continue to circulate as if they were real money.

were not reliable; in order to contrast them with hard cash, they were dubbed "soft" money.

The Panic of 1819 set in when everyone who held bank notes in effect tried to exchange them for cash—at the same time. Obviously, there was not nearly enough cash to go around, and prices plummeted. This in turn drastically affected relationships between debtors and creditors. A man who had borrowed, say, $1,000 before the panic could repay the loan by selling about a ton and a half of cotton at 30 cents a pound. But when the price of cotton dropped to less than 10 cents, the debtor suddenly saw his real debt tripled. He still owed the same number of dollars, of course, but it cost three times as much in goods and work to pay it off. From the point of view of the lender, such a result was a splendid windfall—provided he could collect the money or take the property that had been promised as security for the loan.

One direct effect of the Panic of 1819, then, was to create an intense consciousness of differing economic interests. These interests were quickly translated into political terms, especially in southern and western states, where farmers heavily in debt agitated for relief legislation that would ease their new burden. They wanted their state governments to enable them to use "soft" paper money at face value to pay off debts. The simplest way to do that would have been for the states to issue their own paper money. But the U.S. Constitution prohibited states from issuing their own money. Still, the debtors knew there was a way around that prohibition: The states could charter official banks, and the banks in turn could issue their own notes—lots of them. Those notes would be "soft" money, to be sure, but with the authority of the state behind them, they would be "legal tender" (meaning that a creditor was legally *obliged* to accept them at face value, as if they were actually specie).

These efforts were particularly powerful in Kentucky and in Jackson's Tennessee. Andrew Jackson himself was of course a creditor—a very large-scale creditor. It was in Jackson's personal interest to oppose the issuing of "soft" paper

money that his debtors would surely use to pay him. His Tennessee cronies distrusted *all* banks and favored a "sound" currency. Jackson himself contemptuously dismissed bank notes as "rags" and "trash." Naturally, he opposed relief legislation for the state's debtors. In a hotly contested election for the Tennessee governorship, Jackson fought hard to defeat the candidate who was running on a platform promising relief. But the soft-money candidate won. In Kentucky, too, the debtor faction was able to push through a state bank, the "Bank of the Commonwealth," which printed paper money that was worth only about half what hard money, based on gold, was worth. They then provided that creditors would have to accept the cheap money, thus reducing the value of debts in the state to about half their real value. The Kentucky courts eventually declared the law unconstitutional in 1823. But the money question did not die. The entire system of credit and money supply would remain a principal question for Jacksonian politicians and their constituents.

THE BANK OF THE UNITED STATES The panic also focused attention sharply on the Bank of the United States. This institution—an outgrowth of the old "Hamiltonian" system (see Chapter 6)—had responded to the panic in the only way it could. To keep itself solvent, the Bank had demanded payment, in gold money, for all the state bank paper money it held (and it held a lot). This demand forced the state banks, in turn, to call in all *their* loans to farmers and businessmen.

A number of state and local banks failed as a result. The net effect was to make money scarce, to send farmers and businessmen into bankruptcy—to make a bad situation even worse. And many western politicians discovered that attacking what they called the "monster Bank" was a powerfully effective way to appeal for votes. Thomas Hart Benton, a senator from Missouri, summed up the antibank sentiment per-

Henry Clay (1777–1852) served Kentucky both as a congressman (where he was Speaker of the House) and, after 1831, as a Senator. This picture was painted as an enamel miniature, a pin intended to be worn as a piece of jewelry. With its embellished border, it served as a pretty decoration for a fashionably dressed woman—but also as a political advertisement for a shrewd politician. (Courtesy of the New-York Historical Society)

United States, he ruled, had a right to establish the Bank of the United States, even though the Constitution did not expressly say so—for the simple reason that the government could do whatever was "necessary and proper" to achieve the general results the Constitution aimed at. If such a federal action was legitimate, Marshall reasoned, then no state could be allowed to place any tax or restriction on the Bank, because the "power to tax involves the power to destroy." The decision was the first case in which the Supreme Court had actually decided that a state law was unconstitutional, and this fact alone was enough to make the very existence of the Bank of the United States a raw political issue for the next two decades, one of the defining issues of Jacksonian political life.

THE AMERICAN SYSTEM Some Americans, and the politicians who spoke for them, looked to other features of the Panic of 1819 for their issues. To them it seemed clear that the underlying cause of the panic was not the credit system or the Bank, but American dependence on foreign trade. The obvious way to break this dependence was to encourage the growth of manufacturing in America. And there was a simple way to do this: Create an *internal* market for American goods so rich and thriving that it could break the ties of economic dependence on Europe that were a hangover of the old colonial past.

The principal spokesman for this point of view, Rep. Henry Clay of Kentucky, called his program the "American system." Its ingredients were simple enough, and reminiscent of Hamilton's economic program in some ways. First, raise a tariff to block imports from outside the country—particularly manufactured goods from England. Second, use the powers of government to improve the system of transportation within the United States. Given the protection of the tariff and the creation of an efficient network of transportation, American farmers and manufac-

fectly when he told his supporters, "All the flourishing cities of the West are mortgaged to this money power. They may be devoured by it at any moment."

Some states even tried to tax the Bank out of existence. Maryland passed a heavy tax on the Bank. The Bank refused to pay the tax, so the state sued the Bank's cashier, James McCulloch. The resulting case, *McCulloch* v. *Maryland*, was decided by the Supreme Court in 1819, in one of John Marshall's most significant decisions. The turers would feed and clothe the rich and growing domestic economy. Clay summed it all up in curiously modern-sounding language in 1824: "We must give a new direction to our industry. We must speedily adopt a genuine American policy."

But simple as the program may have sounded, and much as it may have appealed to the bruised patriotism that came out of the War of 1812, Clay's system posed two nearly insoluble problems. First, in the scramble for tariff protection, there was always the question: Who would get the *most* protection? Would it be the farmer who raised sheep, or the manufacturer who spun and wove the wool into cloth? Would it be the ropemakers who created the thousands of miles of lines so essential to the ship transportation of the day, or the people who grew the hemp from which the ropes were made? Like the question of debtor vs. creditor, the tariff issue heightened people's awareness of their conflicting and competing interests, and they used politics as a means of expressing their calculations.

Second, many Americans wanted no tariffs at all. Southerners, in particular, had always based their economic life on the export of tobacco or cotton to European markets and the easy import of European products in exchange. A tariff would wreck their world, forcing them to sell cotton in American markets for lower prices and to buy American manufactured goods for higher prices.

Tariffs and internal improvements raised other, larger problems, too. The idea that the federal government ought to finance roads and canals ran head-on against the old "republican" commitment to a government with severely limited powers. People who devoutly opposed the Bank of the United States as an arbitrary extension of federal power could hardly be expected to swallow the idea of a federally financed road system. And a tariff that was admittedly designed to create federal control of the economy was an alarming prospect to people who were staunchly committed to the Jeffersonian faith that "that government governs best which governs least."

The Missouri Compromise

Finally, behind it all lay the unmentionable issue of slavery—that brooding issue that had been just below the surface of much of the debate on the Constitution but on which the final product had been almost silent. Whatever touched the interests of the Northern and Southern states in different ways touched slavery, even if politicians preferred to keep silent on the problem. If a system of internal improvements diverted western grain shipments away from New Orleans to New York, the economy of the South would suffer. And the plain fact was that slavery had become so central to Southern life that there was no problem—whether it was the tariff or the Bank question—that did not pose some sort of threat to it. It was no accident, then, that the slavery question surfaced in Congress at the same time all the other issues of the Jacksonian period were being defined.

The settlement of the West had brought one new state after another into the Union without controversy, though some were obviously slave states and others free. Louisiana joined in 1812, Indiana in 1816, Illinois in 1818, and Alabama in 1819. There was almost a pattern to it. One new slave state, one new free state. And hardly anyone noticed.

It was a shock, then, when the admission of Missouri to the Union suddenly flared into a political crisis in 1819 and 1820. When the Missouri Bill reached the floor of the House for what might have been routine action, Congressman James Tallmadge of New York proposed a startling amendment: No new slaves could be introduced into the state, and any child born into slavery in Missouri would become automatically free at the age of twenty-five.

The response of the Southerners in the House was immediate and outraged. Congressman

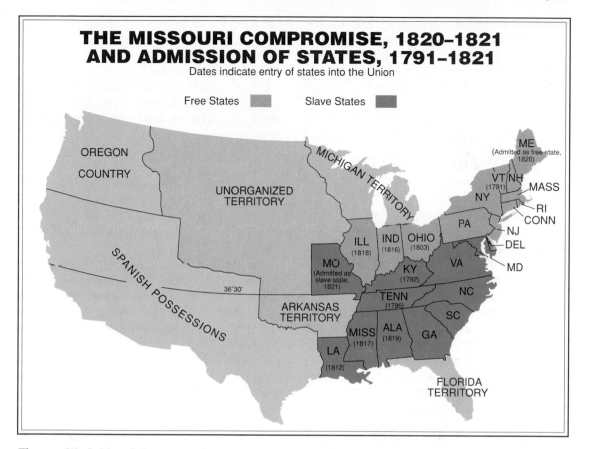

THE MISSOURI COMPROMISE, 1820–1821 AND ADMISSION OF STATES, 1791–1821

Dates indicate entry of states into the Union

Free States   Slave States

OREGON COUNTRY

UNORGANIZED TERRITORY

MICHIGAN TERRITORY

ME (Admitted as free state, 1820)

VT (1791) NH

MASS

NY

RI

CONN

PA

NJ

DEL

ILL (1818)

IND (1816)

OHIO (1803)

VA

MD

SPANISH POSSESSIONS

36°30'

MO (Admitted as slave state, 1821)

KY (1792)

NC

ARKANSAS TERRITORY

TENN (1796)

SC

MISS (1817)

ALA (1819)

GA

LA (1812)

FLORIDA TERRITORY

Thomas W. Cobb, of Georgia, yelled across the floor: "You have kindled a fire which all the waters of the oceans cannot put out, which only seas of blood can extinguish." After bitter debate, the House actually passed the Tallmadge amendment by a slender margin. But no one doubted what the Senate—always the secure nest of Southern power—would do: It defeated the amendment just before the spring adjournment.

This meant the House and Senate versions of the Missouri Bill had to be brought into line before Missouri could become a state. Clay, who was Speaker of the House at the time, found the solution. The northeastern part of Massachusetts, luckily, applied for admission to statehood under the name of Maine. Missouri plus Maine: This would preserve the precious balance of slave and free states. Further, Clay proposed simply

to split the Louisiana Purchase along an arbitrary line of latitude, 36°30', and to prohibit slavery forever north of that line.

The Missouri controversy sent a thrilling shock through the political system. But the settlement—which became known as the Missouri Compromise—seemed to prove that the slavery question could be kept quiet and might even resolve itself peacefully in the long run. In fact, the Compromise established that slavery was *not* going to be an explicit issue in Jacksonian politics but would be kept below the surface. It would influence everything indirectly—tariffs, money questions, internal government, and much else—but it would not be a subject of debates in elections, of bills in Congress, or of presidential speeches and actions. Once more, as in the Constitutional Convention, the problem of slavery had been kept over the political horizon—like some dark and incomprehensible landmark that receded as the country approached it but never went away.

End of the Dynasty

The president who inherited the Panic of 1819 and its consequences was James Monroe, last of the Virginia Dynasty—tall, distinguished, and bewigged. In general, his policy was to have no policy—to regard most of the problems generated by the panic as outside the government's range of action. He also seemed not to understand the urgency of the Missouri question as a political fact of life, and he almost did not sign the bill because he wondered whether Congress had the constitutional authority to prohibit slavery anywhere. Only after his cabinet had unanimously and vigorously endorsed the Missouri Compromise did he approve it. The translation into politics of the effects of the Panic of 1819 had to wait, then, until the elections of 1824 and 1828.

The old rules of succession in the Virginia Dynasty appeared to give the presidency to John Quincy Adams in 1824. He was not a Virginian, of course, but he was the son of a president—a sort of Founding Son—and he had worked his way through the executive branch to the conventional jumping-off point, as Monroe's secretary of state. This time, however, the rules broke down. There were too many new and ambitious men on the scene, too much awareness of conflicting interests and regional identities to allow the one-party system to function smoothly any longer.

The strongest signal that the rules had failed came when the caucus of congressional Republicans met to nominate the party's candidate. Only about a third of the congressmen even took the trouble to show up, and most of those who did were the supporters not of a party position but of a man. They nominated the secretary of the treasury, William Crawford—a Virginia-born Georgian who had the support of old Thomas Jefferson himself. But there was no party discipline. In effect, there was no party. And so several other men went to their state legislatures for nomination as candidates. Adams would run, as a Northern candidate. John C. Calhoun, a third member of the Monroe cabinet, was the candidate of South Carolina. Henry Clay became the first presidential candidate in American history from west of the mountains. He had strong support in his native Kentucky and in neighboring Indiana and Ohio.

Crawford, Calhoun, Adams, and Clay had one thing in common. They were members with full standing in the Republicans' Washington establishment. Each of them might reasonably expect to reunite Jefferson's party, to make it last another generation as *the* national political party. Calhoun withdrew just before the election because he was certain he could become vice president, and so set the stage for a conventional run for the presidency in 1828 and 1832. Crawford suffered a stroke during the campaign, and ended up getting the electoral votes of only Virginia and Georgia. As for Clay and Adams, whichever of them lost would probably join the other's cabinet, hoping to become the next figure in the dynasty. These two candidates even agreed in general on a strong federal program of economic development—including tariffs, internal improvements, and a powerful national bank. It was possible, in short, that the rules could be restored and that a new dynastic generation of presidential leadership could be founded.

But there was a spoiler: Andrew Jackson. The Tennessee legislature nominated him for the presidency late in the election year and with little expectation that he could win. But his campaign caught fire. He took no political positions and announced no program, but he did inspire intense personal loyalty among political workers. And his fame as the Hero of New Orleans guaranteed him a strong popular following in those states where presidential electors were chosen directly by the voters.

The election of 1824 was a political maze. The candidates were five. They were not identified with parties. One was too ill to be president anyway, and another withdrew his name just before the voting took place. Only one-fourth of the eligible voters bothered to cast ballots. And no one won. As in 1800, no candidate commanded a majority of the electoral votes. So the election was thrown into the House of Representatives, where each state had one vote, no matter how many electoral votes it was assigned.

As the strategists for the candidates studied the election map, they confronted a curious mess that made only a few points clear. Jackson had won 99 electoral votes, and Adams 84. But it took 131 to win. When they counted by states—as the votes would occur in the House—Jackson's situation was plain. He had won in ten states out of the twenty-four; if they remained loyal, he needed only three more. Crawford had won in three states, and so had Clay. But the sick Crawford had no real control over his supporters in the House. The key man was obviously the Speaker of the House, Clay, who could not only deliver his own states but could shake loose some of Jackson's and Crawford's. Just as Aaron Burr had held important cards in 1800 (see Chapter 6), Clay held them now, and he played them with more skill than Burr had done. He was courted by all factions, but he finally threw his support to Adams, who in turn named Clay his secretary of state—a political deal that seemed to mean Clay would be the next president after Adams. Jackson's supporters tagged this deal the "Corrupt Bargain."

JOHN QUINCY ADAMS In political reality, the election of 1824 was significant primarily as part of the stage scenery for the next round, 1828. The presidency of John Quincy Adams resembled nothing so much as a four-year campaign between him and Jackson.

In this lengthy jockeying for position, Adams operated at a serious disadvantage, one he inadvertently created for himself. He steadfastly refused to act as a party man. Like all his predecessors in the presidency, John Quincy Adams believed political parties were evil, a symptom of some deep flaw in the American social fabric. He knew that parties had shown real signs of disappearing in the administration of James Monroe: Monroe had been elected to his second term with a virtually unanimous vote—the Federalist party had not even put up a candidate—and his presidency had been dubbed the beginning of an "Era of Good Feeling." President Adams sensed that "the baneful weed of party strife" was being "uprooted." He hoped political parties would disappear for good in his own administration, and that the Era of Good Feeling would become a permanent feature of American politics. If it did, Adams knew he would be in a good position to claim the credit—and to collect his reward in the election of 1828.

So Adams took a calculated gamble. He continued Monroe's policy of appointing old-line Federalists to high office, but he took that policy to an extreme. Adams refused to use his patronage powers to punish his personal opponents or even to reward his supporters. "I shall exclude no person for political opinions or for opposition to me," he said. "My great object will be to break up the remnant of old party distinctions and bring the whole people together in sentiment as much as possible." In his entire term, he removed only twelve men from office.

As president, Adams acted as if he stood not just above party politics but above the people themselves. (Here, too, he was only taking to an extreme an idea of political authority he shared with all his predecessors.) In his inaugural address, Adams recommended to Congress a program of federal activities he knew to be politically unpopular, but he urged Congress to support his program anyway—and not to be "palsied [paralyzed] by the will of our constituents." Like Monroe, he refused to use the federal government to force the removal of the Cherokees. But

John Quincy Adams sat for this formal portrait shortly after the disputed 1824 presidential election had finally been decided in his favor by the House of Representatives. It was a carefully contrived portrait, and each element was intended to convey the image of Adams as a man of culture and practical knowledge: his statesman-like pose, his art collection, the unrolled map of the U.S., and the many books—some shelved, but others lying on Adams's lap and even on the floor. These elements portray a president who was too busy looking after the nation's interests to stoop to petty politics—in short, a man who was not capable of making the "corrupt bargain" by which Adams's opponents accused him of stealing the presidency from Andrew Jackson. (New York State Office of Parks, Recreation and Historic Preservation, Philipse Manor Hall State Historic Site)

on other matters, Adams called for a policy that would make unprecedented use of federal power and money to develop the nation's economy and culture—things that people at the time labeled "internal improvements."

His program would involve building a national system of roads and canals, a national university, even a national astronomical observatory. The program resembled Henry Clay's "American system," but it went beyond anything even Clay had proposed. Adams devoted much of his administration to the pursuit of his program. To a certain extent, he succeeded—particularly with internal improvements. But many

Americans remained deeply suspicious of such aggressive use of federal power. And Adams's own refusal to appoint his friends to political office meant he never created a political base of loyalists who would support him in 1828.

In some respects John Quincy Adams was the best-prepared man ever to become president. The son of a president, he was a Harvard-educated lawyer who became a skilled diplomat in Europe, a U.S. senator, and (under Monroe) the secretary of state. But in one crucial way he was not prepared at all: He sorely miscalculated the temper of American political culture in the 1820s. Adams may have thought of himself as the leader of the nation as a whole, but, as one of his opponents noted, he succeeded in uniting it only in opposition to him.

The Election of 1828

If Andrew Jackson had a campaign issue in 1824, it was simply that he was the outsider, a man of only limited contact with a Washington establishment his followers labeled "aristocratic." The outcome in 1824 seemed to confirm the opposition between Jackson and the center of national political power. Jackson and his supporters went to work at once. They began to emphasize the fact that the "Old Hero" was a man of the people, of humble origins, not "raised in the lap of luxury." His talk was marked by "plain common sense," instead of Adams's "Greek quotations and struggles after eloquence." The image was completed by dramatic use of the 1824 election, when "the people's choice" had been turned back by an unholy alliance between luxury and corruption. Jackson's supporters argued that the true, manipulative face of Adams's aristocratic pretensions had been revealed in the Corrupt Bargain. This, in turn, had been supported in a Congress dominated by what Jackson's party workers called "King Caucus."

What this amounted to was nothing less than a political language, a rhetoric, that pitted the homespun against the refined, the people against conspiratorial tricks in Washington, and the people's leader—General Jackson, who now called himself "Old Hickory"—against an entrenched elite in Washington, Philadelphia, New York, and Boston. It all had the proportions of a myth, pitting the hero against various "monsters" that threatened to "devour" the people and lay waste the republic. It had a lot in common with the myths of the Revolutionary period. But there were two grand differences now. First, the old

enemies—aristocrats and kings or the Terror of the French Revolution—had been foreign; the new ones were domestic, threatening the republic from within. Second, the old heroes had been gentlemen; the new ones would now present themselves as plain men, not just defenders of the people but *embodiments* of the people's experience and will.

But Jackson was as good a politician as he was a general, and he knew perfectly well that it had been cannon, not talk, that had won for him in New Orleans. It would be political organization that would win for him in 1828. A study of the election map that had kept him out of the White House in 1824 bore home several lessons. If Adams could hold onto what he had won then, he would need to pick up only a few more votes to claim the presidency. If Adams could get Pennsylvania and add a few more states like New Jersey and Ohio, then the "man of the people" would lose again. And so Jackson and his strategists set out to build the party organization that, in the end, was their major political accomplishment.

New York was an obvious key, so Jackson courted Martin Van Buren and John Van Ness, one of Van Buren's lieutenants. A central committee was formed in Washington to coordinate state efforts, with Van Ness as its chairman. Newspapers were founded to support Jackson—eighteen in the crucial state of Ohio alone, and many others elsewhere. To hold the South in line, Jackson chose Calhoun as a running mate. And to angle for votes in the Middle West—particularly in old Clay states like Ohio and Kentucky—Jackson's friends went to work on the issue of the tariff. They helped push through what became known as the "tariff of abominations" in the election year of 1828. In it, they conceded limited tariff support to New England manufacturers of cotton and woolen cloth, and of hemp rope. But they gave higher tariff barriers to the people who raised the sheep and the hemp (people who happened to live in crucial states like New York and Ohio). The South opposed the tariff vigorously, of course, but Jackson and his

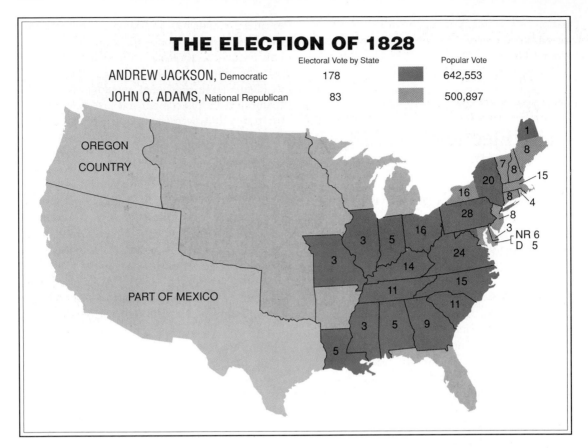

THE ELECTION OF 1828

	Electoral Vote by State		Popular Vote
ANDREW JACKSON, Democratic	178		642,553
JOHN Q. ADAMS, National Republican	83		500,897

supporters knew the South would never turn to Adams.

To kick off the election year, Jackson attended a giant celebration in New Orleans on the anniversary of the battle there. The crowds were given miniature hickory sticks, and over and over he was toasted with the line that became the refrain of his campaign and his career as president: "Andrew Jackson—his Party is the People."

And it all worked. Jackson not only held Pennsylvania but won more than half the electoral votes of New York away from Adams. Twice as many people voted as in 1824, and Jackson had the support of 56 percent of them. The ingredients of victory had been obvious: an expanded electorate; direct election of the presidential electors (only South Carolina still chose them in the legislature); democratic slogans and rhetoric; and a party organization carefully built and controlled by professionals like Van Buren.

Jackson swept into the White House on a wave of democratic feeling combined with his fame as the Hero of New Orleans. He even threw open the president's home to a brawling, muddy-booted crowd that shocked old Washington hands who had grown accustomed to the decorum of the Republican dynasty. But it was difficult to predict what his policies would be. In the campaign, he had taken soft stands on every question and had confined his efforts to building the party and attacking Adams.

Three Jackson Puzzles

The eight years of Jackson's presidency were to be puzzling. One puzzle lay in the role of party itself. The administration very quickly committed

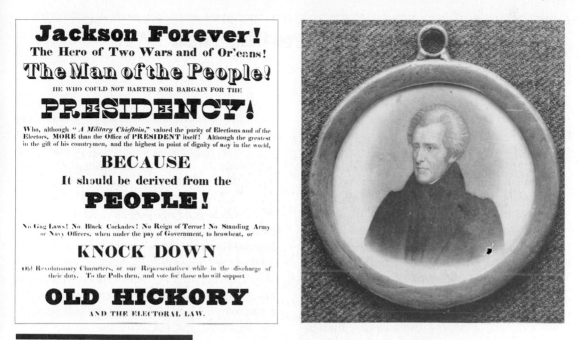

Jackson Forever!

The Hero of Two Wars and of Or'eans!

The Man of the People!

HE WHO COULD NOT BARTER NOR BARGAIN FOR THE

PRESIDENCY!

Who, although " *A Military Chieftain*," valued the purity of Elections and of the Electors, **MORE** than the Office of **PRESIDENT** itself! Although the greatest in the gift of his countrymen, and the highest in point of dignity of any in the world,

BECAUSE

It should be derived from the

PEOPLE!

No Gag Laws! No Black Cockades! No Reign of Terror! No Standing Army or Navy Officers, when under the pay of Government, to browbeat, or

KNOCK DOWN

Old Revolutionary Characters, or our Representatives while in the discharge of their duty. To the Polls then, and vote for those who will support

OLD HICKORY

AND THE ELECTORAL LAW.

Andrew Jackson. The 1828 campaign poster (left) is filled with references to Jackson's heroic past, his moral and political purity, and his identification with "the people." There is no mention of political parties here—and no real political platform. Like the picture of Henry Clay on p. 315, the portrait of Andrew Jackson (right; painted between 1824 and 1828) served both as a piece of women's jewelry and as part of the 1828 campaign—the equivalent of modern-day T-shirts or bumper stickers. (Museum of America Political Life, photo by Sally Anderson-Bruce)

itself to a position that the winners should take the prizes of the contest—public offices. ("To the victor belong the spoils" was the slogan used to explain this practice.) Jackson announced that he intended to replace federal officeholders en masse with his own supporters. But when the dust had settled, and historians could take an actual body count, it turned out that Jackson actually removed fewer bureaucrats than his predecessors had.

A second puzzle lay in Jackson's policies on internal improvements. The darling project of Adams and Clay had been the use of federal power to support roads, canals, and other transportation projects. During the second year of his administration, Jackson vetoed a bill to construct a federal turnpike, the Maysville Road, in Clay's

own Kentucky. The veto had a good deal of sting to it. But when the political talking was finished, Jackson approved more bills for internal improvements than had any president before him.

A third area of seeming contradiction took shape around the problem of the tariff. Here, too, Jackson's position was difficult to pin down. His supporters had helped pass the so-called tariff of abominations of 1828 (in return for crucial political backing), but he himself had proclaimed a vague, "moderate" attitude. Now, as president, Jackson faced a severe challenge. The South Carolina legislature formally denounced the tariff of 1828. Such a denunciation was not unusual, but the legislature went further. It published an *Exposition and Protest*—written anonymously by Jackson's own vice president, Calhoun.

The South Carolinians argued that a state which is convinced a federal law is unconstitutional has the right to "nullify" the law within its own boundaries. If the federal government tried to enforce such a law, the state could go even further and "interpose" state power to protect its own citizens from federal power.

For four years, all the state of South Carolina did was talk and publish. But as the election of 1832 approached, it was clear that Calhoun and Jackson could not get along. Martin Van Buren was chosen as the vice presidential candidate (and presumed successor to Jackson). Now South Carolina acted dramatically. The legislature called a special convention in Charleston. The convention formally nullified the federal tariff and warned that if the president tried to enforce the law, the state might secede from the Union.

Jackson met the Carolina Ordinance of Nullification with a ringing proclamation that insisted on the supremacy of federal law. South Carolina had acted in a way that was "incompatible with the existence of the Union, contradicted expressly by the Constitution, unauthorized by its spirit, inconsistent with every principle on which it was founded and destructive of the great object for which it was formed." But while he thundered, Jackson also offered gifts—as he had always done in making Indian treaties: He actually asked Congress to *lower* the tariff rates.

When the South Carolinians scorned his methods, Jackson went to Congress to ask for a "force bill," giving him the power to send federal troops into South Carolina to collect the tariff. But he continued to offer compromise on the tariff itself. The result was a little comic (except that it foreshadowed a similar and more devastating confrontation a generation later). Congress, on the same day, passed the force bill *and* a new tariff that lowered rates gradually for a nine-year period. The compromise had been supported by both Jackson and Calhoun. Ten days later, South Carolina repealed its nullification of the existing tariff law. But it added one gesture of defiance: It "nullified" the force bill—a law that was a dead letter anyway.

The Bank "War"

On these questions—the "spoils" system, internal improvements, and the tariff—Jackson behaved in roughly the same way: In ringing public statements, he insisted on a tough position, but in practice he compromised, negotiated, and moved with patience and caution. On a personal level, it did not seem so important to him to have his way as to proclaim that he *could* have it if he insisted. Leaving personality aside, however, there was another consistency in his actions that, in effect, redefined the presidency. He and his supporters adopted a public stand on which they did *not* compromise: The president was the leader of his party, the leader of the federal government, and above all, the leader of the people—their defender, patron, and tribune. In his farewell address in 1837, Jackson discussed the tariff question in a way that went to the heart of his idea of what it meant to be president. It was not a question of economic policies or of revenues. It was a question of "powerful interests that are continually at work," interests which sought to "oppress" the people, to "fasten" unjust burdens on them. And to whom could the people look for protection against such sinister designs on their liberty and prosperity? To their only real representative, the president.

This conception of the presidency depended heavily on the individual force of personality of the president himself. Only he could galvanize a mass constituency against supposedly elite interests. This idea came into sharp focus during the election of 1832, on the question of the future of the Bank of the United States.

The Bank issue was an old one—as old as Hamilton's plan for a federalist economy. It became heated during the collapse of credit and banking during the Panic of 1819. Now it came to center stage because of politics. Jackson's opponents were beginning to organize what would finally emerge as a new party, the Whig party. They were looking for an issue. The Bank

The Bank War. President Jackson spoke of the Bank of the United States as a "monster," and his metaphor was taken literally in this political cartoon. A dragon—the Bank—has attacked American society in the dark (note the bed at the right) and is choking a citizen with one of its many tails. President Jackson, himself dressed in bedclothes, is doing battle with the beast, which has another of its tentacles around his left foot. The scene is reminiscent of the story of St. George and the Dragon, and the snakelike dragon was also drawn in such a way as to suggest the serpent in the Garden of Eden—the Devil himself. In either case, Andrew Jackson was the savior of his nation. (Courtesy of the New-York Historical Society, New York City)

of the United States was not scheduled for recharter until after the election of 1832. But the opposition in Congress, led by Clay and Daniel Webster, decided to push through a recharter bill in 1830. They believed they could trap Jackson. If he approved the bill, he would appear to desert "the people," accepting an institution clearly identified with an eastern commercial elite. If he vetoed the Bank, on the other hand, he could be accused of bringing on economic confusion— maybe even another panic. The Bank did help bring some order to the economy, mainly by regulating the amount of credit that state-chartered banks could grant. It had the power, within limits, to either expand or contract credit, thereby promoting speculation or stability.

JACKSON'S VETO AND THE ELECTION OF 1832

Jackson accepted the challenge and made a definite political gamble. In his passionate veto message, he accused the Bank (and its powerful, lordly president, Nicholas Biddle) of being the servant of the rich, the enemy of the poor. And he presented himself and his party (now calling themselves the "Democrats") as the only ones

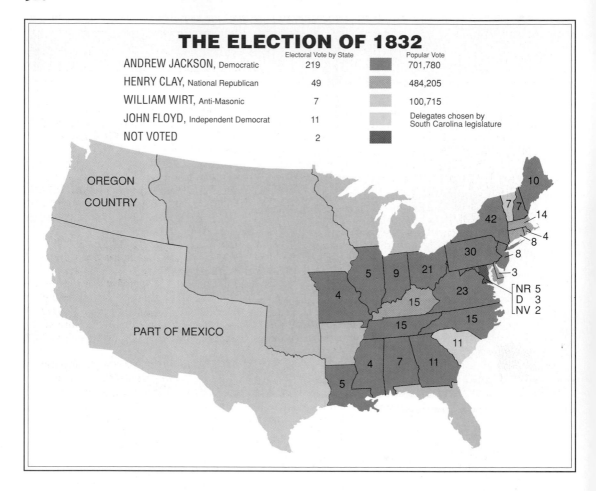

THE ELECTION OF 1832

	Electoral Vote by State		Popular Vote
ANDREW JACKSON, Democratic	219		701,780
HENRY CLAY, National Republican	49		484,205
WILLIAM WIRT, Anti-Masonic	7		100,715
JOHN FLOYD, Independent Democrat	11		Delegates chosen by South Carolina legislature
NOT VOTED	2		

OREGON COUNTRY

PART OF MEXICO

who could protect the people from Biddle and his "monster" interest. The gamble—and the patient party organization that the Democrats had been pursuing for years—paid off. Jackson won a crushing electoral victory (though by a narrower popular margin than in 1828).

The main business of the second Jackson administration was to liquidate the Bank of the United States. The president withdrew federal deposits from the Bank, and provided that only gold—not the notes of the Bank—could be used to pay for public lands. The other principal task was to prepare to pass the party and the presidency to his successor, Van Buren.

The Jacksonian Era

Like George Washington almost half a century earlier, Andrew Jackson came to believe that his personal self-interest was the same as the patriotic interests of his nation—and he was able to persuade a great many of his fellow Americans to agree with him. But there was a difference between Washington's vision and Jackson's. Washington was the undisputed leader of his people, but nobody would have thought that he

Sequoyah

Sequoyah (ca. 1770–1843) is the best-known Cherokee. His name has been given to the giant California redwood trees and to the national park there. His fame stems from his invention of a written Cherokee alphabet—the first written Indian language. Born in Tennessee, the mixed-blood son of a British Indian trader named Nathaniel Gist, Sequoyah was abandoned by his father and raised by his Indian mother. (In adulthood, he also called himself George Guess, a variant of his father's surname.)

Sequoyah never learned to speak English, but he was fascinated with "talking leaves," as the printed pages of white people were commonly known. Around 1810 he determined to devise a written Cherokee language. The task was extremely difficult: Several white missionaries (even one Harvard student) had tried to devise a Cherokee alphabet, but their efforts were defeated by the complex sounds of the language—some made by smacking the lips or clicking the tongue. Sequoyah hit on the idea of dividing the Cherokee language into *syllables*, representing each one with a written symbol. He was able to distinguish some two hundred distinct syllables; by 1821 he had reduced the number to a workable eighty-six. Some of these symbols were represented by Englishlike letters, but these bore no relation to their actual sounds in English: Sequoyah's "D," for example, was pronounced like the English word *a*; and his "A," like the English word "go."

In fact, Sequoyah fervently opposed the assimilationist strategy of Cherokee leaders like The Ridge. He was a traditionalist, a separatist who felt that the Cherokees needed to preserve and strengthen their own indigenous culture, religion, and language. It was his belief that the tribe needed to get away from white people, from Christianity, and from the English language in order to survive. In 1822 he even moved west to Arkansas in order to join the 2,500 Cherokees who had voluntarily gone there in order to flee the white presence. Sequoyah's purpose in devising a written Cherokee language was twofold: to permit Cherokees to communicate with each other without depending on white people's language and to preserve the tribe's rapidly disappearing traditions.

Sequoyah introduced his "syllabary" in 1821, and it quickly caught on at the grassroots level. One white observer wrote in 1824 that "the knowledge of Mr. Guess's Alphabet is spreading through the [Cherokee] nation like fire among the leaves." Sequoyah's invention promised for a time to revitalize Cherokee culture and to become a potent weapon of empowerment and liberation.

By 1828 "Sequoyan" had become so popular that Christian missionaries reluctantly decided to make use of it. They paid for a font of type in "Sequoyan" and for the printing of hymnbooks and catechisms using the new syllabary. Even the *Cherokee Phoenix*, the bilingual newspaper edited by Elias Boudinot, devoted most of its "Sequoyan" portion to Christian material. It was in this misleading context that most white Americans came to know and admire Sequoyah's work.

Sequoyah himself quickly became bitter about what he saw as the co-opting of his great achievement by those who wished to destroy Cherokee culture. In 1829 he moved west once again, from Arkansas to Oklahoma, where the Cherokees had just been granted lands by the U.S. government. Still fascinated by Indian language, the aging Sequoyah began to visit other tribes, hoping to discover some underlying principles of grammar and etymology that might provide the basis for rediscovering a single forgotten culture shared by all Native Americans. Sequoyah died in 1843 while in Mexico, where he had gone in the hope of locating a lost remnant of Cherokees said to have moved there almost 100 years earlier, before the United States had even come into being.

CHRONOLOGY

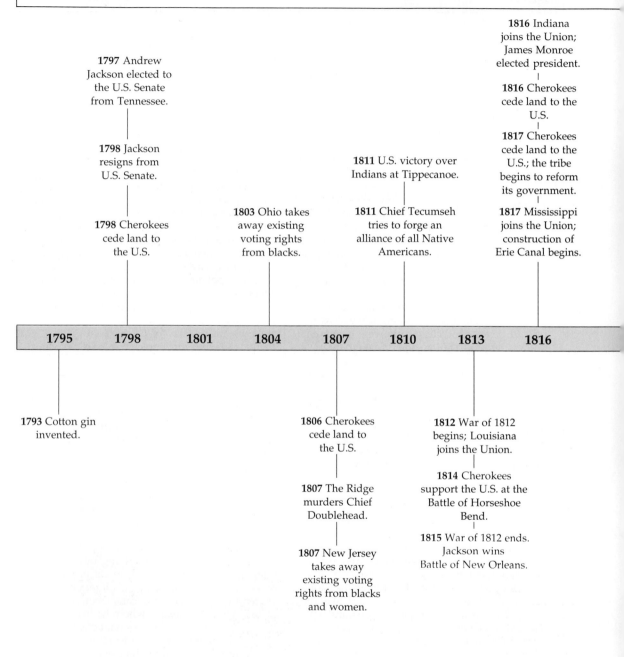

1797 Andrew Jackson elected to the U.S. Senate from Tennessee.

1798 Jackson resigns from U.S. Senate.

1798 Cherokees cede land to the U.S.

1803 Ohio takes away existing voting rights from blacks.

1811 U.S. victory over Indians at Tippecanoe.

1811 Chief Tecumseh tries to forge an alliance of all Native Americans.

1816 Indiana joins the Union; James Monroe elected president.

1816 Cherokees cede land to the U.S.

1817 Cherokees cede land to the U.S.; the tribe begins to reform its government.

1817 Mississippi joins the Union; construction of Erie Canal begins.

| 1795 | 1798 | 1801 | 1804 | 1807 | 1810 | 1813 | 1816 |

1793 Cotton gin invented.

1806 Cherokees cede land to the U.S.

1807 The Ridge murders Chief Doublehead.

1807 New Jersey takes away existing voting rights from blacks and women.

1812 War of 1812 begins; Louisiana joins the Union.

1814 Cherokees support the U.S. at the Battle of Horseshoe Bend.

1815 War of 1812 ends. Jackson wins Battle of New Orleans.

1827 Cherokees adopt a written constitution; Georgia's legislature resolves to take over all Cherokee lands in 1830.

1833 Emergence of a pro-removal faction among the Cherokees.

1821 Sequoyah invents written Cherokee syllabary.

1828 John Ross elected principal chief of the Cherokees; *Cherokee Phoenix* begins publication.

1834 Jackson enters into secret negotiations with the pro-removal faction.

1835 A removal treaty concluded with the pro-removal faction— rejected three times by the tribal council; in December the treaty is "ratified."

1839 Surviving Cherokees arrive in Oklahoma; in June three prominent pro-treaty Cherokees are murdered.

1821 New York takes away existing voting rights from blacks.

1828 Andrew Jackson elected president.

1828 "Tariff of Abominations"

1819	1822	1825	1828	1831	1834	1837	1840

1818 Illinois joins the Union; Connecticut takes away existing voting rights from blacks.

1819 Alabama joins the Union.

1819 Cherokees cede land to the U.S.

1819 Missouri Compromise; Missouri and Maine join the Union (Maine allowing black men to vote)

1819 Panic of 1819.

1819 Supreme Court decides *McCulloch* v. *Maryland*.

1824 John Quincy Adams elected president (Jackson wins the popular vote)

1824 Cherokees establish a National Academy.

1825 Cherokees begin to construct a capital city, New Echota.

1825 Erie Canal completed.

1830 Indian Removal Bill becomes law on May 28; Georgia takes legal control of Cherokee land June 1.

1831 Cyrus McCormick invents the automatic reaper.

1832 Jackson's Bank veto.

1832 Supreme Court decides *Cherokee Nation* v. *State of Georgia* in favor of the Indians; in October, Georgia holds lottery for Cherokee lands.

1832 South Carolina "nullifies" Tariff of Abominations; Congress passes the "Force Bill"

1832 Jackson re-elected president.

1836 U.S. Senate approves the removal treaty.

1837 Pennsylvania takes away existing voting rights from blacks.

1838 Forced Cherokee removal begins— the Trail of Tears.

was *one* of them. Andrew Jackson was the first president to assert that the source of his leadership lay in the fact that he had sprung directly out of the people—that his origins, his dreams and aspirations, his success actually reflected and embodied those of the people writ large. And they surely did. In the quarter-century between 1812 and 1837, thousands of Americans paid homage to Jackson in a singularly personal fashion: They named their male children after him. Even the ill-fated Cherokee leader John Ridge chose to do so.

Andrew Jackson's view of the world was determined by his own remarkable ascent. As a land speculator, a military man, and a politician, he had done remarkably well. Jackson believed he had been able to climb so far because his personal ambition and energy had been strong—stronger than any of the forces that were always there to oppose him. His early poverty, and the lowly social status of his birth, had not prevented him from becoming one of the most powerful men of his time. By the time Jackson became president of the United States, he had decided that his experiences offered a model for the nation, and that the sole legitimate purpose of government was to act as the ultimate guardian of personal ambition and the freedom to pursue wealth and power. When government failed to do so, or when it acted to inhibit that freedom, government became simply another of the powerful forces conspiring to destroy the people's freedom.

Many Americans were eager to accept Jackson's message. A mere generation earlier they had accepted the idea that ambition and self-seeking had to be balanced against the competing claims of order and stability, just as equality had to be limited by the competing claims of hierarchy and status. But now those competing claims turned out to be nothing but the fetters of a corrupt, dying era. Ambition and equality alone were virtues enough to make the nation prosper in the new age that had suddenly dawned. It was therefore necessary to do away with any political restrictions on ambition and equality. Above all, the right to vote had to be open to the rich and the poor alike. And, as we have seen, property qualifications for the franchise were systematically reduced or abolished in the Jacksonian period.

But ambition was mainly for white males. Most Americans of the Jacksonian period would have agreed that it was not appropriate for women, blacks, or Native Americans. All these groups seemed to be excluded from the competitive pursuit of wealth by their very biology and their natural inclinations. Women were "naturally" domestic. Blacks were "naturally" lazy. Indians were "naturally" savage. So it seemed only natural to take from these groups their already limited voting rights at the same time that these rights were being extended to most white men. Formerly, citizenship had been circumscribed by categories of economic status; now it was coming to be circumscribed by categories of gender and race.

In the quarter-century between 1812 and 1837, America developed a political culture that reinforced both the freedom and the limitations of the economic marketplace. The Cherokees' Trail of Tears was a single link, but a crucial one, in a chain of events that connected the expansion of Southern slavery, the growth of Northern commerce and industry, and the emergence of national democracy. Taken together, these developments shaped the generation of American experience dominated by the looming figure of Andrew Jackson—the Jacksonian Era.

Suggestions for Further Reading

THE TRAIL OF TEARS

William G. McLoughlin's splendid *Cherokees and Missionaries, 1789–1839* (1984) is easily the best analysis of Cherokee history and culture in this period. The story of the removal of the southeastern tribes still awaits the book it deserves. One of the best accounts, Thurman Wilkins, *Cherokee Tragedy* (1970), tells the story from the perspective of the Ridge family. Also useful is Dale Van Every, *Disinherited: The Lost Birthright of the American Indian* (1966). Grace Woodward, *The Cherokees* (1966), is a more general history of the tribe. R. S. Cotterill, *The Southern Indians* (1954), describes the world of the Cherokees and the other four "civilized" tribes before their removal. A good account of United States government actions toward all the Native Americans in the West is Ronald N. Satz, *American Indian Policy in the Jacksonian Era* (1975). Mary Young, *Redskins, Ruffleshirts, and Rednecks: Indian Allotments in Alabama and Mississippi* (1961), analyzes the distribution to white "pioneers" of lands that had once belonged to Native Americans.

THE ECONOMY

A good overview of the emergence of a market economy can be found in W. Elliot Brownlee, *Dynamics of Ascent* (1974). The transformation of agriculture in all parts of the nation is described by Paul W. Gates, *The Farmers' Age: Agriculture, 1815–1860* (1960). Caroline F. Ware, *Early New England Cotton Manufacturing* (1934), remains the best account. George R. Taylor, *The Transportation Revolution, 1815–1860* (1951) is already a classic. The construction and operation of the Erie Canal is the subject of Ronald E. Shaw, *Erie Water West* (1966). An extremely valuable analysis of the railroad and canal system is Christopher T. Baer, *Canals and Railroads of the Middle Atlantic States, 1800–1860* (1981). Paul Johnson, *A Shopkeeper's Millenium* (1978), examines some social and institutional consequences of the development of the canal system and the growth of commerce. J. Van Fenstermaker, *The Development of American Commercial Banking, 1782–1837*, traces part of the complex history of banking practices.

THE AGE OF JACKSON

Leonard L. Richards, *The Advent of American Democracy, 1815–1848* (1977), is a fine, brief introduction to the politics of the period. Murray N. Rothbard, *The Panic of 1819* (1962), is the most complete account. Harry Ammon, *James Monroe: The Quest for National Identity* (1971), and Mary W. M. Hargreaves, *The Presidency of John Quincy Adams* (1975), cover those two presidential administrations. Leonard L. Richards, *The Life and Times of Congressman John Quincy Adams* (1986), is an engaging account of Adams's long service in Congress after his presidency. A good, brief life of Jackson is James C. Curtis, *Andrew Jackson and the Search for Vindication* (1976). The major biography of Jackson, however, is the monumental sequence of books by Robert V. Remini: *Andrew Jackson and the Course of American Empire, 1767–1821* (1977), *Andrew Jackson and the Course of American Freedom, 1822–1832* (1981), and *Andrew Jackson and the Course of American Democracy, 1833–1845* (1984). Marvin Meyers, *The Jacksonian Persuasion* (1958), remains valuable. William W. Freehling, *Prelude to Civil War* (1966), is a very good account of the nullification controversy. Robert V. Remini, *Andrew Jackson and the Bank War* (1967), is the best introduction to that episode. Peter Temin, *The Jacksonian Economy* (1967), argues that the business cycle was beyond the control of federal policies advocated by either Jackson or his opponents. Changes in voting practices are well treated in Chilton Williamson, *American Suffrage, from Property to Democracy, 1760–1860* (1960).

CHAPTER 8
THE AGE OF PARTY

THE EPISODE: *The history of American politics has been punctuated by crucial elections that marked turning points. The election of 1800 that brought Thomas Jefferson and the Republicans to power, and the election of 1828 that began what historians call the Age of Jackson, are two examples of such turning-point campaigns. Another example was the election of 1840—but for reasons quite different from those that made the outcomes of the campaigns of 1800 and 1828 memorable. In conventional terms, neither candidate in 1840 was a great political leader. Martin Van Buren, the Democrat, and William Henry Harrison, who ran as a Whig, had no new ideas or programs. As politicians go, they were quite run-of-the-mill. Indeed, the winner of the election would live to serve for only one month as president.*

But the election was an important event, nonetheless, and for reasons that had little to do with either candidate. It was the first presidential election in which the American two-party system was fully and energetically set into motion. The riotous exercise that became known as the Log Cabin Campaign was the first in which both contending parties publicly agreed that the normal situation in a democratic election was: (1) to have two highly organized parties, (2) run by professionals, (3) competing for votes among masses of men, (4) using every possible means of persuasion. This election, in other words, set the standards that would govern national politics in the United States for over the next 150 years.

THE HISTORICAL SETTING: *The significance of the election of 1840 is that it finally laid to rest one of the great failed hopes of the authors of the Constitution. The framers had deplored the concept of political parties and had tried to create a Constitution that would prevent their emergence in national politics. There were party struggles in the 1790s, which this chapter also reviews, but both parties—Federalist and Republican—publicly agreed that having two political parties was a bad thing; the purpose of each was to destroy the other, a purpose the Republicans achieved by 1820. Then, in the 1820s and 1830s two new parties, Democratic and Whig, were shaped. But this time the parties' leaders worked their way to a novel conception of party. Political parties, they decided, were a sign of health in a democracy. This principle generated a new political logic. It justified new kinds of practices by new kinds of politicians. It brought out voters in unprecedented numbers.*

This is the second of two chapters that deal with the politics of the period. Some material discussed here will be somewhat familiar. Our purpose is to look at some of the same facts from a different angle, finding another kind of meaning and significance. What historians think of the "importance" of an event depends not only on the nature of the event but on the kinds of questions they ask about it.

1840: THE LOG CABIN CAMPAIGN

Everyone knew something strange was going on in American politics. All over the country, people found themselves swept up in a new and different kind of presidential campaign. The Whig party's most popular campaign song best captured what was happening:

> What has caused the great commotion, motion, motion, our country through?
> It is the ball a-rolling on.
> For Tippecanoe and Tyler too—Tippecanoe and Tyler too,
> And with them we'll beat little Van, Van, Van.
> Van is a used-up man,
> And with them we'll beat little Van.

When it was all over, no one seemed very clear about what the commotion added up to. But Democrats and Whigs alike agreed that "there never was anything like it." Former president and Whig statesman John Quincy Adams thought the election betokened some deep and mysterious revolution in "the manners and morals" of the American people. The losing candidate, Martin Van Buren, thought the election had been a political "debaucheries" in "which reason and justice" had taken flight. But however anyone looked at it, no matter how strange and bewildering it might appear, one thing seemed clear: The campaign of 1840 had created a new political culture. With it a new kind of mass politics, a politics Americans might embrace or condemn as a new style of democracy, had moved to the center of public life.

At the center of the campaign was an unlikely figure, a sixty-eight-year-old retired general and gentleman farmer, William Henry Harrison, the Tippecanoe in the Whig campaign song. Historical myth has it that Harrison was an obscure figure with no known political views. According to the myth, a bunch of wily Whig politicians turned him into a presidential candidate and sold him to a gullible public as a hero cast in its own image. There is some (but not much) basis for this myth. It is true that in 1835, when Harrison's name was first put forth as a presidential candidate, he had fallen into relative obscurity. But in fact, he was one of the Ohio Valley's most respected and best-known citizens and had enjoyed a long and successful public life.

He was the son of a Virginia gentleman who had been one of the signers of the Declaration of Independence. Harrison had first come to the Ohio country in 1792, when he was only nineteen, to take command of the garrison at Fort Washington that protected Cincinnati. Like many younger sons of well-to-do Virginian planters, he decided to settle in the western territory. He married the daughter of a local official, bought a farm, and entered public life.

There was a lot of room at the top in the West, and Harrison made his way there rapidly. In 1800 President John Adams named him first governor of the Indiana Territory, a post he held for twelve years. He spent one term in the House of Representatives, and in 1827 was elected to the Senate. He left the Senate in 1829 to become minister to Colombia. But (as with Andrew Jackson) it was as an Indian fighter and as a victorious general against the British in the War of 1812 that Harrison became a national figure and a hero of the West. He led the troops that defeated the Prophet at the battle of Tippecanoe in 1811.

In 1835 Harrison had been retired from active public life for nearly five years. His farm at North Bend on the Ohio River proving insufficient to support "his numerous family," his friends secured him the clerkship of the Cincinnati Court of Common Pleas as a kind of pension to support him in retirement. It was, Harrison wrote a friend, "a humble office indeed but still honorable and lucrative." He was only fifty-eight when he retired but seemed content with his standing as a respected elder statesman from the early days of the Republic, presiding at Fourth of July and other patriotic celebrations.

Ironically, it was *Democratic* party maneuverings that first brought Harrison back into the public eye. Democrats were worried about holding onto the White House when Andrew Jackson stepped aside after the customary two terms in office. Some of them began to promote Colonel Richard Johnson, a veteran of the War of 1812 and now a senator from Kentucky, as the successor to Jackson. Johnson's backers did not think he had much chance of gaining the nomination (and some of them did not actually want him to be president). But building Johnson up as a candidate would make him a good running mate for Martin Van Buren, an unheroic easterner, who as Jackson's designated heir was almost certain to be the presidential candidate. As another westerner with military credentials, Johnson might well help the Democrats hold the West.

But the ploy had one unforeseen consequence. It helped turn Harrison into a serious candidate for the Whig nomination. Puffing up Johnson involved rewriting western military history at Harrison's expense. Johnson's backers prepared campaign materials giving Colonel Johnson equal if not the major credit for General Harrison's victory in the Battle of the Thames. They also claimed that Johnson rather than some anonymous soldier had killed Tecumseh. Harrison's friends rushed into print with refutations of these claims. And when Harrison was invited to celebrate what was dubbed "the victory by the American forces under Gen. Harrison and Col. Johnson," he used the opportunity to answer the Democrats' "misrepresentations and slanders." He declined the invitation with a long letter setting the record straight and exposing the political motives behind the Johnson boomlet.

But Harrison also shrewdly sent a copy of his letter to Hezakiah Niles, editor of the *Niles Weekly Register*, one of the most influential and widely distributed

A Van Buren brooch. Political parties in the nineteenth century, like their modern counterparts, used all of the "media" available to them. Instead of television "spots," they put out articles like this mass-produced brooch showing a gentlemanly Martin Van Buren, the Democratic party candidate for president in 1836. The artist has transformed Van Buren's baldness (which might have damaged his media "image") into an asset by using it to emphasize an impossibly high forehead—a suggestion of statesmanlike wisdom. (The American Museum of Political Life, University of Hartford, photo by Sally Anderson-Bruce)

Whig newspapers. Niles promptly printed the letter along with an editorial praising Harrison. Almost immediately a Pennsylvania newspaper extolled "Old Buckeye" as a match for "Old Hickory." And some western Whigs began "circulating political knowledge favorable to the election of the people's candidate for presidency—William Henry Harrison." Quickly, Harrison's candidacy began to take hold.

It did so largely because of the confused state of the opposition to the continuation of Democratic rule. After nearly eight years in office, the Jacksonians had accumulated a lot of opponents. Even though many of these opponents had taken to calling themselves Whigs, as revolutionary leaders had called themselves sixty years before, they did not yet constitute a rival political party. In reality, the opposition was an incoherent mix of organizations and candidates. It had few views in common and no obvious candidate around whom to unite to defeat Van Buren. None of the most prominent opponents—Senators Henry Clay of Kentucky, Daniel Webster of Massachusetts, and John Calhoun of South Carolina—could provide a rallying point for a Whig victory. They all wanted to be president and were as much rivals of each other as they were of Van Buren. And besides, each was too controversial, had too many opponents of his own, and was too regional in appeal to muster the national support needed to wrest the presidency from the Democrats.

For these reasons, Whig politicians began to turn to the hero of Tippecanoe and the Battle of the Thames as the champion who might lead them to victory. They copied the "Hickory Clubs" that had first promoted Andrew Jackson as a presidential candidate, organizing "Tippecanoe Clubs" that conducted lavish celebrations of each of Harrison's military exploits. And they staged popular conventions of supposedly ordinary citizens who would proclaim Harrison their nominee for president. But Harrison was not simply a tool in the hands of politicians. He was an active candidate and a proud man who thought himself just as well suited for the presidency as Andrew

Jackson. He sent out numerous letters judiciously expounding his views on the "true nature of republican government" and embarked on carefully arranged tours of statesmanlike public and ceremonial appearances.

As Harrison took hold as "the people's candidate," Whigs in a number of states turned to him as an essential part of the closest thing to a national strategy that they could muster. The Whigs had no way to select a single candidate. They had initially condemned the Democrats' use of a national nominating convention as an illegitimate usurpation and centralization of power, leaving each state free to nominate its own candidate. Now all they could hope to do was divide and conquer. Harrison would run well in the North and West. Hugh Lawson White of Tennessee, an anti–Van Buren, renegade Democrat might carry some Southern states. Daniel Webster could expect to hold onto a few New England states. If all this happened, maybe Van Buren could be deprived of a majority of the electoral vote. That would throw the election into the House of Representatives, where it might be possible to defeat Van Buren.

The strategy failed. Van Buren won only slightly more than half the popular vote, but he won the electoral vote by a margin of 170 to 124. He actually carried more of New England (four states) than Jackson had in 1832. He won New York and Pennsylvania. And he held onto enough Democratic votes in the South and West to blunt the Whig challenge in the regions that had given Jackson his greatest support. Still, General William Henry Harrison had done very well. He won 73 electoral votes, carrying states in every region except the South. He was a candidate to be reckoned with.

Defeat in 1836 taught the Whigs an important lesson. National organization and unity had elected Van Buren. Without comparable organization and unity, the Whigs would not dislodge the Democrats from national office. The Whigs proved to be quick learners. At a convention held on the Fourth of July 1837, the Whigs of Ohio adopted resolutions calling for a national convention that would enable them to concentrate their energies on a single candidate in the election of 1840. More to the point, even though the convention declared its clear preference for Harrison, it pledged support for any man the Whigs nominated at a national convention. This commitment to unity became even stronger as an economic panic and depression made Van Buren ever more vulnerable. If the opposition could only agree on a candidate, victory would be theirs. In May 1838 the opposition in Congress issued a call for a national convention to be held in Baltimore, Maryland, in December 1839. The group asked Whigs in the various states to resist the temptation to hold state nominating conventions and to pledge to support the nominee of the national convention.

But who should that be? Henry Clay of Kentucky fully expected to be the choice. He was the best known of the opposition leaders. He had worked hard to build a broad base of national support. He seemed the best bet to undercut Democratic strength in the South. Clay adopted a statesmanlike stance of aloof detachment from active campaigning—all the while working tirelessly to make sure that the prize he so coveted would not elude his grasp. But, shrewd as he was, Clay misjudged the determination of his political enemies and underestimated Harrison, who was now a very well known public figure, especially popular in the North and West. And Harrison had few political liabilities. In his 1836 campaign he had carefully avoided taking controversial stands. Instead, he had presented himself to the voters as a statesman

A shawl for Clay. Women could not vote for presidential candidates. But they could talk. And if they wore a brooch or a shawl with a candidate's name and picture on it, they were helping to advertise a party's cause. Henry Clay's supporters manufactured this shawl to try to win votes. It shows an earnest man close to nature, framed by a victor's wreath and a sunburst, and bordered with twining vines and flowers. (The American Museum of Political Life, University of Hartford, photo by Sally Anderson-Bruce)

who had always been fervent in support of "the rights of the people, in the councils of the nation, and in the field, their faithful and devoted soldier."

Harrison's political task was a simple one. All he had to do was protect his standing as a statesman above petty politics and keep his name before the public. His friends sponsored popular meetings that declared their preference for him. Men of affairs from across the country made well-publicized visits to his North Bend farm. And Harrison himself made a few timely and well-publicized speaking tours. It was a strategy calculated to strengthen Harrison's best political card—the idea that he could be elected, and that, deserving as Clay might be, Clay could not.

It proved to be the high card. Thurlow Weed, a young political wizard from New York who was unalterably opposed to Clay, used it to undercut Clay in New York. He arranged for local leaders from across the state to circulate letters declaring

Clay unelectable and extolling Winfield Scott—recently in the news as a hero in a border skirmish with Canada—as someone who might serve as a "new general" around whom the Whigs could rally.

Still, as the delegates gathered in Harrisburg, Pennsylvania, on December 4, 1839, for the Whigs' first national convention, Clay remained confident of victory. He had more support among the individual delegates than either the old or the new general. But the Harrison and Scott forces pushed through a "unit rule" that gave a state's whole vote to anyone receiving a simple majority of the state's delegation. This worked against Clay, since in his states he had large majorities, while Harrison and Scott had only narrow majorities in the states where they were strong. Thus even though Clay led at the end of the first tally, with 103 votes to 91 for Harrison and 57 for Scott, he was stopped short of the majority he needed.

Two adroit maneuvers finally threw the nomination to Harrison. Weed convinced a number of delegates that Clay's greatest strength lay in states the Whigs probably could not win in the general election, while Harrison and Scott were strongest in states like Ohio, Massachusetts, Pennsylvania, and New York, states the Whigs *had* to carry in order to win. Then Thaddeus Stevens of Pennsylvania, a firm Harrison supporter, "accidentally" dropped in front of some Southern delegates a letter Scott had written to curry favor with New York abolitionists. This caused Scott's candidacy to collapse, and the convention closed ranks behind Old Tippecanoe. Henry Clay went into a drunken rage when he learned of his defeat, shouting that he was "always run by my friends when sure to be defeated, and now betrayed . . . when I, or anyone, would be sure of an election." But even Clay submerged his bitterness in the greater interest of Whig victory. He was somewhat placated by Harrison's vow to step aside after a single term and the tacit promise that, next time around, the nomination would indeed belong to Clay.

The Whigs emerged from their first national convention full of confidence. They had finally united behind a single presidential candidate. And they had moved to offset Harrison's major electoral weakness, the South. Harrison had strong support in New England, the Middle Atlantic, and the West. But Van Buren was also strong in New York and Pennsylvania. To be sure of victory, the Whigs had to make enough of an inroad among Southern voters to enable them to carry a few Southern states. Southerners were uneasy about how "sound" Harrison really was on the slavery issue, so the Whigs selected as their vice-presidential candidate John Tyler, a fifty-year-old former governor of Virginia who had served as senator from that state from 1827 to 1836. It was a shrewd move. Tyler would be unlikely to hurt Harrison in the North and West. He was relatively uncontroversial and had been out of national office for four years. Besides, the vice presidency was an office without any power to worry about. But Tyler could be expected to attract to the Whig ticket Southern Democratic voters who did not like Van Buren. In fact, Tyler was a states' rights advocate who had begun his political life as a Jeffersonian Democrat, and he had only finally broken with the Democrats in 1836.

The signs seemed to point to a Whig victory. All they needed was a winning strategy. There seemed no lack of situations the Whigs might turn into political capital.

For nearly eight years a whole range of issues had agitated American politics: tariffs, banks, "hard" and "soft" money, expansion, abolition, internal improvements. One strategy might be to carve a winning program out of at least some of these issues.

But this time the Whigs resolutely rejected such a strategy. Instead, they waged the campaign almost as if these specific issues did not exist. (Partly, of course, they did not have to be very specific in invoking "hard times" as an issue.) They decided Harrison should avoid taking any position on any controversial issue, and initially kept him from making any public comments at all. His campaign managers handled all questions about where he stood. They insisted that since Harrison was a well-established national figure, his position on issues of the day was already known and referred inquirers to his previous statements (knowing full well, of course, that even in those statements Harrison had not taken any clear-cut stands). And the committee only sent him into public to counter the Democrats' ridicule of Harrison as General Mum and to undercut the charge that Harrison was being kept out of the public view because he had become feeble and senile. (Harrison was, at sixty-eight, the oldest man to be elected president until 1980, when Ronald Reagan was elected at age sixty-nine.)

In the end, the Whig presidential campaign deliberately *suppressed* the positions that most of the politicians who now called themselves Whigs and who had united behind Harrison had taken on the various issues of the day. By selecting Harrison, a public figure who was not identified with a firm position on any measures, and then having him keep mum about all controversial issues, the Whigs directed attention away from all the Whig views that the Democrats had so successfully attacked in previous elections. But the strategy had an even more important effect. It kept the focus of the campaign just where the Whigs wanted it—on the "character" of Harrison as an American hero.

The Whig strategy was well designed for a complex political situation. In the first place, there was the problem of the size, diversity, and structure of the American political universe. The presidential electorate was spread out over almost half a continent, and in states and regions with very different and often conflicting interests and concerns. This problem was compounded by the peculiar features of the American electoral system. Even though the presidency was itself a national office (it and the vice presidency are the only national, elective offices in the American system), there was not a single, national electorate. This meant that even though the election for president was a national contest, it really consisted of a set of twenty-five separate state elections. To win the presidency, a candidate had to win enough of the separate state elections to capture a majority of votes in the electoral college. This was a double-edged problem. It required selecting a candidate and putting together a campaign that would not inflame the local jealousies of so many states as to make it impossible to win an electoral majority. But it also required figuring out a way to attract voters in the various states in spite of their different interests.

There were two ways to solve the problem: to focus on the party or to focus on the candidate. Van Buren's triumph in 1836 had been a triumph of party. What had originated in 1828 as a political organization held together by commitment to Andrew Jackson had by 1836 become the Democratic party, held together by loyalty to the party itself as an instrument for gaining national power and furthering the ideals and programs it professed.

The Whigs could not follow a party strategy for a very simple reason. Even though the Whigs had united around Harrison and adopted a common label, there was still no established body of voters that identified itself as Whig in the way that so many voters had come to think of themselves as loyal Democrats. The Whigs' only real option was to copy what the Democrats had originally done—find a "champion" whose character and exploits transcended local differences, a man who could attract the broad following that victory in the electoral college required.

The Whigs cloaked their champion in familiar heroic garb. As an Indian fighter and victorious general in the War of 1812, even in the style of his political nickname, Harrison was presented to the public as a Whig Jackson. After failing in various attempts to find a way that could offset Jackson's heroic appeal, the Whigs had turned to Harrison precisely because he seemed to be someone who could capture that appeal for the Whigs, once Jackson himself was no longer a candidate.

But Harrison was not simply a Jackson clone. The Whigs went back beyond Jackson to another general and president, George Washington, for the full heroic mold in which to cast their hero. They invoked the classical image that had first been used to turn Washington into the godlike Founding Father of the American Republic. They portrayed Harrison as another Cincinnatus, the noble Roman citizen who had taken up arms and office not out of a thirst for personal power and glory, but because his country was in danger. When the task was done, Cincinnatus had voluntarily surrendered the instruments of power and returned to farming and the quiet civilian life.

This portrait of Harrison placed him in a kind of heroic succession, next in a line of American heroes that extended back to the Revolution itself. But the portrait reached even more deeply into American political culture than that. Presenting Harrison to the public as a latter-day Cincinnatus turned the election into a familiar kind of political melodrama—a contest that pitted "virtue" and "liberty" against "corruption" and "tyranny." Casting Harrison as a Cincinnatus also involved casting Van Buren as a special kind of political villain.

The drama the Whigs presented to the voters went like this. Van Buren had gone into office as the pretended "friend of the people" and protector of their liberties. But power, as was its inherent tendency, had corrupted him. He had become a "usurper"—"King Mat." He had turned the government into an instrument of faction and a threat to the sacred liberties of the American people. This was the danger from which Harrison would deliver the American people, just as the first American Cincinnatus, Washington, had saved the country from the corruption and tyranny of King George. Like Cincinnatus and Washington, Harrison had put aside his plow, not because he coveted office and power but out of patriotism and love of liberty. And, again like Cincinnatus and Washington, Harrison would take power reluctantly. He even pledged to surrender it after just one term in office, once his task was complete. This script, of course, was wholly familiar to the American public. In fact, it was a version of the basic script that had shaped political rhetoric at least since the Revolution. And that was precisely the point. The Whigs were trying to lay claim to the nation's most cherished values, to establish their champion as the champion of American liberty.

The hero's home, two versions. The 1840 campaign engraving (top) shows William Henry Harrison at the plow—like the legendary Roman Cincinnatus, ready to be called to the service of the republic. Behind him are the other two essential symbols of his campaign, the cider barrel and the log cabin. Above is a drawing of his actual house at North Bend, Ohio. It exaggerated the grandeur of the house a little, but not nearly so much as the political drawing exaggerated his rustic simplicity. (Cincinnati Historical Society)

This was the "Old Tippecanoe" the Whigs presented to the American public as they began their campaign. But almost immediately they grafted a new and very different kind of symbol onto the campaign, the Log Cabin. Again, the Democrats were partly responsible. On December 11, 1839, a newspaper correspondent printed his own facetious answer to a Clay supporter's exasperated question about how to "get rid of Harrison." The reporter (himself a Democrat) printed this as his answer: "Give him a barrel of hard cider, and settle a pension of two thousand a year on him, and my word for it, he will sit the remainder of his days in his log cabin." Some Democratic editors, trying to exploit the idea that "Old Granny" Harrison was nothing more than a tool in the hand of cynical Whig "managers," reprinted the taunt.

This was the opening the Whigs had been waiting for. Again and again the Democrats had won election by presenting themselves as the party of plain and ordinary folk, of the common man, all the while condemning the Whigs as aristocrats and friends of wealth and privilege. Now the Whigs could turn the tables. In early January 1840, the *New York Daily Whig* replied to the supposed "insult" that had been leveled against the Whig champion. Only "pampered office-holders" who "sneer at the idea of making a poor man president" would consider "log-cabin candidate" a term with which to "reproach" General Harrison. Within a week, other Whig papers joined in. The editor of the Whig paper in Galena, Illinois, told his readers that "Gen. Harrison is sneered at by the Eastern office-holders' pimps, as the 'Log cabin candidate.'" But those who live in log cabins "have a way of taking care of themselves, when insulted, which has sometimes surprised folks."

On January 20, a Harrisburg, Pennsylvania, rally took the next step in the transformation of the Whig campaign. The Whig managers openly presented Harrison to the rally as "The Log-Cabin Candidate." They prepared a huge transparency of what was purportedly Old Tip's log cabin (his original "cabin" had long since been expanded into an impressive sixteen-room house) and placed it next to a barrel of cider and a woodpile. Borrowing from Davy Crockett, they pinned a coonskin cap on the wall.

Whigs all over the country followed suit, and from then on no Whig rally was complete unless it had a display of the log cabin symbols. By May the log cabin had become the official symbol of the campaign. Horace Greeley, chosen by Thurlow Weed to edit the major Whig campaign paper, named it the *Log Cabin*.

Recasting Harrison as a homespun farmer of simple tastes and manly virtues also meant recasting Van Buren as the point-by-point opposite. The Whigs ridiculed the president as a foppish, effeminate dandy, given to extravagant, aristocratic tastes. Davy Crockett in 1836 had already fashioned some potent material for Whig "slang-wangers" (orators whose specialty was slanderous, farfetched ridicule). Crockett had written a scurrilous and largely ghostwritten "biography" of Van Buren which the Whigs now hastily reprinted for service in the 1840 campaign. Crockett portrayed Van Buren as so "laced up in corsets, such as women in town wear, and, if possible, tighter than the best of them. . . . It would be difficult to say from his personal appearance, whether he was man or woman, but for his large red and gray whiskers."

But it was a Pennsylvania congressman, Charles Ogle, who put the finishing touches on the image. Van Buren had asked Congress for an appropriation to improve the White House. For three days in the House, Ogle painted a humorous but lurid

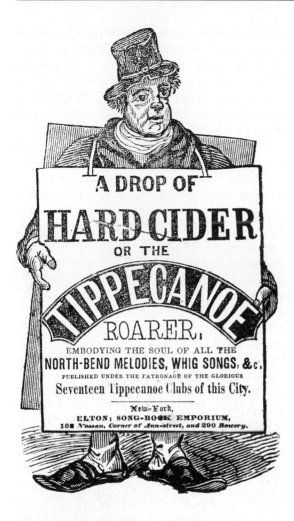

A DROP OF HARD CIDER OR THE TIPPECANOE ROARER,

EMBODYING THE SOUL OF ALL THE NORTH-BEND MELODIES, WHIG SONGS, &c.

PUBLISHED UNDER THE PATRONAGE OF THE GLORIOUS

Seventeen Tippecanoe Clubs of this City.

New-York,

ELTON; SONG-BOOK EMPORIUM,
10■ N'assau, Corner of Ann-street, and 290 Bowery.

The Tippecanoe roarer. This collection of Whig campaign songs was printed in New York's Bowery section. The man wearing the sandwich board is a sterotypical Irishman, and the songbook may be part of a Whig effort to make some inroads on the Democrats' increasingly strong hold on the votes of New York's immigrants. (Cincinnati Historical Society)

picture of Van Buren pandering to his dandified and luxurious tastes while his countrymen suffered under hard times. Ogle took his listeners on a long verbal tour of the "Regal Splendor of the Presidential Palace," a palace he said was already "as splendid as that of the Caesars, and as richly adorned as the proudest Asiatic mansion." He described lavish furnishings and adornments—"silk tassels, gallon, gimp [decorative braiding], and satin medallions." The landscaping, with its hills, was designed, Ogle insisted, "to resemble an Amazon's bosom, with a miniature knoll or hillock on its apex, to denote the n-pple." He was especially scornful of four large mirrors purchased for $2,400. What, he wondered out loud, "would frugal and honest Hoosiers think were they to behold a democratic peacock, in full court costume, strutting by the hour before golden-framed mirrors, nine feet high and four feet and a half wide." The Democrats (and a few Whigs who were offended by its affront to the dignity of the presidential office) condemned Ogle's wildly exaggerated portrait as an "omnibus of lies." But to no avail: The dandified Van Buren became a staple of Whig slogans and

songs. One observer later insisted that Harrison was "sung into the office" with dit-
ties like:

> We've tried your purse-proud lords
>   Who love in palaces to shine.
> But we'll have a ploughman
>   President of the Cincinnatus line.
>
> Let Van from his coolers of silver drink wine,
>   And lounge on his cushioned setee,
> Our man on a buckeye bench can recline,
>   Content with hard cider is he.

The campaign of the "ploughman of North Bend" against the "democratic pea-
cock" immediately took hold, generating "a great commotion" that took even the
Whigs by surprise. Each succeeding rally seemed to top the last—Democrats conceded
that in state after state they had never before "seen such a state of things." To John
Quincy Adams the campaign seemed to generate "a state of agitation . . . never before
witnessed" in the American Republic. A Democratic editor said that "every man,
woman, and child [seemed] to prefer politics to anything else."

The "great commotion" was a measure of how well the Whigs had learned their
political lessons from the Democrats. They whipped up the commotion by appropri-
ating all the techniques that other reform and political groups—especially the Democrats—had invented to appeal to and win the support of "the people." The Whigs
based their campaign on a series of lavish conventions, celebrations, and rallies. In
fact, they turned almost the whole election year into one long Whig rally. They staged
a rally of one sort or another at every possible opportunity—to commemorate Washington's birthday and simultaneously ratify Harrison as the people's candidate, to
mark the victories at Tippecanoe and the Thames, to nominate local Whig candidates,
and, finally, as conventions of "the people" to promote "Tippecanoe and Tyler Too."

A full-blown rally was usually held in a centrally located or principal town or
city and drew people from all the outlying towns, and often, across state boundaries.
Like fair days, these days were set aside as special. As a Whig editor put it, describing
a rally in St. Louis, "The city itself bore, in some respects, the remarkable character
of a Sabbath day. By the Whigs, and even among the Democrats, there was little work
done. The doors of all places of business were closed and nothing was thought of on
this carnival day" but politics and fun.

Planning began weeks in advance. There would be smaller conventions and
rallies in all the outlying communities to select numerous "delegates" to the big convention. As the day approached, the "delegates" were given a rousing send-off. They
then made their way to the convention city with the nineteenth-century version of
parade floats—wagons mounted with log cabins and canoes, with banners and "campaign balls" pasted with the latest slogans extolling Harrison and slurs lampooning
"Van, Van the used-up man."

Convention day really was a kind of political carnival. Cannon and bells
announced the dawn of the big day, calling forth the formal procession to the site
where the speechmaking and banqueting would take place. The procession often
numbered several thousand people and stretched out for a mile or two: a dozen or

A Whig rally. One of the main features of the 1840 campaign was the mass rally. This etching shows a Cincinnati rally held in October. For the occasion, the Whigs built an arch of triumph across the main street. In the background, over a store on the right side of Main Street, is a gigantic cider jug topped by a waving flag and pennant. (Cincinnati Historical Society)

more bands, ranks of dignitaries, veterans who had fought with Old Tip, citizens with banners, on horseback and in carriages, displays of Fort Miegs and other scenes of Harrison's heroism, innumerable canoes, several log cabins, wagons loaded with barrels of cider, other wagons carrying representatives of the various crafts—blacksmiths, for example, with forge and bellows and a banner declaring "We strike for our Country's Good"—and delegation after delegation with banners and the various symbols of the Log Cabin campaign.

No Whig procession was complete without paraders, dressed up in lavish and hilarious costumes, who lampooned Van Buren and the Democrats. And the spectators along the parade route were as much a part of the ritual as the marchers. They cheered and heckled and usually themselves fell into line at the end of the official parade, following the procession. Often, the line of march passed through floral arches and past balconies and embankments filled with "the fairest part of the population" wielding banners and liberty poles inscribed with slogans such as "Harrison Our Protector" and "Harrison: He saved us from the savage tomahawk; may he be the highest in office, and the first in the hearts of his countrymen." One marcher in a Boston rally reported balconies filled with women "with bright eyes and pounding bosoms, waving handkerchiefs, exhibiting flags and garlands, and casting bouquets of flowers upon us."

The procession ended at the "grounds," where a kind of multi-ring oratorical circus would be staged. At the center was the main platform, from which the most prominent speakers (often Whig giants like Henry Clay or Daniel Webster or even Harrison himself) addressed crowds that sometimes numbered in the tens of thousands. At the corners of the grounds were the smaller stands from which various orators simultaneously harangued the crowd. On one stand, local Whig candidates might take turns holding forth, while at another a local citizen (often a veteran from one of Harrison's victories) would extol the virtues and exploits of Old Tip. On still another platform there might be a rising young Whig politician like thirty-one-year-old Abraham Lincoln of Illinois, who had a reputation as an especially effective stump speaker.

One of the platforms on such occasions would feature one of the folk orators, who rarely used the classical political rhetoric of a Webster or Clay. They spoke in the words and accents of ordinary farmers and workingmen, delivering "straight hits from the shoulder." John W. Bear, the best known of these homespun orators, gave over 300 speeches in over a half dozen states. Bear, soon dubbed the "Buckeye Blacksmith," would mount the platform with blacksmith garb and tools. Claiming to have some "dirty work" to do, he would pick up the local Democratic newspaper with his tongs, ridicule it, drop it onto the platform, wipe his feet on it and then wash the "dirt" from his tongs. Once when charged by a heckler that he was not really a blacksmith, Bear quickly hammered out a horseshoe on his anvil. He held it up and, to the great glee of the audience and the chagrin of the heckler, shouted that he would "like to nail it on the jackass who just said I was not a blacksmith."

Such gigantic rallies and conventions were the most dramatic spectacles of the campaign. But they were not the whole of it. Smaller towns had scaled-down versions of them, and villages and hamlets of every size had log-cabin raisings. Almost everywhere the people were subjected to a steady, almost unrelenting stream of Whig oratory. But it was the Whig press that wove all the individual and scattered rallies, speeches, and cabin raisings into a single national commotion. Most newspapers of the day were avowedly political in their affiliations, and consciously partisan in the "news" they chose to print (they often simply ignored the statements of opposition officeholders) and how they printed it. But the Whigs in 1840 went one step beyond journalistic custom. They set up a series of new papers, like Horace Greeley's *Log Cabin*, that were exclusively campaign newspapers. Their sole function was to provide Whig editors with political stories from all across the country. Local Whig editors sent Greeley copies of their own papers, which were filled with lavish accounts of local Whig rallies and speeches. Greeley, in turn, reprinted much of it in the *Log Cabin*, which was itself sent back to the same local editors, who used it to tell their readers about what Whigs in other parts of the country were saying and doing.

The Whig press had found a way to spread word of new campaign techniques, new slogans and songs, and new put-downs of "Little Mat" to Whig organizers across the country. In addition, the Whig press deliberately and very effectively created a sense of unstoppable momentum, inflating figures far beyond plausibility and then circulating those numbers to Whig papers across the land. (The Whig press reported a crowd of 100,000 at a rally in September in Dayton, Ohio, a city of 6,000.) As the campaign progressed, this kind of momentum became the essential "news" story the

A Whig almanac. In this cartoon, Harrison is shown offering "true Hospitality" to well-dressed and well-behaved supporters in front of his Log Cabin. A sneaky Van Buren is trying to bore a hole in the barrel, foppishly telling Andrew Jackson, "I shall Endeavor to stop the supply." And old General Jackson, hiding behind the cabin's open door, is urging him on, saying "Do so, Matty, for by the Eternal it's cursed *Sour*." The viewer is being assured that Van Buren failed, for there are plenty more barrels where this one came from. (Boston Athenaeum)

Whig press told—each rally was reported as the largest that had ever been held in that particular place, and each succeeding rally was reported as exceeding all those that had come before. Thus the campaign press was the essential medium that created a national Whig campaign, the essential instrument by which the crowds at a Whig rally in Kankakee, Illinois, or Barre, Massachusetts, or Little Rock, Arkansas, came to feel they were participants in something far larger than a local event, that they were part of a great national commotion by which "the people" would elect the nation's president.

But the "great commotion" was not simply a triumph of technique. It was equally a matter of content and form. The Whig campaign as a whole integrated three quite distinct popular rituals. First, the various Whig rallies and commemorations fully appropriated symbols and forms that had long characterized ceremonies at presidential and gubernatorial inaugurations, at dedications of monuments marking great events in the nation's history, and on the Fourth of July—which by 1815 had emerged as the "political sabbath" of the Republic. It was already a well-established practice for different political groups to hold separate, competing Fourth of July celebrations, claiming that they were the true carriers of the nation's revolutionary heritage. But what the Whigs did in 1840 was construct the presidential campaign—with its constant evocation of Harrison as a latter-day Cincinnatus, the protector of the nation's liberties and hearths, and the true heir of the spirit of '76—as a yearlong Fourth of July, a continuing national ceremony that celebrated all the grand themes and sacred political values of the American Republic.

Second, the Whig campaign was a ritual of popular political participation that exemplified what seemed to be the full sovereignty of a democratic people. Here again, the Whigs adopted and dramatically extended devices invented by others. The Whigs had originally opposed the use of conventions to select candidates for public office. But in this election they called for "conventions" (rallies) at every possible opportunity. And they used their innumerable conventions to establish the idea that Harrison was in fact "the people's choice" (rather than a candidate selected by scheming, self-interested political bosses or undemocratic political caucuses). In addition, the Log Cabin campaign itself—culminating, of course, in the act of voting—was a ritual enactment of a new, far more democratic conception of the relationship between "the people" and their leaders.

Third, the campaign was also an elaborately staged contest. In fact, many of the forms and much of the language of the campaign were direct imports from the sports and competitions of the day. A common event at many rallies was an actual wrestling match between a Whig and a Democratic "champion." (For some reason, the Whig wrestler always seemed to win.) Many Whig songs and slogans (operating much like the cheers at modern-day athletic contests) incorporated the chants that crowds at log-rollings, plowing contests, horse and foot races, wrestling matches, and cockfights used to urge on the combatants:

> Mum is the word boys,
> Brag is the Game;
> Cooney[1] is the emblem of Old Tip's fame.
> Go it then for cooney—
> Cooney in a cage.
> Go it with a rush, boys
> Go it with a rage.

As Whig and Democratic orators, debaters, and slangwangers vied with each other for the support of the crowds that gathered around them, they were engaging in a form of intellectual sport. It borrowed from court days, when crowds would press

---

[1]*Cooney* is a reference to the raccoons that were the object of "baiting," a popular "sport" of the time.

into local courthouses to watch rival lawyers go at each other. The new sport also imitated popular tale-swappings, in which storytellers would try to outdo each other with ever taller tales. The politicians also incorporated the competitive exchange of "toasts" Americans often practiced at festivals and banquets. Victory, not "truth," was what the competing orators sought. And what the spectators cheered was the contest itself, the struggle of wit and skill between the combatants as they tried to best each other by ridicule, a more telling argument, a clever, unanswerable put-down, a more elaborate pun. They tried, in the language of the day, to "use up" their opponent.

The partisan political press reported these campaign contests as though they were wrestling matches or horse races. In reporting on the debates between Abe Lincoln, the Whigs' champion, and John McClernand, the Democratic champion, a Democratic editor in Springfield, Illinois, insisted that McClernand was routinely "using up A. Lincoln." A Whig editor immediately denounced this as "too simple a lie to tell. Abraham Lincoln used up by John A. McClernard, Bah." And another Whig editor, reporting on some debates between Lincoln and yet another Democratic opponent, asserted: "Mr Lincoln is going it with [such] a perfect rush that all the Democratic nags have come off the field crippled or broken down."

Try as they might, the Democrats were never able to offset the Whig momentum. From the beginning to end, Whig rallies dwarfed Democratic efforts. At the Fourth of July celebrations in Barre, Massachusetts, for example, the Democratic champion, George Bancroft, drew a crowd of 600, whereas more than 5,000 turned out to hear Daniel Webster address the Whig celebration. The Democrats' attempts to put down Harrison as Old Granny or General Mum never took hold. And whenever the Democrats tried to counter Whig ridicule of Van Buren, the Whigs simply "used him up" with another song or slogan.

In the end, the Whig campaign song proved prophetic. The Whigs had "caused a great commotion" that swept Van Buren and the Democrats out of office. The commotion drew a million more people to the polls than had voted in the 1836 election. This was more than 80 percent of the eligible voters (58 percent had voted in the 1836 election). Van Buren in defeat actually got 400,000 more votes than he did in his victory four years earlier. But nearly two-thirds of these million new voters cast their ballots for Old Tip, carrying him to a decisive victory—234 electoral votes to Van Buren's 60. When all the votes were counted, Harrison and the Whigs had won nineteen of the twenty-six states. They carried the crucial Middle Atlantic states of New York and Pennsylvania and swept the Ohio Valley. They even won most of the South.

An embittered Van Buren never became reconciled to what had happened to him. To the end of his life, he remained convinced that the election of 1840 had been some terrible perversion of the democratic politics he himself had done so much to create. But it was the editor of the *Democratic Review* who best summed it up when he sadly lamented, "We have taught them how to conquer us."

DEMOCRACY AND A NEW POLITICS

The election of 1840 gave Americans ample proof that a new kind of political system had emerged. But they could understand their new political system only in comparison with what it had replaced. This required them to think backward in time, to the age of Washington and Jefferson, Madison and Monroe. The same need to understand what had happened also requires us to take a quick look backward—to the making of the Constitution of 1787 and the party struggles between the Federalists and Republicans in the 1790s, the Jeffersonian "Revolution of 1800," the subsequent decline of the Federalist party, and the Federalists' final collapse as a force in national politics after the War of 1812.

These events have been discussed in earlier chapters. But this quick backward look is necessary for a full understanding of the degree to which the new party system of the 1830s and 1840s was really a revolutionary departure from the aims of the Founding Fathers. The deep change that took place in American political life in the years that led to the Log Cabin campaign of 1840 was quiet and nonviolent, but it put the practice of national politics on a footing that the authors of the Constitution would have found shocking, deplorable, and truly revolutionary.

Looking Backward

The Constitution was written by men who hoped to place the national government above the turbulent struggles of political factions and parties. And to the Founding Fathers, this meant keeping elected federal officials (the president and members of Congress) from being chosen by political parties. The clanking, complicated machinery of the electoral college had one main purpose: to prevent political parties from conducting campaigns for the presidency. The framers of the Constitution also supposed that members of the electoral college would be chosen not by voters but by state legislatures. This too, they hoped, would prevent the presidency from becoming a great political plum that might cause politicians to organize factions in support of candidates. The Constitution further provided that senators would be chosen by state legislatures, not the voters, which meant that no federal election involved voters in an area larger than a single congressional district. This, in turn, might keep down what Washington called "the baneful influence of party spirit."

When Thomas Jefferson and James Madison set out to found an opposition party in the 1790s, they seemed on the surface to be rejecting this antiparty attitude. But their Republican party was what might be called an "antiparty party." So was the Federalist party of John Adams and Alexander Hamilton. Republican and Federalist leaders both assumed that only their own party was legitimate, and that the other party was a danger to the health of the Republic. Both Republicans and Federalists had looked forward to the day when their party would triumph, and the other party would be driven out, forever. None of the principal leaders of the political struggles of the period between 1796 and 1820 believed in a two-party system. After his victory in what he called "the Revolution of 1800," Jefferson said, "We are all Federalists, we are all Republicans." What he meant was not that both parties had a useful role to play in American government, but that there was no *need* for political parties. His purpose, and the purpose of his supporters, was a one-party government.

It took them a while, but the Republicans achieved their goal. The Federalist opposition gradually became more and more limited to New England and after the War of 1812, it disappeared. In the election of 1820 the Federalists did not even field a candidate for president. James Monroe was elected by an electoral college count of 231 to 1. The men who cast that electoral vote had been chosen not in a roughhouse party campaign but in a calm and decorous way, and they were chosen not by the voters but by the state legislatures. Little wonder that Monroe could boast that the nation had entered an "Era of Good Feeling." Everything seemed to be working just as the Founding Fathers had planned.

THE COLLAPSE OF THE REPUBLICAN CONSENSUS
James Monroe was the last American president who had participated in the American Revolution—and he was the last to wear one of the symbols of the eighteenth-century gentleman, a wig. The Founding Fathers had made

another grand assumption about politics, closely related to their distaste for political parties. They believed—or insisted that they believed—that to seek office actively was beneath the dignity of a gentleman. A true gentleman was, in their eyes, a man who preferred the quiet retirements of private life. They understood, of course, that this same gentleman had a civic "duty" to serve his country, especially if some foreign or domestic peril was threatening it. In such a case, a gentleman might have to bow to the pleas of his friends and accept public office. In truth, the political leaders of the revolutionary generation really had wanted to be senators and governors and presidents. But their practice was to behave as though they were reluctantly answering the call of duty and saving the nation from the evil schemes of the other party (who, naturally, must not be gentlemen seeking the public good, but corrupt schemers seeking their own private advantage).

The one-party consensus that led to Monroe's winning every state in 1820 might have been comforting to the revolutionary old guard. But four years later it was a shambles. This breakdown in one-party national government was the result not of a new opposition party but of a spirit of personal ambition. Men who had grown up after the Revolution, men who did not wear wigs, proved all too ready to seek office, and to do it very actively. In its complete control over the federal government, the Republican party had no disciplinary control over its own leaders—especially not of men with a strong personal following in a particular state or region. As the election of 1824 approached, factions began to form to support individual candidates: John C. Calhoun of South Carolina, William H. Crawford of Georgia, Henry Clay of Kentucky. John Quincy Adams of Massachusetts thought it would be appropriate if he advanced from secretary of state to president, just as Madison and Monroe had done. The hero of New Orleans, Andrew Jackson, was also convinced that he was just the man for the job. Each of them appealed to his political "friends," who then appealed to their friends. And before anyone knew it, there was a real campaign on.

The party eagle. To help justify a two-party system, politicians of the 1830s and 1840s often recalled the older contests between Republicans and Federalists. And they used many of the same symbols that had gained currency during the period of the first party system. This 1801 Jefferson victory flag used the eagle with spread wings holding a banner, an image that had great currency forty years later. But by the 1830s, such a flag would certainly have included the name of the political party. (The banner in the eagle's mouth proclaims "Jefferson President of the United States of America." The banner coming from the eagle's rear says "John Adams no more.") (The Smithsonian Institution)

It was not a campaign of party against party but a bitter and nasty contest of factions loyal to individual men. There were few significant differences, other than those of personality, among the candidates. They all used the same party label, with slight variations. And faction was only as strong as the determination of a candidate's supporters to elect him. Despite the serious stroke that Crawford suffered during the campaign, his "friends" kept working for his election. They were driven partly by loyalty to a party or a sectional program, but mainly by loyalty to their man. On the other hand, the factions were so ill-defined that politicians could move gracefully

Adams medal. This medal, with a frame of pewter, showed John Quincy Adams as a dignified, thoughtful, even scholarly man, distinctively a gentleman although engaged in politics. He was the first American president to use a middle name; William Henry Harrison was the second. As the son of John Adams, he was also a member of the first father-and-son pair of presidents. William Henry Harrison was a member of the second: His son Benjamin would serve briefly as president after the Civil War and, like his father, die in office. (The American Museum of Political Life, University of Hartford. Photo by Sally Anderson-Bruce)

from one to another, or even straddle. Calhoun decided to drop out, hoping to run another day. He proposed himself as a candidate for vice president, and campaigned to serve with *either* Adams or Jackson, if either of them won. A strong and workable conception of political party would have prevented both the Crawford faction's stubborn insistence on their man and Calhoun's straddle between Jackson and Adams. What had looked in 1820 like one-party politics had suddenly become no-party politics at the national level.

The Founding Fathers would not have been pleased. The absence of well-defined parties in national politics was a sign not of political calm. Instead, it was a signal that a new generation of ambitious political leaders had come forward, ready to mount vigorous campaigns for office. The campaigns were turbulent because a striking new element was added to the presidential election. In 1824, for the first time, the candidates

were appealing to the voters directly. Eighteen of the twenty-four states had decided that presidential electors should be chosen by "the people" instead of the state legislatures. For the first time there was a "popular vote" for president. (The new idea of a popular vote for president, like the idea of political parties, had no basis in the Constitution; most of the men who wrote it would have deplored both concepts.) The outcome of the combination of a new method of voting and a multiplicity of candidates was a confusing nightmare unique in the electoral history of the United States. No candidate won a majority of the electoral votes. The decision in the House of Representatives to choose Adams gave the nation its first "minority" president, for Adams had been chosen by less than a third of the voters. (Jackson had won 42 percent of the popular vote, but his support was heavily concentrated in the South, where he won several states by very large margins.)

Between the confused election of 1824 and the Log Cabin campaign of 1840, a new party system came into being. Historians call it the second party system. National politics passed, in less than a generation, from the one-party consensus of Monroe's administration, through the fragmentation of the Republican party in the 1820s, to the definition of a new two-party system in the 1830s. By 1840, Americans took it for granted that there were two national parties, the Democratic and the Whig, and that each of them would unite behind a single candidate for the presidency. But the change did much more than replace an old party system, the Federalist vs. Republican, with a new Democratic vs. Whig system. The new generation of leaders that came to dominate American politics was more ambitious than that. They set out to redefine the very meaning of the *idea* of political parties. In the process, they drastically redefined the nature and meaning of democracy in America.

A New Kind of Politician

One of the results of the American Revolution had been a modest but real democratization of politics. Before the Revolution, most men who held political office at all levels had had wealth, education, social standing, and family connections. After independence, there were many more men in local and state government who had come from what would have been called "middling" origins and had a middling status: tavernkeepers, artisans, farmers, small merchants, and petty lawyers. But such men tended to advance no further than sheriff or alderman or state legislator. The men who claimed the higher offices in the state and national governments continued to be those with wealth, education, and extensive connections. All the early presidents, from Washington through John Quincy Adams, had the clear markings of a social and economic elite.

In the decades after the War of 1812, this began to change. Andrew Jackson was the first "self-made man" to become president. His successor, Martin Van Buren, was the second. (He was the son of a tavernkeeper in the little town of Kinderhook, New York.) In the Log Cabin campaign of 1840, Harrison became the first president to *pretend* to be a self-made man. The carefully cultivated myth that he had been born in a log cabin was proof that humble origins had become not only acceptable but almost essential to political success.

It was not just presidents who were—or sometimes just pretended they were—self-made men. Henry Clay, whose supporters called him "Harry of the West," went to Kentucky in 1798, at the age of twenty-one. He started more or less from scratch, though he did have good legal training. He made an advantageous marriage, and when only twenty-nine, he was appointed to fill a vacancy in the U.S. Senate caused by a death. Then, in 1810, he was elected to the House of Representatives and was immediately chosen Speaker of the House, though he was only thirty-four and had never been a congressman. Daniel Webster, who eventually would become a towering Whig presence in the Senate, was the son of a modest New Hampshire farming family. Abraham Lincoln, the active young Whig from Illinois who spoke to so many rallies in the campaign of 1840, was from a very poor family. In the end, he would become the legendary model of a politician who had educated himself, reading books by firelight in a rude cabin after a hard day splitting logs for fence rails.

The popular idea of the self-made man had much more reality in political life than in the spheres of commerce, manufacturing, and finance. Most of the wealthy bankers, businessmen, and entrepreneurs of the nineteenth century were born into comfortable or rich families. This has caused historians to be puzzled over how the myth of the self-made man came to be so widely believed. An important part of the answer to the puzzle lies in the new political styles and practices that took shape in the period after 1820. In the new political parties, there really was an abundance of prominent men whose social origins were very modest. The politicians of the day liked to believe that their rise from poverty or obscurity was the realization of a uniquely American dream; and they worked hard to get their supporters to believe it, too. To many people, the fact that a poor boy could grow up to be president was proof that, in America, the same boy could have grown up to be wealthy.

POLITICS AND THE LAW A part of the explanation for the emergence of political leaders from poor backgrounds (real or pretended) had to do with changes in the legal profession. At the beginning of the nineteenth century, it was easy to become a lawyer. Standards for admission to the bar dropped sharply. The change was most pronounced in western states like Jackson's Tennessee, Clay's Kentucky, and Lincoln's Illinois. But the change also occurred in older states like Van Buren's New York and Webster's Massachusetts.

In the past, most men who became lawyers already belonged to elite families. As a career, the law had been a path for the sons of the educated and the wealthy. Now the law was becoming a path *to* wealth and prominence, and one that did not require much education. There were no law schools. Lawyers usually had a minimal amount of training—a few months studying as a clerk to some local practicing lawyer. This short apprenticeship was typically concluded by a brief, oral bar examination that was likely to be no more than a sociable gathering of small-town good old boys, lubricated with whiskey.

At the same time, the tie between law and politics was becoming closer. The expectation of most young men who became lawyers was that the career might well lead them to public office, to fame, and even to dizzying heights of power. But this would depend, at the local and state levels, on their making connections with the right circle of men, the right factions, and the right party organizations. As a result, at the same time that Monroe's presidency seemed to have ended party politics at the national level, politics in the

A Napoleonic Clay. If a political leader could not be depicted as a military hero, there were several conventional alternatives. One was to show him as a Napoleonic figure. In this portrait of Henry Clay, the artist has used his hair to suggest a resemblance to images of Napoleon that were very widely circulated at the time. His right hand is not thrust into his coat, as Napoleon's often was; but it is in about the same position. And the paper he is holding is an 1821 House of Representatives resolution supporting independence for Spain's Latin American colonies. This also had Napoleonic overtones, because Napoleon had taken his armies into half the nations of Europe saying he was going to bring French *liberté* to their people. (In the collection of The Corcoran Gallery of Art, museum purchase, Gallery Fund)

states, counties, and towns was becoming highly organized and partisan. To men who pursued the career of lawyer-politician, loyalty to party was supremely important—much more important than any issue or program. For such men, politics was part of their professional life. For many, like the Van Burens and the Clays and the Lincolns, politics *was* their profession. The political parties were the institutions through which that profession could be pursued. Older leaders like Jefferson and John Adams had believed that politics was something a prominent man might decide to engage in. For the new generation of political professionals, politics was something an ordinary man might do in order to *become* prominent.

A New Theory of Party

The new professional politicians had to come to terms with the American past. They understood very well that their chosen institution, the political party, was something the Founding Fathers had regarded as a kind of prostitution of republican government, an instrument of corruption and demagoguery.

So they began to work out a new theory of politics and parties. No single man made the theory. No single book or speech or magazine summed it up. But gradually, out of the day-to-day and election-to-election practice of the professionals, a new conception of the political party developed. It involved ideas about three basic relationships: (1) of parties to each other, (2) of parties to the constitutional institutions of government, and (3) of parties to the people.

THE TWO-PARTY IDEA During the no-party campaign of 1824, the Albany *Argus*, a newspaper that ardently supported the New York Democratic party which Martin Van Buren was working hard to build and discipline, commented on the history of party in the United States: "From the first organization of the government, this country has been divided into two great parties. . . . We cannot admit that the majority of either have been actuated by any other than the purest, the most patriotic, and the most disinterested motives." To a modern ear, this sounds perfectly

A Roman Van Buren. Martin Van Buren had what a campaign manager today might call an "image" problem. He was not a military hero. And it would have been very difficult to make him look Napoleonic—an alternative to a military pose that was used by some politicians. A second alternative was to look Roman, the choice that Van Buren and his artist agreed on when this picture was made in the 1840s. The cloak is handled like a Roman toga, and the columns and the balustrade are meant to create a setting suggestive of the ancient republic. (National Portrait Gallery, Smithsonian Institution, Washington, D.C.)

normal, if somewhat pious. Today it is a breach of political good manners for a candidate for president to openly question the "patriotism" of an opponent. But to the ears of the Federalist and Republican leaders of the revolutionary generation, the *Argus*'s analysis of party would have sounded downright evil.

But the *Argus*—speaking for Van Buren—was talking about a new idea: that having two parties, both presumed to be full of virtuous, patriotic men, was healthy in a free society. According to the new political logic, one-party government was a bad thing. A single dominant party would always break up into factions, as the Republican party had in 1824. These factions would be tied to the individual personalities of their leaders. Eventually, some leader would be able to build his faction into a party that was strong enough to control the government. Then the whole cycle would have to be repeated, again and again, from one party to many factions, then back again to one party. The only way to prevent this alternation between one-party and no-party politics was to have two permanent parties. Both would be loyal to the Republic. They would compete. Sometimes one would win, sometimes the other. No party could afford to take extreme positions, because that might risk defeat in the next election. The result would be that politics would be kept stable and moderate, in the hands of "sound" men.

What this meant, in turn, was that professional politicians would have to learn that the wild rhetoric of campaigns like the one of 1840 was just a part of the election business. The suggestions that Harrison was a drunkard or Van Buren a man of uncertain sexual identity were only a kind of political theater. No holds were barred, but the lurid charges and countercharges could be forgotten as soon as the campaign ended and the results were in.

The truth, as professionals like Van Buren and Clay and Webster understood, was that the two parties might compete, but they really depended on each other. Democrats did not campaign *for* a program, they campaigned *against* Whigs, and vice versa. Without opposition, no party could survive. There would be no party discipline, no party loyalty. There would be no need for the arts of coalition and compromise that were the career politician's stock-in-trade. Wrestling matches and horse races staged in the rallies of 1840 were symbolic: In the new conception of party, there could no more be a campaign without parties than there could be a one-horse race or a one-man wrestling match.

PARTIES AND THE GOVERNMENT The new political logic tied the administrative machinery of the federal government directly to party. When either party won control of a house of Congress or of the presidency, it could be expected to reward loyal supporters with patronage appointments that would in turn strengthen the party organization. In his inaugural address of 1825, John Quincy Adams had said the national government ought to be above patronage. It ought to give office only to men of "talent and virtue." Washington ought to be a capital city where "the most distinguished men from every section of the country meet to deliberate." Four years later, in his first inaugural, Andrew Jackson made a quite different statement: "The duties of all public officers are so simple that men of intelligence may readily qualify themselves for their performance. . . . No man has any more intrinsic claim to office than another." In 1832, one of his New York supporters, Van Buren's close associate Senator William Learned Marcy, put it more simply: "To the victor belongs the spoils."

Jackson seemed to be talking about democracy, and Marcy about corruption. But in reality they both were talking about the same thing: the use of patronage as a way of enforcing party discipline and rewarding party loyalty. They could talk this way because they knew that to function, the parties needed organization. To organize, they needed people. But most men would work for a party only if they could expect some kind of reward, and since there were not enough elective offices to go around, appointments had to be the currency of party politics. The idea of political "spoils" was not a new one. What was new was the idea that political patronage was legitimate, that it was a good thing that every office from cabinet secretary to local postmaster should depend on party loyalty.

The new logic of party also made the president the leader of his party in Congress. The one-party assumptions of Monroe and John Quincy Adams had meant they had almost no influence over voting in the House and Senate. But a president who clearly identified himself with a party, and

Newspapers were so important to political campaigns that they were sometimes founded just for the election season. These two were published during the elections of 1840 (the lower) and 1848. They endorse not only the presidential and vice presidential candidates, but state and local candidates as well. "Old Rough and Ready" was the nickname of General Zachary Taylor, the Whig candidate of 1848. He is shown leading a heroic charge, mounted on a white horse. (Note that this issue was published in January, almost a year before election day; the campaign was already in full swing.) North Bend was the name of Harrison's town in Ohio—a far cry from Worcester, Massachusetts, where this newspaper was published. (The American Museum of Political Life, University of Hartford)

assumed that there would be an opposition in Congress, could use patronage and other forms of influence to enforce voting along party lines. So the new conception of political parties involved a new conception of the way the separation of powers ought to work in practice. The framers of the Constitution had separated the executive and legislative branches in the belief that each would act as a check or a balance on the other at times. The idea that a president ought to control members of his party in Congress was a recognition that it was parties, not branches of government, that would provide the checks and the balances.

PARTIES AND THE PEOPLE The Whig and Democratic parties both assumed that voting was, and ought to be, universal (at least among white males). They also assumed that one of the main purposes of a political party was to mobilize support among the voters. These two parties were the first truly modern political parties in the world in several important ways. They were permanent organizations, from Washington down to the grass roots. They were staffed by professionals. They went after voters aggressively, using the most up-to-date techniques and "media"—huge picnics with cider and whiskey; newspapers, signs, and handbills; mass-produced banners, engravings, buttons, and gimmicks; wagons carrying blaring bands and mass meetings with as many as five speakers talking at once.

In fact, the parties helped produce an information revolution that was as dramatic as the one brought about in our own time by television and computer technology. In 1790 there were only 75 post offices—one for every 50,000 people. By 1830 there were more than 8,500 post offices—one for every 1,500 people. The result was a flood of mail. In that flood, nothing was more important than newspapers. Between 1790 and 1840 the number of newspapers in the United States increased from 92 to more than 1,400. This meant that during the Log Cabin campaign there was a newspaper for every eligible voter. Almost every one of these newspapers was a party paper, whose columns were devotedly Whig or Democratic.

The professional party leaders understood very well that if they were going to appeal to a great mass of voters, they had to be careful. They could not afford to do or say anything that might alienate the voters or the newspapers or their own party workers. Thus they were reluctant to take clear stands on any issue that might involve serious controversy. Sometimes, as with Harrison in 1840, it meant not taking a stand on *any* issue. One of Martin Van Buren's proudest memories was of a speech he had made on the tariff, not because he had changed anyone's mind but because he had been warmly congratulated afterward both by men who opposed the tariff and men who supported it.

Occasionally, a party might gamble that taking a position on some single question might pay off at the polls. Both Whigs and Democrats took such a gamble in 1832 on the issue of recharter for the Bank of the United States. But in the political norm, both parties tried to keep attention focused on the "character" of their candidates. In order to win a presidential election, both parties needed the votes of hundreds of thousands of Northerners and Southerners, city people and farmers, workers and businessmen, poor people and rich, immigrants and "old-stock" Americans. Putting together a coalition that was diverse enough to win an election required an appeal that would alienate no potential voter. This was another consequence of the new logic of party and democracy.

Jackson and His Party

The role of Andrew Jackson in the development of the new system of political parties was uncertain and even contradictory. The Democratic party wanted to claim him as its great leader. (Democrats today still celebrate an annual Jefferson-Jackson Day with a feast of party unity.) He was, after all, the Old Hero who had defeated the British at New Orleans in the War of 1812. He took on the "monster bank" in the election of 1832 and defeated not only the bank but the Whig challengers. For Democratic candidates for political office in most parts of the country, identifying themselves with Old Hickory was prudent.

But for Andrew Jackson, politics was intensely personal. His fame was older than the Democratic party. He had a stubborn personal pride—arrogance, his enemies would have said—that could override any professional politician's arguments about what might be best for the party.

Whenever Jackson met opposition, he had a tendency to regard it as a personal challenge, and to respond in ways that sometimes ignored his party's interests. Midway through his second term, for example, he provoked a terrific shakeup in his cabinet over just such a personal issue. Peggy O'Neale Eaton, wife of the secretary of war, John Eaton, happened to be the daughter of a tavernkeeper (a signal that not only might the new breed of politicians have modest origins, but that their wives might also). She had also been divorced. When Jackson learned that the

The Eaton affair. In this unfriendly drawing, made in 1834, Peggy O'Neale Eaton is being introduced to President Jackson. This tavernkeeper's daughter is quite elaborately dressed and on her toes, perhaps demonstrating a ballet step. The members of the cabinet all look pretty grim, except perhaps for Van Buren, at the right, who is using a lorgnette to get a better look. (Library of Congress)

wives of other cabinet members were snubbing Peggy Eaton socially, he made an issue of it at a cabinet meeting and forced the resignation of most of the cabinet. A good party man would never have risked party unity over such a trivial social question. Martin Van Buren's loyalty during the quarrel over Peggy Eaton cemented Jackson's personal loyalty to him.

The Eaton affair, probably more than deep political differences, also drove a deep wedge between Jackson and his vice president, John C. Calhoun. Jackson blamed Calhoun (and, even more, Calhoun's wife) for Mrs. Eaton's social distress. When Jackson discovered that Calhoun, way back in 1818, had recommended punishing him for his invasion of Spanish Florida, the break was complete. This probably helped account for Jackson's ferocious response to the nullification movement of 1832 in Calhoun's South Carolina. When Jackson threatened to hang the nullifiers

from the highest tree, he risked alienating Southerners who were committed to the old Jeffersonian notion of states' rights. This would be bad for the party, but Jackson's determination had more to do with people than with party. (For an account of the nullification crisis, see pp. 323–24.)

Jackson responded more or less the same way to the gathering Whig opposition in Congress (at first, a mixed-up coalition with nothing to hold them together except a dislike for the president). He vetoed their bank, campaigned for reelection with this veto as the main issue, and won by a landslide. A good party man would probably have let the bank die a slow death until its existing charter expired in 1836—just in time for another election. But Jackson was aroused, and defined the contest not as a party issue but as a personal struggle to the death between the monster bank and himself. "The bank," he said "is trying to kill me. But I will kill it." Instead of leaving the bank alone, he decided to stop depositing federal funds in it. This may well have been illegal. It was certainly against the cautious advice of many professional party men. His own secretary of the treasury refused to go along, and Jackson had to replace him. (For an account of the bank war, see pp. 324–26.)

Jackson's professional supporters talked a great deal about using the patronage system to distribute offices to loyal Democrats, but he was actually quite restrained in his replacement of Adams's appointees in federal positions with members of the Democratic party. He was much more likely to demand the resignation of a good Democrat who had committed some kind of personal affront to his own sense of dignity. So the spoils of office came more slowly than the party professionals would have liked.

In the final analysis, it is probably more correct to say that the Democratic party unified around Andrew Jackson than that Andrew Jackson unified the party. Jackson was a soldier, but he had spent very little time in the ranks. He had been a field commander, often operating with either no orders or only vague instructions from civilian authorities. He had the habit of imposing his will on other men, in military campaigns, as the master of many slaves, and as a veteran of the dueling grounds. He was also an *old* soldier, older than most of the working politicians who surrounded him. He still tended to think of political struggle the way Jefferson had in 1800, as a total struggle, with truth and justice all on one side, and with the fate of the Republic hanging on the result.

The truth, as party leaders like Van Buren understood, was that in Jackson the party had found an ideal candidate for the new political age, a political "outsider" whose fame had not been earned in government, with few political enemies and no political past. Such a man could be promoted by aggressive, well-organized party campaigns. If the candidate had a colorful past and a vigorous personality, as Jackson did, he could be promoted by his organization as a man who stood above organization, as the champion of the people. This was the formula the Whigs learned

so well in 1840 with Harrison. The same formula would be tried again and again by Whigs and Democrats in the years to come.

And Tyler Too

The second-party system was not going to be perfected by a man like Andrew Jackson, but by a generation of comparatively featureless politicians and bureaucrats. Indeed, the office of president would not be occupied by a man of Jackson's force of personality until Abraham Lincoln came into the office twenty-five years after Jackson, in 1861, to confront the staggering fact of Southern secession and Civil War. Between Jackson and Lincoln would come a succession of one-term presidents, alternating between Whig and Democratic parties with great regularity. Two of these presidents did not live to serve a full term. This sequence of presidents is difficult to memorize, and some of them, like Millard Fillmore, have become the answers to trivia questions, or standing jokes. But these seemingly unimportant men did an extremely important thing: They cemented the two-party system into place with such skill and effectiveness that many Americans are tempted to believe that no nation without such a system can possibly govern itself properly.

THE TRAVAIL OF MARTIN VAN BUREN
The Whig opposition knew it would be difficult to defeat the Democrats in the election of 1836. President Jackson's personal popularity would help his chosen successor, Van Buren. And the Democratic organization was too powerful to confront in a direct contest. So the Whigs settled on a diversionary strategy that looked back to the election of 1824 as its model. They decided to run three sectional candidates: Hugh Lawson White of Tennessee for the South, Daniel Webster of Massachusetts for the Northeast, and William

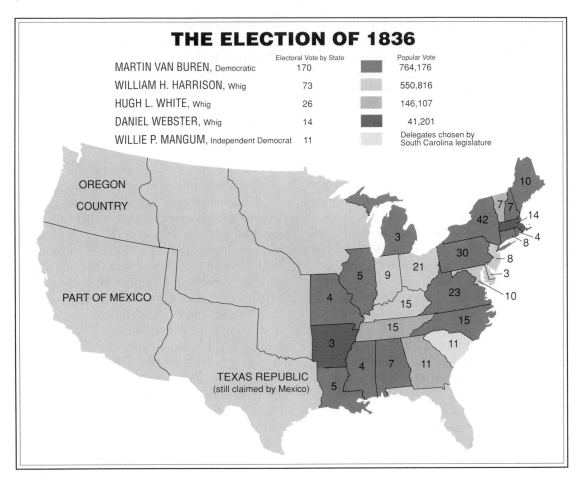

THE ELECTION OF 1836

	Electoral Vote by State	Popular Vote
MARTIN VAN BUREN, Democratic	170	764,176
WILLIAM H. HARRISON, Whig	73	550,816
HUGH L. WHITE, Whig	26	146,107
DANIEL WEBSTER, Whig	14	41,201
WILLIE P. MANGUM, Independent Democrat	11	Delegates chosen by South Carolina legislature

OREGON COUNTRY

PART OF MEXICO

TEXAS REPUBLIC
(still claimed by Mexico)

Henry Harrison of Ohio for the Northwest. They hoped the result would be that no candidate would win a majority of the electoral votes, so the election would be thrown into the House of Representatives, as it had been in 1824. There, with each state casting one vote, the Whigs might have a chance of winning. And if they did not win, they might work out another arrangement like the one that had made John Quincy Adams president.

The popular vote was close—762,000 for Van Buren and 735,000 for all his opponents combined. But the Democrats carried every large state except Virginia, and won the electoral victory, 170 to 124.

The new president took office at a troubled time. A new financial crisis, known as the Panic of 1837, was already under way. The beginnings of the collapse lay in a decision by the Bank of England, the most powerful financial institution in the world, to tighten credit late in 1836. The impact on the American economy was direct and swift. The normal practice for cotton buyers in England was to borrow money to buy American cotton. Now, unable to borrow easily, they did not place their usual orders. The price of cotton fell drastically. Many American brokerage houses went bankrupt, and could not pay *their* large debts to banks. Banks, drained by these failures, were not able to redeem their notes in specie. In

May 1837, New York banks suspended specie payments, and other major banks around the country soon followed suit. This meant outstanding bank notes were suddenly worth much less than their face value. In effect, there was a sudden collapse of the supply of both money and credit. Without money and credit, what had been a long spiral of growth and speculation suddenly became a deep depression.

The causes of the panic had little to do with the actions of the Democratic administration, but the new logic of political parties made everything a partisan issue. The Whigs were quick to blame Van Buren's party for the troubles. (In fact, here were the beginnings of the American political tradition that the party in power claims credit for good times and gets the blame for hard times.) Whigs argued it was no coincidence that the panic came after Jackson's assault on the Bank of the United States. They made much of the fact that just before the election of 1836, the Jackson administration had issued the Specie Circular. This effort to get some control over wild speculation in western lands had required that all payments for public lands be made in gold or silver. This had made bank notes less valuable, since they could not be used by speculators to buy land. In 1837, the sale of public lands shrank to less than a tenth of the sales of 1836.

Van Buren attempted to meet the crisis with a policy that was designed to tighten the supply of money and credit even further. He proposed a new system of public finance that had two main features. First, a system of Independent Treasuries would be established in the large cities. These would hold all federal deposits and conduct government transactions. This would mean that federal funds would not be deposited in any banks, and could not be used as the basis for issuing bank notes. Second, the government would adopt a severe hard-money policy and accept only specie for all taxes, customs duties, or land sales.

In effect, Van Buren was trying to get his party to commit itself to a definite *policy* on an important question. But the nature of the new parties

quickly became clear. The national parties had only one fundamental purpose: the election of presidents. Van Buren had no success getting his program through (and it would not have cured the depression anyway). The Independent Treasury Bill was not passed until the summer of 1840, when the Log Cabin campaign was already under way, and it was repealed a few years later. The provision that the government would accept only specie payments never went into effect.

The economy rebounded slightly in 1838–39 but went into an even steeper decline after 1839. Prices for most commodities fell by an average of about 50 percent, and stayed low until well after the election of 1840. This meant the Democrats entered the campaign of 1840 as the first political party to be saddled (unfairly) with the blame for a depression. In this kind of economic setting, the Whig charges—that Van Buren was a man with a taste for expensive wines who wasted money redecorating the White House—had a bite they would not have had in prosperous times, and the claim that Harrison was a simple farmer who was happy with his homemade cider had a strong appeal. Neither candidate really fitted the picture his party drew. And neither party really had a plan for curing the depression. But the new political logic gave little or no weight to the truth. Van Buren and his party went down to defeat in 1840 as the victims of new methods of party organization and campaigning that they themselves had brought into being. Well might the *Democratic Review* complain, after the election, "We have taught them how to conquer us."

THE WHIG SPLIT The Whig victory was an empty one. The sixty-eight-year-old Harrison died after only a month in office. The political logic that had dictated the choice of "Tyler Too" quickly took its toll on the party. John Tyler had been one of those political choices designed to "unite" different factions of the party long enough to win an election. He was a states' rights advocate of the Calhoun stripe and was opposed to the high tariffs and internal improvements that

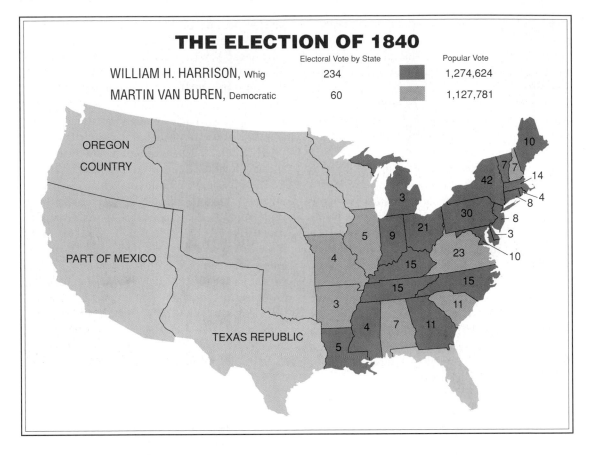

THE ELECTION OF 1840

	Electoral Vote by State		Popular Vote
WILLIAM H. HARRISON, Whig	234		1,274,624
MARTIN VAN BUREN, Democratic	60		1,127,781

OREGON COUNTRY

PART OF MEXICO

TEXAS REPUBLIC

were dear to the hearts of Henry Clay and his followers.

Tyler kept all of Harrison's cabinet appointees—mostly Clay men, and Daniel Webster as secretary of state. But then Tyler began to veto legislation that had the support of most Whigs in Congress—particularly two bills that attempted to create a new version of the national bank. The result was a rift between Tyler and Clay, and a split in the Whig party. A caucus of Whigs in Congress put out a manifesto declaring that the president did not represent his party. All the members of the cabinet, with the exception of Webster, resigned. Clay himself quit the Senate in 1842 to begin a successful two-year campaign for the 1844 nomination as Whig candidate for the presidency, fully expecting to run against Van Buren in a politics-as-usual campaign (for the election of 1844, see pp. 488–89).

Looking Forward

The political landscape of the 1830s and 1840s was in some respects a dull and disappointing one. The kinds of leaders that emerged with the new party system seem to have been primarily interested in office for the sake of office. Or they were, like Jackson, much more intriguing as personalities than as statesmen. As the for the parties themselves, they were perhaps more given to humbug, confidence games, and hoopla than ever before or since. They were more interested in keeping fundamental questions, particularly the question of slavery, out of politics than they were in adopting positions and finding solutions to social or economic problems.

Inauguration day, 1841. This was the moment the Log Cabin campaign had aimed for, Harrison's inauguration day. The artist has chosen to show a fine, clear day, with hatless men without their overcoats. He—or she—has given nonvoting women a fairly prominent role in the picture. Also, though the occasion was civic, the army with its swords, drums, horses, and rifles has an even more prominent place in the picture; its generals played a major role in the politics of the period. (Anne S. K. Brown Military Collection, Brown University)

Little wonder, then, that Abraham Lincoln—who was very much a product of the second-party system—would stand at Gettysburg in 1863 and give all the credit to the Founding Fathers for having created a "government of the people, by the people, and for the people." But for all the eloquence of his statement at Gettysburg, Lincoln was making a fundamental mistake. The generation who made the Revolution had not in fact created a democratic national government. Specifically, they had not wanted presidential elections to be determined by the people. It had been the two succeeding generations of politicians—Van Buren's and Lincoln's—who had really made national politics democratic. For all their faults, the political parties that were shaped during the 1830s and 1840s were perhaps the most important instruments in this process of democratization.

The Whig and Democratic parties would continue down to the middle of the 1850s to be very much like they were established to be: very practical organizations, run by men of limited capacities and aims. The parties did not have very definite programs, and their primary reason for being was to win elections. They very seldom addressed basic, difficult social or economic questions. But the politicians of the period did have one principle and did set themselves one steady goal. The principle was that the meaning of democracy is centered in the way politicians ought to gain power—by winning mass popular

CHRONOLOGY

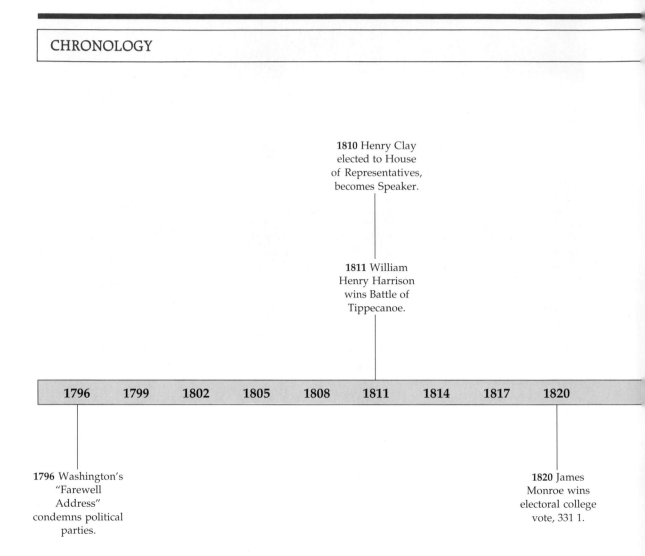

1810 Henry Clay
elected to House
of Representatives,
becomes Speaker.

1811 William
Henry Harrison
wins Battle of
Tippecanoe.

| 1796 | 1799 | 1802 | 1805 | 1808 | 1811 | 1814 | 1817 | 1820 |

1796 Washington's
"Farewell
Address"
condemns political
parties.

1820 James
Monroe wins
electoral college
vote, 331 1.

1840 William Henry Harrison (Whig) wins presidential election. Number of newspapers reaches one for every 400 eligible voters.

1828 Andrew Jackson (Democrat) elected president.

1841 Harrison inaugurated, dies after one month in office. John Tyler (Whig) becomes president. Struggle begins between Tyler and Clay factions for control of Whig Party.

1824 Five candidates compete for the presidency, and none receives an electoral majority. Albany *Argus* endorses concept of two permanent political parties.

1836 Andrew Jackson issues Specie Circular. Martin Van Buren (Democrat) wins presidential election.

1830 Number of post offices reaches one for every 1,500 people.

1842 Clay resigns from Senate to begin two-year campaign for presidency.

1823	1826	1829	1832	1835	1838	1841	1844

1837 Financial panic and depression begins, banks suspend specie payments.

1825 John Quincy Adams made president by House of Representatives.

1832 Jackson vetoes bill to recharter Second Bank of the United States. Jackson re-elected. South Carolina Nullification crises resolved.

1844 James K. Polk (Democrat) wins presidential election.

1839 Whigs hold first major-party national nomination convention, and Harrison is chosen over Clay. Depression worsens after slight recovery in 1838.

1827 William Henry Harrison becomes a U.S. senator.

support in open elections. The goal was to make American politics into the most democratic system the Western world had ever known.

The individual motivations that lay behind this principle and this goal were mostly selfish, shortsighted, and petty. But the historical result was remarkable. It was not really "four score and seven years ago," as Lincoln would say at Gettysburg, that political democracy became the distinctive political fact of American life. It was during Lincoln's *own* political lifetime, during the quarter-century that followed the election of 1824. The men who made it so were not Lincoln's "our fathers," but his own contemporaries, the politicians who had been his colleagues and competitors. And they did it not through lofty means and high purposes, but through rough-and-tumble, pragmatic practices like those that were perfected in the rambunctious Log Cabin campaign of 1840.

Suggestions for Further Reading

1840: THE LOG CABIN CAMPAIGN

R. G. Gunderson, *The Log Cabin Campaign* (1957), is a sprightly account of the election of 1840. Harrison needs a new biography, to replace Freeman Cleaves, *Old Tippecanoe: William Henry Harrison and His Time* (1939). Some useful material is in David Durfee, *William Henry Harrison, 1773–1841: Chronology, Documents and Bibliographic Aids* (1970). The first volume of Arthur M. Schlesinger, Jr., ed., *History of American Presidential Elections* (1971), includes a short account of the 1840 campaign.

A NEW THEORY OF PARTY

Richard P. McCormick, *The Second Party System* (1966), is the best place to begin. It can be supplemented with the same author's *The Presidential Game* (1982). The political theory of parties is neatly laid out in the final chapter of Richard Hofstadter, *The Idea of a Party System* (1970). There are old and powerful traditions among historians, traditions that attempt to see the two parties of the 1830s and 1840s as the political institutionalization of deep ideological divisions. Arthur Schlesinger, Jr., *The Age of Jackson* (1945), argued that the Democrats were the party of the new industrial working class. Marvin Meyers, *The Jacksonian Persuasion* (1960), was an attempt to show that the Democrats really had an ideology, a set of shared social and political beliefs and attitudes. Daniel Walker Howe, *The Political Culture of the American Whigs* (1979), tries to do the same thing for the Whigs. For a more suspicious account of the nature of the new political culture, and its relationship to social and economic change, see Edward Pessen, *Jacksonian America: Society, Personality, and Politics* (1979). Ronald Formisano, *The Transformation of Political Culture: Massachusetts Parties, 1790s–1840s* (1983), has excellent material on the second-party system. The standard account of the expansion of the suffrage is Chilton Williamson, *American Suffrage: From Property to Democracy* (1960). Morton J. Horowitz, *The Transformation of American Law, 1780–1860* (1977), lays the groundwork for a good understanding of the relationship between law and politics.

AND TYLER TOO

James C. Curtis, *The Fox at Bay* (1970), is a careful study of Van Buren's administration. A more general analysis is available in John Niven, *Martin Van Buren: The Romantic Age of American Politics* (1983), and D. B. Cole, *Martin Van Buren and the American Political System* (1984). William Cooper, *The South and the Politics of Slavery, 1828–1856* (1978), contains a thorough discussion of the role of the South in the Tyler administration. But the Tyler administration has not been given a full and careful treatment since O. D. Lambert, *Presidential Politics in the United States, 1841–44* (1939). Clay has not had a full-scale biography in the past thirty years. For the moment, the most convenient approach is through Clement Eaton, *Henry Clay and the Art of American Politics* (1957). The most recent book-length studies of Webster are Sydney Nathans, *Daniel Webster and Jacksonian Democracy* (1973), and Maurice G. Baxter, *One and Inseparable: Daniel Webster and the Union* (1984).

CHAPTER 9
A NEW NORTH

THE EPISODE: *William Lloyd Garrison eventually became famous as an abolitionist. In 1831, he began to publish the most radical antislavery journal in the United States,* The Liberator, *in which he demanded the immediate and unconditional end of slavery. But before he was famous, and before he was an abolitionist, he was—like everyone—part of a family. This chapter begins by exploring his family's history.*

The Garrison family was not important, as historians usually judge importance. The father deserted his wife and children, and the family group was completely broken up by deaths, by "vice," and by economic depressions. The family produced only three girls, who all died young, one boy who grew up to be a drunkard, and William Lloyd Garrison. But, like other families of the period, it was subject to the powerful impacts of social change. Our purpose in looking so closely at the Garrisons is to set the stage for an examination of what amounted to an economic and social revolution that was taking place in the United States during the period between the 1820s and the beginning of the Civil War.

William Lloyd Garrison eventually became a "radical." And radicals are often treated by historians as though they were simply born to be different. Our purpose is to show how Garrison's career was the product not of some mysterious quirk of personality, but of history.

THE HISTORICAL SETTING: *The Garrison family history was a product of deep changes in the ways people produced and exchanged goods and services. An accelerating industrial revolution dramatically increased the impact of the development of the market economy that was discussed in Chapter 7. These changes, in their turn, brought about very significant redefinitions of social class. A new middle class took shape with new institutions, new kinds of organizations, new ideas about what a family was and how it ought to work, new sexual and religious practices, new social expectations and morals, and new culture.*

To some extent, the entire United States was transformed by such changes. But in this chapter, we concentrate on the North, where the transformation was much more rapid and pronounced. In the South, the institution of African-American slavery was molding an increasingly divergent economy, society, and culture. (In the following chapter, we will discuss the history of the South and slavery during the same period.)

We have twin purposes in this chapter: to show how the most unusual individuals—like William Lloyd Garrison—are products of the most common social institution, the family; and to show how explaining the lives of the most insignificant-seeming families—like the Garrisons—can bring about an understanding of social and economic change.

THE GARRISONS: AN ANTEBELLUM FAMILY

William Lloyd Garrison, journalist and reformer, sat up late into the morning of October 14, 1842, keeping a deathwatch over his brother James. At about three o'clock in the morning James died. As William Lloyd told it in a letter a few hours later, James "threw off his mortal habiliments" so gently that at first he seemed only to have dropped off into a quiet sleep. The watching brother took half an hour, at least, to discover his "error."

Then came that rush of relief that softens grief. James Garrison's "release from the flesh" seemed a "consolation" rather than a "sorrow." He had suffered long enough. He had been approaching death, almost courting it, for a long time. A few years earlier, he had tried to kill himself. He had, in William Lloyd's curious word, been "habitancing" toward this final peace for much of his forty-one-year life. Finally, in this dim room in Cambridgeport, just outside Boston, the end had come.

As William Lloyd saw it, James died bravely. In the last hours he had found (at least it seemed so) something that had always escaped him in life: a measure of control over himself. James Garrison appeared to look death steadily in the face, to meet this last struggle as he had met no other before, "with all possible fortitude." He had never been able to master his own weaknesses, and so life had mastered him. But his brother could now see in James Garrison's death a novel triumph of will; finally, there was something to praise: "Death had no power over his spirit."

James had been viewed by all the Garrison family as a hopeless disgrace for years; they called him "Crazy Jem." And he had accepted the role of the family disgrace. In fact, at the end it was this role that provided him with his only real sense of identity: as an almost perfect contrast to his brother.

The career that had led James Garrison to his early death in Cambridgeport had been a fantastic series of defeats and failures. He had been a sailor on every imaginable kind of ship: in the coasting trade from the Caribbean to the maritime provinces of Canada, on a British man-of-war, and on American ships of battle. Along the way, he had been in prisons everywhere—Cuba, Portugal, France. A dozen times and more, he had waked up owning only the tattered clothes on his back. Sometimes he was simply naked and alone. Almost every house of ill fame on the eastern seaboard had taken his money and watched him stagger away the next day, sick and broke.

He had had girls in some ports, men and boys in others. He had been a deserter and a thief, a prisoner and a patient. Finally, he had crept back to Massachusetts, too sick to serve in the navy any more. His brother had taken charge and had sent him to dry out on a small farm in Connecticut owned by relatives. After an uncertain recuperation, James had come to live with William Lloyd. But then had come a final fantastic binge along the Boston docks. And now, death.

Little wonder that William Lloyd Garrison's waking instinct, on the morning after his brother's death, was to plan the funeral as an occasion for making the moral clear:

> I intend that the funeral arrangements and ceremonies shall be as plain, simple and *free* as possible. Liberty of speech shall be given to all who may attend. I shall probably have a testimony to bear against the war system, the navy, intemperance, &c. in connection with James's history.

A few months later, Garrison described the funeral, and added, almost unnecessarily, "My remarks were very pointed."

The brother who lay in the coffin and the brother who made pointed remarks over him could hardly have been more different. William Lloyd Garrison had carefully managed his life, building his character, making himself into almost a model of piety and virtue. He had learned to control every weakness, to deny every temptation, to be always the master of himself. James, in contrast, had *been* mastered—by drink, by women and men, by poverty and illness, and by captains and lieutenants whose cruelty had left him scarred and frightened. Both brothers had been in jails. But William Lloyd always went there because of virtuous stands in virtuous causes; James went for his weaknesses and sins. William Lloyd was a radical in the service of reforms: pacifism, temperance, free speech, antislavery—plus an imposing list of others. James was a radical of vices: drunkenness, thievery, desertion, promiscuity, and licentiousness—plus an imposing list of others. William Lloyd was a drastically upright man; James was just as drastically corrupted.

These contrasts between the Garrison brothers were real, important, and obvious. But there was a veiled similarity in their two lives, less obvious but no less real. The two men, each in his own way, lived lives that were very mobile and uncertain. Both challenged powerful men and institutions—one as a reformer, the other as a chronic misbehaver. For their passions, both men took enormous risks, placing their bodies and their lives in peril. Both had their circles of intimates and friends: one his fellow reformers, the other his shipmates and occasional lovers. But both confronted society at large in angry and provocative ways. As a result, both found themselves branded as outlaws and outcasts. And these lives of uncertainty, opposition, and isolation grew out of an enormous preoccupation with the self that the two brothers shared. Their self-awareness knew almost no limits; nor did their belief that the self was something the individual could make (or destroy) at will. Both were, in short, radical individualists.

The Garrison family took shape in the eighteenth century after the English conquest of Canada during the Seven Years' War. New land was available in Canada for Englishmen to claim and settle. This chance was taken primarily by families that moved up from Massachusetts—families that brought with them the legacies of Puritanism, congregational religion, disciplined lives, and evangelical piety. There were also a few settlers who came directly from England, among them a certain Joseph Garrison, who was alone and ready to start a new family. He married the daughter of one of the Massachusetts immigrants in New Brunswick, and they settled down to the task of having and rearing nine children. Among these nine was Abijah, born in 1773.

Abijah Garrison grew into a tall, strong, ambitious, red-bearded, balding man with a fatefully restless personality. He went to sea and became a pilot in the coasting trade, faring from Newfoundland to the Caribbean. According to family legend at least, he was a skilled navigator and expert seaman. One thing is certain. He somehow managed to educate himself, and he developed a taste for fancy writing. His letters were artful and contrived, full of the excessive sentimentality of the period—full, too, of pretentious language like "a Tempestuous Sky and Enraged Ocean." He could also summon up the rhetoric of religious piety when the occasion seemed to call for it, praying for "a Ray of Divine Light from the Throne of God and Lamb."

This mixture of sentimental romance and religion found a new object in the 1790s. She was a tall, handsome young woman named Frances Maria Lloyd, the daughter of another New Brunswick sailor. Abijah Garrison and Frances Lloyd met for the first time at a religious meeting, a gathering of New Brunswick Baptists. Frances Maria Lloyd Garrison—Fanny, as she came to be called—was a woman of great energy and almost desperate faith. She was as literate as her husband, and capable of some of the same literary flourishes as he. But her capabilities and her flourishings ran to religion more than to romance.

When she met Abijah, she had already suffered for faith. Her father was a Church of England man, an Anglo-Irish immigrant, and a loyal Englishman. He watched in distress in the 1790s as the Anglican establishment in New Brunswick suffered from the energetic efforts of traveling preachers—Baptists, especially—to convert the province to the kind of religion that dominated the newly independent American states down the coast. The threat entered his own house, found his favorite daughter, Fanny, and made her a convert. Her new birth of faith broke the ties of her first birth of the flesh; her father expelled her from his house. Abijah Garrison could call her Blue Jacket, could try to dress her out in romance. But what he had found, above all, was a woman determined to live in faith no matter what the price.

Fanny and Abijah were married in 1798 or 1799 and began a series of moves from place to place in New Brunswick and Nova Scotia. Their first child, a girl, died in infancy; the second, born in 1801, was named James Holley. This was the boy who would grow up to be Crazy Jem. In the first years of the nineteenth century, Abijah Garrison found the going rough. The Napoleonic Wars were making ocean trade difficult and precarious for ships sailing under the British flag. To try to escape what he called "the Ravages of War and the stagnation of business" in Canada, he decided to go to Massachusetts. He chose Newburyport, a prosperous and growing trading and shipbuilding town. He found work readily available, prices cheap, and goods plentiful. As for Fanny, she found Baptists in large numbers, and a couple of rented rooms big enough for her, Abijah, James, and a two-year-old daughter, Caroline. She also found herself pregnant with the child born in December 1805 and named William Lloyd. Jemmy had a trumpet, a toy fife, and a penknife; his father proudly wrote back to New Brunswick that the boy could "Sing a Great many tunes." Things, in short, were good. Wherever he sailed, to Virginia or to Guadeloupe, Abijah Garrison would write home to Fanny: "May God bless you, preserve you in health is the prayer of your affectionate Husband."

Then, at the end of 1807, history closed in on the Garrisons. The Jefferson administration clamped its Embargo on all foreign commerce. Newburyport, like the rest of New England's trading towns, suddenly found itself in a profound depression. Abijah Garrison could no longer find voyages. Fanny, late in 1807, became pregnant again. And Abijah—like millions of other frustrated, unemployed men of all generations—began to spend his time in taverns, drinking with his friends. Sometimes he brought the friends and the drinking home. In the summer of 1808, five-year-old Caroline died. It was all too much for the pregnant Fanny Garrison. One day, when Abijah was at home with some of his mates, she lost her pious temper and shouted the men out of the house. The birth of another daughter in July was not enough to hold the family together—or may have been enough to break it up. Abijah fled, leaving Fanny with James, seven, Lloyd, three, and the infant Maria Elizabeth. Abijah also left behind his sailor's hourglass, with his initials carved into the bottom. But that was all.

For the next three or four years, Fanny Garrison stayed on in Newburyport, working occasionally as a nurse, somehow managing to hold her family together. Then, at about the time the United States finally entered the European wars in 1812, she moved to Lynn, a few miles away. She took James with her, but left Lloyd and Maria Elizabeth with two different families in Newburyport. (Abijah, meanwhile, returned to New Brunswick, where he became an anonymous casualty of the uncertain age. He did write to a cousin in 1814, referring mysteriously to "the Whirl I have taken in the World." But whatever "the Whirl" may have involved, it did not include his family. He never saw Fanny or the children again.)

For the next few years, Fanny Garrison's life took on an unquiet rhythm, alternating between hope and depression. James was troublesome almost from the beginning of the years in Lynn. He was bound out as an apprentice to a cordwainer—a shoemaker who worked with cordovan leather. In his second master's shop, it was the custom to pass a heavy drink of rum mixed with molasses. Soon he was a confirmed drinker. He began a pattern of "sinning," begging his mother for her forgiveness, promising to sin no more, and being encouraged by her to make a new beginning:

> I had never tasted liquor, but was persuaded by my fellow apprentices and likewise my master, to drink a little as it would not hurt me. I took a drink, and it was sweet, and from that fatal hour I became a drunkard.
>
> I soon got so I could take my glass as often as my master, and in a little while it required double that quantity to satisfy my appetite. I was now a confirmed drunkard. It soon reached my mother's ear, that her darling boy, one in whom she had placed strong hopes that he would be a comfort and support to her declining years, one who she had so often prayed to her heavenly father to guide and direct, had fallen before that monster *Rum*. I went, but with feelings I can not describe. She received me kindly, and pointed out in an affectionate and kind manner the path I was pursuing, what the consequences would be to my health, my reputation in this world, the many sufferings it would cause her, and the eternal damnation of my soul in the world to come. I promised to do better, and drink no more.

But the promises failed, and James was soon spending time at a house of ill fame just outside Lynn, a "sink of infamy and vice," where "many, many a poor young girl has lost her reputation."

As if money worries and James's unsteadiness were not problems enough, Fanny Garrison was always "tired with slavish work." Things looked up a little in 1814 when she was able to bring William Lloyd, now nine, to Lynn and apprentice him to a shoemaker. And things looked even brighter the next year when another Lynn shoemaker decided to take a group of workers to the city of Baltimore to open a shoe factory. He invited Fanny and her two boys to join the enterprise.

But the factory failed. By January 1816 Fanny was complaining in letters back to Newburyport that "I walk the streets of Baltimore and feel myself alone." James was "a great trial." William Lloyd was "homesick." Finally, James and William Lloyd both deserted: James to sea after a frightful sequence of jobs, fights, and drinking bouts; Lloyd back to Newburyport. Fanny took up nursing again, working in the suburban mansions of people she called "the Quality," and was proud of "being treated like a lady," for a change.

For the next few years, Fanny Garrison played out a lonely and pathetic drama. She had to put Maria Elizabeth out to work as a servant in Baltimore (where this third daughter died in 1822). She complained constantly of illness and fatigue. She started a diary to record her sinking, gloomy anxieties, her record of blood coughed up from the tuberculosis that flared from time to time, her thoughts of death, dreams of death, and premonitions of death. She also started a prayer group for Baptist women in Baltimore. But even the comforts of the church were denied her. In 1816 she became involved in some sort of controversy by mail with a member of the church in Newburyport where she still kept her membership. She lost, and in 1818 the church voted to deny her the privileges of membership for at least four years. Alone, sick, tired, and afraid, Fanny worked out a simple analysis of her life, which pictured her experience as one of progressive decline and alienation:

> At an early period of life, I was surrounded with every comfort that was necessary, nurtured with peculiar care and tenderness in the bosom of parental affection, blessed with the friendship of an extensive acquaintance, and beloved by all my relations. I had enough to attach me to this world. Gay and thoughtless, vain and wild, I looked forward to nothing but pleasure and happiness.

Her conversion by the Baptists, her marriage, and her migration to Massachusetts had all conspired to spoil the picture:

> But alas! have not my subsequent years taught me that all was visionary? How has the rude blast of misfortune burst over my head, and had it not been for an overruling Providence, I must have sunk under their pressure.

But if she had to learn that this world held only pain, she had also learned that there was a consolation:

> I was taught to see that all my dreams of happiness in this life were chimerical; the efforts we make here are all of them imbecility in themselves and illusive, but religion is perennial. It fortifies the mind to support trouble, elevates the affection of the heart, and its perpetuity has no end.

The ideas were conventional—even clichés—but they fitted. And they were deeply felt. As it happened, there was, finally, only one other human object on which the feelings could really be fastened: the distant, small son in Newburyport, Fanny Garrison's last real hope in "this world."

Whatever the eventual fate of his soul might be, it was this world and not the next that William Lloyd Garrison set out to master at the age of ten, when he went back to Newburyport, back to live in the house of the Baptist deacon who had taken him in when Abijah Garrison deserted the family. He went for a few months to grammar school, but his last hours in a classroom were in his eleventh year. Most of his training was religious. He sang in the choir, read sermons and tracts, and faithfully attended Sunday school and church. Then he took up his second apprenticeship, this time to a cabinetmaker in the nearby town of Haverhill. There was a rebellious streak in William Lloyd—a streak he shared not only with his father and brother but with hundreds of other young apprentices of the day. After only six weeks, he ran away from his master, home again to Newburyport. The master kindly released him from the apprentice's bond. Then, by a stroke of what Garrison always regarded as "Providence," an apprentice's place opened up at a local newspaper, the *Newburyport Herald*. He won the job and settled down quickly to a seven-year apprenticeship.

These years were full of work, learning, ambition, and success. Garrison was able to make himself over from a poor, semiorphaned waif into a man on the threshold of what he believed would be a great career. He read tirelessly, despite being very nearsighted: Shakespeare, contemporary novels and poetry, political books and speeches. He even learned some Latin from a fellow apprentice. He joined a local Franklin Club, where he and other young men of ambition would gather for "improving discussions." He began to dress well, even elegantly. He spent hard-earned apprentice's dollars to have his portrait done in oil at twenty, with his hair arranged in a curling, Byronic style; wearing a high, stiff collar and an elegant shirt; his eyes shown in the brooding, slightly mysterious, insinuating Romantic style so popular in gentlemen's portraits of the period.

Garrison still attended church faithfully, trying to be what his mother had hoped he would be, a "perfect Baptist." But there was a straining, worldly ambition in him, a vague determination that he would somehow earn fame. The ambition and the acute preoccupation with the self were not traits that belonged to Garrison by some sort of genetic mystery. He had absorbed them from his society. The ideal of the self-made man was becoming almost an official part of the creed of middle-class young men in America and England. And Garrison, as a member of the Franklin Club (and, like Franklin, a printer), could hardly have failed to adopt the ideal and the ambition that went with it. He also developed an open-ended sense of possibility, a sense that any man could make himself over into whatever he chose, forsaking parental models, starting from scratch, building whatever type of personality and career he chose. And after all, he *was* a young man, alone, radically free.

When he (mistakenly) thought he was twenty-one, in 1824, Garrison wrote a fervent celebration of his maturity, full of excessive rhetoric in praise of his own "Spirit of Independence," entitled simply "Twenty-One." He saw himself as a young success, destined to fame, free of obligations and involvements. Such a man, he wrote, would

Garrison at 20. Garrison paid hard-earned money to have this portrait painted in Newburyport, Massachusetts, in 1825. He was about to finish his apprenticeship at the local newspaper. He was still quite poor, but dressed himself as a gentleman in anticipation of the great career he already was dreaming of. (Courtesy Essex Institute, Salem, Mass.)

always defy the world, defy wealth, might, power, even defy "lank poverty" or "threatening clouds of dark oppression."

When he was just twenty-three, in the midst of a quarrel with another journalist, he proclaimed in print to all the world:

> If my life be spared, my name shall one day be known so extensively as to render private inquiry unnecessary; and known, too, in a praise-worthy manner. I speak in the spirit of prophesy, not of vainglory—with a strong pulse, a flashing eye, and a glow of the heart. *The task may be yours to write my biography.*

But all this celebration of the free individual and all the blustering about independence could not cut the one tie that still bound him to the memory of real poverty and shame. During his years of apprenticeship, although he lived alone in the home of his master, there was still the persistent tug of his mother. And the tug was in an opposite direction, away from worldly ambition, away from success, away from reputation and fame, from oil portraits and elegant clothes. William Lloyd Garrison viewed his own life as a progress toward self-mastery. His mother saw her experience as a progressive decline, a virtual sinking. And she tried, from Baltimore, to impose at least some of her pathetic, religious version of things on her son.

To begin with, while he was still very young, there were gloomy, mothering cautions:

> Only let me hear that you are steady and go not in the way of bad company, and my heart will be lifted up to God for you, that you may be kept from the snares and

temptations of this evil world. Be a good boy and God will bless, and you have a Mother, although distant from you, that loves you with tenderness.

Fanny Garrison even wrote in 1819 that she was glad he could *not* join her in Baltimore because "you might be led astray by bad company." And James's "fall from Grace" was a concrete and powerful example of what bad company might cause.

Then, as time passed and Fanny Garrison became ill, she introduced the theme of death's approach. Once, when she sent William Lloyd a small trunk full of old clothes, she added a note saying that this might be the last token of love that she would be spared to send. Whenever she wrote him, she detailed her own symptoms and sufferings and described the ravages of epidemics of disease in Baltimore. She signed her letters "Your Mother until Death," or "Adieu, my dear, for I am tired."

When William Lloyd showed the first real signs of worldly ambition and success, such cautionings and lamentings came to a sharp focus. He proudly sent Fanny his first newspaper contributions, which he signed "A.O.B." for "An Old Bachelor." Her first response was to express guarded pleasure: "I am pleased, myself, with the idea, provided that nothing wrong should result from it." Her second was to joke (wittily enough, but with an edge that the seventeen-year-old must have felt): She wondered whether "A.O.B." might not in fact signify "Ass, Oaf, and Blockhead."

The humor went out of her letters a bit later, after Garrison had sent more pieces—verbal explosions on Latin America, Europe, national politics, and even a fictional account of a shipwreck—all written with obvious energy and efficiency in a short period of time. Fanny Garrison was appalled. She drew for Lloyd a clear line between worldly ambition and piety, and she fretted aggressively about what would become of him if he continued to stray across the line:

> Next, your turning author. You have no doubt read and heard the fate of such characters, that they generally starve to death in some garret or place that no one inhabits. Secondly, you think your time was wisely spent while you were writing political pieces. I cannot join with you there, for had you been searching the scriptures for truth, and praying for direction of the holy spirit to lead your mind into the path of holiness, your time would have been more wisely spent, and your advance to the heavenly world more rapid. But instead, you have taken the Hydra by the head, and now beware of his mouth; but as it is done, I suppose you had better go on and seek the applause of mortals. But my Dear L., lose not the favor of God; have an eye single to his glory, and you will not lose your reward.

This reprimand was plain enough to someone who had published his little essays with an almost trembling hope for the "applause of mortals." But it was driven home in the last written words Fanny Garrison ever addressed to her son:

> Now, my dear, I must draw to a close and say that I love you as dear as ever, especially when you consider your dear mother and are trying by your good behavior to soothe her path to the grave.

She asked him, gently, to bring his work for her to see, and signed her full name: "Your affectionate Mother, Frances M. Garrison." Two weeks later, Garrison set out for Baltimore, to make an often-delayed last visit. He found her broken and emaciated and stayed two or three weeks. In a few more weeks she was dead, probably of cancer.

Helen Eliza Benson Garrison. In 1834, Garrison married this daughter of a Connecticut antislavery man, George Benson. During their courtship, he wrote her letters and poems about his mother. During their long and happy marriage, she would quietly share his commitment to reform. As shown in this daguerreotype, made about twenty years after the marriage, she is an almost perfect combination of middle-class respectability and uncompromising principle. (The Bettmann Archive)

Garrison himself wrote and set the type for her obituary in the *Newburyport Herald*: "DIED. In Baltimore, after a long and distressing illness, which she bore with Christian fortitude and resignation, Mrs. Frances Maria Garrison, relict [widow] of the late Capt. Abijah G., formerly of this town."

This obituary and a couple of short poems were all that Garrison published for the next year. He wrote no more "pieces," as though he were trying to reassure his dead mother that he would not become worldly and unsteady. As for his father, Garrison symbolically killed "Abijah G." off with three words of the obituary, *relict*, *late*, and *formerly*, though he had no idea, in fact, whether his father was dead or alive. Maria Elizabeth *was* dead, and Caroline too. James was somewhere, drowning in rum or salt water, God only knew which. Garrison was alone with his printer's trade, his oil portrait, and his ambition.

But he had the company, too, of the memory of Fanny Garrison. Years after she died, when Garrison was courting the woman he was to marry, he wrote his fiancée a remarkable letter about his mother:

> You speak of "a mother's love." An allusion like this dissolves my heart, and causes it to grow liquid as water, I had a mother once, who cared for me with such a passionate regard, who loved me so intensely. How often did she watch over me— weep over me—and pray over me. "O that my mother were living!" is often the exclamation of my heart.

The letter invented a childhood that never had been. For most of the years after Abijah Garrison deserted his family, William Lloyd had not lived with his mother. She did not "care" for him "with passionate regard" or watch and weep over him. But distortion of memory was not his only problem. He added to his letter some lines of poor poetry that revealed a more serious ambiguity:

> She was the masterpiece of womankind—
>   In shape and height majestically fine;
> Her cheeks the lily and the rose combined;
>   Her lips—more opulently red than wine;
> Her raven locks hung tastefully entwined;
>   Her aspect fair as Nature could design;
> And then her eyes! so eloquently bright;
>   An eagle would recoil before their light.

The overt purpose of the poem was to reinforce the picture of his mother as a thing of gentle, caring beauty. But the real effect—an effect that Garrison could hardly have been aware of—was to present a picture of intimidating power: a woman of majestic height (Garrison himself was only a few inches over five feet) and vivid aspect, colored in lurid shades of red, white, and black, with "entwining" locks and with eyes whose light would frighten even an eagle. Little wonder that when Garrison was much older, he would still tell his own children that "I always feel like a little boy when I think of Mother."

When he completed his apprenticeship in December 1825, Garrison's life was a mixture of conflicting purposes and self-images. The center of experience for him was his career. He had mastered his trade. But the trade of printing was only the beginning. His task now was to transform a craft into a vocation—to become not just a printer but an owner and editor, a man of affairs. The path that lay clearly before him was an entrepreneurial one. And since the journalism of the day was very closely associated with politics, his vocation would lead naturally to political involvement, almost as naturally as the careers of lawyers did. Garrison had chosen a calling that was on intimate terms with what his mother fearfully called "this world." And if his life followed the normal pattern, he could expect to deal constantly with the dangerous Hydra of worldly realities: political parties, issues of foreign policy and elections, the pragmatic facts of commerce and legislation, as well as with the economic realities of publishing.

But always there was the conflicting pull of his mother's disdain of the world, her suspicion of power, her mistrust of success, her conviction that the Christian life is, in essence, a life of sacrifice and suffering. In such a world, the only real security and consolation lay in faith, and in the world to come. The issue of Garrison's life was simple: Could the ambitions of the self-made man be reconciled with Fanny Garrison's sacrificial piety? It took Garrison about ten years to come to terms with his dilemma, ten years of movement, frustration, and danger.

His first step was economic. With the help of a loan from his former master, he bought a recently founded newspaper in Newburyport, which he renamed the *Free Press*. He spent about half of 1826 editing and publishing the paper, writing mostly about party politics. His motto was the motto of Massachusetts Federalism: "Our

Country, Our Whole Country, and Nothing But Our Country." And in the pages of the *Free Press* he adopted an almost desperately conservative Federalist line. Already, while still an apprentice, he had written a number of political pieces damning Andrew Jackson, whom Garrison saw as a dueling, gambling, drinking, slaveowning planter.

But Garrison's attachment to the Federalist party went well beyond fear of General Jackson. He resented all the political compromises of the 1820s, the adoption by John Quincy Adams of the "loose" principles of the Jeffersonians. Even when Jefferson died, while most other Federalist newspapers in Massachusetts were willing to forgive him in a quick flurry of bereaved patriotism, Garrison was unbending. Jefferson was still an infidel, and the only acceptable politics was the good, old, true Federalism of the 1790s. So Garrison committed himself to a lost political cause. It cost him subscribers, even in Federalist Newburyport; after six months, his first venture had failed. His choice of his first battleground was political. But in a deeper sense he had been true to his mother's wishes. He had defined politics in moral terms and taken an uncompromising position on the highest principles, regardless of penalty. He had courted the world's rejection, and his courtship was successful.

The next year, Garrison stepped into the tide that was taking thousands of other young men of ambition into the cities, and moved to Boston. He had been to the city at least twice before—once on the way to his deathbed visit to his mother in Baltimore, when he became hopelessly lost and confused; a second time, later, when he had walked the forty miles to the city and arrived with raw and bleeding feet, only to turn around the next day and take the stagecoach back home to Newburyport. This third time, in 1827, he came on a mission, in quest of his own career. He went from one printing establishment to another, ready to hire himself out as a journeyman to any master. But it was several months before an opportunity came his way. He took a position on a struggling newspaper devoted to the cause of temperance, the *National Philanthropist*.

During his months on the *National Philanthropist*, Garrison made a delicate and important transition. He began to write about "the slothfulness and bane of party spirit." He now wrote on issues that he thought went *beyond* the question of party: drunkenness, militarism, gambling, dueling, Sabbath-breaking, and a dozen other disorders in American life. Everywhere he looked, he saw depravity, a host of evils threatening to "subvert the purity of our institutions." And the way to survival, he now saw, lay not through politics but through Christian reform.

What was happening to Garrison was simple: He was becoming a reformer. Like many other Americans, he was being converted to a new type of alternative to the normal channels of parties and government institutions. To be sure, Garrison still wanted to influence politics. But preserving "our institutions," he now decided, demanded something that was *prior* to politics: the reformation of the national character. If men could be saved from drunkenness, kept from prostitutes, exposed to the saving influences of evangelical religion, then (and only then) might they be trusted to elect others to political office. The task of reform was nothing less than the salvation of the national soul, a task well beyond the capacities of party politics.

Reform, as Garrison saw it in the late 1820s, was a difficult and dangerous undertaking. He, and other reformers like him, would have to confront public ridicule and would risk their reputations and their honor. But Garrison was willing to dare it. More than willing, he was delighted. He could now confront the world in a combative spirit. He would be called on for sacrifice. He could view himself in lonely but heroic terms:

> While there remains a tyrant to sway the iron rod of power, or chain about the body or mind to be broken, I cannot surrender my arms. While drunkenness and intemperance abound, I will try to reclaim the dissolute, and to annihilate the progress of vice. I will reprove, admonish and condemn. My duty is plain.

Reform had several advantages for Garrison. As a reform editor and publicist, he could appeal to a constituency that was not local. He would not have to compromise with the prejudices of small towns like Newburyport. He could appeal to a selective audience of people like himself—people of Christian piety and principled energy. Among *them*, he could find a fame that did not require him to satisfy the wishes of "this world." And if triumph came, in time, then it would be honorable. In the meantime, the formula was simple: Take positions that were radical enough to be dangerous (but also radical enough to gain fame) and persist in the faith that the odds could be overcome, the triumph achieved.

Garrison sometimes talked and wrote as though there were only two parties to the reform struggle: on one side was the whole world, full of its disorders, vices, and tyrannies; on the other side was the lone individual, defiant, daring, almost self-created. It was as though the self-made man stepped forth into the world to find a reality so alien to his own virtue that it could be met on no other terms than hostility. But, in truth, something stood between the individual and the world. Reform organizations gave meaning and extension to individual experience. Garrison did not invent reform to solve his vocational problem. He found it. When he came to Boston, new benevolent organizations and societies were being formed in the city at the fantastic rate of one a month.

This organizing fever dated back to the Revolution. But the fever reached its highest pitch just at the time Garrison began his adult career. And, as luck would have it, he chose Boston, the city more in the grip of reform activity than any other in the United States. Garrison lived, soon after he came to Boston, in a boardinghouse full of reformers and Baptist "city missionaries." It was in this boardinghouse that he met the man who had founded the *National Philanthropist*. A steady stream of reformers came to talk to the boarders. Wherever Garrison went to listen to sermons, ministers preached the necessity of reform. If he chose to be a radical, he did so in a movement that was gathering strength, power, and organization.

Garrison sometimes succumbed to the temptation to romanticize himself, to see his role as that of the radical individual facing a series of corrupt powers with only his words as weapons. But this picture was distorted. He became a reformer as a way of *joining*, of gaining membership in an organized community of like-minded people. As a radical reformer, he could be both victim and victor. He could resolve the central difficulty of his young life by satisfying the claims of ambition and piety together.

A Boston mob. In 1835 William Lloyd Garrison was mobbed in Boston. He escaped only when he was placed under arrest for his own protection. The crowd is shown accurately as a combination of "gentlemen," sailors, and stereotyped Irishmen. To the right is another abolitionist, William Thompson, who is escaping in a woman's clothing. (Culver Pictures)

However spiritually rewarding the *National Philanthropist* may have been, it did not satisfy Garrison. He decided to become editor of the *Journal of the Times*, in Bennington, Vermont, where he would work for Adams in the election of 1828—falling back, for the moment, into politics. His editorials for Adams were lukewarm (despite his very intense fear that Jackson might win). And he made the *Journal of the Times* a bit unusual among the small-town newspapers of the day by devoting a great deal of space to the three nonpolitical reforms he had decided were most important: peace, temperance, and antislavery. His months in Bennington amounted to a temporary relapse into party politics. But in the meantime, he was restlessly preparing to define himself as a radical reformer in even more pointed terms.

Garrison was peculiarly vulnerable to other reformers. While he was still in Newburyport, a leader of the pacifist movement gave a lecture there; overnight, Garrison was a pacifist. Every new society in Boston for the suppression of vice caught his attention easily and roused him to the most optimistic kinds of hopes. He was a man in search of movements, a publicist in search of causes, a moralist in search of outrages. So it was with the issue of slavery. Garrison had had little or no direct contact with the institution of slavery. He had never seen a plantation. He had seen very few slaves. But slavery was, in the end, to be his cause. He never lost his interest in universal reform: He kept alive his hopes for evangelism, for women's rights, and for peace. But slavery became, after about 1828, his primary public concern; "abolitionist" became his principal vocation. Slavery could do for Garrison what the peace movement or temperance could not: propel him into fame (and into infamy), threaten his life, send him to jail cells in Baltimore and Boston, and provide him with a cause on which there could be no compromise at all.

Garrison's conversion to antislavery came in 1828 in the same quick way his earlier conversion to pacificism and other reforms had come. Benjamin Lundy, a young Quaker from Ohio, came to Boston to lecture on slavery. He spoke first to an earnest group at Garrison's boardinghouse. Garrison was urgently moved. He made slavery one of the concerns of the *National Philanthropist* and the *Journal of the Times*. After Jackson's victory in the 1828 election, Garrison was out of work and broke; when Lundy invited him to come to Baltimore and serve as coeditor of Lundy's antislavery newspaper, the *Genius of Universal Emancipation*, Garrison jumped at the chance.

When Garrison went to Baltimore, he was in his mid-twenties. He had been a marvelously "steady" boy, and he might have expected to become more successful with the passage of years. But he had failed in his first publishing venture. He had moved through two other editorial positions rapidly and unprofitably. Economically, he was a failure. His financial unsteadiness was more than matched by his growing attraction for unpopular causes and unprofitable reforms. Even before he reached Baltimore, he had decided that Lundy's antislavery position was too cautious. Garrison quickly announced in the *Genius* a radical demand for immediate, unconditional emancipation, by whatever means, at whatever cost, and with whatever consequences. Slavery was a sin, and he would not accept any slow and incomplete solution. He had already reached similar conclusions about drinking and war: He had demanded total prohibition of alcohol, a total end to war. Now he applied the same logic to slavery. Within a few months he was in jail.

Garrison's first imprisonment was connected, by slender threads of history, back to his youth. In the fall of 1829 he printed in the *Genius* a pair of brief items accusing a New England merchant of cruelty and greed. The merchant, who happened to be from Newburyport, and who was engaged in the same coasting trade that Abijah Garrison had plied, had transported some eighty slaves from Baltimore to New Orleans for sale. The venture was entirely legal and commonplace. But Garrison singled the man out for a bitter (and somewhat inaccurate) attack. The result was a suit for libel brought by the merchant against Garrison and Lundy, who were both found guilty and fined. Garrison would not pay his fine, and so was sentenced to six-month jail term.

He was happy. The jail was large, old-fashioned, and relaxed. He could wander around it, eat his meals comfortably with the warden and his family, and had time to write a pamphlet giving *A Brief Sketch of the Trial of William Lloyd Garrison*. But his relaxation, his sense of harmony—almost of ease—were not a result of the physical comforts of jail life, or of the pleasure of writing about his own victimization. Garrison was delighted primarily because all the elements of a new image of himself had at last come neatly together. He had worked out, over the past few years, the main outlines of a new identity. Now, in jail for the first time, these outlines came into

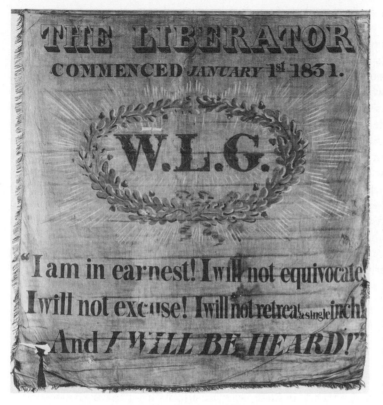

Liberator banner. This fringed banner was hand-lettered to celebrate the beginnings of *The Liberator*. It captures something of Garrison's extreme preoccupation with the self by placing the initials W.L.G. within a conventional wreath and sunburst, and by quoting the thundering sentences that all begin with "I." The designer did not plan the second line very carefully and initially omitted the second *t* in *retreat*. (Massachusetts Historical Society)

dramatic focus, almost as though his life had, for a few weeks at least, an unambiguous dramatic script.

The central theme of the drama was not really slavery, or even reform in general. It was Garrison's realization of his own freedom. As he put it in a joking letter that he proudly dated "Baltimore Jail/May 12, 1830": "I pay no rent—am bound to make no repairs—and enjoy the luxury of independence divested of its cares." He had, in fact, "divested" (literally, "undressed") himself of a good many "cares." He had cast off, one by one, most of the protective rings of identity that men and women ordinarily have. He had no family, no job, no property, no protection of law, no control even over his own body. He had transcended every tie of kinship and institution. He had become, or so it seemed to him, the ultimate master of his own fate and soul. Like many fictional prisoners of his romantic age, Garrison scratched a sonnet onto the wall of his cell, a rhymed celebration of his own transcendent spiritual independence:

> High walls and huge the BODY may confine,
>   And iron gates obstruct the prisoner's gaze,
> And massive bolts may baffle his design,
>   And vigilant keepers watch his devious ways:
> Yet scorns the immortal MIND this base control!
>   No chains can bind it, and no cell enclose:
> Swifter than light, it flies from pole to pole.

In a curious way, this kind of freedom had been the unacknowledged quest of the whole Garrison family for two generations. Abijah's desertion was his way of claiming liberation. James's debauches were his more desperate assertions of freedom. Fanny Garrison's yearnings for the release of death and the perfections of heaven were her version of the search for individual immunity from the world. William Lloyd Garrison found what his brother and parents had failed to find: a way of giving freedom an organized focus in *this* world and not the next, a way of deserting social institutions instead of a wife and children. He could break laws, as his brother did, but his criminality was pious and spiritual, not drunken and fleshly.

Armed with this final sense of his own freedom, his total immunity from the "rude blast of misfortune," Garrison could easily accept the gesture of a wealthy New York merchant who paid his fine after forty-nine days in jail; only his body was dependent on the charity. He could press his radicalism to its logical limit. He had a confident identity now. The old conflict between ambition and piety was laid to rest. He could leave the Baltimore jail and return to Boston to found a new antislavery journal, *The Liberator*, whose first issue appeared on New Year's Day 1831. And in it he could thunder his defiance of the whole world, with a sure sense of who the "I" of the sentences was, and with the words "I will be" set in italics by his own hand:

> *I will be* harsh as truth, and as uncompromising as justice. I am in earnest—I will not equivocate—I will not excuse—I will not retreat a single inch—AND I WILL BE HEARD.

THE SELF-MADE SOCIETY

William Lloyd and James Garrison were curious, idiosyncratic men. Their lives seem to be made up of individual choices and accidents. They do not seem to be *typical* of anything whatsoever. But the life stories of all the Garrisons were products of the same processes of change that were touching the lives of every American during the first half of the nineteenth century. Both William Lloyd and James Garrison would have been regarded as social freaks by most of their contemporaries. But the two brothers were really mirrors, in which the "normal" characteristics of American society can be clearly seen.

At bottom, the life of the Garrison family can be understood as the result of half a dozen processes of change that were transforming American society. The first was an accelerating change in the ways Americans produced, bought, and sold goods and services. The second was an equally drastic change in the ways Americans thought about mobility, about the ways individuals and families moved across the landscape and up or down a ladder of economic and social status. The third change was the spread of another wave of religious revivalism that altered the face of American Protestantism. Fourth, both in practice and in theory, the family became a different kind of social institution. The fifth change was the development of a new sense of the power of people to control and reform their society. Thou-

sands of groups were created whose purpose was to stamp out one kind of evil or another. Finally, in literature and in art, a new set of ideas about the individual and society was shaped by a remarkable generation of intellectuals and writers.

All these developments need to be understood together, for they were in fact closely related. Taken together, they help make sense of the odd, even freakish, experiences of William Lloyd Garrison and his family.

Economic Growth and Transformation

To many Americans who lived during the first half of the nineteenth century, an economic miracle seemed to be happening. Their population increased dramatically, from 5 million in 1800 to 31 million in 1850. Their cities multiplied and spread. Everywhere, there were new machines and new ways of doing things: an engine, or "gin," for removing the seeds from cotton; a mechanical harvester for wheat; canals and railroads; steamboats and textile mills. For most people, there was more to eat, more to wear, bigger houses with bigger rooms. The world seemed to explode with chances and choices: to go west and take up a farm in Ohio or Michigan or Oregon; to invent a machine; to become an educated white-collar worker instead of an illiterate farmer like your father; to marry whomever you chose and live wherever you wanted. Freedom for many Americans was more than an abstract principle of the Declaration of Independence. It seemed to be everywhere, in the concrete details of life. And it seemed to go hand in hand with economic well-being.

There was another side to the coin, though. If there was more wealth every decade, it was owned by fewer and fewer people. In 1800, 10 percent of the families in America owned somewhere between a third and a half of all the land and buildings, and other tangible property. But by 1870 the share that belonged to the richest 10 percent had increased to about two-thirds. And if their other property—stocks, bonds, and other intangibles—was added in, their share of the national pie was even bigger. In the cities, the unequal distribution of wealth was even more striking. In New York in 1845, 4 percent of the people owned 80 percent of the property. In Philadelphia in 1860, 5 percent owned 90 percent.

Yet the evidence is overwhelming that most of the other 90 percent—the 90 percent who owned less than a third of all the wealth—were convinced that the economy was good to them, and that their society was opening up, not closing down, opportunities.

The solution to the puzzle lies in growth. As measured by economists, at least, the American economy was growing so rapidly that most of the people did earn more and own more as time passed. The economy could sustain *both* a growing concentration of wealth in a few rich hands *and* a generally improving situation for a majority of the free population. And the 10 percent who owned two-thirds of the wealth represented many more people in 1850 than it had in 1800— half a million in 1800, over 3 million in 1850. This meant some people did go from poverty to riches. And for every man or woman who made it, there

were thousands of others whose dreams were fed on the successes of a few. When William Lloyd Garrison, poor and practically orphaned, daydreamed about owning a newspaper and being a gentleman, when he bought an oil portrait of himself as a kind of forecast of his future status, he was only hoping the hopes of his generation.

The economic growth that fed the dream of success and prosperity was part of the industrial revolution that had been changing the entire world for at least two centuries. The term "industrial revolution" conjures up a picture of huge factories and complicated machines, but this is not an accurate way of seeing the economic growth of the first half of the nineteenth century. Most production still took place in small shops and in homes.

Much of the change had to do not with machines but with scale. In Cincinnati in the 1840s, a shop for butchering hogs was built. It used no complicated machinery. Its construction was of traditional materials—mostly wood with a little iron. But the work was laid out in an assembly-line fashion, and the result was that a hog could be slaughtered, cleaned, butchered, and barreled in only one minute. Pictures of the construction of the Erie Canal show workers using hand tools and very primitive wood and rope devices. But there were thousands of them, organized into efficient gangs by professional engineers, and the result was a striking increase in efficiency. Hat manufacturers in Danbury, Connecticut, continued to use the traditional "putting-out" system—sending work into rural households to be done by hand, then collecting the results, finishing the hats, and marketing them. But the system could now be organized on a larger and larger scale. The hats could reach bigger markets in shorter times. And the profits would return sooner to Danbury, where they could finance even more systematic organization and marketing. Everywhere, but particularly in the Northern states, the organization of economic activity on a large scale, designed to function at high speed, turned out more and more goods and profits.

An early locomotive. This machine, named the *Atlantic*, was the first steam locomotive to enter Washington, D.C. It was operated by the Baltimore and Ohio Railroad and was built in 1832. To the modern eye, the engine seems frail and even slightly comic. But to the men and women of the 1830s, it was an imposing symbol of power and technological progress. (Library of Congress)

THE RISE OF CORPORATIONS Both the scale and the speed depended on the spread of other forms of organization—of methods of gathering capital, borrowing, and paying. Economic activity became corporate activity. By the time of the War of 1812 the states had already issued almost 2,000 corporate charters. And by the 1820s the state of Massachusetts alone had more corporations than all of western Europe.

The advantages of corporations—from the point of view of those who owned them, at least—were basically two. First, the corporation could, by selling shares of stock or bonds, create a large pool of capital. Second, the corporation limited the liability of any single shareholder. If an individual went bankrupt, he might lose everything—house, furniture, horses, even clothing. But if a corporation failed, the investors would lose only the value of the stock they held. They would not be liable for any of the unpaid debts of the corporation.

THE ADVENT OF THE RAILROAD The large-scale corporations depended heavily on the capacity of producers to get their goods to market rapidly. The Erie Canal, its dozens of imitators, and the steamboats on the Ohio and the Mississippi provided the basic transportation network. But after the 1830s the water and road systems were supplemented by a new invention, the railroad. The workability of the steam locomotive was proved in England in 1829. Within just a few years, the idea caught on in the United States. Short lines were built to connect cities like Charleston or Boston with their surrounding countryside. Then, in the 1840s, a number of major cities were connected not just to the countryside but to each other. In the next decade, rail mileage increased 400 percent, and by 1860 the United States had a total of 30,000 miles of rail lines (about ten times the total canal mileage).

Building the transportation network required corporations, of course. In fact, railroads were among the first billion-dollar corporations in American history. But something more was needed. There was not enough private capital in the country to build the railroads and canals. The crucial missing portion was supplied by governments. The states were especially generous patrons of the canal and railroad companies. All in all, the states went into debt almost $100 million to help finance the construction of rail lines. And what state governments did on such a huge scale, local and county governments imitated wherever they could. Local governments may actually have financed as much as one-fifth of all the rail mileage in the United States before 1860. In 1850 the federal government entered the picture. Congress voted to give almost 4 million acres of land to the Illinois Central Railroad to help it pay for building a line from Illinois to Alabama. By 1860 the federal government had granted away a total of 22 million acres of the public's land to railroad corporations.

POPULATION All these changes demanded people—people to produce the goods, to get them from place to place, and to buy them. The population of the United States increased about 600 percent between 1800 and 1860. Some of this increase was the result of a high birth rate, particularly in rural areas. But the overall birth rate was actually declining, and by the 1840s only a new wave of European immigration could keep the rate of population growth as high as it had been. In the 1840s and 1850s a stream of Irish and German immigrants joined the continuing British immigration. Most of the immigrants were young. And this fact, coupled with the high birth rate of earlier decades, created a population that was dramatically younger than that of Western Europe. By the middle of the century, seven Americans out of every ten were under thirty— as compared to six out of ten in England and five out of ten in France.

The population was both young and mobile. In five towns in western Massachusetts, nine out of ten people who were between the ages of sixteen and twenty in 1850 had left their communities by 1860. The Garrison family's nomadic life—from Canada to Massachusetts, Maryland, and Vermont—was typical of the experience of their contemporaries. And it was typical in another way, too. Most of the people who moved around the country were poor or unskilled, looking for work or for land, and providing a ready pool of cheap labor for commercial and manufacturing enterprises.

On the other hand, the economy also needed a pool of skilled workers. Someone had to design and build the boats and engines. Someone had to add up the columns of figures, keep track of the inventories, pay the bills, and file the receipts. These needs were met by governments, mostly state and local, through the school system. Although public schools had existed in America since the seventeenth century, the first true public school law was passed in Massachusetts in 1837, and was quickly imitated by a number of other states. Most of the schools were only at the elementary level, but most of the people in the northern states attended them and at least learned to read and to do simple arithmetic. For some others, there were more years of school ahead. In 1860, 300 high schools and 137 colleges in the United States were turning out the managers, the accountants, and the engineers needed to tend the new economy.

Skills and education led people more often than not into towns and cities. During the eighteenth century, four port cities had contained more than half the urban population of the nation: Boston, New York, Philadelphia, and Baltimore. After about 1820 the pattern began to change. Boston, Philadelphia, and Baltimore continued to grow, but less rapidly than the population as a whole. Only New York outstripped the national growth rate to become, by the middle of the century, the dominant city. The Hudson River and the Erie Canal gave New York crucial access to the fastest-growing section of the United States, the trans-Appalachian interior.

Irish immigrants. This detail from an 1847 painting shows an immigrant ship being emptied in New York. The Irish immigrants are of both sexes and all ages. In the lower center, a portly gentleman (not an immigrant, his dress and cane suggest) may be negotiating a job with one of the immigrants, who is shown hat-in-hand. At the lower left, another gentleman, in a dandified white waistcoat, is studying a woman, perhaps with a different sort of transaction in mind. The mass of people still on deck suggests how overcrowded the immigrant ships were. (The Museum of the City of New York)

The same reasons that explain the spectacular growth of New York also explain the rise of hundreds of new towns and cities, from the coast to the Mississippi. Where in 1800 there had been only villages or wilderness, new centers like Cincinnati, Rochester, Louisville, Pittsburgh, St. Louis, and New Orleans sprang into life. In 1800 the United States contained only thirty-two cities of the second rank—less than 50,000 inhabitants. By 1860 there were ten times as many. The opening of the agricultural West was an important development, and Americans tend to look to that frontier experience for their myths and their heroes. But migration to the cities was in fact larger than migration westward during the first half of the nineteenth century. Like the rates of growth

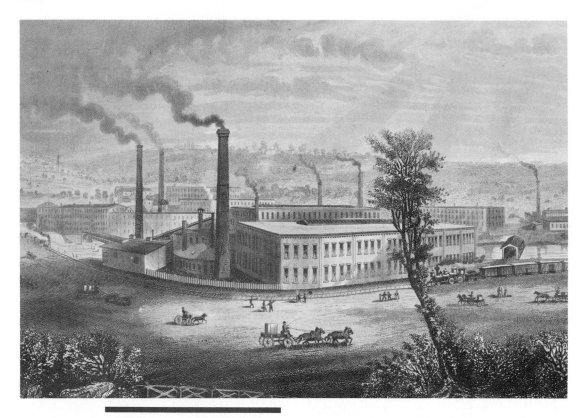

A factory town. Much of the early industrial revolution took place not in great cities but in smaller manufacturing villages, especially in New England. This factory for making scales, in St. Johnsbury, Vermont, was originally built on a river for water power, but it has been transformed by the development of steam power. The artist is also at pains to emphasize the presence of railroad transportation. (Courtesy, The Henry Francis du Pont Winterthur Museum)

of the population and of economic productivity, the increase in the pace of urbanization was more rapid during the decades before 1860 than it had ever been before or would ever be again.

TECHNOLOGY, GROWTH, AND THEIR EFFECTS Here, then, was an incredibly rich economic mixture: enterprises of large scale, using corporate organization and efficient techniques; the most effective system of transportation the world had ever known; a pool of workers who were mobile and willing to work because they were poor and young, or able to work

because they were skilled and educated; governments that helped underwrite ventures for which private capital was unavailable; and cities, old and new, where production and marketing could be concentrated. It was into this mixture that new technological developments were introduced.

Taken by itself, a new machine could have only a limited effect. But combined with all the other ingredients of economic growth, an invention could pay enormous dividends. Robert Fulton demonstrated a steamboat in 1807, but it would not have had such an impact if it had not been for things like the assembly-line hog butchering firm in Cincinnati. Samuel F. B. Morse's

Broadway. This 1834 print shows Broadway, in New York City, looking north from the corner of Canal Street. This is the preindustrial city at its peak of development. Animals are almost as numerous as people. There are hardly any machines in evidence. And the four-story facades are practically uniform, all the way up the long avenue. (Museum of Fine Arts, Boston)

invention of the telegraph in 1840 would have had much less importance if there were not a multitude of intercity commercial messages waiting to be transmitted.

The most spectacular technological changes occurred in the textile industry. Inventions—mostly British—made it possible to spin thread and yarn, and to weave cloth, at rates that were dizzying compared to traditional hand methods. Between the end of the War of 1812 and 1833, the cotton industry produced 16 percent more cloth each year than it had the year before.

The largest textile corporation, the Boston Associates, assembled capital of $600,000 to build cotton mills in Massachusetts towns like Waltham and Lowell. They used new machines as fast as inventors could turn them out. But they also used other, nonmechanical methods: They tapped a cheap labor pool by hiring young girls from rural communities as their primary labor force. (Later, the Irish and other immigrants would largely replace the mill girls. They had more stamina and would work for equally low wages.) The Boston Associates also led the way for other corporations by establishing their own national marketing organization. And they engaged in a program of national advertising that would set a pattern for later large-scale corporations.

The economic change that resulted from all these elements—plus the abundance of land and natural resources—was remarkable. It raised the average standard of living of American workers and their families. On the whole, they probably ate more than any other large population in the world.

But the changes were not all beneficial. The 90 percent of young people who left their Massachusetts towns may not have wanted to go and often did not better themselves when they did move. The skilled shoemaker who lost markets to factory-produced shoes was unhappy. Nearly half the workers of Garrison's Newburyport in the 1850s could testify that their children did not attend the public schools. Skilled workers were better off, to be sure, and there were more of them. The same was true of the shareholders of the new companies. But more numerous were the unskilled workers whose lives had not been improved by economic growth at all. And for the immigrant poor, most of whom stayed in the cities, the death rate was more than twice as high as for rural, native-born, white Americans.

But beneficial or not, economic change reached into every family and into every individual's life. The Garrison family's elation when they first arrived in Massachusetts, where there was plenty of work and low prices, was offset by the economic disasters that broke up the family a few years later. But it would have been difficult to identify an American family that had *not* been touched just as deeply by economic change— whose world would ever be the same again—for better or for worse.

The "Self-Made Man"

The effect of economic growth on people's lives was very often dramatic. Some men whose fathers had been poor became rich. Women whose mothers had minded farmhouses found themselves in cities, married to clerks, or working in mills or shops themselves. Irish peasant boys became saloonkeepers in New York or worked on canal-boats on the Erie. A few boys who had been poor and even orphaned as children actually did grow up to become president of the United States.

As a result, it began to seem to many people that there was no limit to the way a man—though seldom a woman—could make himself into a success. All the restrictions imposed by tradition— poverty or the custom of following a father's trade or being bound to his farm—seemed to drop away in the new rush of opportunity. The popular notion of the "self-made man" supposed that success was everywhere to be had, that opportunity was boundless, that the world was usually fair and rewarded those who deserved success.

The idea of the self-made man found expression in hundreds of books, pamphlets, poems, newspaper articles and editorials, and speeches. But its classic statement was the autobiography written by Benjamin Franklin when he was an old man, published in full only in 1818. Thousands of boys practically memorized Franklin's account of his simple origins. They studied his picture of himself arriving in Philadelphia at seventeen, dressed in old clothes, munching the rolls he had bought with his last money. Then they learned how he had disciplined his character by practicing the virtues of industry, frugality, and sobriety. Franklin's message was plain: If he could do it, there was no reason any other man could not.

The boys and young men who pored over Franklin's life story found the same message in the books they were given to read in the public schools. The idea was reinforced by the fame of Andrew Jackson, the first American president whose lowly beginnings were ever pointed to with pride. And when the boys grew up, they founded Franklin clubs and Franklin societies in almost every town. No American but Washington had more places named after him than Franklin. If Washington was the father of his country, then

Franklin was its kindly ideological uncle, dispensing the advice and encouragement needed by young men on their way up. Garrison's joining the Franklin Club in Newburyport was not an isolated action. It was part of a wave of enthusiasm for enterprise, a faith that anyone could break free of the past, start from scratch, and become rich or famous—or at least respectable.

The ideology of the self-made man was not universal. Many people who belonged to families with old wealth saw it as a threat and complained bitterly about the *nouveaux riches*. The idea of being self-made meant little to most women—except through their husbands' or sons' careers. It meant less than nothing to millions of slaves, for whom the most certain thing of all was that history could *not* be escaped. Poor farmers or immigrants were untouched by it. And the notion of being self-made was bitterly ironic to the thousands of traditional artisans and craftsmen who saw their ways being eroded by the currents of the new economy.

In numerical terms, the idea of the self-made man was a minority idea. It appealed to only a segment of the society, and even within that group it must have weakened as men grew older and the promise of success faded. But the minority to which it appealed was powerful. They could vote, and they did. They clustered in the towns and cities, now clearly the centers of power in the northern states. They had money, and more of it with every passing year. They bought the newspapers and magazines, the novels and poetry. This class of Americans—and there is no more accurate name for it than the middle class—paid the salaries of the ministers and the lecturers. They supported the public schools and sent their children there. In short, they dominated the popular expressions of attitude and opinion. There were other attitudes, of course, and other opinions, but they tended to be voiceless or to express themselves in acts rather than in written words and pictures.

The attitudes of this new middle class seemed utterly confident, even boastful. But there was another side to things. The idea of success implies the possibility of failure. Change could be seen as a gain, but it concealed the threat of rootlessness. Escaping from history might be a good thing, but it could also lead to a world without customs and standards, a world where every man was as good as the next man, but where every action, good or bad, was equally appropriate—if it worked.

The task of the new middle class was to find ways of getting *control* of change, both in their own lives and in their society. They needed to develop new sources of discipline and order. And so they devised new ideas and practices in religion, in their family patterns, and in thousands of clubs and associations they organized to "reform" themselves and other people, to make the world safe for opportunity. Their religion was a new kind of revivalism. Their ideal family was an instrument of restraint and discipline. Their reform movements were designed to turn people whose lives were out of control—slaves or slaveholders, criminals, the insane, drunkards, prostitutes, children—into orderly citizens or, if that failed, into orderly inmates of some well-managed asylum or prison.

Middle-Class Evangelism

Evangelical revivals had always been part of American life. The seventeenth century saw frequent "quickenings" and "awakenings." In the mid-eighteenth century, a greater wave of the "outpouring of God's grace" produced the "Great Awakening." In the 1780s and 1790s came another revival. Older denominations like the Congregationalists and the Presbyterians seemed revitalized, and newer denominations like the Methodists and the Baptists experienced rapid and sustained growth. The energies of Protestantism were so powerful that the movement seemed to deserve the title of the Second Great Awakening. Still, the rate of religious conversions remained so high down through the first half of the nineteenth century that it became difficult to separate one "awakening" from another. American religious experience appeared to be one long evangelical revival, stretching across more than a century, enduring revolution and war, party shifts, and every other change.

The evangelism of the 1820s and the following decades was a religious movement of the new middle class and had some new and distinctive features. Much remained the same, of course. The vocabulary of salvation was still "sin," "grace," "hell," and "heaven." But the ministers and their congregations, the revivalists and their audiences, began to talk and behave differently. And the differences were all related to the hopes and the anxieties of the new social groups that had been generated by economic change.

CHARLES GRANDISON FINNEY Social movements seldom have precise beginnings. But a symbolic beginning for the new evangelism was the conversion, in 1823, of Charles Grandison Finney, who was to become the most spectacularly successful American preacher of the period. He had been born into a farming family that moved out onto the New York frontier at about the time the Erie Canal was begun. In 1823 Finney had moved to a small town not far from Buffalo and was struggling to become a lawyer, hoping, like so many others, to catch the wave of self-made success.

One day he went into the woods, worried about his soul and determined to wrest salvation from God that day or to die a sinner. After hours of struggle, in which he set his will against God's as though in a contest, Finny surrendered. He accepted his damnation as God's will. But the moment of surrender was miraculously transformed into the moment of grace. No sooner did he give up than he was visited by "wave upon wave of liquid love."

The experience altered his life forever, and he began to preach, informally at first, then as a licensed Presbyterian. The conversions he brought about in his little town were spectacular and numerous. He kept to no pulpit but traveled wherever an audience could be assembled. Finally, in 1831 he was invited to Rochester, the booming flour-milling town. The result was a revival that made Finney famous everywhere. From Rochester, the road led to New York, and then out again into whatever communities summoned Finney to save them.

Well before the Rochester revival, other ministers were learning the same strategies. Some preachers, especially in the older denominations, resisted Finney's "New Measures," but most of them gradually became convinced by the most practical test of all: The New Measures worked.

Finney's message, and the New Measures of evangelism, were partly theology, partly pulpit technique, and partly organization. What Finney had learned in his own conversion experience, he thought, was that grace came only when he had given up hope, when he had been willing to deny his own selfish interests and recognize the overriding power and claims of God. Once this had been done, he became free to exercise enormous power as a preacher. Surrendering the self ended by making the self strong, not weak.

The same paradox was part of every conversion, Finney and his associates believed. They demanded that the men and women who came to them become humble and recognize that they were hopelessly damned. But the result, when they truly believed, was that the humble became high, the damned, saved. An evangelical conversion experience was an exercise in religious mobility, in which the converted man or woman could become a kind of self-made Christian. God's help was necessary, of course, but God's help was offered at every moment to every person. Grace was somewhat like success in the ideology of the self-made man: It was there, waiting for anyone who was willing to acknowledge his or her spiritual rags to earn spiritual riches.

TRACTS AND MISSIONARIES Finney and his colleagues communicated their message in language and gestures that were simple, passionate, impatient of theological technicalities, and careless of denominational lines. They were out to reach the largest possible audiences. And they were technologically up-to-date. In important ways, they were adapting the newest methods of manufacturing and marketing. Their sermons were not hand-crafted for local consumers, but were made like interchangeable parts that would work as well in Indiana as in New York or Kentucky, and as well on Baptists as on Methodists or Presbyterians. The evangelists traveled, like the "agents" who were beginning to represent manufacturers in regional "territories." They advertised and promoted, and they measured their success—as entrepreneurs did—by the volume of the conversions they brought about. The new evangelism, like the new world of corporate enterprise, was based on organization. A number of new, interdenominational organizations were founded. The most important were the American Tract Society (which distributed the mass-produced Evangelical Family Library) and the American Home Missionary Society, which sent its missionaries into almost every part of the North and West. By the 1850s, the Home Missionary Society had about 1,000 full-time "agents" in the "field." The Tract Society had over 600 full-time "distributors."

In theory, the revivalists and their powerful organizations wanted to convert everyone. But in practice, their source of strength was the new middle class. In the Rochester revival of 1831, Finney's converts were mainly in the families of lawyers, merchants, manufacturers, and master artisans. Among the poor and the unskilled he was much less successful. And this remained the primary pattern of revivalism throughout the North. Only in periods of economic depression, or in areas where workers were losing jobs to Catholic immigrants, did evangelism make much headway among the poor and the unskilled.

Evangelism made great strides, too, in the West, but its success there was peculiar. To the preachers, the West was a distant problem. It had to be saved not from within, and not by its own people, but by the East, by the missionaries who would carry the evangelical word, distribute the tracts, and record the conversions. In fact, the revivalists tended to look at workers and westerners in somewhat the same way: as populations that needed restraint and discipline.

The new evangelism was also different from the old in the much heavier emphasis it gave to the role of women. Many of the supporters of the missionary and tract societies were women, and the conversion of wives and mothers was often preached as an essential step toward the conversion of entire families. In fact, women were described frequently as being instinctively more virtuous than men. They were pictured, at the most extreme, as the only Christianizing influence that could restrain a society as competitive, as subject to material temptation, and as much in flux as the United States.

Revivalism fitted nicely with the two sides of the ideology of the self-made man. It emphasized the possibility that people could change themselves, and it also seemed to provide a means for quieting anxieties generated by change. It held out hope, but it demanded self-denial, self-control, and self-restraint.

A New Model of Family Life

Wherever industrialization has taken place, whether in the United States, Europe, or other parts of the world, the ways women, men, and their children live together have been deeply altered. In the nineteenth-century United States, a new model of the family began to take shape. It did not emerge in full detail until the twentieth century, and it was as much an ideal as a reality. But the same kinds of people that adopted the idea of the self-made man and provided the memberships for the tract and home missions organizations gradually started to redefine what it meant to be a man or a woman, to bring up a child or manage a home.

A school for young ladies. This daguerreotype, made around 1855, shows a classroom in Boston's Emerson School for Young Ladies. It was founded by George Barrell Emerson (not related to Ralph Waldo Emerson) and was considered a model school. Sending daughters as well as sons off to such schools was a convenient thing to do for middle-class women whose lives increasingly involved active membership in religious, civic, and social organizations. But higher education for women was still extremely rare. (The Metropolitan Museum of Art, Gift of I. N. Phelps Stokes, Edward S. Hawes, Alice Mary Hawes, Marion Augusta Hawes, 1937.)

In objective terms, the most striking development was a decline in the birth rate among native-born white people. The United States entered the nineteenth century with one of the highest birth rates in the Western world—a fact that reflected the easy availability of land more than anything else. Where land was plentiful and cheap, people continued to marry early and to have large numbers of children. But in older, more crowded rural areas, family size began to shrink. And in the towns and cities, it went down even faster. The net result was a reduction, between the beginning of the century and 1860, of almost 30 percent in the number of children for each woman between the ages of sixteen and forty-four.

But the change was not evenly spread through the society. Immigrants continued to have large families. So did people on the frontier. So did many of the poor everywhere, especially in the South. The decline of 30 percent was a national figure. Among the well-off, the educated, and the city dwellers, the drop was even more dramatic.

Some of the reasons for the change are clear. Poor farmers and workers could think of their children as potential economic assets, who could be put to work and needed little or no education. But for well-off town families, who did not expect their children to go into the fields or into shops and mills, children were a costly burden. And there were other, more subtle reasons. New standards of space and privacy in the home made children a greater problem. More and more women were active outside the home, busily taking on roles in clubs, churches, and reform groups. Their time, more than for most women in earlier centuries, was at a premium. Even geographical mobility probably helped cut the birth rate (though it is difficult to tell whether people did not want children because they were on the move, or were on the move because they did not have so many children to take along).

CHANGES IN THE ROLE OF WOMEN

It is easier to determine why the new middle class might want fewer children than it is to know *how* they accomplished their purpose. A part of the explanation lies in the fact that the better-educated simply tended to marry later, and even to remain single. There was some publicity about contraception—though very little. It seems clear that one method was simply to reduce the frequency of sexual intercourse. And with this practice came a striking new set of ideas and attitudes about sex.

The poem "Sugar and spice, and everything nice;/That's what little girls are made of. . . ./ Snips and snails, and puppy dogs' tails;/That's what little boys are made of" first became popular during the 1820s and 1830s. It captured the essence of a new way of thinking about masculinity and femininity. What the poem implied was made clear in hundreds of pamphlets, lectures, and magazine articles: Men were by nature suited to the rough, competitive world. Their nature was tough, their passions more "base," even "animal," than women's. Women, on the other hand, were "naturally" tender, innocent, and purer than men. They were the prime carriers of religious sentiments. They shrank from whatever was "base." And if some did not, there was some kind of deep flaw in their nature. By the middle of the nineteenth century, much of the middle class had probably reached the conclusion that women did not "naturally" enjoy or want sex.

Starting with such assumptions, the role of women in the home, and of home in the lives of children and husbands, could be radically revised. The most popular manual on home life was written in 1841 by Catharine Beecher. Its title, *A Treatise on Domestic Economy*, suggested one of its main arguments. There was an economy of the home as important as the economy of the world. In the world, all was effort, competition, and flux. But the ideal home was a place of refuge and order, a place where men might retreat from their fevered struggles and children might be protected from evil influences.

Within this home of Beecher's and of the many other writers who imitated her—women were to be the central figures. What she proposed was nothing less than a new kind of division of labor. Men made forays into the world of business or industry; women managed the household—deciding on diet, decoration, and the training of children, on religious questions and social practices.

Beecher put heavy emphasis on organization and efficiency. Even more emphatically, she laid down rules for avoiding tempting "stimuli." In fact, everything that might stimulate was to be rigorously suppressed. Food should be bland and served at a moderate temperature, since spices or food that was too hot might stimulate. Clothing should be loose. Tight garments were "stimulating." Coffee, tea, and alcohol were dangerous stimulants. So was sleeping late. Visiting, entertaining, and other kinds of sociability should be kept to a minimum.

The picture of woman as a domestic figure, whose proper place was in the home and whose main role seemed to be repression, was not an idea invented by men to keep women in their "place" (though it could be used that way). The idea belonged to a new social class and was welcomed by both its men and its women. In fact, for some women it was a way of claiming a place where they could be supreme and independent, at least in theory. The "sphere" for women was small. It hardly passed the boundaries of church

An idealized family. This 1840 painting captured the new conception of family life rather well. The husband in the picture is its geometrical center. But in other respects he is almost out of it. Looking off to the side, he is not touching either his wife or his children. The emotional center of the family is the wife, who is holding one child and being grasped by two others. The eldest, a boy, is posed in a way that suggests he will soon become like his father—detached from the home, interested in other things. The elaborate furniture, draperies, and carpet, used to suggest the family's solid economic status, were all mass-produced in factories. (The Brooklyn Museum)

and home. But by comparison with most of their eighteenth-century grandmothers, nineteenth-century women were making a strong bargain: They would leave politics and business to men, in return for a more powerful role in family life.

Oddly, dozens of women like Catharine Beecher made careers *outside* the home as the publicists of the ideal of domesticity. Women's magazines with large circulations made their first appearance. Women's clubs invited women speakers and writers to lecture. An enormous amount—perhaps even most—of magazine writ-

ing, sentimental novels and poetry, and other forms of popular literature was produced by women, for women readers. The idea of women's essentially domestic nature became the stock-in-trade of a new group of women who were either unmarried—as was Catharine Beecher—or who played limited roles in their own homes. Women spoke, wrote, and organized to promote the idea that women were *not* suited to public careers. When Garrison began his career as a reformer, he understood what every other reformer and evangelical preacher understood: The pathetic,

The Seneca Falls Declaration, 1848

A majority of middle-class women seemed happy enough to embrace the new notions of woman's special nature and mission. To many, in fact, this set of ideas was a distinct advance over the old situation, when women were regarded simply as inferior creatures, with no special attributes or special sphere of activity.

But a determined minority of middle-class women was gaining experience as reformers in fields such as abolition, education, and temperance—the same reforms promoted by men like William Lloyd Garrison. And it was inevitable that such women would sooner or later turn their attention to the plight of women themselves and to developing a feminist movement.

This path was illustrated by the careers of Lucretia Mott and Elizabeth Cady Stanton. Both were active in the antislavery movement; Mott was famous as an effective speaker at abolitionist rallies. In 1840 the two women met in London, where they had gone to attend a World Anti-slavery Convention. To their shock, the convention refused to seat women delegates, and they had to sit in the balcony.

From that point on, both were feminists as well as abolitionists. In 1848 they organized a meeting in Seneca Falls, New York, where Stanton lived with her husband and children. The meeting attracted a variety of reformers, male and female. And it issued the most ringing declaration of women's rights ever made in America.

Mott and Stanton, who drafted the declaration, took the Declaration of Independence as their model. They used its organization; a preface consisting of a statement of general principles, followed by a list of the "long train of abuses" of a tyrant. But in the Seneca Falls Declaration, the "inalienable rights" became the rights of "men and women." The tyrant was no longer George III of England but men. And the "long train of abuses" was transformed into a list of "repeated injuries on the part of man toward woman, having in direct object the establishment of an absolute tyranny over her."

The effect was electric. The declaration could be ridiculed—as it was in most of the press. But for anyone who came to it with a sympathetic mind, or for any woman who was ready to be drawn into feminist activity, it was both convincing and exciting.

As writing, the declaration worked because it took the tone of the most hallowed American document of all and changed very little of its stirring language. It began with the same words: "When in the course of human events . . . " And it went on, in familiar language: "We hold these truths to be self-evident: that all men and women are created equal; that they are endowed by their Creator with certain inalienable rights; that among these are life, liberty and the pursuit of happiness."

This much could be accepted even by a woman who was committed to the doctrine of women's separate and special sphere. She could argue that women were entitled to the pursuit of happiness in an equal but separate realm.

But the "train of abuses" set the feminists very much apart from the proponents of middle-class domesticity. The abuses included every law and restraint that made women's status any different from men's. It began with the right to vote. But it went on to claim equality of women's rights in divorce and the rights to hold property, to sue and be sued, to obtain an education, to pursue a career in any profession. Finally, it attacked the new morality of domesticity. Man has, it charged, "created a false public sentiment by giving to the world a different code of morals for men and women."

Mott, Stanton, and the other reformers who adopted the Seneca Falls Declaration represented a militant minority. But they had laid down a standard of feminist reform that could stand, with no essential change, for a hundred years and more.

suffering figure of Fanny Garrison was being replaced by women for whom moral and religious questions demanded organization, even action.

An Age of Reformers

During the last half of the eighteenth century, and especially after the Revolution, Americans had begun to form large numbers of societies and associations to solve the problems of the world. After about 1820, their efforts redoubled. Just as revivalism seemed to develop continuously from the eighteenth century into the nineteenth, so did the impulse to reform everything and everyone in sight. But again, as with evangelical revivalism, there were important differences that separated the reformers of Garrison's lifetime from those of the revolutionary period.

Reformist organizations before the 1820s had tended to address practical problems. During the 1820s the focus began to shift from solving practical problems to reforming *people*. Reformers began to treat every question as though it could be solved only by changing the *character* of the needy or the oppressed.

The new reformers' efforts to rescue and discipline the "lost" people in their society took a bewildering number of shapes. For every social evil, a dozen organizations promoted a solution. But the solutions and the organizations all had some basic things in common.

Nineteenth-century reformers divided the world more or less simply into two kinds of people. On one side were those individuals who were reasonably well-off, literate, white, and Christian, and whose character was marked by discipline, restraint, and a capacity for self-control. Such men and women could be trusted to be citizens in a free society. On the other side were vast numbers who could not be trusted because they were morally crippled and dependent. They might be insane. They might be drunkards like James Garrison, hopelessly lost in their dependence on alcohol. They might be children, who had not yet developed the adult character traits essential to moral citizenship. Or they might be criminals or prostitutes, caught in the grip of systems of vice. They might be women, reduced by dependence to childlike, frivolous moral cripples. They might be slaves, whose "racial inferiority" combined with their enslavement made them incapable of self-control. Every reform movement defined a group of victims in some sort of "bondage."

The reformers agreed that most types of bondage could be broken, most victims rescued and made over into alert, honest, and disciplined citizens. The insane—most of them anyway—could be treated and not merely shut away in misery. Criminals could be taken off the streets and put into prisons, the "sanctuaries" within which their characters could be reformed. Women could be educated and trained to accept the social responsibilities that would teach them good character instead of the nervous frivolity that governed their captive lives. Even blacks, whom most reformers still regarded as racially inferior, could be freed and sent back to their native Africa— the solution favored by many early antislavery reformers.

The new reformers almost always agreed that the final cure lay within the victim. It would do no good simply to break some form of bondage, unless the liberated individual learned to control himself or herself. For many of the reform movements, this implied the creation of a place of asylum where the handicapped, the depraved, or the childlike could be taught. Societies to rescue "fallen" women created homes for lost and "wayward" girls. Prison reformers persuaded state legislatures to build model prisons, the most famous of which was at Auburn, New York. For educational reformers like Massachusetts's Horace Mann, the public school was just such a place of asylum, where children could be made over into mature candidates for responsibility and respectability. For a family reformer like Catharine Beecher, the family itself was an asylum from what she called the "sordid" passions of the world.

The places of asylum and training promoted by the reformers were all fundamentally alike, whether their inmates were children, prostitutes, the insane, or the deaf. Their main preoccupation was with order, regularity, and habit. The idealized schoolroom of the day pictured straight-backed children sitting on benches spaced with geometrical perfection, being put through mechanical paces. The perfect prison, for the proponents of the Auburn system, was one in which every foot of space and every hour of time was perfectly organized, so that the criminal could be habituated to regularity in every feature of life and thus made safe for reentry into the world. The same efficient organization governed Catharine Beecher's model home.

All these common elements made it possible for many men and women to be active in a great variety of reform movements, with no sense of discontinuity. For a woman like Dorothea Dix, whose primary cause was to improve the treatment of the insane, there was no essential difference between that effort and the temperance movement or the "rescue" of prostitutes. William Lloyd Garrison could move easily from temperance to antislavery to pacifism to women's rights and back to slavery, confident that the various middle-class crusades all shared the same basic concerns and techniques.

But for all the similarities among reform movements and their leaders, there were important differences that tended to deepen with time. For the more cautious reformers—men like Charles Finney and Horace Mann—the initial assumption was that society was basically healthy; the problem was to find ways of treating its unhealthy parts. Such reformers could use the institutions already available: churches, schools, governments, and the like. Their reform organizations and their missionary societies were designed to supplement the established order.

But as time passed, an activist minority of people—people like Garrison—reached the conclusion that the disease was deeper than had at first been thought: Society itself was the real problem. For such reformers, a solution more radical than creating better prisons and schools had to be found. This logic created a paradox: Men and women whose personal lives were characterized by a preoccupation with self-discipline, order, and restraint could begin to seek radical alternatives and find themselves treated as dangerous prophets of disorder and confusion. A few years after Garrison began to publish *The Liberator*, he was attacked by a mob in the streets of Boston. Garrison once publicly burned a copy of the Constitution of the United States, and he often used similar provocations, courting abuse and welcoming the publicity that might make converts out of a daring few.

UTOPIAN COMMUNITIES But for most of the men and women who decided that social problems demanded radical strategies, the solution was not confrontation, but withdrawal. The outcome was the creation of dozens of communal societies. Almost every such community was utopian—convinced that its scheme could become the model for the salvation and perfection of the world the members had left behind.

Some of the utopian communities, like New Harmony in Indiana, focused on creating "rational" relationships of production. Others, like villages planned by the Shakers, concentrated more attention on religious piety and asceticism. Some communities, like Oneida, New York, experimented with sexual practices like intercourse without orgasm, and multiple marriage. Others, like Brook Farm in Massachusetts, were built by intellectuals around philosophical notions or cults.

Whatever their tone, the utopian groups all emphasized some scheme of order, planning, and disciplined self-denial. They were willing to be viewed as cranks by their former neighbors and relatives, but their crankiness ran not toward anarchy but toward order. The communities were, in fact, simply taking the most cherished beliefs of the new middle class to a logical and uncompromising conclusion. Within their walls, their own notions of industry, temperance, and self-control reigned supreme.

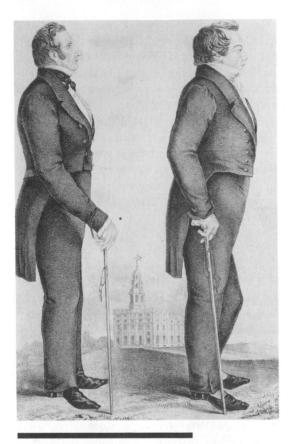

The Smith brothers. Hyrum and Joseph Smith, leaders of the Mormons, were both killed in 1844 in a mob attack on the Mormon settlement in Illinois. In the background is an exaggerated sketch of the Mormon temple of Nauvoo. The artist has tried to make the Smiths look as proper, elegant, and restrained as any middle-class gentleman of the period. (Culver Pictures)

The true solution for Christians was to leave the world behind and make their own, purified society. Smith's converts, under his leadership, migrated from New York to Ohio. Then they moved on to Missouri. By 1839 they had moved again—always under pressure from their neighbors—to Illinois. There, on the Mississippi, they founded a community they named Nauvoo. But in 1844 Smith was killed by an armed mob, and the Mormons were driven out of Nauvoo.

Under the guidance of a new leader, Brigham Young, the Mormons moved on, this time to a place of expansive emptiness. Out in the Great Basin, they tried to found a new state, Deseret, covering much of what is now Nevada, Utah, Arizona, and southern California.

Largely because of their practice of polygamy, the Mormons were objects of scorn and fear. But they shared with all the other utopian experiments of the period—and indeed with most orthodox reformers—an intense concern for order and discipline within their world. One of their leaders, Orson Pratt, summed up the Mormon condemnation of the world in language a Finney or a Garrison might have used: "Wickedness keeps pace with the hurried revolutions of the age. Gross immoralities, drunkenness, whoredoms, robbing, murdering, have engulfed the nations in a deathly ocean of filth." And in Mormon households, a popular writer like Catharine Beecher would have found much to approve of, such as the exclusion of hot drinks, alcohol, and tobacco.

THE MORMONS The most famous and successful community of radical withdrawal was the Church of Jesus Christ of Latter-Day Saints, or Mormons. This first American religion originated in the 1820s with a rural New Yorker named Joseph Smith, who was convinced that he had been given a divine revelation, which he wrote down as the Book of Mormon. It taught that the world as it was presently constituted was thoroughly "anti-Christ" and thoroughly doomed.

New Artists, New Ideas

During the first half of the nineteenth century, the United States produced a remarkable generation of writers, who created what Americans began to describe as a "new" national literature.

This literary explosion began during the first two decades of the century with the work of Washington Irving: first with his comic *Knickerbocker History of New York* (1809) and then, in 1819, with his *Sketch Book*—particularly its tales of Rip Van Winkle and Ichabod Crane. During the 1820s James Fenimore Cooper began to write the novels about his frontier scout, Leatherstocking, that would make him the most successful American writer of his age. The series included *The Last of the Mohicans* (1826), and eventually ran to five novels, each of which only added to Cooper's fame in Europe and in the United States.

Then, between the presidencies of Jackson and Lincoln, a tight-knit group of even more gifted writers appeared. In the 1830s Ralph Waldo Emerson began to publish lectures and essays that would eventually become part of most middle-class libraries. In the 1840s his friend Henry David Thoreau managed to turn a two-year experiment at living alone in the woods into the masterpiece *Walden, or Life in the Woods*. Their acquaintance Nathaniel Hawthorne published classic novels like *The Scarlet Letter* (1850) and *The House of Seven Gables* (1851). His friend Herman Melville completed the momentous *Moby Dick* in 1851. A poet with whom many of these writers would develop a distant and tentative acquaintance, Walt Whitman, published in 1855 the first edition of his *Leaves of Grass*. A young woman who was utterly unknown to all these intellectuals, Emily Dickinson, started at the end of the 1850s to write the powerful poems that were to make her (after she died) at least Whitman's equal in literary reputation and influence.

Thus in about half a century a group of literary monuments had sprung into existence. And these monuments throw some interesting light on the kinds of economic, social, and ideological changes that Americans were undergoing.

The writers experienced the same sorts of change that touched the lives of other Americans. They did not simply observe, in detachment, the emergence of a market economy or the myths and realities of the self-made man. Instead, intellectuals now found *themselves* in the market, part

Nathaniel Hawthorne. This oil portrait of Hawthorne was painted in 1840, before he completed his most famous novels. Hawthorne's first published story was titled "The Gentle Boy," and he quickly became known as "Gentle Hawthorne." But as he aged, his tales took on a bite and a gloom that seem at odds with this painting, which depicts a young man at peace both with himself and his world. (Essex Institute)

of the new economy, and with the same kinds of possibilities of success and failure that every other entrepreneur faced.

Beginning late in the eighteenth century, an explosion of literacy caused a dramatic increase in the size of the potential audience for novels, essays, and poems. Literacy went hand in hand, in the new middle class, with increasing incomes.

In short, the market for literature expanded at least as dramatically as the market for shoes or stoves. The first recognizably modern publishing companies appeared. And they used innovations—like the steam press and aggressive marketing methods—just as other entrepreneurs did. The result was that newspapers, magazines, and books poured into the new market at much cheaper prices.

For talented men (and women as well), this meant that for the first time it was possible for many people to have a successful—even a lucrative—career as a writer. A new kind of intellectual career had opened up, a career that could put intellectuals in touch with a larger public. Writers could become self-made men, or women. They could win fame, recognition, even wealth— all as a result of their own individual efforts, talent, and will. Or they could fail.

It is not surprising, then, that the main preoccupation of American writers—themselves "self-made" or ambitious to be—was the free individual. The typical central figure of their novels, poems, and essays was the singular man or woman whose life was undergoing some sort of radical transformation. In general, American writers portrayed society as a network of customs, laws, and other restraints, against which the individual struggled to win freedom. In fact, the classic American literature of the period often seemed to be a simple celebration of individual freedom and solitude, against the demands of the community and its order.

In Rip Van Winkle, for example, Irving pictured a man who was trapped by his marriage, by his farm, by the web of social custom. Irving had this character undergo a radical transformation. Alone, in nature, Rip encounters a band of sailors, the ghosts of Henry Hudson's Dutch crew. He drinks a mysterious liquor they offer him and sleeps for twenty years. The end result is that Rip Van Winkle returns to his community as a "free" man. He now has no wife, no farm, no obligation to work. He can be what he always wanted to be, an idler and a storyteller. On his own terms, Rip is a success, and he owes his success to no one. Cooper's Leatherstocking fig-

Thoreau's cabin. The title page of the 1854 edition of *Walden* shows Thoreau's house at the pond. The line from the book promises that Thoreau will not dwell on "dejection," but will "brag lustily" about the possibilities of living outside the system of property, custom, and law. The cabin pictured is a bit more snug and permanent-looking than the building Thoreau describes in the book. (New York Public, Rare Book Department, Astor, Lenox and Tilden Foundation)

ure was, like Rip Van Winkle, an individual defined by solitude in the woods. Cooper's novels are about the ways the solitary frontiersman evades the traps set for him by civilization, with all its restraints.

In the essay that probably had the greatest influence on other intellectuals, *Nature* (1836), Emerson precisely sketched out the rules for authentic experience: A person's truest self was to be found only in solitude and only in nature. Thoreau's *Walden* was an even clearer declaration of individual independence from the social order. Its prescription was simple: Only by freeing themselves from society could individuals gain true insights into nature and the self. In society, men could only lead lives of "desperation." Walt Whitman was just as pointed: The longest section of *Leaves of Grass* was the poem he labeled "Song of Myself." And Emily Dickinson's poetry had only one principal subject: the inner experience of the self, the figure she always called simply "I." In the world of her poems—if not in her actual life—society seemed hardly to exist at all.

Emerson summed it all up neatly when he said that the "present age" was "the age of the first person singular." And Emerson gave a name to the preoccupation with the free individual, "transcendentalism." The term was adopted by a number of New England intellectuals, like Thoreau and the founders of the utopian community at Brook Farm. The cumbersome expression meant simply that it was possible for any individual to transcend—literally, get beyond—the social and historical conditions of his or her life. Men and women could transcend all boundaries, customs, and restraints. As a result of this liberation, they could put themselves in spiritual touch with a sublime reality that some people called Nature, others God.

For all their subtlety, writers like Emerson and Thoreau shared much with the celebrators of the self-made man, and with the evangelical revivalists. But (like the ideas of the self-made man and evangelical revivalism) the radical individualism of American writing had another, darker side of doubt. Rip Van Winkle's "freedom" had an enormous price: He had to surrender twenty years of his life. Cooper's scout, no matter how virtuous and skilled he was, was doomed to fail in the long run. It was clear to Cooper and to his readers that society and "progress" would be the inevitable winners, and that Leatherstocking and

Ralph Waldo Emerson. Emerson, shown here as a young man, coined the term "transcendentalism" to explain the preoccupation with the self that dominated much American thought in the 1840s and 1850s. His essay *Nature* was extremely influential among intellectuals of this period. It urged self-study in solitary, unspoiled surroundings, removed from the social order. (Metropolitan Museum of Art)

his Indians belonged only to the past. At the end of Whitman's "Song of Myself," the "I" of the poem dies. Emily Dickinson's "I" dies over and over again in her anguished lyrics. In Emerson's essay *Nature*, the moment when the solitary individual finally achieves mystical union with nature is the moment when he disappears. "I become nothing," Emerson said. "I see all."

Here was a curious contradiction. The same writers who insisted on individual freedom as the essence of life seemed to be saying that freedom led nowhere, or even to death. In fact, the writers of the period seemed to fear the liberated self as much as they celebrated it. But the monumental works of art were only expressing the same contradiction that underlay the idea of the self-made man, evangelical religion, and the reform movements of their day. Both in popular culture and in the work of people like Emerson or Dickinson, the assertion of the self went hand in hand with a dread of "free" individuals.

The solution to the contradiction, both in popular culture and in great literature, was to combine freedom with *inner* restraint. Like the ideal self-made man, the heroes of the novels and poems were men and women of rigid self-control, even asceticism. Thoreau, in *Walden*, wanted little or nothing in a material way. In fact, his description of life at the pond bore a considerable resemblance to the lifestyle laid out by Catharine Beecher in her *Treatise on Domestic Economy*. Emerson's model individual was equally self-denying. Cooper's Leatherstocking wanted no wealth, no property, no sex, no income, and no civilized luxuries. For all his brash language, Whitman's poetic "I" was a man of almost monastic habits of self-denial. Emily Dickinson's poems were filled with repudiations of pleasures of every kind, from money to sex.

And when American writers dealt with liberated individuals who did *not* exercise self-control and restraint, they treated them as tainted men or women, who had to be punished or destroyed. Hester Prynne, in *The Scarlet Letter*, was a woman who had defied Puritan society by committing adultery. The novel is about her gradual and heroic recognition that she *has* sinned and must pay her social debt with a long life of industry, frugality, modesty, and temperance. In *Moby Dick*, Melville drew the same moral lesson, but in more violent terms. Captain Ahab, who commands the whaling vessel *Pequod*, is obsessed with revenge against the mysterious white whale that has cost him a leg. Because of his obsession, he is determined to break all the social and economic rules, to pervert a commercial whaling enterprise. His individual "freedom," which is

Emily Dickinson at 17. Emily Dickinson grew up to be a great poet. Here, however, she was photographed as a very conventional schoolgirl of 17, a student at a "female seminary" in South Hadley, Massachusetts. The photographer has posed her in a rigid way, managing to suggest that she is like any well-brought-up middle-class girl, familiar with books but closer to flowers, passive, and rigidly self-controlled. Years later she would write her most famous sentence of self-description: "I . . . am small, like the Wren, and my Hair is bold, like the Chestnut Bur—and my eyes, like the Sherry in the Glass, that the Guest leaves." (Courtesy Trustees of Amherst College)

radical, has become dangerous. It knows no boundaries or inner restraints. And the outcome is that Ahab brings disaster and death not only upon himself but upon his crew.

When William Lloyd Garrison took up writing as a career, a path to success, he was acting on the same assumptions as an Irving or a Cooper. His assertion of the determined self against all of society was earlier than, and just as powerful as, Thoreau's. He suffered through his mother's warnings about the fatal dangers of worldly success. But he did so in terms that an Emerson or an Emily Dickinson would have understood at once. Garrison's individualism was at bottom a radical version of the tamer individualism of the new middle class. It promised success, morality, and progress, but it feared excess, cynicism, and disorder. And so it demanded rigid self-control and self-denial.

Suggestions for Further Reading

THE GARRISONS

Two modern biographies of William Lloyd Garrison are John Thomas, *The Liberator* (1963), and Walter M. Merrill, *Against Wind and Tide* (1963). But the best approach to the family may still be the four-volume account by Garrison's children, *William Lloyd Garrison, 1805–1879: The Story of His Life as Told by His Children* (1885–89). For students who like to work with documents, the six volumes of *The Letters of William Lloyd Garrison* (1971–81), edited by Walter M. Merrill and Louis Ruchames, are a careful and valuable resource. The most fascinating reading on the family is the autobiography of "Crazy Jem" Garrison, written shortly before his death and edited by Walter M. Merrill as *Behold Myself Once More* (1954).

ECONOMIC GROWTH AND TRANSFORMATION

Douglass C. North, *The Economic Growth of the United States* (1961), is a serious and thoughtful survey. So are the relevant chapters of Elliott Brownlee, *The Dynamics of Ascent* (1985). Albert Fishlow, *American Railroads and the Transformation of the Antebellum Economy* (1965), examines the impact of railroads on economic growth. A detailed study of the railroad and canal system is Christopher T. Baer, *Canals and Railroads of the Middle Atlantic States, 1800–1860* (1981). Anthony F. C. Wallace, *Rockdale: The Growth of an American Village in the Early Industrial Revolution* (1978), has stirred considerable debate about the ways that the coming of mills and factories transformed smaller towns and villages.

TECHNOLOGY, GROWTH, AND THEIR EFFECTS

Stephen Thernstrom, *Poverty and Progress* (1964), was a ground-breaking study of social mobility. David Montgomery's superb essay, "The Shuttle and the Cross: Weavers and Artisans in the Kensington Riots of 1844," *Journal of Social History* (1972), is an excellent introduction to the working-class experience of the period. Among the most valuable books on work and workers are Herbert Gutman, *Work, Culture, and Society* (1976); Alan Dawley, *Class and Community: The Industrial Revolution in Lynn* (1977); and Bruce Laurie, *Working People of Philadelphia, 1800–1850* (1980). Two fine studies of urban development and its consequences are Paul Boyer, *Urban Masses and Moral Order* (1978), and Sam Bass Warner, *The Urban Wilderness* (1972). Paul Johnson, *Shopkeeper's Millennium* (1978), makes a strong case for an intimate relationship between the growth of commerce and industry and the new revivalism. It can be supplemented with Michael Barkun, *Crucible of the Millennium: The Burned-over District of New York in the 1840s* (1986).

THE "SELF-MADE MAN"

Irvin G. Wyllie, *The Self-Made Man in America* (1954), is a very readable introduction to the subject. It can be supplemented with John G. Cawelti, *Apostles of the Self-Made Man* (1965), and Daniel T. Rodgers, *The Work Ethic in Industrial America, 1850–1920* (1981).

MIDDLE-CLASS EVANGELISM

K. J. Hardman, *Charles Grandison Finney* (1987), filled

CHRONOLOGY

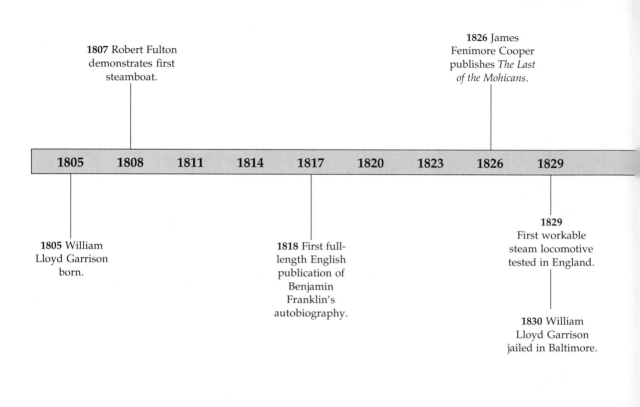

1807 Robert Fulton demonstrates first steamboat.

1826 James Fenimore Cooper publishes *The Last of the Mohicans.*

| 1805 | 1808 | 1811 | 1814 | 1817 | 1820 | 1823 | 1826 | 1829 |

1805 William Lloyd Garrison born.

1818 First full-length English publication of Benjamin Franklin's autobiography.

1829 First workable steam locomotive tested in England.

1830 William Lloyd Garrison jailed in Baltimore.

an important gap. W. G. McLoughlin, *Modern Revivalism* (1957), is still a useful survey, with early chapters that address the Finney period.

CHANGES IN THE ROLE OF WOMEN

Women in the industrial labor force are discussed in Thomas Dublin, *Women at Work: The Transformation of Work and Community in Lowell, Massachusetts, 1826–1860* (1979). Nancy Cott, *The Bonds of Womanhood* (1977), attempts to assess both the costs and the rewards of the ideology of separate spheres for women in New England. The ways that growing up has changed during the course of history is the subject of Joseph Kett, *Rites of Passage: Adolescence in America* (1977). Carl Degler, *At Odds: Women and the Family in America from the Revolution to the Present* (1980), is a readable survey that adequately summarizes the work of many scholars.

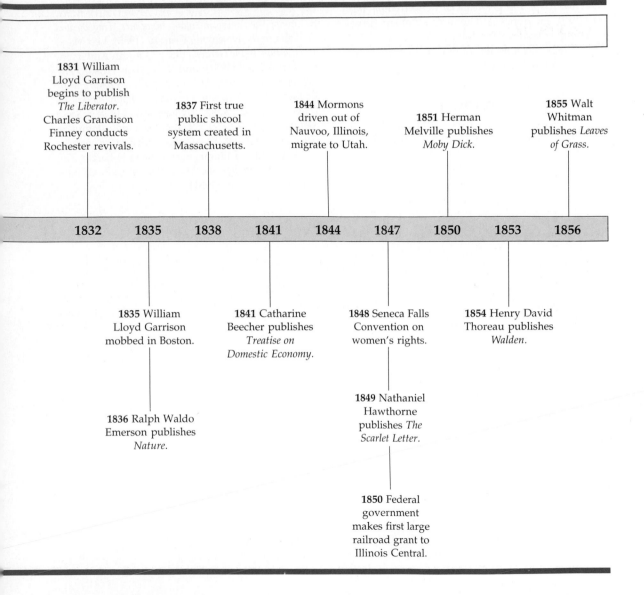

1831 William Lloyd Garrison begins to publish *The Liberator.* Charles Grandison Finney conducts Rochester revivals.

1837 First true public shcool system created in Massachusetts.

1844 Mormons driven out of Nauvoo, Illinois, migrate to Utah.

1851 Herman Melville publishes *Moby Dick.*

1855 Walt Whitman publishes *Leaves of Grass.*

| 1832 | 1835 | 1838 | 1841 | 1844 | 1847 | 1850 | 1853 | 1856 |

1835 William Lloyd Garrison mobbed in Boston.

1841 Catharine Beecher publishes *Treatise on Domestic Economy.*

1848 Seneca Falls Convention on women's rights.

1854 Henry David Thoreau publishes *Walden.*

1849 Nathaniel Hawthorne publishes *The Scarlet Letter.*

1836 Ralph Waldo Emerson publishes *Nature.*

1850 Federal government makes first large railroad grant to Illinois Central.

AN AGE OF REFORMERS

A good place to begin is Ronald G. Walters, *American Reformers, 1815–1860* (1978). C. S. Griffen, *The Ferment of Reform* (1967), is a very thoughtful essay on the ways historians have tried to explain the surge of interest in social problems during this period. Lewis Perry, *Childhood, Marriage, and Reform* (1980), is an interesting interpretation. Stephen Nissenbaum, *Sex, Diet, and Debility in Jacksonian America*

(1989), is a fascinating study. Good places to begin reading on the beginnings of feminism are K. E. Melder, *The Beginnings of Sisterhood* (1977), and Catherine Clinton, *The Other Civil War: American Women in the Nineteenth Century* (1984). An original and provocative interpretation of feminism can be found in William Leach, *True Love and Perfect Union: The Feminist Reform of Sex and Society* (1980). The temperance movement is well treated in I. R. Tyrrell, *Sobering*

Up: From Temperance to Prohibition in Antebellum America (1979). Lawrence A. Cremin's excellent survey, *American Education: The National Experience, 1783–1876* (1980), has a wealth of information on literacy and educational reform.

NEW ARTISTS, NEW IDEAS

The classic study of American writers of the antebellum period is F. O. Mathiessen, *American Renaissance* (1941). Other significant works on writers and intellectuals include Perry Miller, *The Life of the Mind in America* (1965); Henry Nash Smith, *Virgin Land: The American West as Symbol and Myth* (1951); R. W. B. Lewis, *The American Adam: Innocence, Tragedy, and Tradition in the Nineteenth Century* (1955); Leo Marx, *The Machine in the Garden* (1965); Quentin Anderson, *The Imperial Self* (1971); and R. Jackson Wilson, *Figures of Speech: American Writers and the Literary Marketplace, from Benjamin Franklin to Emily Dickinson* (1989). Anne C. Rose, *Transcendentalism as a Social Movement, 1830–1850* (1974), is a good attempt to place Emerson and his colleagues in a social context. A good study of literary nationalism is Larzer Ziff, *Literary Democracy: The Declaration of Cultural Independence in America* (1981).

CHAPTER 10
A NEW SOUTH

THE EPISODE: *The labor of millions of African-American slaves enabled some white people to live lives of a comfort that shaded into luxury and a confidence that shaded into arrogance. But behind the comfort and the confidence, the luxury and the arrogance, there was always a haunting fear that the slaves might rise up and wrathfully strike for their freedom.*

This white nightmare came true on an August morning in 1831 in Southhampton County, Virginia. A slave who became known as Nat Turner led a band of rebels into bloody insurrection. Panic-stricken and enraged white people struck back, brutally murdering African Americans without knowing whether they had taken part in the revolt. Nal Turner himself was able to hide out for two months, but then he was captured, tried, and put to death—asking, poignantly, "Was not Christ crucified?"

THE HISTORICAL SETTING: *Nat Turner's rebellion was not the first slave revolt in North America, but it was the largest and bloodiest. It came at a key moment in the history of American slavery. In the three decades following the American Revolution more and more Southern slaves had been able to gain their freedom by purchasing it or through voluntary manumission by their masters. In fact, by 1810, there were almost 135,000 free blacks in the South (8.5% of the black population). But by the early 1820s, this pattern had reversed itself: In 1830, the percentage of free blacks in the South was* actually less than it had been in 1810.

As they saw the opportunity for emancipation diminish, some blacks became more vehement in their opposition to slavery. In 1822, Denmark Vesey, a former slave who had purchased his freedom, organized a slave revolt in South Carolina that was thwarted only at the last minute when authorities got wind of his plot. And in 1829, David Walker, a North Carolina free black who had moved to Boston, published a passionate appeal to blacks to rise up against slavery.

The retreat from manumission as well as the angry response of blacks to it was a symptom of changes taking place not only in slavery itself but in the place of slavery in Southern life and society. In almost every way—economically, socially, politically, and ideologically—slavery deepened its hold on the South after 1830. By 1850, slavery was no longer a "peculiar institution" that happened to exist in the South; the South itself had become a slave society. Its economy revolved around forms of large-scale agriculture that depended upon slave labor; its society was organized around a system of caste and class in which the divide between slave and master, black and white, was fixed and immutable; its politics centered around the defense of its "peculiar institution" against any and all perceived threats; its ideology extolled slavery, not as a necessary evil, but as a "positive good," the foundation of a noble civilization.

NAT TURNER'S REBELLION

The voice of the spirit had told him the sign would appear in the sky. Now, as Nat Turner looked at the sun on the morning of Saturday, August 13, 1831, he knew this was the signal he had been waiting for. It was a strange phenomenon, one that many people on the east coast of the United States were noticing that day, even though it did not mean to them what it meant to Nat Turner as he worked in the fields of Southampton County, Virginia. First, the sun grew dim in the cloudless sky. Then it began to change colors—turning green, then blue, finally almost white. By the afternoon the sun was looking almost like a silvery mirror. Then, as Nat stared in fascination, on the solar surface appeared a single black spot.

Nat Turner thought he knew exactly what it all meant. The sun had become a mirror of what was about to happen on the earth. Just as a black spot had passed across the sun, so black men would rise up and move across the earth. This was the signal Nat had been waiting for—the signal the spirit had promised him. He knew the time for delay had passed. The massacre must begin. The white people of Southampton County must be killed or put to flight.

Nine days later, fifty-five whites lay slaughtered—forty-two of them women and children. Most were hacked to death with axes. Many had been decapitated. Then vengeful whites struck back. The luckier blacks were captured alive and held for trial; others were simply killed outright by enraged and terrified white men. It was by far the bloodiest uprising in the long history of American slavery. Nat Turner himself managed to evade capture for more than two months, far longer than any of his fellow conspirators. He was finally taken in late October, duly tried and convicted, and publicly hanged on November 11, 1831. It was less than a year after William Lloyd Garrison had begun publishing the *Liberator*.

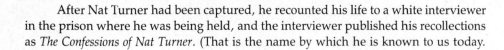

After Nat Turner had been captured, he recounted his life to a white interviewer in the prison where he was being held, and the interviewer published his recollections as *The Confessions of Nat Turner*. (That is the name by which he is known to us today.

Turner's Nat. The poster that offered a $500 reward for the capture of Turner's Nat described him as "between 30 & 35 years old—five feet six or 8 inches high—weighs between 150 and 160 rather bright complexion but not a mulatto—broad-shouldered—large flat nose—large eyes—broad flat fleet rather knock kneed—walk brisk and active—hair on the top of the head very thin—no beard except on the upper lip and tip of the chin. A scar on one of his temples produced by the kick of a mule—also one on the back of his neck by a bite—a large knot on one of the bones of his right arm near the wrist produced by a blow." (Library of Congress)

But he was probably never called Nat Turner during his lifetime, by either black or white people. Like all slaves, he had only a given name—Nat. Slaves normally received last names only when they became fugitives or embroiled in legal proceedings. *Turner* was nothing but the surname of a white man who once happened to "own" him. At most, he would have been spoken of as "Turner's Nat." To call him *Turner* here would be to identify him as a piece of property. It is possible that he had an African name, which white people did not know then and we do not know now. We have chosen to call him *Nat* here.)

Nat was about thirty years old at the time of the massacre. Even in his earliest years, though, he had felt himself to be no ordinary slave but someone who was marked for greatness—or, as he put it, "called to superior righteousness." Nat had taught himself how to read—his parents were both illiterate—and he seemed to "remember" things that had happened before he was born. Around the farm on which his parents worked, his abilities soon became a "source of wonder." More than once Nat had overheard his mother and father tell each other that he was "intended for some great purpose." Even the white man who owned the farm, pious Benjamin Turner, took to displaying the talented young slave to his white friends, and Nat heard them all agree that he was too special to be "of any service to anyone as a slave."

Nat Turner grew up with great expectations and, much like the young William Lloyd Garrison, with a determination to make something of himself. He played with the white children around the farm. His mind was restless. He read every book that came his way. He performed experiments with everyday materials, devising things like paper and gunpowder. When he reached his teens, he decided to adopt a life of "austerity": never to touch alcohol or tobacco, and "studiously" to avoid any kind of carousing with his fellow slaves. Through this program of self-improvement and self-discipline, Nat Turner tried to show others something of his great promise and to prepare himself for the rewards it would bring.

What happened was a bitter disappointment. He hoped to be emancipated at the death of his master. But when Benjamin Turner died, ten-year-old Nat was simply handed on to Turner's son Samuel, who was just setting himself up on a nearby farm of his own. Within a few years, Nat found himself laboring in the fields alongside the half-dozen slaves Samuel Turner used to work his 360-acre farm. For the first time it occurred to him, as a teenager, that he might have to spend his entire life as a field hand. When Nat reached his twenty-first birthday, his future had become clear: "I had arrived to man's estate," he recalled, "and was a slave." The prospect was unbearable.

In his frustration, Nat ran away from his owner. For an entire month he hid in the woods. But for some reason he changed his mind. At the end of the month he voluntarily returned, to resume the drudgery of field work.

But still he held his ambition. It was about this time that Nat discovered his hopes might be fulfilled through religion. His mind fastened on one verse he had read in the Bible: "Seek ye the kingdom of heaven, and all things shall be added to you." The words seemed to promise that if Nat would only concentrate his energy on spiritual matters—the kingdom of heaven—everything else would follow. In order to win the world, he must look to heaven. But what did that involve?

One day, while working alone behind the plow in one of his owner's fields, Nat heard a voice intoning the biblical passage he had been pondering. He was sure the voice was the spirit of God, speaking directly to him as He had spoken ages before to the biblical prophets. From that time on, the divine spirit addressed him regularly. And this confirmed Nat's belief that he was "ordained to some great purpose."

But there were worldly disappointments. About 1822, Nat's young master, Samuel Turner, died, and Nat was sold outside the Turner family, to a neighboring farmer named Thomas Moore. What made this event even more unsettling was the fact that Nat had recently married a slave woman on Samuel Turner's farm, and the couple was now forced to live apart. All in all, it was a vivid display of Nat's inability to control the ordinary course of his life. But he had decided to focus his attention elsewhere. He fasted, he prayed, and he avoided contact with his fellow slaves. And through it all the spirit continued to talk to him, to reassure him that "something was about to happen that would terminate in fulfilling the great promise that had been made to me."

For the time being, though, Nat did not know just how his "great promise" would be fulfilled, and he awaited further revelations. First, the spirit gave him secret understandings of the natural world around him: "knowledge of the elements, the revolution of the planets, the operation of the tides, and changes of the seasons." In essence, Nat was resuming his old program of self-improvement in the only way still open to him—through mystic revelation instead of white men's books.

Little by little, through fasting, prayer, and revelation, Nat sensed that he was being "made perfect" in "true knowledge" and "holiness." At length, he began to speak about his powers to other slaves in the neighborhood, and his strange dignity brought many of them under his spell. On one occasion, Nat's charismatic influence even reached across racial lines to touch a white man. Nat would later recall the incident with pride:

> I told these things to a white man, Ethelred T. Brantley, on whom it had a wonderful effect—and he ceased immediately from his wickedness, and was attacked immediately with a cutaneous [skin] eruption, and blood oozed from the pores of his skin. And after praying and fasting nine days, he was healed.

The spirit even told Nat to baptize this white man. To the shock of other whites, the man agreed:

> And when the white people would not let us be baptized by the church, we went down to the water together, in the sight of many who reviled us, and were baptized by the Spirit. After this, I rejoiced greatly, and gave thanks to God.

But that was to be the only time Nat would achieve even this much impact in the white world, the only time that he would *stop* a white man's blood from flowing.

One day in 1825, Nat had his first vision of racial violence:

> I saw white spirits and black spirits engaged in battle, and the sun was darkened—the thunder rolled in the heavens, and blood flowed in streams. And I heard a voice saying, "Such is your luck, such you are called to see, and let it come rough or smooth, you must surely bear it."

Was race war, then, the "great purpose" for which Nat was chosen? It was a shocking prospect. Nat decided not to tell this terrible vision to his fellow slaves, and for several years he even withdrew from associating with them in order to ponder it, and to understand more fully what he was expected to bear.

Nat looked everywhere for signs—in the sky, in the woods, even in the crops he worked for his master. And slowly, with the aid of his spirit voice, he came to discover strange connections—between heaven and earth, between religious salvation and slave rebellion, between Jesus Christ and Nat Turner.

He learned that what people called the Milky Way was really "the lights of the Savior's hands, stretched forth from east to west, as they were extended on the cross on Calvary for the redemption of sinners." One day, at work in the corn field, Nat found "drops of blood on the corn, as though it were dew from Heaven." And the spirit explained to him that the Milky Way and the blood on the corn were both symbols of Christ's sacrifice:

> The blood of Christ had been shed on this earth, and had ascended to heaven for the salvation of sinners, and was now returning to earth again in the form of dew.

Searching the night sky once again, Nat saw that the stars were arranged to form pictures of men in different poses. Then, walking in the woods, he discovered certain leaves that contained the very same pictures, along with mysterious hieroglyphic markings —all marked in blood. Once more the spirit explained the meaning—

the ominous meaning—of this strange discovery:

> As the leaves on the trees bore the impression of the figures I had seen in the heavens, it was plain to me that the Savior was about to lay down the yoke he had borne for the sins of men—and the Day of Judgment was at hand.

The signs were beginning to become clear. Nat was finally putting together the diverse elements in his life: religion, self-improvement, the promise of greatness, and the bitter, incomprehensible frustration. But what did it all mean for Nat himself? What was his personal role in the tremendous mystery he was coming to unravel? Finally, the answer to that question began to emerge. On May 12, 1828—he would always recall the exact date—Nat heard "a loud noise in the heavens." Then, in fateful language, the spirit spoke again:

> The serpent was loosened [let loose], and Christ had laid down the yoke he had borne for the sins of man, and *I should take it on, and fight against the serpent—for the time was fast approaching when the first should be last, and the last should be first.*

Finally, it was all fitting into place: the patterns in the leaves and the stars, the blood on the corn, the vision of race war, and the abiding question of Nat's own great purpose in life. Christ had not simply laid down his burden of suffering, he had passed it on, to Nat Turner himself. By taking up the cross, Nat would fulfill both Christ's purpose and his own burning ambition.

The "serpent" in Nat's vision was of course the white man, and by doing battle against him, Nat would "redeem" his own black race in both a religious sense and a political one—freeing them simultaneously from the bonds of both sin and slavery. The final result would not be race war but a more just reordering of society—"the first should be last, and the last should be first." Nat himself might die in the struggle, but his death, like Christ's, would only seal his triumph. When a white man visited Nat in jail after the rebellion and asked him whether his approaching execution did not prove his visions had been false and his rebellion useless, Nat was able to respond, simply: "Was not Christ crucified?"

The Day of Judgment was nearly at hand. All that now remained was to discover the details. And even these the spirit promised to reveal. "By signs in the heavens," Nat would learn exactly when to begin his "great work." At the appearance of the first of these signs—but not a day before—he was to reveal to a handful of other slaves the nature of the plan. Until then, he was to keep the project to himself.

The promised signs took almost three years to appear. In the meantime, Nat's owner, Thomas Moore, died, and Moore's widow married a local wheelwright named Joseph Travis. Once again, Nat was forced to change one master and one home for another. Travis was a decent fellow, but that was hardly the point. (When the rebellion finally did get under way, he was the first man to be slaughtered.)

Finally, in February 1831, there was an eclipse of the sun. Nat determined this to be the promised sign—the sign that removed "the seal from my lips." He now revealed his intentions to four trusted black friends who had fallen under the influence of his personality. The four men soon agreed to participate in his great work. The time had come "to slay my enemies with their own weapons," to plan strategy, to convert a private religious vision into a political and military operation.

First, it was necessary to decide on a date to begin the slaughter. Always sensitive to symbols, Nat first proposed July 4—Independence Day—and his friends agreed. But there agreement ended. Up to this time Nat had dealt with private visions, not public strategy, and on these practical questions, the spirit failed to address him.

The questions to be answered were numerous and difficult. How many slaves should be told about the plan? Where should the operation begin? What route should their army follow? How would they get weapons? Should they spare anybody from the slaughter? How could they protect *themselves* against capture by the white troops who were sure to arrive? Above all, what was to be their practical goal? To escape, perhaps into the Great Dismal Swamp some thirty miles to the east? To capture the county seat, Jerusalem? To establish a secure free state in Southampton County? To spread rebellion throughout the South?

Through the spring months of 1831, the five men engaged in long debates and formulated any number of plans. But they could come to no agreement. "The time passed," Nat later recalled, "without our coming to any determination how to commence." Nat himself was so disturbed by this turn of events that he fell ill.

So July 4 came and went, and nothing happened. The conspirators were "still forming new schemes and rejecting them." It was at this confused and discouraged point, on August 13, that Nat was finally jolted into action by a sign too clear to be ignored: This was, of course, the day the sun grew dim and changed colors, and the black spot appeared on its surface. Now Nat knew that the Day of Judgment could be delayed no longer.

Eight days later, on Sunday, August 21, Nat's four associates gathered at a secluded pond in the neighborhood: Hark, Nelson, Sam, and Henry. Hark (his full name was Hercules) brought a pig he had filched from his master. Henry brought some brandy. There were also present two new conspirators, slaves who had not previously been part of the group. Both were well known to the original four. The pig was killed and cooked.

Nat himself did not join this last meal until the middle of the afternoon. The seven men ate and drank (though Nat himself, true to his temperance principles, refused to touch the brandy). After the food was finished, the group continued to sit around the pond and debate their plans—for even at this late hour they had not formulated any clear strategy. There was, however, general agreement that the group could delay no longer—that very night they had to rise up and "kill all the white people."

Jack, one of the newcomers, objected that the scheme was impractical—"their number was too few." Jack's objection seemed reasonable. How could seven unarmed slaves mount a general insurrection? Surely they would be captured and killed before they could accomplish anything.

But Nat was ready to answer this objection. It was not through carelessness, or visionary fanaticism, that he had failed to spread advance word of the rebellion to the slaves in the county. It was hard political calculation. He had carefully weighed the two options available to him, each involving great but different risks. First, he might try to organize the rebellion in advance. He could inform a large number of slaves of his plans, giving them time to prepare emotionally and tactically to murder their masters and join his army. But Nat knew that to do so was to risk betrayal—there was bound to be at least one slave who, out of fear or loyalty, would betray the conspiracy. Nat was aware of the fact that earlier American slave insurrections had been uncovered and stopped in just this fashion before they could even get under way.

Nat was determined above all to maintain secrecy. Until the moment of the actual onslaught, only seven men knew what was going to happen. And these seven were closely related to each other by ties of friendship or kinship. Jack was Hark's brother-in-law. Hark and Nat both worked for the same white man, Joseph Travis. And both Sam and Will were the property of Nathaniel Francis, who was Joseph Travis's brother-in-law. Among such a tight-knit group, the risk of betrayal was minimal.

But by ensuring secrecy, Nat was forced to take the second of his options—and risks. He had to give up the possibility of systematic recruitment and effective organization. He would have to recruit his forces in spontaneous fashion as the group moved on from one farm to another. Their numbers would increase as they went along, he argued. The places Nat planned to attack were all familiar to him. He had lived his entire life in the neighborhood, and his party of insurrectionists was well known to many of the slaves in the region. When these slaves saw their owners actually lying dead, and felt themselves masterless, they would surely join the liberating army. And since the slaves in Southampton County outnumbered the whites, the county would belong to *them*.

So Nat argued, as he and his six friends sat by the pond, watching afternoon turn to dusk, and dusk slip into darkness. Finally, then, it was agreed: That very night they would begin. They would head to the house of Joseph Travis, the master of Nat and Hark. There they would stop and "kill all the white people." Then they would collect weapons and horses, recruit other male Travis slaves—slaves now without a master—to join them, and march on to other farms and plantations. There the scene would be repeated, and their army of recruits would swell to overwhelming proportions. At first, they would spare no white person in their path, whether man, woman, or child—that much was necessary in order to "strike terror and alarm" through the countryside and cause the remaining white people of the county to flee for their lives. Within a day, if all went well, the black army could march unopposed and triumphant into the county seat—a town whose biblical name, Jerusalem, could not have escaped Nat's notice.

The killings had to be brutal, to intensify the general terror. The heads of some victims were to be severed, and the bodies of others dismembered. But Nat also insisted on clear limits: There was to be no torture, no rape, and (except for necessary supplies) no looting. There was no room for indulging in simple revenge or personal gratification. Furthermore, the slaughter would not continue indefinitely. Nat later told a white questioner that "indiscriminate massacre was not their intention after they obtained a foothold. Women and children would afterward be spared, and men too who ceased to resist."

The seven slaves waited at the pond until sometime after midnight. Then they walked the half-mile to the Travis house. But still they hung back. To fortify themselves

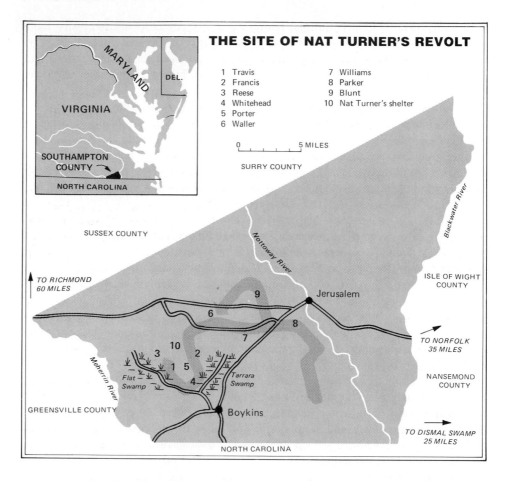

THE SITE OF NAT TURNER'S REVOLT

1 Travis
2 Francis
3 Reese
4 Whitehead
5 Porter
6 Waller
7 Williams
8 Parker
9 Blunt
10 Nat Turner's shelter

0 5 MILES

for the awful things that had to be done, they retreated to an outbuilding that housed the family's cider press, where all of them drank—all except Nat. Then, finally, they returned to the house. It was now about 2 A.M. Nat reported what happened next:

> On returning to the house Hark went to the door with an axe, for the purpose of breaking it open, as we knew we were strong enough to murder the family even if they were awakened by the noise. But, reflecting that it might create an alarm in the neighborhood, we determined to enter the house secretly, and murder them whilst sleeping. Hark got a ladder and set it against the chimney, on which I ascended, and hoisting a window, entered and came downstairs, unbarred the door, and removed the guns from their places.
>
> It was then observed that I must spill the first blood. Armed with a hatchet, and accompanied by Will, I entered my master's chamber. It being dark, I could not give him a death blow; the hatchet glanced from his head, he sprang from the bed and called his wife. It was his last word—Will laid him dead with a blow of his ax, and Mrs. Travis shared the same fate as she lay in the bed.

The murder of his family, five in number, was the work of a moment. Not one of them awoke. There was a little infant sleeping in a cradle, that was forgotten until we had left the house and gone some distance, when Henry and Will returned and killed it.

In military formation, the troop now marched a few hundred yards to the property of the nearest neighbor, Salathiel Francis. Nat sent Sam to knock on the door and announce he had a letter for Mr. Francis. As soon as the door opened, Francis's head was smashed with hatchets and clubs. Quickly now and silently, the army moved to the next house, the home of a widow, Piety Reese, and her son William, who was Jack's master. This time the door was not locked. The men entered quietly and killed the widow Reese in her bed. But the noise woke her grown son. "Who is that?" he called out. These were his last words. Finally, the killers turned on the Reeses' overseer, whom they mistakenly left for dead—the first white to survive the terror. Before they left, Jack celebrated his liberation by putting on his dead master's socks and shoes. It was a gesture that would be repeated several times in the hours to come.

At dawn—about 5:30—the troop reached the farm that had belonged to Samuel Turner, Nat's former master. This time, Nat abandoned stealth and trickery and simply stormed the farmhouse. Will broke open the door with an axe, and quickly the list of the dead was lengthened by three: Mrs. Turner, a female visitor, and the white overseer. Nat was well known among the Turner slaves, and here, if anywhere, he could expect new recruits. He did get a few. One man celebrated his liberation by putting on the clothes of the dead overseer. Another was less elated, and seems to have joined only under a threat of death from Nat's men. It was a bad sign. Four raids had netted only six recruits. If this was the result at Turner's, then what could Nat expect at other farms where he was less well known? He could take some comfort in the fact that his army now had nine horses and a few guns to go with their precarious arsenal of axes, swords, and hoes.

Nat now moved his mounted men on northward, headed toward Barrow Road, which led to the town of Jerusalem. The next farm north belonged to another widow, Catherine Whitehead, and was the largest farm Nat had yet attacked. Here for the first and last time, Nat Turner killed.

Out in a field near the main house, the rebels found Mrs. Whitehead's son, a young Methodist minister. Will finished him with an axe. Then the army moved on the main house, where they quickly slaughtered three of Mrs. Whitehead's daughters, a young grandchild, and the old mistress herself.

Nat waited outside as these murders were finished. But, like it or not, he had his own desperate baptism to perform: He had to come face to face with slaughter. One of the Whitehead daughters, Margaret, had been able to sneak out of the house and hide herself. Nat saw her, and she ran wildly into a nearby field. He chased her down and began to swing at her with a small sword he was now carrying. For some reason, the sword would not finish off the screaming woman, and he had to pick up a fence post and finally club her to death.

The Whitehead farm had twenty-five slaves, and Nat could reasonably hope for some recruits. But his luck was even worse here than it had been at Turner's. Three of the adult male slaves ran away to the woods, and Nat could persuade only two of those who remained to join his campaign of terror. One of the slaves, an old house servant, had even managed to save the life of a fifth Whitehead daughter by hiding her under a mattress and convincing Nat's men that she was not at the house.

The August dawn had now become full day. It was a Monday, and every farm family in the neighborhood would be awake and at work. Before the day was over, Nat Turner would know the answer to two very crucial questions: How many of Southampton County's 10,000 blacks would join him? and Would the county's 6,000 white people flee, or would they resist? The answer to the first question would depend on Nat's ability to persuade. The answer to the second would hang on the success of his deliberate, calculated tactic of terror. He knew one thing for certain. He had to get scores, even hundreds, of recruits. The only alternative was collapse.

Already there were ominous signs of failure. The very next house Nat raided was empty. The family had been warned by its own slaves—who in turn had been told what was happening by slaves from the Travis place, site of the first killings. And there were few recruits. Months later, after the rebellion had been crushed, a local white man summed up the problem accurately enough:

> They did not find one dozen efficient recruits along their whole route of slaughter. They certainly made many more [than twelve], but instead of being of any service, most of them had to be guarded, by some two or three of the principals [rebel leaders], furnished with guns—with orders to shoot the first men who endeavored to escape.

If Nat Turner's few guns and the precious energies of his lieutenants had to be put to such uses, his chances of success were frail indeed. And if he came upon more empty houses, whose white occupants had been warned, could a force of mounted and well-armed whites be far away? Sadly, from his point of view, the first whites to flee had not even seen the bloodied and headless bodies he was counting on to generate terror. He had almost reached the road leading east to Jerusalem. But a terrible burden of fatigue and uncertainty had to lie behind the flat and understated judgment Nat remembered making at this point: "I understood, then, that the alarm had already spread."

It had been spread first by slaves. A boy had run all the way from the Travis farm—the first that had been attacked—to warn Travis's brother-in-law, Nathaniel Francis. Francis, not convinced, had decided to ride off to see for himself. His mother had followed. When Nat's men arrived at about 9 A.M., they killed an overseer, a female visitor and her child, and two young Francis nephews. One of these boys, a

---

Governor Floyd's journal. John Floyd was governor of Virginia during Nat Turner's revolt. This is a page of his journal from September 1831. The entry for the 27th, as well as attacking the *Liberator*, speaks of Floyd's willingness to recommend mercy in the case of three slaves sentenced in Southampton County and of his inability to do so because of the "forms of our infamous [state] constitution." (Virginia State Library)

Twenty sixth day. It is raining the wind
from the South East — the rain continued
all day. I have been busily employed
sending off arms to different counties this
morning, but the rain put a stop to
that operation—

Twenty seventh day. It is cloudy &
cool. Wind South west—

I have received the record of the trial
of three slaves, for treason &c in Southampton,
one recommended to mercy, which
I would grant, but the forms of our
infamous constitution makes it necessary
before the Governor does any act involving
discretionary power, first to require
advice of Council — and in this case
I cannot do so, because, there is
not one member of the Council
of State in Richmond. wherefore the
poor wretch must loose his life by
their absence from their official duty.

I have received this day another
number of the "Liberator" a News-paper
printed in Boston, with the express
intention of inciting the slaves and
free negroes in this and the other
States to rebellion and to murder

SLAVERY AND SOUTHERN SOCIETY

On the day Nat Turner's rebellion began, a group of sweaty riders galloped into Richmond, the state capital, with the news. Shouting, they rushed to the mansion of the governor, John Floyd. He immediately put the militia of the entire state on alert and sent companies of cavalry and artillery off to Southampton County, with bugles blaring and guns at the ready. Floyd and many others in Virginia were convinced that a massive uprising of slaves had begun. Roadblocks were put up around many towns, and black slaves were arrested everywhere, for little or no reason.

In the days that followed, the governor calmed down a little, and so did other white Virginians. Then, ten days after the rebellion, Floyd made a remarkable entry in his diary: "Before I leave this government, I will have contrived to have a law passed gradually abolishing slavery in this state." And if he could not accomplish that, he would at least get a law that would prohibit slavery west of the Blue Ridge Mountains—more than half of Virginia. For a brief moment, it seemed that the outcome of Nat Turner's rebellion might be the end of slavery in Virginia, the oldest and still the most important slave state of all. It seemed possible, briefly, that Nat Turner *had* been able to win freedom for his people.

Floyd was not the only Virginian who wanted to be rid of slavery. Many members of the legislature shared his wish. Some of them were gentlemen whose dream was of a modern commercial and industrial South; they were convinced that slavery kept them in bondage to economic underdevelopment. And there were others—mostly from the western part of the state, where slavery had not yet become important—who feared it, although not for moral reasons or out of any concern for blacks. Like most other Americans, they were racists, and they simply did not want African Americans living in their midst, either as slaves or as free people. These westerners also disliked slavery because they were convinced it inevitably brought with it aristocracy, an extreme social division between wealthy planters and ordinary white people. Both anti-slavery groups, the gentlemen interested in economic development and the westerners, agreed on one thing. If slavery actually ended, the freed slaves would have to be transported out of the country and "colonized" in Africa. The South could then become white, democratic, and prosperous.

The question was, did the opponents of slavery in Virginia have enough power to overturn the rule of the eastern planters who had always

Governor John Floyd. Governor Floyd, though favoring gradual emancipation at the time of the 1831–32 debate in Virginia, soon afterward took a strong proslavery position. (Virginia State Library)

run the state? John Floyd, for one, was determined. Just before the legislature met in Richmond in December, he said, "I will not rest until slavery is abolished in Virginia." And a number of the legislators were equally determined. They began a debate that was the most serious and important discussion of slavery ever to have occurred in a Southern state.

In their debate, the Virginia legislators talked about the economic benefits and drawbacks of slavery, and its general political consequences. But the very specific and terrifying fact of the rebellion hovered in the background and occasionally broke the surface. One legislator drew a conclusion that was clearly in the minds of many Virginians: Every slave was a potential Nat Turner. Could a "deluded and drunken handful"

of rebels like Nat Turner's band possibly have created panic throughout Virginia? this legislator asked. "No," came his answer. "It was the suspicion eternally attached to the slave himself, the suspicion that a Nat Turner might be in every family, that the same bloody deed could be acted over at any time in any place, that the materials for it were spread through the land, and always ready for a like explosion." The only solution, he argued, was to abolish slavery and send the freed slaves far away.

The debate was exciting to Virginians. People flocked to the galleries to listen, and a Richmond newspaper published the entire proceedings from week to week. As the paper's editor described it, "We now see the whole subject ripped up and discussed with open doors, and in the presence of a crowded gallery and lobby. And nothing else could have prompted it, but the bloody massacre in the month of August."

The debate wore on through January and into February 1832. Antislavery legislators won no important vote. In the end, they lost key votes in the Virginia House and Senate by about the same margins. In the lower house, fifty-eight members, almost all from the western part of the state, voted in favor of a bill that provided for gradual emancipation, money compensation for slaveholders, and colonization. But seventy-three voted no, and the bill lost. In the Senate, a later vote was eighteen to fourteen against even *considering* any sort of antislavery measure. In the end, the legislators decided to accept the judgment of one of the proslavery speakers, that slavery "is our destiny, and the moment has never yet been when it was possible for us to free ourselves from it." Philosophical arguments had made little dent in the hard realities of Southern life. The members from the west, who cast forty-nine of the antislavery votes, owned only 102 slaves. The eastern members, who provided sixty-seven of the proslavery votes, owned a total of over 1,000 slaves.

The slender and fleeting chance that Virginia might actually abolish slavery passed quickly.

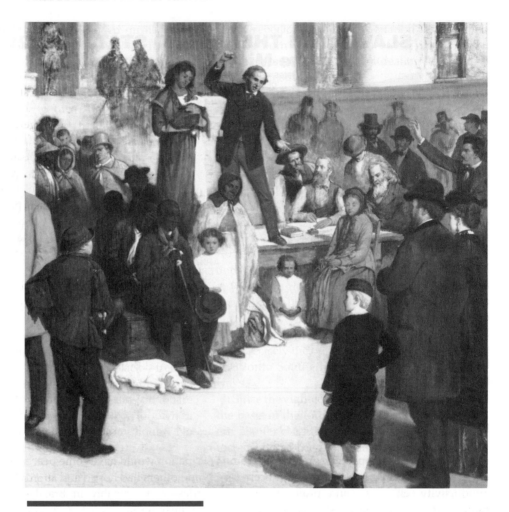

The slave auction. This detail of a painting by an anti-slavery artist depicts an auctioneer calling for bids on a mother and child. Slaves were sold for many reasons—as punishment, for profit, or to pay taxes and settle debts left at a planter's death. They usually were sold at auctions in which buyers would inspect the slave "goods," which were then sold to the highest bidder. Many slaveholders accepted the auction as a necessary part of the system, but antislavery critics considered it to be the ultimate symbol of the degradation visited upon the slave. (Missouri Historical Society)

The economic rent on slaves in the South *increased* during the crucial period between the 1820s and the Civil War. By the 1850s a planter who had brought a slave to maturity could sell him or her for well over twice the money he had spent feeding and sheltering his "property." Slavery was not only viable, it was increasingly viable.

It was also a profitable way of investing money. A planter who bought and maintained slaves, not to sell again but to use as a labor force, could realize a profit from this investment. The net rate of return on slaves, male and female, seems to have averaged about 10 percent a year. This was not true every year, and it was not true when the land itself was poor (hence the pressure to find new, good land). But it was true on average all across the South. More important, this rate of return on investment was equal to any other major investment the planter might make—in railroads or canals, or even in one of the spanking new Yankee cotton mills in Massachusetts. Slavery was not only viable, it was as profitable as any other capital investment of that period.

SLAVERY AND COTTON The South had already developed a strong export economy in the colonial period. Its cash crops—mainly tobacco, rice, and indigo—had all used slave labor. But it was the dramatic growth of cotton as the South's most important cash crop that stamped slavery so firmly on the Southern economy and society. In 1790 only slightly more than 3,000 bales of cotton were produced. By 1830, production had expanded to nearly 1 million bales. By 1860, cotton production exceeded 4 million bales and accounted for an astonishing two-thirds of all United States exports.

As noted in Chapter 7, several things lay behind this dramatic growth. First, Eli Whitney's invention of the cotton gin in 1793 made it easy to separate the cotton seed from the fiber. The end of the Napoleonic Wars opened up a booming international market for American agricultural produce after 1815. By the 1830s both England and New England had developed a textiles industry that was capable of producing enormous quantities of cheap cotton cloth. Finally, rich new land in Georgia, Alabama, Mississippi, and Louisiana was opened up to cotton cultivation, as the Native-American populations were systematically removed to the West.

All these cash crops, and especially cotton and sugar (which became important in Louisiana in the 1840s), depended on slave labor for their profitability. They were all crops that benefited enormously from what economists call "economies of scale": The larger the plantation and the greater the number of slaves in the labor force, the higher the rate of profit. By 1850, for example, the productivity of slave labor in the cotton and sugar economy—the value of the crops produced in relation to the cost of slave labor itself—was almost eight times what it had been at the end of the eighteenth century, when slaveholders had complained of how uneconomical the institution was and had begun to talk of getting rid of it.

Fluctuations in the price of cotton also led Southern planters to an ever greater reliance on increasing numbers of slaves. Cotton prices nearly tripled between 1831 and 1836. Southern planters rushed to increase their production and take advantage of the enormous profits. They pushed into Alabama, Georgia, Mississippi, Arkansas, Louisiana, and Texas, where the soil was rich and land was plentiful and inexpensive. But when cotton prices declined, the pressures to expand production only increased more. Falling prices demanded even more land and more slaves if profit was to stay high. Planters pushed all available land into cotton production and intensified their search for new lands. By the late 1840s, in fact, many planters in the states along the Mississippi Valley found that it was more profitable to import corn and wheat for their slaves' food than to take any of their own land out of cotton cultivation.

The dramatic growth of cotton as the South's major cash crop and the nation's leading export had several important consequences. It fostered a mystique among Southern planters and politicians about the importance of cotton to the nation and the world. "King Cotton," many came to believe, was the foundation of all the progress of the modern world: It sustained the prosperity and civilization of the South. Northern merchants and manufacturers depended on it for their wealth. It fueled the industrial revolution in England and France. In all, then, it fostered the absolute conviction among planters and politicians that continued prosperity depended on the continuing expansion of cotton production. From the 1830s on, Southerners constantly sought ways to find new lands for cotton cultivation. And if the production of cotton had to expand, so did the slave system it depended on.

The slave system had become just as important to Southern market capitalism as the textile factories were to the emergent industrial system of New England. The planters now had to calculate the possibilities of profit and loss in larger and more precise terms. The pressure to produce more efficiently and more consistently bore down on them heavily—and, through them, onto their African-American labor force. It became more important than ever that slave labor be disciplined and submissive.

There were variations in the South between old tobacco areas and new cotton-producing areas, between upland regions, where agriculture centered on grain and livestock production, and the lower South of single-crop production for export. But through all the variations ran a consistent thread. The large plantations—rice, cotton, or sugar—that produced for external markets were the plantations that had to function most efficiently. And on them, slavery was at its most brutal. In one Southern state after another, the need for a disciplined and submissive slave labor force produced slave codes even more severe than the one passed in Virginia just after Nat Turner's rebellion. These codes prohibited slaves from owning property, going about at night, assembling in groups, preaching, traveling without a written pass, or bearing arms. In most places after 1830, it was even against the law for whites to teach blacks to read or write.

Slavery as a Social System

Nat Turner's rebellion, the Virginia debate, the cotton boom, the slave codes—all pointed to the same fact. Slavery was not just a labor system, it was a *social* system that involved the legal status of the slave and the master; the organization of labor; patterns of landholding and land use; and religion, both white and black.

This complex and all-inclusive character is what has caused so much dispute about slavery—dispute that has lasted for more than a century since the emancipation of blacks during the Civil War. In particular, historians have argued vehemently about how masters treated their slaves.

Some have argued that slavery was a cruel and brutal system—though admitting the existence of some humane masters. They point to the meager cotton dresses, shirts, and pants, the crude huts and furnishings, and the protein-poor diets masters gave their slaves. Most of all, they point to the often sadistic and brutal forms of punishment—whipping, chaining, branding, maiming, and killing—to which some masters subjected their slaves.

Other historians have argued that in actual practice slavery was relatively mild—though admitting that there were plenty of abuses. They suggest that whippings were relatively infrequent, and that many masters did not resort to it at all. They argue that many slaves were better off than many Southern poor whites, and better off than much of the working class of industrial Europe and the North. They point out that slave housing was at least as good as that of most poor whites, and that the slave diet, especially when it was supplemented by produce from the slaves' garden plots and by game and fish, was considerably better. They argue that on many plantations, children, the sick, and the elderly were better taken care of than were the children, sick, and aged in the working classes of free society.

VARIETIES OF SLAVE EXPERIENCE In practice, slavery differed considerably according to the size of the plantation or farm, the nature of the crop work, and the place the slave lived. Slavery in the older, eastern states of Virginia, North Carolina, and South Carolina, and in border states like Maryland, Kentucky, and Tennessee often had a milder character than slavery on the generally larger, more efficient, and more productive cotton and sugar plantations of Alabama,

Mississippi, and Texas. There, work was often harder, and both the heat and the treatment more brutal. In fact, masters in the eastern and border states used "sale down the river" as both a threat and a punishment for slaves they considered disobedient or unruly.

On small farms where there were only a few slaves, they might do a wide variety of jobs—much like hired hands in the free states. Like Nat Turner, they might move from farm to farm, belong to a series of owners. But a majority of slaves belonged to large, essentially self-contained black communities on a single plantation, to which their families might be attached for generations. Many of the slaves on the Cameron family's plantations in North Carolina in the 1850s, for example, were descended from slaves who had been in the family since the 1770s.

But in spite of the numerous guises slavery could take, all slaves had one thing in common. They were chattel—property. Like horses or land, they could be bought and sold, claimed for payment of a debt, transferred, and inherited. The law, at least in theory, offered slaves some protection. It was a crime for a master *wantonly* to maim or kill a slave. Still, slaves had no legal standing as persons. They had no access to the courts. They could not charge whites with a crime, bring a suit, or testify in court against whites. Slave marriages and families had no legal standing or protection. Like Nat Turner's marriage, they could be broken up simply by a master's decision to sell one of his slaves.

In formal, legal ways, slavery in the American South was harsher and more complete than anywhere else in the Western Hemisphere. But in actual practice, it could often be considerably milder. Many of the prohibitions were loosely or only sporadically enforced. Some slaves were taught to read and write, and some, like Nat Turner, continued to teach themselves. Slaves were sometimes able to gather in their own religious, familial, and festive ceremonies. Many had a small garden plot and a few animals to tend. Most probably had some personal possessions beyond the clothes, shelter, and rations provided

A servant in the Carroll family. This photograph from around 1855 depicts a maid in a prominent Louisiana planter's household. Here the conventions of formal portraiture are used to depict a house slave, suggesting something of the complex and often ambiguous nature of the relations between the wealthiest planters and the slaves in their household. Does the photograph capture the slave's pride of place within the household? Does it convey the esteem in which her mistress might have held her personal servant? Or does it mainly provide the planter himself with a flattering portrait of the wealth and grandeur of his own household? (Louisiana State Museum)

by masters. Still, they had no rights in any of these things. A master could always confiscate their possessions, and slaves who were sold usually had to leave everything behind. The only rights, finally, were the masters' rights in their slave property.

Slaves engaged in a number of different kinds of labor and worked under all sorts of conditions. They served as valets and personal maids, wet nurses and nannies, cooks and butlers, grooms

CHAPTER 11
EXPANSION AND THE CRISIS OF THE UNION

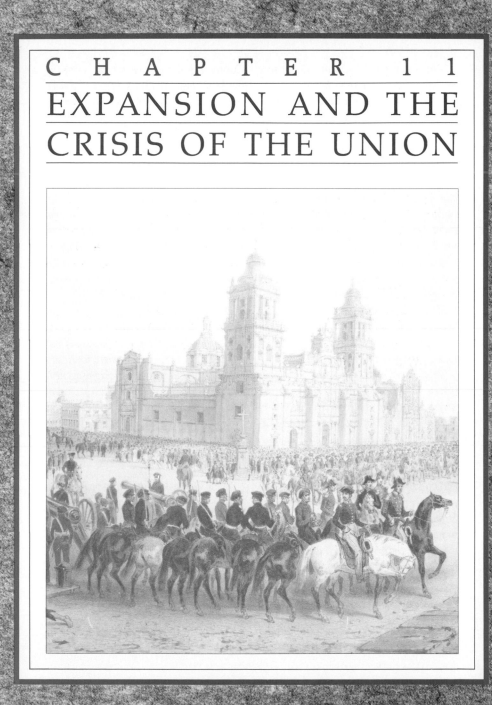

THE EPISODE: *The dramatic episode we have chosen for this chapter is not a type that historians usually have in mind when they talk about an "event." It is a work of fiction, Harriet Beecher Stowe's novel* Uncle Tom's Cabin.

Nevertheless, an enormous number of Americans who lived through the 1850s and 1860s would have said that the publication of Uncle Tom's Cabin *was an event of enormous significance. During the Civil War, Stowe visited Abraham Lincoln in the White House, and he is supposed to have said that her book had been one of the causes of the war. Hundreds of thousands of other people would have agreed, saying that reading* Uncle Tom's Cabin *had changed their attitudes toward the great issue of slavery.*

This chapter examines the novel not just as a piece of literature, but as part of the history of the greatest crisis the Union has endured. All of Stowe's most legendary characters are here—Uncle Tom himself, the beautiful and daring Eliza, the consummately cruel Simon Legree, the pathetically angelic Little Eva. But our purpose is not just to understand how Stowe's story worked as a novel. The historian's problem is to understand what it was about the book that caused so many people to read and reread it with such passion and to believe that a work of fiction might actually have changed the course of history.

THE HISTORICAL SETTING: *The astonishing popularity of Uncle Tom's*

Cabin was not caused by the nature of the book itself. It was a result of a deep change in the attitudes of white Americans, North and South, toward slavery. For many decades, most Northerners had considered slavery to be a Southern matter. They knew full well that it was a dangerous and potentially divisive matter. But for more than half a century— from the debates in the Constitutional Convention of 1787 to the early 1850s— political leaders had managed either to suppress the question of slavery or to find acceptable compromises when the question did reach the surface of politics.

But in the 1850s an increasing number of Northerners became determined to do something about slavery. If they could not eradicate it in the states where it already existed, then they would try to prevent it from spreading into the territories west of the Mississippi. And for an increasing number of people in the South, pushing slavery westward became a purpose so urgent that they would leave the Union rather than give it up.

These changes in attitude set the stage for the explosive success of Uncle Tom's Cabin. *This chapter analyzes why millions of free Americans changed their minds about slavery, became convinced that the Union could not remain half slave and half free, and were ready to risk cruel and bloody war to settle the issue. The grapes of wrath had been stored, the vintage made ready, and the terrible, swift sword waited not far ahead.*

UNCLE TOM'S CABIN

The two men were talking business when a beautiful young woman walked into the room. Conversation stopped; one of the men, a coarse-looking individual, looked her over. The woman blushed deeply as the coarse man's eyes moved quickly from her rich, silky hair and her darkly beautiful face to her delicate hands and shapely figure. Embarrassed and frightened, the young woman quickly left the room.

The business conversation resumed, but now it turned to the young woman. The coarse-looking man's interest in her was not sexual—it was economic. The woman, despite her light skin and European features, was an African-American slave, and the property of the other man in the room, a gentleman farmer in whose Kentucky home this conversation was taking place. And the coarse-looking man, Haley, was a slave trader. "By Jupiter, there's an article, now!" he exclaimed to the woman's owner. "Capital, sir—first chop! Come, how will you trade about the gal?—What shall I say for her? What'll you take?"

"She is not to be sold," the owner answered. "I say no, and I mean no." Eliza Harris, the beautiful young woman whom Haley wanted to purchase, was the personal servant of the gentleman farmer's wife, and he explained that she "would not part with her for her weight in gold." In fact, he did not want to sell any of his slaves. He was a kindly man, and he had always treated them well. But he had succumbed to the lure of financial speculation; his investments had failed, and he was deeply in debt. His notes of indebtedness had fallen into the hands of the slave trader, and now he had no choice but to give in to Haley's demands. Already he had agreed to sell one of his best slaves, a strong middle-aged farmhand named Tom, right-hand man on the farm and a beloved figure. But now Haley insisted on adding another slave in order to satisfy the debt. And because the gentleman farmer would not part with his wife's beautiful servant, Eliza, Haley finally accepted a substitute: Eliza's five-year-old son. He realized the child would fetch a good sum from one of his regular customers, a man who "buys up handsome boys to raise for the market."

"I would rather not sell him," the gentleman farmer argued halfheartedly. "I'm a humane man, and I hate to take the boy from his mother." But Haley assured him that it was possible to avoid an unpleasant scene of separation. "These yer screechin' screamin' times are *mighty* unpleasant," he agreed, "but as I manages business, I generally avoids 'em, sir." The trick was simple—just "get the girl off for a day, or a week, or so. Then the thing's done quietly—all over before she comes home. These critters an't like white folks, you know; they gets over things, only manage right." The trader assumed a confidential air as he discussed his business techniques.

> "Now, they say that this kind o' trade is hardening to the feelings; but I never found it so. Fact is, I never could do things up the way some fellers manage this business. I've seen 'em as would pull a woman's child out of her arms, and set him up to sell, and she screechin' like mad all the time. Very bad policy—damages the article—makes 'em quite unfit for service sometimes. . . . It's always best to do the humane thing, sir; that's been *my* experience."

So it was settled: Haley would take the farmhand Tom and Eliza Harris's little boy.

These two slaves could not have been more different. The boy looked just like his mother: His skin was almost white, and his silky hair hung in pretty curls around his dimpled face. The other slave, Tom, had glossy black skin, woolly hair, and African features. He was a large man, powerfully built and accustomed to manual labor. And he, too, was an exceptional slave: He was deeply religious, and completely trustworthy. He carried a pass that permitted him to travel freely. In fact, he had recently been entrusted to go by himself on a business trip to Cincinnati, a trip on which he carried home $500 in hard cash. Cincinnati was in the neighboring state of Ohio—a free state—and when Tom was offered the opportunity to remain there with the money and thus gain his own freedom, he had refused. "Master trusted me, and I couldn't" was his only explanation.

Tom cried when he learned he was to be sold and separated from his family. But once again, he refused to escape. "No, no," he sobbed,

> "I an't going. If I must be sold, or all the people on the place . . . , why, let me be sold. I s'pose I can b'ar it as well as any on 'em. Mas'r always found me on the spot—he always will. I have never broke trust and I never will."

But Eliza Harris, whose son was to be taken away, felt differently. She was determined to run off with her child before the boy's new owner could take him from her. Even pious Uncle Tom approved her decision. "It's her right!" he exclaimed. "'T'aint in *natur* for her to stay."

Eliza scrawled a hasty note to her mistress:

> O, Missis! dear Missis! don't think me ungrateful—don't think hard of me. I heard all you and master said tonight. I am going to try to save my boy—you will not blame me! God bless and reward you for your kindness!

And she was on her way. Before dark, the mother and child had walked all the way to the Ohio River—the border between Kentucky and free Ohio.

But as night approached, the two refugees were forced to pause at the edge of the river. There was no bridge, and even the ferry had canceled its usual run. It was late February, and the water was high and turbulent. Even worse, large cakes of ice were shifting to and fro in the water, forming a great, undulating raft that extended almost—but not quite—to the bank near where Eliza was waiting. The river surely could not be crossed.

The sky was almost dark when Eliza spotted a familiar man approaching. It was Haley, the slave trader. The most important moment in Eliza's life had come, and her reaction was quick and instinctive:

> She caught her child, and sprang towards [the river bank]. The trader caught a full glimpse of her just as she was disappearing down the bank, and throwing himself from his horse, he was after her like a hound after a deer. In that dizzy moment her feet scarce seemed to touch the ground, and a moment brought her to the water's edge. Right on behind her [Haley] came; and, nerved with strength such as God gives only to the desperate, with one wild and flying leap, she vaulted sheer over the turbid current by the shore, on to the raft of ice beyond. It was a desperate leap—impossible to anything but madness and despair, and Haley instinctively cried as she did it.
>
> The huge green fragment of ice on which she alighted pitched and creaked as her weight came on it, but she stayed there not a moment. With wild cries and desperate energy she leaped to another and still another cake—stumbling—leaping—slipping—springing upwards again! Her shoes are gone—her stockings cut from her feet—while blood marked every step; but she saw nothing, felt nothing, till dimly, as in a dream, she saw the Ohio side, and a man helping her up the bank.

Eliza was in Ohio now, on free soil. For the time being she was safe. The trader could not possibly follow her until the next day. In the meantime, a sympathetic man directed Eliza and her child to a nearby house. "Go there," he urged; "they're kind folks. That's no danger but they'll help you—they're up to all that sort o' thing." "The Lord bless you," Eliza answered. She picked up the little boy and walked rapidly toward the house—and freedom.

It was all fiction, of course—the first eight chapters of *Uncle Tom's Cabin*, a novel that was to outpace its author's modest expectations, both for its length and for its popularity. *Uncle Tom's Cabin* finally ran to forty-five chapters, appearing weekly in an antislavery magazine over a ten-month period between June 1851 and April 1852. Within three weeks of its publication in book form in March 1852, 20,000 copies were sold. The printer was desperately running three power presses around the clock, and he hired 100 bookbinders—all in a vain effort to keep up with the unexpected public demand. Within a year, more than 300,000 copies had been sold—an unprecedented figure for an American book. By the end of the decade, *Uncle Tom's Cabin* had been set to music and had been published in a special children's edition. Pictures of its characters and its scenes (including Eliza's escape across the ice) were sold in the form of lithographs, playing cards, and even on dishes and wallpaper.

But *Uncle Tom's Cabin* had a political impact as well as a literary and commercial one. In fact, its publication did as much as anything that happened during the 1850s to help reshape the political consciousness of the North. In 1850 most Northerners thought of slavery merely as an unfortunate fact of life about the South. Ten years later, they had come to feel it to be an intolerable stain on the entire nation. And many of them looked back on their reading of *Uncle Tom's Cabin* as the event that had changed their feelings. When the author of the book visited Abraham Lincoln in the

wish for a war to the finish and no idea how fierce the Mexican resistance would be. Now came a secret offer from Santa Anna, who was still living in forced exile in Cuba. If the United States would allow him to "escape" and return to Mexico, he would see to it that Polk's strategy worked. The Americans decided to trust him. What they got was not the deal they had bargained for, but a Santa Anna who rallied his people to a heroic resistance.

For their part, the Mexicans were both proud and confident—at least the well-off and educated Mexicans who had access to government and the press. The year before the war began, a writer in *La Voz del Pueblo* in Mexico City boasted that Mexico's soldiers were hardened professionals who would easily turn back the American armies:

> Nuestros soldados han nacido bajo las cureñas de los cañones, se han mecido al estallido de la artillería; su educación, su alimento, su vivir ha sido la guerra. ¿Cómo podrán resistirlos los que han pasado su vida en el ocio de la paz? . . . México debía armarse y hacer una grande expedición terrestre y marítima para forzar los Estados Unidos a adoptar unánimemente la religión católica apostólica y romana, a sangre y fuego.[2]

The strident tones of American Manifest Destiny had found their echoes among some Mexican leaders.

Once war began, the United States' opening move was to march an army of about 2,000 from Kansas to Santa Fé. This army, led by General Stephen W. Kearney, took Santa Fé easily and set out for its second objective, San Diego and Los Angeles. But even before Kearney could arrive,

the American settlers of California, led by Captain John C. Frémont, had organized a rebellion of their own and proclaimed the "Bear Flag Republic."

Zachary Taylor, who sported the nickname Old Rough and Ready, crossed the Rio Grande into Mexico and finally met and defeated an army that Santa Anna was rushing northward, at the town of Buena Vista in February 1847. Santa Anna gave up any further effort to dislodge Taylor in order to meet a new and more serious American threat. An American army was moving by sea toward Vera Cruz, with the obvious intention of mounting an overland attack on the capital of Mexico. The Americans were commanded by General Winfield Scott—Old Fuss and Feathers he was called, because he wore ornate uniforms and insisted on a strict discipline.

After a siege, Scott forced Vera Cruz to surrender. Then he began a long and difficult campaign, moving across rough terrain toward Mexico City and meeting stiff and skilled resistance in battle after battle. Finally, in September 1847, he was at the fortress of Chapultepec, just south and west of the capital. The garrison consisted largely of the teenage cadets of the Mexican military academy. But the boys fought with desperate heroism—easily matching that of the hardened American frontiersmen at the Alamo—and died to a man. Scott's artillery now had a clear command of the capital. Santa Anna, after some complicated negotiations, agreed to the Treaty of Guadalupe Hidalgo. In the treaty, Mexico accepted the Rio Grande border, and ceded California and New Mexico to the United States. In return, the United States agreed to pay Mexico the modest sum of $15 million and to take care of any claims American citizens might have against Mexico as a result of the war.

The war was a mild one for the Americans. It cost them 3,000 casualities, but they increased their territory by more than one-third. Like the War of 1812, this one also had its heroes, its myths, and its slogans. It gave the Marines the first line of their hymn, "From the halls of Montezuma." It thrust new presidential contenders

---

[2]Our soldiers were born under the stocks of the cannons, they have been rocked to the crack of the artillery. Their education, their nourishment, their life has been war. How can those who have spent their lives in the idleness of peace resist them? Mexico should arm herself and conduct a great expedition, by land and sea, to force the United States, in blood and fire, to unanimously adopt the apostolic Roman Catholic religion.

General Winfield Scott's entry into Mexico City. In March 1847 the American army captured Mexico City. This print appeared in a history of the war by George W. Kendell, who was one of the first reporters to go into battle with an army. (Library of Congress)

into the national spotlight: Scott, Taylor, and Frémont. It yielded the slogan "Remember the Alamo." And it gave a pair of young officers, Ulysses S. Grant and Robert E. Lee, their first real experience of war—an experience they would take into battle again fifteen years later.

Polk had fulfilled America's Manifest Destiny with skill and determination. When he left office in 1849, the United States had spread its dominion over all the territory between the oceans, north of Mexico and south of Canada. But his expansionism had once again injected slavery into politics and unleashed forces of division far more powerful than anyone had imagined. The contrast between Polk's aggressive southwestern expansion and his willingness to settle for less than all of Oregon angered many Northerners, who already viewed Polk with suspicion. When, during the Mexican War, Polk asked Congress for money for "adjustment of a boundary" between Mexico and the United States, David Wil-

mot, a Democratic representative from Pennsylvania, introduced an amendment that would make it "an express and fundamental condition" that slavery be forever excluded from any territory gained from Mexico. A rider attached to an insignificant bill by an obscure first-term congressman, the Wilmot Proviso—though never enacted—had an enormous political impact and pushed the slavery controversy to a much higher plane.

Slavery and Expansion

It is ironic that when the antislavery movement concentrated on the states where slavery existed, it made little headway, but when the focus shifted to the territories where slavery did not yet exist, the issue became so explosive it eventually split

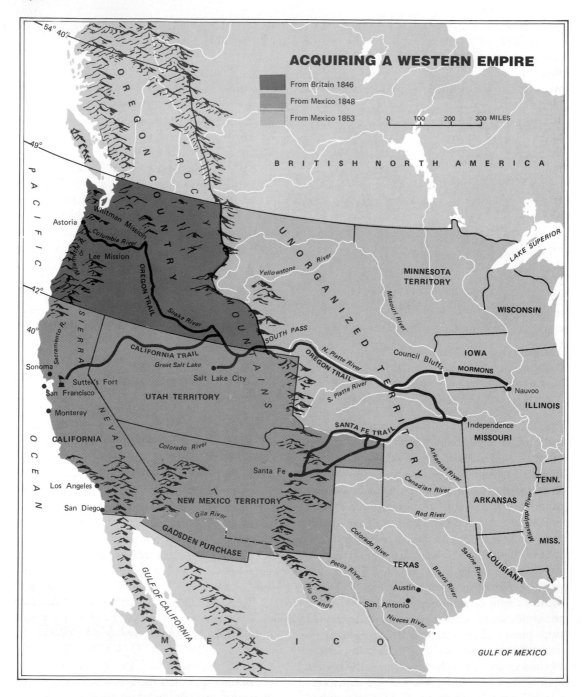

ACQUIRING A WESTERN EMPIRE

From Britain 1846
From Mexico 1848
From Mexico 1853

0   100   200   300 MILES

the nation apart. There are several reasons for this. The Constitution clearly denied Congress the authority to abolish slavery in the states. But the territories were a different matter: They belonged to the whole nation. The precedents of the Northwest Ordinance and the Missouri Compromise seemed to give Congress the authority to prohibit slavery in the territories.

It was primarily racism that kept most Northerners from embracing abolitionism. Like Miss Ophelia, most Northerners had a deep, almost visceral antipathy to African Americans. They were no more eager than Southerners to have blacks as free and equal members of their society. To them, abolitionism threatened to turn millions of blacks loose on white society, a prospect that during the 1830s provoked dozens of Northern mobs to attack abolitionists and free blacks, killing one white abolitionist and dozens of blacks. When Wilmot introduced his proviso, most Northerners were still perfectly content to let slavery remain in the states where it already existed. They still denounced abolitionists as fanatical "amalgamationists" hell-bent on destroying the Union. Nonetheless, many had become convinced that slavery was the direct antithesis of all that they associated with freedom. In its essence, slavery robbed people of their labor, the very instrument by which free men and women determined their own destinies.

The question of slavery in the territories divorced race from the issue of slavery and made the "slavery question" a matter of fundamental principle, far removed from the reality of America's black slaves. For Northerners and Southerners alike, the territories represented the future. The conflict over slavery in the territories thus became a struggle for control of the future. Most slaveholders believed their way of life could endure and thrive only if they had full freedom to take their slave property into the open territories. To deny them that right, they believed, was to deprive them of the foundation of their present prosperity and their dreams for the future. To the citizens of the free states, the open territories also symbolized an open future, full of opportunity. But many now considered the expansion of slavery to be incompatible with their own freedom to make the best life their talent and labor would allow. They feared that slavery would jeopardize their future if it was permitted to enter the territories they themselves might want to go into. Slavery seemed to them to give slaveholders an unfair advantage in "the race of life": With only their own labor, how could they possibly compete with the labor and capital the planter could extract from his slaves?

SLAVERY AND POLITICS: THE ELECTION OF 1848

The encroachment of slavery on ordinary politics was unmistakable in the elections of 1848. Expansion had led the Democrats to victory in 1844, but in 1848 it left them in disarray. The sectional fissures were deep, and in many Northern states, feuding between antislavery and conservative Democrats wracked the party. In spite of his success in carrying out his program, Polk was forced to step aside, and the Democrats nominated Lewis Cass of Michigan. Cass, firmly opposed to the Wilmot Proviso, argued that the people in the territories should decide the issue. This "popular sovereignty," he insisted, was in accord with the American tradition of local autonomy. Besides, it would remove the whole problem from national politics.

The Whigs were split between "conscience" Whigs, who were increasingly antislavery and anti-South, and "cotton" Whigs, who did not want to disrupt the alliance between Southern planters and Northern merchants and textile manufacturers. But with the Democrats even more bitterly divided, the Whigs had a good chance to regain the presidency. Again they turned to a military hero and nominated General Zachary Taylor, who had spent most of his adult life on the frontier fighting Native Americans. The Whigs did not even adopt a party platform. Any position they might take was sure to antagonize voters, so they decided to stand for nothing. The tactic worked, and Taylor won the election.

If the major parties' desperate avoidance of the territorial issue was testimony to the power of that issue, the most ominous sign of how the question was beginning to disrupt ordinary politics was the emergence of a new political party. In August several thousand reformers, Democrats, and conscience Whigs gathered in Buffalo, New York, and established the antislavery Free-Soil party. The party nominated Martin Van Buren for the presidency and called for an end to the expansion of slavery, a homestead act, internal improvements, and a new tariff. The new party's significance lay less in its electoral success or failure than in the range of people and ideas it brought together. It drew humanitarian reformers who until now had condemned politics as unprincipled and sordid and had worked outside the political arena, and it drew young politicians who were willing to stake their careers on antislavery. Perhaps most revealing of all, the new party attracted some established Whig and Democratic politicians who had always thought of themselves as loyal party men; now they had decided to cast their lot with a political party that was as much an instrument of a moral crusade as it was an electoral machine.

THE CRISIS AND COMPROMISE OF 1850

The politics of avoidance could not work forever. It had elected Taylor, and for three years Congress simply left the new territories unorganized. But avoidance was no longer possible when, in 1849, nearly 80,000 "forty-niners" flocked to California after the discovery of gold at Sutter's Mill. California had to have some kind of civil organization. President Taylor, though a Southern slaveholder, was a staunch Unionist. A military man, he believed in firm action and decided that it was time to put the territorial issue to rest. He devised a straightforward plan to skip the territorial stage and have the people of the territories won from Mexico adopt constitutions and apply directly for statehood.

Southern leaders were shocked. By September, Californians had already ratified a Free-Soil constitution and New Mexico was about to follow suit. If the antislavery forces were permitted to keep slavery out of California and New Mexico, how could they be stopped from keeping it out of all future territories? If California and New Mexico came into the Union as free states, power might shift so decisively to the North that slavery in the South itself would be endangered. All over the South, alarmed Southerners held rallies denouncing the attack on their institutions and rights. Amid threats of secession, Southern leaders called for a convention in Nashville to plan a concerted response to the threat they faced.

The vehemence of the Southern response alarmed Unionists everywhere. Henry Clay, "the Great Pacificator," the border-state senator who had worked out the Missouri Compromise, began work on a new compromise, designed to settle the full range of issues by giving each side some of what it wanted. He proposed that California be admitted as a free state but that New Mexico and Utah be organized as territories without any restrictions on slavery. He proposed that the interstate slave trade be prohibited from operating in the nation's capital, but that slavery there be abolished only if the people of the District of Columbia and Maryland agreed and if slaveholders were compensated for their slaves. Finally, he called for a stringent federal law requiring the return of fugitive slaves to their masters.

For months, debate over the compromise raged, drawing forth the best rhetorical efforts of two generations of political leaders. Clay urged Northerners to drop their insistence on the abstract Wilmot Proviso and be content with California and the probability that New Mexico would eventually become a free state. To the dying Calhoun, so sick he had to have his speech read for him, the compromise would solve nothing. He insisted that the Union could be preserved only if the political balance between North and South was made permanent and the South's rights to take its slaves into the territories and have its runaway property returned were guaranteed. If the North could not agree, he warned, "tell us so and let the states we both represent agree to separate and part in peace. If you are unwilling we should part in peace, tell us so, and we shall know what to do when you reduce the question to submission or resistance."

Daniel Webster rose to answer Calhoun. He spoke, he began, "not as a Massachusetts man, not as a Northern man, but as an American. I speak today for the preservation of the Union. Hear me for my cause." He too pleaded for the

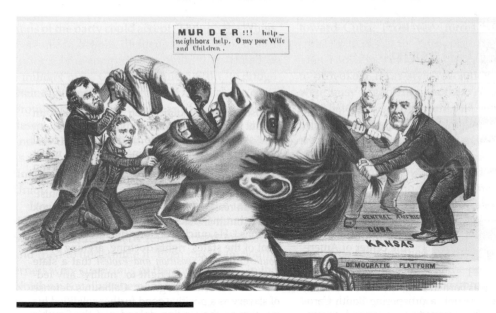

MURDER !!! help—neighbors help, O my poor Wife and Children.

Forcing slavery down the throat of a Free-Soiler. In this Free-Soil cartoon, the Democrats—Stephen Douglas and Franklin Pierce on the left, James Buchanan and Lewis Cass on the right—are shoving both slavery and black people down the throat of a white Free-Soiler. Neither Free-Soilers nor their opponents were above trying to exploit white racial prejudices for their own political advantage. (Courtesy of the New-York Historical Society)

North to give up its adherence to the Wilmot Proviso, and he pleaded with the South to surrender its talk of secession. Now it was time for the other flank to speak. William Seward, an antislavery Whig from New York, condemned the compromise as morally "wrong and essentially vicious." The Constitution, he argued, did not protect slavery in the territories because there was "a higher law than the Constitution" that had preserved the land for liberty and justice.

Brilliant and moving oratory was not enough to pass Clay's "omnibus bill." On July 31, Free-Soilers, antislavery Whigs, and Southern "fire-eaters" (proslavery extremists) combined in a parliamentary ploy that ripped the compromise to shreds, piece by piece. A dejected Clay surrendered leadership of the compromise forces to Senator Stephen Douglas of Illinois. Douglas broke the bill into separate measures and secured

a different majority for each item of the compromise. The sudden death of President Taylor, who had opposed the compromise, removed the threat of veto, and by September the major measures had been signed into law by President Millard Fillmore.

All over the country people celebrated. The crisis had been resolved, the Union saved. In New Orleans a huge rally applauded the compromise and honored its architects; in New York a hundred leading merchants set up a Union Safety Committee to strengthen support for the measure; in the Middle West, Whigs and Democrats swore to stand by the compromise. Stephen Douglas vowed "never to make another speech on the slavery question. Let us cease agitating, stop the debate, drop the subject. If we do this, the Compromise will be recognized as a final settlement."

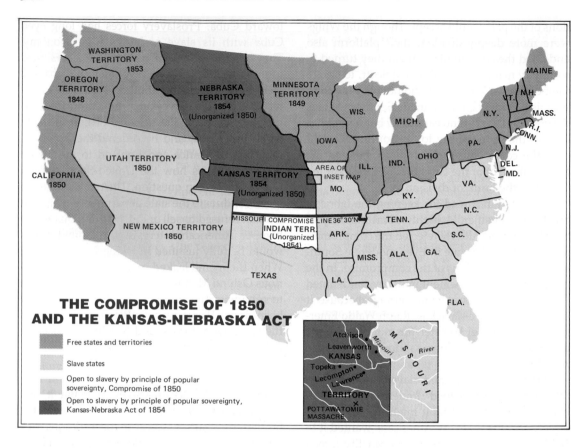

THE COMPROMISE OF 1850
AND THE KANSAS-NEBRASKA ACT

that destiny demanded development, and development demanded railroads. However, it made the most sense to put the Pacific railroad through lands that were already settled, organized, and surveyed. The preferred Southern route lay fully within existing states and organized territories, whereas the Northern route went through a huge expanse of unorganized territory. As chairman of the Senate committee on the territories, Douglas introduced a bill to organize the Nebraska Territory (the huge tract that lay between Iowa and Missouri and the Utah Territory) without reference to the issue of slavery. But under the Missouri Compromise of 1820 (see Chapter 7), slavery was excluded from the territory Douglas wanted to organize, and Southern senators blocked the bill. Douglas agreed to amend the bill in a way that would repeal the Missouri Compromise and divide the territory in two—the

southern portion, Kansas, apparently to be slave and the northern portion, Nebraska, to be free. Douglas's maneuver worked: The Kansas-Nebraska Bill passed both houses and Pierce signed it into law.

The reaction in the North was vehement. Antislavery leaders condemned the act as a monstrous plot by slaveholders to spread slavery into all the territories of the Union, while moderates condemned the repeal of the Missouri Compromise as the "violation of a sacred pledge." Douglas had known that tampering with the Missouri Compromise would "raise a hell of a storm." But he was confident that he could ride it out and that the controversy would quiet down once people began to reap the benefits of the bill and see the wisdom of the formula of popular sovereignty. He was dead wrong. Because Douglas himself considered slavery in the territories a bogus issue, he failed to realize how deeply many Northerners and Southerners had come to feel about it.

"BLEEDING KANSAS" The rush to control Kansas began. New England emigrant aid societies sent more than a thousand settlers into Kansas, while Southern promoters sponsored a large proslavery migration. Initially, there were probably more pro- than antislavery voters in Kansas. But the proslavery forces were not going to leave anything to chance. On the eve of the territorial election, nearly 5,000 proslavery voters crossed from Missouri into Kansas and used intimidation, force, and fraud to steal the election. When this fraudulently elected legislature—which Pierce, under intense proslavery pressure, let stand—convened, it expelled the few antislavery legislators who had been elected and made it a felony to challenge the existence of slavery in Kansas. The outraged Free-Soilers countered with their own "free state convention," drew up a constitution, and proceeded to elect their own territorial legislature. Popular sovereignty had not solved the issue; it had established two implacably hostile governments in Kansas, neither of which had a clear claim to legitimacy.

Pierce did nothing to solve the problem. Extremists on both sides began to arm themselves. Many of the "border ruffians" who crossed into Kansas carried guns, and antislavery groups all over the North sent rifles to the antislavery settlers. In a territory near anarchy, with people on both sides living in terror of what the other might do, it was only a question of time before real violence occurred. In May 1856, a proslavery marshal led a posse into the antislavery stronghold of Lawrence to arrest two local officials for "treason." The posse destroyed the press of the antislavery newspaper and burned many of the buildings in the town. Later, abolitionist John Brown retaliated with a raid on the proslavery town on Pottawatomie Creek. Brown and his seven men dragged five unarmed men from their cabins, killed them with axes, and mutilated their bodies.

The violence even spilled over into Congress. Senator Charles Sumner of Massachusetts delivered a fiery speech on "the crime against Kansas," singling out Senator Andrew Butler of South Carolina for special abuse. Sumner's attack outraged Butler's nephew, Preston Brooks, a congressman from South Carolina, who came up behind Sumner one day when the Senate was not in session and caned him into insensibility. Fistfights broke out between individual congressmen, and some men even began to come to sessions armed. Pierce sent a new governor to Kansas, who was able to put a lid on the violence there. But "Bleeding Kansas" had already had a profound effect on American politics.

The Rise of the Republican Party

For nearly twenty years the contest between two national parties had structured American politics. In 1856 that system fell apart. The Whig party had barely survived the election of 1852, and the Kansas-Nebraska Act effectively destroyed it as a national party. Almost all the Southern Whigs had joined their Democratic counterparts to support the bill, and almost all the Northern Whigs had opposed it. They could no longer stay in the same party. Most of the Southern Whigs became Democrats, making the South increasingly a one-party region. The situation in the North was more chaotic. Anti-Nebraska Whigs were cut loose from their own party but could hardly join the Southern-dominated Democratic party. Kansas had also driven many antislavery Democrats from their party. By the fall of 1854, the old political groupings were disintegrating, and people were coming together in new ways under a bewildering range of labels. The most important of these was the Republican party, which sprang up in a number of different places, drawing together Free-Soilers, anti-Nebraska Democrats, and conscience Whigs.

were fighting not only to ward off Yankee aggression but to expand and enhance a civilization that in their eyes appeared far finer and nobler than the money-grubbing materialism of the so-called free society of the Yankee North. They saw themselves as true Southern patriots cast in the American revolutionary tradition of Patrick Henry. By the early 1850s they had begun to dream of an independent slaveholding republic and to work as hard as they could to bring it about. In 1860 they had been working for nearly a decade to alert the Southern people to the true nature of Yankee tyranny and to lead them out of the Union and into a republic that would let Southern civilization expand and flourish as it was destined to do.

So long as the Democrats held national power and so long as the South controlled the Democratic party, the radicals failed to gain broad support for secession. But after 1856 the logic of events—the rise of a Republican party that spoke of an "irrepressible conflict" and talked of the day when the whole society would be free of the sin of slavery; a Democratic party that had essentially repudiated the *Dred Scott* decision; and a Northern population that made a martyr of a madman who had tried to provoke a slave insurrection—such events made the radicals' arguments more and more compelling. With the triumph of the Black Republicans, it seemed clear that the time for the South to rise against the tyranny that was determined to deprive it of its rights and liberty had come. The secessionists were well prepared to seize the moment, and they did. The day of wrath and judgment that Augustine St. Clare has warned of and that Abraham Lincoln later referred to as "this mighty scourge of war" was close at hand.

Suggestions for Further Reading

UNCLE TOM'S CABIN

Uncle Tom's Cabin is readily available in several paperback and hardcover editions. The best discussion of this novel is the opening chapter of Edmund Wilson, *Patriotic Gore: Studies in the Literature of the American Civil War* (1961). Stowe's novel is criticized for its racist assumptions in James Baldwin, *Notes of a Native Son* (1971). Edward Wagenknecht, *Harriet Beecher Stowe* (1965), is a good short biography. Charles H. Foster, *The Rungless Ladder: Harriet Beecher Stowe and American Puritanism* (1954), discusses the theological sources of the novel. Milton Rugoff, *The Beechers* (1981), tells the story of that extraordinary family. Jeanne Boydston et al., *The Limits of Sisterhood: The Beecher Sisters on Women's Rights and Woman's Sphere* (1988), contains an excellent set of documents. Robert H. Abzug, *Passionate Liberator: Theodore Dwight Weld and the Dilemma of Reform* (1980), is a biography of the abolitionist who managed to embroil the Beecher family in the antislavery issue.

EXPANSION IN THE 1840s

Albert K. Weinberg, *Manifest Destiny* (1935), is the classic account of American expansionism. Charles G. Sellers, Jr., *James K. Polk: Continentalist, 1843–1846* (1966), is a relatively sympathetic account. Otis Singletary, *The Mexican War* (1960), and K. Jack Bauer, *The Mexican-American War* (1974), provide good one-volume treatments of the Mexican War. William R. Brock, *Parties and Political Conscience* (1979), establishes the political context of sectional conflict during the 1840s. The story of Mexico's attempt to govern and retain its northern territories is admirably treated in Donald J. Weber, *The Mexican Frontier, 1821–1846: The American Southwest Under Mexico* (1982). The Southern understanding of the politics of slavery and expansion is well covered in William Cooper, *The South and the Politics of Slavery, 1828–1856* (1978).

THE 1850s

David Potter, *The Impending Crisis, 1848–1861* (1976), is the best introduction to the events of this decade. Michael F. Holt, *The Political Crisis of the 1850s* (1978), is a recent analysis of changing party alignments. For the Compromise of 1850, see Holman Hamilton, *Prologue to Conflict* (1964). Eric Foner, *Free Soil, Free Labor, Free Men* (1970), is an important book about the political ideology of the early Republican party. The enforcement of the Fugitive Slave Law is the subject of Stanley Campbell, *The Slave Catchers* (1968). Biographies of two contrasting figures also illuminate some of the key events of the period: Robert W. Johannsen, *Stephen A. Douglas* (1973), and Stephen P. Oates, *To Purge This Land with Blood: A Biography of John Brown* (1970). Don E. Fehrenbacher, *Prelude to Greatness* (1962), deals with Abraham Lincoln during the 1850s. Dwight Dumond, ed., *Southern Editorials on Secession* (1931), and Harold C. Perkins, ed., *Northern Editorials on Secession*, 2 vols. (1942), provide a good sampling of newspaper opinion on the crisis of the Union.

CHAPTER 12
"HIS TERRIBLE, SWIFT SWORD"

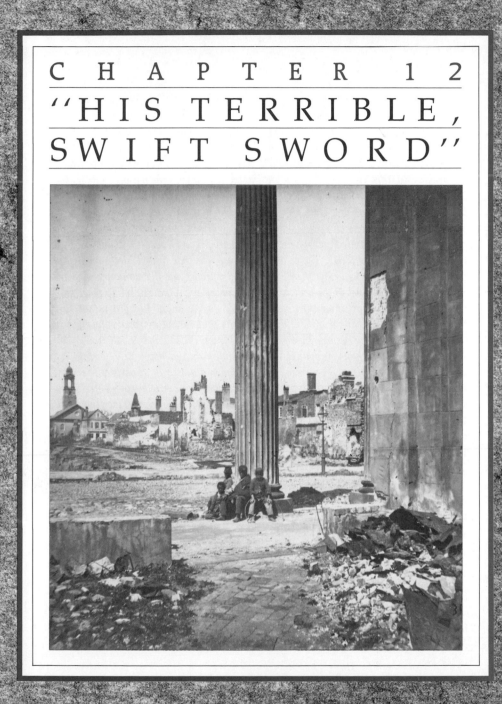

THE EPISODE: *If the importance of historical figures can be measured by the amount of attention that historians and biographers pay to them, then Abraham Lincoln was surely the most important American. In this chapter, we look in some detail at several crucial moments and themes in his career as president.*

The first is the secession crisis, which the new president confronted when he took office in March of 1861. The second is Lincoln's attempt to define the Civil War as the ultimate test of the principles of republican government, an attempt he began soon after the war started and that climaxed at Gettysburg, Pennsylvania, in 1863, when he said that the cause of the Union was the cause of "government of the people, by the people, for the people." The third is his halting, tentative effort to confront the question of slavery and the relationship between the preservation of the Union and freedom for African Americans. The fourth is his assassination and the public mourning that followed, which made it clear that he had become the symbol, in the North at least, of both Union and liberty.

We chose these moments and themes not only because they are intrinsically interesting and important, but because they also reveal much about a transformation in the man. When he ran for president in 1860, Abraham Lincoln was a folksy, practical, politically shrewd Illinois politician with a flair for words. If he had died then, nothing he had done would have made him more than a footnote to history. When he did die less than five years later, most Americans would agree that he was the nation's savior, the Great Emancipator, the embodiment of their highest national aspirations.

THE HISTORICAL SETTING: *Abraham Lincoln did not cause the Civil War. In a sense, the war caused him—made him into the leader and the monumental memory he became. Understanding what happened to Abraham Lincoln after 1861 means understanding what happened to the nation during the decade and a half of Civil War and Reconstruction.*

The momentous questions he confronted during every day of his two terms as president were the same questions that were also confronted by American men and women, North and South, white and African American. Would there be war? If the war came, who would fight and what would be the strategies of battle? Who would prevail, and how? And what would be the political, economic, and social fate of millions of African Americans held in slavery, not only in the states that formed the Confederacy but in several states that remained loyal to the Union? And when the war was over, if the Union did endure, how would the Confederate states be returned to their rightful place in it?

ABRAHAM LINCOLN: FROM POLITICS TO MARTYRDOM

As the winter of 1860–61 ended, the new president came quietly, even somewhat secretly, into Washington to take his oath of office. He was about to face a reality no other American president had had to face: a divided Union. And no one, not even men who had agreed to serve in his cabinet, not even the political friends who had helped engineer his nomination and win his election, knew what his strategies and policies would be. Most people who thought about Abraham Lincoln at all thought of him as a western lawyer, as a pretty good stump speaker, and—above all—as a shrewd politician. And they were, in the main, right. Lincoln had shown a remarkable ability to find moderate positions about slavery, positions he knew were not far from the opinions of the Northern voters who had elected him.

No one could have predicted that four years later, a murdered Abraham Lincoln would leave the capital as the greatest national hero since George Washington. When his body returned westward, back to Illinois, it was no longer the political figure, or even the political leader, that people mourned. It was a dedicated, heroic martyr to what Lincoln had managed to define as a national crusade. He had managed to transform an ugly civil war into a spiritual struggle for principles much higher than the political unity of a nation. His death put the seal on that transformation.

He began his presidency by playing a complicated political "game," as he some-times called it. The game became war. And war changed Abraham Lincoln. The change was not complete: The shrewd politician remained always a part of him. But he began to see the war as something more than politics, more even than battle and suffering. Part of him began to think of it as a religious experience, in which a nation that seemed to have been chosen by God for special blessings was now being put through a special trial and punishment. He began to insist more and more that the war was a kind of blood sacrifice demanded by God as a payment for the long sin of slavery. And when, at the war's end, he paid with his own blood, dramatic proof seemed to be given that his redefinition of the war was correct.

As Lincoln prepared to take office, the political situation was so delicate and so dangerous that even his practical skills had only a slender chance. Seven states in the lower South had already seceded and had established a new federal government for

Abraham Lincoln, 1860 and 1865.
The first portrait shows Lincoln in June 1860, at the opening of his presidential campaign. (Library of Congress) The second, taken just four days before his assassination, reveals the psychological and physical toll the Civil War had extracted from Lincoln. (McLellan Lincoln Collection, Brown University, John Hay Library)

themselves, the Confederate States of America. Several states in the upper South, particularly Virginia, Maryland, and Kentucky, were poised to join the new Confederacy. All the federal officials in the seceded states had either given allegiance to the Confederacy or had been replaced by secessionists. The Confederacy had taken over almost all the federal property within its borders—the post offices, the customs and land offices, even the forts and arsenals. All that remained of visible federal authority were two forts. One was Fort Pickens, far off in Pensacola, Florida; the other was Fort Sumter in Charleston Harbor, in the heart of secession country.

Then, as inauguration day approached, there was a strange lull. Everyone waited to see what Lincoln would do. He made no public statements. The only prediction anyone could hazard was that his actions would be—characteristically—cautious, secretive, and essentially political. In Lincoln's mind, the best direction things could go was clear: Secession would somehow be stopped without violence; the Union would be restored. And this would be done without compromising the basic Republican position on slavery in the western territories. The problem was, did he have the means and the power to work out such a political solution?

The answer would surely lie with Virginia. If he could manipulate events carefully enough so that Virginia stayed in the Union, then surely Maryland and Kentucky, probably Tennessee and Missouri, would follow Virginia's lead. Time would take its toll on the weak and isolated Confederacy. Good sense might win out, and one by one the seceding states could come back into the Union.

At this point, Lincoln saw the problem in terms that were legal, political, and constitutional. It was illegal for any state to secede. He had no doubt of that. But it was equally unconstitutional for the federal government to interfere at all with slavery in any of the states. The political bargain he wanted was for the upper South to accept this political settlement, remain in the Union, and keep their slave system as long as they could make it last.

But it was a tricky situation. If Lincoln did anything that even seemed hostile, he might provoke the border states and the upper South, especially Virginia, into joining the Confederacy, leaving the Union in a much more vulnerable position if and when war came. But he could not simply ignore secession: The people who had elected him expected Lincoln to stand up to the slave power, not give in to it. Should he try to get national institutions going again and send Republican postmasters, judges, and customs officials into the Confederacy? Should he try to reclaim federal property? What about Fort Pickens and Fort Sumter? There had already been one crisis over Fort Sumter. On December 26 Major Robert Anderson had moved his Union garrison out of Fort Moultrie, far out in the harbor into Sumter. But outraged South Carolinians had demanded the total evacuation of federal troops. After three days of vacillation, President Buchanan had rejected the Confederate demand and the first Sumter crisis had died down. But Fort Sumter had become an important symbol: To the North it was an emblem of the endurance of the Union; to the South it was a galling sign of Yankee aggression.

Lincoln announced his policy in his first act as president, his inaugural address. He began by reassuring the South. His administration would not "directly or indirectly interfere with the institution of slavery where it exists." Lincoln then flatly declared that the Union remained unbroken. "No state," he insisted, "can lawfully get out of the Union; and acts of violence within any state or states against the authority of the United States are insurrectionary." He warned that he would use "the power confided to me to hold, occupy, and possess the property and places belonging to the government." But then, his resolve to defend the Union unmistakable, he assured the South that there would be "no bloodshed or violence unless it be forced upon the national authority." He would deliver the mails only if the South wanted them delivered, and he would not "force obnoxious strangers into the South to carry out Federal business." Even though he had "the strict legal right" to do so, he would "forgo, for the time, the use of such offices" because any attempt to do otherwise "would be so irritating and so nearly impracticable."

Finally, Lincoln insisted again on his peaceful intentions. "In your hands, my dissatisfied fellow countrymen, and not mine, is the momentous issue of Civil War— the government will not assail you. You can have no conflict, without being yourself the aggesssors."

Lincoln was carefully walking a political tightrope, trying to avoid as long as possible any action that would set events on an irreversible course to war. His policy was designed to buy some political time to get his administration set up and to let Unionist sentiment in the South regroup. But the policy was also aimed toward making sure that if war *did* come, the responsibility for starting it would lie not with Lincoln but with "his dissatisfied fellow countrymen." It would be easier to rally the political support needed to wage war if the Confederacy rather than Lincoln was seen as the aggressor. Also, if Lincoln started the war, all the remaining slave states would probably join the Confederacy, and then Britain and France, leaping at the chance to split the American empire, might formally recognize the Confederacy as a separate nation.

Lincoln's policy of "masterly inactivity," as the *New York Times* dubbed it, rested on the assurance of his military advisers that Fort Sumter could hold out indefinitely and stand as a continuing symbol of the unbroken Union. But the day after Lincoln delivered his inaugural address, Major Anderson sent the surprising word that his provisions would last only four to six weeks. He would have to surrender Fort Sumter unless 70,000 troops were sent to relieve him.

So Sumter would have to be reinforced or evacuated. Neither alternative was very desirable in political terms. Sending military relief would certainly bring civil war. It would surely drive the upper South and quite possibly the border states as well into the Confederacy. But evacuation also had political risks. It would probably avoid war for a time and might help Southern Unionists. But it might push reunion ever further away by confirming the secessionists' claim that the North lacked the will to fight, thus strengthening their political grip on the Confederate states. The impact of evacuation on Northern opinion could be even more disastrous. Most Northerners, and especially the Republican majority that had elected Lincoln, would surely consider evacuation a betrayal of his pledge to "hold and possess" federal property. This might so discredit him as a political leader that his capacity to govern would collapse. And that, Lincoln feared, would lead to the collapse of the Republican party, the political force that had finally succeeded in wresting the federal government away from the slave power. Everything the Republicans had fought for during six long years would be lost forever.

Lincoln proceeded cautiously. He asked each of the members of his cabinet for a written response to the suggestion that provisions only, not fresh troops, be sent to Fort Sumter. Only one man, Postmaster General Montgomery Blair, urged that course. The others feared that even this would lead to war. Secretary of State William Seward argued most vehemently against sending provisions, insisting that the evacuation of Sumter was the only possible way, short of war, to end the crisis and restore the Union. Lincoln listened to the debate but did not express a firm position of his own. Those around him certainly thought he had accepted the overwhelming opinion of his cabinet that the fort would have to be surrendered. In fact (unknown to Lincoln), Seward privately assured some Confederate commissioners who had come to Washington to demand recognition of the Confederacy that Sumter *would* be evacuated. The commissioners knew that Lincoln could not possibly accept their demand for recognition, but they hoped to use his formal refusal to prove their contention that his real intent was hostile. Arguing that Sumter was about to be evacuated, Seward persuaded the commissioners to delay asking for an immediate answer to their demand. He himself favored evacuation and was dead certain that the inexperienced Lincoln would follow his seasoned advice.

But Lincoln had not decided to pull out of Fort Sumter. Seward and the others had misread his silence as an endorsement of evacuation. (Lincoln usually listened to advice, but he rarely revealed his own intentions until he was ready to act.) Though it seemed likely that Sumter would have to be abandoned, Lincoln was reluctant to take the step and played for more time. He had ordered the troops waiting aboard ship in Pensacola Harbor to move into Fort Pickens. This quiet, relatively unprovocative act might let him turn Pickens into the symbol of an unbroken Union. He sent Stephen Hurlbut, a Charleston-born friend, to South Carolina to find out how strong the Union sentiment there really was.

But the clamor for action was mounting. The rumors of an impending evacuation of Sumter were eroding Lincoln's support, and disillusionment over his "weakness" and "inaction" began to set in. "The country feels no more assurance as to the future than it did on the day Mr. Buchanan left Washington," the *New York Times* editorialized. "The people want something to be decided on—some standard raised—some policy put forward which shall serve as a rallying point for the abundant but discouraged loyalty of the American heart." Lincoln's old friend Senator Lyman Trumbull, of Illinois, introduced a resolution into the Senate declaring that it was "the duty of the President to use all the means in his power to hold and protect the property of the United States."

Hurlbut reported back that Unionism was utterly dead in South Carolina and all but extinct in other seceding states. He was sure that the Confederacy would accept nothing but "unqualified recognition of absolute independence," and he believed that nothing done "by the government will prevent the possibility of armed collision." Major Anderson in the meantime sent back word that he could hold out no longer than April 15. So on March 29 Lincoln ordered that an expedition to provision Sumter be prepared, "to be used, according to circumstance."

Still, the president hesitated. For weeks he had waited for word from Pensacola, but when it finally came, on April 6, it was not what Lincoln had hoped to hear. The order to garrison Fort Pickens, sent by sea rather than land, had taken a long time to get there. When it finally had arrived, it had not been obeyed! The captain of the troopship, acting on orders issued under Buchanan, would not take orders from the army and refused to act until a navy superior told him to. Now lack of supplies would force the surrender of Sumter before Pickens could be established as the symbol of the Union. And so, finally, Lincoln sent a message to Governor Pickens of South Carolina, informing him that "an attempt will be made to supply Fort Sumter with provisions only, and that if such attempt be not resisted, no effort to throw in men, arms, or ammunition will be made without further notice, or in case of an attack upon the fort." On April 9 the expedition, carrying provisions for a year, set forth with an armed escort.

Lincoln's message to Governor Pickens surprised and angered Southern leaders, who thought that Seward had spoken for Lincoln when he had promised the evacuation of Sumter. But secessionists were also becoming impatient with the inactivity of *their* leaders. The United States flag fluttering above the fort, in full view of Charlestonians, was a continuing affront to the idea of Southern independence. The Confederates acted. At 4:30 A.M. on April 12, 1861, before the relief expedition had time to arrive, shore batteries opened fire on Fort Sumter. The next day Major Anderson withdrew his forces, and on the following day, April 14, Lincoln, declaring that the South had fired the first shot, issued a call for 75,000 volunteers to put down the insurrection.

Lincoln's efforts to avoid the war had been political—naturally enough, for the situation *was* political until one side or the other began to shoot. And the political task had suited his personality and his talents. Now, confronted with a war that quickly became more deadly and more enduring than anyone on either side expected, what would Lincoln do? What was there in his character that would emerge under the intense pressure of armed conflict?

Initially, some of his work was still mainly political. He had to organize the government for war. He had to take full control of his party, which was as yet merely a loose electoral coalition. Few Republicans felt much loyalty to the "little Illinois lawyer," as Secretary of State William Seward had once called Lincoln. He had become president through a combination of adroit maneuvering and accident. Now he had

Mary Todd Lincoln (1818–82) encouraged her husband's political ambitions and fully supported his presidential aspirations. But her White House years were especially difficult. Born in Kentucky, she was suspected of disloyalty to the Union. Washington society condemned her as both a crude westerner and an excessively extravagant hostess. The death of her son Willie in 1862 and the assassination of her husband undermined her physical and mental health. In her last years, she was a desperate and pathetic woman bordering on insanity. (Lilly Library, Indiana University, Bloomington)

to spend enormous amounts of time handing out the favors and the offices that would create political loyalties.

But in the midst of the politics, a new Lincoln began to find his voice. He developed a special way of talking about the war—no longer as a war for the Union, or just as a combat forced on the government by a few hotheads in the South. In his language, the war gradually became a test of the principles of freedom and democracy—for white people, at least. On July 4, in a message calling Congress into special session, Lincoln stated the argument he was to use for the next four years: that the struggle was not between North and South, or between Union and secession, but a struggle for the rights of the people. The real issue, he declared,

> embraces more than the fate of these United States. It presents to the whole family of man the question whether a constitutional republic, or a democracy—a government of the people, by the same people—can or cannot maintain its territorial integrity against its domestic foes. It presents the question whether discontented individuals, few in number, can arbitrarily break up their government and thus practically put an end to free government upon the face of the earth.

These brief words summarized a brilliant rhetorical strategy. There were three interlocking steps. First, identify the Union cause as the cause of "the people," the cause of democracy. Second, make the outcome a test case of the cause of democracy not just in the United States but for the whole world, the "family of man." Third, make the outcome the *ultimate* test case: If democracy cannot survive here and now, then it can never survive anywhere.

From that July 4 address to the end of the Civil War in 1865, Abraham Lincoln continued to insist on these principles. They were somewhat illogical: There was no sound reason why democracy might not fail in the United States and still succeed in other places. And they were somewhat unrealistic: There was in fact little or no democracy for the "family of man" in the world. But neither logic nor realism was at stake for Lincoln. He understood the necessity of enabling his countrymen to believe they were embarked on an ennobling crusade. And he plainly came to believe it himself.

Lincoln's definition of the war got its most famous statement two years later, in November 1863. He traveled to Gettysburg, Pennsylvania, where the Union armies had turned back a Confederate advance in one of the bloodiest battles of the war just three months earlier. Lincoln's speech came at the end of a long ceremony dedicating a military cemetery. This short address came to represent his greatest performance as a writer, speaker, and ideological leader of his people. His strategy had not changed. He still defined the war as a war for democracy, for all the world, and for all time. But the tactics had become even more skillful.

First, Lincoln sanctified democracy by making it into an *inheritance*. "Four score and seven years ago," he began, "our fathers brought forth on this continent a new nation, conceived in Liberty, and dedicated to the proposition that all men are created equal." No more skillful sentence was ever written by an American president. "Four score and seven years" sounded much more ancient and more holy than "eighty-seven." And "our fathers brought forth . . . conceived . . ." was the language of procreation and birth. It stood in superb dramatic contrast to the place of death he had come to dedicate. Again, the logic and the accuracy were questionable. The United States was already heavily populated by immigrants whose "fathers" had not "brought forth" the nation at all. And it was equally true that the fathers who had "conceived" the nation included a great many slaveholding Virginians and South Carolinians. But once again, logic and realism were not what counted. Lincoln was making the war into an act of faith.

In his next paragraph—and the Gettysburg Address consisted of only two paragraphs—he began to make this religious message clear. The first sentence used the words *dedicate, consecrate,* and *hallow*: "But in a larger sense, we cannot dedicate, we cannot consecrate, we cannot hallow, this ground. The brave men, living and dead, who struggled here, have consecrated it." (Those brave men, of course, were all Union soldiers, for nothing in Lincoln's way of defining the struggle could admit Confederate dead to a share in the "unfinished work . . . so nobly advanced.") The issue was, in the end, dedication—not the dedication of a cemetery but the need for dedication of those who lived on to complete the work. And so Lincoln ended with a ringing plea that "we here highly resolve that these dead shall not have died in vain—that this nation, under God, shall have a new birth of freedom—and that government of the people, by the people, for the people, shall not perish from the earth."

❧

Lincoln had, by the force of his words more than by any other means, made the war into a crusade. But while he worked out the definition of the crusade as a struggle to defend democracy for all time, a nagging, often private dilemma would not go away. Lincoln's fine speech at Gettysburg did not mention the problem of slavery. Was that part of the crusade? Did "our fathers" include African-American fathers? Did "a new birth of freedom" include freedom and some measure of equality for slaves? This part of Lincoln's drama was never settled with anything like the clarity and coherence of his mighty assertion of liberty and democracy as the real stakes of war. But his halting, indecisive attempts to confront the issue of slavery are still a central thread in the story of his movement toward heroic martyrdom.

While Lincoln was defining the war as democracy's struggle for survival, other men around him wanted a different, more radical definition. For them, slavery *was* the issue. Charles Sumner, a Massachusetts senator and the leader of the abolitionist wing of the Republican party, insisted that Lincoln strike immediately at slavery—both as an act of justice and as a military measure to weaken the Confederacy. Frederick Douglass, the leading black abolitionist, declared that "the innermost logic of events will force it upon them in the end: that the war is a war for and against slavery." A leading white abolitionist, Wendell Phillips, spoke in even more demanding terms to the North: "Seize the thunderbolt God has forged for you, and annihilate the system that has troubled your peace for seventy years."

But Lincoln hung back. He knew that somehow slavery was the "root of the rebellion." And he knew he did not like it. He could not remember a time when he did not believe that "if slavery is not wrong, nothing is wrong." At the same time, he shared the view of most Northern white voters that black people were racially inferior to whites. Even if he considered fighting the war *against* slavery, he could not conceive of it as a war *for* black freedom and equality. He was also deeply convinced that the Constitution did not give him any power to interfere with slavery within the states.

Most of all, the idea of emancipating slaves by executive order went against Lincoln's political instincts. He knew that a leader who defied public opinion might lose his capacity to lead at all. He had not been elected on an abolitionist platform (and no Republican could have been elected that way). The support he enjoyed early in the war came to him as the friend of the Union, perhaps as the friend of democracy and liberty for whites, but not as the friend of black slaves. Most of all, Lincoln feared that the political outcome of any attempt to emancipate the slaves would be to drive the border states, especially Kentucky, into the Confederacy. "To lose Kentucky," he said, "is nearly the same as to lose the whole game. Kentucky gone, we could not hold Missouri, nor, as I think, Maryland. These all against us, the job on our hands is too large for us. We would as well consent to the separation at once, including the surrender of this capital."

But Frederick Douglass was right: The "innermost logic of events" did keep forcing the question of slavery to the surface. In the most practical way, military commanders operating in places like Missouri and Maryland had to deal with the status of slaves. Twice, in August 1861 and then again in May 1862, Union generals in the field issued orders declaring the slaves of rebels or slaves who had come within Union battle lines free. Lincoln quickly and unambiguously canceled both orders, to the dismay of abolitionists in the North.

Lincoln was in trouble. And he groped for a solution. He proposed the old idea of "colonization"—sending freed slaves out of the country. He even had agents scouting out suitable land in Central America. He promoted the idea of encouraging slaveholders to give up their slaves voluntarily, in return for federal government compensation.

Lincoln and his cabinet. Lincoln selected his cabinet carefully, making sure that the many factions of his party were represented. From left to right: Edwin M. Stanton, secretary of war; Salmon P. Chase, secretary of the treasury; Lincoln; Gideon Welles, secretary of the navy; Caleb Smith, secretary of the interior; William H. Seward, secretary of state; Montgomery Blair, postmaster general; Edward Bates, attorney general. (Gift of Mrs. Chester E. King, National Portrait Gallery, Smithsonian Institution, Washington, D.C.)

But he was beginning a private journey toward a new policy. During the spring of 1862, he slipped down into the telegraph room of the White House. It was the only place he could hide from the nagging politicians and office seekers who dogged his tracks all day. There he wrote out a draft proclamation of emancipation, which he put away to use in case he needed it.

It waited for two months, until July 1862. He continued to try to rally support for his plan for voluntary, gradual, and compensated emancipation followed by colonization. But the support did not come quickly enough nor in great enough strength. On July 13 Lincoln hinted to two members of his cabinet that emancipation might become a "military necessity." A week later, on July 21, he called the rest of the cabinet together to read them his draft of an emancipation proclamation. The cabinet was stunned by the policy change. They argued the question back and forth while the president listened. Finally, he was persuaded to wait again. The Union was still losing battle after battle. At home and in Europe, a proclamation might seem to be only a clumsy attempt to draw public attention away from the military blundering and defeats. Back into Lincoln's desk drawer went the draft, to wait for at least a Union victory.

While he waited, the president suffered, publicly and privately. In public, he was accused of being "an Ass for the Slave Power to ride." Horace Greeley, editor of the influential Republican paper the *New York Tribune*, printed an open letter to the president: "On the whole face of this wide earth, Mr. President, there is not one determined, intelligent champion of the Union cause who does not feel that all attempts to put down the Rebellion and at the same time uphold its inciting cause are preposterous and futile."

The *Tribune* letter gave Lincoln a chance to restate, in the clearest possible way, his continued analysis of the relationship between the war and slavery. He did wish, he wrote in reply, that "all men everywhere be free." But—and the "but" was the same one that had dogged him since his election—"My paramount object is to save the Union and is *not* either to save or to destroy Slavery. If I could save the Union without freeing any slave I would do it, and if I could save it by freeing all the slaves, I would do it, and if I could do it by freeing some and leaving others alone, I would also do that."

That answer might satisfy some, even most, Northerners. But the private suffering was harder to deal with. Lincoln had begun to brood over the meaning of the war—especially of the Union defeats—in a way that went far beyond politics and public opinion. After one particularly disastrous military failure, he sat in his study at night and thought about God. "We are whipped again." That much was clear. If God was all powerful, as Lincoln devoutly believed He was, then why did the slaveholders keep winning? Maybe God had something in mind that neither Union nor Confederacy could know. "God wills this contest, and wills that it should not end yet," he thought. "By His mere quiet power, He could have either saved or destroyed the Union without human contest." Alone, at night, Lincoln began to wonder whether he "might be an instrument in God's hands for accomplishing a great work." He even began to look for some kind of sign from God.

The sign—or something like it—came on the battlefield. The Confederates invaded Maryland at summer's end, in 1862. This time they were stopped cold. The Union commander wired that he had won a great victory, a statement Lincoln soon learned was somewhat exaggerated. But he proclaimed the victory anyway. Lincoln went to his cabinet and told them he had made a covenant with God that when victory came in Maryland, he "would consider it an indication of the Divine Will" that he should "move forward in the cause of emancipation."

The next day, September 22, 1862, Lincoln issued his Emancipation Proclamation. He had come only a little distance. The proclamation did not free a single slave until New Year's Day 1863, and then it declared only that the slaves in Confederate territory were to be freed. Since most of that territory was still very firmly in the hands of the Southerners, the proclamation could hardly be enforced. In fact, the proclamation suggested a very odd paradox: that slavery was illegal in rebel states but still perfectly all right in Union states like Kentucky or Missouri—in the city of Washington itself, if it came to that.

But Lincoln had done one decisive thing. He had settled one question firmly that no one had considered settled before. If the Union won the war, then slavery in the American South would effectively come to an end. Now the war was not just a war for the Union but against slavery. It was not yet a war *for* African-American rights—and it never would become quite that. But it was a very different thing from the intricate political "game" it had been when the president took office.

Abraham Lincoln's sense that the Civil War had some sort of deep, religious meaning deepened over the next year and a half. The casualty lists grew to appalling proportions on both sides. But the months and the battles favored the Union, whose armies now advanced in the unanticipated role of liberating armies for black slaves. No one, including Lincoln, had any clear idea what liberation might mean in fact and in practice. But Frederick Douglass's "logic of events" had done its work. When on March 4, 1865, Lincoln again climbed the steps of the Capitol to deliver his second inaugural address, the end was in sight. He knew everything he said would be studied with care by men and women, blacks and whites, in the North and in the South. And so he tried once more to say what the war signified, to give some explanation of the reasons he thought the nation had to endure what it was going through.

When the war had begun almost four years earlier, he began, no one on either side had guessed that it would last so long, or that it would be transformed into a war against slavery. But that had been God's will. He had given the Americans this long and "terrible war," perhaps as a punishment for the "offense" of slavery. "Fondly do we hope, fervently do we pray," Lincoln went on, "that this mighty scourge of war may speedily pass away." His language had the accents of the Old Testament prophets. And he did not hold back: "Yet if God wills that it continue until all the wealth piled by the bondsman's two hundred and fifty years of unrequited toil shall be sunk, and until every drop of blood drawn with the lash shall be paid by another drawn with the sword, as was said three thousand years ago, so still must be said, 'the judgements of the Lord are true and righteous altogether.'"

But in the religious world of Abraham Lincoln and of most of his countrymen, North and South, the Lord did not only judge, he forgave. So Lincoln ended with a plea that echoed more the New Testament than the Old. "With malice toward none; with charity for all; with firmness in the right as God gives us to see the light, let us strive to finish the work we are in; to bind up the nation's wounds, to care for him who shall have borne the battle, and for his widow, and his orphan—to do all which may achieve a just and lasting peace, among ourselves and with all nations." Here were the words so central to the New Testament: *charity, light, care, peace*. When he lay dead a few weeks later, the vocabularies of both testaments would echo back over him, and he would be compared to Moses, then to Jesus.

At Appomattox Courthouse in Virginia on April 9, 1865, Robert E. Lee surrendered his Army of Northern Virginia to Ulysses S. Grant. By April 14—which was Good Friday—it had all begun to sink in: Armed resistance in the South was practically over. The sadness that had seemed to weigh so heavily on Lincoln lifted a bit. That night, he and his wife would go to the theater. A new English comedy, *Our American Cousin*, had just opened at Ford's Theater, and the Lincolns were in just the right mood for such a play. During the third act, John Wilkes Booth, a member of the famous Booth family of actors, slipped into the president's box, pointed a derringer at Lincoln's head, and pulled the trigger. Lincoln slumped forward, with the bullet that had passed through his brain now lodged just behind his right eye. He probably never knew what had happened. He was carried, deeply unconscious, to a house across the street. All through the night, the hopeless vigil of the doctors, of high government officials, and of Lincoln's son, Robert, continued. Then, at 7:22 in the morning, Lincoln died. The secretary of war, Edwin Stanton, was heard to mutter, "Now he belongs to the ages."

Stanton was right. What now began was a drama of grief that seemed almost boundless. War and victory had made Lincoln a hero. Now death transformed him into a near-saint. "The heart grows sick and faint," wrote the *Washington National Republican* on this day before Easter. "The pen almost refuses to trace the details of the tragedy." Crowds had gathered in the rain outside the house where Lincoln lay dying. At 7:30 "the tolling of bells announced to the lamenting people that he had ceased to breathe. His great and loving heart was still." Immediately, the streets were crowded with "people, men, women, and children, thronging the thoroughfares. It seemed as if everyone was in tears." As the bells tolled, offices, government buildings, and stores all closed. The black crepe of mourning replaced the red, white, and blue bunting that only a few days earlier had been put up to celebrate Lee's surrender. It was the same everywhere. As the telegraph hurried the news over the land, people gathered in the streets to express and share their horror, bewilderment, and grief.

To many, the loss was personal—something that had happened directly to them, not just to the nation. Some could barely contain their rage and struck out at anyone who uttered anything against the fallen president. Black freedmen were numbed by the word that the president was dead. One young girl remarked that she thought she could "never love God anymore." Walt Whitman expressed his sense of loss in a poem. News of the assassination had come to him just as the lilacs, portent of spring, rebirth, and renewal, had come into blossom:

> When lilacs last in the dooryard bloom'd
> And the great star early droop'd in the western
>   sky in the night,
> I mourn'd, and yet shall mourn with ever-returning spring.
> Ever-returning spring, trinity sure to me you bring,
> Lilac blooming perennial and drooping star in the west,
> And thought of him I love.

The press and public orators struggled to find ways to comprehend and interpret the tragedy. What dumbfounded the people, wrote the *New York Herald*, was that such a thing could have happened to the American Republic. The real "horror of the deed," the *Boston Transcript* insisted, was "the fact that the victim was the kindliest and most magnanimous of great magistrates and seemed to fall martyr to his own goodness." In Lincoln's hometown, a newspaper that had not always supported the president described the event this way:

> Just in the hour when the crowning triumph of his life awaited him; . . . when he could begin clearly to see the promised land of his longings—the restored Union— the assassin's hand at once put a rude period to his life and to his hopes. As Moses of old, who had led God's people through the gloom and danger of the wilderness, dies when on the eve of realizing all that his hopes had pictured, so Lincoln is cut off just as the white wing of peace begins to reflect its silvery radiance over the red billows of war.

As the first shocked grief poured forth, plans for the funeral and burial were made. Several groups laid claim to the body. The City Council in Springfield, Illinois,

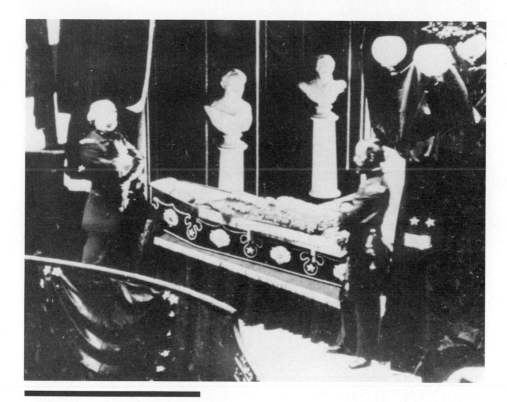

Lincoln lies in state. Lincoln's open casket lay in state for two days in the Capitol rotunda. (UPI/Bettmann Archives)

insisted that Springfield "should be the final resting place for all of him that remains mortal." New York papers urged construction of a monument that would contain his remains. The Commission of Public Monuments in Washington declared that the body ought to be deposited in the vault that had been prepared for George Washington under the rotunda of the Capitol. But the distraught widow insisted (as had Washington's family) that "his dust shall lie among his own neighbors and kin." Lincoln would be returned to Springfield for burial, but not directly and immediately as Mary Lincoln wanted. Her husband also belonged to the public. Secretary of War Stanton, in charge of the official arrangements, thought it was important that as many people as possible have a chance to take part in the farewell to Lincoln.

At noon on Wednesday, April 19, the official funeral service took place in the East Room of the White House. At the same hour, people all over the country gathered in their churches for simultaneous services. Lincoln's pastor eulogized the president and pointed to the belief in the "justness and goodness of God" that had been "an anchor to his soul" and had "emboldened him in his path of duty." Then a procession, led by an African-American regiment, followed by half a dozen other military units, thirty bands, and then another African-American regiment, carried the body past a vast crowd of blacks and whites, soldiers and wounded veterans, to the Capitol, where the open casket lay in state for two days. "The procession of saddened faces came pressing forward at the rate of three thousand persons per hour. The Rotunda, which

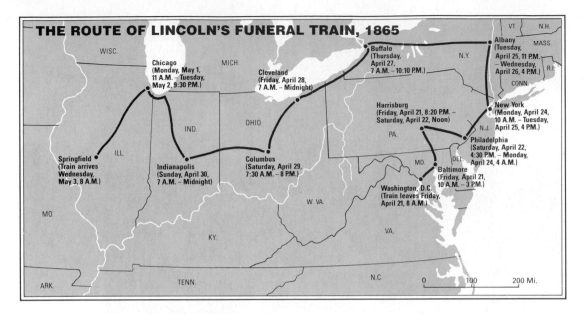

THE ROUTE OF LINCOLN'S FUNERAL TRAIN, 1865

Chicago (Monday, May 1, 11 A.M. – Tuesday, May 2, 9:30 P.M.)

Cleveland (Friday, April 28, 7 A.M. – Midnight)

Buffalo (Thursday, April 27, 7 A.M. – 10:10 P.M.)

Albany (Tuesday, April 25, 11 P.M. – Wednesday, April 26, 4 P.M.)

Harrisburg (Friday, April 21, 8:20 P.M. – Saturday, April 22, Noon)

New York (Monday, April 24, 10 A.M. – Tuesday, April 25, 4 P.M.)

Springfield (Train arrives Wednesday, May 3, 8 A.M.)

Indianapolis (Sunday, April 30, 7 A.M. – Midnight)

Columbus (Saturday, April 29, 7:30 A.M. – 8 P.M.)

Philadelphia (Saturday, April 22, 4:30 P.M. – Monday, April 24, 4 A.M.)

Baltimore (Friday, April 21, 10 A.M. – 3 P.M.)

Washington, D.C. (Train leaves Friday, April 21, 8 A.M.)

WISC. MICH. N.Y. VT. N.H. MASS. R.I. CONN. IND. OHIO PA. ILL. N.J. MD. DEL. MO. W. VA. VA. KY. N.C. TENN. ARK.

0   100   200 Mi.

Rotunda, which was lighted only by a sort of twilight hue, was filled with solemn stillness, unbroken save by the rustling of the dresses of female mourners, and occasionally a deep sigh from some of those passing the coffin."

Then, on April 21, a nine-car funeral train left Washington for the long journey back to Springfield. The train retraced the route that just four years earlier had carried Lincoln to his inauguration. It stopped in ten cities along the way. Everywhere it was the same: a procession through the city, ceremonies in a hall where the body lay in state, throngs of people filing past the coffin to get a last glimpse of the "face of our great friend." In Philadelphia 100,000 people joined the procession; 300,000 more looked on, as the hearse bearing the casket made its way to Independence Hall, "the Temple of American Liberty," to lie in state. When the body arrived at the hall, three women placed a cross of pure white flowers on the casket. It was, according to the silk streamer attached to it, "A Tribute to our Great and Good President Fallen a Martyr to the Cause of Human Freedom—'In my Hand No Price I Bring, Simply My Cross to Cling.'"

In every city, banners along the route that the procession took proclaimed their messages: "His Memory, like the Union he Preserved, is not for a day, but for all time"; "God's noblest work, an honest man"; "Weep, generous nation, weep; the sad, swift removal of him whom Heaven indulgent sent to man. Too good for earth, to Heaven art thou fled, and left the Nation in tears." At numerous ceremonies, Lincoln's second inaugural address was read again and again. Orators and clergymen tried to capture the meaning of the man and the tragedy. Lincoln's "death, which was meant to sever the Union beyond repair, binds it more firmly than ever," George Bancroft declared. "The country may need this imperishable grief, to touch its inmost feelings.

Lincoln's funeral train. This nine-car train carried Lincoln across the land to his grave in Springfield, Illinois. (Culver Pictures)

The grave that receives the remains of President Lincoln, receives a martyr to the Union, and the monument which arises over his body will bear witness to the Union."

Not only the cities mourned. As the train passed through hamlet, countryside, and town, it went through arches with banners and emblems, past bands playing requiems, and regiments of militiamen and Union soldiers. Everywhere, at every hour and in every kind of weather, people thronged to see the train. At midnight, in Syracuse, New York, 35,000 people stood in a drenching rain as the train passed by. During the nights, all along the way, a "pillar of fire" guided the cortege as "at every crossroads the glare of innumerable torches illuminated the whole population from age to infancy, kneeling on the ground, their clergymen leading them in prayers and hymns."

After twelve days and more than 1,600 miles, the funeral train reached Springfield, Illinois. At ten in the morning on May 3, the casket was closed, carried to the waiting hearse, and taken by one last procession to Oak Ridge Cemetery.

The long journey was over. Stanton had said that Lincoln belonged to the ages. As the funeral train had made its way across the nation, the people themselves had poured out on him the accumulated grief of four years of war and taken possession of him. "Give him place, oh, ye prairie," the Reverend Henry Ward Beecher had said as the cortege passed through New York. "Ye winds that move over the mighty prairies of the west, chant his requiem. Ye people, behold the martyr, whose blood pleads for

The execution of the conspirators. John Wilkes Booth, killed trying to resist capture, escaped trial for the assassination of Lincoln. But four others were tried and, on July 7, 1865, publicly executed. One of them, Mary E. Surratt, in whose boardinghouse some of the plotting had taken place, was probably innocent of any involvement in the crime, a victim of the hysteria and desire for revenge that Lincoln's assassination provoked. (Culver Pictures)

fidelity, for law, for liberty." From Lincoln's words and acts, out of their own needs, from historical myth and their religious traditions, they had transmuted the Lincoln many of them had once ridiculed and condemned into Lincoln the martyr—the good and pure Lincoln, who had befriended the lowly slave, and sacrificed himself for liberty and the Union. "Washington the Father, Lincoln the Savior of his Country" countless banners along the way proclaimed.

CIVIL WAR AND RECONSTRUCTION

When Lincoln summoned the North to combat, few people were really surprised—war talk had been going on for a long time. But neither side was at all ready for war. The United States scarcely had a military establishment: Its army existed mainly to fight Native Americans and consisted of about 20,000 soldiers scattered in remote frontier forts. Its navy was made up of about ninety ships, most of which were obsolete, out of commission, or in foreign ports. In addition, Americans were largely an agricultural people, living in a huge, sparsely populated, decentralized society.

Building and Equipping Armies

The first task was to create armies. There was no shortage of men willing to fight. Northerners and Southerners both greeted the call to arms with naive enthusiasm. All over the nation, men, many scarcely more than boys, rushed to volunteer. The big question was "not who shall go to the wars, but who shall stay at home." Local communities themselves organized companies, platoons, and regiments. With a motley assort-ment of uniforms and weapons, with fiery speeches, and with knapsacks crammed with cakes and mementoes from wives, mothers, and sweethearts, the volunteers went off to war, flushed with idealism, eager to serve the sacred cause of Union or Southern independence. Death did not frighten them. Each side expected its valor in a righteous cause to bring quick victory. If death did come, it would be heroic: "And for life," wrote one young man in words many on both sides would have echoed, "if the Nation will take me, I do not see that I can put myself—experience and character—to any more useful use."

The flood of volunteers had to be turned into disciplined armies. There was not much to build on. Their only military experience was the musters of local militias, to which most able-bodied white men had gone each month for a little haphazard drill, a lot of speechmaking, and even more drinking. More serious was the lack of an adequate and experienced officer corps. Of the 1,000 officers with any formal military training (about three-quarters of whom joined the Confederacy), none had ever commanded more than a few battalions. At the company and regimental levels (and often even at higher levels), command was often conferred because of political connections or local prominence rather than military competence. Throughout the war, but especially in the first two years, the war efforts of both sides

531

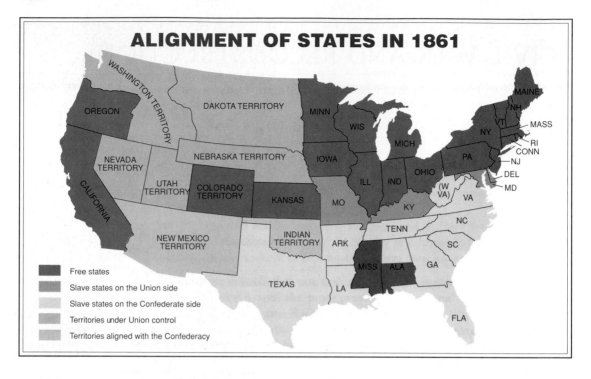

ALIGNMENT OF STATES IN 1861

- Free states
- Slave states on the Union side
- Slave states on the Confederate side
- Territories under Union control
- Territories aligned with the Confederacy

Confederate volunteers. With the outbreak of hostilities both sides had to scramble to build armies from new volunteers and from any existing prewar militia companies. Both sides greeted the outbreak of war with confidence and enthusiasm. Here the Sumter Light Guards, which became part of the 4th Georgia Infantry Regiment, stand at review in April of 1861. (Library of Congress)

and particularly the North were plagued by wildly incompetent officers.

Creating and fielding armies also demanded kinds of economic and governmental organization that neither side had. Both sides and particularly the North possessed considerable resources, but in 1861 neither economy (especially the South's) was designed for feeding, equipping, and transporting large armies. The North's textile mills, for example, produced hundreds of thousands of yards of cloth each year, but this cloth was still turned into finished clothing (like uniforms) in small workshops. And the nearly 10,000 miles of Southern railroad (as much railway, in proportion to population, as the North had) did not constitute a genuine transportation system, since few of the railroads were hooked up to each other.

There was a similar lack of administrative machinery. Except for the postal service, the federal government played only a small role in people's lives. With a minuscule military establishment, no federal taxes or national banking system, and no educational or welfare agencies, the experienced officials or bureaucratic mechanisms needed to prepare for and conduct war did not exist. Near-chaos reigned for much of the first year. Leroy P. Walker, the Confederacy's first secretary of war (whose filing system consisted of piling papers on a chair), turned away tens of thousands of volunteers because he did not know what to do with them. The Union's first secretary of war, Simon Cameron, like Walker a political appointee with no relevant experience, was equally unable to cope with the flood of recruits and military contracts. As a result, corrupt profiteers had a heyday, getting exorbitant prices for often worthless equipment. One large lot of Northern uniforms, for example, was made of "shoddy," a cheap cotton fabric that disintegrated in a hard rain.

Not until well into the second year of the war did many of these problems begin to get worked out. Lincoln shipped Cameron off to a relatively innocuous ambassadorship in Russia and replaced him with Edwin Stanton, who ran the War Department from then on with incorruptible efficiency. Confederate President Jefferson Davis, too, found more competent personnel, and by 1862 the Confederacy had an ordinance chief who was able to procure 20 million cartridges for a 400,000-man army. (When the Confederacy declared war, it had only 20 cartridges per soldier.)

Jefferson Davis. Though a reluctant secessionist, Davis (1808–89) was a firm and unrelenting champion of the Confederacy. Like Lincoln, he was often vilified by opponents who objected to his handling of the war. Imprisoned for two years after the war, he remained a believer in the righteousness of the Southern cause to the end of his life. He refused to request official amnesty and never regained United States citizenship. (The Museum of the Confederacy, Richmond, Virginia. Photo by Katherine Wetzel)

Strategy—Theory and Practice

Economic strength and military power go hand in hand, and when war began, the North seemed to have an overwhelming economic advantage. Its population of 22 million was more than double that of the South; its industrial output and its overall wealth were more than ten times that of the South. It even outstripped the agricultural South in the production of food. Jefferson Davis (a West Point graduate who would have preferred to lead the Confederate armies rather than head its government) chose a defensive strategy to offset the North's enormous economic advantage. It would cost far less in men and resources to force the Union to fight in the South than it would to invade the North. Davis's strategy was to have the Confederate army fight close to its economic base and use the military advantages of defense, familiar territory, and short supply lines to win a few major battles. The North, Davis believed, would find the price of victory too high and would grant the Confederate States of America independence, just as a war-weary and frustrated

The battle of the ironclads. In an attempt to break the Northern naval blockade, the Confederacy devised the first "ironclad" vessel, a wooden ship plated with armor. In March 1862, the first battle of the ironclads took place, a standoff between the Confederate *Merrimac* and the Union *Monitor*. By the end of 1864, the Union navy had more than seventy ironclads in commission. (National Gallery of Art)

Britain had granted the American colonies their independence.

Northern strategy, not surprisingly, was almost the mirror opposite. By the nature of its paramount goal—to save the Union—the North had to go on the offensive. Only if the South was thoroughly defeated, Lincoln and his military advisers believed, could it be forced to give up its claim to independence. Lincoln knew that even with its economic superiority the North faced a task that would strain its will and resources to the utmost. And he recognized, too, the link between economic and military strength. To strangle the South economically, he declared a naval blockade, hoping to keep the Confederacy from importing the war materials it needed. On the military front, he planned a two-pronged attack. In the West, Northern armies would invade and try to cut the Confederacy in two, while in the East, they would strike at the Southern capital of Richmond.

These were the grand designs. But geography and the conventions of military doctrine shaped how they were put into practice. Until the last year of the war, almost all the fighting in the East took place in the narrow area between the Blue Ridge Mountains and the Atlantic Ocean and between the James and Potomac rivers, the narrow corridor between Richmond and Washington. In the thinking of the day, capital cities had great military, political, and symbolic significance. According to strategic doctrine, capturing the enemy's capital could itself bring victory, and loss of one's own might well bring defeat.

The war in the West was very different. There, the changing border between Union and Confederacy stretched for over a thousand miles. In this vast theater, warfare took many forms. The long border exposed both sides to quick strikes and raids. Along the Missouri and Kansas border, a marauding guerrilla warfare of the most brutal sort took place. (Indeed, Jesse and Frank James, the most notorious bandits in American history, got their start as members of William C. Quantrill's Confederate guerrilla band.) In the West, too, the Mississippi, Tennessee, and Cumberland rivers opened up avenues into the heart of the Confederacy.

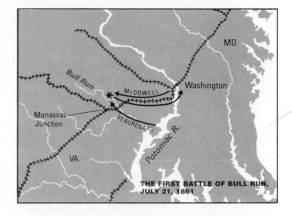

THE FIRST BATTLE OF BULL RUN, JULY 21, 1861

The Struggle Begins

If the war could be won (or lost) quickly, as a lot of people on both sides expected it would be, then the decisive action would surely come in the East. If the war had to be fought in the heartland beyond the Appalachian Mountains—in Kentucky, Tennessee, or Mississippi—then it would be long and bitter.

During the first spring and early summer of war, 1861, not much happened on the battlefields. Both sides were getting ready. Then Lincoln decided to try for the quick victory that would end the war. He ordered General Irvin McDowell, who commanded about 30,000 inexperienced troops, to march south from Washington toward the Virginia town of Manassas, to do battle with a smaller Confederate army commanded by General P. G. T. Beauregard. In mid-July McDowell moved. Beauregard waited just south of a muddy little creek (or "run" as country people called it) named Bull Run. The two armies met on July 21. Several times the federal soldiers charged Beauregard's lines. Each time, they were driven back. Then Beauregard ordered a counterattack. The heat, the clamor, and the unexpectedly heavy casualties all took their toll on the

young and green federal soldiers. The Union forward units panicked and ran back across Bull Run. The panic spread, and before it was over, McDowell had to retreat all the way to Washington.

The retreating soldiers brought only a few of their dead and wounded. But they also brought a blunt, wordless message. The war would not be won and lost in a few weeks in northern Virginia. It would be long and bloody. The first force of Union volunteers had enlisted for three months. Now Lincoln set out to raise a force of hundreds of thousands, recruited not for a few weeks but for three years. The Confederate leaders began the same grim task.

The winter of 1861–62 was another season of regrouping, supply, and training on both sides. And when the war heated up again, it was in the West, and it was savage. The Confederate armies in Kentucky were grouped around Bowling Green in the east and Columbus in the west. A Union commander, Ulysses S. Grant, received permission to move south from Illinois to drive a wedge between the armies and try to gain control of the Tennessee River. He succeeded in capturing two Confederate forts just inside Tennessee before the Confederate commanders could get their armies in position to challenge his advance. Then he quickly headed southward up the river. By early April he had reached Pittsburg Landing, near the Mississippi border and a crucial rail junction at Corinth, Mississippi.

Meanwhile the two Confederate forces in the West, split by Grant's maneuver, had fallen back, abandoning the western half of Tennessee. The two armies, one commanded by Beauregard, the other by Albert Sidney Johnston, came together in northern Mississippi. Sooner or later they and Grant's force would have to meet. The Southern commanders decided to strike at Grant before Union reinforcements, racing down from Louisville, could reach him. They attacked near a Tennessee country church called Shiloh on April 6.

The struggle was ferocious. The Confederate generals had 55,000 troops to throw at Grant, who had about 40,000 men. The first day ended in stalemate, but the corpses piled up. Then Grant's reinforcements arrived, and after the second day, the Southerners had to break off their attack.

Neither army had been broken or destroyed at Shiloh. But two things were now clear. First, the Confederate forces had not been able to drive Grant's threatening army out of the Deep South. Second, the war was going to be more savage than even Bull Run had hinted it would be. On the fields and in the woods at Shiloh, 13,000 Union soldiers and 10,000 of the Confederacy's best troops lay dead. Many thousands of others on both sides were wounded. Victory was now a question of which side could stand the carnage longer, could continue to pour men and guns into one titanic battle after another, and could go on hauling away the wagonloads of the dead and wounded.

Strategically, the Union was very close to accomplishing a major goal: controlling the Mississippi. In April 1862, the same month as Shiloh, Flag Officer—soon to be Admiral—David Farragut captured Mobile and New Orleans for the Union. A little later, he had moved up the Mississippi to Baton Rouge. Grant took Corinth, Union forces occupied Memphis, and now most of the river was theirs, except for the strong Confederate fortress at Vicksburg.

While the Union attack in the West went forward, the war in the East became a bloody standoff. Neither the Union's failures nor the Confed-

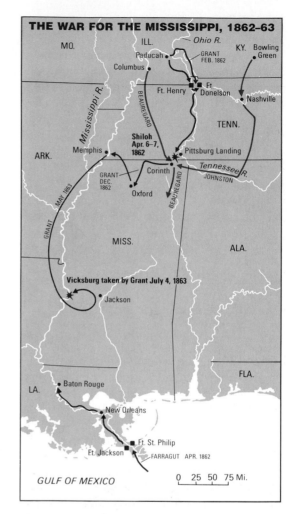

eracy's successes were decisive enough to bring either side within sight of final victory or defeat.

The main Union army in Virginia, the Army of the Potomac, was now commanded by young George B. McClellan, who had convinced Lincoln to let him try to take Richmond, not by land this time but by sea and up the peninsula between the York and James rivers—that same peninsula where Charles, Lord Cornwallis, had surrendered to George Washington in 1781. Confederate armies led by a new commander, Robert E. Lee, and his ablest lieutenant, General Thomas J. "Stonewall" Jackson, met the threat and turned McClellan back. The major battles of the campaign lasted seven days and cost Lee 20,000 dead, McClellan 15,000. But Lee had won. The Army

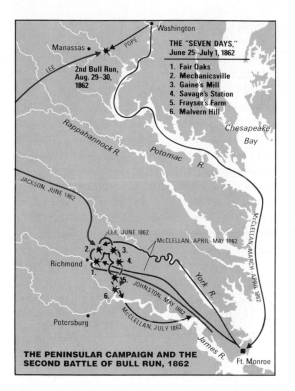

THE "SEVEN DAYS,"
June 25–July 1, 1862

1. Fair Oaks
2. Mechanicsville
3. Gaine's Mill
4. Savage's Station
5. Frayser's Farm
6. Malvern Hill

THE PENINSULAR CAMPAIGN AND THE
SECOND BATTLE OF BULL RUN, 1862

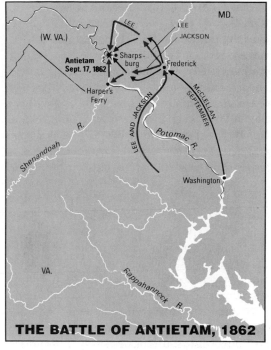

THE BATTLE OF ANTIETAM, 1862

of the Potomac was driven back down the peninsula.

Lincoln ordered McClellan's army home to Washington, determined to attack Richmond overland. But Lee and Jackson now moved north, hoping to defeat other Union forces near Washington before McClellan's army could complete its withdrawal and regroup. And they succeeded. A second battle near Manassas, the Second Battle of Bull Run, August 29–30, 1862, was the most decisive Confederate victory yet.

Now Lee took the offensive. He moved his army into Maryland, knowing that the federal army would have to place itself between him and the capital, leaving Virginia's farmers free to take in the fall harvest without the presence of massive Union armies. McClellan moved out to meet the threat and threw an army of almost 90,000 at Lee's 50,000 near Sharpsburg, Maryland, at a stream called Antietam Creek.

On September 17 Lee's men and McClellan's fought three pitched battles on the same field. The Confederate lines bent under overwhelming pressure. Then, when it was clear that one more Union assault would bring a massive defeat, Jackson rushed to Lee with reinforcements. Still, McClellan might have won with one more charge. But he held back and even gave Lee another day to withdraw.

Antietam was the bloodiest single day of the war. At its end, 13,000 men in Union blue and almost 11,000 in Confederate gray lay dead. Lincoln called it a victory and used it as the occasion for the Emancipation Proclamation. But he mourned McClellan's failure to follow up on his apparent advantage, and he relieved McClellan as commander. In the East, as in the West, some things had become clear, at least for the time being. Neither side had an overwhelming advantage in the field. The Union was not able to manage a successful offensive against Richmond. But neither was Lee able to operate successfully outside Virginia. Any Union commander who wanted to defeat Lee had to be prepared to accept appalling casualties and keep attacking, again and again.

Such an officer was the man Lincoln chose to replace McClellan, General Ambrose E. Burnside. Burnside shocked Lee and Jackson by driving his Army of the Potomac across the Rappahannock River, near Fredericksburg, Virginia, and attacking strong Confederate positions on the high ground near the town. The Confederates held. Burnside sent his men again up the heights. Again they failed. The bewildered general commanded another attack. Another failure. And by the end of the battle, Burnside had lost 12,000 men in his disastrous effort. The two exhausted armies dug in for a winter of waiting on the opposite shores of the Rappahannock.

The next spring, another new general, "Fighting Joe" Hooker, took charge of the Army of the Potomac. But his luck against Lee was no better than McClellan's or Burnside's had been. Hooker tried moving upriver, then across the Rappahannock, to outflank Fredericksburg. Lee and Jackson met him at Chancellorsville, in early May 1863, and defeated him decisively. But by now the Confederacy was so weakened that no Southern general could assemble the supplies and fresh troops necessary to take decisive advantage of any victory. Once more, Lee had won, but he had won only time and stalemate. And time and stalemate were now clearly the allies of the Union.

War, Diplomacy, and Northern Morale

The fortunes of war are not made only on the battlefield. From the perspective of long-range strategy, the Union's successes in the West put it in a fairly strong position. But it did not seem that way to the Northern people. The Civil War was the first American war to get vivid daily newspaper coverage, and it was in the eastern theater that the most dramatic, closely watched, and highly publicized fighting took place. There in the early years of the war the North took a

pounding, and this was far more important than Union victories in the West at Shiloh and Corinth in shaping the politics and diplomacy that could determine the outcome of the war.

Diplomacy played an important part in the Confederacy's overall strategy. From the outset, Davis hoped to secure recognition and support from the European powers, especially England and France. The South's confidence that Britain would come to its aid lay in the importance of its cotton to the English economy. Nearly 20 percent of Britain's population was dependent on textiles for its livelihood; cotton goods made up over 40 percent of its exports, and it got more than 80 percent of its raw cotton (700 million pounds per year) from the South. This situation, and the fact that Britain's own imperial designs in the Western Hemisphere would be well served if the American Union fell apart, brought that country very close to recognizing the Confederacy. As it was, in thinly disguised fashion Britain supplied the South with blockade-running ships and, at the risk of provoking war with the North, had even taken orders for two ironclad rams that could easily have broken the Northern blockade. Still, prudence and certain hard economic facts—the fact that Britain, having stockpiled a great deal of cotton before hostilities, had not yet felt much of an economic pinch; the fact that its merchants were profiting handsomely from trade with both sides; the fact that it imported a great deal of Northern wheat—dictated caution. Though leaning heavily toward the Confederacy, the British government chose to look carefully before it leaped; it waited to see how the war was going before it did anything that might provoke the North's open hostility. Lincoln knew that the British had their eyes trained on the battlefield. That was one of the reasons he so hastily proclaimed Antietam a major victory and issued the Emancipation Proclamation. He hoped to swing British public opinion behind the Northern cause.

Those at home also watched the eastern theater with concern. Northern morale—the willingness of the people of the North to endure the suffering of war—was almost as important for Northern victory as what happened on the battlefield. Lincoln knew that one of his greatest tasks was to keep up support for the war, and he tried at every point to strengthen commitment to the Union as a cause worthy of any sacrifice. Moreover, Confederate strategy was aimed directly at Northern morale. Davis expected Southern independence to come from the Confederacy's ability to hold off defeat until a weary Northern public turned against the war. The strategic importance Lee attached to the destruction of a Northern army lay in the impact he hoped it would have on Northern and foreign opinion.

Lincoln was acutely aware of how precarious Northern morale was in the summer and fall of 1862. Enthusiasm for the war had waned with the end of any hope for a quick victory, and many people were beginning to wonder if there would be any victory. Discontent with the administration's conduct of the war was mounting, and the war weariness threatened to slip into opposition to the war itself. Already there were those who argued that the North should stop fighting and negotiate with the Confederacy about rejoining the Union. Lincoln issued his Emancipation Proclamation partly to line up antislavery fervor solidly behind the administration and to draw more blacks into the Union's war effort. He considered the organized opposition to the war to be a form of treason and jailed some of its leaders. If things in the East kept going as they were, the North's will to fight might well give out.

Leadership and Opposition in Wartime

As the war ground on inexorably, opposition to Lincoln and Davis mounted. Northerners and Southerners increasingly blamed the seeming weakness and incompetence of their respective leaders for the hardship, suffering, and frustration they had to endure. Throughout the war, opponents portrayed Lincoln as a well-meaning but hapless bungler. To many Southerners, Davis seemed petty, aloof, bogged down in detail, and incapable of strong leadership. But oddly enough, Lincoln and Davis were also accused of being *too* forceful and were vilified as dictators and tyrants.

In large measure, the charge of tyranny reflected the fact that the war had led to an unprecedented centralization of government power on both sides. In 1863 the North reinstituted a national banking system. The Confederate and Union governments both levied new forms of taxation. The North imposed duties on most goods and adopted an income tax, while the South introduced a tax that required each planter and farmer to contribute 10 percent of his produce to the government. By early 1863 both sides had turned to conscription to help fill their armies. The opposition to the draft was intense, especially because the conscription acts contained exemption clauses that let the rich avoid the draft by hiring substitutes.

Finally, both presidents used executive authority in unprecedented ways. Lincoln used his authority as commander in chief to initiate limited emancipation, and Davis used executive authority to impress slaves for work on military projects. Both Lincoln and Davis at times suspended the right of habeas corpus so that those suspected of aiding the enemy could be arrested and detained without trial. (In the North, more than 13,000 were detained in this way.) From an administrative point of view, these were all pragmatic measures dictated by military necessity, but to the Northerners and Southerners who experienced them, they were forms of centralization and regimentation—tyranny—that went against long-standing traditions of local autonomy.

Lincoln and Davis also found it increasingly difficult to muster the unified support needed to carry out the policies necessary for victory. The Republican party itself was divided, and Lincoln constantly had to try to balance the conflicting demands of moderates and radicals in his own camp. Most Northern Democrats had initially lined up behind the war effort, but partisan politics quickly reasserted itself. The Demo-

Draft riot in New York City, 1863. Violent riots broke out in New York and other Northern cities in reaction against Abraham Lincoln's conscription policies. Most of the rioters were workers who were especially angered because men with enough money could buy their way out of being drafted. The riots were only one manifestation of widespread dissatisfaction with Lincoln's administration. In the South, Jefferson Davis also met with major resistance to his policies. (Library of Congress)

crats, even while supporting the war, subjected Lincoln's leadership and policies to unrelenting attack. Finally, the growing war weariness sapped support for the war effort itself. By the summer of 1864, the North, with its overwhelming economic and military strength, was on the brink of triumph. But war weariness was so strong that Lincoln thought it likely that Northern voters would repudiate him in the fall elections and elect General George McClellan on a Democratic "peace" ticket instead. Lincoln was rescued by the fall of Atlanta, his own political skills, and his ability to provide the Northern public with a sense of the higher, sacred meaning of the war. He won a solid victory, gaining the support he needed to see the cause through to victory.

There was far less opposition to the war effort in the Confederacy than in the Union. But Jefferson Davis had even greater problems getting the support he needed than Lincoln did. Many planters, though steadfastly loyal to the Confederacy, opposed Davis's policies and did all they could to evade or subvert them. Davis's efforts also ran afoul of the doctrine of states' rights. His own vice president, Alexander Stephens, led the opposition to Davis's alleged usurpations of state sovereignty, and the governors of Georgia and North Carolina continually obstructed Davis's efforts to develop and carry out a unified policy. This dissension and disaffection proved insurmountable, even for one as singlemindedly dedicated to Southern independence as Jefferson Davis.

The Struggle Climaxes

At the end of April 1863, Grant had put the Mississippi River town of Vicksburg under heavy siege. The situation was critical. If Vicksburg fell, as it must if not given massive support from the East, then Confederate communications with the states west of the river would be cut. Lee had to decide whether to send an army west to raise the siege. He decided on another, daring strategy, designed to try for a victory that might force the Union to move part of Grant's forces east. So once more Lee invaded, this time not just into Maryland, but into Pennsylvania.

As Lee moved north, Hooker moved too, keeping his army between the enemy and Washington. But Hooker did not attack. Chancellorsville had been a painful lesson. He finally asked Lincoln to remove him from command, and the hapless Army of the Potomac now received yet another new commander, George G. Meade. With Lee about ten miles inside Pennsylvania, Meade moved in on the rear of the advancing Confederates.

On July 1, 1863, Lee sent a brigade of infantry into the town of Gettysburg, hoping to seize shoes for his army. The infantry stumbled onto some Union cavalry units, and there was a brief skirmish. Messengers on both sides rode away toward their main armies, asking for quick reinforcements. Neither commander had chosen Gettysburg as a battlefield. But Lee could not keep moving northward once the Army of the Potomac had found him and was at his rear, able to cut him off from Virginia. The Union commander, Meade, could not give Gettysburg to Lee. The town was just too important. It was a junction for a dozen different roads, one of them leading straight into Baltimore.

All day long on July 1, both armies rushed men toward Gettysburg. Lee was a bit closer, so he managed to get 25,000 soldiers into action on that first day. Meade managed to move up about 20,000. The Union's forward units fought and fell

Ulysses S. Grant (Library of Congress)

back, then fought again. (One Northern unit, after ferocious fighting, retreated in a panic through the town of Gettysburg, to take up new positions on Cemetery Hill. As they rushed sweating and frightened past the gates of the town's cemetery there, some of them may have noticed a small sign, a memory of more peaceful days. It read, "All persons found using firearms in these grounds will be prosecuted with the utmost rigor of the law." The good citizens of Gettysburg wanted their dead to sleep in peace.)

At the end of the first day's fighting, Meade's soldiers had fallen back into tight and powerful defensive positions on the long hook-shaped ridge south and west of Gettysburg. Time was on his side. Every hour, he could expect fresh men and supplies. Lee was reluctant to attack because he did not know where the rest of the great Army of the Potomac was, or how long it would take it to fall upon him. But he was encouraged by the success of his men on that first day, when they had seemed able to drive the Union troops back toward the ridge top with ease. In fact, Lee was fighting a war of morale, hoping

Robert E. Lee (Cook Collection, Valentine Museum)

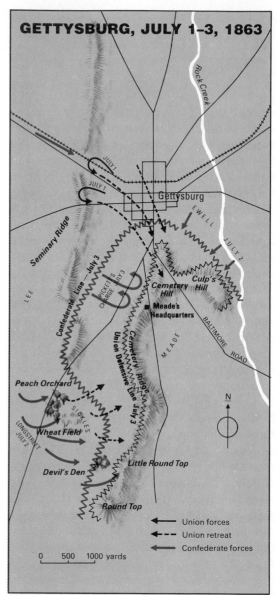

he could break the spirit of the Union soldiers at Gettysburg and that a victory here would damage the Union's will to continue the war.

So Lee decided to try to turn both Union flanks on July 2. He ordered General Richard Ewell to take Cemetery Hill, on the Union right, "if practicable." But Ewell, who commanded the corps that Stonewall Jackson had once led, was not willing to risk his men. He was certain that the enemy was securely dug in on the hill and had a lot of artillery ready to fire into his advancing troops. So he held back.

Lee also ordered a larger force, commanded by General James P. Longstreet, to attack the Union left and to try to take the hills, known as Little Round Top and Round Top, at the southern end of Cemetery Ridge. Longstreet's desperate charge fell short and only succeeded in driving some Union cavalry units off the forward slopes of the ridge.

Lee's hope had been that attacks by Ewell and Longstreet would tempt Meade to move forces out of the center of his line, to defend its open flanks. Meantime, he was massing almost the entire Confederate artillery in the center, ready for an assault on the third day. Despite Ewell's decision not to attack Cemetery Hill, and despite Longstreet's bloody and costly failure, Lee decided to go ahead with his plan. In fact, given the state of battle and the state of the war, he probably had no choice but to launch an all-out attack.

By noon on July 3 the Confederates had everything ready. About 143 cannon were massed near the center of the field. At 1:00, Lee ordered them to fire. They were answered by a barrage of equal ferocity from the heights. It was the single heaviest exchange of artillery of the entire war. But as the exchange wore on, two things happened. The Confederate guns dug themselves more deeply into the earth on each recoil, pointing their barrels higher. Their shots began to fly above the Union positions, where the infantry crouched behind defenses they had dug for themselves the day before. Second, Union commanders, understanding that a massive infantry assault would soon be coming, ordered their artillery gradually to fall silent and wait. In fact, Meade had anticipated Lee's strategy, and was ready for the assault on his center. He had placed a lot of artillery there and had some of his best and toughest troops defending that part of the line.

Lee and his generals may have been convinced they had a good chance to break the Union's lines. Or Lee may have felt he had no choice but to continue his attack, no matter what. He could hardly take up a defensive position this deep into enemy territory. And he could not retreat without dooming Vicksburg to surrendering to Grant. Whatever the reason, Lee ordered 13,000 men, commanded by General George Pickett, to charge Cemetery Ridge. Pickett formed his men in parade-ground order and sent them forward. The Union artillery opened up, followed by a withering fire from a strong center held by some of the most seasoned troops in the Army of the Potomac. And still the Confederates came. A few of them actually reached Union breastworks along the ridge line. But only a few. The rest were dead or wounded on the field, and the few who did make it to Union lines had no choice but to die, surrender, or run back down the slope under the same deadly fire.

As the charge began, Pickett had had three brigade commanders. Two were now dead and the third badly wounded. The thirteen colonels

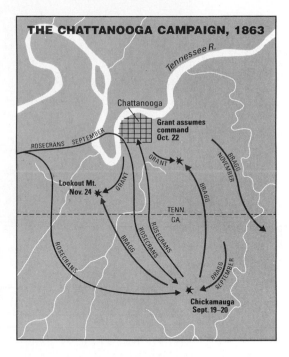

in his division were all dead. And three-fourths of his men were dead, wounded, or captured.

All in all, the Confederate armies had lost between 25,000 and 30,000 men at Gettysburg. (Lee had lost seventeen generals in the three days of battle.) Meade had lost about 23,000 men. But he had held. And on the day of Pickett's dreadful charge, the news came to both sides that Vicksburg had fallen to Grant.

The Struggle Ends

The end was all but inevitable, but still the fighting and dying continued. Union troops occupied Chattanooga, Tennessee, in August. Then a Union force moved down into Georgia. They were beaten there in the fierce battle of Chickamauga, one of the few fights in which the Confederates outnumbered the Union troops. But the

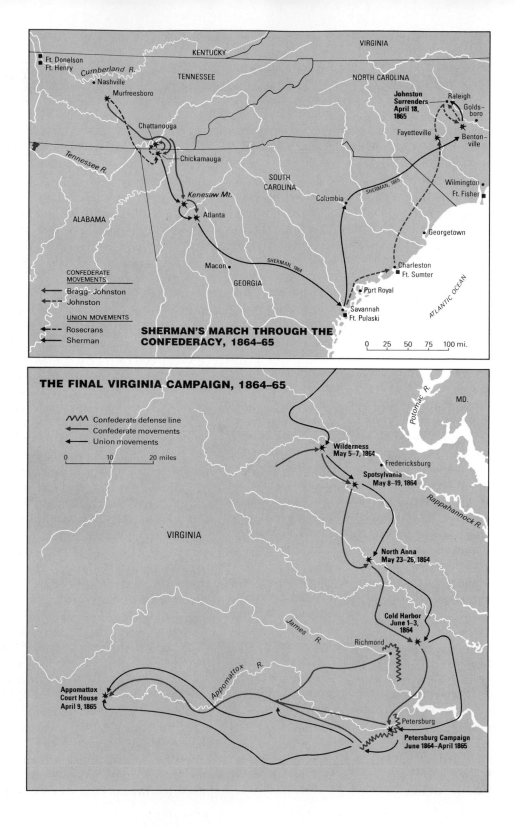

SHERMAN'S MARCH THROUGH THE CONFEDERACY, 1864–65

KENTUCKY

VIRGINIA

TENNESSEE

NORTH CAROLINA

Ft. Donelson
Ft. Henry

Cumberland R.

• Nashville

Murfreesboro

Chattanooga

Tennessee R.

Chickamauga

Johnston Surrenders April 18, 1865

Raleigh

Golds-boro

Fayetteville

Benton-ville

Wilmington
Ft. Fisher

SHERMAN, 1865

SOUTH CAROLINA

Columbia

Kenesaw Mt.

ALABAMA

Atlanta

Macon

SHERMAN, 1864

GEORGIA

Georgetown

Charleston
Ft. Sumter

Port Royal

Savannah
Ft. Pulaski

ATLANTIC OCEAN

CONFEDERATE MOVEMENTS

⟶ Bragg–Johnston

⟶ Johnston

UNION MOVEMENTS

⟶ Rosecrans

⟶ Sherman

0 25 50 75 100 mi.

THE FINAL VIRGINIA CAMPAIGN, 1864–65

Potomac R.

MD.

ᴧᴧᴧᴧ Confederate defense line
⟶ Confederate movements
⟶ Union movements

0   10   20 miles

Wilderness
May 5–7, 1864

Fredericksburg

Spotsylvania
May 8–19, 1864

Rappahannock R.

VIRGINIA

North Anna
May 23–26, 1864

Cold Harbor
June 1–3, 1864

James R.

Richmond

Appomattox Court House
April 9, 1865

Appomattox R.

Petersburg

Petersburg Campaign
June 1864–April 1865

544

victory counted for little. A month later, in the Battle of Chattanooga, Grant's army drove the South off its positions on the ridges and mountains around the city.

Once the Union armies had taken unchallenged control of Chattanooga, Atlanta lay before them, and then the sea. The South, already divided along the Mississippi, could now be split a second time by a line of soldiers stretching from Kentucky across Tennessee and Georgia to the Atlantic. This mission was not to be Grant's. Lincoln called him east to take command of the Army of the Potomac. The West was left under the command of William Tecumseh Sherman.

In the spring of 1864, the end drew nearer—though still it would not come. Grant embarked on the most vicious offensive of the war, attacking Lee day after day in May in a terrible struggle known as the Wilderness Campaign. The Southerners fell back, but they continued to kill with deadly skill. They cost Grant 55,000 casualties in a little less than a month. But they suffered 30,000 of their own, losses they could no longer afford.

Meanwhile, in May, Sherman had begun his move southeastward from Chattanooga. It took him three months to reach Atlanta, but reach it he did. Then he set off on one of the most remarkable military marches in history. He ordered his men to advance along a front fully sixty miles wide, feeding off the countryside and destroying civilian property as they went. By December he was in Savannah.

For nine months the armies of Grant and Lee had been entrenched around Richmond, Grant waiting, Lee unable to attack. Defeat for the Confederacy was becoming more and more obvious with every dispatch from Georgia. Then Grant finally moved to surround Lee's force. The Confederate army, now numbering only about 25,000, made a desperate lunge westward, trying to escape encirclement, but it failed. Lee surrendered his army at Appomattox Court House, Virginia, on April 9, 1865. There were a few days more of scattered fighting in the Carolinas. But the war had finally ended. So had the lives of 600,000 soldiers.

The Toll of Total War

In the North, there was an outpouring of jubilation, then a sense of completion and deliverance that was sealed in the ritual of mourning and transfiguration that carried Lincoln to his martyr's grave. To the ex-slaves, it was also time for jubilation—the day of deliverance longed for and promised in so many spirituals. Among the defeated whites of the South, especially those of the planter class, there was shock and disbelief, fear and uncertainty; their ordeal, it seemed, was far from over. All around them was chaos and destruction—no money, little food, a society and economy in shambles. Many wondered how or if they would survive and what might become of them. Would their lands be seized? Would they be tried and hanged as traitors, especially now that some Southern fanatic had killed the seemingly magnanimous Lincoln? Some also experienced an overpowering sense of loss. Not only had the Confederate armies been defeated, Southern civilization seemed also to have been destroyed. It was more than some could bear. On June 17 Edmund Ruffin, an early and vehement secessionist, who had been chosen to pull the lanyard that opened fire on Fort Sumter, made a final entry in his diary: "I here proclaim my unmitigated hatred to Yankee rule and the perfidious, malignant, and vile Yankee Race." Then he placed the muzzle of his gun in his mouth and pulled the trigger with a forked stick.

The final push to the bloody end had made clear what the decisive year of 1863 had already suggested. This was a war unlike any previous war. The Civil War has been called the first modern war, for good reasons. It was the first railroad war, with unprecedented quantities of troops and supplies transported over unprecedented distances. While Sherman conducted his siege of Atlanta, sixteen trains rushed him 1,600 tons of supplies each day. In addition, the huge armies—ten times the size of any previous units—using

Mary Boykin Chesnut

Mary Boykin Chesnut wrote one of the most revealing pieces of Southern literature to come out of the Civil War era, a book first published under the title *A Diary from Dixie* in 1905, nearly forty years after the events it described. Chesnut was in a particularly strong position to observe the Confederacy as it rose, fell in defeat, and disintegrated. Born into a well-known South Carolina family, she also married into one of the most prominent families of the South. As was customary for the scion of such a family, her husband, James Chesnut, Jr., entered politics, becoming a U.S. senator in 1858 and serving throughout the war as a chief aide to Jefferson Davis, whose wife was one of Mary Chesnut's closest friends. Stationed close to the heart of the Confederacy—she was in Washington as the nation divided, in Charleston for the firing on Fort Sumter, and in the Confederate capital of Richmond during much of the war—Chesnut kept an extensive journal filled with notations about the people and events that came to her attention.

Though a keen and often detached observer of her class and culture, Chesnut still held the attitudes of the planter elite. Her faith in the righteousness of the Confederate cause never wavered, and although she condemned slavery as a curse that had brought her society to its destruction, she viewed blacks with the paternalistic condescension common to her class. But

Mary Chesnut was only partly an insider. Intelligent, well-educated, and informed, she was nonetheless excluded from the masculine world of power and politics. Even while basking in the social attention her femininity bestowed on her, she resented her position on the periphery of things. Her journal gave her a vicarious sense of participation and superiority, as she gazed down on the masculine world and condemned and criticized its folly and hypocrisy.

A Diary from Dixie was fashioned in the 1870s and 1880s from a deliberate reworking of the original journals. Chesnut began to think of herself as a writer only after the war. She wrote partly to try to help recoup the family fortunes, partly to relieve the pain of the collapse of her world, and partly out of a compulsion to preserve the South that once had been. She first tried her hand at fiction, writing but never publishing three novels before turning to her Civil War journals as the source for her "big book" about the South and the Civil War.

Filled with gossip, romance, and the ordinary events that happen even in wartime, Chesnut's book retained the day-to-day randomness of a true diary. At the same time, it possessed the coherence and sense of theme and direction that only hindsight and Chesnut's conscious literary intentions could give it. The result was an extraordinary document about the Civil War but strongly shaped by Reconstruction. Her work kept alive the pain of the South's defeat. Throughout the *Diary*, life goes on, but the war keeps intruding, with its death, uncertainty, and destruction. A sense of sadness and loss begins to punctuate the book, a sense that in spite of the righteousness of its cause, the Confederacy is doomed and its civilization is ending.

Picture: National Portrait Gallery, Smithsonian Institution, Washington, D.C.

new technologies of destruction—trench warfare, repeat-loading rifles—had brought about an unprecedented mass slaughter. As Walt Whitman wrote in 1863, "The heart grows sick of war after all, when you see what it really is—every

once in a while I feel so horrified and disgusted—it seems to me like a great slaughterhouse and the men mutually butchering each other."

But what more than anything else set the Civil War apart from earlier wars was its character as

The destruction of Charleston, South Carolina. As the Union armies pressed into the South, they left much of it in ruins, visiting a destruction upon the civilian population that few other Americans have ever experienced. (Library of Congress, Brady Collection)

a total war. Wars traditionally had been fought by professional armies, which jockeyed for territory until some kind of negotiated settlement was reached. Partly because of the new technologies of war and partly because each side was fighting for a principle it would not compromise, the Civil War became the first total war in modern times. It pitted not just two armies, but two societies—each by the end fully mobilized for the effort—against each other. Victory came not with the taking of territory but with the destruction of the other society's capacity to fight. Sherman grasped the brutal logic of total war. As he put it, as he embarked on his march to the sea, "We are not only fighting hostile armies, but a hostile people. We must make old and young, rich and poor, feel the hand of war." And victory and defeat were themselves total: A destroyed South held on until it was forced into unconditional

surrender. At the end, the Confederacy was in no position to negotiate a peace—it surrendered because it could no longer carry on.

The War and Slavery

After four long years, the war had once and for all determined that the American Republic could not be divided. But the society that had to be reunited was very different from the one that had split apart in 1861. As Lincoln had written to a Southern Unionist in early 1864, "The nation's condition is not what either party, or any man, devised or expected." The Emancipation Proclamation had formally ended slavery in the Confederacy, and the Thirteenth Amendment, proposed by Lincoln in 1864 and ratified in

December of 1865, had made freedom universal. But well before these acts and well before hostilities ended, the institution of slavery had started to fall apart, due to the "friction and abrasion" of war. By the end of 1861, runaways to the Union armies were treated as "contraband" of war, rather than returned to their masters. As early as 1862 the Northern fleet had captured the Sea Islands off the Carolina and Georgia coasts, and the slaves there had been freed.

Masters tried to keep news of the approach of the Northern armies and the progress of the war from their slaves, but slaves devised ways of finding out anyway. In Forsythe, Georgia, a slave who was responsible for bringing the newspaper to his mistress always showed it to the local black preacher before he delivered it. House servants often overheard their masters talking and returned to the quarters with information about the whereabouts of the Union armies. More than once, a master awoke to find that many if not all of his slaves had slipped away in the night to become "contraband." As it marched through Georgia, Sherman's army became a veritable army of liberation (somewhat ironically, since Sherman himself had not opposed slavery and was deeply prejudiced against African Americans). After the collapse of the Confederacy, actual freedom came by direct announcement to the slaves by former masters, the grapevine, or federal officials.

By the summer of 1865 most slaveholders had relinquished their slave property. But they still held onto the attitudes that had justified holding African Americans in bondage. They thought of blacks as childlike people, whom they had fed, clothed, housed, and cared for. And most had convinced themselves that their own slaves were loyal and happy, content with the lot to which their race had consigned them. The former masters thus had great difficulty even imagining blacks as anything but a dependent and subservient people. Masters were perplexed, angered, and even hurt when their slaves (often led by personal or house servants, who had been considered most loyal) left them, refused to work, or stole tools and food.

The response of the ex-slaves to their new status was similarly confused and complex. Word of emancipation penetrated many places slowly and often in a garbled way. A few slaves wondered if emancipation meant that they now belonged to Lincoln. When slavery ended, there was nothing definite to take its place. The freedmen possessed a number of agricultural and other skills, but they were a people suddenly released from bondage, with few personal possessions and no money, property, or housing. It was not at all clear what they should do, where they should go, or how they could feed, clothe, and shelter themselves. Some set off for places from which they had been sold, hoping to reunite with their families. Others stayed where they were, working for their former masters or for nearby planters. Others, essentially refugees of war, roamed about and flocked to Union encampments in search of food, shelter, and protection.

In spite of all the confusion and uncertainty, the ex-slaves possessed a clear and definite idea of the difference between slavery and freedom. They asserted their sense of freedom in subtle ways. A rural and agricultural population tied to land and place, most were reluctant to leave areas they regarded as home. But, refusing to stay in quarters that reminded them of their previous situation, they often moved to huts scattered around their former master's lands. Some moved to a neighboring planter's land to demonstrate that the tie to their former master had indeed been broken. For many, simply the act of moving, whatever the distance, was a gesture of liberation, a deliberate exercise of the choice and freedom that had been denied them under slavery.

Many blacks resisted contracting for their labor, a refusal many whites condemned as a sign of laziness and irresponsibility. But many freedmen were suspicious of anything that seemed to bind them and their labor to any white man. Possession of their labor had been one of the essential marks of their enslavement. Indeed, many thought themselves justified in taking food, tools, and mules from their former masters as payment morally due them for their previous labor. But land was probably the most important

Freed African Americans in Richmond, Virginia. A major problem after the war was the future of the former slaves. Slavery ended without any clear sense of what was to take its place. All over the South, freed men and women drifted to the cities in search of work or simply to test their newfound freedom. (Library of Congress)

token of freedom—a parcel of land that was their own. Again and again, blacks during Reconstruction pleaded for land, "forty acres and a mule," that would enable them to establish their independence and set up households where husbands and wives could work for themselves and rear and protect their children.

LINCOLN'S PLAN Reunion required more than just returning the seceded states to full and equal participation in the nation. It also meant reconstructing a society in which slavery no longer existed and determining what kind of freedom the ex-slaves would have. Lincoln had begun to plan for the aftermath of war well before the end of the fighting. He hoped to restore political relations as quickly and with as little animosity as possible. On December 8, 1863, he issued a proclamation specifying that whenever voters equal to 10 percent of the eligible voters of 1860 took an oath swearing future loyalty to the Constitution, the Union, and the acts freeing the slaves, a state could set up a republican form of government and resume ordinary political operations. (As blacks had not been eligible to

vote in 1860, Lincoln's proclamation excluded black suffrage.) The Republican leaders in Congress wanted a much tougher procedure, one that would guarantee what they considered true loyalty to the Union. In July 1864, Congress passed the Wade-Davis Bill, which Lincoln pocket-vetoed. The bill required action by 50 percent of the eligible electorate. More important, it contained provisions for an "ironclad" oath—a pledge of past as well as future loyalty—which was designed to bar all former secessionists and Confederate officeholders from political participation.

Lincoln was not unmindful of the troubling question of the freedmen, nor was he unaware of the tricky relationship between race and the politics of reunion. But just as he had initially subordinated slavery to the task of preserving the Union, he now placed highest priority on reestablishing normal political relations. He thought Reconstruction could be best achieved if the question of the freedmen was separated from the process of political reunion: If the ordinary political machinery was reestablished, the nation would be better able to work out what the freedman's place in American society should be. Lincoln had always been reluctant to push for civil and social equality for blacks, partly because of his awareness of the depth of American racism and partly because he shared some of that prejudice. Still, at the time of his death, he had begun to work on the problem of the freedmen and on the politics of that problem. When Louisiana drew up its constitution in 1864, he urged the governor to consider giving the vote to "some of the colored people," especially "the very intelligent and those who have fought gallantly in our ranks." (Altogether, nearly 178,000 black troops, many of them ex-slaves, served in the Union armies.) On March 3, 1865, he signed a bill creating a Freedmen's Bureau. The bill gave federal protection and aid to ex-slaves and contained a limited provision for giving them land, a provision that looked forward to the possible establishment of a landholding black yeomanry.

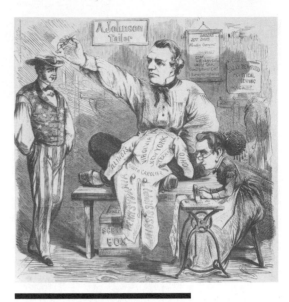

Andrew Johnson. When Tennessee seceded in June 1861, Johnson—alone among Southern senators—refused to resign and join the Confederacy. Lincoln appointed him military governor of Tennessee. His staunch Unionism and his effectiveness in restoring civilian rule to Tennessee made him a logical choice as Lincoln's running mate in 1864. This political cartoon favorable to Johnson depicts him as the leader needed to repair the torn fabric of the Union. (American Antiquarian Society)

Reconstruction: 1865–77

PRESIDENTIAL RECONSTRUCTION UNDER JOHNSON Lincoln's successor, Andrew Johnson, fully intended to carry out the policy Lincoln had begun. But he operated at a severe disadvantage. As is the case with most vice presidents, Johnson was chosen with no expectation that he would ever be president. He was selected because he was a Democrat and a staunch Union man from the border state of Tennessee. These very attributes, plus the fact that he had once owned slaves, heightened Republicans' suspicion of him and made them all the more eager to keep control of Reconstruction in the hands of Congress. In addition, he lacked the political power Lincoln had amassed through his adroit dispensing of favors and patronage. Even more important, Johnson lacked the stature—the legitimacy—Lincoln had acquired as the head of state who had seen the Union through to victory and the first president since Andrew Jackson to win

reelection. And even with all these assets, Lincoln had run into stiff opposition to his approach to Reconstruction.

Congress was not in session when Johnson took office, and he proceeded to carry out his own plan for Reconstruction by executive action, without consulting the Republican leaders of Congress. Here, too, he partly followed Lincoln's example. Lincoln had jailed opponents to the war, ended slavery in the Confederate states, and instituted a draft—all by executive action. He had launched Reconstruction by proclamation and vetoed the Wade-Davis Bill because he opposed its more stringent conditions and thought Reconstruction was properly an executive function. So Johnson charged ahead. He renewed the promise of amnesty to most ex-Confederates, and he set three conditions for a rebel state's reentry into the political system: The state had to nullify its ordinance of secession, accept the Thirteenth Amendment, and repudiate all Confederate debts. Johnson insisted that the states had never legally been out of the Union and hence retained the power to set their own rules on who could vote. He also assured Southern leaders that Congress was constitutionally bound to accept these governments. Under the leadership of many ex-Confederates, the South moved quickly. When Congress came back into session in December, it was presented with a fait accompli: All but Texas had set up state governments firmly under the control of former slaveholders and Confederate leaders and had sent senators and representatives to Washington to claim their seats in the new Congress.

Johnson and most white Southerners thought political reconstruction was substantially complete. Johnson's major goal was political reunion. He was unconcerned about the freedmen. He rescinded General Sherman's Special Field Order of January 1865, which had set aside a thirty-mile strip along the South Carolina coast to be distributed in forty-acre plots to the freedmen, and ordered the land returned to its previous white owners. But the planters also wanted to create a society as close as possible to the antebellum South, a goal in direct conflict with the freedmen's aspirations for land and independence. (After Johnson's reversal of Sherman's order, one freedman declared, "They will make freedom a curse to us, for we have no home, no land, no oath, no vote.")

As soon as the ex-slaveholders found themselves regaining local power, they moved rapidly to reestablish their economic and social dominion, to return the freedmen to a position of social subordination and keep them as a cheap source of plantation labor. Mississippi, South Carolina, and Alabama enacted Black Codes (the other states followed in early 1866), which severely restricted black freedom. In general, the codes were designed to do two things: to maintain white supremacy and to secure a black labor supply. Some codes barred blacks from jury service or testifying against whites; others restricted them to agricultural labor; still others forbade

them from renting land or carrying firearms, or imposed curfews on them. The most far-reaching codes, however, were the vagrancy laws, under which unemployed African Americans who could not pay their fines for vagrancy could be bound out to work for whomever paid the fine.

To many in the North, the new South that Johnson's Reconstruction had ushered in seemed frighteningly similar to the old South. Most of the ex-Confederates seemed right back in power. They filled the state legislatures. And the former vice president of the Confederacy, six former cabinet members, nine generals, and more than fifty members of the Confederate legislature had been elected to the national Congress by the reconstructed states. Moreover, the Black Codes seemed to have reestablished slavery under another name. As the *Chicago Tribune* thundered, "We tell the white men of Mississippi that the men of the North will convert the state of Mississippi into a frog pond before they will allow any such laws to disgrace one foot of soil over which the flag of freedom waves."

Northerners were divided over what they wanted out of Reconstruction, and few were eager to grant equality to blacks. (Twelve Northern states still refused to give the franchise to blacks.) Still, they had opposed slavery, fought and won a war that had come about partly because of slavery, and they did not want to see it restored under some new guise. But most upsetting of all, those who had led the rebellion—those responsible for the terrible war—refused to acknowledge defeat. Mississippi had rejected the Thirteenth Amendment, South Carolina refused to nullify its ordinance of secession, and members of the old slavocracy demanded seats in Congress. It seemed as if Reconstruction was about to deprive the North of the victory for which so many of its men had died.

When the new Congress returned to Washington, it refused to seat the senators and representatives from the former Confederate states. It moved to take Reconstruction policy into its own hands and set up a Joint Committee on Reconstruction headed by two strong-willed radical Republicans, Representative Thaddeus

Stevens of Pennsylvania and Senator Charles Sumner of Massachusetts. They believed that the Reconstruction of the nation would not be completed until the revolution in Southern society brought about by the end of slavery was completed. For Sumner, this required granting full citizenship and political rights to the freedmen, while for Stevens it involved using government lands and confiscating the plantations of the old planter aristocracy to give the freedmen the land to establish themselves as independent farmers. Even the moderate members of Congress were alarmed by what was happening in the South: Unless there was "some legislation by the nation for his protection," Senator Trumbull of Illinois insisted, the ex-slave would be "abused and virtually re-enslaved."

Concern for the freedmen was certainly not the only thing that motivated Republicans in Congress. Johnson's Reconstruction threatened them with the loss of their political power, and many Republicans were more concerned with holding onto political power than with the rights of blacks. With the end of slavery, Southern representation in the House of Representatives would be increased by about twenty seats, since for purposes of apportionment a slave had been counted as only three-fifths of a person. Republicans feared that the exclusion of Southern blacks from the vote would ensure the election of unreconstructed rebels, who would join with pro-Southern Democrats to drive the Republicans from power. Black suffrage might be essential for the establishment of any real freedom for the ex-slaves, but it also seemed essential for keeping the Republicans in power. In fact, it was not until the Republicans began to lose power in the North in 1870 that they passed the Fifteenth Amendment, granting suffrage to African-American males in the North and South.

CONGRESSIONAL RECONSTRUCTION But Stevens and Sumner were not yet in control of Congress. Moderates like Senator John Sherman of Ohio were still in the ascendancy. They did not want to throw out the governments orga-

nized under Johnson, but they did want to give some protection to the freedmen. Congress enacted two pieces of legislation. It extended the Freedmen's Bureau, the agency that had been set up to help the transition out of bondage by providing relief, setting up schools, and helping freedmen find employment. It also passed the Civil Rights Act of 1866 that granted the rights of citizenship to the ex-slaves and gave federal courts jurisdiction over all cases involving those rights. President Johnson promptly vetoed both acts. The moderates then countered with the Fourteenth Amendment, a complex measure designed to give some basic protection to the ex-slaves in a form that the moderates hoped the South would accept. The amendment contained the basic features of the Civil Rights Act, but it also reduced the political power of the old Southern elite by barring from public office anyone who had ever sworn fidelity to the Constitution and then participated in rebellion. At the same time, the amendment did not directly require black suffrage; it only threatened to reduce Southern representation if blacks were not permitted to vote. Nor did it contain any provision for the confiscation or redistribution of lands. It was clear, however, that the Republican Congress would not accept any state back into the Union that did not ratify the amendment.

President and Congress were now at complete loggerheads. Johnson denounced the amendment and even urged Southerners to reject it. He decided to take the issue of Reconstruction directly to the voters in the upcoming congressional elections. Contrary to custom, Johnson went on the political hustings, denouncing the Republican Congress and further polarizing the issue. But his campaign was a disaster, and the voters overwhelmingly repudiated his policies. The Republicans, now increasingly under the influence of Sumner and Stevens, won more than two-thirds of the seats in both houses, enough to override any presidential veto.

Most of the members of the newly constituted Southern legislatures were firmly opposed to the Fourteenth Amendment, which would remove many of their members from office. But white

A Freedman's Bureau school. The Freedman's Bureau was the central federal agency set up to help former slaves make the transition to life after slavery. One of its main goals was to set up schools, often staffed with women from the North, many of whom had been active supporters of the antislavery movement. (Library of Congress)

Southerners were also angry and felt a deep sense of betrayal. Many had complied with Lincoln's and Johnson's requirements in good faith, only to have new and harsher conditions imposed on them in what seemed like an all-too-familiar resurgence of Yankee tyranny. Amid fiery denunciations of fanatical South-hating Republicans, all the Southern states except Tennessee rejected the Fourteenth Amendment, further infuriating the Republicans in Congress. "The last one of the sinful ten has flung back into our teeth the magnanimous offer of a generous nation" was how Representative John Garfield of Ohio saw it. It was now two years after the end of the fighting, and North and South were further from reconciliation than ever. In his last major speech, Lincoln had pleaded for Americans to "bind up the nation's wounds"; two years of Reconstruction politics had only poured salt on them.

RADICAL RECONSTRUCTION An aroused Republican Congress came to Washington in December 1866 determined to impose a harsh new style of Reconstruction on a dismayed and angered South. They moved quickly to consolidate their power and to ensure that neither the courts nor the president thwarted their will. When the Supreme Court issued a ruling that seemed to challenge the validity of the military courts of the Freedmen's Bureau, they reduced the size of the Court, depriving Johnson of the chance to make any appointments to it. When in 1868 the Court seemed about to challenge the Reconstruction Acts the radicals had passed, they took jurisdiction over such matters away from the Court. But it was Johnson's power that the Republicans were most determined to check. The election had given them the votes to nullify his veto power. The Republicans were equally determined to nullify his use of executive authority, especially his powers as commander-in-chief (the powers Lincoln had used so effectively during the war to bypass Congress). They enacted legislation that required all military orders, including those of Johnson, to go through General Grant. The Republicans were also worried that Johnson would try to use federal patronage to create a political machine that would be loyal to him. To thwart this possibility, they passed a Tenure of Office Act, designed to prevent Johnson from firing people opposed to his policies. They even used this act to try to remove Johnson from office. In August of 1867, Johnson suspended the secretary of war, Edwin Stanton (who worked closely with the radicals). When the Senate refused to agree to Stanton's removal, Johnson ordered Stanton to vacate his office. The Republicans responded by voting articles of impeachment in the House of Representatives. The subsequent Senate vote to convict him failed by one vote.

In the spring and early summer of 1867, the radical Republicans drew up a plan of military reconstruction. Lincoln and Johnson had argued that since secession itself was illegal, the Confederate states had never really been out of the Union. But the radicals insisted that by rebelling, the states had forfeited their statehood, committing "state-suicide," as Sumner called it. Congress accordingly declared the Johnson governments illegal and divided the conquered South into five military districts. The commander of each district, with the aid of the army, would prepare the states for readmission by registering all adult black males and all white males not disenfranchised under the provisions of the Fourteenth Amendment. All voters were required to take a stringent oath of loyalty. Once legitimate voters had been certified—approximately 700,000 blacks and 650,000 whites were registered under these provisions, and probably between 100,000 and 200,000 whites were disenfranchised—the usual steps for setting up a state would take place. Then, if Congress accepted the state's constitution and the state legislature passed the Fourteenth Amendment, the state would be readmitted to the Union. By June 1868, seven states, all clearly under the control of Republican-dominated "Reconstruction" governments, were accepted back into the Union; by early 1870 the remaining states were also admitted and the Union was formally restored.

For three years, much of the drama of Reconstruction had taken place in Washington. But as the states returned to the Union under the radical formula, the battle shifted to the South. The North finally had "reconstructed" states it could accept as legitimate, full-fledged members of the Union. But to many white Southerners these governments were never legitimate, and they were determined to do whatever it took to undermine them. To them, radical Reconstruction was an unmitigated nightmare, and it left a century-long legacy of bitterness. There was, first, the tyranny—the imposition by military force of governments and rulers that they themselves would never have chosen. It was a long-standing American axiom that government rested on the consent of the governed, and Southerners had certainly never consented to the kinds of governments that military Reconstruction forced on them. But to most white Southerners, the greatest of the horrors of radical Reconstruction was that it subjected them to "Negro rule."

The "Negro rule" of radical Reconstruction was a myth. In no state did blacks dominate or control the government. There was not a single elected black governor, and only in South Carolina was there ever a black legislative majority. Moreover, the range of ability, education, and competence among black officeholders was not wildly different from the range among most white officeholders in the North or South. The Reconstruction governments certainly contained corruption, but they were no more corrupt than their "lily-white" counterparts before or after the war. Although black suffrage was essential for keeping these regimes in power, their electoral base, especially in the beginning, extended beyond the ex-slaves. Many former Whigs, Southern Union men, and antisecessionists initially allied themselves with the new Republican governments. Many whites in nonslaveholding regions who had always resented the rule of the planter elite

"Of Course He Wants to Vote the Democratic Ticket." The efforts to "redeem" the South from Republican rule centered around attempts to neutralize the political effects of black enfranchisement. This Republican cartoon depicts the intimidation often used to keep blacks from voting or to get them to vote against the Republicans. (The Bettmann Archive)

voted for and participated in the Reconstruction governments. These governments were in many ways reform governments. But they spent comparatively little time trying to achieve social equality between whites and blacks. Instead, they concentrated on such things as public education and eliminating the undemocratic features of the antebellum political system, by which the planter elite had maintained its dominion—things that benefited poor whites as well as the freedmen.

"REDEEMING" THE STATES But this is not how the former slaveholders and old planter elite saw radical Reconstruction. Illiterate black field hands who could vote while former planters could not, blacks who held office, "uppity" ex-slaves who mocked their former masters, black soldiers who now patrolled whites—all these things in the eyes of the former slaveholders turned radical Reconstruction into "Black Reconstruction." "Negro rule" became the galling symbol of all the horrors of radical Reconstruction,

of all they had lost, of the defeat they had suffered and the degradation they now felt. They struck back against the Reconstruction governments with all the means at their disposal. They appealed to white supremacy to draw support of the poorer whites away from the Republicans, casting themselves as saviors who would "redeem" the South from the twin specter of black rule and Yankee domination. In states like Tennessee, Virginia, and North Carolina, where white voters held a clear majority, the "redeemers" gained control by 1871. For the most part they relied on the ballot box for victory, but in some areas they used intimidation and violence against blacks and their allies.

Where the racial balance was even or blacks held a majority, the battle for control was often violent. Carpetbaggers (whites from the North) and scalawags (white Southerners who collaborated with the Yankees) were ostracized and boycotted. Blacks were threatened with loss of jobs, credit, and access to lands for sharecropping. Secret organizations like the Ku Klux Klan were set up. Striking at night, dressed in robes and

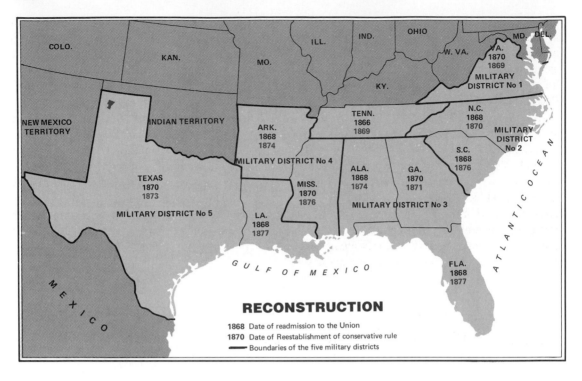

RECONSTRUCTION

1868 Date of readmission to the Union
1870 Date of Reestablishment of conservative rule
━━━ Boundaries of the five military districts

hoods, they beat, mutilated, and often murdered their victims. Directing their attacks mostly against scalawags and black leaders, they tried to terrorize blacks into withdrawing from political activity. The campaign of terror shocked Northerners and a number of Southerners. Two "force bills" and a Ku Klux Klan Act were passed by Congress, and in 1871 President Ulysses S. Grant initiated federal prosecutions in Mississippi. In South Carolina, Grant placed a few counties under martial law. But the laws were unevenly enforced and violence continued. "White legions," semimilitary organizations that intimidated whites into voting Democratic and forcibly kept blacks from voting, helped redeem Texas, Arkansas, and Alabama. As the 1875 Mississippi election approached, whites were determined to keep blacks and Republicans away from the polls, and the governor feared a bloodbath if he used black militia to oversee the elections. When he asked for federal help, the Grant administration refused, declaring that "the whole public are tired of these annual autumnal outbreaks in the South." The Democrats swept to power, aided by

the white legions, and Mississippi too joined the ranks of the redeemed.

THE END OF RECONSTRUCTION By 1876 only Louisiana, South Carolina, and Florida remained "unredeemed." Even there the hold of Reconstruction was precarious, dependent on the continuing presence of federal troops. The election of 1876 removed this prop, largely because most Northerners (at best minimally interested in the welfare of the ex-slaves) no longer cared very much about what was happening in the South. In his inaugural address of 1869, Ulysses S. Grant called for "peace," which most Northerners took to mean relief from the turmoil of Reconstruction politics. The election of 1872 indicated how rapidly Northern concerns were shifting. Many liberal Republicans who had been staunch in their concern for black rights, including Charles Sumner, turned against the Republican party and supported the Democratic nominee, Horace Greeley, himself an old Whig-Republican, who focused his campaign largely on the corruption of the Grant administration. By the mid-1870s, Northerners were more preoccupied with the politics of corruption and agrarian discontent, and with the problems of inflation, tariffs, and railroads, than with Reconstruction.

The election of 1876 resulted in a bizarre deadlock between Rutherford B. Hayes, the Republican nominee, and his Democratic opponent, Samuel J. Tilden. In exchange for the disputed electoral votes of South Carolina, Florida, and Louisiana, Hayes, who had narrowly lost the popular vote to Tilden, promised to remove all remaining federal troops from the South, thus putting a symbolic end to the Reconstruction that in all essential respects had already come to an end.

The end of Reconstruction did not mean a sudden end to all black gains or rights. African Americans continued to vote and even to hold a few offices, and they fought hard to preserve their schools and to hold onto whatever land they had. But continuing intimidation, white unity, and the indifference of the North isolated the ex-slaves politically and made their rights increasingly vulnerable. In his second inaugural address, Lincoln had linked the survival of the Union to the fate of the slaves. Slavery had ended and "the mighty scourge of war" was lifted, but twelve years of Reconstruction had made it clear that white Americans were far from ready to make good on the promise of emancipation.

Suggestions for Further Reading

ABRAHAM LINCOLN

The literature on Abraham Lincoln is voluminous. Benjamin Thomas, *Abraham Lincoln* (1952), is a good single-volume biography; it is somewhat surpassed by Stephen B. Oates, *With Malice Toward None: The Life of Abraham Lincoln* (1977) and *Abraham Lincoln: The Man Behind the Myths* (1988). Lawanda Cox, *Lincoln and Black Freedom* (1981), is a very useful study of the decision for emancipation. David Donald, *Lincoln Reconsidered* (1958), and Richard Current, *The Lincoln Nobody Knows* (1951), provide refreshing perspectives on Lincoln as a politician. Edmund Wilson, *Patriotic Gore* (1962), treats Lincoln's mystical attachment to the Union and his deepening religious sentiments during the war. David Potter, *Lincoln and His Party in the Secession Crisis* (1942), remains the best study of the subject. John Hope Franklin, *The Emancipation Proclamation* (1963), is a succinct history of how the document came about; Allan Nevins, *Lincoln and the Gettysburg Address* (1954), is a solid account of that famous oration. Ralph Borreson, *When Lincoln Died* (1965), is a detailed account of Lincoln's assassination and funeral. T. Harry Williams, *Lincoln: Selected Speeches and Letters* (1960), is an excellent sampling of the president's own writings.

CIVIL WAR

An excellent overview of the period is James McPherson, *Ordeal by Fire* (1982). The same author's *Battle Cry of Freedom* (1988) covers much the same ground, but in a somewhat more readable fashion. James G. Randall and David Donald, *The Civil War and Reconstruction* (2nd ed., 1961), is an older work but is still a useful survey. An excellent study of secession in one state is Michael P. Johnson, *Toward a Patriarchal Republic: The Secession of Georgia* (1977).

Two fine recent studies of the armies and battles of the war are Michael Barton, *Good Men: The Character of Civil War Soldiers* (1981), and Gerald F. Linderman, *Embattled Courage: Combat in the Civil War* (1977). William S. McFeely, *Grant: A Biography* (1981), is essential reading. Sherman's Georgia campaign is discussed in rich detail in *March to the Sea and Beyond* (1985). The causes of Northern victory and Confederate defeat are discussed in David Donald, ed., *Why the North Won the Civil War* (1960); Richard E. Beringer, Herman Hattaway, Archer Jones, and William N. Still, Jr., *Why the South Lost the Civil War* (1986); and Herman Hattaway and Archer Jones, *How the North Won* (1983). The life of the common soldier is the subject of Bell Irvin Wiley's pioneering works, *The Life of Johnny Reb* (1943) and *The Life of*

CHRONOLOGY

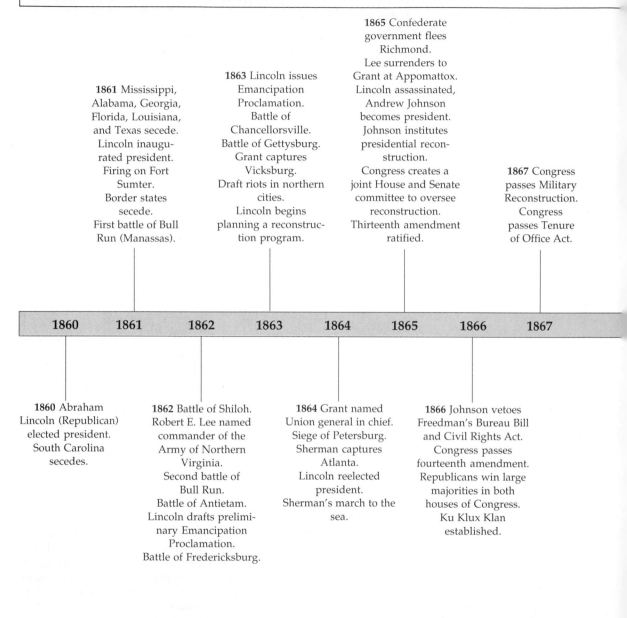

1865 Confederate government flees Richmond. Lee surrenders to Grant at Appomattox. Lincoln assassinated, Andrew Johnson becomes president. Johnson institutes presidential reconstruction. Congress creates a joint House and Senate committee to oversee reconstruction. Thirteenth amendment ratified.

1863 Lincoln issues Emancipation Proclamation. Battle of Chancellorsville. Battle of Gettysburg. Grant captures Vicksburg. Draft riots in northern cities. Lincoln begins planning a reconstruction program.

1861 Mississippi, Alabama, Georgia, Florida, Louisiana, and Texas secede. Lincoln inaugurated president. Firing on Fort Sumter. Border states secede. First battle of Bull Run (Manassas).

1867 Congress passes Military Reconstruction. Congress passes Tenure of Office Act.

| 1860 | 1861 | 1862 | 1863 | 1864 | 1865 | 1866 | 1867 |

1860 Abraham Lincoln (Republican) elected president. South Carolina secedes.

1862 Battle of Shiloh. Robert E. Lee named commander of the Army of Northern Virginia. Second battle of Bull Run. Battle of Antietam. Lincoln drafts preliminary Emancipation Proclamation. Battle of Fredericksburg.

1864 Grant named Union general in chief. Siege of Petersburg. Sherman captures Atlanta. Lincoln reelected president. Sherman's march to the sea.

1866 Johnson vetoes Freedman's Bureau Bill and Civil Rights Act. Congress passes fourteenth amendment. Republicans win large majorities in both houses of Congress. Ku Klux Klan established.

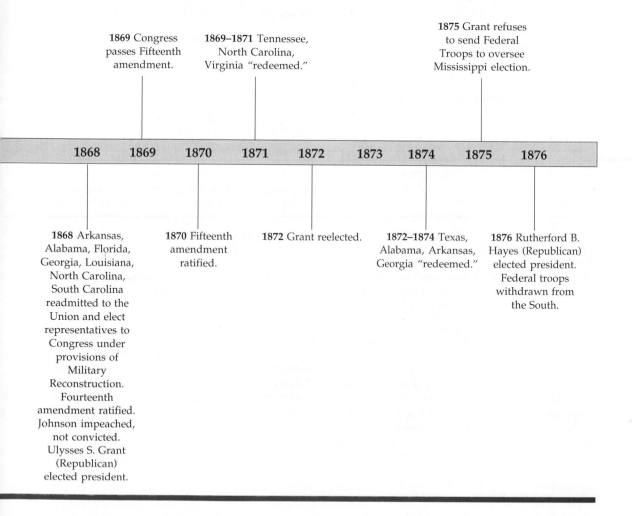

1869 Congress passes Fifteenth amendment.

1869–1871 Tennessee, North Carolina, Virginia "redeemed."

1875 Grant refuses to send Federal Troops to oversee Mississippi election.

| 1868 | 1869 | 1870 | 1871 | 1872 | 1873 | 1874 | 1875 | 1876 |

1868 Arkansas, Alabama, Florida, Georgia, Louisiana, North Carolina, South Carolina readmitted to the Union and elect representatives to Congress under provisions of Military Reconstruction. Fourteenth amendment ratified. Johnson impeached, not convicted. Ulysses S. Grant (Republican) elected president.

1870 Fifteenth amendment ratified.

1872 Grant reelected.

1872–1874 Texas, Alabama, Arkansas, Georgia "redeemed."

1876 Rutherford B. Hayes (Republican) elected president. Federal troops withdrawn from the South.

Billy Yank (1952). Allan Nevins, *The War for the Union*, 4 vols. (1959–71), Bruce Catton, *This Hallowed Ground* (1956) and *Centennial History of the Civil War* (1961–65), and Douglass Southall Freeman, *R. E. Lee*, 4 vols. (1934–35), provide full, readable accounts of the military history of the Civil War. T. Harry Williams, *Lincoln and the Radicals* (1942), argues that Lincoln and the radicals were in continuing opposition; whereas Hans L. Trefousse, *The Radical Republicans* (1968), stresses their cooperation. Emory L. Thomas, *The Confederate Nation* (1979), is a good single-volume treatment. Charles Ramsdell, *Behind the Lines in the Southern Confederacy* (1944), discusses the internal political conflicts within the Confederacy. The lives of African-American women are treated in Jacqueline Jones, *Labor of Love, Labor of Sorrow* (1985). Other valuable works on blacks and the war include Benjamin Quarles, *The Negro in the Civil War* (1953); James McPherson, ed., *The Negro's Civil War* (1965); and Dudley Cornish, *The Sable Arm: Negro Troops in the Union Army* (2nd ed., 1987). James L. Roark, *Masters without Slaves* (1977), describes the breakdown of the plantation system during the war and Reconstruction.

Politics and ideology in the North are the subjects of Earl J. Hess, *Liberty, Virtue, and Progress: Northerners and Their War for the Union* (1988); Eric Foner, *Politics and Ideology in the Age of the Civil War* (1980); and Dale Baum, *The Civil War Party System* (1984).

George Frederickson, *The Inner Civil War* (1965), and Edmund Wilson, *Patriotic Gore* (1962), provide superb discussions of the intellectual impact of the war. Ralph Andreano, ed., *The Economic Impact of the American Civil War* (1962), contains a number of important articles assessing the economic dimensions of the war. James L. Roark, *Masters Without Slaves* (1977), analyzes the plight of Southern planters during the Civil War and Reconstruction.

RECONSTRUCTION

John Hope Franklin, *Reconstruction After the Civil War* (1961), Kenneth M. Stampp, *The Era of Reconstruction* (1965), and W. E. B. du Bois, *Black Reconstruction* (1935), are valuable general treatments of Reconstruction. Herman Belz, *Reconstructing the Union* (1969), is a solid treatment of national policy; W. McKee Evans, *Ballots and Fence Rails* (1966), is a superb study of the politics of Reconstruction on the local level in North Carolina. Lawanda Cox and John Cox, *Politics, Principle, and Prejudice* (1965), and William Gillette, *The Right to Vote* (1969), treat race and politics in North and South during the period. Eric McKitrick, *Andrew Johnson and Reconstruction* (1966), is a thorough study of early presidential Reconstruction. William S. McFeely, *Grant* (1981), is the best study of Grant's presidency. William S. McFeely, *Yankee Step-Father: General O. O. Howard and the Freedmen* (1968), is a useful study of the Freedmen's Bureau. Allen Trelease, *White Terror* (1967), analyzes the role of the Ku Klux Klan and white terrorism in defeating Reconstruction. C. Vann Woodward, *Reunion and Reaction* (1951), and William Gillette, *Retreat from Reconstruction* (1980), describe the end of Reconstruction.

LIFE DURING THE CIVIL WAR AND RECONSTRUCTION

The story of blacks in Reconstruction is explored in several works. The most notable are Joel Williamson, *After Slavery* (1966); Thomas Hold, *Black over White* (1977); Willie Lee Rose, *Rehearsal for Reconstruction* (1964); and Leon Litwack, *Been in the Storm So Long* (1979). Other important books on Reconstruction and its impact are Paul D. Escott, *Many Excellent People* (1985); Eric Foner, *Nothing But Freedom* (1983); and Stephen Hahn, *The Roots of Southern Populism* (1983). Morgan Kousser and James McPherson, eds., *Region, Race, and Reconstruction* (1982), is a valuable collection of essays.

Collections of documents include Frank Moore, ed., *Rebellion Record*, a twelve-volume compilation put together in the 1860s and reprinted in a modern edition in 1977; Francis T. Miller, *The Photographic History of the Civil War*, 10 vols. (1957), is the most extensive of the many collections of Civil War photographs. Frank Freidel, ed., *Union Pamphlets of the Civil War* (1967), provides a valuable collection of Northern writings. See also Harold Hyman, ed., *The Radical Republicans and Reconstruction* (1967). C. Vann Woodward, ed., *Mary Chesnut's Civil War* (1981), and Robert Myers, *The Children of Pride* (1972), provide invaluable insight into Southern life during the war. Rupert S. Holland, ed., *The Letters and Diary of Laura M. Towne* (1970), is a superb collection of letters from a young woman who went to the South Carolina Sea Islands to teach the ex-slaves.

THE DECLARATION OF INDEPENDENCE

In Congress, July 4, 1776. *The unanimous Declaration of the thirteen United States of America.*

When in the Course of human events, it becomes necessary for one people to dissolve the political bands which have connected them with another, and to assume among the powers of the earth, the separate and equal station to which the Laws of Nature and of Nature's God entitle them, a decent respect to the opinions of mankind requires that they should declare the causes which impel them to the separation.—

We hold these truths to be self-evident, that all men are created equal, that they are endowed by their Creator with certain unalienable Rights, that among these are Life, Liberty and the pursuit of Happiness.—

That to secure these rights, Governments are instituted among Men, deriving their just powers from the consent of the governed,—

That whenever any Form of Government becomes destructive of these ends, it is the Right of the People to alter or to abolish it, and to institute new Government, laying its foundation on such principles and organizing its powers in such form, as to them shall seem most likely to effect their Safety and Happiness. Prudence, indeed, will dictate that Governments long established should not be changed for light and transient causes; and accordingly all experience hath shown, that mankind are more disposed to suffer, while evils are sufferable, than to right themselves by abolishing the forms to which they are accustomed. But when a long train of abuses and usurpations, pursuing invariably the same Object evinces a design to reduce them under absolute Despotism, it is their right, it is their duty, to throw off such Government, and to provide new Guards for their future security.—

Such has been the patient sufferance of these Colonies; and such is now the necessity which constrains them to alter their former Systems of Government. The history of the present King of Great Britain is a history of repeated injuries and usurpations, all having in direct object the establishment of an absolute Tyranny over these States. To prove this, let Facts be submitted to a candid world.—

He has refused his Assent to Laws, the most wholesome and necessary for the public good.—

He has forbidden his Governors to pass Laws of immediate and pressing importance, unless suspended in their operation till his Assent should be obtained; and when so suspended, he has utterly neglected to attend to them.—

He has refused to pass other Laws for the accommodation of large districts of people, unless those people would relinquish the right of Representation in the Legislature, a right inestimable to them and formidable to tyrants only.—

He has called together legislative bodies at places unusual, uncomfortable, and distant from the depository of their public Records, for the sole purpose of fatiguing them into compliance with his measures.—

He has dissolved Representative Houses repeatedly, for opposing with manly firmness his invasions on the rights of the people.—

He has refused for a long time, after such dissolutions, to cause others to be elected; whereby the Legislative powers, incapable of Annihilation, have returned to the People at large for their exercise; the State remaining in the mean time exposed to all the dangers of invasion from without, and convulsions within.—

He has endeavored to prevent the population of these States; for that purpose obstructing the Laws for Naturalization of Foreigners; refusing to pass others to encourage their migrations hither, and raising the conditions of new Appropriations of Lands.—

He has obstructed the Administration of Justice, by refusing his Assent to Laws for establishing Judiciary powers.—

He has made Judges dependent on his Will alone, for the tenure of their offices, and the amount and payment of their salaries.—

He has erected a multitude of New Offices, and sent hither swarms of Officers to harrass our people, and eat out their substance.—

He has kept among us, in times of peace, Standing Armies without the Consent of our legislatures.—

He has affected to render the Military independent of and superior to the Civil power.—

He has combined with others to subject us to a jurisdiction foreign to our constitution, and unacknowledged by our laws; giving his Assent to their Acts of pretended Legislation:—

For quartering large bodies of armed troops among us:—

For protecting them, by a mock Trial, from punishment for any Murders which they should commit on the Inhabitants of these States:—

For cutting off our Trade with all parts of the world:—

For imposing Taxes on us without our Consent:—

For depriving us in many cases, of the benefits of Trial by Jury:—

For transporting us beyond Seas to be tried for pretended offences:—

For abolishing the free System of English Laws in a neighbouring Province, establishing therein an Arbitrary government, and enlarging its Boundaries so as to render it at once an example and fit instrument for introducing the same absolute rule into these Colonies:—

For taking away our Charters, abolishing our most valuable Laws, and altering fundamentally the Forms of our Government:—

For suspending our own Legislatures, and declaring themselves invested with power to legislate for us in all cases whatsoever.—

He has abdicated Government here, by declaring us out of his Protection and waging War against us.—

He has plundered our seas, ravaged our Coasts, burnt our towns, and destroyed the lives of our people.—

He is at this time transporting large Armies of foreign Mercenaries to compleat the works of death, desolation and tyranny, already begun with circumstances of Cruelty & perfidy scarcely paralleled in the most barbarous ages, and totally unworthy the Head of a civilized nation.—

He has constrained our fellow Citizens taken Captive on the high Seas to bear Arms against their Country, to become the executioners of their friends and Brethren, or to fall themselves by their Hands.—

He has excited domestic insurrections amongst us, and has endeavoured to bring on the inhabitants of our frontiers, the merciless Indian Savages, whose known rule of warfare, is an undistinguished destruction of all ages, sexes and conditions.

In every stage of these Oppressions We have Petitioned for Redress in the most humble terms: Our repeated Petitions have been answered only by repeated injury. A Prince, whose character is thus marked by every act which may define a Tyrant, is unfit to be the ruler of a free people.

Nor have We been wanting in our attentions to our British brethren. We have warned them from time to time of attempts by their legislature to extend an unwarrantable jurisdiction over us. We have reminded them of the circumstances of our emigration and settlement here. We have appealed to their native justice and magnanimity, and we have conjured them by the ties of our common kindred to disavow these usurpations, which, would inevitably interrupt our connections and correspondence. They too have been deaf to the voice of justice and of consanguinity. We must, therefore, acquiesce in the necessity, which denounces our Separation, and hold them, as we hold the rest of mankind, Enemies in War, in Peace Friends.—

We, Therefore, the Representatives of the united States of America, in General Congress, Assembled, appealing to the Supreme Judge of the world for the rectitude of our intentions, do, in the Name, and by the Authority of the good People of these Colonies, solemnly publish and declare, That these United Colonies are, and of Right ought to be, Free and Independent States; that they are Absolved from all Allegiance to the British Crown, and that all political connection between them and the State of Great Britain, is and ought to be totally dissolved; and that as Free and Independent States, they have full Power to levy War, conclude Peace, contract Alliances, establish Commerce, and to do all other Acts and Things which Independent States may of right do.—

And for the support of this Declaration, with a firm reliance on the protection of divine Providence, we mutually pledge to each other our Lives, our Fortunes, and our sacred Honor.

John Hancock
(MASSACHUSETTS)

New Hampshire
Josiah Bartlett
William Whipple
Matthew Thornton

Massachusetts
Samuel Adams
John Adams
Robert Treat Paine
Elbridge Gerry

Delaware
Caesar Rodney
George Read
Thomas McKean

New York
William Floyd
Philip Livingston
Francis Lewis
Lewis Morris

New Jersey
Richard Stockton
John Witherspoon
Francis Hopkinson
John Hart
Abraham Clark

North Carolina
William Hooper
Joseph Hewes
John Penn

Maryland
Samuel Chase
William Paca
Thomas Stone
Charles Carroll of Carrollton

South Carolina
Edward Rutledge
Thomas Heywood, Jr.
Thomas Lynch, Jr.
Arthur Middleton

Rhode Island
Stephen Hopkins
William Ellery

Connecticut
Roger Sherman
Samuel Huntington
William Williams
Oliver Wolcott

Pennsylvania
Robert Morris
Benjamin Rush
Benjamin Franklin
John Morton
George Clymer
James Smith
George Taylor
James Wilson
George Ross

Virginia
George Wythe
Richard Henry Lee
Thomas Jefferson
Benjamin Harrison
Thomas Nelson, Jr.
Francis Lightfoot Lee
Carter Braxton

Georgia
Button Gwinnett
Lyman Hall
George Walton

THE CONSTITUTION OF THE UNITED STATES OF AMERICA

We the People of the United States, in Order to form a more perfect Union, establish Justice, insure domestic Tranquility, provide for the common defence, promote the general Welfare, and secure the Blessings of Liberty to ourselves and our Posterity, do ordain and establish this Constitution for the United States of America.

> The preamble establishes the principle of government by the people and lists the six basic purposes of the Constitution.

ARTICLE I LEGISLATIVE DEPARTMENT

Section 1. All legislative Powers herein granted shall be vested in a Congress of the United States, which shall consist of a Senate and House of Representatives.

Section 2. The House of Representatives shall be composed of Members chosen every second Year by the People of the several States, and the Electors in each State shall have the Qualifications requisite for Electors of the most numerous Branch of the State Legislature.

> Representatives serve two-year terms. They are chosen by those electors (that is, voters) who are qualified to vote for members of the lower house of their own state legislature.

No Person shall be a Representative who shall not have attained to the Age of twenty-five Years, and have been seven Years a Citizen of the United States, and who shall not, when elected, be an Inhabitant of that State in which he shall be chosen.

> The number of representatives allotted to a state is determined by the size of its population. The 14th Amendment has made obsolete the reference to "all other persons"—that is, slaves.

Representatives and direct Taxes shall be apportioned among the several States which may be included within this Union, according to their respective Numbers, <u>which shall be determined by adding to the whole Number of free Persons, including those bound to Service for a Term of Years, and excluding Indians not taxed, three-fifths of all other Persons.</u> The actual Enumeration shall be made within three Years after the first Meeting of the Congress of the United States, and within every subsequent Term of ten Years, in such Manner as they shall by Law direct. The Number of Representatives shall not exceed one for every thirty Thousand, but each State

> A census must be taken every ten years to determine the number of representatives to which each state is entitled. There is now one representative for about every 470,000 persons.

Source: House Document #529. U.S. Government Printing Office, 1967.
Note: The Constitution and the amendments are reprinted here in their original form. Portions that have been amended or superseded are underlined. The words printed in the margins explain some of the more difficult passages.

shall have at Least one Representative; <u>and until such enumeration shall be made, the State of New Hampshire shall be entitled to chuse three, Massachusetts eight, Rhode Island and Providence Plantations one, Connecticut five, New York six, New Jersey four, Pennsylvania eight, Delaware one, Maryland six, Virginia ten, North Carolina five, South Carolina five, and Georgia three.</u>

When vacancies happen in the Representation from any State, the Executive Authority thereof shall issue Writs of Election to fill such Vacancies.

The House of Representatives shall chuse their Speaker and other Officers; and shall have the sole Power of Impeachment.

Section 3.   The Senate of the United States shall be composed of two Senators from each State, <u>chosen by the Legislature thereof,</u> for six Years; and each Senator shall have one Vote.

Immediately after they shall be assembled in Consequence of the first Election, they shall be divided as equally as may be into three Classes. The Seats of the Senators of the first Class shall be vacated at the Expiration of the second Year, of the second Class at the expiration of the fourth Year, and of the third Class at the Expiration of the sixth Year, so that one third may be chosen every second Year; and if Vacancies happen by Resignation, or otherwise, <u>during the Recess of the Legislature of any State, the Executive thereof may make temporary Appointments until the next Meeting of the Legislature, which shall then fill such Vacancies.</u>

No Person shall be a Senator who shall not have attained to the Age of thirty Years, and been nine Years a Citizen of the United States, and who shall not, when elected, be an Inhabitant of that State for which he shall be chosen.

The Vice President of the United States shall be President of the Senate, but shall have no Vote, unless they be equally divided.

The Senate shall chuse their other Officers, and also a President pro tempore, in the absence of the Vice President, or when he shall exercise the Office of President of the United States.

The Senate shall have the sole Power to try all Impeachments. When sitting for that Purpose, they shall be on Oath or Affirmation. When the President of the United States is tried, the Chief Justice shall preside: And no Person shall be convicted without the Concurrence of two thirds of the Members present.

Judgment in Cases of Impeachment shall not extend further than to removal from Office, and disqualification to hold and enjoy any Office of Honor, Trust or Profit under the United States: but the Party convicted shall nevertheless be liable and subject to Indictment, Trial, Judgment and Punishment, according to Law.

Section 4.   The Times, Places and Manner of holding Elections for Senators and Representatives, shall be prescribed in each State by the Legislature thereof; but the Congress may at any time by Law make or alter such Regulations, except as to the Place of chusing Senators.

The Congress shall assemble at least once in every Year, <u>and such Meeting shall be on the first Monday in December,</u> unless they shall by Law appoint a different Day.

Section 5.   Each House shall be the Judge of the Elections, Returns and Qualifications of its own Members, and a Majority of each shall constitute a Quorum to do

Margin notes:

"Executive authority" refers to the governor of a state.

The Speaker, chosen by and from the majority party, presides over the House. Impeachment is the act of bringing formal charges against an official. (See also Section 3.)

The 17th Amendment changed this method to direct election.

The 17th Amendment also provides that a state governor shall appoint a successor to fill a vacant Senate seat until a direct election is held.

The Vice President may cast a vote in the Senate only to break a tie.

The president *pro tempore* of the Senate is a temporary officer; the Latin words mean "for the time being."

No President has ever been convicted on charges of impeachment. In 1868 the Senate fell one vote short of the two-thirds majority needed to convict Andrew Johnson. Thirteen other officials—eleven federal judges, one senator, and one secretary of war—have been impeached; five of the judges were convicted.

Elections for Congress are held on the first Tuesday after the First Monday in November in even-numbered years.

The 20th Amendment designates January 3 as the opening of the congressional session.

Business; but a smaller number may adjourn from day to day, and may be authorized to compel the Attendance of absent Members, in such Manner, and under such Penalties as each House may provide.

Each House may determine the Rules of its Proceedings, punish its Members for disorderly Behavior, and with the Concurrence of two thirds, expel a Member.

Each House shall keep a Journal of its Proceedings, and from time to time publish the same, excepting such Parts as may in their Judgment require Secrecy; and the Yeas and Nays of the Members of either House on any question shall, at the Desire of one fifth of those Present, be entered on the Journal.

Neither House, during the Session of Congress, shall, without the Consent of the other, adjourn for more than three days, nor to any other Place than that in which the two Houses shall be sitting.

Section 6. The Senators and Representatives shall receive a Compensation for their Services, to be ascertained by Law, and paid out of the Treasury of the United States. They shall in all Cases, except Treason, Felony and Breach of the Peace, be privileged from Arrest during their Attendance at the Session of their respective Houses, and in going to and returning from the same; and for any Speech or Debate in either House, they shall not be questioned in any other Place.

No Senator or Representative shall, during the Time for which he was elected, be appointed to any civil Office under the Authority of the United States, which shall have been created, or the Emoluments whereof shall have been encreased during such time; and no Person holding any Office under the United States, shall be a Member of either House during his Continuance in Office.

Section 7. All Bills for raising Revenue shall originate in the House of Representatives; but the Senate may propose or concur with Amendments as on other Bills.

Every Bill which shall have passed the House of Representatives and the Senate, shall, before it become a Law, be presented to the President of the United States; If he approve he shall sign it, but if not he shall return it, with his Objections to that House in which it shall have originated, who shall enter the Objections at large on their Journal, and proceed to reconsider it. If after such Reconsideration two thirds of that House shall agree to pass the Bill, it shall be sent, together with the Objections, to the other House, by which it shall likewise be reconsidered, and if approved by two thirds of that House, it shall become a Law. But in all such Cases the Votes of both Houses shall be determined by Yeas and Nays, and the Names of the Persons voting for and against the Bill shall be entered on the Journal of each House respectively. If any Bill shall not be returned by the President within ten Days (Sundays excepted) after it shall have been presented to him, the Same shall be a Law, in like Manner as if he had signed it, unless the Congress by their Adjournment prevent its Return, in which Case it shall not be a Law.

Every Order, Resolution, or Vote to which the Concurrence of the Senate and House of Representatives may be necessary (except on a question of Adjournment) shall be presented to the President of the United States; and before the Same shall take Effect, shall be approved by him, or being disapproved by him, shall be repassed by two thirds of the Senate and House of Representatives, according to the Rules and Limitations prescribed in the Case of a Bill.

Each house of Congress decides whether a member has been elected properly and is qualified to be seated. (A quorum is the minimum number of persons required to be present in order to conduct business.) The House once refused admittance to an elected representative who had been guilty of a crime. The Senate did likewise in the case of a candidate whose election campaign lent itself to "fraud and corruption."

Congressmen have the power to fix their own salaries. Under the principle of *congressional immunity*, they cannot be sued or arrested for anything they say in a congressional debate. This provision enables them to speak freely.

This clause reinforces the principle of separation of powers by stating that, during his term of office, a member of Congress may not be appointed to a position in another branch of government. Nor may he resign and accept a position created during his term.

The House initiates tax bills but the Senate may propose changes in them.

By returning a bill unsigned to the house in which it originated, the President exercises a *veto*. A two-thirds majority in both houses can override the veto. If the President receives a bill within the last ten days of a session and does not sign it, the measure dies by *pocket veto*. Merely by keeping the bill in his pocket, so to speak, the President effects a veto.

The same process of approval or disapproval by the President is applied to resolutions and other matters passed by both houses (except adjournment).

These are the *delegated*, or *enumerated*, powers of Congress.

Duties are taxes on imported goods; *excises* are taxes on goods manufactured, sold, or consumed within the country. *Imposts* is a general term including both duties and excise taxes.

Naturalization is the process by which an alien becomes a citizen.

Government *securities* include savings bonds and other notes.

Authors' and inventors' rights are protected by copyright and patent laws.

Congress may establish lower federal courts.

Only Congress may declare war. *Letters of marque and reprisal* grant merchant ships permission to attack enemy vessels.

Militia refers to national guard units, which may become part of the United States Army during an emergency. Congress aids the states in maintaining their national guard units.

This clause gives Congress the power to govern what became the District of Columbia, as well as other federal sites.

Known as the *elastic clause*, this provision enables Congress to exercise many powers not specifically granted to it by the Constitution.

This clause concerns the slave trade, which Congress did ban in 1808.

Section 8. The Congress shall have Power to lay and collect Taxes, Duties, Imposts and Excises, to pay the Debts and provide for the common Defence and general Welfare of the United States; but all Duties, Imposts and Excises shall be uniform throughout the United States;

To borrow money on the credit of the United States;

To regulate Commerce with foreign Nations, and among the several States, and with the Indian Tribes;

To establish an uniform Rule of Naturalization, and uniform Laws on the subject of Bankruptcies throughout the United States;

To coin Money, regulate the Value thereof, and of foreign Coin, and fix the Standard of Weights and Measures;

To provide for the Punishment of counterfeiting the Securities and current Coin of the United States;

To establish Post Offices and post Roads;

To promote the Progress of Science and useful Arts, by securing for limited Times to Authors and Inventors the exclusive Right to their respective Writings and Discoveries;

To constitute Tribunals inferior to the superior Court;

To define and punish Piracies and Felonies committed on the high Seas, and Offenses against the Law of Nations;

To declare War, grant Letters of Marque and Reprisal, and make Rules concerning Captures on Land and Water;

To raise and support Armies, but no Appropriation of Money to that Use shall be for a longer Term than two years;

To provide and maintain a Navy;

To make Rules for the Government and Regulation of the land and naval Forces;

To provide for calling forth the Militia to execute the Laws of the Union, suppress Insurrections and repel Invasions;

To provide for organizing, arming, and disciplining the Militia, and for governing such Part of them as may be employed in the Service of the United States, reserving to the States respectively, the Appointment of the Officers, and the Authority of training the Militia according to the discipline prescribed by Congress;

To exercise the exclusive Legislation in all Cases whatsoever, over such District (not exceeding ten Miles square) as may, by Cession of particular States, and the acceptance of Congress, become the Seat of the Government of the United States, and to exercise like Authority over all Places purchased by the Consent of the Legislature of the State in which the Same shall be, for the Erection of Forts, Magazines, Arsenals, dock-Yards, and other needful Buildings;—And

To make all Laws which shall be necessary and proper for carrying into Execution the foregoing Powers, and all other Powers vested by this Constitution in the Government of the United States, or in any Department or Officer thereof.

Section 9. The Migration or Importation of such Persons as any of the States now existing shall think proper to admit, shall not be prohibited by the Congress prior to the Year one thousand eight hundred and eight, but a tax or duty may be imposed on such Importation, not exceeding ten dollars for each Person.

The privilege of the Writ of Habeas Corpus shall not be suspended unless when in Cases of Rebellion or Invasion the public Safety may require it.

No Bill of Attainder or ex post facto Law shall be passed.

No capitation, or other direct, Tax shall be laid, unless in Proportion to the Census of Enumeration herein before directed to be taken.

No Tax or Duty shall be laid on Articles exported from any State.

No Preference shall be given by any Regulation of Commerce or Revenue to the Ports of one State over those of another; nor shall Vessels bound to, or from, one State, be obliged to enter, clear, or pay Duties in another.

No Money shall be drawn from the Treasury, but in Consequence of Appropriations made by Law; and a regular Statement and Account of the Receipts and Expenditures of all public Money shall be published from time to time.

No Title of Nobility shall be granted by the United States: And no Person holding any Office of Profit or Trust under them, shall, without the Consent of the Congress, accept of any present, Emolument, Office, or Title, of any kind whatever, from any King, Prince, or foreign State.

Section 10.   No State shall enter into any Treaty, Alliance, or Confederation; grant Letters of Marque and Reprisal; coin Money; emit Bills of Credit; make any Thing but gold and silver Coin a Tender in Payment of Debts; pass any Bill of Attainder, ex post facto Law, or Law impairing the Obligation of Contracts, or grant any Title of Nobility.

No State shall, without the Consent of the Congress, lay any Imposts or Duties on Imports or Exports, except what may be absolutely necessary for executing its inspection Laws: and the net Produce of all Duties and Imposts, laid by any State on Imports or Exports, shall be for the Use of the Treasury of the United States; and all such Laws shall be subject to the Revision and Controul of the Congress.

No State shall, without the Consent of Congress, lay any duty of Tonnage, keep Troops, or Ships of War in time of Peace, enter into any Agreement or Compact with another State, or with a foreign Power, or engage in War, unless actually invaded, or in such imminent Danger as will not admit of delay.

ARTICLE II   EXECUTIVE DEPARTMENT

Section 1.   The executive Power shall be vested in a President of the United States of America. He shall hold his Office during the Term of four Years, and, together with the Vice President, chosen for the same Term, be elected, as follows.

Each State shall appoint, in such Manner as the Legislature thereof may direct, a Number of Electors, equal to the whole Number of Senators and Representatives to which the State may be entitled in the Congress: but no Senator or Representative, or Person holding an office of Trust or Profit under the United States, shall be appointed an Elector.

The Electors shall meet in their respective States, and vote by Ballot for two persons, of whom one at least shall not be an Inhabitant of the same State with themselves. And they shall make a List of all the Persons voted for, and of the Number of Votes for each; which List they shall sign and certify, and transmit sealed to the Seat of

---

Marginal notes:

The *writ of habeas corpus* permits a prisoner to appear before a judge to inquire into the legality of his or her detention.

A *bill of attainder* is an act of legislation that declares a person guilty of a crime and punishes him or her without a trial. An *ex post facto* law punishes a person for an act that was legal when performed but later declared illegal.

The object of Clause 4 was to bar direct (per person) taxation of slaves for the purpose of abolishing slavery. The 16th Amendment modified this provision by giving Congress the power to tax personal income.

States are hereby forbidden to exercise certain powers. Some of these powers belong to Congress alone; others are considered undemocratic.

States cannot, without congressional authority, tax goods that enter or leave, except for a small inspection fee.

Federal officials are ineligible to serve as presidential electors.

The 12th Amendment superseded this clause. The weakness of the original constitutional provision became apparent in the election of 1800, when Thomas Jefferson and Aaron Burr received the same number of electoral votes. The 12th Amendment avoids this possibility by requiring electors to cast separate ballots for President and Vice President.

the Government of the United States, directed to the President of the Senate. The President of the Senate shall, in the Presence of the Senate and House of Representatives, open all the Certificates, and the Votes shall then be counted. The Person having the greatest Number of Votes shall be the President, if such Number be a Majority of the whole Number of Electors appointed; and if there be more than one who have such Majority, and have an equal Number of Votes, then the House of Representatives shall immediately chuse by Ballot one of them for President; and if no Person have a Majority, then from the five highest on the List the said House shall in like Manner chuse the President. But in chusing the President, the Votes shall be taken by States, the Representation from each State having one Vote; a quorum for this Purpose shall consist of a Member or Members from two thirds of the States, and a Majority of all the States shall be necessary to a Choice. In every Case, after the Choice of the President, the Person having the Greatest Number of Votes of the Electors shall be the Vice President. But if there should remain two or more who have equal Votes, the Senate shall chuse from them by Ballot the Vice President.

The Congress may determine the Time of chusing the Electors, and the Day on which they shall give their Votes; which Day shall be the same throughout the United States.

A naturalized citizen may not become President.

No person except a natural born Citizen, or a Citizen of the United States, at the time of the Adoption of this Constitution, shall be eligible to the Office of President; neither shall any Person be eligible to that Office who shall not have attained to the Age of Thirty-five Years, and been fourteen Years a Resident within the United States.

The Vice President is next in line for the presidency. A federal law passed in 1947 determined the order of presidential succession as follows: (1) Speaker of the House; (2) president *pro tempore* of the Senate; and (3) Cabinet officers in the order in which their departments were created. This clause has been amplified by the 25th Amendment.

In a Case of the Removal of the President from Office, or of his Death, Resignation, or Inability to discharge the Powers and Duities of the said Office, the same shall devolve on the Vice-President, and the Congress may by Law provide for the Case of Removal, Death, Resignation or Inability, both of the President and the Vice President, declaring what Officer shall then act as President, and such Officer shall act accordingly, until the Disability be removed, or a President shall be elected.

The President shall, at stated Times, receive for his Services, a Compensation, which shall neither be encreased nor diminished during the Period for which he shall have been elected, and he shall not receive within that Period any other Emolument from the United States, or any of them.

Before he enter on the Execution of his Office, he shall take the following Oath or Affirmation:—"I do solemnly swear (or affirm) that I will faithfully execute the Office of the President of the United States, and will to the best of my Ability, preserve, protect and defend the Constitution of the United States."

This clause suggests written communication between the President and "the principal officer in each of the executive departments." As it developed, these officials comprise the Cabinet—whose members are chosen, and may be replaced, by the President.

Senate approval is required for treaties and presidential appointments.

Section 2.   The President shall be Commander in Chief of the Army and Navy of the United States, and of the Militia of the several States, when called into the actual Service of the United States; he may require the Opinion in writing, of the principal Officer in each of the executive Departments, upon any subject relating to the Duties of their respective Offices, and he shall have Power to Grant Reprieves and Pardons for Offenses against the United States, except in Cases of Impeachment.

He shall have Power, by and with the Advice and Consent of the Senate, to make Treaties, provided two thirds of the Senators present concur; and he shall nominate, and by and with the Advice and Consent of the Senate, shall appoint Ambassadors, other public Ministers and Consuls, Judges of the supreme Court, and all other

Officers of the United States, whose Appointments are not herein otherwise provided for, and which shall be established by Law: but the Congress may by Law vest the Appointment of such inferior Officers, as they think proper, in the President alone, in the Courts of Law, or in the Heads of Departments.

The President shall have Power to fill up all Vacancies that may happen during the Recess of the Senate, by granting commissions which shall expire at the End of their next Session.

Without the consent of the Senate, the President may appoint officials only on a temporary basis.

Section 3. He shall from time to time give to the Congress Information of the State of the Union, and recommend to their Consideration such Measures as he shall judge necessary and expedient; he may, on extraordinary Occasions, convene both Houses, or either of them, and in Case of Disagreement between them, with Respect to the Time of Adjournment, he may adjourn them to such Time as he shall think proper; he shall receive Ambassadors and other public Ministers; he shall take Care that the Laws be faithfully executed, and shall Commission all the Officers of the United States.

The President delivers a "State of the Union" message at the opening of each session of Congress. Woodrow Wilson was the first President since John Adams to read his messages in person. Franklin D. Roosevelt and his successors followed Wilson's example.

Section 4. The President, Vice President and all civil Officers of the United States, shall be removed from Office on Impeachment for, and Conviction of, Treason, Bribery, or other high Crimes and Misdemeanors.

ARTICLE III   JUDICIAL DEPARTMENT

Section 1. The judicial Power of the United States, shall be vested in one supreme Court, and in such inferior Courts as the Congress may from time to time ordain and establish. The Judges, both of the supreme and inferior Courts, shall hold their Offices during good Behaviour, and shall, at stated Times, receive for their services, a Compensation, which shall not be diminished during their Continuance in Office.

Federal judges hold office for life and may not have their salaries lowered while in office. These provisions are intended to keep the federal bench independent of political pressure.

Section 2. The judicial Power shall extend to all Cases, in Law and Equity, arising under this Constitution, the Laws of the United States, and Treaties made, or which shall be made, under their Authority;—to all Cases affecting Ambassadors, other public Ministers and Consuls;—to all Cases of admiralty and maritime Jurisdiction;—to Controversies to which the United States shall be a Party;—to Controversies between two or more States;—between a State and Citizens of another state;—between Citizens of different states;—between Citizens of the same State claiming Lands under Grants of different States, and between a State, or the Citizens thereof, and foreign States, Citizens or Subjects.

This clause describes the types of cases that may be heard in federal courts.

The 11th Amendment prevents a citizen from suing a state in a federal court.

In all Cases affecting Ambassadors, other public Ministers and Consuls, and those in which a State shall be Party, the supreme Court shall have original Jurisdiction. In all the other Cases before mentioned, the supreme Court shall have appellate Jurisdiction, both as to Law and Fact, with such Exceptions, and under such Regulations as the Congress shall make.

The Supreme Court handles certain cases directly. It may also review cases handled by lower courts, but Congress in some cases may withhold the right to appeal to the highest court or limit appeal by setting various conditions.

The trial of all Crimes, except in Cases of Impeachment, shall be by Jury; and such Trial shall be held in the State where the said Crimes shall have been committed; but when not committed within any State, the Trial shall be at such Place or Places as the Congress may by Law have directed.

The 6th Amendment strengthens this clause on trial procedure.

Section 3. Treason against the United States, shall consist only in levying War against them, or in adhering to their Enemies, giving them Aid and Comfort. No

Treason is rigorously defined. A person can be convicted only if two witnesses testify to the same obvious act or if he or she confesses in court.

Person shall be convicted of Treason unless on the Testimony of two Witnesses to the same overt Act, or on Confession in open Court.

Punishment for treason extends only to the person convicted, not to his or her descendants. ("Corruption of blood" means that the heirs of a convicted person are deprived of certain rights.)

The Congress shall have Power to declare the Punishment of Treason, but no Attainder of Treason shall work Corruption of Blood, or Forfeiture except during the Life of the Person attainted.

ARTICLE IV   RELATIONS AMONG THE STATES

States must honor each other's laws, court decisions, and records (for example, birth, marriage, and death certificates).

Section 1.   Full Faith and Credit shall be given in each State to the public Acts, Records, and judicial Proceedings of every other State. And the Congress may by general Laws prescribe the Manner in which such Acts, Records and Proceedings shall be proved, and the Effect thereof.

Each state must respect the rights of citizens of other states.

The process of returning a person accused of a crime to the governmental authority (in this case a state) from which he or she has fled is called *extradition*.

The 13th Amendment, which abolished slavery, makes this clause obsolete.

Section 2.   The Citizens of each State shall be entitled to all Privileges and Immunities of Citizens in the several States.

A Person charged in any State with Treason, Felony, or other Crime, who shall flee from Justice, and be found in another State, shall on demand of the executive Authority of the State from which he fled, be delivered up, to be removed to the State having Jurisdiction of the Crime.

No Person held in Service or Labour in one State, under the laws thereof, escaping into another, shall, in Consequence of any Law or Regulation therein, be discharged from such Service or Labour, but shall be delivered up on Claim of the Party to whom such Service or Labour may be due.

A new state may not be created by dividing or joining existing states unless approved by the legislatures of the states affected and by Congress. An exception to the provision forbidding the division of a state occurred during the Civil War. In 1863 West Virginia was formed out of the western region of Virginia.

Section 3.   New States may be admitted by the Congress into this Union; but no new State shall be formed or erected within the Jurisdiction of any other State; nor any State be formed by the Junction of two or more States, or parts of States, without the Consent of the Legislatures of the States concerned as well as of the Congress.

The Congress shall have Power to dispose of and make all needful Rules and Regulations respecting the Territory or other Property belonging to the United States; and nothing in this Constitution shall be so construed as to Prejudice any Claims of the United States, or of any particular State.

A *republican* form of government is one in which citizens choose representatives to govern them. The federal government must protect a state against invasion and, if state authorities request it, against violence within a state.

Section 4.   The United States shall guarantee to every State in this Union a Republican Form of Government, and shall protect each of them against Invasion; and on Application of the Legislature, or of the Executive (when the Legislature cannot be convened) against domestic Violence.

ARTICLE V   AMENDING THE CONSTITUTION

An amendment to the Constitution can be proposed (a) by Congress, with a two-thirds vote of both houses, or (b) by a convention called by Congress when two-thirds of the state legislatures request it. An amendment is ratified (a) by three-fourths of the state legislatures or (b) by conventions in three-fourths of the states. The twofold procedure of proposal and ratification

The Congress, whenever two thirds of both Houses shall deem it necessary, shall propose Amendments to this Constitution, or, on the Application of the Legislatures of two thirds of the several States, shall call a Convention for proposing Amendments, which, in either Case, shall be valid to all Intents and Purposes, as part of this Constitution, when ratified by the Legislatures of three fourths of the several States, or by Conventions in three fourths thereof, as the one or the other Mode of Ratification may be proposed by the Congress: Provided that no Amendment which may be made prior to the Year One thousand eight hundred and eight shall in any Manner affect the first and fourth Clauses in the Ninth Section of the first Article; and that no State, without its Consent, shall be deprived of its equal Suffrage in the Senate.

ARTICLE VI GENERAL PROVISIONS

All Debts contracted and Engagements entered into, before the Adoption of this Constitution, shall be as valid against the United States under this Constitution, as under the Confederation.

This Constitution, and the Laws of the United States which shall be made in Pursuance thereof; and all Treaties made, or which shall be made, under the Authority of the United States, shall be the supreme Law of the Land; and the Judges in every State shall be bound thereby, any Thing in the Constitution or Laws of any State to the Contrary notwithstanding.

The Senators and Representatives before mentioned, and the Members of the several State Legislatures, and all executive and judicial Officers, both of the United States and of the several States, shall be bound by Oath or Affirmation, to support this Constitution; but no religious Test shall ever be required as a Qualification to any Office or public Trust under the United States.

> reflects the seriousness with which the framers of the Constitution regarded amendments. Over 7,000 amendments have been proposed; only 26 have been ratified.

> The *supremacy clause* means that if a federal and a state law conflict, the federal law prevails.

> Religion may not be a condition for holding public office.

ARTICLE VII RATIFICATION

The Ratification of the Conventions of nine States shall be sufficient for the Establishment of this Constitution between the States so ratifying the Same.

DONE in Convention by the Unanimous Consent of the States present the Seventeenth Day of September in the Year of our Lord one thousand seven hundred and eighty-seven and of the Independence of the United States of America the Twelfth. In Witness whereof We have hereunto subscribed our Names.

> The Constitution would become the law of the land upon the approval of nine states.

G° *WASHINGTON*
Presid^t and deputy from
VIRGINIA

Attest: *William Jackson,* Secretary

Delaware
Geo: Read
Gunning Bedford, jun
John Dickinson
Richard Bassett
Jaco: Broom

Maryland
James McHenry
Dan: of St Thos Jenifer
Danl Carroll

Virginia
John Blair
James Madison Jr.

North Carolina
Wm Blount
Richd Dobbs Spaight
Hu Williamson

South Carolina
J. Rutledge
Charles Cotesworth Pinckney
Charles Pinckney
Pierce Butler

Georgia
William Few
Abr Baldwin

New Hampshire
John Langdon
Nicholas Gilman

Massachusetts
Nathaniel Gorham
Rufus King

Connecticut
Wm Saml Johnson
Roger Sherman

New York
Alexander Hamilton

New Jersey
Wil: Livingston
David Brearley
Wm Paterson
Jona: Dayton

Pennsylvania
B Franklin
Thomas Mifflin
Robt. Morris
Geo. Clymer
Thos. FitzSimons
Jared Ingersoll
James Wilson
Gouv Morris

AMENDMENTS

[The date following each amendment number is the year of ratification.]

AMENDMENT 1   (1791)

Establishes freedom of religion, speech, and the press; gives citizens the rights of assembly and petition.

Congress shall make no law respecting an establishment of religion, or prohibiting the free exercise thereof: or abridging the freedom of speech, or of the press; or the right of the people peaceably to assemble, and to petition the Government for a redress of grievances.

AMENDMENT II   (1791)

States have the right to maintain a militia.

A well regulated Milita, being necessary to the security of a free State, the right of the people to keep and bear Arms, shall not be infringed.

AMENDMENT III   (1791)

Limits the army's right to quarter soldiers in private homes.

No Soldier shall, in time of peace, be quartered in any house, without the consent of the Owner, nor in time of war, but in a manner to be prescribed by law.

AMENDMENT IV   (1791)

Search warrants are required as a guarantee of a citizen's right to privacy.

The right of the people to be secure in their persons, houses, papers, and effects, against unreasonable searches and seizures, shall not be violated, and no Warrants shall issue, but upon probable cause, supported by Oath or affirmation, and particularly describing the place to be searched, and the persons or things to be seized.

AMENDMENT V   (1791)

To be prosecuted for a serious crime, a person must first be accused (*indicted*) by a grand jury. No one can be tried twice for the same crime (*double jeopardy*). Nor can a person be forced into self-incrimination by testifying against him- or herself.

No person shall be held to answer for a capital, or otherwise infamous crime, unless on a presentment or indictment of a Grand Jury, except in cases arising in the land or naval forces, or in the Militia, when in actual service in time of War or public danger; nor shall any person be subject for the same offence to be twice put in jeopardy of life or limb; nor shall be compelled in any criminal case to be a witness against himself, nor be deprived of life, liberty, or property, without due process of law; nor shall private property be taken for public use, without just compensation.

AMENDMENT VI   (1791)

Guarantees a defendant's right to be tried without delay and to face witnesses testifying for the other side.

In all criminal prosecutions, the accused shall enjoy the right to a speedy and public trial, by an impartial jury of the State and district wherein the crime shall have been committed, which district shall have been previously ascertained by law, and to be informed of the nature and cause of the accusation; to be confronted with the witnesses against him; to have compulsory process for obtaining witnesses in his favor, and to have the Assistance of Counsel for his defense.

AMENDMENT VII   (1791)

In suits at common law, where the value in controversy shall exceed twenty dollars, the right of trial by jury shall be preserved, and no fact tried by a jury, shall be otherwise reexamined in any court of the United States, than according to rules of the common law.

A jury trial is guaranteed in federal civil suits involving more than twenty dollars.

AMENDMENT VIII   (1791)

Excessive bail shall not be required, nor excessive fines imposed, nor cruel and unusual punishments inflicted.

AMENDMENT IX   (1791)

The enumeration in the Constitution, of certain rights, shall not be construed to deny or disparage others retained by the people.

The listing of specific rights in the Constitution does not mean that others are not protected.

AMENDMENT X   (1791)

The powers not delegated to the United States by the Constitution, nor prohibited by it to the States, are reserved to the States respectively, or to the people.

Limits the federal government to its specific powers. Powers not prohibited the states by the Constitution may be exercised by them.

AMENDMENT XI   (1798)

The Judicial power of the United States shall not be construed to extend to any suit in law or equity, commenced or prosecuted against one of the United States by Citizens of another State, or by Citizens or Subjects of any Foreign State.

A state cannot be sued by a citizen of another state in a federal court. Such a case can be tried only in the courts of the state being sued.

AMENDMENT XII   (1804)

The Electors shall meet in their respective states and vote by ballot for President and Vice-President, one of whom, at least, shall not be an inhabitant of the same state with themselves; they shall name in their ballots the person voted for as President, and in distinct ballots the person voted for as Vice-President, and they shall make distinct lists of all persons voted for as President, and of all persons voted for as Vice-President, and of the number of votes for each, which lists they shall sign and certify, and transmit sealed to the seat of the government of the United States, directed to the President of the Senate;—The President of the Senate shall, in presence of the Senate and House of Representatives, open all the certificates and the votes shall then be counted;—The person having the greatest number of votes for President, shall be the President, if such number be a majority of the whole number of Electors appointed; and if no person have such majority, then from the persons having the highest numbers not exceeding three on the list of those voted for as President, the House of Representatives shall choose immediately, by ballot, the President. But in choosing the President, the votes shall be taken by states, the representation from each state having one vote; a quorum for this purpose shall consist of a member or members from two-thirds of the states, and a majority of all the states shall be

Revises the process by which the President and Vice President were elected (see Article II, Section 1, Clause 3). The major change requires electors to cast separate ballots for President and Vice President. If none of the presidential candidates obtains a majority vote, the House of Representatives—with each state having one vote—chooses a President from the three candidates having the highest number of votes. If no vice presidential candidate wins a majority, the Senate chooses from the two candidates having the highest number of votes. The underlined portion was superseded by Section 3 of the 20th Amendment.

necessary to a choice. <u>And if the House of Representatives shall not choose a President whenever the right of choice shall devolve upon them, before the fourth day of March next following, then the Vice-President shall act as President, as in the case of the death or other constitutional disability of the President:</u>—The person having the greatest number of votes as Vice-President, shall be the Vice-President, if such number be a majority of the whole number of Electors appointed, and if no person have a majority, then from the two highest numbers on the list, the Senate shall choose the Vice-President; a quorum for the purpose shall consist of two-thirds of the whole number of Senators, and a majority of the whole number shall be necessary to a choice. But no person constitutionally ineligible to the office of President shall be eligible to that of Vice-President of the United States.

AMENDMENT XIII   (1865)

Abolishes slavery.

Section 1.   Neither slavery nor involuntary servitude, except as a punishment for crime whereof the party shall have been duly convicted, shall exist within the United States, or any place subject to their jurisdiction.

Section 2.   Congress shall have power to enforce this article by appropriate legislation.

AMENDMENT XIV   (1868)

This section confers full civil rights on former slaves. Supreme Court decisions have interpreted the language of Section 1 to mean that the states, as well as the federal government, are bound by the Bill of Rights.

A penalty of a reduction in congressional representation shall be applied to any state that refuses to give all adult male citizens the right to vote in federal elections. This section has never been applied. The underlined portion was superseded by Section 1 of the 26th Amendment. (This section has also been amplified by the 19th Amendment.)

Any former federal or state official who served the Confederacy during the Civil War could not become a federal official again unless Congress voted otherwise.

Section 1.   All persons born or naturalized in the United States, and subject to the jurisdiction thereof, are citizens of the United States and of the State wherein they reside. No state shall make or enforce any law which shall abridge the privileges or immunities of citizens of the United States; nor shall any State deprive any person of life, liberty, or property, without due process of law; nor deny any person within its jurisdiction the equal protection of the laws.

Section 2.   Representatives shall be apportioned among the several States according to their respective numbers, counting the whole number of persons in each State, excluding Indians not taxed. But when the right to vote at any election for the choice of electors for President and Vice-President of the United States, Representatives in Congress, the Executive and Judicial officers of a State, or the members of the Legislature thereof, is denied to any of the male inhabitants of such State, being <u>twenty-one</u> years of age, and citizens of the United States, or in any way abridged, except for participation in rebellion, or other crime, the basis of representation therein shall be reduced in the proportion which the number of such male citizens shall bear to the whole number of male citizens twenty-one years of age in such state.

Section 3.   No person shall be a Senator or Representative in Congress, or elector of President and Vice-President, or hold any office, civil or military, under the United States, or under any State, who, having previously taken an oath, as a member of Congress, or as an officer of the United States, or as a member of any State legislature, or as an executive or judicial officer of any State, to support the Constitution of the United States, shall have engaged in insurrection or rebellion against the same, or given aid or comfort to the enemies thereof. But Congress may by a vote of two-thirds of each House, remove such disability.

Section 4. The validity of the public debt of the United States, authorized by law, including debts incurred for payment of pensions and bounties for services in suppressing insurrection or rebellion, shall not be questioned. But neither the United States nor any State shall assume or pay any debt or obligation incurred in aid of insurrection or rebellion against the United States, or any claim for the loss or emancipation of any slave; but all such debts, obligations and claims shall be held illegal and void.

Makes legal the federal Civil War debt, but at the same time voids all Confederate debts incurred in the war.

Section 5. The Congress shall have power to enforce, by appropriate legislation, the provisions of this article.

AMENDMENT XV   (1870)

Section 1. The right of citizens of the United States to vote shall not be denied or abridged by the United States or by any State on account of race, color, or previous condition of servitude.

Gives ex-slaves the right to vote.

Section 2. The Congress shall have power to enforce this article by appropriate legislation.

AMENDMENT XVI   (1913)

The Congress shall have power to lay and collect taxes on incomes, from whatever source derived, without apportionment among the several States, and without regard to any census or enumeration.

Allows Congress to levy direct taxes on incomes.

AMENDMENT XVII   (1913)

The Senate of the United States shall be composed of two Senators from each State, elected by the people thereof, for six years; and each Senator shall have one vote. The electors in each State shall have the qualifications requisite for electors of the most numerous branch of the State legislature.

Provides for election of senators by the people of a state, rather than the state legislature.

When vacancies happen in the representation of any State in the Senate, the Executive authority of such State shall issue writs of election to fill such vacancies: *Provided*, That the legislature of any State may empower the executive thereof to make temporary appointments until the people fill the vacancies by election as the legislature may direct.

This amendment shall not be so construed as to affect the election or term of any Senator chosen before it becomes valid as part of the Constitution.

AMENDMENT XVIII   (1919)

Section 1. After one year from the ratification of this article, the manufacture, sale, or transportation of intoxicating liquors within, the importation thereof into, or the exportation thereof from the United States and all territory subject to the jurisdiction thereof for beverage purposes is hereby prohibited.

Legalizes prohibition—*that is, forbidding the making, selling, or transporting of intoxicating beverages. Superseded by the 21st Amendment.*

Section 2. The Congress and the several States shall have concurrent power to enforce this article by appropriate legislation.

Section 3.   This article shall be inoperative unless it shall have been ratified as an amendment to the Constitution by the legislatures of the several States, as provided in the Constitution, within seven years from the date of the submission hereof to the States by the Congress.

AMENDMENT XIX   (1920)

Gives women the right to vote.

The right of citizens of the United States to vote shall not be denied or abridged by the United States or by any State on account of sex.

Congress shall have power to enforce this article by appropriate legislation.

AMENDMENT XX   (1933)

The "lame duck" amendment allows the President to take office on January 20, and members of Congress on January 3. The purpose of the amendment is to reduce the term in office of defeated incumbents—known as "lame ducks."

Section 1.   The terms of the President and Vice-President shall end at noon on the 20th day of January, and the terms of Senators and Representatives at noon on the 3d day of January, of the years in which such terms would have ended if this article had not been ratified; and the terms of their successors shall then begin.

Section 2.   The Congress shall assemble at least once in every year, and such meeting shall begin at noon on the 3d day of January, unless they shall by law appoint a different day.

Section 3.   If, at the time fixed for the beginning of the term of the President, the President elect shall have died, the Vice-President elect shall become President. If a President shall not have been chosen before the time fixed for the beginning of his term, or if the President elect shall have failed to qualify, then the Vice-President elect shall act as President until a President shall have qualified; and the Congress may by law provide for the case wherein neither a President elect nor a Vice-President elect shall have qualified, declaring who shall then act as President, or the manner in which one who is to act shall be selected, and such person shall act accordingly until a President or Vice-President shall have qualified.

Section 4.   The Congress may by law provide for the case of the death of any of the persons from whom the House of Representatives may choose a President whenever the right of choice shall have devolved upon them, and for the case of the death of any of the persons from whom the Senate may choose a Vice-President whenever the right of choice shall have devolved upon them.

Section 5.   Sections 1 and 2 shall take effect on the 15th day of October following the ratification of this article.

Section 6.   This article shall be inoperative unless it shall have been ratified as an amendment to the Constitution by the legislatures of three-fourths of the several States within seven years from the date of its submission.

AMENDMENT XXI   (1933)

Repeals the 18th Amendment.

Section 1.   The eighteenth article of amendment to the Constitution of the United States is hereby repealed.

Section 2. The transportation or importation into any State, Territory, or possession of the United States for delivery or use therein of intoxicating liquors, in violation of the laws thereof, is hereby prohibited.

States may pass prohibition laws.

Section 3. This article shall be inoperative unless it shall have been ratified as an amendment to the Constitution by conventions in the several States, as provided in the Constitution, within seven years from the date of the submission hereof to the States by the Congress.

AMENDMENT XXII (1951)

Section 1. No person shall be elected to the office of the President more than twice, and no person who has held the office of President, or acted as President, for more than two years of a term to which some other person was elected President shall be elected to the office of the President more than once. But this Article shall not apply to any person holding the office of President when this Article was proposed by the Congress, and shall not prevent any person who may be holding the office of President, or acting as President, during the term within which this Article becomes operative from holding the office of President or acting as President during the remainder of such term.

Limits a President to two full terms or one term plus two years of a previous President's term.

Section 2. This article shall be inoperative unless it shall have been ratified as an amendment to the Constitution by the legislatures of three-fourths of the several States within seven years from the date of its submission to the States by the Congress.

AMENDMENT XXIII (1961)

Section 1. The District constituting the seat of Government of the United States shall appoint in such manner as the Congress may direct:

By giving the District of Columbia three electoral votes, Congress enabled its residents to vote for President and Vice President.

A number of electors of President and Vice-President equal to the whole number of Senators and Representatives in Congress to which the District would be entitled if it were a State, but in no event more than the least populous State; they shall be in addition to those appointed by the States, but they shall be considered, for the purposes of the election of President and Vice-President, to be electors appointed by a State; and they shall meet in the District and perform such duties as provided by the twelfth article of amendment.

Section 2. The Congress shall have power to enforce this article by appropriate legislation.

AMENDMENT XXIV (1964)

Section 1. The right of citizens of the United States to vote in any primary or other election for President or Vice-President, for electors for President or Vice-President, or for Senator or Representative in Congress, shall not be denied or abridged by the United States or any State by reason of failure to pay any poll tax or other tax.

Forbids the use of a poll tax as a requirement for voting in federal elections.

Section 2. The Congress shall have power to enforce this article by appropriate legislation.

AMENDMENT XXV   (1967)

Outlines the procedure to be followed in case of presidential disability.

Section 1.   In case of the removal of the President from office or of his death or resignation, the Vice-President shall become President.

Section 2.   Whenever there is a vacancy in the office of the Vice-President, the President shall nominate a Vice-President who shall take office upon confirmation by a majority vote of both Houses of Congress.

Section 3.   Whenever the President transmits to the President pro tempore of the Senate and the Speaker of the House of Representatives his written declaration that he is unable to discharge the powers and duties of his office, and until he transmits to them a written declaration to the contrary, such powers and duties shall be discharged by the Vice-President as Acting President.

Section 4.   Whenever the Vice-President and a majority of either the principal officers of the executive departments or of such other body as Congress may by law provide, transmit to the President pro tempore of the Senate and the Speaker of the House of Representatives their written declaration that the President is unable to discharge the powers and duties of his office, the Vice-President shall immediately assume the powers and duties of the office as Acting President.

Thereafter, when the President transmits to the President pro tempore of the Senate and the Speaker of the House of Representatives his written declaration that no inability exists, he shall resume the powers and duties of his office unless the Vice-President and a majority of either the principal officers of the executive department or of such other body as Congress may by law provide, transmit within four days to the President pro tempore of the Senate and the Speaker of the House of Representatives their written declaration that the President is unable to discharge the powers and duties of his office. Thereupon Congress shall decide the issue, assembling within forty-eight hours for that purpose if not in session. If the Congress, within twenty-one days after receipt of the latter written declaration, or, if Congress is not in session, within twenty-one days after Congress is required to assemble, determines by two-thirds vote of both Houses that the President is unable to discharge the powers and duties of his office, the Vice-President shall continue to discharge the same as Acting President; otherwise, the President shall resume the powers and duties of his office.

AMENDMENT XXVI   (1971)

Lowers the voting age to eighteen.

Section 1.   The right of citizens of the United States, who are eighteen years of age or older, to vote shall not be denied or abridged by the United States or any state on account of age.

Section 2.   The Congress shall have the power to enforce this article by appropriate legislation.

INDEX

Page numbers in italic refer to art.